LIBER MEMORIALIS
PROFESSOR JAMES C. BRADY

AUSTRALIA

LBC Information Services
Sydney

CANADA AND THE USA

Carswell

NEW ZEALAND

Brooker's
Wellington

SINGAPORE AND MALAYSIA

Thomson Information (S.E. Asia)
Singapore

LIBER MEMORIALIS
PROFESSOR JAMES C. BRADY

edited by

OONAGH BREEN
JAMES CASEY
ANTHONY KERR

DUBLIN
ROUND HALL SWEET & MAXWELL
2001

Published in 2001 by
Round Hall Ltd
43 Fitzwilliam Place
Dublin 2

Typeset by
Gough Typesetting Services
Dublin

Printed by
MPG Books, Cornwall

ISBN 1-85800-215-X

A catalogue record for this book
is available from the British Library.

TABLE OF CONTENTS

Preface ix

Tabula Amicorum xi

List of Contributors xiii

Bibliography – Professor James C. Brady xv

Table of Cases xvii

Table of Legislation xxxix

Address at the Funeral Mass for Jim Brady on June 19, 1998
  JOHN J. (SEÁN) BALLANCE 1

**Anti-Seizure Statutes in Art Law: The Influence of "La Danse" on
  French Law**
  LEILA ANGLADE 3

**Grating Expectations? The Protection of Legitimate Expectations in
  European Community Law and in Autochthonous Irish Law**
  GAVIN BARRETT 17

**Children These Days – Section 117 of the Succession Act 1965 and
  the Moral Obligations of Parenthood**
  OONAGH BREEN 72

Unbundling Constructive Trusteeship
  JOHN BRESLIN 94

Part Performance Lives!
  JOHN F. BUCKLEY 115

**Assignment of Debts and the Rule in *Dearle v. Hall*: The Journey
  from Equity to Law – and Back Again**
  DERMOT CAHILL 121

Injunctions and Freedom of Expression
JAMES CASEY 139

Judicial Discretion and the Planning Injunction
TOM COONEY 148

**Is There Still a Use for Trusts in Tax/Wealth Preservation
Planning?**
ANNE CORRIGAN 172

Regulating the Anti-Dismissal Injunction
KEVIN COSTELLO 188

**Succession Rights under the European Convention on
Human Rights**
SUZANNE EGAN 203

**"A False, Mawkish and Mongrel Humanity"? The Early History
of Employers' Liability in Ireland**
D.S. GREER 227

"What's in a Name?" – Taxonomy and the Law
RONAN KEANE 254

Recent Developments in the Law on the Limitation of Actions
ANTHONY KERR 261

Quia Emptores in Ireland
ANDREW LYALL 275

Prayers Unanswered: How Contract Law Views Religion
PAUL ANTHONY McDERMOTT 295

Extramural Pursuits of the Eighteenth-Century Bench
W.N. OSBOROUGH 317

The Eighteenth-Century Origins of the Irish Doctrine of Graft
ALBERT POWER 326

**Statute of Limitations (Amendment) Act 2000 and Actions for
Child Sexual Abuse**
PAUL WARD 344

The Reform of Irish Land Law
J.C.W. WYLIE 371

Appendix I   The James C. Brady Memorial Trust 383

Appendix II Memorial Trust Fund Contributors 384

Subject Heading Index 387

PREFACE

James C. Brady – Jim to family, friends and colleagues – taught Property and Equity in the Faculty of Law at University College Dublin for 30 years. From 1978 until his untimely death in June 1998 he held the Chair of Equity and the Law of Property. The affection and respect successive generations of students felt for him were legendary, a tribute to both his scholarship and his skill in conveying it. Nor could anyone have failed to admire the courage with which he faced (or perhaps faced down) the multiple sclerosis which afflicted him for the last 20 years of his life. The books and articles which he produced during that period, despite increasing physical difficulties, are eloquent testimony to that courage.

The Faculty of Law invited the three undersigned to find ways to commemorate Jim Brady's distinguished service. We opted for two separate projects, the first being a trust fund to provide *inter alia* an annual Equity prize in Jim's memory (details may be found in Appendix I). The success of our appeal for funds is abundant evidence of the affection and respect mentioned above. We also conceived the idea of this volume of essays, contributed by friends and colleagues from within and without the UCD Law Faculty. We hope, and believe, that this *Liber Memorialis* will furnish a permanent literary commemoration of Jim Brady's academic career and achievements.

We are most grateful to the contributors for all their efforts, particularly for their promptness in meeting deadlines. Ms Caoilfhionn Gallagher BCL deserves our thanks for her valuable assistance in preparing the text for publication. And we are grateful to the publishers for their courtesy, efficiency and patience.

Oonagh Breen
James Casey
Anthony Kerr

St. Patrick's Day, 2001

TABULA AMICORUM

Jennefer Aston
Kevin Boyle
John J. and Ann Breen
His Honour Judge John F. Buckley
The Hon. Mr. Justice Declan Budd
The Hon. Miss Justice Mella Carroll
Robert Clark
Anne Corrigan
Art Cosgrove
Brian Cosgrove
Hilary Delany
Alan Dowling
Patrick J.M. Durcan
Eugene P. Fanning
William D. Finlay
The Hon. Mr. Justice Joseph Finnegan
Paul Gallagher
Noel Gaughran
C.A. Gearty
The Hon. Mr. Justice Hugh Geoghegan
John T. Gibbons
Dermot Gleeson
Marie A. Griffin
Patrick Groarke
Eamonn G. Hall
David Hayton

The Hon. Mr. Justice Daniel Herbert
Gerard Hogan
G. Brian Hutchinson
Owen A. MacCarthy
Felix McEnroy
Imelda Maher
Alan Mitchell
Gerry Murphy
The Hon. Mr. Justice Aindrias Ó Caoimh
Patrick O'Connor (Mayo)
Donal O'Donoghue
T. John O'Dowd
James O'Reilly
Andrew O'Rorke
John S. O'Sullivan
John J. Power
Patrick G. Quinn
Mary Redmond
Laurence K. Shields
Vincent Shields
The Hon. Mr. Justice T.C. Smyth
Noel Joseph Travers
Patrick Anthony Wallace
G.F. Whyte
The Law Society of Ireland

LIST OF CONTRIBUTORS

Leila Anglade is a lecturer in the Law of Arbitration and International Commercial Transactions at University College Dublin.

John J. (Seán) Ballance OBE, an architect and engineer, is the founder and principal of a firm of project managers.

Gavin Barrett is a lecturer in European Law at University College Dublin.

Oonagh Breen is a lecturer in Equity and Land Law at University College Dublin.

John Breslin is a statutory lecturer in Banking and Financial Services Law at University College Dublin.

John Buckley is a judge of the Circuit Court and a member of the Law Reform Commission's Working Group on Land Law and Conveyancing Law.

Dermot Cahill is a lecturer in European Law and Corporate Finance Law at University College Dublin.

James Casey is professor of law at University College Dublin.

Tom Cooney is a lecturer in Planning and Development and Medical Law at University College Dublin.

Anne Corrigan is a lawyer in Arthur Cox Solicitors and a lecturer in Revenue Law at University College Dublin.

Kevin Costello is a lecturer in Employment and Administrative Law at University College Dublin.

Suzanne Egan is a lecturer in Human Rights Law at University College Dublin.

Desmond Greer is professor of Common Law at Queen's University, Belfast.

Ronan Keane is the Chief Justice of Ireland and former President of the Law Reform Commission.

Anthony Kerr is a statutory lecturer in Labour Law at University College Dublin.

Andrew Lyall is a statutory lecturer in Land Law and Legal Anthropology at University College Dublin.

Paul McDermott is a lecturer in Criminal Law and Tort at University College Dublin.

Nial Osborough is professor of Jurisprudence and Legal History at University College Dublin.

Albert Power is director of education and training at The Institute of Chartered Accountants in Ireland.

Paul Ward is a lecturer in Family Law and Tort at University College Dublin.

John Wylie is professor of law at Cardiff University and a Consultant
    with A & L Goodbody, Solicitors.

BIBLIOGRAPHY – PROFESSOR JAMES C. BRADY 1940–1998

BOOKS

Religion and the Law of Charities in Ireland (Belfast, 1975).
Limitation of Actions in the Republic of Ireland with Anthony Kerr (1st ed., Dublin 1984; 2nd ed., Dublin, 1994).
Succession Law in Ireland (1st ed., Dublin, 1989; 2nd ed., Dublin, 1995).

CHAPTERS IN BOOKS

"Equity without the Equity Lawyers" in *Essays in Honour of Ben Beinart*: Volume I (Juta & Co.: South Africa, 1978) [also published in (1977) *Acta Juridica* 125].
Chapter XXIV: "Legal Developments 1801-79" pp. 451–482 in W E Vaughan (ed.), *New History of Ireland: Volume V – Ireland Under the Union* (Oxford, 1989).
"Aspiring Students, Retiring Professors and the Doctrine of Legitimate Expectation" in *Essays in Honour of Geoffrey Hand* (Dublin, 1996) [also published in (1996) XXXI *Irish Jurist* (ns) 133 –144].

PERIODICALS

"The Demise of the Discretionary Trust" (1967) 18 *N.I.L.Q.* 343.
"Belfast Association for Employment of Industrious Blind v. Commissioner of Valuation for Northern Ireland" (1968) 19 *N.I.L.Q.* 312.
"Some problems touching the nature of bequests for masses in Northern Ireland." (1968) 19 *N.I.L.Q.* 358.
"Charitable Purposes and Rating Exemption in Ireland" (1968) 3 *Irish Jurist* 215.
"An English and Irish View of Proprietary Estoppel" (1970) 5 *Irish Jurist* 47.
"A Case of Promissory Estoppel in Ireland" (1970) 5 *Irish Jurist* 296.
"Northern Ireland Commissioner of Valuation v. Fermanagh Protestant Board of Education" (1970) 21 *N.I.L.Q.* 193.
"English Law and Irish Land in the Nineteenth Century" (1972) 23 *N.I.L.Q.* 24.

"Legal Certainty: The Durable Myth" (1973) 8 *Irish Jurist* 18.

"The House of Lords, Charities and Rating Relief in Northern Ireland" (1973) 24 *N.I.L.Q.* 106.

"The Rates (Northern Ireland) Order 1972, Article 41" (1973) 24 *N.I.L.Q.* 440.

"Public Benefit and Religious Trusts: Fact or Fiction" (1974) 25 *N.I.L.Q.* 174.

"The Law of Charity and Judicial Responsiveness to Changing Social Need" (1976) 27 *N.I.L.Q.* 198.

"Equity without the Equity Lawyers" (1977) *Acta Juridica* 125.

"English Law in the Republic of Ireland" (1978) 6 *Univ. Tas. L.R.* 60.

"The 'Favour Testament' in Irish Law" (1980) XV *Irish Jurist* 1.

"A recent case of dependent relative revocation" (1981) 75 *G.I.L.S.I.* 5.

"Adverse Possession in Particular Circumstances" (1982) 4 *D.U.L.J.* 79.

"Trusts, Law Reform and the Emancipation of Women" (1984) 6 *D.U.L.J.* 1.

"Judicial Pragmatism and the Search for Justice Inter Partes" (1986) XXI *Irish Jurist* 47.

"A Limitations Conundrum" (1986) 80 *G.I.L.S.I.* 21.

"Adverse Possession and The *Animus Possidendi*" (1986) 80 *G.I.L.S.I.* 141.

"Periodic Tenancies and the Running of Time" (1986) 80 *G.I.L.S.I.* 253.

"Constructive Trusts, Constitutional Rhetoric and the Non-Owning Spouse" (1991) 42 *N.I.L.Q.* 1.

"A Rare Case of Cy Près" (1994) 16 *D.U.L.J. (ns)* 153.

"Solicitors' Duty of Care in Drafting Wills" (1995) 46 *N.I.L.Q.* 434.

"Aspiring Students, Retiring Professors and the Doctrine of Legitimate Expectation" (1996) XXXI *Ir. Jurist (ns)* 133.

TABLE OF CASES

IRELAND

Abrahamson v. Law Society of Ireland [1996] 1 I.R. 403; [1996]
  2 I.L.R.M. 481 .... 50, 51, 52, 67, 70
Aga Khan v. Firestone and Firestone [1982] I.L.R.M. 31 296
Allied Irish Banks v. Fagan, unreported, High Court, November 10, 1995 296
Association of General Practitioners Ltd. v. Minister for Health [1995]
  1 I.R. 382 53
Attorney General v. Hamilton [1993] 2 I.R. 250 142
Attorney General v. Jameson [1904] 2 I.R. 644 (K.B.); [1905] 2 I.R. 218
  (Ir. C.A.) 378
Attorney General v. Lee, unreported, Supreme Court, October 23, 2000 198
Attorney General v. Southern Industrial Trust Ltd. (1957) 94 I.L.T.R. 161 268
Attorney General for England and Wales v. Brandon Book Publishers Ltd.
  [1986] I.R. 597 .... 140–142, 144
Attorney General (McGarry) v. Sligo County Council [1991] 1 I.R. 21 .... 160, 162
Attorney General (S.P.U.C. (Ireland) Ltd.) v. Open Door Counselling Ltd.
  [1988] I.R. 593 142
Attorney General (S.P.U.C. (Ireland) Ltd.) v. Open Door
  Counselling Ltd. [1994] 2 I.R. 338 142
Avenue Properties Ltd. v. Farrell Homes Ltd. [1982]
  I.L.R.M. 21 .... 149, 150, 152, 153, 157

Behan v. Bank of Ireland [1998] 2 I.L.R.M. 507 366
Bell v. G.N. Railway Co. (1890) L.R. (Ir.) 428 355
Bignold v. James Haigh (1870) B.P.P. xv, 449 239
Boland v. Phoenix Shannon plc [1997] E.L.R. 113 190
Bolger v. O'Brien [1999] 2 I.L.R.M. 372 .... 270, 352, 354
Boylan v. Dublin Corporation [1949] I.R. 60 256
Boyle v. Lee & Goyns [1992] 1 I.R. 555 .... 117, 119
Boyle v. Lysaght [1787] 1 Ridg. P.C. 384 289
Brady v. Fitzgerald (1848) 12 Ir. Eq. R. 273 293
Brady's Estate, Re [1920] 1 I.R. 710 331
Bray v. Bray, unreported, High Court, Hamilton J., February 25. 1977 78
Brennan v. Western Health Board, unreported, High Court,
  Macken J., May 18, 1999 272
Browne v. Sweeney and Mc Carthy, unreported, High Court, Lavan J.,
  July 5, 1996; [1998] 2 I.L.R.M. 141 (S.C.) 84, 85, 86, 92

Buckley v. Holland Clyde Ltd., unreported, High Court,
  Kenny J., 1969 149
Bus Éireann v. SIPTU *The Irish Times*, June 17, 1993 197
Byrne v. Ireland [1972] I.R. 241 169
Byrne v. Southern and Western Railway Company, unreported, Court of Appeal,
  February 1884 355

C(IA) dec'd, In the Estate of; C. and F. v. W.C. and T.C. [1989]
  I.L.R.M. 815 (S.C.) 77, 91
Campbell v. Brennan (1889) 23 I.L.T.R. 84 249
Campus Oil Ltd. v. Minister for Energy (No. 2) [1983] I.R. 88 .... 145, 195–201
Cannon v. Minister for the Marine [1991] 1 I.R. 82; [1991]
  I.L.R.M. 261 .... 49, 50, 55
Carbery Milk Products Ltd. v. Minister for Agriculture and others
  (1988–1993) 4 I.T.R. 492 (judgment of April 23, 1993) 18, 50
Carlos v. Congested Districts Board [1908] 2 I.R. 91 246
Carroll Shipping Ltd. v. Matthews Mulcahy & Sutherland Ltd., unreported,
  High Court, McGuinness J., December 18, 1996 271
Casey v. Irish Intercontinental Bank [1979] I.R. 364 .... 116, 117
Cassidy v. Shannon Castle Banquets and Heritage Centre, unreported,
  High Court, July 30, 1999 196
Cavan County Council v. Eircell Ltd., unreported, High Court, Geoghegan J.,
  March 10, 1999 .... 149, 152
Celtic Ceramics Ltd. v. Industrial Development Authority [1993]
  I.L.R.M. 248 272
Coffey v. Hebron Homes Ltd., unreported, High Court, O'Hanlon J.,
  July 27, 1984 150
Collins v. Dublin Bus, unreported, Supreme Court, October 22, 1999 273
Collins, Mary Francis, dec'd, In the Estate of; Joseph O'Connell and Alma
  O'Connell v. Governor and Company of the Bank of Ireland Trustee
  Co. Ltd. [1998] I.L.R.M. 203, 465
Conlan v. Carlow County Council [1912] 2 I.R. 535 127
Connolly v. RTÉ [1991] 2 I.R. 446 .... 144, 145
Conroy v. Garda Commissioner [1989] I.R. 140 .... 53, 57
Conway v. Belfast & Northern Counties Railway Co. (1875)
  I.R. 9 C.L. 498 246
Cork Corporation v. O'Connell [1982] I.L.R.M. 505 .... 60, 148, 151
Cosgrave v. Legal Aid Board [1991] 2 I.R. 43 59
Courtney v. Radio 2000 Ltd. [1997] E.L.R. 199 .... 189, 190
Coyne, Lessee of, v. Smith (1826) Batty 90 293
Cramp v. Robert Rowan & Co 1874 B.P.P. xiii, 146 239
Cremins v. Minister for Defence, unreported, High Court, O'Donovan J.,
  February 17, 1999 .... 350, 351
Cullen v. Toibín [1984] I.L.R.M. 577 142
Curley v. Galway Corporation, unreported, High Court, Kelly J.,
  December 14, 1998 158
Curran v. Cadbury (Ireland) Ltd [2000] 2 I.L.R.M. 343 355

D(J) v. D(D) [1998] 1 Fam. L.J. 17 184–186
Daly v. Minister of the Marine, unreported, High Court, O'Sullivan J.,
    February 25, 1999 .... 50, 59
Darkin v. Brookfield & Doagh Spinning Co. 1859 (Sess. 1) B.P.P. xii, 221 239
Darkin v. Foster Connor (1857) (Sess. 2) B.P.P. xvi, 259 239
Darkin v. Francis Ritchie & Sons 1857 (Sess. 1) B.P.P. iii, 617 239
Darkin v. Francis Ritchie & Sons 1857 B.P.P. xvi, 260 239
Darkin v. Herdman's of Sion Mills Reports of the Inspectors of Factories for
    the half year ending 31st October 1854; 1854 B.P.P. xv, 275 .... 235, 239, 241
Darkin v. James Kennedy & Son 1856 B.P.P. xviii, 362 239
Darkin v. James Kennedy & Son 1857-1858 B.P.P. xviv, 751 239
de B. (J.H.) dec'd, In the Estate of [1991] 2 I.R. 105 92
Delacherois v. Delacherois (1859) 8 Ir. C.L.R. 1, Irish Ex. Ch., on appeal at
    (1864) 11 H.L.C. 62 .... 276, 281
Dempsey v. Ward [1899] 1 I.R. 463 326
Dillon v. Irish Cement, unreported, Supreme Court, November 26, 1986 151
Dolan v. Cooke, unreported, High Court, Morris J., January 20, 2000 151
Doran v. Thompson [1978] I.R. 223 369
Dowd v. Kerry County Council [1970] I.R. 97 272
Doyle v. Grangeford Precast Concrete Ltd. [1998] E.L.R. 261 .... 189, 190
Draycar Ltd v. Whelan [1993] E.L.R. 119 197
Drohan v. Drohan [1981] I.L.R.M. 473 .... 262, 263
Dublin Corporation v. Garland [1982] I.L.R.M. 104 151
Dublin Corporation v. Kevans, unreported, High Court, Finlay P.,
    July 14, 1980 .... 151, 154, 155, 161
Dublin Corporation v. Lowe & Signings Holdings Ltd., unreported,
    High Court, Morris J., February 4, 2000 151
Dublin Corporation v. Maiden Posters Sites [1983] I.L.R.M. 48 159
Dublin Corporation v. McGowan [1993] 1 I.R. 405 151
Dublin Corporation v. Mulligan, unreported, High Court, Finlay P.,
    May 6, 1987 .... 153, 154, 159, 160, 165, 166, 170
Dublin Corporation v. Regan Advertising Ltd. [1986] I.R. 171 (H.C.);
    [1989] I.R. 61 (S.C.) 148
Dublin Corporation v. Sullivan, unreported, High Court, Finlay P.,
    December 21, 1984 151
Dublin County Council v. Crampton Builders Ltd., unreported, High Court,
    Finlay P., March 10, 1980 149
Dublin County Council v. Elton Homes [1984] I.L.R.M. 297 150
Dublin County Council v. Kirby [1985] I.L.R.M. 325 151
Dublin County Council v. Macken, unreported, High Court, O'Hanlon J.,
    May 13, 1994 150
Dublin County Council v. Matra Investments Ltd. (1980) 114 I.L.T.R. 306 153
Dublin County Council v. O'Riordan [1985] I.R. 159; [1986]
    I.L.R.M. 104 .... 150, 151
Dublin County Council v. Sellwood Quarries Ltd. [1982] I.L.R.M. 23 156
Dublin Port and Docks Board v. Britannia Dredging [1968] I.R. 136 200
Duff v. Minister for Agriculture (No. 2) [1997] 2 I.R. 22 (S.C.) 32, 50

Duff v. Minister for Agriculture (No. 2), unreported, High Court, Laffoy J.,
    March 25, 1999 32
Duggan v. An Taoiseach [1989] I.L.R.M. 710 .... 51, 52, 54, 66
Dun Laoghaire Corporation v. Parkhill Developments [1989] I.R. 447;
    [1989] I.L.R.M. 235 150
Dunne v. Electricity Supply Board, unreported, High Court, Laffoy J.,
    October 19, 1999 272

Edenfell Holdings, Re [1999] 1 I.R. 458 94
Educational Company of Ireland Ltd v. Fitzpatrick [1961] I.R. 323 201
Egan v. Minister for Defence, unreported, High Court, Barr J.,
    November 28, 1998 .... 45, 54, 56
Emmens v. Elderton (1853) 4 H.L.C. 624; 10 E.R. 106 188
Eogan v. University College Dublin [1996] 2 I.L.R.M. 702 .... 56, 63
Esso Petroleum Co. Ltd v. Fogarty [1965] I.R. 531 .... 200, 202
Eyre v. Dolphin (1813) 2 Ball & Beatty 290 326

F.M. v. T.A.M. (1972) 106 I.L.T.R. 82 .... 77, 78, 79
Fakih v. Minister for Justice [1993] 2 I.R. 406 .... 19, 52, 53, 57, 59, 63, 68
Fennelly v. Assicurazioni S.P.A. & General Underwriting Agreements Ireland Ltd.
    (ex tempore) High Court, Costello J., March 12, 1985
    (see (1985) 3 I.L.T. (n.s.) 73) 188–190, 193, 194, 196
Fitzpatrick v. O'Connor, unreported, High Court, Costello J.,
    March 11, 1988 149
Flynn v. Great Northern Railway (1955) 89 I.L.T.R. 46 192
Foley v. Irish Land Commission [1952] I.R. 118 268
Foley v. Musgrave Cash and Carry Ltd., unreported, Supreme Court,
    December 20, 1995 258
Foster v. Hornsby (1853) 2 Ir. Ch. Rep. 426 200
Frederick Inns Ltd., Re [1994] 1 I.L.R.M. 387 111
Fusco v. Aprile, unreported, High Court, Morris J., June 6, 1997. 156

Gabbett v. Lawder (1883) 11 L.R. Ir. 295 326
Gallagher v. Minister for Defence [1998] 4 I.R. 457 .... 270, 350, 351
Garda Representative Association v. Ireland [1989] I.L.R.M. 1 59
Gee v. The Irish Times, *The Irish Times*, June 28, 2000 .... 189, 190
Ghneim v. Minister for Justice, *The Irish Times*, September 2, 1989,
    Hamilton P. 39, 56
Gilheaney v. Revenue Commissioners [1998] I.R. 150 .... 54, 65
Gleeson v. Feehan (No. 1) [1993] 2 I.R. 113 263
Gleeson v. Feehan (No. 2) [1997] 1 I.L.R.M. 522 .... 263, 265
Glencar Exploration v. Mayo County Council, unreported, High Court,
    Kelly J., August 20, 1998 51
Glynn v. Rotunda Hospital, unreported, High Court, O'Sullivan J.,
    April 6, 2000 272
Goodman v. Pocock (1850) 15 Q.B. 576; 117 E.R. 577 188
Goodwin v. Giesler (1794) Irish Term Reports 371 325

Gordon v. Phelan (1881) 15 I.L.T.R. 70 275

H. v. M. [1983] I.L.R.M. 519 265
H.(J.) dec'd, Re the goods of [1984] I.R. 599 .... 80, 92
H.(J.) v. A.I.B. [1978] I.L.R.M. 203 81
Harte v. Kelly [1997] E.L.R. 125 .... 189, 190
Heffernan v. O'Herlihy, unreported, High Court, Kinlen J.,
    April 3, 1998 366
Hegarty v. O'Loughran [1990] 1 I.R. 148 .... 267, 349, 364, 365
Hegarty v. P.J. Hegarty and Sons, *The Irish Times*, January 21, 1998 194
Hempenstall v. Minister for the Environment [1993] I.L.R.M. 318 64
Hildige v. O'Farrell (1880) 6 L.R. Ir. 493 245
Hogan v. Fitzgerald (1825) 1 Hud. & Br. 77 292
Hogan v. Jones [1994] 1 I.L.R.M. 512 .... 271, 272
Hogg v. Keane [1956] I.R. 155 354
House of Spring Gardens Ltd. v. Point Blank Ltd. [1986] I.R. 611 140
Howard v. The Commissioners of Public Works [1994] 1 I.R. 101 162
Howlin v. Power, unreported, High Court, McWilliam J., May 5, 1978 119
Hughes v. Moy Contractors Ltd. (No. 1)., unreported, High Court, Carroll J.,
    July 29, 1999 272
Hughes v. Moy Contractors Ltd. (No. 2), unreported, High Court, Morris P.,
    January 25, 2000 272

International (Factors) Ireland Ltd. v. Midland International Ltd., unreported,
    High Court, Lynch J., December 9, 1993 .... 122, 126
Irish Equine Foundation Ltd. v. Robinson [1999] 2 I.L.R.M. 289 267
Irish Shell v. Elm Motors [1984] I.L.R.M. 198

Jones v. Kearney (1841) 4 Ir. Eq. 74 326

Keating v. Weir & Son, *The Irish Times*, February 13, 1999 190
Kelly v. Cullen, unreported, Supreme Court, July 27, 1998 274
Kelly v. Hennessy [1995] 3 I.R. 253 355
Kelly v. Park Hall School [1979] I.R. 340 .... 116, 117
Kennedy v. Baxendale (1871) I.R. 5 C.L. 74 234
Kennedy v. Ireland [1987] I.R. 587 143
Kennedy v. Kennedy, unreported, High Court, January 12, 1984 296
Kenny v. Kelly [1988] I.R. 457 .... 53, 66
Kerwick v. Minister for Defence, unreported, High Court, O'Donovan J.,
    March 19, 1999 .... 350, 351
Kieran v. McCann [1920] 1 I.R. 99 342
Kirwan v. Cullen (1854) 2 Ir. Ch. Rep. 322 311

Lambert v. Lewis, unreported, High Court, Gannon J., November 24, 1982 151
Latchford v. Minister for Industry and Commerce [1950] I.R. 33 67
Leech v. Reilly, unreported, High Court, O'Hanlon J., April 26, 1983 158
Lonergan v. Salter Townshend [2000] E.L.R. 15 .... 189, 190, 195

Loubrough v. James Panton & Co. Ltd. [1965] I.R. 272 200
Lynch v. Fitzgerald [1938] I.R. 382 142

M. v. Drury [1994] 2 I.R. 8 .... 143, 144
McAuley v. Clarendon (1858) 8 Ir. Ch. Rep. 121 326
McCann v. Jurys Hotel Group, *The Irish Times*, June April 9, 1999 189
MacCarthy v. Murphy, unreported, High Court, McCracken J.,
    February 10, 1998 354
McCracken v. Dargan (1856) 1 I.J. (ns) 404 .... 240, 243
McCracken v. Dargan and Haughton Reports of the Inspectors of Factories
    for the half year ending 31st October 1856; 1857 (Sess. 1)
    B.P.P. iii, 559 .... 243, 244
McD. v. N. [1999] 4 I.R. 301 .... 81, 89–92,
McDonnell v. Ireland [1998] 1 I.R. 134 369
M'Evoy v. Waterford Steamship Co. (No. 2) (1886) 18 L.R. Ir. 159 249
M'Evoy v. Waterford Steamship Co. (No. 1) (1885) L.R. Ir. 291 250
McGee v. Attorney General [1974] I.R. 284 143
McGregor, Robert, & Sons (Ireland) Ltd. v. The Mining Board, unreported,
    High Court, Carroll J., October 5, 1998 272
Mackey v. Scottish Widows Fund Assurance Society (1876) I.R. 10 Eq. 114 201
McMullen v. Clancy, unreported, High Court, McGuinness J.,
    September 3, 1999 368
MacNamara v. Electricity Supply Board [1975] I.R. 1 .... 257, 258
Mahon v. Butler [1998] 1 I.L.R.M. 284 .... 148, 152
Martin v. Kearney (1902) 36 I.L.T.R. 117 .... 265, 266
Meath County Council v. Thornton & Thornton Waste Disposals Ltd.
    unreported, High Court, O'Hanlon J., January 14, 1984 .... 150, 162
Metropolitan Properties Ltd. v. O'Brien [1995] 1 I.R. 467 380
Monaghan County Council v. Brogan [1987] I.R. 333 151
Moore v. Attorney General [1927] I.R. 569 .... 200, 201
Morris v. Garvey [1983] I.R. 319 .... 150, 153
Mulally v. Bus Éireann [1992] 2 I.L.R.M. 722 355
Mulhall v. Haren [1981] I.R. 364 116
Murphy v. Attorney General [1982] I.R. 241 215
Murphy v. Ireland [1996] 2 I.L.R.M. 461 369

National Irish Bank Ltd. v. Radio Telefís Éireann [1998] 2 I.R. 465 140
Nesbit v. Tredennick (1808) 1 Ball & Beatty 29 326
Noonan v. Dublin Distillery Co. (1893) 32 L.R. Ir. 399 .... 248, 250
Norris v. Attorney General [1984] I.R. 36 143
Norton v. Kearon (1871) I.R. 6 C.L. 126 245

O'B v. S [1984] I.R. 316 213
O'Brien v. Egan (1880) 5 L.R. Ir. 633 326
O'Brien v. Keogh [1972] I.R. 144 268
O'Brien v. Manufacturing Engineering Co. Ltd. [1973] I.R. 334;
    108 I.L.T.R. 105 268

O'Connor & Spollen Concrete Group Ltd. v. Frank Harrington Ltd.
  unreported, High Court, Barr J., April 26, 1983 .... 155, 156, 165, 166
O Domhnaill v. Merrick [1984] I.R. 151 .... 268, 272, 363, 364, 365
O'Leary v. Minister for Finance [1998] 2 I.L.R.M. 321 .... 65, 66
O'Malley v. Aravon School, unreported, High Court,
  August 13, 1997 189

Patterson v. Murphy [1978] I.L.R.M. 85 148
Pesca Valentia Ltd. v. Minister for Fisheries [1990] 2 I.R. 205 .... 52, 58, 64
Phelan v. BIC (Ireland) Ltd. [1997] E.L.R. 208 .... 190, 196
Pluck v. Digges (1828) 2 Hud. & Br. 1, (1832) 5 Bli. N.S. 31, 5 E.R. 219
  (Exchequer Chamber, Ir.), 2 Dow. & Cl. 180, 6 E.R. 695
  (British House of Lords) 275, 291–294
Polycell Products Ltd. v. O'Connell [1959] Ir. Jur. Rep. 34 200
Porter v. French (1847) 9 Ir. C.L.R. 519 292
Potts v. Plunkett (1859) 9 I.C.L.R. 290 232
Primor plc v. Stokes Kennedy Crowley [1996] 2 I.R. 459 .... 272, 273
Purtill v. Athlone UDC [1968] I.R. 205 .... 257, 258

Quinton v. Frith (1868) Ir. Eq. 396 339

Rainsford v. Limerick Corporation, unreported, High Court, Finlay P.,
  July 31, 1979 272
Reidy v. National Maternity Hospital, unreported, High Court, Barr J.,
  July 31, 1997 271
Reynolds v. Malocco [1999] 2 I.R. 203 .... 146, 147
Richardson v. Murphy [1899] 1 I.R. 248 200
Roberts v. Mayne (1859) 8 Ir. Ch. R. 523 292
Robinson v. Chariot Inns Ltd. [1986] I.L.R.M. 21 150
Rogers v. Smith, unreported, Supreme Court, July 16, 1970 302
Rohan v. Bord na Mona [1990] 2 I.R. 425 359
Rooney v. Connolly [1987] I.L.R.M. 258 .... 258, 259
Rooney v. Cork Corporation (1881) 7 Ir. L.R. 191 200
Rowe v. Law [1978] I.R. 55 203
Ryan v. Connolly, unreported, High Court, February 29, 2000 369

S.P.U.C. (Ireland) Ltd. v. Coogan [1989] I.R. 734 142
S.P.U.C. (Ireland) Ltd. v. Grogan [1989] I.R. 753 142
S.P.U.C. (Ireland) Ltd. v. Grogan (No. 4) [1994] 1 I.R. 46 142
S.P.U.C. (Ireland) Ltd. v. Grogan (No. 5) [1998] 4 I.R. 343 142
Shaughnessy v. Boston Scientific, *The Irish Times*, January 19, 1999 189
Shortt v. Data Packaging Ltd. [1994] E.L.R. 251 190
Silver Tassie Co. Ltd. v. Beirne (1956) 90 I.L.T.R. 90 199
Sinclair v. Gogarty [1937] I.R. 377 .... 145, 146, 200
Smith v. Beirne *The Irish Times*, January 30, 1953; (1954) 88 I.L.T.R, 24 201
Smith v. Ireland [1983] I.L.R.M. 380 18
Southern Mineral Oil Ltd., unreported, Supreme Court, July 22, 1997 273

Stafford v. Roadstone Ltd. [1980] I.L.R.M. 1 .... 152, 157
State (Byrne) v. Frawley [1978] I.R. 326 215
State (Haverty) v. An Bord Pleanála [1988] I.L.R.M. 545 149
Staunton v. St. Lawrence's Hospital, unreported, High Court,
     February 21, 1986 67
Steen v. Bridget Jordan (1857) (Sess. 1) B.P.P. iii, 620 239
Steen v. Nicholas Kenny (1859) (Sess. 2) B.P.P. xiv, 450 239
Superwood Holdings plc v. Scully, unreported, Supreme Court,
     November 4, 1998 272

Tara Prospecting Ltd. v. Minister for Energy [1993]
     I.L.R.M. 771 .... 49, 51, 62, 63, 64
Tassan Din v. Banco Ambrosiano [1991] 1 I.R. 569 103
Toal v. Duignan (No. 1) [1991] I.L.R.M. 135 .... 363, 364
Toal v. Duignan (No. 2) [1991] I.L.R.M. 140 .... 363, 364
Tobin v. Redmond (1861) 11 Ir. Ch. R. 445 292
Truck and Machinery Sales Ltd. v. General Accident Fire and Life Assurance
     Corporation plc, unreported, High Court, Geoghegan J.,
     November 12, 1999 272
Tuohy v. Courtney [1994] 3 I.R. 1 .... 267, 268, 269
Turner v. Robinson (1860) Ir. Ch. Rep. 117 200

Vaughan v. Cork & Youghal Rly. Co. (1860) 12 I.C.L.R. 297 .... 231, 232
Verit Hotel and Leisure (Ireland) Ltd, In re, unreported, High Court,
     O'Donovan J., July 27, 2000 272
Verschoyle v. Perkins (1847) 12 Ir. Eq. R. 72 .... 279, 288
Vogel v. Cheeverstown House [1998] 2 I.R. 496 199

Walker v. Williamson (1794) Ir. T. Rep. 271 292
Walsh, Lessee of, v. Feely (1835) Jones 413 293
Webb v. Ireland [1988] I.R. 353; [1988] I.L.R.M. 565 .... 17, 18, 50, 51, 52, 56, 66
Weeland v. RTÉ [1987] I.R. 662 145
Whearty v. Agriculture Credit Corporation Ltd., unreported, High Court,
     McCracken J., October 31, 1997 271
White v. McInerney Construction Ltd. [1995] 1 I.L.R.M. 373 152
Whitely v. Minister for Defence [1998] 4 I.R. 442 .... 270, 271, 350, 351, 352, 356
Whyte v. Meade (1840) Ir. Eq. R. 420 .... 306, 307
Wiley v. Revenue Commissioners [1989] I.R. 350 (H.C.) 54, 56, 66
Wiley v. Revenue Commissioners [1993] I.L.R.M. 482 (S.C.) 18, 58

UNITED KINGDOM

Abney v. Miller (1743) 2 Atk. 593 .... 329, 330, 342
Acheson v. Fair (1843) 2 Dr. & War. 512 331
Acton's (Sir Robert) Case (1570) 3 Dyer 288b, 72 ER 647 281
Adderley v. Clavering (1789) 2 Cox C.C. 192 333

Addis v. Clement (1728) 2 P. Wms. 456 .... 328, 329
Agip (Africa) Ltd. v. Jackson [1990] Ch. 265; [1991]
    Ch. 547 (C.A.) 97, 98, 101, 107
Allcard v. Skinner (1887) 36 Ch. D. 145 .... 307, 308, 309
Allen v. New Gas Co. (1876) 1 Ex. D. 251 246
American Cyanimid v. Ethicon [1975] 1 A.C. 396 .... 195, 198, 200
Archer v. Moss [1971] 1 All E.R. 747 367
Atkinson v. Newcastle and Gateshead Waterworks Co. (1877) 2 Ex. D. 441 245
Attorney General of Hong Kong v. Ng Yuen Shiu [1983]
    2 A.C. 629 .... 53, 54, 56, 59, 67
Attorney General of Hong Kong v. Reid [1994] 1 A.C. 324 94
Attorney General v. Blake [2000] 3 W.L.R. 625 139
Attorney General v. Guardian Newspapers Ltd. (No. 2) [1990] 1 A.C. 109 140
Attorney General v. Guardian Newspapers Ltd. [1987] 1 W.L.R. 1248 140

Baden v. Sociètè Genéralé pour Favouriser le Développement et de l'industrie en
    France S.A. [1992] 4 All E.R. 161 .... 96–99, 104–107, 113
Bank of America v. Arnell [1999] Lloyd's Law Rep. Banking 399 99
Bankgesellschaft Berlin AG v. Makis, unreported, Queen's Bench Division,
    Cresswell J., January 22, 1999 104
Barclays Bank plc v. O'Brien [1994] 1 A.C. 180 109
Barnes v. Addy (1874) 9 Ch. App. 244 .... 95, 96, 98, 104
Bartonshill Coal Co. v. Reid (1858) 3 Macq. 266 245
BCCI v. Akindele [1999] B.C.C. 669 110
BCCI v. Akindele [2000] 4 All E.R. 221 (C.A.) 110–113
Belmont Finance Corporation v. Williams Furniture Ltd. (No. 2)
    [1980] 1 All E.R. 393 111
Birch v. Wright (1786) 1 T.R. 378, 99 E.R. 1148 291
Biss, Re: Biss v. Biss [1903] 2 Ch. 40 .... 341, 342
Blake v. Blake (1786) 1 Cox C.C. 266 335
Blenkinsop v. Ogden [1898] 1 Q.B. 783 .... 236, 237
Blewitt v. Millett (1774) 7 Brown P.C. 120 330
Bloomfield v. Eyre (1845) 8 Beav. 250 339
Bonnard v. Perryman [1891] 2 Ch. 269 146
Boscawen v. Bajwa [1995] 4 All E.R. 769 108
Bowen v. Hall (1881) 6 Q.B.D. 333 255
Brandt, William, sons of & Co v. Dunlop Rubber Company [1905]
    A.C. 454 129
Breen v. Amalgamated Engineering Union [1971] 2 Q.B. 175 .... 49, 68
Brinks Ltd. v. Abu Saleh, The Times, October 23, 1995 .... 100, 101
Butterfield v. Forrester (1809) 11 East 60, 103 E.R. 926 231

Campbell v. Walker (1800) 5 Ves. 677 342
Cann v. Cann ((1687) 1 Vernon 480 .... 334, 335
Caswell v. Worth (1856) 25 L.J.Q.B. 121 .... 240, 242
Cinnamond v. British Airports Authority [1980] 2 All E.R. 368 37
Civil Service Unions v. Minister for the Public Service [1985] A.C. 319 45

Clarke v. Holmes (1862) 7 H. & N. 937, 158 E.R. 751 232
Coe v. Platt (1851) 6 Exch. Rep. 752; (1852) 7 Exch. Rep. 460 and 293;
    155 E.R. 1030 .... 239, 245
Commission for the New Towns v. Cooper (Great Britain) Ltd.
    [1995] Ch. 259 116
Compaq Computer Ltd. v. Abercorn Group [1991] B.C.C. 484 ..... 122, 131, 133, 137
Cooper v. Cooper (1874) L.R. 7 H.L. 53 265
Cordwell v. Mackrill (1766) 2 Eden 344 .... 334, 335
Cotterrell v. Samuel Report of the Inspector of Factories for the quarter ending 30th
    September, 1840, 1841 B.P.P. x, 168–169 230
Couch v. Steel (1854) 3 El. & Bl. 402, 118 E.R. 1193 .... 240, 245
Council of Civil Service Unions v. Minister for Civil Service [1985]
    1 A.C. 374 .... 52, 54, 56, 68
County and District Properties v. Lyell [1991] 1 W.L.R. 683 273
Cowan de Groot Properties Ltd., v. Eagle Trust plc. [1992] 4 All E.R. 700 99
Credit Lyonnais Bank v. Burch [1997] 1 All E.R. 144 309
Crop v. Norton (1740) 2 Atk.74 329

Dalrymple v. Dalrymple (1811) 2 Hag. Con. 54; 161 E.R. 665 301
Dawson v. I.R.C. [1990] A.C. 1 172
Dearle v. Hall (1823) 3 Russ. 1; [1824–1834] All E.R.28 121–138
Denmark Productions Ltd. v. Boscobel Productions Ltd. [1969]
    1 Q.B. 699 .... 191, 193
Denny Gasquet & Metcalfe v. Conklin [1913] 3 K.B. 177 129
Doctor Barnardo's Homes v. Special Income Tax Commissioners
    [1921] 2 A.C. 1 266
Doel v. Sheppard (1856) El. & Bl. 856, 119 E.R. 700 .... 242, 243
Doherty v. Allman (1878) 3 App. Cas. 709 199
Dormer v. Fortescue (1744) 3 Atk. 123 339
Dubai Aluminium Co. Ltd. v. Salaam [1999] Lloyd's Rep. 415 .... 100, 104
Dunn v. Crawford & Smith Report of the Inspector of Factories for the
    quarter ending 30th September, 1840, 1841 B.P.P. x, 186 230
Dunne v. English (1874) L.R. 18 Eq. 524 342

Eagle Trust plc v. SBC Securities Limited [1992] 4 All E.R. 488 107
Edwards v. Lewis (1747) 3 Atk. 538 330
El Ajou v. Dollar Land Holdings [1993] 3 All E.R. 717 (Ch. D.);
    [1993] B.C.L.C. 735 .... 105, 107
El Ajou v. Dollar Land Holdings [1994] 2 All E.R. 685 (C.A.);
    [1994] 1 B.C.L.C. 464 104,106
Emmens v. Elderton [1853] 4 HL Cas. 624; 10 E.R. 642 190
Erlanger v. New Sombrero Phosphate Co. (1887) 3 App. Cas. 1218 369
Ewings v. Tisdal (1847) 1 Exch. 295 190

Fairman v. Perpetual Investment Building Society [1923] A.C. 74 256
Findlay, Re [1985] A.C. 318 .... 67, 68

Findlay v. Secretary of State for the Home Department [1995]
    A.C. 3187 64
Fitzpatrick v. Sterling Housing Association Ltd. [1999]
    4 All E.R. 705 .... 220, 221, 224
Fitzroy v. Cave [1905] 2 K.B. 364 123
Forster v. Baker [1910] 2 K.B.636 127
Foster v. Cockerell (1835) 9 Bl.N.S. 332 125
Fry, ex p. [1954] 2 All E.R. 118 60
Fulbrook v. Berkshire Magistrates Court (1970) 69 L.G.R. 75 60

Giddings v. Giddings (1826) 3 Russell 241 331
Goodman v. Pocock [(1850) 15 Q.B. 576; 117 E.R. 577 190
Gorringe v. Irwell India Rubber and Gutta Percha Works (1887)
    34 Ch. D. 128 130
Grace, ex p. (1799) 1 Bos. & Pul. 376 .... 339, 341, 342
Griffin v. Griffin (1804) 1 Sch. & Lef. 352 339
Griffiths v. Earl Dudley (1882) 9 Q.B.D. 357 .... 249, 253
Groves v. Lord Wimborne [1898] 2 Q.B. 402 .... 245, 251

H.T.V. v. Price Commission [1976] I.C.R. 170 56
Haigh v. Brooks (1839) 10 Ad. & E. 309, 113 E.R. 119 298
Hamilton v. Denny (1809) 1 Ball & Beatty 199 342
Hardman v. Johnson (1815) 3 Merivale 347 335
Haseldine v. C.A. Daw & Co. Ltd. [1941] 2 K.B. 343 256
Heinl v. Jyske Bank (Gibraltar) Ltd. [1990] Lloyd's Law Rep.
    Banking 511 .... 101, 102, 103
Herrington v. British Railways Board [1972] A.C. 877 257
Holliday, Re [1922] 2 Ch. D. 698 279
Hollis v. Edwards (1683) 1 Vern 189 115
Holt v. Heatherfield Trust Ltd. [1942] 1 All E.R. 404 .... 129, 130, 133
Holt v. Holt (1670) 1 Chan. Cas. 190 .... 327, 342
Houghton v. Fayers [2000] 1 B.C.L.C. 511 111
Howard v. Howard [1945] 1 All E.R. 91 184
Hughes v. Department of Health and Social Security [1985] A.C. 776;
    [1985] 2 W.L.R. 866 68
Hutchinson v. York, Newcastle & Berwick Rly. Co. (1850) 5 Ex. 343,
    155 E.R. 150 232

"Ikarian Reefer, The", see National Justice Campania Navicra v. Prudential
    Assurance Co Ltd. [1993] Lloyd's Rep. 68 103
Indermaur v. Dames (1866) L.R. 1 C.P. 274 .... 255, 256, 258
International Factors Ltd. v. Rodriguez [1979] Q.B. 351 126

James, ex p (1803) 8 Ves. 337 342
Jenison v. Lord Lexington (1719) 1 P. Wms, 555; 2 Eq. Cas. Ab. 430 pl. 10;
    24 E.R. 515 292
Johnathon v. Tilley, unreported, Peter Gibson L.J., June 30, 1995 105

Johnstone v. Cox (1881) 16 Ch. Div. 571 131

Karak Rubber Co. Limited v. Burden (No. 2) [1972] 1 All E.R. 1210 96
Keech v. Sandford (1726) Sel. Cas. Chan. 61; 2 Eq. Cas. Abr. 741;
    Cas. Temp. King. 61; 25 E.R. 233; 1 Wh. & Tud. Leading Cases 39;
    [1158–1774] All E.R. 230 .... 326–328, 330, 331, 337, 342
Kennedy v. DeTrafford [1896] 1 Ch. D. 762; [1897] A.C. 180 342
Killick v. Flexney (1792) 4 Brown P.C. 161 342

Lacey, ex p. (1802) 6 Ves. 625 342
Lansing Linde v. Kerr [1991] I.C.R. 428 198
Law v. Jones [1974] Ch. 112 116
Lawrence v. Maggs (1759) 1 Eden 453 333
Lee v. Lord Vernon (1776) 5 Brown P.C. 10 .... 331, 332
Lee v. McGrath [1882] 10 L.R. (Ir) 313 (C.A.) 130
Lindsay Petroleum Co. v. Hurd (1874) L.R. 5 P.C. 221 369
Lipkin Gorman v. Karpnale [1991] 2 A.C. 548 108
Lock v. Lock (1710) 2 Vernon 666 .... 328, 333
Long v. Hepworth [1968] 1 W.L.R. 1299 348
Loraine v. Loraine & Murphy [1912] P. 222 184
Lowry v. Reid [1927] N.I. 142 118–120

McCafferty v. Metropolitan Police District Receiver [1977] 1 W.L.R. 1073 270
McCausland v. Duncan Lawrie [1997] 1 W.L.R. 38 116
McInnes v. Onslow-Fane [1978] 1 W.L.R. 1520 55
McLoughlin v. O'Brian [1983] 1 A.C. 410 355
Marchant v. Morton Down [1901] 2 K.B. 829 .... 122, 125, 131
Maritime Electric Co. Ltd. v. General Dairies Ltd. [1937] A.C. 610 64
Marsh v. National Autistic Society [1993] I.C.R. 453 .... 191, 192
Mason v. Day (1711) Prec. Chan. 319 340
Milsington (Lord) v. Musgrave and Portmore (1818)
    3 Maddock 491 343
Montagu's Settlement, Re [1992] All E.R. 308; [1987]
    Ch. 264 .... 104–106, 109, 114
Moore & Hulme's Contract, Re [1912] 2 Ch. 105 291
Moreton v. Hardern (1825) 4 B. & C. 223, 107 E.R. 1042 230
Morgan v. Morgan (1737) 1 Atk. 489 339
Morgan, Re: Pilgrem v. Pilgrem (1881) 18 Ch. D. 84 331

National Justice Campania Naviera v. Prudential Assurance Co Ltd.
    ("The Ikarian Reefer") [1993] Lloyd's Rep. 68 103
Neale v. Mackenzie (1836) 1 M. & W. 747, 150 E.R. 635 291
Neville Estates v. Madden [1962] Ch. 832 295
Newburgh v. Bickerstaffe (1684) 1 Vernon 295 339
Newfoundland Government v. Newfoundland Railway Co. (1883)
    App. Cas. 198 126
Nightingale v. Lawson (1785) 1 Brown 440 333

Norris v. Le Neve (1743) 3 Atk. 26; (1744) 4 Brown 465 (H.L.) 335, 336, 337

O'Herlihy v. Hedges (1803) 1 Sch. & Lef. 123 326
O'Neill v. Murphy [1936] N.I. 16 .... 297–301, 310, 311
O'Reilly v. Mackman [1983] 2 A.C. 237 50
Owen v. Williams (1773) 2 Ambler 734 330

Palmer v. Young (1684) 1 Vernon 276 341
Pannet v. McGuinness & Co. [1972] 2 Q.B. 599 259
Pfeiffer Weinkellerei v. Arbuthnot Factors Ltd. [1988]
    1 W.L.R. 150 .... 122, 131–133, 137
Phillips v. Phillips (1885) 29 Ch. D. 673 331
Pickering v. Vowles (1783) 1 Brown 197 332
Pierson v. Shore (1737) 1 Atk. 479 340
Pluck v. Digges (1828) 2 Hud. & Br. 1, (1832) 5 Bli. N.S. 31, 5 E.R. 219
    (Exchequer Chamber, Ir.), 2 Dow. & Cl. 180, 6 E.R. 695 (HL) 275
Polly Peck International plc v. Nadir [1992] 4 All E.R. 769 97
Priestley v. Fowler (1837) 3 M. & W. 1, 150 E.R. 1030 .... 229–231, 235, 247

R. v. Inland Revenue Commissioners, ex p. Preston [1985] 2 W.L.R. 836 64
R. v. Inland Revenue Commissioners, ex p. Unilever [1998] S.T.C. 681 .... 56, 65
R. v. Liverpool Corporation, ex p. Liverpool Taxi Fleet Operator's Association
    [1972] 2 Q.B. 299 56
R. v. Minister for Agriculture, Fisheries and Foods ex p. Offshore Fisheries
    Ltd. [1995] All E.R. 714 .... 45, 60, 68
R. v. North East Devon Health Authority, ex p. Coughlan [2000]
    3 All E.R. 850 .... 50, 51, 57, 58, 65, 68–71
R. v. Secretary of State for the Home Department, ex p. Hargreaves
    [1997] 1 W.L.R. 906 65
R. v. Secretary of State for the Home Department, ex p. Khan
    [1984] 1 W.L.R. 1337 .... 57, 68, 69
R. v. Secretary of State for the Home Department, ex p. Mowla
    [1992] 1 W.L.R. 70 67
R. v. Secretary of State for the Home Department, ex p. Ruddock
    [1987] 1 W.L.R. 1482 68
R. v. Secretary of State for Health, ex p. US Tobacco International Inc.
    [1992] 1 All E.R. 212 64
R. v. Secretary of State for Transport, ex p. Richmond upon Thames LBC
    [1994] 1 W.L.R. 74 67
Rakestraw v. Brewer (1728) 2 P. Wms. 511 .... 338, 339
Randall v. Russell (1817) 3 Merivale 190 .... 335, 336
Ravenscroft v. Rederiaktiebolaget Transatlantic [1991] 3 All E.R. 73 355
Rawe v. Chichester (1773) 2 Ambler 715 .... 327, 331
Rhodes v. Allied Dunbar Pension Services [1987] 1 W.L.R. 1703 133
Ridge v. Baldwin [1964] A.C. 40 52
Roebuck v. Mungovin [1994] 2 A.C. 224 273
Rose and Frank v. Crompton [1943] 2 K.B. 261 302

Royal British Bank v. Turquand (1856) 6 E. & B. 327 112
Royal Brunei Airlines v. Tan [1995] 2 A.C. 378 (P.C.);
    [1995] 3 W.L.R. 64 .... 97–105, 113
Rumford Market Case *see* Keech v. Sandford
Rushworth's Case (1676) 2 Freeman 14 327

Saunders v. Vautier (1841) Cr. & Ph. 240 378
Schmidt v. Secretary of State for Home Affairs [1969] 2 Ch. 149 .... 49, 55
Seabourne v. Powell (1686) 2 Vernon 10 .... 327, 338
Selangor United Rubber Estates Ltd v. Craddock [1968] 2 All E.R. 1073 .... 96, 97
Selsey (Lord) v. Rhodes (1824) 2 Sim. & Stu. 49 343
Sergie, Re [1954] N.I. 1 376
Shelley's Case (1581) 1 Co. Rep. 88b. 76 E.R. 199 376
Sir Robert Acton's Case (1570) 3 Dyer 288b, 72 ER 647 281
Skipper and Tucker v. Holloway and Howard [1910] 2 K.B. 630 127
Smith v. Baker & Sons [1891] A.C. 325 .... 249, 251
South Tyneside Metropolitan B.C. v. Svenska International [1995]
    1 All E.R. 545 108
Southend-on-Sea Corporation v. Hodgson [1962] 1 Q.B. 416 64
Steadman v. Steadman [1976] A.C. 536 .... 118, 119
Stone v. Theed (1787) 2 Brown 243 .... 326, 332–334
Stubbings v. Webb [1993] 1 A.C. 498 .... 345, 347, 348, 353–356, 362
Sudely v. Attorney General [1897] A.C. 11 266

Taster v. Marriott (1768) 2 Ambler 668 330
Taylor v. Wheeler (1706) 2 Vernon 564 338
Thellusen v. Woodford (1799) 4 Ves. 227; (1805) 11 Ves. 112 378
Thomas v. Pearce, unreported, Court of Appeal, February 10, 2000 103
Tiverton v. Wearwell [1975] Ch. 146 116
Torkington v. Magee [1902] 2 K.B. 427; [1903] W.N. 60 128
Treacy, Re [2000] N.I. 330 .... 68, 69
Tulk v. Moxhay (1848) 2 Ph. 744. 41 E.R. 1143 380
Twinsectra Ltd. v. Yardley [1999] Lloyd's Law Rep. Banking 4381 99

U. v. W. (Attorney General Intervening) [1997] 3 W.L.R. 739 219

Vaughan v. Menlove. (1837) 3 Bing. N.C. 468, 132 E.R. 490 230
Verney v. Verney (1750) Ambler 88 .... 328, 333

Walley v. Walley (1687) 1 Vernon 484 342
Walter & Sullivan v. J. Murphy & Sons Ltd. [1995] 2 Q.B. 584 127
Westdeutsche Landesbank v. Islington London Borough Council
    [1996] A.C. 669 108
Western Fish Products v. Penwith District Council [1981] 2 All E.R. 204 64
Wheeldon v. Burrows (1878) Ch. D. 31 379
Whitby v. Mitchell (1890) 44 Ch. D. 85 .... 377, 378
White v. Chief Constable of the South Yorkshire Police [1999] 1 All E.R. 1 355

White v. White (1804) 9 Ves. 554 334
Wilkinson v. Downton [1897] 2 Q.B. 57 348
Williams v. Atlantic Assurance Co. Ltd. [1933] 1 K.B. 81 127
Williams v. Holland (1833) 10 Bing. 112, 131 E.R. 848 230
Williams, Re [1917] 1 Ch. 1 127
Wilson v. Merry and Cunningham (1868) L.R. 1 Sc. & Div. 326 .... 245, 246
Witter v. Witter (1730) 2 P. Wms. 99 340

Yaxley v. Gotts [2000] 1 All E.R. 711 .... 118, 119

COURT OF JUSTICE OF THE EUROPEAN UNION

Agazzi Léonard v. Commission (Case 181/87) [1988] E.C.R. 3823 44
Alpha Steel Ltd. v. Commission (Case 14/81) [1982] E.C.R. 749 41
Algera v. Common Assembly (Joined Cases 7/56 and 3-7/57) [1957]
    E.C.R. 39 23
Amylum v. Council (Case 108/81) [1982] E.C.R. 3107 28
Angelo Tomadino SNC v. Amministrazione delle Finanze dello Stato
    (Case 84/78) [1979] E.C.R. 1801 34
Blackman v. European Parliament (Case T–33/89) [1993] E.C.R. II–249 42
Cambo Erbo Industrial SA v. EU Council (Case T–472/93) [1995]
    E.C.R. II–421 42
Climax Paper Converters v. Council (Case T–155/94 [1996]
    E.C.R. II–877 34
CNTA S.A. v. Commission (Case 74/74) [1975] E.C.R. 533 .... 25, 35, 43
Commission v. Council (Officials' Salaries) (Case 81/72) [1973]
    E.C.R. 575 .... 28, 31
Compagnie Continentale de France v. Council (Case169/73) [1975]
    E.C.R. 117 42
Compagnie Industrielle et Agricole du Comté de Loheac v.
    Council and Commission [1977] E.C.R. 6456 33
Continental Produkten-Gesellschaft Erhardt Renken–Renken GmbH v.
    Hauptzollamt München-West (Case 246/87) [1989] E.C.R. 200 42
Continentale Produkten-Gesellschaft v. Hauptzollamt München-West
    (Case 246/87) [1989] E.C.R. 1151 39
Cornée v. COPALL (Case 196/88) [1989] E.C.R. 2309 33
Costa v. ENEL (Case 6/64) [1964] E.C.R. 585 18
De Dapper v. Parliament (Case 29/74) [1975] E.C.R. 35 25
Deboeck v. Commission (Case 90/74) [1975] E.C.R. 1123 25
Decker v. Caisse de Pension des Employés Privés (Case 129/87)
    [1988] E.C.R. 6121 38
Delacre v. Commission (Case C–350/88) [1990] E.C.R. I–395 41
Delauche v. Commission (Case 111/86) [1987] E.C.R. 5345 39
Diversinte SA and Iberlacta SA v. Administración Principal de Aduanas de la
    Junquera (Joined Cases C–2360/91 and C–261/91) [1993]
    E.C.R. I 1885 .... 36, 38

Driessen en Zonen v. Minster van Verkeer em Waterstaat (Cases C–13 to
    C–16/92) [1993] E.C.R. I–4751 35
Duff v. Minister for Agriculture and Food (Case 63/93)
    [1996] E.C.R. I–576 .... 29, 31, 32, 43
Edeka Zentrale AG v. Germany (Case 245/81) [1982] E.C.R. 2745 44
Einfuhr und Vorratsstelle Getreide v. Mackprang (Case 4/1975) [1975]
    E.C.R. 607 .... 28, 43
Elliniki Radiophonia Tileorassi AE v. Plioroforissis and Kouvelas
    (Case C–260/89) [1991] E.C.R. I–2925 59
Epichiriseon Metalleftikon Viomichanikon kai Naftiliakon AE v. Council
    (Case C–121/86) [1989] E.C.R. 3919 39
Eugénio Branco Lda v. Commission (Case T–142/97) [1988]
    E.C.R. II–3567 45
Faust v. Commission (Case 52/81) [1982] E.C.R. 3745 43
Fédération Charbonnière de Belgique v. High Authority (Case 8/55)
    [1954 to 1956] E.C.R. 245 23
Ferriere San Carlo SpA v. Commission (Case 344/84) [1987] E.C.R. 4435 38
Finsider SpA v. Commission (Joined Cases 63 and 147/84) [1985]
    E.C.R. 2857 .... 29, 33
Firma Anton Dürbeck v. Hauptzollamt Frankfurt am Main-Flughafen
    (Case 112/80) [1981] E.C.R. 1095 36
Firma Gebrüder Dietz (Case 126/76) [1977] E.C.R. 2431 46
FRUBO v. Commission (Case 71/74) [1975] E.C.R. 563 40
Hauer v. Rheinland Pfalz (Case 44/79) [1979] E.C.R. 3727 24
Hauptzollamt Krefeld v. Maizina GmbH (Case 5/82) [1982] E.C.R. 4601 40
Hauptzollamt Hamburg-Jonas v. Firma P. Krücken (Case 316/86)
    [1988] E.C.R. 2213 40
Héretiers d'Edmond Ropars v. Council of the European Union (Case T–429/93)
    (Judgment of the Court of First Instance (First Chamber) of
    June 21, 2000 25
Holtbecker v. Commission (Case T–20/91) [1992] E.C.R. II–2599 .... 38, 56
Hoogovens v. High Authority (Case14/61) [1962] E.C.R. 511 27
IFG-Interkontinentale Fleischhandelsgesellschaft GmbH v. Commission
    (Case 68/77) [1978] E.C.R. 353 36
Industrias Pesqueras Campos v. Commission (Case T–551/93) [1996]
    E.C.R. II–247 45
Ireland v. Commission (Case 239/86) [1987] E.C.R. 5271 29
Ireland v. Commisson (Case 325/85) [1987] E.C.R. 5041 29
Italy v. Commission (Case 14/88) [1989] E.C.R. 3677 38
Klensch v. Luxembourg Secretary of State for Agriculture (Case 202/85)
    [1986] E.C.R. 3477 59
Laboratoires Pharmaceutiques Bergaderm S.A. v. Jean-Jacques Goupil, Judgment
    of the Court of Justice, July 4, 2000 48
Lageder SpA v. Amministrazione delle Finanze (Joined Cases C– 31 to C–44/91)
    [1993] E.C.R. I 1761 40
Land Rheinland-Pfalz v. Alcan Deutschland (Case C–24/95) [1997]
    E.C.R. I–1591 40

Lefebvre and others v. Commission (Case T–571/93) [1995]
  E.C.R. II–2385 40
Maizena v. Council (Case 139/79) [1980] E.C.R. 3393 37
Marcato v. Commission (Case 37/72) [1973] E.C.R. 361 25
Mavridis v. European Parliament (Case 289/81) [1983] E.C.R. 1731 .... 19, 24
Meiko-Konservenfabrik v. Germany (Case 224/82) [1983] E.C.R. 2539 37
Merkur Aussenhandel GmbH v. Commission (Case 97/76) [1977]
  E.C.R. 1063 26
Merkur v. Commission (Case 97/76) [1977] E.C.R. 1063 43
Mulder and others v. Council and Commission sub. nom. Mulder II
  (Joined Cases C–104/89 and C–37/90) [1992] E.C.R. I–3061 .... 25, 34, 45–48
Mulder v. Minister von Landbouw en Visserij (Case 120/86) [1988]
  E.C.R. 2321 .... 24, 26, 32, 34, 45, 46, 47
Nakajima All Precision Co. Ltd. (Case C–69/89) [1991] E.C.R. I–2069 64
Officine Elettromeccaniche Ing A Merline v. High Authority (Case 108/63)
  [1965] E.C.R. 1 22
Opel Austria v. Council (Case T–115/94) [1997] E.C.R. II– 39 35
Oryzomyli Kavallas v. Commission (Case 160/84) [1986] E.C.R. 1633 42
Pardini v. Ministero del Commerciao con l'Estero (Case 338/85) [1988]
  E.C.R. I–2041 43
Parti Ecologiste "Les Verts" v. European Parliament (Case 294/83) [1986]
  E.C.R. 1339 21
Pastätter v. Hauptzollamt Bad Reichenhall (Case C–217/89) [1990]
  E.C.R. I–4585 47
Pesquerias v. Commission (Joined Cases C–258 and 259/90) [1992]
  E.C.R. I–2901 34
R. v. Kent Kirk (Case 63/83) [1984] E.C.R. 2689 .... 36, 59
Racke (Firma A.) v. Hauptzollamt Mainz (Case 98/78) [1979] E.C.R. 79 36
Rijn-Schelde-Verolme Maschinefabrieken en Scheepswerven NV (RSV) v.
  Commission (Case 223/85) [1987] E.C.R. 4617 39
Road Air B v. Inspecteur der Invoerrechten en Accijnzen (Case C–310/95)
  [1997] E.C.R. I–100 36
Roquette Frères SA v. Council (Case 138/79) [1980] E.C.R. 3333 37
San Marco Impex Italiano SA v. Commission (Case T–451/93) [1994]
  E.C.R. II–1061 41
Savma v. Commission (Case 264/81) [1984] E.C.R. 3915 38
Sideradia v. Commission (Case 67/84) [1985] E.C.R. 3983 45
Sociedade Agro-Pecuària Vicente Nobre Lda v. Council (Case 253/86)
  [1988] E.C.R. 2725 41
Sofrimport Sarl v. Commission (Case C–152/88) [1990] E.C.R. I–2477 34
Spagl v. Hauptzollamt Rosenheim (Case C–189/89) [1990] E.C.R. I–4539 47
Spitta & Co. v. Hauptzollamt Frankfurt am Main-Ost (Case 127/78)
  [1979] E.C.R. 171 36
S.P.U.C. (Ireland) Ltd. v. Grogan (Case C–159/60) [1991] E.C.R. I–4685 142
Thyssen v. Commission (Case 188/92) [1983] E.C.R. 372 40
Töpfer & Co. GmbH v. Commission (Case 112/77) [1978]
  E.C.R. 1019 .... 26, 29, 40

Tromeur v. Council of the European Union and Commission of the European
    Union (Case T–537/93) (Judgment of the Court of First Instance
    (First Chamber) of June 21, 2000 25
Unifrigo Gadus Srl and CPL Imperial 2 SpA v. Commission of the European
    Communities (Joined Cases T–10/97 and T–11/97) [1997]
    E.C.R. II–2231 .... 29, 40, 45
Union Nationale des Coopératives Agricoles de Céréales and others v.
    Commission (Case 95/75) [1975] E.C.R. 1615 42
Usines de la Providence v. High Authority (Case 29/63) [1965]
    E.C.R. I–1591 40
Van den Bergh en Jurgens v. Commission (Case 265/85) [1987]
    E.C.R. 1155 .... 19, 39
Van Gend en Loos NV v. Commission (Joined Cases 98/83 and 230/83)
    [1984] E.C.R. 3763 40
Von Deetzen v. Hauptzollamt Hamburg-Jonas (Case 170/86) [1988]
    E.C.R. 2355 47
Wachauf v. Germany (Case 5/88) [1989] E.C.R. 2609 59
Weingut Gustav Decker KG v. Hauptzollamt Landau (Case 99/78)
    [1979] E.C.R. 101 36
Westzucker v. Einfuhr und Vorratsstelle für Zucker (Case 1/73) [1973]
    E.C.R. 723 27
Zuckerfabrik Franken GmbH v. Germany (Case 77/81) [1982] E.C.R. 681 24

EUROPEAN COURT OF HUMAN RIGHTS

Abdulaziz, Cabales & Balkandali v. United Kingdom (1985)
    7 E.H.R.R. 471 209
Airey v. Ireland (1980) 2 E.H.R.R. 305 208
Belgian Linguistics (No. 2) (1968) E.H.R.R. 252 .... 282, 210
Berrehab v. Netherlands Series A, No. 138; (1999) 11 E.H.R.R. 322 221
Camp & Bourimi v. The Netherlands Application No. 28369, admissibility
    decision of September 8, 1997; Report of the Commission adopted on
    April 23, 1997 .... 217, 218
Cossey v. United Kingdom Series A, No. 184; (1991) 13 E.H.R.R. 622 224
Fredin v. Sweden (1991) Series A, 192; (1991) 13 E.H.R.R. 784 210
G. v. The Netherlands (1993) 13 E.H.R.R. 38 219
Handyside v. United Kingdom, Series A, No. 24; (1976) 1 E.H.R.R. 737 208
Inze v. Austria (1987) Series A, No. 126, 10 E.H.R.R. 394 .... 213, 214, 218, 219
Johnston v. Ireland (1987) 9 E.H.R.R. 203 .... 212–214, 219, 223, 224
Keegan v. Ireland Series A, No. 290; (1994) 18 E.H.R.R. 342 221
Kerkhoven v. Netherlands Commission, admissibility decision,
    May 19, 1992 .... 222, 225
Kroon v. Netherlands Series A, No. 297-C; (1995) 19 E.H.R.R. 263 221
Lawless v. Ireland (1979) Series B., para 408; (1979-80) 1 E.H.R.R. 15 208
Marckx v. Belgium (1979) Series A 31; (1979)
    2 E.H.R.R. 330 .... 206, 210–219, 221, 222

National Provincial Building Society v. United Kingdom [1997] S.T.C. 1466 27
Norris v. Ireland (1991) 13 E.H.R.R 737 208
Open Door and Dublin Well Woman v. Ireland (1992) 15 E.H.R.R. 244 142
Powell & Rayner v. United Kingdom (1990) 12 E.H.R.R. 355 209
Rees v. United Kingdom Series A, No. 106; (1987) 9 E.H.R.R. 56 222
Saucedo Gomez v. Spain (Application No. 37784/97, admissibility decision,
    January 19, 1998 225
Sheffield and Horsham v. United Kingdom (1999) 27 E.H.R.R. 163 209
Soering v. United Kingdom Series A, No. 161; (1989) 11 E.H.R.R. 439 224
Tyrer v. United Kingdom Series A, No. 26; (1980) 2 E.H.R.R. 1 224
Vermeire v. Belgium (1991) Series A No. 214-C, 81 .... 215, 216, 218
X v. United Kingdom (1997) 24 E.H.R.R. 143 .... 222, 223, 225

AUSTRALIA

Attorney-General for New South Wales v. Quin (1990) 170 C.L.R. 1 .... 64, 67
Australian Broadcasting v. Bond (1990) 170 C.L.R. 321 70
Automatic Fire Sprinklers Pty. Ltd. v. Watson (1976) 72 C.L.R. 435 191
Beach Petroleum NL v. Abbott Tout Russell Kennedy, unreported,
    New South Wales Court of Appeal, November 5, 1999 100
Commonwealth v. John Fairfax and Sons Ltd. (1980) 147 C.L.R. 39 141
Consul Development Pty v. DPC Estates Pty (1974–1975)
    132 C.L.R. 373 102
Equitcorp v. Finance v. Bank of New Zealand [1993] N.S.W.L.R. 50 107
Gertsch v. Atsas, unreported, Supreme Court of New South Wales,
    Foster A.J., October 1, 1999 .... 99, 104
Koorootang Nominees Pty Ltd. v. Australia and New Zealand Banking
    Group Ltd. [1998] V.R. 16 109
Macquarie Bank Ltd. v. Sixty-Fourth Throne Pty Ltd. [1998] 3 V.R. 133 109
Minister of Ethnic Affairs v. Teoh (1995) 128 A.L.R. 353;
    183 C.L.R. 273 .... 57, 67
Salemi v. MacKellar (No. 2) (1977) 137 C.L.R. 396 53
Stamp Duties Commissioner (Queensland) v. Livingston [1965]
    A.C. 694 .... 259, 266

CANADA

Apotex Inc. v. Canada (Attorney General) (2000) 188 D.L.R. (4th) 145 .... 49, 68
Bartel et al. and Holmes, Re (1982) 16 Man. R. (2d) 29 .... 78, 88, 92
Canada Assistance Plan, Re (1991) 83 D.L.R. (4th) 297 67
Frame v. Smith (1987) 42 D.L.R. (4th) 81 368
Furey v. Conception Bay Centre Roman Catholic School Board (1993)
    104 D.L.R. (4th) 455 67
Hall v. Hall's Estate (1981) 10 Man. R. (2d) 168 86
Harrison v. Evans Estate [1987] 8 E.T.R. 53 82

Hodgkinson v. Simms [1994] 3 R.C.S. 377 368
Karabin, Re (1955) 62 Man. R. 334 88
LAC Minerals v. International Corona Resouirces Ltd. (1989) 61 D.L.R.
     (4th) 14 368
M.(K.) v. M.(H.) (1992) 96 D.L.R. (4th) 289 .. 344–346,356, 357, 361, 362, 365–370
Mason v. Westside Cemeteries Ltd. (1996) 135 D.L.R.
     (4th) 361 .... 315, 316
Patterson v. Lauritsen et al. (1984) B.C.L.R. 182 .... 79, 83, 84
Radcliffe, Re [1977] 1 A.C.W.S. 658; [1977] A.C.W.S.J. 159595 1 .... 82, 83
Steinberg Simmonds v. Rehn et al., Re (1969) 3 D.L.R. (3d) 565
     (Manitoba Q.B.) 78, 82
Tataryn v. Tataryn (1994) 116 D.L.R. (4th) 193 81
Walker v. McDermott [1931] 1 D.L.R. 662 .... 78, 79
Zecevic v. The Russian Orthodox Christ the Saviour Cathedral, unreported,
     Ontario High Court, Gray J., August 10, 1988 .... 302, 303

FRANCE

de Cujas, In re, *Cass. Civ.* June 19, 1963 JDI1964.555 8
Gentili di Giuseppe case, (Court of Appeals of Paris, June, 1999,
     unpublished) 11, 12
Newhouse, In re, *Cour de Cassation, Chambre Criminelle*
     June 4, 1998 .... 11, 12
Shchukina, In re, Decision of the Vice President of the Tribunal de Grande Instance,
     Paris, March 5, 1993 7
Sovereign Immunity, In re, *Cass. Civ.* April 15, 1986. (1986) 75 *Rev. Cr. Dr. Int. Pr.*
     723, note Gouchez 8

GERMANY

Bundesverfassungsgericht (1981) BverfGE 128 27
Oberverwaltungsgericht Berlin (1957) 72 DVBI 505-506 27

NEW ZEALAND

Allardice v. Allardice (1910) 29 N.Z.L.R. 959; [1911] A.C. 730 .... 78, 80, 84
Allen v. Manchester [1922] N.Z.L.R. 218 80
Biddle v. Bentley [1967] N.Z.L.R. 1047 .... 303, 304
Bosch v. Perpetual Trustee Co. Ltd. [1938] A.C. 463 .... 79, 80, 84
Bradley v. Attorney General [1988] 2 N.Z.L.R. 454; (1988)
     7 N.Z.A.R. 193 .... 67, 68
Daganayasi v. Minister of Immigration [1980] 1 N.Z.L.R. 355 .... 62, 70
Daniels v. Thompson [1998] 3 N.Z.L.R. 22 .... 367, 369
Downsview Nominees Ltd. v. First City Corporation Ltd. [1993] A.C. 295 94

Equiticorp Group v. Attorney-General [1996] 3 N.Z.L.R. 586 107
Goodwin, Re [1958] N.Z.L.R. 320 79
H. v. H. [1997] 2 N.Z.L.R. 700 .... 344, 358, 367
H. v. R. [1996] 1 N.Z.L.R. 299 .... 344, 347, 358, 368
Holmes (dec'd), Re [1936] N.Z.L.R. 26 93
Khalon v. Attorney General [1996] 1 N.Z.L.R. 458 67
Leonard, Re [1985] 2 N.Z.L.R. 88 .... 76, 78, 84
McGregor, Re [1961] N.Z.L.R. 1077 86
P. v. T. [1997] 2 N.Z.L.R. 688 .... 344, 358, 359
Ray v. Moncrieff [1917] N.Z.L.R. 234 .... 83, 84, 86
Rough, Re [1976] 1 N.Z.L.R. 604 77
S. v. G. [1995] 3 N.Z.L.R. 681 .... 345, 346, 349, 354, 356, 357, 362, 367, 369
Smith (dec'd), Re (1991) 8 F.R.N.Z. 459 87
T. v. H. [1995] 3 N.Z.L.R. 37 .... 346, 356, 359, 361
Westpac Banking Corp. v. Savin [1985] 2 N.Z.L.R. 41 99

SOUTH AFRICA

Administrator, Transvaal and others v. Traub and others (1989) (4) S.A. 731 62

UNITED STATES

Ausseresses' Estate, Re (1960) 178 Cal. App. 487 75
Bible Speaks, Re The (1989) 869 F. (2d) 628 312
Caspari v. The First German Church of the New Jersualem (1882) 12
    Mo. App. 293 309
Conor v. Stanley (1887) 72 Cal. 556; 14 P. 306 305
D., Mary v. D., John (1989) 264 Cal. Rptr. 633 (Cal. App. 6 Dist.) 356
De Rose v. Carswell (1987) 242 Cal. Rptr. 368 (Cal. App. 6 Dist.) 356
Evans v. Eckelman (1990) 365 Cal.Rptr. 605 367
Florida Star v. B.J.F. (1989) 491 U.S. 524 139
Gilmore v. Lee (1908) 237 Ill. 402 305
Good v. Zook (1901) 116 Iowa 582; 88 N.W. 376 .... 305, 306
Hammer v. Hammer (1978) 418 N.W. (2d) 23 (Wis. App.) 356
Honigman's Will, Re (1960) 8 N.Y. 2d. 244, 168 N.E. 2d 676 75
Linkletter v. Walker (1965) 381 U.S. 618 215
Marx v. McGlynn (1882) 88 N.Y. 357 311
Near v. Minnesota (1931) 283 U.S. 697 139
Nebraska Press Association v. Stuart (1976) 427 U.S. 539 139
New York Times Co. v. Sullivan (1964) 376 U.S. 254 139
New York Times Co. v. United States (1976) 427 U.S. 713 139
Pando v. Fernandez (1984) 127 Misc. (2d) 224; 485 N.Y.S. (2d) 162 298–301
Pendarvis v. Gibb (1927) 328 Ill. 282, 159 N.E. 353 75
People v. Museum of Modern Art (In re Grand Jury Subpoena Duces Tecum)
    (1999) 93 N.Y. (2d) 729, 697 N.Y.S. (2d) 538,719 N.E. (2d) 897 10

Petersen v. Bruen (1990) 727) P. (2d) 18 (Nev.) 356
Raymond v. Ingram (1987) 737 P. (2d) 314 (Wash. App.) 356
Riggs v. Palmer (1889) 115 N.Y. 506, 22 N.E. 188 164
Snepp v. United States (1980) 44 U.S. 507 139
Stambovsky v. Ackley (1991) 19 A.D. (2d) 254, 572 N.Y.S. (2d) 672 .... 313, 314
Tyson v. Tyson (1986) 727 P. (2d) 226 356
United States v. Satan and his Staff (1971) 54 F.R.D. 282 315
Whatcott v. Whatcott (1990) 790 P. (2d) 578 (Utah App.) 356

TABLE OF LEGISLATION

IRELAND

Constitution of Ireland
Art. 28.4.3° 142
Art. 40 .... 143, 144
Art. 40.3.1° 268
Art. 40.3.2° 140, 268
Art. 40.6.1° 140
Art. 40.6.1°i 144
Art. 41 .... 143, 144
Art. 43 13

Acts of the Oireachtas 1922–2001
Administration of Estates Act 1959 .... 265, 266
Adoption Act 1952 87
Adoption Act 1964 87
Civil Service Regulation Act 1956
    s. 17 65
Companies Act 1963
    s. 60 96
    s. 99 135
    s. 316A 113
Companies Act 1990
    s. 109 113
Courts of Justice Act 1936
    s. 38(3) 263
Criminal Justice Act 1994
    s. 31 113
    s. 31(6) 113
    s. 31(7) 113
    s. 31(8) 113
Electronic Commerce Act 2000
    s. 10(1)(b) 375
European Communities Act 1972
    s. 2(1) 18
European Communities Act 1992
    s. 2 18

Family Law Act 1995 .... 73, 183, 185
      s. 35 186
      s. 35(5) 186
Family Law (Divorce) Act 1996 .... 73, 185
      s. 14(1)(c) 183
      s. 14(1)(d) 183
Family Law (Judicial Separation) Act 1989 73
Finance Act 1984
      s. 106 178
      s. 108 178
      s. 108(1)(d) 178
Industrial Relations Act 1990 197
Judicial Separation and Family Law Reform Act 1989 183
Landlord and Tenant Act 1931 382
Law Reform Commission Act 1975
      s. 4(2)(c) 372
Law Reform (Personal Injuries) Act 1958 248
Local Government (Planning and Development Act) 1963 160
      s. 4 163
      s. 24 163
Local Government (Planning and Development) Act 1976
      s. 27 .... 148–153, 155, 157, 159,
                                                  161–163, 165, 166, 168–171
      s. 27(1) 149, 152
      s. 27(2) 149, 152
      s. 27(3) 149, 151
      s. 27(4) 150
      s. 27(6) 152
      s. 30 154
      s. 31 154
Local Government (Planning and Development) Act 1992
      s. 19(4)(g) 148
Local Government (Planning and Development Act) 2000
      s. 160 148
      s. 160(1) 152
      s. 160(6) 152
Occupiers' Liability Act 1995 257
Payment of Wages Act 1991 192
      s. 5 192
      s. 5(1) 193
      s. 5(2) 193
      s. 5(5)(c) 192
Redundancy Payments Act 1967 201
Redundancy Payments Act 1991 201
Registration of Title Act 1964
      s. 123 376
Status of Children Act 1987 73

Statute of Limitations 1957 .... 269, 345, 347, 349
    s. 2(1) 345
    s. 2(2)(a)(i) 367
    s. 5 369
    s. 11 .... 267, 268
    s. 11(2) 369
    s. 13(2) 262, 264
    s. 24 .... 263, 266
    s. 45 262–264
    s. 45(1) 262, 263
    s. 48 .... 261, 353, 359, 360
    s. 48A 360, 363
    s. 48(1)(a) 360
    s. 48(1)(b) 360
    s. 48(1)(b)(i) 360
    s. 48(1)(b)(ii) 360
    s. 48(7) 360
    s. 48(7)(a)-(c) 360
    s. 49 359
    s. 49(1)(a) 353
    s. 71 366
    s. 71(1)(b) 366
Statute of Limitations (Amendment) Act 1991 .... 270, 345, 247, 349, 364
    s. 2 .... 350, 355
    s. 2(1) 270, 350, 356, 361
    s. 2(1)(a) 350
    s. 2(1)(b) 350
    s. 2(1)(c) 350
    s. 2(1)(d) 350
    s. 2(1)(e) 350
    s. 2(2) 271, 350, 361
    s. 2(2)(a) 350, 351, 355
    s. 2(2)(b) 350, 351, 355
    s. 2(3) 350, 361
    s. 2(3)(a) 350, 358
    s. 2(3)(b) 350, 358
    s. 3(1) 348, 349, 350
    s. 5(1) 353
    s. 6 348
Statute of Limitations (Amendment) Act 2000 (No. 13 of 2000) 262, 344–370
    s. 2 360
    s. 3 .... 363, 365, 366
    s. 5 369
Succession Act 1965 .... 87, 203, 212, 264, 265, 374
    s. 13 266
    s. 90 203
    s. 117 .... 72–93, 213

Succession Act 1965—*contd.*
    s. 120 .... 87, 90, 93
    s. 126 .... 262, 264
Taxes Consolidation Act 1997
    s. 574 193
    s. 576 174
    s. 577 174
    s. 577(3) 174
    s. 579 174
    s. 795 173
    s. 796 173
    s. 806 173
    s. 807(5) 173

Rules of Court
Circuit Court Rules 1950 (S.I. No. 179 of 1950) 151
    O. 67A 151
Circuit Court Rules (No. 1) 1995 (S.I. No. 215 of 1995) 151
Rules of the Superior Courts 1986 (S.I. No. 15 of 1996) 151
    O. 84, r. 26(5) 53
Rules of the Superior Courts (No. 1) 1996 (S.I. No. 5 of 1996) 150, 151
    O. 103 151
    O. 103, r. 8 150

UNITED KINGDOM

Accumulations Act 1800 378
Accumulations Act 1892 378
Administration of Estates Act 1925 .... 372, 374
Civil Bill Act 1836
    s. 1 230
Coal Mines Regulation Act 1887
    s. 70 236
Commission on Sales of Land Act (N.I.) 1972 372
Common Law Procedure Act 1854 126
Common Law Procedure Amendment Act (Ireland) 1853
    (16 & 17 Vict., c. 113) 269
Common Law Procedure Amendment Act (Ireland) 1870 234
Companies Act 1948
    s. 95 135
Companies Act 1985
    s. 399 315
Conveyancing Act 1881 373
    s. 6 379
    s. 44 291
Conveyancing Act 1911 373

County Officers and Courts (Ireland) Act 1877
  s. 52 234
Deasy's Act *see* Landlord and Tenant Law Amendment, Ireland, Act 1860
Dublin Port and Docks Act 1869 245
Employers' Liability Act 1880 .... 231, 248–252
  s. 1(1) 248
  s. 5 236
  s. 6(1) 250
  s. 6(2) 250
  s. 82 236–238
Factories Act 1955
  s. 103 238
Factories Act (N.I.) 1965 238
Factory Act 1833 .... 229, 233–235
Factory Act 1844 .... 233–235, 239, 240, 242, 245
  s. 20 235
  s. 21 .... 235, 240–243
  s. 24 .... 233, 234, 240, 243
  s. 25 233
  s. 60 .... 234–236, 240, 241
Factory Act 1856 .... 242, 244, 245
  s. 4 243
  s. 5 243
  s. 43 243
Factory and Workshop Act 1878
  s. 82 236
Factory and Workshop Act 1895
  s. 13 236
Factory and Workshop Act 1901
  s. 136 236
Fatal Accidents Act 1846 230
Finance Act 1992 127
Fines Act (Ireland) 1851
  s. 13 235
Fines and Recoveries (Ireland) Act 1834
  s. 39 377
Land Charges Act 1925 .... 372, 373
Land Charges Act 1972 373
Land Registration Act 1925 .... 372, 373
Land Registration Act 1997 373
Landlord and Tenant (Covenants) Act 1995 381
Landlord and Tenant Law Amendment, Ireland Act 1860 294
  s. 3 .... 275, 292
  s. 16 381
Law of Property (Miscellaneous Provisions) Act 1989
  s. 2 120
  s. 2(1) 116, 119

Law of Property (Miscellaneous Provisions) Act 1989—*contd.*
    s. 2(8) 116
Law of Property Act 1925 (15 Geo. 5, c. 20) 372, 373, 377
    s. 40 116
    s. 40(1) 116
    s. 40(2) 116
    s. 136(1) 121, 122, 128, 129, 130, 132, 133, 134, 136, 137
Law Reform (Miscellaneous Provisions) Act (N.I.) 1948 248
Limitation Act 1980 270
    s. 11(1) 348
    s. 14 350
    s. 14(2) 350
Local Land Charges Act 1975 373
Local Registration of Title (Ireland) Act 1891 374
Metalliferous Mines Regulation Act 1872
    s. 13 236
Occupiers' Liability Act 1957 257
Perpetuities Act (N.I.) 1966 377
Perpetuities and Accumulations Act 1964 377
Prescription Act 1832 .... 374, 379
Prescription (Ireland) Act 1858 379
Probate and Letters of Administration (Ireland) Act 1859
    s. 15 266
Rent Act 1977 .... 220, 221
    s. 3(1) 220
Salmon Fishery Act (Ireland) Act 1863
    s. 45 236
Settled Land Act 1882 373
    s. 63 378
Settled Land Act 1884 373
    s. 6 378
Settled Land Act 1890 373
Settled Land Act 1925 373
Supreme Court of Judicature Act 1873 (36 & 37 Vict., c. 57) 121–125
    s. 25(6) 121, 122, 127, 128, 131
Supreme Court of Judicature (Ireland) Act 1877
    (40 & 41 Vict, c. 57) 121–125, 201
    s. 27 .... 123, 126
    s. 28(6) 121, 122, 126–134, 136, 138
    s. 60 234
Town Tenants (Ir.) Act 1906 382
Trustee Act 1893 .... 374, 379
Trustee Act 1925 .... 129, 374
Trustee Act (N.I) 1958 .... 379s
Trusts of Land and Appointment of Trustees Act 1996 .... 377, 379
Variation of Trusts Act 1958 379
Workmen's Compensation Act 1906 231

Wills Act 1837 .... 203, 374

Pre-1800
17 Edw. 2, c. 6 *De Prærogative Regis* 279
18 Edw. 1, cc. 1, 2 *Quia Emptores* 1290 (Statute of Westminster III) 275–294
21 Edw. 1, 1293 .... 282–285, 291
34 Edw. 3, c. 15 279
44 Edw. 3, fo. 14 280
56 Geo. 3, c. 88
10 Hen. 7, c. 22 (Ir.) *Poyning's Law* 282
33 Hen. 8 280
8 & 9 Wm. 3, c. 5 290
Bill of Rights 1689 286
Middlesex Registry Act 1708 373
Registration of Deeds Act (Ir.) 1707 373
Settlement of Ireland Act 1634 (10 Chas. 1, sess. 1., c. 3, Ir.) 289
Settlement of Ireland Act 1634 (10 Chas. 1, sess. 3., c. 2, Ir.) 289
Settlement of Ireland Act 1634 (10 Chas. 1, sess. 3., c. 3, Ir.) 289
Settlement of Ireland Act 1639 (15 Chas. 1, sess. 2., c. 6, Ir.) 289
Settlement of Ireland Act 1665 (17 & 18 Chas. 2, c. 2, Ir.) 289
Settlement of Ireland Act 1695 (7 Wm. 3, c. 3., Ir.) 289
Statute of Distributions (Ireland) 1695 265
Statute of Frauds 1677 .... 116, 119, 299
        s. 4 119
Statute of Frauds 1694 .... 117, 119
        s. 4 119
Statute of Uses (Ireland) 1634 376
Statute of Wills 1540, (32 Hen. 7), c. 16 74
Yorkshire Registry Act 1703 373
Yorkshire Registry Act 1734 373

Scotland
Succession Act 1964 75

Secondary Legislation
Property (N.I.) Order 1978 372
Property (N.I.) Order 1997 372
        Art. 34 280
Registration of Title Order 1989 (S.I. No. 1347) 373
Wills and Administration Proceedings Order (N.I.) Order 1994 372

E.U.
E.C. Treaty (Treaty of Rome) 22, 24
        Art. 230 29
        Art. 289 48
European Coal and Steel Community Treaty 23, 24

Community Directive 75/159/EEC 32
Council Directive 93/7 14
    Art. 2 14
    Art. 4.5 14
Council Directive 2000/21 *(Directive on Electronic Commerce)*
    Art. 9(2) 375
    Art. 9(2)(a) 375
Council Regulation 2707/72 34
Council Regulation 1078/77 .... 45, 48
Council Regulation 1697/79
    Art 5(2) 29
Council Regulation 856/84 32
Council Regulation 857/84 46
Council Regulation 962/88 34
Council Regulation 764/89 47

AUSTRIA

Carinthian Hereditary Farms Act 1903 214

CANADA

Testator's Family Maintenance Act 1924 79

FRANCE

Constitution of 1958
        Preamble 8
New Code of Civil Procedure 6
    s. 808 6
    s. 809 6
Law No. 94-679 10
    Art. 61 .... 10, 11, 12, 13

NEW ZEALAND

Family Protection Act 1955 77
    s. 33 86
Statutes Amendment Act 1947 86
Testator's Family Maintenance Act 1900 76

TRINIDAD AND TOBAGO

Condominiums Act 1981 381

UNITED STATES

New York Arts and Cultural Affairs Law
    Art. 12.03 .... 10, 12
Louisiana, La Code Civ.
    Art. 1493 75
Uniform Commercial Code
    s. 2-610a 193
    s. 2-723 193
Uniform Probate Code §2–302 76

INTERNATIONAL CONVENTIONS

European Convention on Human Rights and Fundamental Freedoms 204–226
    Protocol 1 205
        Art. 1 .... 8, 206, 211–214
        para. 1 206
        para. 2 206
    Protocol 4 205
    Protocol 6 205
    Protocol 7 205
    Protocol 11 .... 204, 205
        Art. 8 .... 206–213, 216–218, 221, 222, 223–226
        Art. 8(1) 207
        Art. 14 .... 206, 207, 209–212, 214, 216–218, 222
        Art. 26 (amended by Protocol 11:I) 204
        Art. 27 (amended by Protocol 11:I) 204
        Art. 33 205
        Art. 35 205
        Art. 46 205
    Protocol 12 .... 205, 209
    Statute of the Council of Europe 205
        Art. 3 205
        Art. 8 205
UNIDROIT Convention on Stolen or Illegally Exported Cultural Objects 15
    Art. 1 15
    Art. 4(1) 15
    Art. 4(2) 15

ADDRESS AT THE FUNERAL MASS FOR JIM BRADY ON JUNE 19, 1998

JOHN J. (SEÁN) BALLANCE

"How slow the shadow creeps, but when t's past
how fast the shadows fall, how fast, how fast.
Loss and Possession, Death and Life, are one,
but there falls no shadow, where there shines no sun"[1]

I celebrate that shining of the sun, which was the life of my friend Jim Brady.

There was a steel town in the North of England called Consett, and people commonly referred to "the Consett men" – who were inured to work in the steel mills, and as a result were considered the toughest men in England. Well Jim was from an even grimmer apprenticeship; he was a Newry Christian Brothers' man. Jim pretended to scorn the old place but he actually had a secret affection for it. He claimed, that as a result of the threat of the leather strap, we left the school with three great gifts:

(1) dornán Gaeilge, "a fistful of Irish";

(2) an ability to spell any word in the English language; and finally,

(3) a venomous hatred of Colonialism.

Jim always said that Nelson Mandela must have gone to a Christian Brothers School.

At the Abbey in Newry, Jim was a tremendous worker, but he had one serious delusion. He thought he had great prospects of playing for Manchester United or Newcastle and never quite recovered from the disappointment. Whatever about his soccer ambitions, Jim shone even in a gifted school group, which has since produced in the academic world alone, three Law Professors,[2] one English Professor,[3] one History Professor and the current President of University College Dublin.[4]

---

[1] Hilaire Belloc, *"For a Sundial"*.
[2] The late Professor Brady, Professor James Casey, UCD and Professor Kevin Boyle, University of Essex.
[3] Professor Brian Cosgrove, NUI Maynooth.
[4] Professor Art Cosgrove.

When Jim and I first visited Queen's University Belfast to get lodgings, Jim was at that stage interested in a medical career. He loved to tell the story of our encounter with a famous landlady Mrs. O'Toole who offered Jim a room, with its own skeleton. Jim always wondered if the skeleton had been seized from a penniless student or actually was the penniless student.

Because of eye problems Jim had to redirect his talents from Medicine to Law. But he did confide in me that while double vision was a severe disadvantage in Medicine, it was an extremely useful asset in the Law.

Jim suffered with multiple sclerosis for over 20 years and, as you all know, he fought it in every way for all that time. He worked right up to the end at the very limit of his physical strength. He had a healthy scepticism for all things medical and loved the story, from my brother Tommy, that the only certainty of a quick death was for the doctors in Daisy Hill Hospital Newry, to give a patient the "all clear".

Jim never succumbed to self-pity, but he did discuss with me his one fear of being totally hospitalised. I think that the manner of his leaving had the mercy of God about it.

> *"Cowards die many times before their deaths*
> *the valiant never taste of death but once"*[5]

Jim Brady was a valiant man. But there are other brave ones as well who supported him in his work and in his life and above all, who loved him. His incomparable wife, Joan, his children, Sinéad, Imogen and Damian and his sorrowing mother, Sarah. His sisters Mary, Theresa, and Lilian and his brother Michael. Joan's mother, Bridget, and Joan's brother, Patsy, and her sister Maura and all their families.

For my own part all I can do is to quote from Emerson, "a friend, may well be recognised as *the* masterpiece of Nature."[6] I have lost a masterpiece.

---

[5] Shakespeare, *Julius Caesar*, Act II, Scene II, Lines 33-34.
[6] Ralph Waldo Emerson, *"Nature"*.

ANTI-SEIZURE STATUTES IN ART LAW: THE INFLUENCE OF "LA DANSE" ON FRENCH LAW

LEILA ANGLADE

In the autumn of 1905, Paris was in a state of shock: a new generation of painters on exhibition at the famous "*Salon d'Automne*" had caused an outrage.[1] The works of Matisse, Marquet, Roualt, Puy, Valtat, Vlaminck and Derain, because of their unusual and powerful use of colours, were described as pictorial aberrations and unspeakable fantasies. Criticism was also directed at the painters themselves whose "deranged minds" had created such "wild" or "savage" monstrosities: they were called the "*Fauves*", literally the "wild beasts" because of their untamed use of colour. Yet, for Matisse, the "*Salon*" was to be one of the most important points in his career. While the most conservative art critics were outraged by Matisse's "*Open Window*", it certainly attracted the attention of the most adventurous collectors. It was around the same time that Matisse started his relationship with Gertrude, Leo and Michael Stein, who were all avid American collectors of modern daring talents. Through the Stein family, Matisse was introduced to a new world of enlightened art connoisseurs and wealthy patrons. Soon after, Matisse started a series of exhibitions around the world. Amongst the greatest admirers of his work was a man who was to play a crucial part in Matisse's career: Sergei Shchukin.[2]

Shchukin was an extremely wealthy and extravagant Moscow textile industrialist with a devouring passion for art. He had transformed his home in Moscow, the Trubetskoy Palace,[3] into a gigantic museum for his extraordinary and diverse collection, which he had started in the 1880s. He had begun purchasing Matisse's paintings in 1906 and soon became Matisse's biggest patron. In the spring of 1908, Matisse exhibited some of his paintings in Moscow where they were received with great enthusiasm, which prompted Shchukin to invest even more in Matisse's talent. In 1909, Shchukin commissioned two very large murals for the gigantic staircase in the Trubetskoy Palace. The two murals represented allegories of music and dance. They are simply entitled "*La Musique*" and "*La Danse*". They are still considered today as masterpieces of

---

[1] See for example *Matisse Artbook* (New York, Dorling Kindersley, 1999), see also *Le Monde* February 25, 1993. For an account of the 1905 Salon and its atmosphere see *Le Monde* October 30, 1999.

[2] On the work of Matisse around that time see *Le Monde* October 12, 1992.

[3] The palace is located close to the Kremlin.

modern art. Shchukin was a collector with a vision and, by 1914, his collection of impressionist and modernist paintings was one of the finest in the world. He had gathered over 450 paintings in his palace-museum. The collection included, in addition to the paintings by Matisse,[4] works by Monet, Cezanne, Pissaro, Renoir, Degas, Van Gogh, Gauguin, Derain, Picasso[5] and many others.[6]

At the onset of the Russian revolution, in February 1917, Shchukin did not feel threatened by the changes brought to Russia by its new leaders. In fact, Shchukin was known for his liberal views and he welcomed the Russian revolution with open arms. Shchukin's view of the new Russia was that of a utopian aesthete. He informed the new Russian authorities that he intended to donate his entire collection to the city of Moscow. The authorities were initially very interested in his proposal and an official commission was set up to examine the feasibility of the project. Shchukin himself was a member of that commission. The commission completed its work and proposed that the entire Kremlin be transformed into an oversized museum which would easily accommodate the Shchukin collection in a prominent position. The project, however, was not to be realised: in October 1917, Lenin and the Bolsheviks took power and Lenin set up his headquarters in the Kremlin. Soon after the Bolshevik revolution, Shchukin became very wary of the new masters of the Kremlin. In the summer of 1918, he fled Russia with his wife and his younger daughter, a three-year-old girl named Irina,[7] and the family settled in Paris. A few months after Shchukin's installation in France, the precious collection was nationalised by the Bolsheviks[8] and became the "public property of the Federal Socialist Republic of Russia".[9] The decree nationalising the collection was signed by Lenin himself.[10] Shchukin never received any compensation for the nationalisation of his collection. The collection was ultimately split between the Pushkin and the Hermitage Museums. Shchukin never saw it again. He died in Paris in 1936.[11]

Shchukin's daughter, Irina, subsequently tried to reclaim ownership of the

---

[4] Shchukin purchased 39 paintings from Matisse.

[5] Shchukin owned 51 Picassos and 17 Gauguins.

[6] In the Trubetskoy palace, each painting was assigned a dedicated space. Picasso was displayed in a vaulted cabinet, the music room hosted the paintings of the impressionists, and the dining room was dedicated to Gauguin, while the pink salon was reserved for Matisse. Shchukin opened his house for public viewing every Sunday. The success was immense. Moscovites queued every Sunday outside the Trubetskoy palace to glimpse Shchukin's latest acquisitions. See *Le Monde* February 25, 1993.

[7] Shchukin's elder daughter stayed in Moscow to keep an eye on the precious collection. See *Le Monde* February 25, 1993.

[8] The collection was nationalised on October 18, 1918. See *Agence France Presse*, June 16, 1993.

[9] Reported in *Agence France Presse*, June 13, 2000.

[10] See *Le Monde*, March 1, 1993.

[11] See *Le Monde*, February 25, 1993.

collection. In 1954, 34 paintings by Picasso from the Shchukin collection left Russia for the first time. They were exhibited by an affiliate of the French Communist Party in Paris. Irina Shchukina requested the *Tribunal de Grande Instance* in Paris to issue an injunction to seize the paintings. The Paris tribunal declined to hear the case on the grounds of lack of jurisdiction. The tribunal's decision was criticised as being an "act of complacency" towards the Soviet government. However, as a result of Ms. Shchukina's action, the Picasso exhibition was cancelled and the paintings were repatriated to Russia in a hurry. Picasso himself used strong words to condemn the legal action started by Ms. Shchukina. He suggested sarcastically that the Count of Paris (heir to the French throne) should follow her example and try to reclaim ownership of the Chateau de Versailles. Irina Shchukina's claim, however, had an important consequence: western galleries and museums wishing to exhibit some of the paintings from the Shchukin collection would first ask her permission to show the paintings. Ms. Shchukina always granted such permission. In 1993, in light of Russia's new political situation, Ms. Shchukina also wrote to President Yeltsin, asking him to rehabilitate the memory of her father, to reunite the collection in a single place and to give her a "symbolic indemnity". President Yeltsin did not respond.

In Paris, in February 1993, the Pompidou Centre was getting ready to present a retrospective of Matisse's work between 1905 and 1917. The museum was to exhibit 130 paintings. The French organisers of the exhibition were particularly happy that the Pushkin and the Hermitage Museums had agreed to lend some of Matisse's masterpieces which had very rarely been shown outside Russia. Among the works lent by the Russian museums were "*La Danse*" and some twenty other paintings from the Shchukin collection. The exhibition was inaugurated by President Mitterrand on February 23, 1993 and it was to be opened to the public on February 24, 1993.

A few days before the opening to the public, Irina Shchukina, who was still living in Paris, asked the *Tribunal de Grande Instance* in Paris to issue a series of injunctions with respect to the Shchukin paintings on display at the Pompidou Centre.[12] In essence, Ms. Shchukina claimed that the paintings had never lawfully become the property of the Russian museums and that she was the real owner of the paintings by virtue of her father's will. She first asked the President of the tribunal in Paris to issue an interim order to have the paintings belonging to her late father's collection immediately removed from the walls of the Pompidou Centre, where they were displayed. She also claimed that the Shchukin paintings could not be reproduced in the exhibition's catalogue without her permission. She therefore asked the tribunal to issue, as a second interim measure, an injunction to have the 40,000 catalogues of the Matisse

---

[12] The various attempts by Ms. Shchukina to obtain the recognition of her grievances are detailed *in Le Monde*, February 25, 1993.

exhibition printed by the Pompidou Centre seized. These two injunctions were sought as *"référés"* orders (conservatory interim measures), prior to the full hearing of another legal action directed at the Pushkin and Hermitage museums for the seizure of the paintings.[13] On February 25 and 26, 1993 Ms. Shchukina served the directors of the Pushkin and the Hermitage Museums inside the Charles de Gaulle airport in Paris.[14]

A first hearing took place in February 1993 with respect to the immediate removal of the paintings from the exhibition and the seizure of the exhibition's catalogues.[15] At the hearing, Ms. Shchukina's lawyer announced that his client had decided to abandon her interim request to have the paintings removed from the Matisse exhibition. Nevertheless, Ms. Shchukina maintained her request to have the catalogues seized. Ms. Shchukina argued that the paintings had been unlawfully nationalised in 1918 and that neither her father nor his heirs had ever relinquished their right of ownership over the collection. The Pompidou Centre on the other hand, argued that in view of the nationalisation decree of 1918, the Russian state was the current owner of the paintings and that Ms. Shchukina had no valid claims over the paintings by virtue of her position as her father's heir.

On March 5, 1993, the *Juge des Référés* refused to grant the injunction to seize the catalogues and decided that the conditions mentioned in Articles 808 and 809 of the New Code of Civil Procedure with respect to the granting of a *référé* were not met. The tribunal's ruling was based on Articles 808 and 809 of the New Code of Civil Procedure, which establish the conditions for the granting of a *référé* order. Articles 808 and 809 of the New Code of Civil Procedure provide that:

> "Art. 808. In all cases of urgency, the president of the tribunal [...] may order, in summary proceedings [(*'en référé'*)], any measures which do not come up against any serious challenge or which are justified by the existence of a dispute.

> Art. 809. Even in the presence of a serious challenge, the president may always prescribe, in summary proceedings [(*'en référé'*)], the conservatory measures which are called for, either to prevent an imminent harm or to put an end to an obviously illicit disturbance.

> In the cases where the existence of the obligation is not seriously contestable, he may grant a provision to the creditor or order the specific performance of the obligation, even if it consists in a mandatory specific performance obligation [(*'obligation de faire'*)]."

---

[13]The paintings were to be displayed in a Matisse exhibition in Essen at the end of June 1993.

[14]Details on the unusual circumstances of the service of the two Russian museum directors may be found in *Le Monde*, March 1, 1993.

[15]*Audience de référé* under Article 808 of the New Code of Civil Procedure.

The judge decided that to grant an order seizing of the catalogues, she would have to investigate issues relating to the substance of the dispute which she could not decide as a matter of law. The *référé* judge could not rule on the legality of the nationalisation decree which was not within her jurisdiction as a "*Juge des Référés*". The tribunal stated:

> "It is not within the realm of the *Juge des Référés* to assess [...] whether the manner in which the Soviet State, now the Russian State, [...] violates French public policy so seriously that it should not produce any effect in France".[16]

The tribunal found that Ms. Shchukina could not establish that she was the owner of the paintings. It therefore concluded that Ms. Shchukina could not validly request the seizure of the catalogues.

Despite the decision of the *Tribunal des Référés*, Ms. Shchukina, having failed to secure interim relief, maintained her action at the *Tribunal de Grande Instance* of Paris against the Russian museums with respect to the seizure of the paintings at the end of the Matisse exhibition and their safekeeping within the limits of French territory.[17] The hearing at the *Tribunal de Grande Instance* of Paris took place on May 12, 1993. Ms. Shchukina explained that she did not wish that the paintings be returned to her since her father had always intended to donate the collection to the City of Moscow. Ms. Shchukina explained that she wanted to obtain satisfaction from the Russian State on a certain number of substantial issues: she requested the abrogation of the Decree which had nationalised her father's collection, the reunion of the collection in a single dedicated Museum (possibly the Trubetskoy Palace), with the name of her father clearly displayed on each painting alongside the notice "Shchukin donation". She also claimed the Trubetskoy Palace should be given back to her family. She mentioned that the palace could host a foundation, set up by the Shchukin family, in aid of young Russian artists. Finally, Ms. Shchukina wished to receive a "symbolic indemnity" which could be equivalent to one per cent of the current insured value of the paintings.[18] Ms Shchukina based her claim *inter alia* on the French Revolution Declaration of Human Rights of August 26, 1789. Article 17 of that Declaration provides:

> "Property being a sacred and inviolable right, no one shall be deprived of

---

[16]Decision of the Vice President of the *Tribunal de Grande Instance* of Paris of March 5, 1993, unpublished.

[17]Ms. Shchukina's attorney also indicated that she intended to start an action in Germany during the Essen exhibition.

[18]Which, given the value of the paintings, would represent several million pounds. See *Le Monde*, February 25, 1993.

it, unless required by a public necessity, legally acknowledged, and under the condition of a just and prior compensation."

The Declaration of 1789 is not itself in the French constitution, but the Preamble to the Constitution of 1958 refers to it specifically. The Preamble to the 1958 Constitution provides that:

"The French People solemnly proclaims its attachment to human rights and principles of national sovereignty defined by the Declaration of 1789, confirmed and completed by the preamble to the Constitution of 1946."

Ms. Shchukina argued that the Soviet nationalisation of her father's collection was contrary to the Declaration of Human Rights reaffirmed in the Preamble to the French Constitution of 1958. Consequently, Ms. Shchukina claimed that the nationalisation of the collection without any fair indemnity was a violation of French public policy. Ms. Shchukina's lawyer also mentioned Article 1 of Protocol No. 1 of the European Convention on Human Rights which states that:

"Every natural or legal person is entitled to the peaceful enjoyment of his possessions except in the public interest and subject to the conditions provided for by law and by the general principles of international law.[…]"[19]

Ms. Shchukina based her claim to ownership of the paintings on both her father's will and French private international law rules since, under French case law, the inheritance of movable property is governed by the law of the domicile of the deceased.[20]

On June 16, 1993, the tribunal refused to grant the order of seizure and declined jurisdiction over the case.[21] The tribunal based its ruling on the principle of sovereign immunity of the Russian state. The tribunal found that the nationalisation of the collection was the act of a sovereign state, on which the French court could not rule. The fact that this act of state might have resulted in spoliation did not deprive it of its sovereign character. The tribunal stated that: "The spoliating nature of the nationalisation does not change its nature as an act of sovereignty". The tribunal concluded by applying the principle of sovereign immunity to the conservatory measure requested by Ms. Shchukina. The

---

[19] On the application of Article 1 of Protocol No.1 of the European Convention on Human Rights to Cultural Property see Renold, "A landmark decision in Art Law by the European Court of Human Rights", (2000) 5 *Art Antiquity and Law* 73.
[20] See for example, *Cass. Civ.* June 19, 1963 JDI 1964.555.
[21] The decision is consistent with French case law. See *Cass. Civ.* April 15, 1986. (1986) 75 *Rev. Cr. Dr. Int. Pr.*723, note Gouchez.

tribunal stated that "in the absence of a waiver of its immunity by the State, this tribunal cannot order against it a conservatory measure, even such a limited one". Ms. Shchukina did not appeal the decision.[22]

This court saga, however, had consequences that Ms. Shchukina had probably not foreseen. Following the Shchukina case, the Russian museums became increasingly worried about exhibiting their collections outside Russia. They sought guarantees that the paintings they would lend could not be seized while on exhibition abroad.[23] The Russians became increasingly worried as they were faced with an increasing number of claims from original owners particularly in respect of war trophies removed from Germany at the end of the Second World War.[24] Archives released by the Russians in the early 1990s revealed that at the end of the Second World War, special Russian units accompanied by art specialists took entire collections of artworks, paintings in particular, held by German museums and individuals. On the orders of the KGB, these objects were hidden in the cellars of the museums in Moscow and Saint Petersburg. This war treasure was, until the *Perestroika*, a well-kept secret.[25] In fact, many in the West believed that the objects had been destroyed by the bombings over Germany at the end of the war.[26] Most of these works had not been seen since the Second World War.

Russian officials publicly declared that if nothing was done to protect objects loaned by Russia to western museums against threats of seizure, then Russia would simply stop lending its artworks for exhibitions outside its national territory.[27] Concomitantly, all over the world, holocaust victims were increasingly trying to reclaim what had been stolen from them during the Second World War.[28] The French museums became increasingly worried that foreign art institutions would feel at risk when lending their paintings for French exhibitions. The French government was caught between two competing con-

---

[22] See the case note by Ruth Redmond-Cooper in (1996) 1 *Art Antiquity and Law* 73.

[23] See *Le Monde,* February 25, 1993.

[24] A significant percentage of the war treasure that the Russians brought back from Germany had been previously looted by the Germans themselves from the various European countries they had occupied.

[25] See, for example, the history of the Dutch Koenig collection which had disappeared during the war. In 1992, the Russian Ministry of Culture disclosed that it held a large part of the collection. The collection had been looted by the Nazis in 1941 and stocked in Dresden during the war. It had disappeared at the end of the war. See *Agence France Presse,* April 22, 1995, March 8, 1995, September 17, 1997 and March 5, 1997.

[26] See in particular, *Le Monde,* December 22, 1993, March 31, 1995, *International Herald Tribune,* April 29-30, 2000.

[27] See for example the statement of Mr. Piotrovski, the Director of the Hermitage Museum, reported *in Le Monde*, June 18, 1993.

[28] In response to claims relating to Russian trophy art, the Russian Parliament adopted a law declaring that the artwork confiscated by the Red Army in Germany at the end of the Second World War was the property of Russia. See *Le Monde*, December 26, 1997.

cerns: the right of owners of cultural property to reclaim objects illegally taken from them and the ability of French museums to continue their public mandate.

The response of the French government to those concerns was swift. On August 8, 1994[29] France adopted Law No. 94-679 which included a provision guaranteeing foreign art institutions that cultural objects they would loan for public exhibitions in France would be immune from seizure while on French territory. Article 61 of the law provides:

> "Cultural objects loaned by a foreign power, a foreign public or cultural entity, which are to be exhibited to the public in France, cannot be seized while they are loaned to the French State or to any legal person designated by it.
>
> A decree[30] issued jointly by the Minister of Culture and the Minister of Foreign Affairs fixes, for each exhibition, the list of cultural objects, determines the duration of their loan and identifies the exhibition organisers."

The new anti-seizure French statute is, however, not broadly drafted and applies to a limited number of cases. It is, for example, narrower than its American counterparts. The New York exemption statute, for instance, which is found in Article 12.03 of the New York Arts and Cultural Affairs Law states:

> "No process of attachment, execution, sequestration, replevin, distress or any kind of civil seizure shall be served or levied upon any work of fine art while the same is en route to or from, or while on exhibition or deposited by a non-resident exhibitor at any exhibition held under the auspices or supervision of any museum, college, university or other non-profit art gallery, institution or organisation within any city or county of this state for any cultural, educational, charitable or other purpose not conducted for profit to the exhibitor, nor shall such work of fine art be subject to attachment, civil seizure, levy or sale, for any cause whatever in the hands of the authorities of such exhibition or otherwise."[31]

Obviously, the French government did not want to adopt a broad anti-seizure statute which would have prevented the seizure in France of all artwork belonging to private or public foreign owners. Such a statute would have resulted in total immunity for foreign art owners, irrespective of their legitimacy, not

---

[29]Published in the French Official Journal of October 19, 1994.

[30]*Arrêté.*

[31]For the application of the Statute to a criminal seizure see *People v. Museum of Modern Art (In re Grand Jury Subpoena Duces Tecum)* (1999) 93 N.Y. (2d) 729, 697 N.Y.S. (2d) 538, 719 N.E. (2d) 897.

only to display but also to import into France artworks looted, stolen or of other dubious provenance.[32] For that reason the scope of application of the statute is quite limited and in order to benefit from it, a number of conditions have to be met.

The first condition is that the objects must fall into the category of "cultural objects". That term is not defined by the statute and has not been explained either by any other decree relating to the statute or by any court. However, to date, the joint decrees issued under this statute have covered the loan of paintings, statues, antique furniture or artefacts, rare books and photographs.

The second condition is that the lender of the object be foreign. Obviously, the statute does not intend to protect domestic lenders. In fact, a number of claims against the French museums have been upheld by French courts.[33]

The third condition relates to the identity of the lender. The statute only applies if the lender is a state or a public entity such as a public museum, or else a cultural institution. The latter refers to private museums or collections such as the Frick or Barnes collections. Article 61 does not therefore apply to private owners or to commercial entities such as commercial art galleries, auctioneers, banks or insurance companies which have also been the target of seizures.[34]

The fourth condition is that the objects be loaned temporarily to be exhibited to the public. This would obviously exclude sales or donations of these objects in France.

The fifth condition is that the objects be loaned to the French state or to a legal person designated by the French state. Obviously, Article 61 was clearly designed for the benefit of the French public and private museums. The statute therefore excludes loans to private persons. It is unclear, however, whether commercial art galleries could benefit from it. The statute does not exclude this specifically. However to date, all decrees issued under Article 61 have concerned loan to French museums. Article 61 also grants the French State discre-

---

[32] See, for example, the *Newhouse* case decided by the French Supreme Court for the Franz Hals, *Cass. Crim.*, June 4, 1998.

[33] See, for example, the *Gentili di Giuseppe* case (Court of Appeals of Paris, June 2, 1999, unpublished) against the *Musée du Louvre* in which the Court of Appeals of Paris ordered the *Musée du Louvre* to return a series of paintings by Tiepolo to the Gentili di Giuseppe heirs. More recently, on November 1998, the estate of another famous art collector, Alphonse Kahn, filed a criminal complaint against the Pompidou Centre with respect to a painting by George Braque. See *Le Monde*, April 27, 1999.

[34] A French case against an American art gallery is indicative of the current attitude of French courts with respect to seizure of artworks in the hands of commercial art galleries. On June 4, 1998, the French Supreme Court (*La Cour de Cassation*) rendered a decision with respect to the possible indictment of a New York art gallery which was exhibiting in France a painting from the Schloss collection, a well-known Jewish collection looted by the Germans. The French courts not only allowed the painting, a Franz Hals, to be seized, but they also decided that a criminal action against the New York gallery owner could proceed for possession of looted artworks. See *Cour de Cassation, Chambre Criminelle* June 4, 1998.

tion with respect to the identity of the institution organising the exhibition. Any French museum willing to exhibit cultural objects protected by Article 61 would first have to clear it with the French government, even before a decree is issued in their favour.

The sixth condition is the making of a special decree issued jointly by the Minister of Culture and the Minister of Foreign Affairs. Even if all the above conditions are met, the statute does not automatically apply. The organisers of the exhibition have to request the issuance of the decree and provide the two Ministers with an exact list of the objects covered by the decree as well as a list of the organisers of the exhibition.

Finally, the application of the statute is also limited in time. The decree issued under the statute is only valid for the duration of the loan of the objects to the organisers of the exhibition. Should objects be loaned to France twice in the same year, they would have to be protected by two separate decrees.

It is unclear whether the French statute would apply to criminal as well as civil seizures. The wording of the statute, however, may be broad enough to encompass criminal as well as civil seizures.[35]

Since its adoption in 1994, the French anti-seizure statute has been widely used. In fact, most of the objects on loan from Russian museums exhibited in France since October 1994 are protected by a decree issued under Article 61. The Russian Federation, however, has not been the sole beneficiary of the protection granted under Article 61. Interestingly, museums from Turkey, Norway, Holland, England, Romania, Canada, Germany, Spain, Ireland, Sweden, Switzerland, Macedonia, Israel, Taiwan, Poland and the United States, among others, have also requested that certain of their cultural objects be protected by the French anti-seizure statute.[36]

The French statute may be in conflict, if not with the letter, at least with the spirit of a number of legal instruments either adopted or having force in France. It is however, interesting to note that since its adoption in 1994, the validity of the French anti-seizure statute has never been challenged, despite an increasing number of court cases involving holocaust victims trying to reclaim their

---

[35] Interestingly, current cases of claims and seizures attempted against museums or galleries with respect to Nazi-looted art are now of a criminal nature. See in particular the *Franz Hals* case, above, n.34, and the *Braque* case, above, n.33, in France. In the United States, a criminal subpoena in New York was sought to detain two paintings by Egon Schiele which had been borrowed by the MoMA from the Leopold Foundation in Vienna. In September 1999, the New York Supreme Court quashed the subpoena which, according to the court, was in contradiction to the anti-seizure statute contained in Article 12.03 of the New York Arts and Cultural Affairs Law. Federal proceedings, however, are still under way. For a complete account of the New York Schiele saga see Martha Lufkin, "The subpoena heard round the world: The Schiele Case and other Legal Immunities for Art Loaned into the US" (1999) 4 *Art Antiquity and Law* 363.

[36] See for example, Decree of January 14, 2000, Decree of January 11, 2000, Decree of December 22, 1999, Decree of December 1, 1999, Decree of August 30, 1999, Decree of May 12, 1999.

looted artworks from museums around the world and from Russia in particu-lar.[37]

The French anti-seizure statute is certainly contrary to the spirit in which the French government has recently tried to facilitate the return of Second World War looted art to holocaust survivors and their families. In 1997, the French Prime Minister Lionel Jospin issued an Edict[38] creating a new Commission chaired by Mr. Mattéoli ("the Mattéoli Commission") to study in depth the looting of Jewish assets during the Second World War. The Commission's role was to make proposals and to recommend the adoption of measures with re-spect to looted Jewish assets which still have not been returned to their legiti-mate owners.[39] On the recommendation of the Mattéoli Commission, the French government put in place an entirely new procedure, outside the realm of ordi-nary judicial courts, to facilitate the fair and speedy settlement of claims from holocaust survivors and their families.[40] Until now, the anti-seizure statute has never been challenged with respect to looted art. This apparent acceptance as a *"fait accompli"* of the French anti-seizure statute may nevertheless be explained. In April 2000, the Mattéoli Commission released its final report. The work of the Commission revealed that many artworks looted in France were still in the hands of German, Austrian and Russian museums. Consequently, a number of initiatives and joint working-groups have been put in place by the French gov-ernment to reach a settlement of all outstanding cases with those three coun-tries.[41] The Russians have recently publicly expressed their good will in that respect. They have in particular started acknowledging publicly the fact that hundreds of artworks taken from Germany at the end of the Second World War

---

[37] It is interesting to note that the French anti-seizure statute is not incompatible with the French constitution since, unlike Article 43 of the Irish constitution, the French constitution does not guarantee citizens the protection of their property.

[38] Edict of the Prime Minister of March 25, 1997.

[39] On December 31, 1997, the Commission released its first progress report. A second progress report recommended putting in place a special simplified procedure in order to examine and satisfy outstanding recovery claims in an efficient manner. See *Mission d'étude sur la spolia-tion des Juifs de France: Rapport genéral* (La Documentation Française, Paris, 2000). The French government adopted the recommendation of the Commission and in an edict of Septem-ber 10, 1999 created an entirely new procedure, outside the ordinary court system, for those recovery claims. Article 1 of the Edict specifies that the purpose of the new commission, called the Drai Commission, is:

"to examine individual claims emanating from victims or their families in order to indem-nify them for the damages they have sustained as a result of the looting of properties which occurred by the operation of the anti-Semitic laws adopted during the Occupation, by the [Germans] as well as by the Vichy authorities."

[40] Edict of September 10, 1999.

[41] See Mattéoli *Final Report* (La Documentation Française, Paris, 2000) p.83. In order to facili-tate the return of missing artworks, the final report advocates the establishment of cross border governmental bodies with Germany, Austria and Russia. A permanent working group for cul-tural property is being created with Russia and another cross border body has been put in place with Germany.

were still in their possession, most of them in boxes or in the cellars of Russian museums. They have also announced that they will provide access to Russian archives containing Nazi documents relating to looted artwork.[42] It is therefore possible that potential claimants, who could try to challenge the validity of the anti-seizure statute, have put their claims on hold in expectation of a diplomatic settlement between the two governments. In May 2000, Russian legislation was passed which should enable Russian holocaust victims or their families to institute claims.[43]

The French anti-seizure statute could also be, in certain cases, in conflict with the European Council Directive 93/7 of March 15, 1993 on the return of cultural objects unlawfully removed from the territory of a Member State.[44] More specifically, Article 61 of the Law No. 94-679 could be contrary to Articles 2 and 4.4 of the Directive. Article 2 of the Directive provides that:

> "Cultural objects which have been unlawfully removed from the territory of a Member State shall be returned in accordance with the procedure and in the circumstances provided for in this Directive."

Article 4 of the Directive puts in place a series of co-operation procedures between member states to facilitate the return of cultural objects under Article 2. Article 4.5 is of particular interest in light of the existence of the French anti-seizure statute. Article 4.5 provides that:

> "Member States' central authorities shall co-operate and promote consultation between the Member States' competent national authorities. The latter shall in particular: ... 5. *Prevent, by the necessary interim measures, any action to evade the return procedure.* [Emphasis added]"

A simple hypothetical illustrates the difficulties which could be generated by the conflict between the two legal regimes. One could easily imagine a situation where a German museum would loan artworks to a French museum for an exhibition and would obtain the protection of a Decree under Article 61 of Law No. 94-679. What would be the response of French courts if, during the exhibition, a Dutch museum claimed that the paintings were stolen from Holland by the Nazis and asked a French court for the immediate seizure of the paintings under Article 4.5 of the Directive?[45]

Finally, the French anti-seizure statute may not be compatible with the UNIDROIT Convention of June 24, 1995, on Stolen or Illegally Exported

---

[42] See *The Art Newspaper*, No. 108, November 2000.
[43] See *The Art Newspaper*, No. 108, November 2000.
[44] (1993) O.J. L. 74.
[45] The Nazis plundered Holland's museums and art collections during the war.

Cultural Objects, signed by France.[46] According to its Article 1, the Convention is intended to apply:

> "to claims of an international character for:
> (a) the restitution of stolen cultural objects;
> (b) the return of cultural objects removed from the territory of a Contracting State contrary to its law regulating the export of cultural objects for the purpose of protecting its cultural heritage (hereinafter 'illegally exported cultural objects')."

In addition, Article 3(1) of the Convention provides that "the possessor of a cultural object which has been stolen shall return it". The obligation to return stolen objects applies even where the possessor of the stolen object did not or could not have known that the object had been stolen.[47] Obviously, the French anti-seizure statute could be in conflict with the UNIDROIT Convention in situations where artworks protected by an Article 61 decree were the object of a claim before a French court to have them returned under Article 3(1) of the UNIDROIT Convention. The provisions of the UNIDROIT Convention prevail over a decree under Article 61 of the 1994 Law, since Article 55 of the 1958 French Constitution provides that:

> "The treaties or conventions regularly ratified or approved have, from the moment when they are published, an authority which supersedes that of the laws, on the condition, for each convention or treaty, that they be applied by the other party."

CONCLUSION: THE QUEST FOR "*LA DANSE*" CONTINUES

The Shchukin family has not brought any other actions in France since the adoption of the new statute. However, the family has not given up its crusade against the Russian museums. In June 2000, after the death of his mother, Ms. Shchukina's son, Mr. Delocque-Fourcaud, applied to an Italian court for the seizure of "*La Danse*", which was on temporary exhibition in Rome.[48] The painting was part of an exhibition on the theme of "One Hundred Treasures of

---

[46]For a commentary on the Convention, see the research paper by Marina Schneider "The UNIDROIT Convention on Stolen or Illegally Exported Cultural Objects" UNIDROIT Rome (1995). See also Valentin, "The UNIDROIT Convention on the International Return of Stolen or Illegally Exported Cultural objects" (1999) 4 *Art Antiquity and Law* 107.

[47]Article 4(1) of the UNIDROIT Convention. The *bona fide* possessor is nevertheless entitled to payment of fair compensation under Article 4(1) and 4(2) of the Convention.

[48]The *Art Newspaper*, No. 105, July-August 2000.

the Hermitage Museum". Nearly half of the artworks loaned by the Hermitage museum for the Rome exhibition came from the Shchukin collection. Mr. Delocque-Fourcaud, however, sought only the seizure of a single painting out of the 45 from the Shchukin collection on exhibition, as a symbolic action in order to attract public attention to the plight of his family.[49] The Hermitage Museum responded to the action by asserting that Mr. Delocque-Fourcaud's claims were totally unjustified. The museum also declared that the French courts had already rejected these claims. The Italian court ordered an expert report with respect to the nature of the agreements signed between the Russian museum and the Italian organisers of the exhibition.[50] The judge, however, never got the opportunity to render a decision on the case since the Russians rushed "*La Danse*" back to Saint Petersburg before the first hearing was to take place.[51]

---

[49] *Agence France Presse* June 9, 2000.
[50] *Agence France Presse* June 13, 2000.
[51] *The Art Newspaper*, No. 105, July-August 2000.

GRATING EXPECTATIONS? THE PROTECTION OF LEGITIMATE EXPECTATIONS IN EUROPEAN COMMUNITY LAW AND IN AUTOCHTHONOUS IRISH LAW

GAVIN BARRETT

1. INTRODUCTION

The writings of the late Professor James Brady over the course of his career spanned a considerable range of topics, primarily but not exclusively concentrated in the fields of equity, charities and succession. In seeking a suitable topic upon which to write a contribution in a volume dedicated to his memory, the student or practitioner of European Community law finds at least one topic which readily proposes itself.[1] This is the subject of legitimate expectation – a subject the growing importance of which in recent years Professor Brady focussed a perceptive eye upon.[2] It would perhaps be more accurate to say that Professor Brady focussed his attention on *one* of the doctrines of legitimate expectation which exist in Irish law. There are in fact now two such doctrines. One of them – the doctrine of legitimate expectation which Professor Brady examined – is the form of legitimate expectation which has recently come to prominence in various jurisdictions throughout the common law world. It has attained a particular prominence in Ireland since the famous decision of the Supreme Court in *Webb v. Ireland*[3] – the case concerning the discovery of the Derrynaflan hoard. It would probably be somewhat invidious (at least at this point of this essay) to term this the "common law" doctrine of legitimate expectation, since equity lawyers have tended to claim the doctrine as further proof that equity is not past the age of childbearing.[4] Thus for the purposes of

---

[1] My thanks are due to my colleagues Professor Jim Casey for originally suggesting the topic of legitimate expectation to me, Oonagh Breen for pointing me towards some useful material on the Irish doctrine of legitimate expectation and to John O'Dowd for calling some very recent decisions in this area from elsewhere in the common law world to my attention. Finally, my thanks also to Madeleine Coumont de Bairéid for her invaluable help in transforming this essay from a well-nigh illegible scrawl to an immaculately typed manuscript.

[2] See here Professor Brady's article "Aspiring Students, Retiring Professors and the Doctrine of Legitimate Expectation" (1996) 31 *Ir. Jur. (ns)* 133.

[3] [1988] I.R. 353.

[4] Professor Brady regarded the recent emergence of the doctrine as "further evidence of equity's

this chapter (and for want of a better name) it is intended to refer to this doctrine by the rubric of the "autochthonous" doctrine of legitimate expectation. I am conscious of the potential of this name to mislead. It is as well to remind ourselves, therefore, that the doctrine is not "autochthonous" to the Irish legal system as such, but rather to the whole common law tradition, since it is the fruit of the intellectual exertions not merely of Irish judges, lawyers and academics, but of those of their colleagues in other jurisdictions such as Canada, Australia, New Zealand and, above all, England.

A second reason why the use of the word "autochthonous" gives us some cause to pause is that, as mentioned above, there is a second doctrine of legitimate expectation in Irish law. This second doctrine forms just as much part and parcel of Irish law as the doctrine which I have somewhat arbitrarily styled the "autochthonous" doctrine. This second doctrine is the general principle of European Community law of legitimate expectation. Its standing as part of Irish law is unquestionable,[5] and indeed it should be noted that this latter doctrine was relied upon – albeit unsuccessfully – in at least one case before the Irish courts which predated the recent upsurge in cases concerning the autochthonous doctrine.[6] For the purposes of clarity, this second doctrine will be referred to in this chapter as the "Community law" doctrine of legitimate expectation.

The above-described doctrines are distinct and differ in a number of respects, although there has been at least some degree of cross-fertilisation between the two in the past, and there seems to be no good reason why this should not continue to be the case in the future.[7] As Delany has pointed out:

---

vital role in the modern legal system" (See Brady, *loc. cit.,* above, n. 2 at p. 133) a view with which Finlay C.J. would certainly have been in accord since he asserted in *Webb* that the doctrine was "but an aspect of the well-recognised equitable concept of promissory estoppel ... whereby a promise or representation as to intention may in certain circumstances be held binding on the representor or promisor." (See [1988] I.R. 353 at 384). Whether Professor Brady would have been in accord with the views of the learned Chief Justice on this point, however, seems less clear to this writer. (See Brady, *loc. cit.,* above, n. 2 at p. 144).

[5] Thus s. 2(1) of the European Communities Act 1972 (as amended by section 2 of the European Communities Act 1992) provides that "from the 1st day of January 1973, the treaties governing the European Communities and the existing and future acts adopted by the institutions of those Communities and by the bodies competent under the said treaties shall be binding on the State and shall be part of the domestic law thereof under the conditions laid down in those treaties." Note also the words of the European Court of Justice in the landmark case of *Costa v. ENEL* (Case 6/64) [1964] E.C.R. 585 at 593:
    "By contrast with ordinary international treaties, the EEC Treaty has created its own legal system which, on the entry into force of the Treaty, became an integral part of the legal systems of the Member States and which their courts are bound to apply."

[6] *Smith v. Ireland* [1983] I.L.R.M. 300. This case was first called to light by Delany in "The Doctrine of Legitimate Expectation in Irish Law" (1990) 12 *D.U.L.J. (ns)* 1 at 5.

[7] See text, below. Note that in his concurring judgment in *Wiley v. Revenue Commissioners* [1993] I.L.R.M. 482 at 493, a case which concerned the autochthonous concept, O'Flaherty J. had regard to authorities both on the autochthonous doctrine and on the Community law doctrine of legitimate expectation. Hamilton J. (as he then was) did the same in *Carbery Milk Products Ltd. v. Minister for Agriculture and others* (1988-1993) 4 I.T.R. 492 (judgment of April 23, 1993).

"while the origins of the principle of legitimate expectations in European Community law and the doctrine of legitimate expectations in English law owe little or nothing to each other, the preconditions for their operation have many common features and they both seek to ensure the protection of expectations legitimately created, whether by the institutions of the European Communities or by various types of government authorities or administrative bodies."[8]

Thus the two doctrines have in common "an attribution of legal consequences to reliance by private parties upon the conduct or representations of public authorities."[9]

It has been said of the Community principle of legitimate expectation that it may be invoked by any individual who is in a situation in which it appears that the conduct of the administration has led him to entertain reasonable expectations or justified hopes.[10] Such a definition seems appropriate whether one is discussing either the Community principle or the autochthonous doctrine.[11] Another observation which also applies both in relation to the community principle and the autochthonous is that:

"the expectations which a person can derive from a policy are not merely a matter for factual analysis. They will depend on a normative view of the expectations which an individual can be said to derive from the original policy, combined with an interpretative judgment as to whether the legislative framework will, in some way, be jeopardised by holding the administration to the original policy, even in relation to those already accepted by it."[12]

This seems acceptable only insofar as it is borne in mind that two distinct, albeit extensively conceptually overlapping, doctrines are being dealt with. On a more general note, Schwarze has observed that:

"today a prolific interaction between Community law and national law is developing: law traditions common to the Member States have provided a basis and an inspiration for the Community's legal order. Community law in turn is now beginning to inspire national laws."

(See "Sources of European Administrative Law" Chapter 9 of Martin (ed.), *The Construction of Europe – Essays in Honour of Emile Noël*, (Kluwer Academic Publishers: Dordrecht, 1994) 183 at 195).

[8] Delany, *loc. cit.,* above, n.6, at p. 6.
[9] Wyatt, "European Community Law and Public Law in the United Kingdom" in Markesinis (ed.) *The Gradual Convergence* (Oxford, 1994) 188 at 194 to 195.
[10] Vaughan, *Law of the European Communities* (2nd ed., London, 1990) at para. 1266 relying on the words of the Court of Justice in cases such as *Mavridis v. European Parliament* (Case 289/81) [1983] E.C.R. 1731 at para. 21 thereof and *Van den Bergh en Jurgens v. Commission* (Case 265/85) [1987] E.C.R. 1155 at para. 44 thereof.
[11] *cf.,* however, *Fakih v. Minister for Justice* [1993] 2 I.R. 406 discussed in the text, below.
[12] Craig, "Legitimate Expectations: A Conceptual Analysis" (1992) 108 *L.Q.R.* 79.

Both doctrines also require examination of a similar range of issues, including "the question of what makes an expectation or privilege reasonable or legitimate, whether it is an expectation of a fair hearing and being allowed to put one's case, or of receiving the privilege or benefit sought, the factors which give right rise to a legitimate expectation such as an established practice, a promise or undertaking given or a series of rules or guidelines which may give rise to an expectation that a certain result will follow".[13] An effort is therefore made to examine these questions in relation to the two doctrines which form the subject of this essay, although the emphasis placed on individual issues in this piece varies with the doctrine being examined, since so too do the emphases in the relevant bodies of case-law. Hence the question of whether there can be such a thing as substantive legitimate expectation has caused major difficulty in the case of the autochthonous doctrine, but has provoked relatively little controversy in so far as concerns the Community principle of legitimate expectation. The time spent in answering such questions is well spent, for such doctrines constitute a subject of study of some importance. It is perhaps stating the obvious to point out that in an era in which the role of government has expanded to encompass authorising, licensing, financing, administering and delegating a vast array of human activities, any doctrine which is concerned with the rights of individuals and companies interacting with the State is obviously likely to be of correspondingly increased significance.[14] Furthermore, insofar as the erstwhile "zone of immunity" around governmental activities has been contained or is being reduced,[15] – and it seems fair to say that the attribution of immunity to governmental activities seems increasingly less tolerable as their scope has become increasingly broad – doctrines such as those which form the subject of this chapter have had a significant role to play, and seem likely to continue to do so. They thus constitute an important element of Irish administrative law.

One should not make the mistake of exaggerating similarities between the Community and the autochthonous doctrines. Without delving too much into topics which form the substance of the remainder of this essay, one difference which may be pointed out, for example, is that the relative importance of the Community principle in the Community legal system and that of the autochthonous doctrine within the Irish system have not been the same to date. Schwarze has asserted that "European Community law is primarily made up of rules of administrative law, drawn in particular from the area of law governing the management of the economy" and observed that "the European Commu-

---

[13] Delany, *loc. cit.*, above, n.6 at p. 3.
[14] See on this point Baldwin and Horne, "Expectations in a Joyless Landscape" (1986) 49 *M.L.R.* 685 at 685-686.
[15] See here de Smith, Woolf and Jowell, *Judicial Review of Administrative Action* (5th edition, London, 1995) at p.9 and Delany "Significant Themes in Judicial Review of Administrative Action" (1998) 20 *D.U.L.J. (ns)* 73.

nity, already described by the European Court of Justice as a Community based on law, could more precisely be termed a Community based on administrative law".[16] There may be some exaggeration here, but it is certainly true to say that, to date, administrative law principles have played a vastly more significant role in the Community legal system than have administrative law principles in the domestic Irish legal system. Furthermore, within the Community law system of administrative law, the Community law principle of legitimate expectation has enjoyed a more prominent and long-established role than has the autochthonous principle in domestic Irish administrative law. (The number of cases in which the doctrine of legitimate expectation has been invoked before the European Court of Justice now runs into the high hundreds).[17]

Of course, the Community law principles of legitimate expectation can be relied upon not alone before the European Court of Justice but, in an appropriate case, before Irish courts as well. However, the reality is that this Community law principle has remained to date both in academic writing and in practice a relatively unexplored concept both in academic writings and in judgments emanating from this jurisdiction to date. The first part of the article therefore is primarily dedicated to an examination of the Community law principle. The autochthonous doctrine will be discussed in the second part.

2. THE COMMUNITY LAW PRINCIPLE OF LEGITIMATE EXPECTATION

(a) Introduction

It may perhaps be an unexpected feature of a regime so influenced by the laws of the civil law jurisdictions that Community administrative law (and within it, the general principles of Community law, and within these again, the legal rules relating to the principle of legitimate expectation) is largely constituted by judge-made law.[18] The legal principles here have been created "on an incre-

---

[16] Schwarze, "Sources of European Administrative Law" Chapter 9 of Martin (ed.), *The Construction of Europe – Essays in Honour of Emile Noël*, 183 at 183. The description by the European Court of the Community as one based on law has been applied by the court in a number of cases, among them *Parti écologiste "Les Verts" v. European Parliament* (Case 294/83)[1986] E.C.R. 1339 at para. 23 of the judgment.

[17] See Usher, *General Principles of EC Law* (London, 1998) at p. 52. Note also that Schwarze dedicates over 300 pages of his seminal volume *European Administrative Law* (Office for Official Publications of the European Communities/ Sweet and Maxwell, 1992) to a chapter entitled "Legal Certainty and Protection of Legitimate Expectations."

[18] It is interesting, however, to note that this is also true of French administrative law and the approach of the Conseil d'État in that jurisdiction. See Bell, Boyron and Whittaker, *Principles of French Law* (Oxford, 1998) at pp. 28 to 29. Note that Community administrative law is not entirely unwritten. Within certain policy areas, such as the competition and anti–dumping regimes, special codes of administrative procedure have been developed. (See Schwarze, "Developing Principles of European Administrative Law" [1993] *P.L.* 229 at 230 to 231).

mental, *ad hoc* basis in the light of the concrete needs of the cases under consideration."[19] The unwritten nature of the rules at issue here gives rise to the advantage of flexibility, but has also created an element of uncertainty as to some of the applicable legal norms.

(b) The Provenance of Legitimate Expectation in EC Law: General Principles of Community Law

General principles of law have been described as a source of Community law. They are an unwritten source of law – a concept which exists in the Community legal system just as in others – hence the observation of the European Court of Justice that "the fact that a principle is not mentioned in written Community law is not sufficient proof that it does not exist."[20] General principles of law have been characterised as the particular response of the European Court of Justice to the problem that in no legal system is it possible for legislation or other written sources of law to provide an answer to every question which comes before the courts.[21] Thus in Community law, general principles fulfil the same role played out *e.g.,* by the myth of the common law in common law systems or *e.g.,* in Irish constitutional jurisprudence by rights derived from, *inter alia,* Article 40.3 of the Constitution. In Hartley's vivid phrase they are what the European Court of Justice uses:

> "to cloak the nakedness of judicial law-making: the idea is that, if a ruling can be shown to be derived from a principle of sufficient generality as to command common assent, a firm legal foundation for the judgment will be provided."[22]

It has been said that more use is made by the European Court of Justice of general principles of law than is made by other international tribunals. Akehurst has argued that the main reason for this is the fact that in many respects Community law bears more resemblance to municipal law in structure and content than it does to ordinary international law, even though the Communities were created by international treaties. Thus, like municipal law, Community law creates rights for individuals, and further, the institutions of the Community bear a certain degree of resemblance to the institutions of a state.[23] Another reason for recourse to general principles is the reality that the Treaty of Rome

---

[19] Schwarze, *loc. cit.,* above, n.18 at p. 229.
[20] See the judgment of the European Court of Justice in *Officine Elettromeccaniche Ing A Merlini v. High Authority* (Case 108/63) [1965] E.C.R. 1 at 10.
[21] Hartley, *The Foundations of European Community Law* (4th ed., Oxford, 1998) at p. 130.
[22] *ibid.*
[23] See Akehurst, "The Application of General Principles of Law by the Court of Justice of the European Communities" [1981] *BYIL* 29 at 31.

(or EC Treaty) shares with national constitutions the features that it cannot be exhaustive, and that it is exceedingly difficult to amend.[24] Last and certainly not least is the particular feature of the EC Treaty that it was written as a *traité cadre* (framework treaty) which tends to merely set broad goals and principles, leaving it to secondary legislation and to the jurisdiction of the court to bridge any gaps which might exist in its provisions.[25]

The necessity for a gap-filling device was encountered by the Court of Justice even before the Treaty of Rome came about, when it was realised in the early days of operation of its older sister treaty, the European Coal and Steel Community (ECSC) Treaty, that the Treaty rules and secondary legislation lacked the comprehensiveness which was needed in order to enable the court to decide disputes which arose before it. Already, in the early case of *Fédération Charbonnière de Belgique v. High Authority*[26] Advocate General Lagrange pointed out that the Court of Justice could not be absolved from the duty of giving judgment in a case before it merely because of a lacuna in Community law.[27] Implicit acceptance of such opinions was a feature of the later landmark decision of the European Court of Justice in *Algera v. Common Assembly* (also decided under the ECSC Treaty) in which the court accepted the principle of the revocability of administrative decisions which were vitiated by illegality (in this case the decision to appoint the claimants to the staff of the Assembly). In the court's own words, this case involved:

> "a problem of administrative law which is familiar in the case-law and learned writing of all the countries of the Community, but for the solution of which the Treaty does not contain any rules. Unless the Court is to deny justice it is therefore obliged to solve the problem by reference to the rules acknowledged by the legislation, the learned writing and the case-law of the member countries."[28]

Apart from their role as a source of principles to plug the gaps in the written corpus of Community law, general principles fulfil at least two other major roles. Their second function is to operate as guidance as to how Treaty provisions and secondary legislation (*i.e.* acts which are adopted by the Community

---

[24] See Charlesworth and Cullen, *European Community Law* (London, 1994) at p. 97. Indeed, the process of amendment of the EC Treaty is far more difficult than that required to amend national constitutions. The Treaty of Rome has of course the feature in common with many national constitutions that its provisions are the highest-ranking legal rules within a particular legal system.

[25] See Schwarze, "Sources of European Administrative Law" Chapter 9 of Martin (ed.), *The Construction of Europe – Essays in Honour of Emile Noël*, 183 at 191.

[26] Case 8/55 [1954 to 1956] E.C.R. 245 at 277 to 278.

[27] A case first highlighted by Usher in "The Influence of National Concepts on Decisions of the European Court" [1975-6] 1 *E.L. Rev.* 359.

[28] Joined Cases 7/56 and 3-7/57, [1957] E.C.R. 39 at 55.

institutions in order to implement the Treaties) ought to be interpreted. The end effect of interpretation in the light of such principles is often to ensure the validity of the relevant secondary Community legislation. This task has been described as the most frequent use to which general principles of Community law are put.[29]

The third role of general principles of Community law is to control the actions both of Community institutions and of national authorities. This control is exercised in one of three ways.

The first is that general principles act as criteria for determining the legality (and hence validity) of acts both of the Community institutions and of the Member States (including, it should be noted, that of legislation).[30] In other words, the general principles are a vital element in the process of judicial review in Community law. Questions of legality can come before the Court in a number of ways: (a) in a direct action for annulment aimed at challenging the validity of a measure; (b) if a so-called plea of illegality is raised (*i.e.,* if, in the course of proceedings concerned with something else, the argument is raised that a particular act should not apply because it is invalid)[31] – either in a direct action before the Court of Justice or else in the course of national proceedings and the preliminary reference procedure is employed so as to bring the matter before the Court of Justice;[32] or (c) in the context of a claim for damages.[33]

The Court of Justice has pointed out that a violation of a principle (here legitimate expectations) "does not automatically mean that the disputed measure is void."[34] Rather, the remedy awarded will depend on the circumstances

---

[29] Usher, *General Principles of EC Law* (London, 1998) at p. 122.

[30] See, for a case concerning Community secondary legislation, *e.g., Hauer v. Rheinland-Pfalz* (Case 44/79) [1979] E.C.R. 3727, and for a case concerning national legislation, see *e.g., Zuckerfabrik Franken GmbH v. Germany* (Case 77/81) [1982] E.C.R. 681. Akehurst has argued in the past that the relative lack of democratic legitimacy at European level has justified the Court of Justice in reviewing secondary legislation of the Community according to standards as strict as those used in many Member States in reviewing delegated legislation. If Akehurst is correct in this, then standards of review of the Court of Justice should be expected to be relaxed somewhat in the wake of the coming into force of the Treaty of Amsterdam, given the expansion in the powers of the European Parliament which was effected by that Treaty. However, it is not clear that any change has occurred in the approach of the Court of Justice since the coming into force of the Amsterdam Treaty. (See Akehurst, "The Application of General Principles of Law by the Court of Justice of the European Communities" [1981] *B.Y.I.L.* 29 at 50 to 51).

[31] See generally Hartley, *op. cit.,* above, n.21 at pp. 327 to 329 and at ch. 14 thereof.

[32] There have been numerous instances of the European Court of Justice holding a Community measure to be invalid on a preliminary reference from a national court because the measure in question breached a general principle of Community law. A prominent example is the *Mulder* case (Case 120/86) [1988] E.C.R. 2321 in which a Community measure (a Council Regulation) was held invalid because it breached the principle of the protection of legitimate expectation.

[33] As to which, see text below. See generally here, Usher, *op. cit.,* above n.29 at pp. 123 *et seq.*

[34] *Mavrides v. European Parliament* (Case 289/81) [1983] E.C.R. 1731.

of the case.[35] *Semble* that annulment of a measure on the grounds that it violates a general principle will not be granted by the court unless an applicant can show that the breach involved made a difference to his or her case.[36]

The second method of control of Community institutions and national authorities flows from (and to some extent overlaps with) the first. General provisions (such as legitimate expectations) operate as guidance as to how powers granted by Community law ought appropriately to be exercised. As Vaughan has pointed out, the obligation to comply with the general principles of Community law follows from the fact that a failure to do so might lead to an annulment of the measure sought.[37]

The third method of control of Community institutions lies in the fact that breach of general principles of Community law may in certain circumstances give rise to a right to damages on the part of the offended individual. This possibility emerged in the case of *CNTA v. Commission*,[38] a case which involved the principle of legitimate expectations. Here, liability was imposed on the Community because the Commission had violated the legitimate expectations of a trader by failing to allow a transitional period before abolishing a system for compensatory amounts applicable to rape and colza seeds, so that even seeds changing hands under already existing contractual arrangements now failed to attract the compensatory amounts. A number of limitations should be noted here. First, and perhaps self-evidently, a prerequisite to the obtaining of damages for breach of one's legitimate expectations will be the existence of a causal connection between loss suffered and the breach of the relevant expectation.[39] Secondly, the *CNTA* judgment itself is a good illustration of the

---

[35] The Court suggested that in certain circumstances such a breach would justify the award of damages if the person concerned has suffered injury as a result – see further the text, below. See also Schwarze, *European Administrative Law* (Luxembourg/London, Office for Official Publications of the European Communities/Sweet and Maxwell, 1992) at p. 953.

[36] This argument is put forward by Usher, *op. cit.,* above, n. 29 in reliance on the judgment of the Court of Justice in *Deboeck v. Commission* (Case 90/74) [1975] E.C.R. 1123 which however involved a lesser breach of Community law than that of a general principle. See also *De Dapper v. Parliament* (Case 29/74) [1975] E.C.R. 35 and *Marcato v. Commission* (Case 37/72) [1973] E.C.R. 361. Hartley has argued, however, that serious violations of the law will be investigated by the European Court of Justice of its own motion, so that it will be irrelevant whether or not the applicant has an interest. (See Hartley, *op. cit.,* above, n. 21 at pp. 421 to 422).

[37] Vaughan, *op. cit.,* above, n.10 para. 1209 at n.2.

[38] Case 74/74 [1975] E.C.R. 533.

[39] See *Héritiers d'Edmond Ropars v. Council of the European Union* (Case T–429/93) (Judgment of Court of First Instance (First Chamber) of June 21, 2000) and *Tromeur v. Council of the European Union and Commission of the European Union* (Case T–537/93) (Judgment of Court of First Instance (First Chamber) of same date), two of the most recent cases to come before the Court concerning legitimate expectation, and both of which involved claims for damages somewhat similar to those at issue in the earlier case of *Mulder II* (discussed in the text below) in which damages had been awarded for breach of the claimant's legitimate expectations. In *Ropars* and *Tromeur*, both claimants were unsuccessful, however, the claimants – unlike Mulder – having been unable to demonstrate the existence of any intention to resume milk production which had been frustrated by a Commission Regulation.

point that, in general, a limit will be placed on the damages recoverable for breach of the principle of legitimate expectations. Compensation will be limited to the positive damage suffered as a result of the expectation. It will not extend to compensation for any loss of profit which results from the disappointment of the expectation.[40] Thirdly, not just any breach of a general principle will suffice to give rise to liability in damages. Where questions of economic policy are concerned, only a sufficiently serious or flagrant breach of a general principle will suffice to give rise to liability in damages. Thus there are instances of a claimant succeeding in having a measure declared invalid on the basis that it violates the general principle of legitimate expectation, and yet failing to obtain any damages in respect of loss caused by this breach.[41]

Where are general principles of Community law derived from? The two most important sources of general principles are, respectively, the Treaties establishing the Communities and the various legal systems of the Member States (the provenance of the principle of legitimate expectations being, as shall be seen presently, the latter). In the former case,

> "the Court declares that a specific provision in one of the Treaties is an application of some more general principle which is not itself laid down in the Treaty. This is then applied in its own right as a general principle of law...When the Court looks to national law for inspiration, it is not necessary that the principle should be accepted by the legal systems of all the Member States. It would be sufficient if the principle were generally accepted by the legal systems of most Member States, or if it was in conformity with a trend in the Member States, so that one could say that the national legal systems were developing towards it. It must again be emphasised, however, that whatever the factual origin of the principle, it is applied by the European Court as a principle of Community law, not national law."[42]

Thus a general principle of Community law has an existence separate and independent from that of the same principle in a national legal system (or systems) which may have inspired it.[43]

---

[40] See further on this point, *August Töpfer & Co. GmBH v. Commission* (Case 112/77) [1978] E.C.R. 1019.

[41] The famous *Mulder* saga, discussed in part in the text below, is a case in point. A good discussion both of the issues here, and of the issues which arose in the *Mulder* cases is to be found in Usher, *op. cit.,* above, n.29 at pp. 128 to 132.

[42] Hartley, *op. cit.,* above, n.21 at pp. 130 to 131.

[43] Notwithstanding the great influence which continental concepts of administrative law, particularly French law, have had on the judicial remedies provided for and the expressions used in the Treaties, the court has always emphasised the specific character of European Community law as a separate and independent legal system. (See here Schwarze in "Sources of European Administrative Law" Chapter 9 of Martin (ed.), *The Construction of Europe – Essays in Honour of*

(c) Legitimate Expectations as a General Principle of Community Law

The origins of the Community doctrine of legitimate expectation are to be found in the legal systems of the Member States rather than in the Treaties. The concept of legitimate expectation seems to be one which exists in all of the Member States of the Community, although the exact content of the doctrine may vary from state to state.[44] It is also an approach to problem-solving which has featured in the jurisprudence of the European Court of Human Rights as well as in European Community law.[45] Insofar as the protection of legitimate expectations in Community law is concerned, it has, as Nolte has observed, the reputation of being "made in Germany", with legal writers having tended to ascribe its origins (at least in the way in which it is commonly formulated) to the German law doctrine of protection of legitimate expectations or "Vertrauensschutz" (a doctrine the importance of which vastly increased in the German legal system in the 1950s, as a result of decisions of Administrative Courts of the Länder, the reasoning in which was later confirmed by the Federal Constitutional Court, the Bundesverfassungsgericht).[46] While it can occasionally be difficult to determine the precise provenance of principles endorsed by the European Court of Justice,[47] it is certainly true to say (as Schwarze has observed) that the Opinions of the Advocates-General tend to be particularly marked by those legal systems with which they are personally familiar, and that the Opinions of Advocates General Roemer and Reischl in the *Westzucker*

Emile Noël, 183 at 194). Nevertheless the occasionally strong influence of individual national legal systems, in particular, in the derivation of general legal principles, should not be overlooked. The comment has been made that even when a general principle is present in legal systems throughout the Community, the form in which it is adopted by the European Court of Justice will usually be based primarily on the concept as it exists in one Member State in particular. (Charlesworth and Cullen, *op. cit.,* above, n. 24 at p. 98).

[44] Schwarze, *European Administrative Law op. cit.,* above, n.35 at pp. 874 to 937; Craig, "Substantive Legitimate Expectations in Domestic and Community Law (1996) 55 *C.L.J.* 289 at 304.

[45] See *e.g.,* the judgment of the European Court of Human Rights in *National Provincial Building Society and others v. United Kingdom* [1997] S.T.C. 1466, a decision commented on in Oliver, "A Negative Aspect to Legitimate Expectations" [1998] *P.L.* 558.

[46] See in particular the decision of the Oberverwaltungsgericht Berlin (1957) 72 DVBl 505-506, that of the Bundesverfassungsgericht at (1981) 59 BverfGE 128, 164 to 167, and see generally Nolte, "General Principles of German and European Administrative Law – A Comparison in Historical Perspective" (1994) 57 *M.L.R.* 191 in particular at p. 203 *et seq.* See also Usher, "The Influence of National Concepts on Decisions of the European Court" (1975-6) 1 *E.L. Rev.* 359 at 363 to 364; and Charlesworth and Cullen, *op. cit.,* above, n.24 at p. 122.

[47] In this regard, note the observation of Advocate General Lagrange in *Hoogovens v. High Authority* (Case 14/61) [1962] E.C.R. 511 at 570 that "the Court in so far as it invokes national laws (as it does to a large extent) to define the rules of law relating to the application of the Treaty, is not content to draw on more or less arithmetical 'common denominators' between the different national solutions, but chooses from each of the Member States those solutions which, having regard to the object of the Treaty, appear to it to be the best or, if one may use the expression, the most progressive. That is the spirit, moreover, which has guided the Court hitherto." For authorities to similar effect, see Vaughan, *op. cit.,* above, n.10, para. 1220 at n. 9.

and *Isoglucose* cases are clearly modelled on the German case law on "Vertrauensschutz".[48] In both of these cases, the Opinion of the Advocate General was followed by the court in its judgment.[49]

The court has not always clearly distinguished in the language which it has used between legitimate expectation and the related principles of vested rights and legal certainty.[50] However, insofar as vested rights are concerned, it may be noted that the decision of the European Court of Justice in *Commission v. Council (Officials' Salaries)* [51] has been described as the *locus classicus* of legitimate expectations in Community law in particular because the case did *not* appear to involve the protection of any "established rights" but rather merely that of an expectation.[52] In this case, the European Court of Justice held that a 1972 Council Decision to apply for a period of three years a particular system for calculating Community staff salaries was binding – and this prevented the valid adoption by the Council of a subsequent Regulation departing from its terms. In reaching this decision, the court took account of the particular relationship which existed between the employer and the staff and expressly relied upon "the rule of protection of the confidence that the staff could have that the authorities would respect undertakings of this nature."[53]

As for the relationship between the principles of legitimate expectation and legal certainty,[54] the concepts appear to be linked. Indeed it is sometimes said

---

[48] See *Westzucker v. Einfuhr und Vorratsstelle für Zucker* (Case 1/73) [1973] E.C.R. 723 and *Amylum v. Council* (Case 108/81) [1982] E.C.R. 3107 and see generally Schwarze, *op. cit.,* above, n.35, pp. 939 to 940.

[49] In contrast, Schwarze has observed the influence of English legal thinking in the Opinion of Advocate General Warner in *Commission v. Council (Officials' Salaries)* (Case 81/72) [1973] E.C.R. 575. Note, however, that in this particular case the Court did not follow the Opinion of the Advocate General in its judgment.

[50] See *Westzucker v. Einfuhr und Vorratsstelle für Zucker* (Case 1/73) [1973] E.C.R. 723 first noted in this context in Usher, "The Influence of National Concepts on Decisions of the European Court" [1975-6] 1 *E.L. Rev.* 359 at 364.

[51] Case 81/72 [1973] E.C.R. 575

[52] Usher, *loc. cit.,* above, n.46, p. 364.

[53] It should be explained that the French term "protection de la confiance légitime" was originally translated into English as "protection of legitimate confidence." Fears that the use of the word "confidence" would cause confusion led to the use of the expression "legitimate expectation" becoming the preferred label for the doctrine, however. See Opinion of Advocate General Warner in *Einfuhr und Vorratsstelle Getreide und Futtermittel v. Mackprang* (Case 4/1975) [1975] E.C.R. 607 at 622 (cited in Usher, *op. cit.,* above, n.29 at p. 54). (It may be noted in passing that it is a frequently encountered obstacle to easy comprehension of the general principles that what may effectively be the same principle is sometimes given several names in the jurisprudence of the court. (See Usher, *op. cit.,* above, n.29 at pp. 8 to 9).

[54] This is a principle the operation of which is somewhat complex in practice, but which at its most basic requires that legal rules (both Community rules and national rules in areas covered by Community law) be brought to the attention of those whom they affect and be clear and predictable as regards their effects so that persons affected are capable of knowing with certainty from when their legal position is affected. For two cases involving Ireland which raised the principle

that the principle of legitimate expectation springs from that of legal certainty.[55] Schwarze has therefore gone only as far as saying that legitimate expectation "appears to be an expression ... of legal certainty, which is equal in rank in the hierarchy of rules" and has summarised the position in the following terms:

> "the overall impression is that although the European Court of Justice in certain individual cases applies the principles of legal certainty and of the protection of legitimate expectations separately from each other, it nevertheless assumes that, in theoretical terms, there is a close correlation between the two with one being derived from the other. Here, legal certainty in many cases is used as a legal principle based on objective criteria, whilst the recognition of legitimate expectations serves to protect subjective rights."[56]

This view now finds support in judgments of the Court of Justice in which the Court has described the legitimate expectation principle as the corollary of the principle of legal certainty. [57]

Whatever its origins, the principle of legitimate expectation is now "undeniably part of Community law".[58] Indeed in the case of *Töpfer v. Commission* the court went so far as to state that by virtue of the principle of legitimate expectation forming part of the Community legal order, failure to respect a legitimate expectation would be a breach of the Treaty within the meaning of Article 230.[59] The large number of cases in which the doctrine is invoked has already been adverted to. Legitimate expectation is by now one of the principles of Community law which is most often relied upon before the European

---

of certainty, see *Ireland v. Commission* (Case 325/85) [1987] E.C.R. 5041 and *Ireland v. Commission* (Case 239/86) [1987] E.C.R. 5271. See generally here the list of authorities cited by Vaughan, *op. cit.,* above, n.10, para. 1243, n. 1 and n. 2.

[55] Edward and Lane, *European Community Law: An Introduction* (2nd ed., Edinburgh, 1995) at para. 154. The first author, it should be noted, is a judge of the European Court of Justice. Charlesworth and Cullen refer to legitimate expectations as a "sub-principle" of legal certainty. (*op. cit.,* above, n.24 at p. 126).

[56] Schwarze, *op. cit.,* above, n.35 at pp. 946 and 947, respectively.

[57] See here *e.g.,* the judgment of the European Court of Justice in *Duff and others v. Minister for Agriculture and Food, Ireland, and the Attorney General* (Case 63/93) [1996] E.C.R. I 576, discussed in the text, below.

[58] See Opinion of Advocate General Lenz in *Finsider SpA v. Commission* (Joined Cases 63 and 147/84) [1985] E.C.R. 2857 at 2865

[59] Case 112/77 [1978] E.C.R. 1019. Note that protection for the legitimate expectation of individuals or firms is sometimes provided for in Community legislation. See *e.g.,* Article 5(2) of Council Regulation (EEC) 1697/79 of July 24, 1979 on the post-clearance recovery of import duties or export duties which have not been required of the person liable for payment on goods entered for a customs procedure involving the obligation to pay such duties. This was discussed in *Unifrigo Gadus Srl and CPL Imperial 2 SpA v. Commission of the European Communities* (Joined Cases T–10/97 and T–11/97) [1998] E.C.R. II–2231.

Court of Justice.[60] It must be said, however, that it is undoubtedly often raised in cases where it seems clear that it will not succeed as an argument. Indeed – perhaps somewhat paradoxically, notwithstanding the widespread reliance on the principle by litigants – it must be said that it is only very seldom that the protection of legitimate expectations has ultimately benefited any of them.[61] Success stories, as Sharpston has observed, are rare,[62] and the court, while continuously emphasising the need to protect the individual's legitimate expectations in individual cases, often goes on to conclude those same cases by deciding that no legitimate expectation was raised on the facts, or, if one was, that it was not violated in this particular case.[63] The large number of decisions of this kind may be due to the fact that the court is aware of the consequences of its decisions and does not wish to reach decisions which would place undue strain on the Community institutions unless a significant injustice has been done. Furthermore, several commentators have noted the difficulty in discerning any clear pattern to those few cases in which the litigant does succeed in pleading breach of legitimate expectations, although certain points about the doctrine have gradually become much clearer.[64]

(d) Examining the Community Doctrine of Legitimate Expectation: What is a "Legitimate" Expectation for the Purposes of the Community Principle?

The principle of legitimate expectation in Community law is an administrative law principle: the kind of legitimate expectation protected by Community law arise only *vis-à-vis* administrative authorities, be they Community institutions or national administrations. As Sharpston has noted:

> "such legitimate expectations can only be generated in a regulated environment and arise, indeed, out of the presence of such regulation. In a completely non-regulated economic environment, there would be no administrative authorities to raise producers' and traders' hopes in the continuance of a particular pattern of regulation."[65]

---

[60] See here Usher, *op. cit.,* above, n.35 at pp. 52 and 125.
[61] Schwarze, *op. cit.,* above, n.35 at p. 950.
[62] Sharpston, "Legitimate Expectations and Economic Reality" (1990) 15 *E.L. Rev.* 103 at 132.
[63] Schwarze, *op. cit.,* above, n.35 at p. 1171. Sharpston, *loc. cit.,* above, n.62 at p. 160, has commented that the court has a tendency to begin by formulating a broad principle on which it seems as though traders may successfully rely; and then going on to whittle down its potential applicability so that in the end, the trader loses.
[64] See *e.g.,* Schwarze, *op. cit.,* above, n.35 at p. 949 and Sharpston, *loc. cit.,* above, n.62 at p. 160.
[65] Sharpston, *loc. cit.,* above, n.62 at p. 104.

As if to underline this point, the majority of cases concerning the Community principle have arisen in highly regulated economic sectors such as agriculture and steel.[66] It may be added that, in practice, the principle usually applies in situations concerning an individual decision. However, as some of the cases discussed in the present text demonstrate, it can also apply in respect of the exercise of more broadly applicable powers.[67]

Trade, of course, takes place in an environment of constantly changing factors such as prices, and the fact and level of demand or supply. The question therefore arises why changes in the regulatory environment should not simply be regarded as another factor the risk of which should be borne by the producer or trader. The answer seems to be that in a sense, the principle of legitimate expectations can be regarded as representing the Community legal system's choice as to the appropriate degree of play to be allowed to various countervailing forces. On the one hand, economic policy dictates that there are many factors which a trader should accept as a "risk of the game", including, to some extent, the risk of changes in market regulation, and further requires some degree of freedom on the part of regulatory bodies so as to enable them to respond effectively to market changes. On the other hand, it is also clear that there is a degree of legal certainty without which any forward planning of economic activity by traders or producers will be rendered excessively difficult. In other words, there is a point at which the potential for shifting of regulatory goalposts discourages participation in the market to the ultimate detriment of society.[68] Thus "if the regulatory authorities are perceived as too arbitrary, or too given to making sudden and frequent changes to the regulatory framework, certain types of business will vote with their feet, if necessary, and move elsewhere."[69] The general principle of legitimate expectation shows where the Community legal system draws a line in the sand between these two sets of interests. Careful note should be made of the point, however, that it is not *market* uncertainty that the trader or producer is intended to be protected or insured from by the Community doctrine, but rather *regulatory* uncertainty.

One case illustrating some of the above considerations is that of *Duff and others v. Minister for Agriculture and Food, Ireland, and the Attorney General*.[70] Duff and his fellow small farmers were induced to borrow money and

---

[66] Sharpston, *loc. cit.*, above, n.62 at p. 104.

[67] See *e.g. Commission v. Council (Officials' Salaries)* (Case 81/72) [1973] E.C.R. 575 (discussed in the text above).

[68] It will be noted that the factors weighing in one direction or the other are both economic and legal. As Sharpston has observed, "for both legal reasons (an estoppel-type argument) and economic reasons (sometimes the economic agent should be able to rely on the administration not changing the rules in the middle of the game), a doctrine of legitimate expectation is attractive." (Sharpston, "European Community Law and the Doctrine of Legitimate Expectations: How Legitimate and For Whom?" (1990) 11 *J. Intl. L. Bus.* 87 at 89).

[69] Sharpston, "Legitimate Expectations and Economic Reality" (1990) 15 *E.L. Rev.* 103 at 106.

[70] Case 63/93, [1996] E.C.R. I 576.

develop their farms. They made their plans under the Irish implementation of a 1972 Community Directive,[71] making investments which could only be justified by increasing their output and selling it at a price which would give a reasonable return. These plans needed a period of time to be put into effect. However, before their plans yielded profits, the Council introduced the milk superlevy system,[72] and Duff and his co-litigants were given reference quantities (*i.e.*, milk production quotas) based only on their pre-development output – with the result that having incurred heavy expenditure, they could not now get an outlet for the sale of their increased milk production. They argued that this situation violated their legitimate expectations, and more particularly, that the 1972 Directive had been a signal that they could increase their milk production and would receive a special reference quantity. The Court of Justice rejected this argument, however, holding that:

> "the principle of the protection of legitimate expectations may be invoked as against Community rules only to the extent that *the Community itself* has previously created a situation which can give rise to a legitimate expectation.
>
> Neither the Community rules on development plans, nor the terms or purpose of those plans, nor the context in which the plaintiffs in the main proceedings adopted their development plans indicate that the Community created a situation providing producers who were implementing a development plan with reasonable grounds to expect that a special reference quantity ... would be allocated and that they would therefore be exempted in part from the restrictions established by the additional levy scheme."[73]

Unfortunately for themselves, therefore, Duff and his co-litigants fell on the wrong side – if perhaps only just – of the line drawn by the European Court of Justice. For, to paraphrase a comment in the Opinion of Advocate General Slynn in the *Mulder* case,[74] in order to rely successfully on the principle of legitimate expectation, one must establish a situation which "crosses the line between what is merely "hard business luck" and what is "unreasonable treatment." In *Duff*, the court implicitly took the view that this case fell into the former category. Thus Duff and his co-litigants were to be regarded as indirect victims of a change in the market situation (which the Community rule-making

---

[71] Community Directive 75/159/EEC of April 17, 1972 on the Modernisation of Farms.

[72] The rules governing this system were set out in Regulation EEC/856/84.

[73] Emphasis added.

[74] Case 120/86 [1988] E.C.R. 2321. The claimants ultimately fared better in the Irish Supreme Court, albeit on different grounds. (See *Duff v. Minister for Agriculture (No. 2)* [1997] 2 I.R. 22 and the subsequent High Court judgment in the same case by Laffoy J. of March 25, 1999 in which the quantum of damages was assessed).

bodies had to be free to respond to) rather than as victims of unreasonable treatment by the Community legislature. Put another way, Duff *et al* were expected to foresee the possibility of unfavourable market trends and the need of the Community institutions to react to such trends.[75]

(e) Factors Which Go Towards Making an Expectation "Legitimate" in Community Law

A number of factors may be derived from the case law of the Court of Justice – which is not always as clear as the following description may suggest – as necessary in order to justify the protection of a legitimate expectation. Summarised, and somewhat roughly grouped, these are as follows:

(i) Conduct Justifying the Expectation

Some conduct on the part of the Community or of a Member State justifying legitimate expectations is required. A mere expectation that the Community institutions will act in a particular way is thus not enough (probably because the court does not wish to assume the role of dictating policy choices to Community institutions – or to allow litigants to do so).[76]

The conduct required on the part of the Community or Member State may take a number of forms. It may consist of (i) an instrument conferring benefits; (ii) a consistent administrative practice (which will obviously be used to justify a legitimate expectation in the continuation of a situation which already exists); or (iii) written or oral statements or representations.

A good example of (i) an instrument conferring benefits giving rise to legitimate expectations[77] is provided by legislative provisions which require special account to be taken of certain situations or persons. Such provisions can

---

[75] See also the similar case of *Cornée and others v. COPALL and others* (Case 196/88) [1989] E.C.R. 2309. The case of *Finsider SpA v. Commission* (Joined Cases 63 and 147/84) [1985] E.C.R. 2857 is also analogous. This case involved an unsuccessful attempt by the claimant – a steel company – to have a production quota decision by the Commission annulled because it prevented Finsider benefiting from a restructuring programme including the bringing into service of a new mill, and the Commission had earlier delivered a favourable opinion on both the programme and the mill, and indeed made the grant the investment aids to Finsider to this opinion being favourable. The court held that the decision had not violated Finsider's legitimate expectations. The case is discussed by Sharpston, *loc. cit.,* above, n.69 at p. 128 *et seq.*

[76] See *e.g., Compagnie Industrielle et Agricole du Comté de Loheac and others v. Council and Commission* [1977] E.C.R. 6456 where the Community institutions were alleged to have failed, in setting sugar intervention prices, to take into consideration the different harvesting and selling times for sugar in Guadaloupe and Martinique (which are French overseas departments) to those in Europe itself. However appropriate it might have seemed that such considerations be taken into account, the Court of Justice were not prepared to bring the doctrine of legitimate expectations into play here. (See further here Sharpston, *loc. cit.,* above, n.69 at p. 110).

[77] As to which see generally Vaughan, *op. cit.,* above, n.10 at paras 1287 to 1300.

create legitimate expectations that these persons or situations will be so treated absent an overriding public interest. A case involving this phenomenon was *Sofrimport Sarl v. Commission.*[78] This concerned Regulation 2707/72, which gave the Commission power to take protective measures regarding the importation of certain goods. The regulation contained a provision, however, which laid down that account should be taken of the special position of goods in transit – a measure obviously intended to ensure that traders would not be excessively prejudiced by any protective measures taken by the Commission. In 1988, the Commission took protective measures under Regulation 2707/72. It suspended all licences for the importation of apples from Chile (such licences being necessary to engage in this trade). The instrument which the Commission used to effect this suspension, however,[79] made no special provision for goods in transit. The applicant company, which held such a licence and whose goods were already in transit when the suspending measure was adopted, therefore brought an action for annulment. The Court of Justice duly annulled the protective measure, holding that the failure of the Commission to make any special provision for goods in transit was a violation of the claimants' legitimate expectation.

The normal rule, however, is that a legitimate expectation will not be created in a situation which can be altered by a Community institution exercising its discretionary powers – including its power to legislate. This is a point which applies with particular force in regulating areas which involve constant attention so as to enable a flexible response to market change.[80] It is worth noting, in this context, the observation by Usher that in the famous milk quota cases (such as *Mulder*[81]) that "the expectation that was protected was not that the rules would remain unchanged when the outgoers returned to milk production,

---

[78]Case C–152/88, [1990] E.C.R. I–2477.

[79]*Viz.,* Regulation 962/88.

[80]*Pesquerias v. Commission* (Joined Cases C–258 and C–259/90) [1992] E.C.R. I–2901 and *Climax Paper Converters v. Council* (Case T–155/94) [1996] E.C.R. II – 877 and see Usher, *op. cit.,* above, n.29, pp. 58 to 59. Note, however, the particular situation described in *Angelo Tomadino SNC v. Amministrazione delle Finanze dello Stato* (Case 84/78) [1979] E.C.R. 1801 where it was held that if in order to deal with individual situations the Community institutions had laid down specific rules enabling traders, in return for entering into certain obligations with the public authorities, to protect themselves – insofar as it concerned transactions definitively undertaken – from the effects of necessarily frequent variations in rules, the principle of respect for legitimate expectations then prohibited those institutions from amending those rules without laying down transitional measures (unless the adoption of such a transitional measure was contrary to an overriding public interest). This is somewhat exceptional. In general, the European Court of Justice has been reticent in holding that legitimate expectations require transitional measures to be adopted so as to protect contracts agreed but not yet executed before the change in rules came into force.

[81]See *Mulder v. Minister van Landbouw en Visserij* (Case 120/86) [1988] E.C.R. 2321; *Mulder and others v. Council and Commission ("Mulder II")* (Joined Cases C–104/89 and C–37/90) [1992] E.C.R. I–3061. These cases are discussed in the text below.

but that they should not be penalised compared with the producers for having participated in a Community scheme."[82]

Insofar as draft legislation is concerned, the form which draft legislation takes will give rise to no legitimate expectation that in its ultimate form the legislation will be the same or similar, since of course the possibility always exists that legislation will be amended during the process leading to its adoption.[83]

The Community Principle of Legitimate Expectation and the Issue of Retroactive Legislation

A particular kind of legislation which raises issues concerning the legitimate expectations of individuals or businesses is that of retroactive legislation. A distinction is generally drawn between "true" retroactivity or retroactivity *strictu sensu* – which is where a rule is adopted which applies to events which have already taken place – and "apparent" retroactivity, which concerns the immediate application of new rules to pre-existing situations (*e.g.,* where new quota rules are imposed with immediate effect, thereby affecting the goods delivery of which was agreed under a contract signed prior to the new rules coming into effect).[84] Many cases concerning the Community doctrine involve issues of apparent retroactivity, for "a person may have planned his or her actions on the basis of one policy choice made by the administration, and seek redress when the chosen policy alters, even though this alteration is only prospective and not retrospective.'[85]

One issue which arises which concerns *apparently retroactive rules* is that of transitional measures. For a failure to adopt such measures may violate the legitimate expectations of an individual or trader, creating an entitlement, in an appropriate case, to damages.[86] On the other hand, the chances of a legitimate expectation of transitional arrangements being held to exist depend very much on the market which is being discussed.[87] The general position is encapsulated

---

[82] Usher, *op. cit.,* above, n.29 at p. 59.

[83] See *Driessen en Zonen v. Minister van Verkeer en Waterstaat* (Cases C–13 to C–16/92) [1993] E.C.R. I–4751. Note that it is not always the case that rules which have not yet entered into force are incapable of giving rise to legitimate expectations. In *Opel Austria v. Council* (Case T–115/94) [1997] E.C.R. II–39, a legitimate expectation was held to exist that the Council would not introduce measures contrary to the European Economic Area Agreement once the Community had deposited its instruments of approval of the Agreement and the date of entry into force of the Agreement was known.

[84] "Apparent" retroactivity is sometimes called secondary retroactivity (as distinct from "primary" – *i.e.,* true – retroactivity. (See *Bowen v. Georgetown Hospital* (1988) 488 U.S. 204 cited in Craig in "Substantive Legitimate Expectations in Domestic and Community Law" (1996) 55 *C.L.J.* 289 at n. 46).

[85] Craig, *loc. cit.,* above, n.84 at p. 305.

[86] As was held to be the case in *CNTA SA v. Commission* (Case 74/74) [1975] E.C.R. 533.

[87] See *Firma Gebrüder Dietz v. Commission* (Case 126/76) [1977] E.C.R. 2431 where the Court

in Sharpston's observation that:

> "the European Court has ... tended to reject arguments for transitional measures, citing variously the overriding public interest, a reasonable fear that making a transitional period available would destroy the whole point of the change in legislation and its oft-repeated tenet that prudent traders should have realised that change was imminent".[88]

Truly retroactive laws are looked upon with disfavour from both a legal and economic standpoint. Viewed in legal terms, they are felt to be a threat to the rule of law, which requires that situations ought to be judged in the light of legal rules which obtain when they occur so that individuals and businesses may plan their affairs in awareness of what the legal consequences of their actions will be.[89] From the economic viewpoint, they tend to have a negative effect on business and investor confidence in legal systems in which they are allowed. If truly retroactive laws are to be permitted at all in the Community legal system it is therefore obvious that that they can be allowed only under the most strictly controlled circumstances. In its case law, the European Court of Justice has ruled out the retrospective imposition of criminal liability.[90] However, the rule is not so rigid in non-criminal cases, where it has been held that:

> "although in *general* the principle of legal certainty precludes a Community measure from taking effect at a point in time before its publication, it may *exceptionally* be otherwise where the purpose to be achieved so demands and where the legitimate expectations of those concerned are duly respected."[91]

---

of Justice refused to hold that an international sugar trader had any legitimate expectation that transitional arrangements be provided for when alterations – which stemmed from currency fluctuations – were made in the Community system laying down the rules governing monetary compensation amounts for such traders. The attitude seems to have been that such changes were foreseeable in a situation of fluctuating exchange rates and it was up to the traders themselves to take measures to protect themselves against any consequent changes.

[88] Sharpston, *loc. cit.,* above, n.69 at p. 144. See *e.g., Merkur Aussenhandel GmbH v. Commission* (Case 97/76) [1977] E.C.R. 1063, *IFG-Interkontinentale Fleischhandelsgesellschaft GmbH v. Commission* (Case 68/77) [1978] E.C.R. 353, *Hans Spitta & Co. v. Hauptzollamt Frankfurt am Main-Ost* (Case 127/78) [1979] E.C.R. 171 and *Firma Anton Dürbeck v. Hauptzollamt Frankfurt am Main-Flughafen* (Case 112/80) [1981] E.C.R. 1095.

[89] See generally here Chapter 3 of Waldron, *The Law* (London, 1990).

[90] See here *R. v. Kent Kirk* (Case 63/83) [1984] E.C.R. 2689 where the court observed that the principle that penal provisions may not have retroactive effect "takes its place among the general principles of law whose observance is ensured by the Court of Justice." (See para. 22 of the court's judgment).

[91] *Racke (Firma A.) v. Hauptzollamt Mainz* (Case 98/78) [1979] E.C.R. 79 at para. 20 (emphasis added). See also *e.g., Weingut Gustav Decker KG v. Hauptzollamt Landau* (Case 99/78) [1979] E.C.R. 101, *Diversinte SA and Iberlacta SA v. Administración Principal de Aduanas de la Junquera* (Joined Cases C–260/91 and C–261/91) [1993] E.C.R. I–1885 and *Road Air BV v.*

These conditions are occasionally met. One of the most prominent examples of this happening was in the *Isoglucose* cases, the factual basis of which concerned the introduction by regulation of production quotas for isoglucose, a natural sweetener which competed with sugar. Isoglucose manufacturers succeeded in having the original regulation declared void by the Court of Justice for procedural reasons not relevant in the present context.[92] The Council's response was to adopt a new regulation reintroducing the production quotas and making them retrospective so as to cover the interregnum brought about by the court's judgment. When the isoglucose producers brought a challenge against this latter regulation in turn, seeking to have it declared void, the court applied the above-quoted test to uphold the new regulation, notwithstanding its retroactivity. The court felt that the legitimate expectations of the isoglucose producers (who were a limited number of traders who were very well informed both about the isoglucose market and about likely legislative developments) had been respected in this case, since they had many reasons to expect that the system would be retrospectively reimposed. To be contrasted with the *Isoglucose* cases is the case of *Firma Meiko-Konservenfabrik v. Germany*,[93] which concerned an attempt by the Commission to change retrospectively the rules concerning qualification for certain financial assistance to sweet cherry producers. This was done by imposing a requirement that certain contracts be forwarded to national authorities by a now expired date. The result was that the applicants were deprived of the opportunity of qualifying for the aid in circumstances which (unlike those in the *Isoglucose* cases) the court held could not reasonably have been anticipated. The legislation was therefore held invalid, *inter alia*, because the legitimate expectations of the applicants had been breached.[94]

Inspecteur der Invoerrechten en Accijnzen (Case C–310/95) [1997] E.C.R. I–100. The Community principle has been compared unfavourably with the autochthonous doctrine by Oliver as "quite contrary to the spirit of the common law" on the basis of the *Racke* rule (see Oliver, "A Negative Aspect to Legitimate Expectations" [1998] *PL* 558) although the contrast drawn between the two doctrines there seems unconvincing to the present writer. See in regard to the autochthonous doctrine here, *Cinnamond v. British Airports Authority* [1980] 2 All E.R. 368 and the commentary thereon by France in "Legitimate Expectations in New Zealand" (1990) 14 *N.Z.U.L.R.* 123 at 133.

[92] See *e.g., Roquette Frères SA v. Council* (Case 138/79) [1980] E.C.R. 3333 where the court declared Regulation 1293/79 void because the obligation (at that time laid down in Article 43 of the Treaty of Rome) on the Council of Ministers to consult the Parliament before making a regulation in this field had not been respected. See also *Maizena v. Council* (Case 139/79) [1980] E.C.R. 3393.

[93] Case 224/82 [1983] E.C.R. 2539.

[94] Sharpston (*loc. cit.,* above at n.69 at p. 143) has applauded this decision since "no ordinary degree of economic caution would have sufficed to warn [the traders] of the likelihood, the nature or the detail of the retroactive change subsequently introduced and thus to invalidate their expectations in the aid scheme as originally established." On the occasional restriction by the European Court of Justice of the "retrospective" effect of its own judgments in deference to the legitimate expectations of those who have acted on the basis of what was previously generally understood to be the law, see Mengozzi, *From the Treaty of Rome to the Treaty of Amsterdam* (2nd ed., The Hague/London: Kluwer, 1999) at 208 to 211.

It should be noted that clear and unequivocal reasons will be required to be given in order to justify retrospective effect.[95] Thus where regulations are not expressly stated to be retroactive and, in addition, reasons given for this retro-activity, the test set down in these cases will be used to avoid a retroactive interpretation. Again, if the factual reasoning offered for the retroactivity is defective, there will be no need to demonstrate a violation of legitimate expectations in order to have retrospective legislation annulled.[96]

As regards legitimate expectations engendered by consistent administrative practices, a good example of this is provided by *Ferriere San Carlo SpA v. Commission,*[97] where the claimant company, which had been fined by the Commission for selling steel in excess of a delivery quota, was held to have had a legitimate expectation of the continuation of the Commission's general practice in the previous two years of allowing over-quota sales which had been made for the purposes of running down stocks. A 1983 general decision extending the life of the steel quota system was held not to have clearly indicated a modification of the previous practice. Nor had the company been individually informed of a modification of the practice in good time before the sale was made. The Commission decision to fine the company was therefore annulled by the court. The *San Carlo* case seems to illustrate the point that where a consistent administrative practice is adopted by an authority, producers and traders are entitled to expect continued adherence to that practice, unless and until the authority indicates (whether by legislative provision or by individual warning) that this will no longer be the case.[98]

The exercise on one occasion of a discretion will not, of course, be regarded as constituting a consistent practice.[99] Nor will a legitimate expectation be deemed to have been raised where an individual is effectively on notice that an alteration of the relevant practice is imminent. (It should be explained that changes in the law at European level are often preceded by discussions between the Commission and producers or traders likely to be affected by the alteration. These negotiations may be regarded as having alerted these parties

---

[95] See *e.g. Diversinte SA and Iberlacta SA v. Administración Principal de Aduanas de la Junquera* (Joined Cases C–260/91 and C–261/91) [1993] E.C.R. I–1885 where the court held a regulation invalid because the regulation's statement of reasons (which merely made the point that the regulation's provisions were being introduced as a matter of urgency in order to avoid speculation) did not make it possible to review the question of whether the retrospective effect was justified.

[96] *Savma v. Commission* (Case 264/81) [1984] E.C.R. 3915.

[97] Case 344/85 [1987] E.C.R. 4435.

[98] See also *Decker v. Caisse de Pension des Employés Privés* (Case 129/87) [1988] E.C.R. 6121 and *Italy v. Commission* (Case 14/88) [1989] E.C.R. 3677. There can be no legitimate expectation in the continuance of an illegal practice, however. (See *e.g. United Kingdom v. Council* (Case 68/86) [1988] E.C.R. 855).

[99] See *e.g. Holtbecker v. Commission* (Case T–20/91)[1992] E.C.R. II–2599.

that a change in the existing system is imminent.[100]) Finally, a word may be added insofar as the effects of administrative *inactivity* are concerned. There is no expectation that any decision-making process will have a particular result, and normally, the mere fact that a long time is taken in reaching a decision will *not* give rise to a legitimate expectation as to the eventual outcome of that decision.[101] Nor will the passage of time while negotiations are under way with the authority in question give rise to a legitimate expectation.[102] On the other hand, in certain limited circumstances, the passage of time accompanied by inactivity may give rise to a claim of legitimate expectation of the continuation of the status quo – such as where past conduct of the administrative authority has given reasonable grounds to the individual concerned to believe that the authority now regards a particular situation as lawful.[103]

Insofar as concerns (iii) written or oral statements or representations, these can take the form of information given, statements made or pledges undertaken. In essence, however, what is looked for in order to support a legitimate expectation is a precise or specific assurance to the individual concerned. Thus in *Delauche v. Commission*[104] it was held by the court that mere general statements by the Commission to the effect that the number of women with positions of responsibility should be increased would not give rise to any legitimate

---

[100] See here Sharpston, "Legitimate Expectations and Economic Reality" (1990) 15 *EL Rev.* 103 at 147 and, by the same writer, "European Community Law and the Doctrine of Legitimate Expectations: How Legitimate and For Whom?" (1990) 11 *J. Intl. L. Bus.* 87 at 99. The topic of what, for the purposes of the legitimate expectations principle, an individual is regarded as being "on notice" of will be returned to in the text, below.

[101] See *Epichiriseon Metalleftikon Viomichanikon kai Naftiliakon AE v. Council* (Case C–121/ 86)[1989] E.C.R. 3919 and *Continentale Produkten-Gesellschaft v. Hauptzollamt München-West* (Case 246/87) [1989] E.C.R. 1151. See more generally, Vaughan, *op. cit.,* above, n.10, para. 1282. Contrast the decision, concerning the autochthonous doctrine, of Hamilton P. in *Ghneim v. Minister for Justice,* a case dealt with in n. 180 below.

[102] See here Sharpston, "Legitimate Expectations and Economic Reality" (1990) 15 *E.L. Rev.* 103 at 159.

[103] The administrative authority must, however, be aware of all the material facts of the situation. See generally *Rijn-Schelde-Verolme Maschinefabrieken en Scheepswerven NV (RSV) v. Commission* (Case 223/85) [1987] E.C.R. 4617. This was a state aids case in which the Court of Justice took the view that the delay which occurred before the Commission prohibited aid granted to a Dutch shipbuilding concern in 1982, (the Commission decision was published only in 1985), combined with the fact that the Commission had earlier approved similar such aid, and that the Commission was very familiar with the underlying situation meant that the prohibition violated a legitimate expectation that the Commission would not require the Dutch authorities to obtain repayment of the aid. Sharpston has described the circumstances of this case as "fairly exceptional", however (*loc. cit.,* above, n.102 at pp 132 to 133).

[104] Case 111/86 [1987] E.C.R. 5345. See also *Van den Bergh en Jurgens v. Commission* (Case 265/85) [1987] E.C.R. 1155 where frequent public statements by the Commission to the effect that Christmas butter schemes were an inappropriate means to achieve lasting cuts in butter stocks were held not to give rise to a legitimate expectation that no further scheme would be organised by the Commission, partly because they involved no specific undertaking never to institute such a scheme again.

expectation on the part of the claimant that she would be promoted. And in *Lefebvre and others v. Commission*[105] even letters addressed to the applicants were held not to give rise to any legitimate expectation, since the undertaking they contained – *viz.*, to take into account the position of small and medium-sized enterprises in formulating a particular legislative proposal relating to bananas – could not be regarded as a precise assurance.

Even precise or specific assurances by Community officials not to apply the law will not give rise to a legitimate expectation.[106] Nor will acts of national authorities which breach Community law, at least where the Commission has declared that these acts violate Community law.[107] In this regard, it should be noted that where a document is inaccurately completed, the initial reaction of the national authorities to that document (*e.g.*, in accepting it) will not normally give rise to a legitimate expectation.[108] The court has also been unsympathetic to attempts by individuals or companies to rely on the legitimate expectation principle so as to ensure the continuance of erroneous calculations of entitlements by Community institutions which have previously led to traders making profits.[109]

---

[105] Case T–571/93 [1995] E.C.R. II–2385.

[106] *Thyssen v. Commission* (Case 188/82) [1983] E.C.R. 372 which involved an alleged promise by senior Commission officials not to impose a fine on Thyssen if it exceeded its sales quota. Although the court held that no legitimate expectation of not being fined had been aroused since "no official can give a valid undertaking not to apply Community law", it did recognise that Thyssen had been misled by reducing the size of the fine to a token amount and ordering the Commission to bear its own costs; *FRUBO v. Commission* (Case 71/74) [1975] E.C.R. 563. *cf.*, however, *Usines de la Providence v. High Authority* (Case 29/63) [1965] E.C.R. I–1591 where liability in damages was created on the part of the ECSC High Authority by the making of promises by its officials to make unlawful payments over a period of time, because this demonstrated a lack of care on the part of the High Authority.

[107] *Land Rheinland-Pfalz v. Alcan Deutschland* (Case C–24/95) [1997] E.C.R. I–1591. See generally here, Usher, *op. cit.,* above, n.29 at p. 63. This point is obviously an important one in the field of state aids, as to which see generally Sharpston at 132 to 133. Vaughan has gone so far as to assert that "a wrongful act on the part of a Community institution or one of its officials, or a practice of a Member State which does not conform to Community rules, may never give rise to a legitimate expectation under Community law." (*Op. cit.,* above, n.10, para. 1283, and note the authorities cited at nn. 1 to 3). See in this regard *e.g.*, *Hauptzollamt Hamburg-Jonas v. Firma P. Krücken* (Case 316/86) [1988] E.C.R. 2213 and *Hauptzollamt Krefeld v. Maizena GmbH* (Case 5/82) [1982] E.C.R. 4601 and *Alois Lageder SpA v. Amministrazione delle Finanze* (Joined Cases C–31 to 44/91) [1993] E.C.R. I–1761. A parallel can be drawn here with the unwillingness of national courts to applying the autochthonous doctrine of legitimate expectations to legitimise *ultra vires* action on the part of administrative authorities *i.e.* by making promises to act or refrain from acting in a way which is *ultra vires* the body in question. See on this point Hogan and Morgan, *Administrative Law in Ireland* (3rd ed., Dublin, 1998) at 865.

[108] *Van Gend en Loos NV and Expeditiebedriff Wim Bosman BV v. Commission* (Joined Cases 98/83 and 230/83) [1984] E.C.R. 3763, *Unifrigo Gadus and CPL Imperial 2 SpA v. Commission* (Joined Cases T–10/97 and T–11/97) [1998] E.C.R. II–2231.

[109] *Firma August Töpfer & Co. v. Commission* (Case 112/77) [1978] E.C.R. 1019.

(ii) The Requirement of an Expectation

Secondly, and perhaps somewhat self-evidently, in order for the principle of legitimate expectation in Community law to apply, an expectation must have been generated. The requirement of this expectation is a subjective test in the sense that the expectation must be a concrete one which was genuinely held by an individual (who must not have acted in a way inconsistent with his holding this expectation[110]) but the standard required is objective in certain other respects.[111] An expectation is not legitimate unless a prudent individual would have had it. Thus if an expectation allegedly created by the conduct of an administrative authority is unreasonable or incapable of fulfilment, then it will not be regarded as a legitimate expectation for the purposes of Community law.[112] Nor will an expectation be regarded as legitimate if its subsequent frustration was foreseeable. Vaughan has summarised the position in relation to this objective element of the legitimate expectations principle by observing:

> "no legitimate expectation can be claimed if a change in the law is foreseeable or if frequent changes in the position is a characteristic feature of a given economic situation; if a prudent and discriminating trader could have foreseen the adoption of a Community measure likely to affect his interest (which may arise where legislation provides for its future amendment); if a decision may be subject to review in accordance with the legislation on the basis of which it was adopted; or if the situation can be altered at any time by decisions taken by the Community institutions within the limits of their discretionary powers."[113]

One of the most important elements to note here is that in deciding whether the legitimate expectations of an individual have been breached, regard will be had to the knowledge and information which ought to be available to the prudent and informed business person.[114] The standard applied is what a well-

---

[110] In *Alpha Steel Ltd. v. Commission* (Case 14/81) [1982] E.C.R. 749, the claimant firm failed in its attempt to plead that legitimate expectations on its part had been created by a particular Commission decision regarding steel quotas, since it had brought an action seeking the annulment of the decision in question.

[111] Schwarze, *op. cit.,* above, n.35 at p. 951.

[112] *San Marco Impex Italiano SA v. Commission* (Case T–451/93) [1994] E.C.R. II–1061. It should be noted that it may be reasonable to hold a belief which is in actual fact erroneous. (See Sharpston, *loc. cit.,* above, n.102 at p. 158).

[113] Vaughan, *op. cit.,* above, n.10, para. 1285, and the case-law cited therein, in particular *Sociedade Agro-Pecuària Vicente Nobre Lda v. Council* (Case 253/86) [1988] E.C.R. 2725, which concerned legislation which made specific provision for the possibility of future changes. Note also the comment in *Delacre and others v. Commission* (Case C–350/88) [1990] E.C.R. I–395 at 462 that "traders cannot have a legitimate expectation that an existing situation which is capable of being altered by the Community institutions in the exercise of their discretionary powers will be maintained."

[114] See *e.g. Delacre and others v. Commission* (Case C–350/88) [1990] E.C.R. I–395.

informed, experienced trader would have anticipated. A high level of awareness of market realities is therefore presupposed. Thus "if the underlying economic situation and the regulatory situation are plainly out of step with one
another, an economic agent cannot have a reasonable – let alone legitimate –
expectation that sudden regulatory changes will not be made."[115] The prudent
trader is also aware of the rules governing the relevant market sector, so that
any expectation which conflicts with those rules will not be regarded as legitimate.[116] A high level of monitoring of Commission activities is also an attribute of the prudent trader,[117] as is awareness of the latest contents of the
Official Journal.[118] One might quibble with the standard of knowledge expected. It is not always clear that such a level of knowledge is likely to be
reached in practice – by small economic operators in particular. On the other
hand, as Sharpston has commented, "the logic is unassailable: a trader should
not be able to place himself in a better position by not taking care than he
would have been in had he exercised all due care."[119] Further, one should be
aware in this context and in others (as the Court of Justice undoubtedly is) that
the doctrine of legitimate expectations entails serious consequences for a far
wider range of persons than merely a particular claimant when it is deployed
against the Community legislative or administrative organs. As Usher has observed, "the exercise of legislative and administrative discretion may be subject to severe constraints in situations where a legitimate expectation has been
created."[120]

---

[115] Sharpston, *loc. cit.,* above, n.102 at p. 120.

[116] Illustrated by *Compagnie Continentale France v. Council* (Case 169/73) [1975] E.C.R. 117
(where knowledge of the UK's Act of Accession to the European Economic Community was
expected of a French trader) Cf. *Cambo Erbo Industrial SA v. EU Council* (Case T–472/93)
[1995] E.C.R. II–421 (where awareness was expected of the possibility that Community intervention prices for Spanish sugar might change sooner than a transitional period for price align-
ments provided for in the Spanish Act of Accession). See also *Blackman v. European Parliament*
(Case T–33/89) [1993] 249 II–E.C.R. (no legitimate expectation stemmed from failure of Community administration to bring insurance rules which were publicly available to the attention of
claimant). *cf.,* however, *Oryzomyli Kavallas v. Commission* (Case 160/84) [1986] E.C.R. 1633
(where a series of factors combined to make obtaining knowledge of the relevant rules practically impossible) and see generally Usher, *op. cit.,* above, n.29 at pp. 60 to 61).

[117] See *e.g.* in this regard the case of *Continentale Produkten-Gesellschaft Erhardt–Renken GmbH
v. Hauptzollamt München-West* (Case 246/87) [1989] E.C.R. 200 where it was held that a
prudent and informed trader would be aware that an antI–dumping investigation was underway,
and therefore aware that anti–dumping duties could be imposed, when entering into contracts
with suppliers.

[118] Seen in *Union Nationale des Coopératives Agricoles de Céréales and others v. Commission
and Council* (Case 95/75) [1975] E.C.R. 1615 in which the court distinguished unfavourably
the legitimate expectations of claimants who had entered into contracts after the publication in
the Official Journal of a regulation modifying the method of calculating monetary compensation amounts *vis-à-vis* the expectations of those who had entered into such contracts prior to
publication.

[119] *Loc. cit.,* above, n.102 at p. 150.

[120] *Op. cit.,* above, n.29 at p. 57.

The standards of reasonableness and foreseeability will vary according to the circumstances of the case – context counts for much in setting the required standard of knowledge and awareness. As the court stated in the *Duff* ruling,

> "It is settled case-law that in the sphere of the common organisation of the markets, whose purpose involves constant adjustments to meet changes in the economic situation, economic agents cannot legitimately expect that they will not be subject to restrictions arising out of future rules of market or structural policy..."[121]

To take one example, the policy area of agriculture – or more accurately, the various Community financial mechanisms and systems which operate in agriculture-related fields – has as its subject matter a volatile market where change has been described as the normal state of affairs.[122] In practice, a good proportion of the legitimate expectations cases which have come before the court have been brought in this area. Here, not only is it the case that the Court of Justice usually gives the Community institutions wide freedom to manoeuvre in managing the market, and is therefore little inclined to impose restrictions on them via the legitimate expectations principle,[123] but the court has also firmly adhered to the position that speculative undertakings (by which is meant attempts to take advantages of weaknesses in the Community system to make a profit, rather than actions in the normal course of business) will be entered into at the trader's own risk.[124] In this way, the Court has refused to allow the legitimate expectations principle to be used to make Community institutions in effect the insurers of last resort for such activities.

An area in which the court, for understandable reasons, has shown itself, if anything, to be even less inclined to allow the doctrine of legitimate expectations to be deployed is that of the Community's external trade relations.[125] A

---

[121] *Duff and others v. Minister for Agriculture and Food, Ireland, and the Attorney General* (Case 63/93) [1996] E.C.R. I–576.

[122] Sharpston has observed that "the inexpert do not play in this market which provides considerable opportunities for speculative gains – and also losses.", *loc. cit.*, above, n.102 at p. 118.

[123] Sharpston, *loc. cit.*, above, n.102 at p. 108. Some idea of the Court's approach can be gained from its observation in *Merkur v. Commission* (Case 97/76) [1977] E.C.R. 1063 that liability in respect of losses suffered by traders as a result of measures adopted in relation to the monetary compensatory amounts system would be imposed on the Community only were the Commission to abolish monetary compensatory amounts in a particular sector with immediate effect and without either giving notice or adopting transitional measures – and even then, only in the absence of an overriding public interest. (See also Usher, *op. cit.*, above, n.29 at p. 59). Although stringent, these criteria appear to have been met in the earlier case of *Comptoir National Technique Agricole v. Commission* (Case 74/74) [1975] E.C.R. 533.

[124] See *e.g. Pardini v. Ministero del Commercio con l'Estero* (Case 338/85) [1988] E.C.R. I–2041, *Einfuhr– und Vorratstelle für Getreide und Futtermittel v. Mackprang* [1975] E.C.R. 607. See further here Hartley, *op. cit.*, above, n.21 at pp. 145 to 146.

[125] See *OHG Firma Werner Faust v. Commission* (Case 52/81) [1982] E.C.R. 3745, *Edeka Zentrale*

restrictive approach has also been adopted in the field of anti-dumping, at least in any cases with policy implications.[126]

(iii) Reliance on the Expectation

Thirdly, in order for the general Community law principle of legitimate expectations to be successfully invoked, the individual must have acted on the basis of the expectation, or at least to have refrained from acting on the basis of it. Merely hoping that the existing situation will continue will not result in entitlement to protection under the principle of legitimate expectation.[127] Nor will an alteration in one's position which is due to factors other than the expectation (which would be shown to be the case, for example, if the individual altered his or her position before the conduct raising the expectation occurred).[128]

(iv) Absence of Misconduct

A fourth factor, reflecting the point that nobody can rely on a situation caused by their own violation of Community law may be stated in negative terms. This is that no legitimate expectation will be given to any individual or firm where the conduct of the Community or national administrative body results from a failure on the part of that individual or firm to provide timely or accurate infor-

---

AG v. Germany (Case 245/81) [1982] E.C.R. 2745. In these cases, the entry into a commercial agreement between the Community and China was held to have the result that no informed trader was entitled to expect that existing patterns of trade would be respected – so that no legitimate expectations were violated subsequently by what amounted to an almost complete prohibition of mushroom imports from Taiwan at very short notice by the Commission.

[126] See further Sharpston, *loc. cit.,* above, n.102 at pp. 116 to 118.

[127] See further Sharpston, *loc. cit.,* above, n.102 at p. 158. It is perhaps because of this requirement of alteration in the claimant's position that Craig has argued that:

"the case law of the ECJ indicates that the individual must be able to point either to a bargain of some form which has been entered into between the individual and the authorities, or to a course of conduct or assurance on the part of the authorities which can be said to generate the legitimate expectation."

(See Craig, "Substantive Legitimate Expectations in Domestic and Community Law" (1996) 55 *C.L.J.* 289 at 307). However, since the alteration in the claimant's position seems to be required even when the expectation relied upon has been generated by consistent behaviour by an administrative body, perhaps as far as it is necessary to go on this point is to endorse Sharpston's observation that:

"legitimate expectations are most likely to be created as a result of discussions with the administration which put the administration on notice that a trader intends to avail himself or herself of a particular provision and which lead the trader to commit himself or herself reasonably and irrevocably to a particular course of action. If possible, therefore, the competent authorities should be duly notified."

Sharpston, "European Community Law and the Doctrine of Legitimate Expectations: How Legitimate and For Whom?" (1990) 11 *J. Intl. L. Bus.* 87 at 102.

[128] See *Agazzi Léonard v. Commission* (Case 181/87) [1988] E.C.R. 3823 and see generally authorities cited by Vaughan, *op. cit.,* above, n.10 at para. 1301.

mation as to a state of affairs.[129] It has further been held that a manifest breach
of the relevant rules by a party seeking to rely upon the principle of legitimate
expectation will prevent any such reliance.[130]

(v) A Weighing Up of Interests

Finally, in each case there will be a weighing up of the interests of the person in
having his or her legitimate expectation protected against the public interest in
having the relevant public authority free to act in whatever way it deems most
appropriate.[131] This aspect is one of the ways in which the Community doctrine most closely resembles the autochthonous doctrine in Irish law under
which a public body will be entitled to change its position where objective
considerations exist which justify it in so doing.[132]

As regards the Community principle of legitimate expectations, perhaps
one of the most useful examples of this weighing up of interests took place at
each stage in the course of the famous *Mulder* series of judgments.[133] The
facts which gave rise to the Mulder cases stemmed from the need of the Community to cut milk production. Under a scheme with this objective, which was
introduced by a 1977 Regulation,[134] producers were permitted to cease production of milk for a period, in exchange for which they received a premium
for the non-marketing of milk. Mulder took advantage of this scheme, agreeing
in 1979 to cease production for a period of five years. Subsequently, further

---

[129] See *e.g.* the judgment of the European Court of First Instance in *Unifrigo Gadus Srl and CPL Imperial 2 SpA v. Commission of the European Communities* (Joined Cases T–10/97 and T–11/97) [1998] E.C.R. II–2231 (where the competent national authorities were misled by incorrect declarations made by an exporter to the effect that particular consignments of cod originated in Norway).

[130] See *e.g. Eugénio Branco Lda v. Commission* (Case T–142/97) [1988] E.C.R. II–3567 in which it was held that a recipient of European Social Fund assistance who had not implemented a training programme in accordance with the conditions on which a grant of assistance by the Commission had been made could not rely on the principle of protection of legitimate expectations with a view to securing final payment of the full amount of assistance initially granted. (See also *e.g.*, *Sideradria v. Commission* (Case 67/84) [1985] E.C.R. 3983 and *Industrias Pesqueras Campos v. Commission* (Case T–551/93) [1996] E.C.R. II–247 and see Usher, *op. cit.,* above, n.29 at pp. 61 to 62).

[131] See Craig, *loc. cit.,* above, n.127 at p. 307; Schwarze, *op. cit.,* above, n.35 at p. 953.

[132] See *e.g. Egan v. Minister for Defence,* unreported, High Court, Barr J., November 24, 1988 ("new situation" created by numerous applications for early retirement from air corps); *Council of Civil Service Unions v. Minister for the Public Service* (the "GCHQ" case) [1985] A.C. 319 (considerations of national security justified departure from previous practice). Note also the balancing of interests carried out by Sedley J. in *R. v. Minister for Agriculture, Fisheries and Foods ex parte Hamble (Offshore) Fisheries Ltd.* [1995] 2 All E.R. 714.

[133] *Mulder v. Minister van Landbouw en Visserij* (Case 120/86) [1988] E.C.R. 2321; *Mulder and others v. Council and Commission ("Mulder II")* (Joined Cases C–104/89 and C–37/90) [1992] E.C.R. I–3061.

[134] Council Regulation 1078/77 of 17 May 1977.

measures to control Community milk production were introduced. Thus in 1984, the milk superlevy system was created. Under a Regulation of that year,[135] milk producers were given milk-quotas based on the previous year's production (*i.e.* that of 1983). Mulder, having ceased to produce milk for the previous five years, now decided that he wanted to resume production in 1984. However, he could obtain no quota from the Dutch authorities, because he had produced no milk at all in 1983.

In practical terms, what this meant was that the bargain Mulder had entered into with the authorities in 1979 was now being used to exclude him entirely from engaging in milk production. Mulder therefore sought the annulment of the 1984 Regulation, arguing that he had an expectation of being allowed to re-enter the market and resume production under the same conditions as those which had obtained when he had entered the arrangement in 1979.

The European Court of Justice held that a producer who had voluntarily ceased production could not expect to resume production under the same conditions on re-entering the market. Rather, such an individual should be aware that the rules relating to the market might change during the period and he or she could not expect to be exempt from these changes. However, Mulder was not without a legitimate expectation. The court held that:

> "where such a producer, as in the present case, has been encouraged by a Community measure to suspend marketing for a limited period in the general interest and against payment of a premium he may legitimately expect not to be subject, upon the expiry of his undertaking, to restrictions *which specifically affect him precisely because he availed himself of the possibilities offered by the Community provisions.*"[136]

More specifically, there had been nothing in the 1977 instrument to indicate that taking up the bargain which it offered might entail a complete bar to resuming milk production. The court therefore held that such an effect frustrated the producer's legitimate expectations that the effect of the 1977 arrangements would be limited. In consequence, the 1984 Regulation was annulled.

The first *Mulder* case is illustrative of a number of points examined elsewhere in this article – the fact that the Community principle of legitimate expectations extends to the protection of substantive rights, and additionally the regard which is had in establishing what is a legitimate expectation to the factors which ought to be within the ken of the prudent and informed trader. It is also illustrative of the balance which the court seeks to achieve between the

---

[135] Council Regulation 857/84 of 31 March 1984.
[136] *Mulder I*, above, n.133 at para. 24 of the judgment of the Court of Justice. Emphasis added.

interest of the public and those of the individual. The court's judgment made it clear that the Community legislature *was* free to alter the rules governing the milk market – but not to the extent of excluding entirely from the market those producers who availed of the earlier scheme. In other words, as Usher has put it:

> "the expectation that was protected was not that the rules would remain unchanged when the outgoers returned to milk production, but that they should not be penalised compared with other producers for having participated in a Community scheme."[137]

Further examples of the kinds of balancing of interests which can occur in cases concerning legitimate expectations were provided by subsequent cases concerning essentially the same factual scenario. Following the first *Mulder* case,[138] another Regulation was adopted by the Council in 1989,[139] granting a quota to those farmers who found themselves in a situation similar to that of *Mulder,* with this quota being based on 60 per cent of the quantity of milk produced in the year before they took part in the agreement to cease production. This Regulation was challenged in turn before the court on the basis that it violated producers' legitimate expectations because the figure of 60 per cent was too low.[140] Here again, the Court of Justice upheld the challenge. The court took the view that it *had* been lawful for the Community legislature to seek to ensure that producers who availed of the 1977 scheme gain no advantage over producers who had not. The hands of the Community legislature were therefore not tied to the extent that such producers had to be restored to the situation in which they had been in 1977. Some regulatory response to a changing market environment was permitted, and these producers could not escape that merely by virtue of having availed of the 1977 arrangement. However, the court took the view that the quota reduction which had now been applied to the former category of producers had been excessive, being over twice the size of the highest quota reduction applied to those who had not availed of the 1977 scheme. Here again, the claimants were effectively being penalised merely for having participated in a Community scheme. The court therefore annulled the offending Regulation.

The final balancing exercise between public and individual interest – albeit

---

[137] Usher, *op. cit.,* above, n.29 at p. 59.
[138] And also that in the similar case of *Von Deetzen v. Hauptzollamt Hamburg-Jonas* (Case 170/86) [1988] E.C.R. 2355.
[139] Council Regulation 764/89.
[140] *Spagl v. Hauptzollamt Rosenheim* (Case C–189/89) [1990] E.C.R. I–4539; *Pastätter v. Hauptzollamt Bad Reichenhall* (Case C–217/89) [1990] E.C.R. I–4585.

one of a somewhat different nature – was yet to come. Subsequent to the above mentioned cases, yet another Regulation was adopted, giving the relevant producers an improved quota. Mulder, however, now brought a claim for damages against the Council and Commission under what is now Article 288 of the EC Treaty in respect of his losses during the period before which this final Regulation was introduced.[141] When the matter came before the court in *"Mulder II"*, the court acknowledged that both the 1984 Regulation denying Mulder any quota at all, and the 1989 Regulation which had introduced the 60% rule had indeed violated the claimant's legitimate expectations. However, the court was willing to award damages only in relation to the former violation. This was because of the court's application of the rule that in a legislative field such as the one in question which was characterised by need for the exercise of a wide discretion, the Community could not incur liability unless the institution concerned had manifestly and gravely disregarded the limits on the exercise of its powers.[142] The court felt that in adopting the 1989 Regulation the Community legislature *had* taken account of the higher public interest – *viz.,* the higher public necessity of not jeopardising the fragile stability that obtained in the milk products sector – without gravely and manifestly disregarding the limits of its discretionary power in this area. It had gotten the balance wrong, and had violated the claimant's legitimate expectations for a second time, but on this occasion, its behaviour did not give rise to liability in damages, although (as has already been seen) it was sufficient to have the offending measure annulled.[143]

---

[141] Formerly Article 215. This was *Mulder and others v. Council and Commission ("Mulder II")* (Joined Cases C–104/89 and C–37/90) [1992] E.C.R. I–3061.

[142] In contrast, however, in relation to policy areas in which a Community institution or Member State has considerably reduced or even no discretion, mere infringement of the law may be sufficient to establish the existence of a sufficiently serious breach. (See now Case C–352/98P *Laboratoires Pharmaceutiques Bergaderm SA v. Jean-Jacques Goupil* Judgment of the Court of Justice of July 4, 2000).

[143] The facts which gave rise to the *Mulder* saga are still resulting in cases coming before the Court of Justice at the time of writing. Two of the latest cases to come before the court, *Héritiers d'Edmond Ropars and others v. Council of the European Union* (Case T–429/93) (Judgment of Court of First Instance (First Chamber) of June 21, 2000) and *Tromeur v. Council of the European Union and Commission of the European Union* (Case T–537/93) (Judgment of Court of First Instance (First Chamber) of same date), both of which involved claims for damages somewhat similar to those at issue in *Mulder II*. Both were unsuccessful, however, the claimants having been unable to demonstrate the existence of any intention to resume milk production at the time of the expiry of their undertakings not to market milk pursuant to Regulation 1078/77. As is noted in the text above, the cases are thus illustrative of a perhaps self-evident prerequisite to the obtaining of damages for breach of one's legitimate expectations – the existence of a causal connection between loss suffered and the breach of the relevant expectation.

3. An Adolescent Cousin? The Autochthonous Doctrine of Legitimate
Expectation in the Light of the Foregoing

(a) Introduction – The Origins of the Autochthonous Doctrine

The autochthonous doctrine of legitimate expectation – described judicially as involving the question of "whether in all the circumstances it would be unfair or unjust to allow a party to resile from a position created or adopted by him which at that time gave rise to a legitimate expectation in the mind of another that the situation would continue and might be acted upon by him to his advantage"[144] – has had a striking rise to prominence in the case-law since the 1980s. The writers of the leading Irish text on administrative law have observed that "apart from the doctrine of proportionality, there is, perhaps, no other principle which has so rapidly given rise to so much litigation or which has so quickly become embedded in the fabric of the legal system."[145] The origins of the autochthonous doctrine in common law systems have occasionally been ascribed to European Community law.[146] If this is true at all, however, it seems to have been so at most only at a sub-conscious level. The doctrine was cited for the first time in a common law context in Lord Denning's judgment in *Schmidt v. Secretary of State for Home Affairs,*[147] a case which preceded UK accession to the (then) European Economic Community in 1973 by some years. The concept of legitimate expectation was, according to Lord Denning, one which "came out of my own head and not from any continental or other source."[148] From these beginnings, its use has spread across the common law world, including to Ireland.[149]

It has been accurately observed that the English and Commonwealth case

---

[144] Barr J. in *Cannon v. Minister for the Marine* [1991] I.L.R.M. 261.

[145] Hogan and Morgan, *Administrative Law in Ireland* (3rd edition, Dublin, 1998) at 858. Chapter 15 of this book contains an outstanding analysis of the autochthonous doctrine of legitimate expectations.

[146] See here *e.g.* Mackenzie Stuart "Recent Developments in English Administrative Law – the Impact of Europe?" in Capotorti (ed.), *Du Droit International au Droit de l'Integration, Liber Amicorum P. Pescatore* (Baden-Baden, 1987) at 417 where Mackenzie Stuart describes legitimate expectations "as a novelty in English law which lacks discernible English parentage." He continues "to find the true ancestry one does not have to go far beyond the channel." (Quoted in Hogan and Morgan *op. cit.,* above, n.145 at p. 859).

[147] [1969] 2 Ch. 149. This was followed by his dissenting judgment in *Breen v. Amalgamated Engineering Union* [1971] 2 Q.B. 175 which also made reference to legitimate expectation.

[148] In a letter to Forsyth quoted by that writer in "The Provenance and Protection of Legitimate Expectations" (1988) 47 *C.L.J.* 238 at 241.

[149] See the judgment of Costello J. in *Tara Prospecting Ltd v. Minister for Energy* [1993] I.L.R.M. 771 at 783. See regarding developments in other jurisdictions *e.g.*, France, "Legitimate Expectations in New Zealand" (1990-1991) 14 *N.Z.U.L.R.* 123 and Hlophe "Legitimate Expectation and Natural Justice: English, Australian and South African Law" (1987) 104 *S.A.L.J.* 165. In relation to the Canadian courts see *e.g.* the recent decision on the Canadian Federal Court of Appeal in *Apotex Inc. v. Canada (Attorney General)* (2000) 188 D.L.R. (4th) 145.

law appears to have developed with little explicit reference to European parallels, but in this jurisdiction at least, there has been some degree of reference to European Community law authorities. The extent of their influence on the autochthonous doctrine should not, at the same time, be overestimated, but it is probably fair to say that the existence of a parallel doctrine may well have acted in a certain measure as a consolidating influence insofar as the autochthonous doctrine is concerned.[150] Perhaps because of the early involvement of Lord Denning in the establishment of the doctrine in English law, the autochthonous doctrine of legitimate expectations is sometimes said to be an equitable doctrine. Indeed in *Webb* itself, Finlay C.J. went so far as to assert that the doctrine of legitimate expectation, "is but an aspect of the well-recognised equitable concept of promissory estoppel (which has been frequently applied in our courts), whereby a promise or representation as to intention may in certain circumstances be held binding on the representor or the promisor."[151] This was a statement which was later relied upon by Barr J. in *Cannon v. Minister for the Marine* where he held that "the concept of legitimate expectations being derived from an equitable doctrine, must be reviewed in the light of equitable principles".[152] And yet the case for the autochthonous doctrine being either an aspect of promissory estoppel or indeed an equitable doctrine at all seems far from having been convincingly made out. Indeed, fair arguments to the contrary effect can be made.[153] In the first place, legitimate expectation is a public law doctrine – in other words, a doctrine which is directed at protecting the individual against unfair administrative decision-making.[154] Secondly, it is a doctrine the application of which appears to be capable of being denied on the basis of policy considerations relating to good administration which post-

---

[150] Here see both the High Court judgment of Murphy J. in *Duff v. Minister for Agriculture* [1997] 2 I.R. 22 and the observations of Hamilton J. in *Carbery Milk Products Ltd. v. Minister for Agriculture* (1988-93) 4 I.T.R. 492. For a recent United Kingdom case in which careful regard was had to the Community law principle of legitimate expectations in determining the scope of the autochthonous doctrine, see the judgment of the Court of Appeal (delivered by Lord Woolf M.R.) in *R. v. North East Devon Health Authority, ex parte Coughlan* [2000] 3 All E.R. 850.

[151] *Webb v. Ireland* [1988] I.R. 353 at 384.

[152] [1991] I.L.R.M. 261 at 266. See more recently the decision of O'Sullivan J. in *Daly v. Minister of the Marine* unreported, High Court, February 25, 1999, where the learned judge observed that "it is clear and not disputed that the relief granted on the basis of legitimate expectation is an equitable remedy."

[153] For a list of some such arguments, see Hogan and Morgan, *op. cit.*, above, n.145 at pp. 897 to 900.

[154] *See O'Reilly v. Mackman* [1983] 2 A.C. 237 at 275 and the authorities cited by Hogan and Morgan, op. cit., above, n.145 at p. 860, n. 11. Note that the public law remedies are discretionary. In *Abrahamson v. Law Society of Ireland* [1996] 2 I.L.R.M. 481, McCracken J. distinguished the doctrine of legitimate expectation from that of promissory estoppel, by observing, *inter alia*, that the latter doctrine "is usually, although not exclusively, related to matters of private law rather than public law."

date the facts of the case.[155] Thirdly, it requires no existing contractual (or other similar) relationship in order to apply.[156] Fourthly, unlike promissory estoppel, legitimate expectations act as a sword as well as a shield, in that legitimate expectations may give rise to a cause of action in respect of which a court will award damages.[157] These are all factors which appear to distinguish it from promissory estoppel. In any case, it should not be forgotten that, for better or for worse, the traditional rule is that there is no place for estoppel in public law.[158] Rather than in equity, the rationale for creating a doctrine of legitimate expectation lies in the fact that it is the interest of good administration that these interests be shielded. This is a view which finds support in the recent judgment of the Court of Appeal in *R. v. North East Devon Health Authority, ex parte Coughlan*[159] where Lord Woolf M.R. described the doctrine of legitimate expectations as "a distinct application of the concept of abuse of power." Thus France has observed that:

"legitimate expectations finds its origin in procedural impropriety, and in particular is most often seen as being the means by which the potential strait-jacket of rights and privileges is broken. The great developments of

---

[155] See text below.

[156] *cf.* however, the judgment of Kelly J. in *Glencar Exploration v. Mayo County Council* (unreported, High Court, August 20, 1998) where he asserted at 66 of the judgment that "there was no legitimate expectation such as is contended for and *even if there was, damages would not be available as a remedy in respect of it because of the absence of a contractual or similar relationship between the parties.*" (Emphasis added.) The only support adduced by Kelly J. for this proposition was his assertion that the cases in which damages have been awarded such as *Webb* and *Duggan* were "distinguishable from this case because the applicants there were in long-term contractual or equivalent relationships with the respondents and the wrongs done were akin to a breach of contract. There is no such equivalent relationship between the parties to this litigation." With respect, the facts of *Webb* did not involve any such relationship, but rather (as Finlay C.J. described it in his judgment in that case) a "transaction" whereby a hoard of treasure was deposited in the National Museum and accepted on behalf of the State. *Duggan* is also a poor authority, since properly viewed, the facts of that case probably did not raise an issue of legitimate expectations at all. (See further n. 165 below.) In neither *Webb* nor *Duggan* was any suggestion made that the award of damages for breach of a legitimate expectation was conditional on the existence of a "long-term contractual or equivalent relationship."

[157] Damages were awarded by the Supreme Court in *Webb v. Ireland* [1988] I.R. 353 and in the High Court case of *Duggan v. An Taoiseach* [1989] I.L.R.M. 710, in both cases purportedly for violation of legitimate expectations. The judgment of McCracken J. in *Abrahamson v. Law Society of Ireland* [1996] 2 I.L.R.M. 481 at 498 also indicates that damages may be awarded for breach of an individual's legitimate expectations. See also the judgment of Kelly J. in *Glencar Exploration v. Mayo County Council* (unreported, High Court, August 20, 1998) discussed in n. 156 above.

[158] See in this regard the judgment of Costello J. in *Tara Prospecting v. Minister for Energy* [1993] I.L.R.M. 771 at 789. This point is referred to again in the text below, and further authorities are cited there.

[159] [2000] 3 All E.R. 850. Lord Woolf gave the judgment for the Court of Appeal (Sedley and Mummery L.JJ. concurring with his opinion).

Ridge v. Baldwin[160] and subsequent cases were seen to be imperilled by the idea that the imposition of the requirements of natural justice might be restricted to situations where there was present an established interest or right."[161]

Similarly, Baldwin and Horne have attributed the basis of the legitimate expectations doctrine to:

> "the notion that statutory powers are not given to public bodies to be exercised capriciously. Reasonable and fair action thus involves a modicum of consistency. Certain types of actions will create legitimate expectations on this basis".[162]

As is the case with the Community principle of legitimate expectations, the case law concerning the autochthonous doctrine is far from entirely consistent. In the case of the autochthonous doctrine, this is probably for a number of reasons. First, as was observed by McCracken J. in *Abrahamson v. Law Society of Ireland*, "it is only to be expected that in an evolving concept there will be contradictory judgments."[163] Secondly, it must be acknowledged that there has been a tendency in some cases to use the language of legitimate expectation in order to bring about an outcome which is consonant with the requirements of justice, when, properly analysed, the case does not raise an issue of legitimate expectation at all. The prime example of this is the Supreme Court decision in the *Webb* case itself, which, it is submitted, has been correctly characterised as having really been a private law case involving the application of the principles of promissory estoppel, with any reference to notions of legitimate expectation having been superfluous.[164] *Webb* is not by any means the sole example of this phenomenon, however.[165] A third reason why there are

---

[160] [1964] A.C. 40.

[161] See France, "Legitimate Expectations in New Zealand" (1990-1991) 14 *N.Z.U.L.R.* 123.

[162] Baldwin and Horne, "Expectations in a Joyless Landscape" (1986) 49 *M.L.R.* 685 at 702. In *Fakih v. Minister for Justice* [1993] 2 I.R. 406 at 423, O'Hanlon J. described the doctrine of legitimate expectations as a "manifestation of the duty to act fairly", although he also quoted the observations made by Finlay C.J. in *Webb v. Ireland* [1988] I.R. 353, (quoted in the text above) without making any criticism of them. See also the judgment of Lord Diplock in *Council of Civil Service Unions v. Minister for Civil Service* [1985] 1 A.C. 374 at 408-409 to which reference is made by Keane J. (as he then was) in *Pesca Valentia Ltd. v. Minister for Fisheries* [1990] 2 I.R. 205.

[163] [1996] 1 I.R. 403 at 422.

[164] [1988] I.R. 353. See Hogan and Morgan, *op. cit.*, above, n.145 at pp. 872 and 889.

[165] Another prominent case in which the legitimate expectations doctrine was used as the basis of the decision when the facts would not seem to have given rise to such an issue is the High Court decision in *Fakih v. Minister for Justice* [1993] 2 I.R. 406, which is examined below. See also *e.g. Duggan v. An Taoiseach* [1989] I.L.R.M. 710, a High Court decision to the effect that two civil servants had a legitimate expectation to continue in posts to which they had been ap-

inconsistencies in the case law is that there has been an element of retrenchment from the broadest interpretations of the legitimate expectation doctrine by many judges, perhaps in trepidation of what are felt to be its unclear implications.[166] This topic will be revisited below.

(b) Factors Which Go Towards Making an Expectation "Legitimate" under the Autochthonous Doctrine

Some examination of the factors which go towards making an expectation "legitimate" in Irish law may be thought worthwhile.[167] The notion of upholding legitimate expectations has generally been taken to require the protection of more than merely enforceable legal rights.[168] But there has been some judicial discussion of whether the word "legitimate" is so broad as to be merely a syno-

---

pointed for a certain period, when it could have been decided on the point that the executive had no power to suspend the operation of the Farm Tax Office (since it was established by a statute and the Government cannot, acting alone, alter a statute). In *Conroy v. Garda Commissioner* [1989] I.R. 140 a retired Garda was held to have had a legitimate expectation that he would receive a full pension, when the doctrine of legitimate expectations seemed inapplicable on the facts. *Conroy* really seemed to raise issues of innocent misrepresentation. See Hogan and Moran, *op. cit.,* above, n.145 at pp. 885 and 887. *Kenny v. Kelly* [1988] I.R. 457 (in which a declaration was granted to the applicant that she was entitled to a place in the Arts Faculty in University College Dublin in 1987, on foot of representations made to her by an official in the university admissions office) is a judgment which is clearly based primarily on the doctrine of promissory estoppel. The last line of the judgment ("whichever legal approach is adopted, the applicant is entitled to a declaration ...') seems to indicate that subsidiary reliance was placed on the doctrine of legitimate expectations. This is certainly how the case was interpreted by Professor Brady (see Brady *loc. cit.,* above, n.2 at pp. 134 to 137).

It can be argued (although the point is far more debatable here) that the case was an inappropriate one for the application of the doctrine of legitimate expectations (and indeed for the grant of a declaration) since it is not clear that it involved a public law issue. Indeed Barron J. himself acknowledged that the public law/private law divide had raised its head here by observing that the case could have been an appropriate one for an order under Order 84, Rule 26(5) of the Rules of the Superior Courts, 1986, that proceedings should continue as if they had been begun by plenary summons, had such a timely application for such an order been brought. See however, on the public law/private law divide and the difficulties which it raises, Hogan and Morgan, *op. cit.,* above, n.145, Chapter 14.

[166] See O'Hanlon J.'s observation in *Fakih v. Minister for Justice* [1993] 2 I.R. 406 at 423 where he observed that legitimate expectations "may have some of the characteristics of the "unruly horse" which were associated with the plea of public policy". See also the similarly unenthusiastic equine analogy drawn by the same judge in *Association of General Practitioners Ltd. v. Minister of Health* [1995] 1 I.R. 382 at 393–394 where he expressed the fear that if the autochthonous doctrine were "allowed its head" uncertainty in contract law and property law, *inter alia,* could result.

[167] See generally Delany, "The Doctrine of Legitimate Expectation in Irish Law" (1990) 12 *D.U.L.J.* (ns) 1 at 6 to 8.

[168] *Attorney General of Hong Kong v. Ng Yuen Shiu* [1983] 2 A.C. 629. The suggestion in at least one Australian case that the doctrine added little if anything to the concept of a right was one which was never taken up in this hemisphere. See the judgment of Barwick C.J. in *Salemi v. MacKellar (No. 2)* (1977) 137 C.L.R. 396 cited in Delany, *loc. cit.,* above, n.167.

nym for "reasonable" or whether it signifies a concept which is somewhat narrower in meaning. Initial indications pointed in the direction of the words "legitimate" and "reasonable" being interchangeable.[169] Lord Diplock, in the *G.C.H.Q.,* case expressed a preference for the use of the description:

> "a 'legitimate expectation' rather than a 'reasonable expectation' in order thereby to indicate that it has consequences to which effect will be given in public law, whereas an expectation or hope that some benefit or advantage would continue to be enjoyed, although it might well be entertained by a 'reasonable' man, would not necessarily have such consequences."[170]

The same general approach seems to have been adopted by Blayney J. in his High Court judgment in *Wiley v. Revenue Commissioners,*[171] in which he observed of the applicant, who had asserted that he had a legitimate expectation to certain excise duty repayments, that:

> "at best, all he could have believed was that he had a good chance of getting it because he had got it twice before. And no doubt that would have been a reasonable belief. But it fell far short of being a legitimate expectation."[172]

The terms "legitimate" and "reasonable" are occasionally used interchangeably by the Irish courts.[173] For the sake of terminological clarity, however, it is probably better to adhere to the distinction drawn by Lord Diplock. It should be understood that drawing this distinction is a question of labelling, however, not of substance.[174] In other words, it offers no conceptual guidance to what constitutes a legitimate expectation, telling us no more than that a legitimate expectation is a reasonable expectation in relation to which judges will be pre-

---

[169] See the speech of Lord Fraser in *Attorney General of Hong Kong v. Ng Yuen Shiu* [1983] 2 A.C. 629.

[170] *Council of Civil Service Unions v. Minister for the Civil Service* [1985] 1 A.C. 374 at 408–409.

[171] [1989] I.R. 350 at 355. This judgment was appealed unsuccessfully to the Supreme Court: [1993] I.L.R.M. 482.

[172] For further examples of cases in which the applicants had what appear to have been perfectly reasonable expectations which were nonetheless held not to involve situations of legitimate expectations, see *e.g., Egan v. Minister for Defence* unreported, High Court, Barr J., November 24, 1988 and the judgment of Costello J. in *Gilheaney v. Revenue Commissioners* [1998] I.R. 150.

[173] See *e.g.,* the judgment of Finlay C.J. in *Webb v. Ireland* [1988] I.L.R.M. 565 at 384 and that of Hamilton P. in *Duggan v. An Taoiseach* [1989] I.L.R.M. 710 at 727.

[174] Hence the observation by France in "Legitimate Expectations in New Zealand" (1990-1991) 14 *N.Z.U.L.R.* 123 at 142 that "the distinction seems simply an attempt to stress that a legitimate expectation is a reasonable expectation that will be given judicial protection. This is circular and unhelpful, particularly when it is remembered that remedies are discretionary.'

pared to exercise their discretion to grant a remedy. However, as with the Community principle of legitimate expectations, it is possible to garner from the case-law some idea of the elements which the courts will require to be present before the autochthonous doctrine of legitimate expectation will be deployed in favour of an individual or business whose expectations have been disappointed.[175]

(i) Conduct Justifying the Expectation

We may begin here by noting that, as is the case with the Community principle, some conduct on the part of an administration justifying a legitimate expectation will normally be called for.

In the case of the autochthonous doctrine, however, the requirement of conduct justifying an expectation does not always seem to have been seen as an absolute one throughout the common law world – at least insofar as concerns legitimate expectations as to the *procedure* by which a decision will be taken. There have been a number of decisions of the United Kingdom courts in which it has been decided that a particular interest is important enough that an applicant should not be refused it without having some procedural rights afforded to him.[176] Indeed this is the context in which legitimate expectations first emerged as a concept in the common law. Here, the rights did not depend on any promise or practice by the decision-making body.[177] These cases are few in number, however, and date from an early period in the evolution of the autochthonous doctrine.

The conduct normally required for the purposes of the autochthonous doctrine bears strong similarities to that required under Community law in order to engage the Community principle of legitimate expectations. Hence the conduct may consist of:[178]

---

[175] It is perhaps stating the obvious to point out that an applicant may be held to have had a legitimate expectation in a particular case which falls short of all that the applicant is contending for. (See *Cannon v. Minister for the Marine* [1991] 1 I.R. 82.) The result in such a case may be that the expectation is not regarded as having been disappointed, with the result that the applicant does not succeed.

[176] As in *Schmidt v. Secretary of State for Home Affairs* [1969] 2 Ch. 149 and *McInnes v. Onslow-Fane* [1978] 1 W.L.R. 1520. Note the observation by Lord Denning at 170 of *Schmidt* that "it all depends on whether he has some right or interest, or, I would add, some legitimate expectation, of which it would not be fair to deprive him without hearing what he has to say." See also Craig, "Legitimate Expectations: A Conceptual Analysis" (1992) 108 *L.Q.R.* 82 to 83.

[177] See here Singh, "Making Legitimate Use of Legitimate Expectation" (1994) 144 *N.L.J.* 1215 at 1215.

[178] See here Baldwin and Horne, "Expectations in a Joyless Landscape" (1986) 49 *M.L.R.* 685 at 702.

(i)   an express or implied undertaking to behave in a particular way in exercising a power;[179]

(ii) the adoption of a consistent practice. In other words, if a practice continues for a sufficiently long period of time, this may be regarded as justifying a legitimate expectation that this practice will continue.[180] The logic here appears to be that such prior behaviour will have some kind of precedent value, or, put otherwise, that such a pattern of conduct in the past will be taken as amounting to a representation that others in a similar situation will also have legitimate expectations.[181] The latter analysis was clearly that which Barr J. had in mind in *Egan v. Minister for Defence*[182] when he held that there was no legitimate expectation that the plaintiff – an officer in the air corps – would be granted early retirement, enabling him to take a civilian job. Barr J. based his decision on his view that "such a practice, however firmly entrenched it may have been in the life of the permanent defence force, did not amount to an implied promise or representation ... made by the Minister to the officer corps...that permission to retire would be granted in every case as of course."[183]

(iii) the publication of rules or policies which it is known by the authority will

---

[179] As in *Webb v. Ireland* [1988] I.L.R.M. 565 where the promise was express. See also e.g., *Attorney General of Hong Kong v. Ng Yuen Shiu* [1983] 2 A.C. 629 and *R. v. Liverpool Corporation ex parte Liverpool Taxi Fleet Operators' Association* [1972] 2 Q.B. 299.

[180] See here *e.g., Eogan v. University College Dublin* [1996] 2 I.L.R.M. 702, *Egan v. Minister for Defence* above, n.172, *Wiley v. Revenue Commissioners* [1989] I.R. 350 (H.C.) where Blayney J. took the view that the doing of something on two occasions only could not constitute a practice. Compare *Holtbecker v. Commission* (Case T–20/91) [1992] E.C.R. II–2599 as regards the Community law principle. See also *Council of Civil Service Unions v. Minister for Civil Service* [1985] 1 A.C. 374 (the *"GCHQ"* case) where, were it not for the exigencies of national security, the applicants would have been held to have had a legitimate expectation that unions and employees would be consulted in relation to certain matters, such right having arisen by virtue of consistent practice. Note Lord Fraser's observation that "legitimate expectations, or reasonable expectations may arise either from an express promise given on behalf of a public authority or from the existence of a regular practice which the claimant can reasonably expect to continue." (See [1985] 1 A.C. 374 at 401). See also *H.T.V. v. Price Commission* [1976] I.C.R. 170 (which involved a practice of interpreting a so-called "Price Code" in a particular manner, and the Court of Appeal decision in *R. v. Inland Revenue Commissioners ex. parte Unilever* [1998] S.T.C. 681. Hogan and Morgan, *op. cit.*, above, n.145 at p. 880 also refer to the case of *Ghneim v. Minister for Justice* (reported in the *Irish Times* of September 2, 1989) where Hamilton J. was of the view that a delay of a year and a half in reaching a decision as to whether the applicant should have permission to stay in Ireland beyond the date stipulated in his entry visa (for the purposes of facilitating the completion of his studies in Ireland) could give rise to a legitimate expectation. Contrast the effect of delay in reaching a decision for the purposes of the Community law principle of legitimate expectations (as to which see text at n.101 above *et seq.*).

[181] Singh, "Making Legitimate Use of Legitimate Expectation" (1994) 144 *N.L.J.* 1215.

[182] Unreported, High Court, Barr J., November 24, 1988.

[183] *ibid.* at 15.

be relied upon. In this case, the relevant public body will have set out the criteria for the application of policy in a certain area, an applicant will have relied on these criteria, and the public body will now be seeking to apply different criteria.[184]

There have also been a number of cases where the courts decide that a particular interest is important enough that an applicant should not be refused it without having some procedural rights afforded to him

(ii) The Requirement of an Expectation

Again, as is the case with the Community law principle, a subjective expectation on the part of the individual concerned is required before the autochthonous doctrine of legitimate expectations will apply. Forsyth has drawn attention to the "self-evident and fundamental" and yet "often overlooked" point that:

> "whether an expectation exists or not, is simply a question of fact: what did the person concerned actually expect? If that person did not in fact expect anything then, even if others did expect something, that person's expectation, being non-existent, cannot be protected."[185]

The existence of a subjectively held expectation will not suffice in and of itself to make an expectation a legitimate one, however. As is the case with the Community law doctrine, certain further objective requirements concerning the nature of the expectation must be met. The issue of whether the protection afforded by the autochthonous doctrine goes further than the protection of mere procedural (as opposed to substantive) legitimate expectations – a controversy which has largely passed the Community doctrine by[186] – is a subject which has some relevance to this heading. It is a topic which is examined below.

Other requirements which may be dealt with under this rubric include the limitation that there cannot be a legitimate expectation of something which

---

[184] As in *e.g., R. v. Secretary of State for the Home Department ex parte Khan* [1984] 1 W.L.R. 1337. An Irish case involving this situation, although an unsatisfactory one, is *Fakih v. Minister for Justice* [1993] 2 I.R. 406.

[185] Forsyth, *loc. cit.,* above, n.148 at p. 376. The point seems to have been overlooked in *Fakih v. Minister for Justice* [1993] 2 I.R. 406. A more deliberate (but no less incorrect) overlooking of this requirement occurred in the Australian High Court case of *Minister of Ethnic Affairs v. Teoh* (1995) 128 A.L.R. 353. The assertion in this case that personally entertaining an expectation is unnecessary and that it is enough that the expectation be reasonable was described by Forsyth as wrong and confusing legitimate expectations with the duty to act fairly.

[186] A point which was alluded to by Lord Woolf. in *R. v. North East Devon Health Authority ex parte Coughlan* [2000] 3 All E.R. 850 at 873 where he observed that "this is not a live issue in the common law of the European Union, where a uniform standard of full review for fairness is well established".

would be *contra legem*,[187] or more specifically, a legitimate expectation of anything which would be contrary to the requirements of the Constitution.

The *contra legem* point is exemplified by the rejection by the Supreme Court of the appellant's case in *Wiley v. Revenue Commissioners*, for this rested in part on the court's view that recognising the contended-for legitimate expectations (of a recipient of excise duty) would have required the respondent statutory authority to take a decision which would have been *ultra vires*.[188]

The point as to expectations which run contrary to the requirements of the Constitution is exemplified in the High Court judgment in *Pesca Valentia Ltd. v. Minister for Fisheries,* where Keane J. (as he then was) rejected any idea that the plaintiffs had a legitimate expectation that no legislative changes affecting in a fundamental way their right to fish would be adopted, observing:

> "no such 'estoppel' could conceivably operate so as to prevent the Oireachtas from legislating or the executive from implementing the legislation when enacted."[189]

In this regard, it should be noted that the principle of the separation of powers will operate as a more important restraint on the operation of the autochthonous doctrine than will be the case insofar as concerns the Community principle of legitimate expectations. In other words, the Community principle is a more powerful one, capable of prevailing against legislative intent, either at Community or, within certain limits, at national level. In part, this is due to the fact that the separation of powers principle is generally of more limited application at Community level in any case.[190] But in part, it is also due to the higher status of the doctrine in Community law. General principles of Community law rank more highly in the hierarchy of Community legal norms than does Community legislation, which has the effect that such legislation can and has been held invalid by the European Court of Justice by reason of its failure to respect legitimate expectations or any other recognised general principle of Community law. Nor should it be forgotten that *national* legislation which comes within

[187] *cf.,* however, the judgment of Hamilton P. (as he then was) in *Conroy v. Garda Commissioner* [1989] I.R. 140. Compare the position in Community law, dealt with in the text above at n. 106 *et seq.*

[188] See on this point *e.g.* the judgment of Finlay C.J. at 488. Note also the observation by Lord Woolf M.R. in *R. v. North East Devon Health Authority, ex parte Coughlan* [2000] 3 All E.R. 850 at 873 that it was "axiomatic that a public authority which derives its existence and its powers from statute cannot validly act outside those powers".

[189] [1990] 2 I.R. 205 at 323. Hogan and Morgan, *op. cit.*, above, n.145 at pp. 883–884, discuss the decision of Keane J. on this point.

[190] Thus, for example, the powers of the primary "executive" organ of the Community – the Commission – stretch across the legislative, executive and judicial fields of government. See for an examination of this area, Craig and de Búrca, *European Union Law: Text, Cases and Materials* (2nd ed., Oxford, 1998) at 49-56.

the scope of Community law (and this means national laws which either apply Community law norms or which constitute permissible derogations from Community law standards) may be held inapplicable on the grounds that it violates general principles of Community law – including the principle of legitimate expectation.[191] In contrast, reliance on the autochthonous doctrine of legitimate expectation against Irish legislation (or indeed against executive acts which comply with the legislation authorising them at the expense of the reasonable expectations of individuals) will continue to be precluded unless, or until such time, as the principle of legitimate expectation is accorded the status of a constitutional principle in Irish law.[192]

(iii) Reliance on the Expectation

Is an element of detrimental reliance by an individual on the undertaking necessary? In Community law, as we have seen, the answer is "yes".[193] There is authority in favour of the view that the approach under the autochthonous doctrine is the same.[194] The approach is not entirely uncontroversial. Hogan and Morgan, although they agree that expectation depends on prior knowledge, have argued that detrimental reliance on the expectation is not needed since the interests of consistency, good administration and equal treatment which underlie the doctrine may require that the decision-maker abide by its previous practice.[195] It may be argued, however, that, given that the essence of the doctrine

---

[191] See generally here cases such as *Klensch v. Luxembourg Secretary of State for Agriculture* (Case 202/85) [1986] E.C.R. 3477, *R. v. Kent Kirk* (Case 63/83) [1984] E.C.R. 2689, *Wachauf v. Germany* (Case 5/88) [1989] E.C.R. 2609 and *Elliniki Radiophonia Tileorassi AE v. Pliroforissis and Kouvelas* (Case C–260/89) [1991] E.C.R. I–2925. See further Craig and de Búrca, *op. cit.*, above, n.190 at pp. 317–331 and Usher, *op. cit.*, above, n.29 at pp. 132–137.

[192] As to such a possibility, see Hogan and Morgan, *op. cit.*, above, n.145 at pp. 887–889.

[193] See text, above.

[194] *Garda Representative Association v. Ireland* [1989] I.L.R.M. 1, *Cosgrove v. Legal Aid Board* [1991] 2 I.R. 43. Note also *Daly v. Minister for the Marine* (unreported, High Court, O'Sullivan J., February 25, 1999) where it appeared to work to the applicant's disadvantage that finding him to have the legitimate expectation he claimed would have made him "the beneficiary of an unpaid for advantage which cost him nothing".

[195] Hogan and Morgan, *op. cit.*, above, n.145 at pp. 869–898. See also *Attorney General of Hong Kong v. Ng Yuen Shiu* [1983] 2 A.C. 629 where there appears to have been no detrimental reliance and yet the doctrine of legitimate expectations was applied. *Fakih v. Minister for Justice* [1993] 2 I.R. 406 involved a conscious purported application of the doctrine of legitimate expectation by O'Hanlon J. in the absence of detrimental reliance (see in this regard in particular p. 423 of the judgment) but the case is not a very strong authority. *Fakih* has been described as probably having really involved an application of the principle that it is in the interests of good and orderly administration that, in the absence of good reasons to the contrary, an administrator should be bound to agreed procedures (Hogan and Morgan, *op. cit.*, above, n.145 at p. 869). This seems an accurate characterisation, since the facts of the case did not show even advance knowledge of any applicable procedures on the part of the applicants, let alone any detrimental reliance.

of legitimate expectation is the attainment of a balance between fulfilling the need of the individual for fairness and legal certainty on the one hand, and the need to assure sufficient flexibility to decision-makers to carry out their task on the other, it is difficult to see what unfairness is being inflicted on an individual by changing a policy on which in any case he has not placed any reliance.

(iv) Absence of Misconduct

Although the relevance of misconduct is not a point which seems to have attracted as much attention in the context of the autochthonous legitimate expectation doctrine as it has in Community law, it should be noted that insofar as the autochthonous doctrine is invoked for the purposes of obtaining public law remedies, declarations or injunctions, these remedies are all discretionary. Lack of utmost good faith, or of full disclosure on the part of the applicant may therefore result in a denial of relief[196] as may any conduct of the applicant which is not considered satisfactory by the court.[197]

(v) A Weighing Up of Interests

Perhaps the most obvious point to make about the autochthonous doctrine of legitimate expectation is that it, like its parallel principle in Community law, involves a balancing exercise. For both doctrines involve balancing on the one hand the interest of the individual in securing the optimum level of fairness and certainty in decision-making in public law matters (and indeed the societal interest in according an individual or business this degree of fairness) and on the other hand, the societal interest in maintaining maximum flexibility on the part of decision-makers to react to the changing needs of circumstance. There may be instances where the public interest in a fresh exercise of a discretion will outweigh the injustice suffered by an individual (or business) who has relied on an earlier representation that the discretion will be exercised in favour of a particular result.[198] The process of attaining a balance between the sometimes competing interests of consistency and flexibility in policy manifests itself in a number of ways. Thus, for example, a necessary and sometimes explicit part of the application both of the autochthonous doctrine of legitimate expectation and of the Community principle will be an examination of whether some overriding public interest has justified the change of policy which is alleged to have violated an expectation.[199] Insofar as the autochthonous doctrine

---

[196] See *e.g., Cork Corporation v. O'Connell* [1982] I.L.R.M. 505.

[197] *Ex p. Fry* [1954] 2 All E.R. 118, *Fulbrook v. Berkshire Magistrates Court* (1970) 69 L.G.R. 75.

[198] See Lewis, "Fairness, Legitimate Expectations and Estoppel" (1986) 49 *M.L.R.* 251 at 252.

[199] See here concerning the autochthonous doctrine, Craig, "Legitimate Expectations: A Concep-

is concerned, there has been controversy on where this balancing act should be carried out: should it go to the issue of whether there is a legitimate expectation,[200] or should it come into play only after the legitimacy of the expectation has been established?[201] It is not intended to attempt to resolve this debate here. Suffice it to point out that whichever view is correct, a balancing process is involved.[202]

In the context of the autochthonous doctrine, one way in which it has been sought to establish the boundary between what we may roughly call private and public interest has been the approach of some judges of denying legitimate expectation a substantive aspect and asserting that it is capable only of affecting the procedure by which decisions are reached.

(vi) The Procedure v. Substance Debate

Forsyth has observed that:

> "expectations divide broadly into two groups: *procedural expectations* – where procedural justice of one form or another is expected – and *substantive expectations* – where a favourable decision of one kind or another is expected."[203]

Put simply, therefore, the distinction between procedure and substance is the difference between the process which a decision-maker uses to reach a conclusion and the conclusion itself. Although "substantive due process" is said to be a concept which is gaining increasing acceptance, the idea has met with uneven levels of acceptance in the context of the autochthonous doctrine of le-

---

tual Analysis" (1992) 108 *L.Q.R.* 79 at 97 and concerning the Community doctrine, see *e.g.,* Schwarze, *op. cit.,* above, n.35 at pp. 952–953.

[200] A view adopted by Sedley J. (as he then was) in *R. v. Ministry for Agriculture, Fisheries and Foods ex parte Hamble* [1995] 2 All E.R. 714.

[201] A view advocated by Craig. See here and on this point generally, Craig, "Substantive Legitimate Expectations in Domestic and Community Law" (1996) 55 *C.L.J.* 289 at 300–304.

[202] In the case of the autochthonous doctrine, it may be that further potential for disagreement lies in the as yet apparently unresolved question of whether the departure from the previous representation has to be objectively justified or merely justified in the view of the decision-maker, (or somewhere between these two extremes – *e.g.* justified in the view of the decision-maker, which view must be reasonable). See on this point Singh, *"Making Legitimate Use of Legitimate Expectation"* (1994) 144 *N.L.J.* 1215 at 1216.

[203] Forsyth, "Wednesbury Protection of Substantive Legitimate Expectations" [1997] *P.L.* 375 at 376. Similarly, Craig has taken the concept of procedural legitimate expectations to denote "the existence of some species of process right, whether in the form of natural justice, fairness or a related idea of consultation" and the concept of substantive legitimate expectations to refer to where the applicant seeks "a particular benefit or commodity, whether this takes the form of a welfare benefit, a licence or one of the myriad other forms which such claims can assume". See Craig, "Substantive Legitimate Expectations in Domestic and Community Law" (1996) 55 *C.L.J.* 289 at 290.

gitimate expectations – principally due to a reluctance on the part of the judiciary to be seen to interfere excessively in the operation of other branches of government.[204]

There is no doubt that the doctrine of legitimate expectation can be relied upon in order to secure procedural rights.[205] The outcome here is that the relevant decision may still go against the person affected, but it will be required to follow a procedure which is fair. Thus "at the least, a legitimate expectation will normally be protected by the imposition of obligations of procedural fairness. The content of the fairness requirement will vary according to the circumstances."[206] It should be noted that even a substantive expectation may be afforded procedural protection by the courts.[207]

A conservative view of the legitimate expectation doctrine is that it affords no more than procedural protection. Viewed in this way, the doctrine of legitimate expectation can be described as being about no more than achieving an acceptable middle ground between a general obligation to consult prior to the taking of a decision, and the total freedom to change policy.[208] The clearest statement of the conservative position by an Irish court to date has been that of Costello J. in the High Court case of *Tara Prospecting v. Minister for Energy* where, after reviewing the authorities, he came to the following conclusions in the context of a challenge to the exercise of a ministerial discretion. They are of general interest and hence worth quoting at length:

> "(1) There is a duty on a minister who is exercising a discretionary power which may affect *rights* or *interests* to adopt fair procedures in the exercise of the power. Where a member of the public has a *legitimate expectation* arising from the minister's words and/or conduct that (a) he will be given a hearing before a decision adverse to his interests will be taken or (b) that he will obtain a benefit from the exercise of the power then the

---

[204] See Delany, "Significant Themes in Judicial Review of Administrative Action" (1998) 20 *D.U.L.J.* (n.s.) 73 at 75. On the topic of a constitutional right of substantive due process, see by the same writer, "The Doctrine of Legitimate Expectation in Irish Law" (1990) 12 *D.U.L.J.* (n.s.) 1 at 19 to 20.

[205] See here *e.g.,* the judgment of Costello J. in *Tara Prospecting v. Minister for Energy* [1993] I.L.R.M. 771.

[206] France, "Legitimate Expectations in New Zealand" (1990-1991) 14 *N.Z.U.L.R.* 123 at 142. France gives the example of *Daganayasi v. Minister of Immigration* [1980] 1 N.Z.L.R. 355, where the New Zealand Court of Appeal held that the complainant had a legitimate expectation not only to make submissions on her proposed deportation, but also the right to see reports held by the Minister who was making the decision.

[207] See *e.g. Administrator, Transvaal and others v. Traub and others* (1989) (4) S.A. 731. Note also the observations of Costello J. to this effect in *Tara Prospecting Ltd. v. Minister for Energy* [1993] I.L.R.M. 771 at 788.

[208] To adapt phraseology first employed by France, "Legitimate Expectations in New Zealand" (1990-1991) 14 *N.Z.U.L.R.* 140 at 141.

minister also has a duty to act fairly towards him and this may involve a duty to give him a fair hearing before a decision adverse to his interests is taken. There would then arise a correlative right to a fair hearing which, if denied, will justify the court in quashing the decision.

(2) The existence of a legitimate expectation that a *benefit* will be conferred does not in itself give rise to any legal or equitable right to the *benefit itself* which can be enforced by an order of *mandamus* or otherwise. However, in cases involving public authorities, other than cases involving the exercise of statutory discretionary powers, an equitable right to benefit may arise from the application of the principles of promissory estoppel to which effect will be given by appropriate court order.

(3) In cases involving the exercise of a discretionary statutory power the only legitimate expectation relating to the conferring of a benefit that can be *inferred* from words or conduct is a conditional one, namely, that a benefit will be conferred provided that at the time the minister considers that it is a proper exercise of the statutory power in the light of current policy to grant it. Such a conditional expectation cannot give rise to an enforceable right to the benefit should it later be refused by the minister in the public interest.

(4) In cases involving the exercise of a discretionary statutory power in which an explicit *assurance* has been given which gives rise to an expectation that a benefit will be conferred no enforceable equitable or legal right to benefit can arise. No promissory estoppel can arise because the minister cannot estop either himself or his successors from exercising a discretionary power in the manner prescribed by parliament at the time it is being exercised."[209]

As exemplified by the judgment of Costello J. in *Tara Prospecting*, Irish courts have often refrained from advancing beyond the procedural aspect of legitimate expectation and holding that legitimate expectation can give rise to substantive, rather than merely procedural fairness.[210] Instead, driven by concerns

---

[209] [1993] I.L.R.M. 771 at 788 to 789.
[210] See in this regard also the judgment of Shanley J. in *Eogan v. University College Dublin* [1996] 1 I.R. 390, where the doctrine is quite clearly regarded as having procedural implications only. Note also *Fakih v. Minister for Justice* [1993] 2 I.R. 406, where O'Hanlon J. upheld the right of the applicant asylum-seekers to rely on the doctrine of legitimate expectation so as to have their claims for asylum determined by reference to procedures set out in a letter sent to the representative of the UN High Commissioner for Refugees by an official of the Department of Justice. However, O'Hanlon J. noted "I accept that the legal status of applicants, or the question of their legal entitlement to remain in Ireland, are not governed in any way by the terms of the letter and that it is of benefit to the applicants only in relation to the manner in which their

that administrative discretion might be fettered[211] – or as a judge in another jurisdiction has put it "that it will entail curial interference with administrative decisions on the merits by precluding the decision-maker from ultimately making the decision which he or she considers most appropriate in the circumstances"[212] – there has been a frequent (though far from universal) tendency to draw back from taking the step of upholding substantive legitimate expectations.

On the one hand, such concerns demonstrate an awareness of the reality that the doctrine of substantive legitimate expectations threatens to overwhelm the traditional approach that there is no room for estoppel in public law.[213] On the other hand, such a conservative approach to the doctrine of legitimate expectation (which even the European Court of Justice – famously slow in practice to allow reliance on the Community principle of legitimate expectations – has never applied in Community law) reduces the autochthonous doctrine of

---

claims to rights of asylum are to be processed". (See [1993] 2 I.R. 406 at 424.) See also the earlier High Court decision of Keane J. in *Pesca Valentia Ltd. v. Minister for the Fisheries and Forestry* [1990] 2 I.R. 205. Such judgments repeat sentiments also expressed in English cases such as *R. v. Secretary of State for Health ex parte US Tobacco International Inc.* [1992] 1 All E.R. 212 and *Findlay v. Secretary of State for the Home Department* [1995] A.C. 3187.

[211] The argument that a public body should not fetter its own judgment is sometimes put in terms of the *ultra vires* rule, the argument here being that if a public body fetters its own discretion, it will be held to have acted beyond its powers. Craig has criticised the merits of this *ultra vires* approach as a comprehensive framework for looking at the question of substantive legitimate expectation, describing it as failing to take any account at all of another value recognised in our legal system – that of legal certainty. See Craig, "Substantive Legitimate Expectations in Domestic and Community Law" (1996) 55 *C.L.J.* 289 at 299.

[212] Mason C.J. in *Attorney-General for New South Wales v. Quin* (1990) 170 C.L.R. 1 at 23.

[213] Hence the assertion (quoted in the text above) by Costello J. in *Tara Prospecting Ltd. v. Minister for Energy* (which concerned the exercise of a ministerial discretion) that "no promissory estoppel can arise because the minister cannot estop either himself or his successors from exercising a discretionary power in the manner prescribed by parliament at the time it is being exercised." (See [1993] I.L.R.M. 771 at 789). It should be noted that Costello J. was, however, prepared to countenance the application of the principles of promissory estoppel "in cases involving public authorities, other than cases involving the exercise of statutory discretionary powers". See also in relation to this estoppel point the judgment of Costello J. in *Hempenstall v. Minister for the Environment* [1993] I.L.R.M. 318. See further Singh, *loc. cit.,* above, n.202 at p. 1215 where he cites as cases in support of this rule *Maritime Electric Co. Ltd v. General Dairies Ltd* [1937] A.C. 610, *Southend-on-Sea Corporation v. Hodgson* [1962] 1 Q.B. 416 and *Western Fish Products v. Penwith District Council* [1981] 2 All E.R. 204. Note also Lewis' description of the House of Lords as having paid "lip service" to the principle that estoppel did not apply to public bodies in its judgment in *R. v. Inland Revenue Commissioners ex parte Preston* [1985] 2 W.L.R. 836 (Lewis, "Fairness, Legitimate Expectations and Estoppel" (1986) 49 *M.L.R.* 251 at 252). Finally, by way of contrast it is interesting to note Schwarze's description of the judgment of the European Court of Justice in *Nakajima All Precision Co. Ltd.* (Case C–69/89) [1991] E.C.R. I–2069 as having integrated the legal argument of estoppel into already existing legal concepts and notices at Community level, "in particular those of legal certainty and the protection of legitimate expectations." (See Schwarze, "Sources of European Administrative Law" Chap. 9 of Martin (ed.), *The Construction of Europe – Essays in Honour of Emile Noël*, 183 at 192).

legitimate expectation to a shadow of what it could be and goes against the increasing tendency on the part of the courts to ensure not alone that fair procedures are adhered to, but also that a fair result or outcome is arrived at.[214] Such an approach to legitimate expectation arguably either clears the way for unreasonable and unfair decisions or puts an undesirable degree of pressure on a court confronting such decisions to prevent them by recourse to other doctrines which fetter discretion to an extent similar to that which it would supposedly be objectionable for the legitimate expectation doctrine to fetter it – *e.g., via* judicial review for unreasonableness,[215] or *via* the notion of contracts or agreements being entered into to exercise statutory powers in a particular way, or of promissory estoppels operating.[216]

---

[214] See here Delany, "Significant Themes in Judicial Review of Administrative Action" (1998) 20 *D.U.L.J.* (ns) 73 at 75-77.

[215] See here *e.g., R. v. Inland Revenue Commissioners ex parte Unilever* [1996] S.T.C. 681 and *R. v. Secretary of State for the Home Department ex parte Hargreaves* [1997] 1 W.L.R. 906. Both of these decisions are analysed in Forsyth, "Wednesbury Protection of Substantive Legitimate Expectations" [1997] *P.L.* 375 and Foster, "Legitimate Expectations and Prisoners' Rights: The Right to Get What You Are Given" (1997) 60 *M.L.R.* 727. See now the judgment of the Court of Appeal (delivered by Lord Woolf MR) in *R. v. North East Devon Health Authority, ex parte Coughlan* [2000] 3 All E.R. 850 at 880 *et seq.* where the concept of legitimate expectations is distinguished from that of unreasonableness and the view taken that both legitimate expectations and Wednesbury unreasonableness are categories of abuse of power.

[216] In *Gilheaney v. the Revenue Commissioners* [1998] I.R. 150, a case in which a decision not to promote the applicant was challenged, Costello J. acknowledged that a statutory provision (s. 17 of the Civil Service Regulation Act 1956 which empowered the Minister for Finance to enter into "arrangements" for the purpose of, *inter alia*, fixing the terms of employment and of promotion of civil servants) involved the possibility of a Minister entering into arrangements even with a serving civil servant whose original appointment had been the result of the exercise of a statutory power and was not contractual. However, Costello J. noted the further power conferred on the Minister by the same statutory provision to vary and cancel arrangements made for the promotion of a civil servants, and held that "this [latter] discretionary power cannot be fettered by contract. This means that the only *intra vires* contract which could be entered into was one which allowed the respondents to vary or cancel its terms and I can find no evidence of an intention to enter into such an unusual contract."

In the subsequent case of *O'Leary v. Minister for Finance* [1998] 2 I.L.R.M. 321, however, (which concerned the same statutory provision) it was held by Quirke J. on the facts that a s.17 contract had been created "on the basis of an understanding that generally it is not in the interest of the public service that the statutory powers [*i.e.,* to vary or cancel it] would be exercised". Apparently taking the view that the doctrines of legitimate expectations, estoppel and contract all applied, Quirke J. went on to hold "I am satisfied that Mr. O'Leary has a legitimate expectation that he will receive the benefits of the contract into which he entered with [the Minister] and that the latter is estopped from denying Mr. O'Leary the benefits arising from the contract or 'arrangement' (and the exercise of the statutory power by the first respondent)". Thus a combination of contract, estoppel and legitimate expectation were used to prevent the Minister resiling from an arrangement reached with the applicant. In other words, they were used to fetter a Ministerial discretion. Quirke J. seemed to feel that the doctrines of estoppel and legitimate expectation alone sufficed, holding "I make no finding as to whether or not the first named respondent has in fact exercised his statutory power to cancel or vary the terms of the benefit which was conferred upon Mr. O'Leary. If he has not done so, then contractual rights against [the Minister] may also be vested in Mr. O'Leary but in my judgment it

Not all judgments of the Irish courts have viewed the autochthonous doctrine of legitimate expectation as confined to ensuring protection for procedural rights. The seminal Supreme Court judgment in *Webb v. Ireland*[217] is one in which the opposite approach was adopted. In this case Chief Justice Finlay described the effect of the unqualified assurance give by the director of the National Museum to Webb as being "that the State cannot now go back on the assurance. It must be given effect to in the form of a monetary award of an amount which is reasonable in the light of all the relevant circumstances." However, the authority of this judgment is lessened by the fact that no real consideration was given in *Webb* to the question now at issue: *viz.,* whether the doctrine of legitimate expectation can operate to protect substantive expectations or whether it should be confined to procedural expectations. Furthermore, the judgment of the Chief Justice is arguably even further weakened because of its almost certainly incorrect characterisation of legitimate expectation as an aspect of promissory estoppel.

Webb was expressly followed by Hamilton P. in the High Court case of *Duggan v. An Taoiseach,*[218] where the learned judge held that "if a person establishes that he has a legitimate expectation of receiving a benefit or privilege, the courts will protect his expectation by judicial review as a matter of public law".[219] Again, as in *Webb,* an award of damages was made to the applicants, who, in this case, were civil servants who had been disappointed in their expectation that temporary promotions to a higher grade would be made permanent. Again, however, as in *Webb,* no real consideration was given to the procedural/substantive legitimate expectations issue now being discussed.[220]

In two further High Court decisions, *Kelly v. Kenny*[221] and *O'Leary v. Minister for Finance,*[222] the doctrine of legitimate expectation was also invoked as a ground for holding the applicant to be entitled to a substantive benefit. In both cases, however, alternative grounds for finding the existence of this entitlement were relied upon.[223] Once again, no thought seems to have been de-

---

matters little because I see no reason why contractual rights should not co-exist with rights arising out of the doctrine of 'legitimate expectation' or the equitable concept of promissory estoppel." [1998] 2 I.L.R.M. 321 at 343.

[217] [1988] I.R. 353.

[218] [1989] I.L.R.M. 710.

[219] *ibid.* at 727.

[220] The above-quoted statement by Hamilton P. in *Duggan* was adopted by Blayney J. in the subsequent case of *Wiley v. Revenue Commissioners* [1989] I.R. 350 at 355 but again with no real consideration being given to the procedural / substantive legitimate expectation issue. The Supreme Court judgments in the same case were much less sympathetic to the idea of substantive legitimate expectations. [1994] 2 I.R. 160.

[221] [1988] I.R. 457. Judgment of Barron J.

[222] [1998] 2 I.L.R.M. 321. Judgment of Quirke J.

[223] *Viz.,* in *Kelly,* the ground of promissory estoppel, and in *O'Leary,* both the ground of promissory estoppel and that of contract.

voted to the question of whether the doctrine of legitimate expectations could actually give rise to substantive as opposed to merely procedural rights.

One case in which the procedural/substantive issue was clearly at the forefront of the deciding judge's mind, however, was the High Court case of *Abrahamson v. Law Society* where, after considering a number of authorities such as *Tara Prospecting*, McCracken J. asserted that:

> "where the legitimate expectation is that a benefit will be secured, the courts will endeavour to obtain that benefit or to compensate the applicant, whether by way of an order of mandamus or by an award of damages, provided that to do so is lawful."[224]

Abrahamson is probably the strongest authority that exists in favour of the existence of a substantive aspect to the doctrine of legitimate expectation in autochthonous Irish law.[225] Overall, however, it must be said that there is, relatively speaking, a regrettable dearth of reasoned analysis by Irish courts on this issue. At least equally regrettable, in this writer's view, however, is the fact in so many Irish cases a highly restrictive approach has been exhibited towards the notion of substantive legitimate expectation.

The issue is one which has attracted considerable judicial attention in other common law jurisdictions. In these jurisdictions, as might be expected, the existence of procedural legitimate expectation has frequently been acknowledged.[226] In some cases this has been accompanied by a refusal to acknowledge the existence of substantive legitimate expectation.[227] In other cases, however, a very different view has been taken. Thus some decisions seem to be situated at least some distance along the road of recognising substantive legiti-

---

[224] [1996] 2 I.L.R.M. 481 at 498.

[225] It is worth mentioning at least in passing, however, that where Irish courts have dealt with decision-making which does not involve the exercise of a statutory discretion, a similar less inhibited approach has been adopted to the idea of what in effect has seemed to amount to the vindication of substantive legitimate expectation. See *Latchford v. Minister for Industry and Commerce* [1950] I.R. 33 and *Staunton v. St. Lawrence's Hospital* unreported, High Court, February 21, 1986. Both of these cases are discussed in Hogan and Morgan, *op. cit.*, above, n.145 at pp. 890 to 893.

[226] See *e.g., Attorney-General of Hong Kong v. Ng Yuen Shiu* [1983] 2 A.C. 629, and *Re Findlay* [1985] A.C. 318.

[227] See *e.g.,* the English case of *R. v. Secretary of State for Transport, ex p. Richmond upon Thames LBC* [1994] 1 W.L.R. 74, the Canadian cases of *Re Canada Assistance Plan* (1991) 83 D.L.R. (4th) 297, *Furey v. Conception Bay Centre Roman Catholic School Board* (1993) 104 D.L.R. (4th) 455, the New Zealand cases of *Bradley v. Attorney General* [1988] 2 N.Z.L.R. 454, *Khalon v. Attorney General* [1996] 1 N.Z.L.R. 458 and the Australian case of *Minister for Immigration and Ethnic Affairs v. Teoh* (1995) 183 C.L.R. 273 although *cf.* the earlier Australian case of *Attorney-General for New South Wales v. Quin* (1990) 170 C.L.R. 1. Note also the dicta of Ralph Gibson L.J. in *R. v. Secretary of State for the Home Department, ex p. Mowla* [1992] 1 W.L.R. 70 at 88-89.

mate expectation.[228] Others are unambiguously in favour of the concept of legitimate expectations giving rise to substantive rights.[229] The most recent decisions in other jurisdictions paint a picture which differs markedly from the approach of the courts in the Irish Republic. Hence, notwithstanding the conservative approach previously adopted by the House of Lords in cases such as *In re Findlay,*[230] *Council of Civil Service Unions v. Minister for Civil Service* (the *"GCHQ"* case)[231] and *Hughes v. Department of Health and Social Security* [232] the English Court of Appeal has now moved unambiguously in the direction of accepting the existence of legitimate expectations in its carefully reasoned judgment in *R. v. North East Devon Health Authority, ex p. Coughlan.*[233] Given the influence which previous decisions of the English Courts have had on the development of the doctrine of legitimate expectation in the common law world, the decision in *Coughlan* is likely to prove something of a turning point. Certainly in his recent Northern Ireland High Court decision in *Re Treacy and Another,*[234] Kerr J. (although finding no legitimate expectation had arisen on the facts of this case) paid careful regard to *Coughlan* and expressly refused to accept that the courts in Northern Ireland have set their face against the concept of substantive legitimate expectation.

---

[228] *e.g., R. v. Secretary of State for the Home Department, ex p. Khan* [1984] 1 W.L.R. 1337 (legitimate expectation held to have been created that only criteria laid out in a Home Office circular would be regarded as relevant when an application to adopt a child from overseas was being processed). This judgment can be contrasted with the Irish High Court judgment O'Hanlon J. in *Fakih v. Minister for Justice* [1993] 2 I.R. 406 (as to which see above). See also *R. v. Secretary of State, ex p. Ruddock* [1987] 1 W.L.R. 1482 (where Taylor J., in a case concerning telephone tapping, held that the legitimate expectation doctrine imposed a duty to act fairly. This duty was not, as the respondent had argued, confined to the mere right to be heard – a right which was clearly not going to apply anyway in a case which involved a decision to intercept telephone messages – even if most of the cases involved this latter right).

[229] See *R. v. Ministry for Agriculture, Fisheries and Foods, ex p. Hamble (Offshore) Fisheries Ltd.* [1995] 2 All E.R. 714, *R. v. Secretary of State for the Home Department, ex p. Ruddock* [1987] 1 W.L.R. 1482. See the New Zealand case of *Bradley v. Attorney General* (1988) 7 N.Z.A.R. 193 (where Smellie J. held that the plaintiff had a legitimate expectation "that in due course he would be promoted'). And note the earlier (albeit dissenting) judgment of Lord Denning in *Breen v. Amalgamated Engineering Union* [1971] 2 Q.B. 175.

[230] [1985] 1 A.C. 318 (legitimate expectation of a prisoner seeking parole envisaged at most as being of a particular type of hearing, *viz.,* an individual hearing). See judgment of Lord Scarman in [1985] A.C. 318 at 388.

[231] [1985] A.C. 374. Trade union held to have had legitimate expectation to be consulted in advance of an instruction which prohibited workers at GCHQ from belonging to a trade union.

[232] [1985] A.C. 776, where what was at issue were retirement ages and the House of Lords seemed unsympathetic to the idea of taking legitimate expectation beyond issues of procedural fairness. See in particular here the judgment of Lord Diplock at [1985] 2 W.L.R. 866 at 875.

[233] [2000] 3 All E.R. 850 and see also the note thereon by Elliot in (2000) 5 *J.R.* 27.

[234] [2000] N.I. 330. *cf.,* the judgment of Evans. J. A. in the Canadian Federal Court of Appeal in *Apotex Inc. v. Canada* (2000) 188 D.L.R. (4th) 145 at 183, in which, in a very brief paragraph, he appears to reject the approach of the English Court of Appeal and to take the view that the doctrine does not have a substantive aspect.

It is to be hoped that the Irish courts will arrive at a position on legitimate expectation similar to that adopted by the Court of Appeal in *Coughlan*. It has been observed that the restrictive definition of the doctrine adopted in some cases (*viz.*, confining the autochthonous doctrine to questions of procedural impropriety) is sometimes achieved by "the definitional device of limiting the description of the actual expectation"[235] Yet it is clear that the interest of the individual in a situation where he or she has been led to believe that a discretion will be exercised in a particular way by a public authority will normally relate to the substantive question of how that discretion is exercised, and not to the question of whether he or she will be consulted if the authority decides to go back on its word. Assuming that securing fairness in decision-making is the ultimate objective of this doctrine, why should it be regarded as fair to frustrate a legitimate expectation that something will be done but unfair to frustrate a legitimate expectation that a hearing will be granted before the final decision is made?

In this regard, Craig has made the point that the cogency of the "no fettering" argument is overstated. Policies must be allowed to develop, and in this sense:

> "it is correct to say that they cannot be fettered. One cannot therefore ossify administrative policy, which may alter for a variety of reasons, including experience gleaned from the operation of the previous policy, change of political outlook, or new technological developments. Nevertheless the 'no fettering' theme must be kept within bounds. Where a representation has been made to a specific person, or where conditions for application of policy in a certain area have been published and relied on, then the public body should be under a duty to follow the representation or the published criteria. This does not prevent it from altering its general policy for the future, but it should not be allowed to depart from the representation or pre-existing policy in relation to an individual who *has* relied, unless the overriding public interest requires it, and then only after a hearing."[236]

The same writer has observed that:

> "in the case of changes of policy the court would not be preventing the agency from adopting a new substantive policy ... nor would it be dictating the content of that policy. It would be deciding that if legitimate ex-

---

[235] France, *loc. cit.*, above, n.149 at p. 137.

[236] Craig, "Legitimate Expectations: a Conceptual Analysis" (1992) 108 *L.Q.R.* 79. It is on the basis of this logic that Craig welcomed decisions such as that of the Court of Appeal in *R. v. Secretary of State for the Home Department, ex p. Khan* [1984] 1 W.L.R. 1337 where a broad approach was adopted to the meaning of legitimate expectation.

pectations really could, both practically and normatively, be held to have been generated by the earlier policy, then that policy should continue to apply to the relevant individuals in circumstances where the public interest was not thereby jeopardised."[237]

These are weighty arguments, which await an appropriate degree of consideration in a judgment of an Irish court. However, it is submitted that it would be an undesirable emasculation of the autochthonous doctrine were it (unlike its counterpart in Community law) to be confined to mere surface formalities, leaving decision-makers in the public law field free to disregard solemn undertakings given by them in the most unfair manner. The objective of securing fairness in decision-making – the origin of the autochthonous doctrine – arguably demands more than a doctrine conferring only procedural benefits – a doctrine which has been rightly derided by one commentator as merely giving the individual or business the right to get what they are given.[238] As Delany has argued, "clearly for the doctrine to be of real value it must extend beyond an expectation of being heard; procedural guarantees will not always adequately depend and vindicate substantive legitimate expectations".[239] Cases like *Abrahamson, Treacy* and *Coughlan* may be read as indicating that in the courts of both Ireland and the United Kingdom, the tide is turning or has already turned in favour of substantive legitimate expectations. It is submitted that this is an approach favoured not only by authority, but by the interests of justice, and an approach for which precedent exists in that field of Irish law which is comprised of European Community law.

---

[237] *Loc. cit.*, above, n.237 at p. 95. A further fear, which sometimes receives judicial expression, is that legitimate expectations may enable bodies to extend their powers by making representations which could then be held to bind them. One solution to this is to adopt the position that a legitimate expectation would not be created if the relevant representation was outside the powers of the relevant public body or the relevant officer of that body. (For a discussion of this point, see Craig, "Legitimate Expectations: A Conceptual Analysis" (1992) 108 *L.Q.R.* 29 at 87–89).

[238] Foster, "Legitimate Expectations and Prisoners' Rights: the Right to Get What You Are Given." (1997) 60 *M.L.R.* 727. Hence the comment of Deane J. in *Australian Broadcasting v. Bond* (1990) 170 C.L.R. 321 at 366 to the effect that "it would be both surprising and illogical if fair procedures involved mere surface formalities and left the decision-maker free to make a completely arbitrary decision" and the observation by Cooke J. in *Daganayasi v. Minister for Immigration* [1980] 2 N.Z.L.R. 130 that "fairness need not be confined to procedural matters". In relation to both of these comments see further Delany, "Significant Themes in Judicial Review of Administrative Action" (1998) 20 *D.U.L.J. (ns)* 73 at 77.

[239] Delany, "The Doctrine of Legitimate Expectation in Irish Law" (1990) 12 *D.U.L.J.* (n.s.) 1 at 22.

4. CONCLUSION

Fourteen years ago, the point was made that:

> "to create a new property in the public interest state is not to attack the discretions that govern the enjoyment of governmentally-created wealth. It is however, to demand that those discretions should be used fairly and reasonably and not exceeded or abused.
>
> In Britain the new property has arrived, albeit in struggling fashion. The courts have taken some steps on the procedural front to protect those affected by largesse but they have not gone far enough".[240]

If one substitutes "Ireland" for "Britain," the validity of the above statement seems to hold good for the present day state of law in this jurisdiction, at least insofar as the autochthonous doctrine of legitimate expectations is concerned. So too does the authors' call on the courts to construe statutes in a manner that respects public and private interests, to keep discretionary powers within their proper bounds and to eschew restrictions on the notion of legitimate expectations that owe more to formalism or legalism than to life's realities. Arguably, the most significant contribution which could be made in this respect is the acknowledgement and proper development by the Irish courts of the substantive side of the autochthonous doctrine of legitimate expectations. In this regard as in others, much useful guidance is to be found in the wealth of jurisprudence which has now accumulated in respect of the principle of legitimate expectations in Community law, some of the broad outlines of which at least have been distilled in this essay.[241]

---

[240] Baldwin and Horne, "Expectations in a Joyless Landscape" (1986) 49 *M.L.R.* 685 at 710.

[241] It is instructive in this regard to note the importance attributed by Lord Woolf in his judgment in *R. v. North East Devon Health Authority, ex p. Coughlan* [2000] 3 All E.R. 850 to the position adopted by the European Court of Justice in relation to the concept of substantive legitimate expectations (note in particular paras 77 and 79 of the judgment). This is proof, were any needed, of the potential for useful cross-fertilisation between the national and Community law ideas in this area of the law.

CHILDREN THESE DAYS – SECTION 117 OF THE SUCCESSION ACT 1965 AND THE MORAL OBLIGATIONS OF PARENTHOOD

OONAGH BREEN

1. Introduction

*"… How sharper than a serpent's tooth it is
To have a thankless child!"*[1]

King Lear said it all in relation to the trials and tribulations of parenthood. While the children of the twenty first century undoubtedly differ immensely from those who inhabited Shakespeare's world, in terms not only of life expectation but also in their expectations of life in general, not that much has changed in the 400-year-period since the Bard of Stratford turned his attentions to the domestic problems caused by a parental decision to disinherit a child or to favour one sibling over another.

Perhaps the biggest change in this jurisdiction has been the restriction upon the ease with which a parent can cut a child out of his or her will. Statutory intervention in the form of section 117 of the Succession Act 1965 has, if anything, added a further weight to a parent's conscience – seemingly, even thankless children have a right, in certain circumstances to share in their parents' estate. It would appear that the moral obligations of parenthood are expansive and enduring, as in true Peter Pan fashion, section 117 "children" never grow up.

Twenty years ago, a writer in the *Irish Jurist* justified his in-depth analysis of the section 117 case law on the basis that "from a lawyer's point of view the discretionary provisions relating to children are arguably more arresting as they bring with them the prospect of some intriguing questions of interpretation and adjudication".[2] The passage of time has done little to dampen this prospect. If anything, Ireland's evolution as a prosperous nation with a flourishing economy has been reflected in society's changing values and mores. The last decade alone has borne witness to this with the enactment of legislation dealing with

---

[1] *King Lear*, Act I, Scene IV, Lines 274–275.

[2] Cooney, "Succession and Judicial Discretion in Ireland: The Section 117 Cases" (1980) 15 *Ir. Jur. (n.s.)* 62.

realities of family life – ranging from illegitimacy to judicial separation and divorce.[3] The concepts of "moral duty" and "proper provision" are not immutable[4] and in light of recent judicial authorities it may be that the time is ripe to review our notion of a testator's right to do what he will with his own.

This article proposes to consider the scope of a testator's moral duty to provide for his children under section 117 of the Succession Act 1965; the factors the court takes into consideration in the exercise of its statutory discretion in this regard and the inheritance consequences of a child's bad behaviour towards his/her parent in light of recent pronouncements by the Supreme Court.

2. THE MORAL OBLIGATIONS OF PARENTHOOD – A COMPARATIVE ANALYSIS

Legal systems, in different jurisdictions and at various epochs have grappled with the question of whether a child has an inherent right to inheritance upon the death of a parent. Provision on death for one's children may be viewed by most as a moral duty binding on the conscience of a just parent. Not every jurisdiction, however, views this as a legal duty which should be enforced by means of either legislation or court intervention, especially where the testator has clearly expressed his intention to exclude a child from his bounty.[5] In some legal systems, however, the moral duty is given such a priority that legislation makes it incumbent upon parents to make provision for their children out of their estate.[6] Between these polar extremes lies the method adopted by the Irish Succession Act 1965 whereby a disappointed child, while not having an absolute right to a share in the estate, may make an application to the court where he feels that the testator, in breach of his moral duty, has not made proper provision for him.[7] The court in its discretion may order that such provision be made for the child out of the estate as it thinks just, on condition that such provision does not interfere with a surviving spouse's legal share.[8]

---

[3] See, for instance, the Status of Children Act, 1987; the Family Law (Judicial Separation) Act 1989; the Family Law Act 1995 and the Family Law (Divorce) Act 1996.

[4] As Oliver Wendell Holmes Jr. once said, "A word is not a crystal, transparent and unchanging, it is like the skin of a living thought and may vary greatly in color and content according to the circumstances and time in which it is used."

[5] The clearest example of this approach undoubtedly is found in the United States. See below.

[6] Notably countries where the Napoleonic Code is followed. See below.

[7] References throughout this article to the testator or the use of male pronouns in general have been simply adopted to improve readability. Where reference is made to the masculine gender readers may assume a reference to the feminine gender, or to both.

[8] The full text of section 117 provides as follows:

"(1) Where, on application by or on behalf of a child of a testator, the court is of opinion that the testator has failed in his moral duty to make proper provision for the child in accordance with his means, whether by his will or otherwise, the court may order that such provision shall be made for the child out of the estate as the court thinks just.

(a) The Early Origins of Family Provision

The Romans introduced the concept of freedom of testation with the objective of enabling a testator better to provide for his offspring than the laws governing intestate succession at the time allowed.[9] From the twelfth century onwards in England (and by force in Ireland contrary to the dictates of Brehon law) the feudal law system brought with it the concept of primogeniture. Under this system the land automatically went to the eldest son, not because as a child he had a right to it, but rather because he was viewed as more competent to fulfil the incidents and services of tenure than were his younger siblings. It has been noted[10] that a predominant objective of the Statute of Wills in 1540[11] was to empower a testator to disinherit an incompetent eldest son so that the land could instead be devised to someone better able to conserve the family wealth and prestige.

(b) The Modern Approaches: From Legitim to Testamentary Autonomy

In more modern times, legislatures have tackled the issue of offspring's inheritance in diverse ways – reflecting to a certain extent public opinion on testamentary freedom. Thus in continental law systems such as France, Spain,[12] and Sweden,[13] a system known as the *legitim* operates whereby it is virtually impossible to disinherit one's children.[14] Under what is essentially a system of

---

(2) The court shall consider the application from the point of view of a prudent and just parent, taking into account the position of each of the children of the testator and any other circumstances which the court may consider of assistance in arriving at a decision that will be as fair as possible to the child to whom the application relates and to the other children. (3) An order under this section shall not affect the legal right of a surviving spouse or, if the surviving spouse is the mother or father of the child, any devise or bequest to the spouse or any share to which the spouse is entitled on intestacy."

[9] As Maine has commented in *Ancient Law* (new ed., London, 1930) at p. 215, "It will be found that Wills were never looked upon in the Roman community as a contrivance for parting Property and Family ... but rather as a means of making a better provision for the members of a household than could be secured through the rules of Intestate succession."

[10] Morton, "The Theory of Inheritance" (1894 -95) 8 *Harvard Law Review* 161 at 164; High, "The Tension between Testamentary Freedom and Parental Support Obligations: A Comparison between the United States and Great Britain" (1984) 17 *Cornell International L.J.* 321 at p. 323.

[11] 32 Hen VIII c 16.

[12] In Spain a maximum of two thirds of the estate can be made subject to the legitim principle. In contrast to the other countries where forced heirship applies, Spanish testators may utilise the concept of "mejora" in respect of half the reserved estate to favour one or more of the forced heirs. See Le Van, "Alternatives to Forced Heirship" (1977) 52 *Tul. L.R.* 29 at p. 34.

[13] In Sweden, any will which favours third parties over the testator's children to the extent that the latter would be left with less than half of what they would have received if an intestacy had occurred, will be considered invalid.

[14] It has been noted that in France there is what is described as "a theoretical possibility of disinheritance where the beneficiary has committed certain scandalous conduct" but in reality this would only be relied on in cases of murder or the unlawful killing of the testator. See Hudson and Barbalich, "Succession Law in France and Italy" (1991) 135 *Solicitors Journal* 1032.

forced heirship, children are guaranteed a fixed proportion of their parent's estate, regardless of its size or any past provision made for them during the testator's lifetime. Thus, in France the civil code provides that the testator's freedom to deal with his estate is limited by the number of children he has. The free portion, known as the *"quotité disponible"*, which the testator may dispose of as he pleases, is half if there is one child, one-third if there are two and only one-quarter if there are three children or more. The remainder must be divided equally among the children alive at the testator's death, or where there is a deceased child *per stirpes* amongst his or her issue. Closer to home, the Scottish Succession Act 1964 provides for a legitim (quaintly referred to there as "the bairn's part") to apply in relation to personal property whereby upon the death of a parent, a child is entitled to a third share in the net movable estate if there is a surviving spouse or a half share if no spouse remains.[15]

In complete contrast to this, the law of most states[16] of the United States of America provide that if a testator wishes to disinherit his children, he is entirely within his legal rights to do so. Such a decision is unassailable by disappointed beneficiaries in the absence of a claim relating to undue influence or lack of testamentary capacity on the part of the testator at the time of the will's execution. The respect for freedom of testation in America is such that a parent may deliberately disinherit his children. The extent of this freedom has been subject to much criticism by American commentators who point out that in today's society of second families, it is quite easy for a child to be deprived of his inheritance when upon remarriage, his natural parent dies and the family wealth therefore becomes that of the new spouse who may, without fear of challenge, cut the first family out of the will.[17] Indeed, the only statutory safeguard[18] which children in the United States have against disinheritance rests in the pretermission statutes found in nearly all States. The purpose of these stat-

---

[15]215 *Dáil Debates* Col. 2037 (Second Stage); Dainow, "Restricted Testation in New Zealand, Australia and Canada" (1938) 36 *Michigan Law Review* 1107 at 1116.

[16]The State of Louisiana is the exception to this rule. Harking back to its French roots, it operates a forced share provision for children. While originally this applied to all children, the scope of this right has been restricted following a constitutional amendment such that since 1 July 1990 forced heirship protection applies only to (a) children under the age of 23 and (b) mentally infirm or disabled children (La. Civ. Code art.1493). See Waggoner et al, *Family Property Law* (New York, Foundation Press, 1991) at p. 511; Dukeminier & Johanson, *Wills, Trusts and Estates* (6th ed., New York, Aspen Law & Business, 2000) at p. 537.

[17]Batts, "I didn't ask to be Born: The American Law of Disinheritance and a Proposal for Change to a System of Protected Inheritance" (1990) 41 *Hastings Law Journal* 1197; Brashier, "Disinheritance and the Modern Family" (1994) 45 *Case W. Res.* 84 at p. 163.

[18]The most commonly availed of non-statutory challenges to wills in the United States arise in the form of challenges to the mental competency of the testator at the time the will was executed and claims to have the will set aside on grounds of undue influence – see *Pendarvis v. Gibb*, 328 Ill. 282, 159 N.E. 353 (1927) and *Re Honigman's Will*, 8 N.Y. 2d 244, 168 N.E. 2d 676 (1960) on the issue of mental competency and *Re Ausseresses' Estate*, 178 Cal. App. 487 (1960) on the issue of undue influence.

utes is to protect children from unintentional disinheritance. This may occur, for instance, where a child is born or adopted after the will has been executed and the testator neglects to amend the will in light of the new arrival.[19]

(c) The Irish Approach

> "In a country such as ours which recognises the very special position of the family "as a moral institution possessing inalienable and imprescriptible rights, antecedent and superior to all positive law", a so-called freedom of testation is a paradox which cannot be defended on any ground."

So stated Brian Lenihan, the then Minister for Justice, introducing the provisions of section 117 during the second reading of the Succession Bill to the Dáil in 1965.[20] Rejecting the legitim system as being unduly rigid, the House opted for a system based on judicial discretion, very similar in nature to that employed in New Zealand and Canada. Indeed, the Minister made express reference to New Zealand's Testator's Family Maintenance Act 1900 noting that its interpretation had involved the courts in considering the scope of the moral duty owed by the deceased to the applicant. According to the Minister, the moral duty of a testator to make proper provision for his children by will or otherwise became a legal duty under section 117, thereby enabling the court to make a legal decision as to its fulfilment.[21]

Thus, two novel concepts presented themselves to the Irish courts following the enactment of section 117, namely, the existence of a "moral duty" on parents to make "proper provision" for their children, which would be legally enforceable.

3. THE CONCEPT OF MORAL DUTY

> "It may be as difficult, as it is unwise, to attempt to state as a general principle where the line between duty and no duty is to be drawn. Each case in a sense calls for the making of a value judgment."[22]

---

[19] §2-302 Uniform Probate Code 1990 (as amended in 1993) sets out the rules regarding the share of the estate that an omitted after-born or after-adopted child should take. The basic share equals the amount which the child would have been entitled to had the parent died intestate where there was no child living at the date of the will's execution. Where living children were provided for under the will, the code provides that "(iii) to the extent feasible, the interest granted an omitted after-born or after-adopted child under this section must be of the same character, whether equitable or legal, present or future as that devised to the testator's then-living children under the will."

[20] 215 *Dáil Debates* Col. 2017–2018.

[21] 217 *Dáil Debates* Col. 133 (Committee Stage).

[22] McMullin J. in *Re Leonard* [1985] 2 N.Z.L.R. 88 at 93 (C.A.).

Three years after the coming into force of the Succession Act, the High Court handed down its decision in *F.M. v. T.A.M.*, the *locus classicus* on section 117, in which Kenny J. attempted to elaborate on the moral duty imposed upon a parent to provide for his children and the factors which the court should take into consideration in determining whether that duty had been breached.[23] According to the High Court, the test is an objective test – the fact that the testator believes that he has fulfilled his duties is not conclusive. Rather the court will look at five circumstances in particular in making its decision on the matter, namely,

(a) the amount left to the surviving spouse or the value of the legal right if the survivor elects to take it;

(b) the number of the testator's children, their ages and their positions in life at the date of the testator's death;

(c) the means of the testator;

(d) the age of the child whose case is being considered and his or her financial position and prospects in life; and finally

(e) whether the testator had already made proper provision for the child during his lifetime.

Subsequent case law has elaborated on the application of these principles. Thus, the Supreme Court in *In the Estate of IAC Deceased; C. and F. v. W.C. and T.C.*,[24] while affirming the general principles laid down in *F.M. v. T.A.M.*,[25] qualified them by placing the burden of proof on the child to show a positive failure in this moral duty, Finlay C.J. noting that the onus of proof in such a case is relatively high. Comparative support for such an approach can be found in the New Zealand decision of *Re Rough* where it was held that the fact that a will may be "less than completely fair from a moral point of view" is not sufficient to warrant court intervention in the testator's disposition of his estate.[26] Neither is it enough to show that in comparison with other siblings the award to the applicant might be viewed as "ungenerous" or that the court might consider the provision to be not as great as it might have been. Only where a positive breach of moral duty is established will the court move on to consider what variation should be made to the terms of the testator's will so as to make proper provision.

---

[23] *F.M. v. T.A.M.* (1972) 106 I.L.T.R. 82.
[24] *In the Estate of IAC Deceased; C. and F. v. W.C. and T.C.* [1989] I.L.R.M. 815 at 819.
[25] (1872) 106 I.L.T.R. 82.
[26] [1976] 1 N.Z.L.R. 604 at 607 (S.C., Palmerston North) where the court dismissed an application under the Family Protection Act 1955 by the testator's children from his first marriage, describing them as being "in reasonable financial circumstances" at the testator's death and leaving the "modest estate" to his second wife instead.

So what is the extent of this moral duty with which parents are burdened to do right by their children? It should be noted at the outset that the relationship of parent/child *per se* does not of itself create a moral duty to leave anything by will to the child.[27] The converse, however, equally holds true so that the fact that a parent is estranged from his children during his lifetime does not prevent them from making an application for provision out of his estate.[28] How then should the scope of moral duty be determined? Certainly the *F.M.* factors go some way towards creating a framework for examining an application. The persona cast upon a parent on his deathbed by the court invariably takes the form of a "judicious father of a family seeking to discharge his … parental duty",[29] or in the words of Edwards J. in *Allardice v. Allardice*, the duty which a "just but not a loving … father owes towards his … children."[30] Indeed, the factors borne in mind by other jurisdictions bear a very strong resemblance to those employed by the Irish courts in examining the question of breach of moral duty under section 117.[31]

One may, however, rightly fear that the construction of such a judicious testator who "at the point of death accommodates his preferences to his moral duty" will result in a "statutory post-mortem, metamorphosis of the testator into a paragon of wisdom and justice who is seldom encountered on the Clapham omnibus."[32] This may be particularly pointed in cases where there is mutual bad feeling between the parent and child or where a parent feels let down by the conduct or behaviour of a child. In such cases, seeing matters through the eyes of the testator, it may be very difficult, if not virtually impossible to behave as perhaps only Solomon would. Given human nature, this raises the question as to how absolute a standard should a parent's moral duty to a child be? This is a question to which we will return in light of the recent decisions of the Irish Supreme Court.

---

[27] *ibid.* at 87; *Bray v. Bray* unreported, High Court, Hamilton J., February 25, 1977.

[28] *Re Steinberg Simmonds v. Rehn et al.* (1969) 3 D.L.R. (3d) 565 (Manitoba Q.B.) where at 569 Matas J., in rejecting counsel's claim that the lack of a relationship between the applicants and their father prevented them claiming against his estate, stated "this argument is based on the false premise that a father who has deserted his children while they are infants may expect to receive fulsome affection and regard from them in their adult years… . I am satisfied that the character and conduct of the applicants are not such as to disentitle them to the benefit of an order under the Act".

[29] Duff J. in *Walker v. McDermott* [1931] 1 D.L.R. 662 at 663 (S.C.).

[30] (1910) 29 N.Z.L.R. 959 at 973.

[31] Compare, for instance, *Re Leonard* [1985] 2 N.Z.L.R. 88 at 92, where Richardson J. commented that in considering an application by a disappointed child beneficiary, "the size of the estate and the existence of any other moral claims on the testator's bounty are highly relevant and due regard must be had to ethical and moral considerations, and to contemporary social attitudes as to what should be expected of a wise and just testator in particular circumstances." The "prudent and just parent" mentioned in s. 117(2) is placed in a similar position as a result of the guidelines laid down by Kenny J. in *F.M.*

[32] Scollin J. in *Re Bartel et al. and Holmes* (1982) 16 Man. R. (2d) 29 at 32.

4. PROPER PROVISION

The concept of moral duty cannot be divorced from the notion of proper provision, for it is where a parent fails to make such provision either by will or otherwise that the court will find a breach of moral duty, enabling it to vary the terms of the testator's will in favour of the applicant. The exact meaning of "proper provision", however, has furrowed many a judicial brow both inside and out of this jurisdiction. What constitutes "proper provision", how it differs from "adequate provision", and whether it is needs based are just some of the pertinent issues which have arisen in this respect.

There is agreement among judges to the extent that proper provision goes beyond adequate provision. In *Walker v. McDermott*[33] the majority of the Canadian Supreme Court defined "proper maintenance and support" in the context of the Testator's Family Maintenance Act 1924.[34] Duff J. (Newcombe J. concurring) stated that:

> "It cannot be limited to the bare necessities of existence... If the Court comes to the decision that adequate provision has not been made, then the Court must consider what provision would be not only adequate, but would be just and equitable also; and in exercising its judgment upon this, the pecuniary magnitude of the estate and the situation of others having claims upon the testator, must be taken into account."[35]

Similarly, the New Zealand courts are of the opinion that "need" is not the appropriate yardstick. As the Privy Council pointed out in *Bosch v. Perpetual Trustee Co. Ltd.*:

> "The amount to be provided is not to be measured solely by the need of maintenance. It would be so if the Court were concerned solely with adequacy. But the Court has to consider what is proper maintenance..."[36]

It follows that being the least well off sibling in the family is not an automatic guarantee that the court will provide that applicant with the largest share of the estate.[37] While comparisons between the case law of our Commonwealth neigh-

---

[33][1931] 1 D.L.R. 662 (S.C.).

[34]The Act empowers the Court to make "adequate provision for the proper maintenance and support" of, *inter alia,* the testator's children "as the Court thinks adequate, just and equitable in the circumstances".

[35]*op. cit.* at p. 663.

[36][1938] A.C. 463 at 478 (P.C.) followed in *Re Goodwin* [1958] N.Z.L.R. 320 at 323 (C.A.).

[37]*Patterson v. Lauritsen et al.* (1984) 58 B.C.L.R. 182 (B.C.S.C.) where having reviewed the financial status of four children, Spencer J. found that the applicant was the worst off of the four. However the learned judge stated that this did not call for the applicant to receive any

bours and ourselves in relation to the principle of moral duty hold good and
were in fact envisaged by the Minister for Justice at the time of enactment of
the succession legislation,[38] a little more caution is called for when comparing
jurisprudence on the definition of "proper provision". Kenny J. referred to the
literal differences in his judgment in *F.M.* in the following way:

> "The concept underlying the legislation in New Zealand, New South Wales
> and England is that a testator owes a duty to make reasonable provision
> for the maintenance of his widow and of his dependants. Our Succession
> Act, however, is based on the idea that a testator owes a duty to leave part
> of his estate to his widow (the legal right share) and to make proper pro-
> vision for his children in accordance with his means. It is not based on a
> duty to provide maintenance for his widow nor is it limited in its applica-
> tion to children who are dependent on him. The cases decided on the
> New Zealand, New South Wales and English Acts of Parliament are,
> therefore, of little assistance."[39]

In spite of Kenny J.'s efforts to distance himself from cases such as *Allardice*[40]
and *Bosch*[41] on the grounds of the different basis underlying the Acts, in terms
of sentiment and practice, there seems to be very little difference between the
Irish concept of "proper provision" and that of "adequate provision to make
proper maintenance and support". Under both regimes, the means of the testator are considered alongside any other moral obligations which may have bound
him at the date of his death in addition to the status of the children, their standard of living and the provision made for them in the past by the testator. It is
submitted that sufficient similarities abound to justify a meaningful comparative analysis on the question as to the extent to which the bad behaviour of a
child towards a parent can whittle away the moral duty of the latter under section 117.

---

greater share that the others commenting that the former's life was "shaped by the way in which
he has chosen to live" and ruled that the children should share in the estate equally.

[38] 217 *Dáil Debates* Col. 133, stating, "[t]he reason why we use the phrase 'moral duty' is because
there is already a core of precedents along this line in New Zealand ... Moral duty is read into
the New Zealand legislation by the courts there."

[39] *F.M. v. T.A.M.* (1972) 106 I.L.T.R. 82 at 86. *c.f. Re the goods of J.H. dec'd* [1984] I.R. 599
where Barron J. cited the cases of *Allen v. Manchester* [1922] N.Z.L.R. 218 and *Bosch v. Perpetual Trustee Company Limited* [1938] A.C. 463 with approval.

[40] [1911] A.C. 730, affirming 29 N.Z.L.R. 959 (P.C.).

[41] [1938] A.C. 463.

5. What Constitutes Disqualifying Conduct on The Part of Section 117 Applicants?

"I have purposely excluded my son, John, from any share of my Estate...for the following reason: ... my older son John [has] acted in various ways to disrupt my attempts to establish harmony in the family. Since John was 12 years old he has been a difficult child for me to raise. He has turned against me and totally ignored me for the last 15 years of his life. He has been abusive to the point of profanity; he has been extremely inconsiderate and has made no effort to reconcile his differences with me. He has never been open to discussion with a view to establishing ourselves in unity. [My son Edward is respectable and I commend him for his warm attitude towards me, his honesty and his co-operation with me.]"[42]

How many parents have shared the evident frustration expressed by Alex Tartaryn's will against his son, John? An unappreciative child is one thing but an openly hostile child is quite another matter. One must feel some sympathy for parents, who might well feel that their only way of having the last word on their children's behaviour or the way in which they have chosen to live their lives is through the terms of their will and the provisions which they make (or don't make, as the case may be) for their offspring. Does the same moral duty, incumbent on parents under section 117, apply where bad relations exist between the parties? Can a child's conduct act as a factor disqualifying it from the benefits of its parent's estate? How should the court approach a case where the parent is as much to blame for the hostility as is the child?

(a)   Lack of Love and Affection

Lack of love and affection is not a sufficient justification for a testator to exclude his children from his bounty. In *J.H. v. AIB*,[43] McWilliam J. held that the deceased had a moral duty to provide for his children, both of whom suffered from depressive illness, in spite of the lack of contact between the parties following his estrangement from his wife. In finding that the court in that instance had no obligation to attribute blame for the state of affairs existing between the parties at the date of the testator's death, the learned judge commented that the moral duty imposed on the deceased by section 117 endured "however neglected, thwarted or aggrieved [the testator] may have felt."[44] The Supreme Court of British Columbia has taken a similar view in perhaps more extreme

---

[42] *Tataryn v. Tataryn* (1994) 116 D.L.R. (4th) 193 at 195–196 (S.C.).
[43] [1978] I.L.R.M. 203 (H.C.).
[44] *ibid.* at 207. On the effect of bad relations between the parties *cf. McD. v. N.* [1999] 4 I.R. 301.

circumstances. In *Harrison v. Evans Estate*,[45] the court held that a testator, who separated from the plaintiff's mother when the plaintiff was one and whose attempts at contact with his daughter during her life had been rejected and spurned, failed in his moral duty to her when he made the following provision for her in his will:

> "I leave nothing to my daughter, Marilyn Heizmann as she was only an infant when she left my care, custody and control and I have seen her only a few times since and there is no natural love and affection as between father and daughter."

Despite the plaintiff's lack of knowledge of her father and the fact that she never acknowledged his cards, or telephoned or contacted him on the birth of her children, the court held that this failure on the part of the daughter was as a result of her mother's intervention and that the testator owed her a moral duty at the date of his death to make adequate provision for her proper maintenance. Desertion by a testator of his children, therefore, while it may rob him of their affections, does not relieve him of his moral duty to provide for them by will or otherwise.[46]

Of course, sometimes a parent's very knowledge of his child may be the reason why he wishes to disinherit him or perhaps favour another sibling over him as a sign of his displeasure with the renegade or misfit. The courts have been scrupulous in rooting out these attempted objective justifications for dispensing with a parent's moral duty to provide. Thus in *Re Radcliffe*,[47] the testator who considered his adopted son to be a failure, left his estate instead to two nieces whom he last seen in 1919 and 1940 respectively and to a nine-year-old son of a friend of the testator. The evidence revealed a pitiful picture of a 49-year-old son who had been made to feel inadequate and unwanted from a very early age by his father. Ridiculed and humiliated by his father, he had experienced little or no success in any line of work, and at the date of the testator's death was unemployed with no assets other than his furniture and was $1200 in debt. In the words of McKay J., "[c]learly, he is a man who has had a difficult time in fighting the battle of life."[48] The court held that notwithstanding his obvious lack of regard for his son,[49] the testator had failed in his moral duty towards him. McKay J. commented that if the deceased was to act as a just father, he should have recognised that his only son "for whatever

---

[45] [1987] 8 E.T.R. 53 at 55 (B.C.S.C.).
[46] See also *Re Steinberg Simmonds v. Rehn et al.* [1969] 3 D.L.R. (3d) 565 at 569.
[47] [1977] 1 A.C.W.S. 658; [1977] A.C.W.S.J. 159595 1 (B.C.S.C.).
[48] *ibid.* at 7.
[49] The court categorised the testator's decision to omit the petitioner, his only child, from his will as "one more vindictive act of rejection by the testator." *ibid.* at 6.

reason" was unable to adequately maintain himself and should, therefore, have made provision for him.[50]

The case of *Radcliffe* is an extreme example of perhaps an unreasonable parent. The petitioner, undoubtedly, was no Einstein or entrepreneur and patently his father's hopes and dreams were sorely dashed with a middle-aged son who could not keep a job and for whom the high point of his working career had been his employment as a statistician at the Montreal Olympic Games in 1976, since which date he had been unemployed. When considered in the context of the following cases, however, the testator's disappointment in his son is out of all proportion to the problems he had caused.

(b) Alternative Lifestyles – Sex, Drugs and Prodigal Children

There have been a number of authorities where the reason cited by a testator for disinheriting a child has been the latter's dependence on either drugs or alcohol. Faced with an application for variation of the will by the disappointed beneficiary, a common thread can be seen to exist in the judgments adopted by the various courts. In *Ray v. Moncrieff*,[51] for instance, Chapman J. refused to make additional provision for the applicant out of his father's will. Distinguishing the applicant, a 44-year-old "chronic drunkard" from someone who might need extra provision above the other siblings on account of being "maimed or insane", Chapman J. justified his decision, stating:

> "When he gets money he drinks, and I cannot help seeing that in whatever way any allowance might be safeguarded this propensity would not be cured or lessened by treating this applicant as incapable of restraining himself."[52]

The situation seems to be that if a parent clearly explains in the will the reason for making less or no provision for a particular child, and those reasons are rational and not motivated by maliciousness, but are in keeping with the views of society as a whole, a judge will be very hesitant to vary the terms of the will. A good example of this approach is the Canadian case of *Patterson v. Lauritsen*,[53] where the testatrix's expressed reasons for omitting the plaintiff from her will at the date of its execution were that he "was living with a homosexual and she thought he was a drug addict." The court found no evidence of addiction to drugs. However, the plaintiff was an alcoholic homosexual, who, at the date of his mother's death, had been unemployed in excess of 14 years.

---

[50] *ibid.* at p. 17.
[51] [1917] N.Z.L.R. 234 (S.C. Wellington).
[52] *ibid.* at 235.
[53] (1984) 58 B.C.L.R. 182.

In granting the plaintiff an equal share in his mother's estate along with his siblings, the court drew on the wisdom of the Privy Council decisions in *Bosch*[54] and *Allardice*.[55] Accordingly, the court's task was not to make a new will for the testator but rather to take care to appreciate the motives which swayed him in the disposition of his property or the justification which might be apparent for his decisions. It held that the deceased clearly abhorred the plaintiff's alcoholism, and had had occasion to fear him in his inebriated state in the past. The evidence showed, however, that by the end of his mother's life, the plaintiff was drinking less. With regard to his homosexuality as a factor for cutting him off, the court commented,

> "that although [the testatrix] was entitled to her own view against the plaintiff's homosexuality, the fact of homosexuality in today's society is not a factor which would justify a judicious parent, acting wisely, disinheriting a child."[56]

Given that the two reasons stated in the will were the plaintiff's homosexuality and his addiction to drugs, the court held that the testatrix had failed in her moral duty towards the plaintiff. It is implicit in the case that if the plaintiff had been an unreformed drug addict at the date of the testatrix's death, the result would have been different.

In light of both *Moncrieff* and *Patterson*, it is instructive to consider the most recent Irish authority in this respect. In contrast to *Patterson*, at the time of his mother's death the plaintiff in *Browne v. Sweeney and McCarthy*[57] was an unreformed drug addict. The background to the case revealed a "riches to rags" story of wasted privilege, making Eamonn Browne the modern day equivalent of the prodigal son. An unemployed separated father of three with serious financial difficulties, Eamonn sought relief under section 117 when his mother made no provision for him in her will which left the bulk of her estate, valued in excess of £300,000, to charity. During his parents' lifetime Eamonn had been afforded an excellent education, including financial support for two different university courses, while his father had made openings for him in the family business and set him up in his own business, none of which resulted in

---

[54] [1938] A.C. 463.
[55] [1911] A.C. 730.
[56] (1984) 58 B.C.L.R. 182 at 185. The notion of changing society mores has been considered in other cases. It would seem that regardless of the testator's prejudices the court has a duty to take on board contemporary social attitudes. If the testator's ideals, which result in the disinheritance of a child, are viewed as outdated this will feature in the court's deliberations. See *Re Leonard* [1985] 2 N.Z.L.R. 88 where the court made provision for the testator's daughters whom he had omitted from his will on account of their married status, which he saw as terminating any duty he owed to them, despite his failure to financially assist any of them prior to their marriages.
[57] Unreported judgment of Lavan J., High Court, July 5, 1996; [1998] 2 I.L.R.M. 141 (S.C.).

the long-term gainful employment of the plaintiff. Upon his father's death in 1986, his mother divided the estate, valued in excess of £1 million, between her four children so that they might share in it when they needed it rather than upon her death. To this end, the plaintiff received £275,000 in 1987. By the date of his mother's death, however, he had entirely dissipated his inheritance on a lifestyle of drugs and alcohol. The plaintiff claimed that the testatrix had failed in her moral duty when, in spite of full knowledge of his circumstances, she proceeded to leave her money to charity on the basis that she had made proper provision for all her children during her lifetime.

In rejecting the plaintiff's application in the High Court Lavan J. pointed to the fact that the straitened circumstances in which Eamonn now found himself were brought about by his own actions. It could not be argued, he continued, that by not making further provision for her son in her will as a result of his changed circumstances that the testatrix had therefore failed in her moral duty. Focusing on the scope of such a duty, the learned judge stated,

> "[T]he question which must be raised is when exactly is a parent's moral duty to a child discharged? Is a parent expected to continue supporting a child financially throughout their lives and even after their death? Surely not, save in the case where the child is mentally or physically disabled. There must come a time when a parent having made provision for a child during their lifetime, that such a child is then established in life and so relieving the parent of their moral duty."[58]

By a majority, the Supreme Court dismissed the plaintiff's appeal, holding that he had failed to positively establish that his mother had failed in her moral duty towards him. Keane J. (Lynch J. concurring) pointed to the generous provision made in the past for the plaintiff and held that the testatrix was within her right to leave the plaintiff out of her will on the grounds that past financial gifts had not produced good results. The fact that the plaintiff had not taken drugs or alcohol in the past five years was held to be irrelevant to the discharge of his mother's duty to him, as it only occurred subsequently to her death. In formulating guidelines for the future, Keane J. had the following advice to offer:

> "The Court in applications of this nature, cannot disregard the fact that parents must be presumed to know their children better than anyone else. In many cases that obvious fact would be of little weight where it is established that a child has been treated in a manner which points clearly to a failure of moral duty on the part of the testator. It is of considerable significance, however, in a case such as the present where, even on the

---

[58] *ibid.* at p. 30.

most favourable view of the plaintiff's case, it cannot be suggested that he was treated with anything other than generosity and support by both his parents. ..."[59]

In his dissenting judgment Barron J. referred to Eamonn as "a feckless character and known to be such by his mother."[60] Notwithstanding this, the learned judge construed the legislation to mean that the testatrix had a moral duty, in accordance with her means, to properly provide for her son so as to enable him to meet his responsibilities. He noted that at the time of her death the testatrix knew her son to be an unreformed addict with dependants whom he was incapable of supporting. While he did not deserve more, proper provision, according to Barron J., required the testatrix, who had the wherewithal to alleviate his need, to do so. The fact that the plaintiff's application sought funds only to better the position of his children and not himself was recognition by him of this fact. While stating that it was the moral duty to the plaintiff and not his dependants that was in issue, Barron J. was prepared to find in Eamonn's favour on the basis that the ultimate beneficiaries should be his children and not himself. It is notable that the majority expressly disagreed with Barron J.'s interpretation as to the scope of beneficiaries covered by section 117.[61]

It is interesting to briefly compare the outcome in *Browne* with that of the Canadian courts in *Hall v. Hall's Estate*,[62] where the High Court allowed an application by the 22-year-old daughter of the testator for further provision from his will notwithstanding the fact that she had dissipated her $20,000 trust fund which she had inherited on her eighteenth birthday under the terms of the will.[63] The court held that a wise and just parent would be willing to fund her in a "small business course" which would go some way towards equipping her for making her way in the world, adding that after the completion of her studies that "she would have to make it on her own."[64] *Hall* is reconcilable with the

---

[59] [1998] 2 I.L.R.M. 141 at 150 -151.

[60] [1998] 2 I.L.R.M. 141 at 152.

[61] *ibid.* at 151, *per* Keane J. Support for the majority line excluding grandchildren from the definition of "child" can be found in other jurisdictions with similar legislation to Ireland. See *Ray v. Moncrieff* [1917] N.Z.L.R. 234 at 235, considering section 33 of the Family Protection Act 1908 and *Re McGregor* [1961] N.Z.L.R. 1077 at 1081 (Wellington C.A.). Note, however that since the passing of New Zealand's Statutes Amendment Act 1947 grandchildren are now entitled to make an application in their own right for provision from their grandparents' estate.

[62] (1981) 10 Man. R. (2d) 168 (Manitoba Q.B.).

[63] According to the court, in the space of four years the applicant had spent almost half her fund on alcohol, friends and dental bills while she devoted her time, upon dropping out of high school, to vegetating and joining a travelling circus. At the time of her application, she was unemployed and had "started to re-orient herself towards a better life." *ibid.* at 170.

[64] *ibid.* at 174 – 75. These sentiments of there being a limit to the amount of provision which a parent must provide echo precisely those made by Lavan J. in the High Court in *Browne*. The difference between the two cases being that Eamonn had exhausted the bounty to which he was morally entitled whereas Marian Gaye Hall had not yet scraped the bottom of the barrel.

majority view in *Browne* in so far as in the latter Eamonn had had many bites at the cherry and still failed to make anything of himself, thereby justifying the testatrix's decision not to throw good money after bad.

(c) Criminal Conduct and Lesser Evils

Like most other jurisdictions, the Succession Act 1965 expressly provides that a child should not profit from his crime in so far that if convicted of certain criminal offences against his parent, section 120 of the Act will result in him losing any inheritance due to him under the terms of the will.[65] Thus, in cases where an attempt is made on a parent's life (regardless of its success) or where an attack on a parent incurs a sentence of two years or more, the convict will be prohibited by statute from making an application under section 117. Understandably, society would not look kindly on one who had hastened his parent's demise being enabled to claim a share of the estate the tangibility of which he had expedited.

Not all criminal acts perpetrated by a child, however, will justify a parent in the exclusion of the former from their will. It may be that such conduct does not directly affect the testator and while obviously distressing to the parent, the court may simply view it as evidence of the divergence of opinion between the parent and child as to how the latter should live their life. Thus, in *Re Smith (Dec'd)* the New Zealand courts held that criminal conduct which does not directly affect the will maker and which merely created "the normal disappointment and anguish of a mother at her son's wrongdoing" would not exclude an applicant from provision or diminish the provision which should be made for an applicant with an otherwise good case.[66]

(d) When the Going gets Rough – Hostile Relations

It may frequently be the case, however, that one's progeny will not go so far as to murder you but in their own inimitable way make your life a living hell such that a parent, while not being subject to the type of conduct mentioned in sec-

---

[65]The salient provisions of section 120 of the Succession Act 1965 provide as follows:
"(1) A sane person who has been guilty of the murder attempted murder or manslaughter of another shall be precluded from taking any share in the estate of that other, except a share arising under a will made after the act constituting the offence, *and shall not be entitled to make an application under section 117.*
(4) A person who has been found guilty of an offence against the deceased, or against the spouse or any child of the deceased (including a child adopted under the Adoption Acts, 1952 and 1964, and a person to whom the deceased was in loco parentis at the time of the offence), punishable by imprisonment for a maximum period of at least two years or by a more severe penalty, shall be precluded from taking any share in the estate as a legal right *or from making an application under section 117.*" (emphasis added).
[66](1991) 8 F.R.N.Z. 459 at 463.

tion 120, may nevertheless wish to exclude a child from sharing in the estate. The case law on this matter makes interesting reading.

The Canadian courts have held in *Re Karabin* that the existence of a strained or bad relationship between a parent and child "whittled down very considerably" the moral duty owed by the testator to the applicant.[67] The applicant followed her mother to Canada ten years after the latter had moved there to begin a second relationship which resulted in two children. The evidence before the court revealed that the relationship between mother and daughter was "checkered in character", which too often was one of "remoteness and estrangement".[68] The applicant was engaged in black market activities including bootlegging and her manner of living along with the suspicious sources of her income were a constant cause of friction between the parties. Freedman J. held that the disturbed pattern of their relationship was a factor which he could take into consideration in appraising the extent of the testatrix's moral duty. He qualified this in one significant way, however, stating:

> "[S]ince it is [a] moral duty that must be appraised, the testatrix cannot be the one to judge thereof according to her own opinion of the character or conduct of the applicant, even if formed in all good faith. This is the function of the court, which must consider the matter objectively and in light of all the circumstances."[69]

It follows from this that while a child's appalling conduct may reduce the extent of the moral duty owed by a parent, it does not obliterate it. Moreover, it is not an absolute defence for the executor to say that the conduct justified the deceased in cutting off the child, as only the court can reach this conclusion. The impact of this is very clear from the Canadian case of *Re Bartel et al.* where the deceased left her entire estate to the Cancer Society, thereby disinheriting her son and daughter.[70] Her motives are entirely understandable when viewed against the background of the bad relations between the parties. The original cause for the animosity had arisen from the applicants' displeasure over the devolution of their grandmother's estate. Initially willed in their favour, the deceased's mother changed her mind on her deathbed and willed it to her daughter instead with the intention that her grandchildren would inherit it on the demise of their mother. While their grievances at this change in their fortunes were eventually settled without trial, in the words of Scollin J. "this truce did nothing to disperse the acrid haze of the battle."[71] In the last five

---

[67] (1955) 62 Man. R. 334 at 337 (Manitoba Q.B.).
[68] *ibid.*
[69] *ibid.* at 339.
[70] (1982) 16 Man. R. (2d) 29 (Manitoba Q.B.).
[71] *ibid.* at 31.

years of their mother's life, the applicants never once visited her nor allowed her to have any contact with her grandchildren. Even when she was dying in hospital, her children kept their distance. Mrs Bartel, while deeply hurt, accepted the situation. The evidence indicated that her only retaliation in private was to place a newspaper over a cabinet to hide the photographs of her children and grandchildren and their former gifts to her. Arguably, in such circumstances it is more a case of the children disowning the parent than *vice versa*. To expect that Mrs Bartel would be favourably disposed towards her children in her will would be to demand her to be a testatrix of superhuman character, impervious to her cruel treatment by her children. In giving judgment that half of the charitable bequest should be divided equally between the applicants, Scollin J. nevertheless held that from his objective perspective, the deceased had undoubtedly played some part in the change of her mother's will and in light of the trust imposed by the grandmother to provide for the applicants:

> "... a wise and just testator would not die leaving an overwhelming charitable bequest conceived in revenge and with no provision even for grandchildren; but would, instead, have balanced the merit of that major bequest against a real, if reluctant, duty to see to a reasonable measure of maintenance and support for imperfect dependants."[72]

The final case of significance in this regard is the recent pronouncement of the Supreme Court in *McD. v. N.*[73] Its importance lies in the very thorough scrutiny given by Barron J. for the court on the issue of moral duty and the extent to which account may be taken of bad feeling between a parent and child. James McD., a widower, died in 1993, leaving a substantial farm holding and survived by two sons. In death he left all his property to Mary N., his niece by marriage, with a token £5,000 to the applicant Peter McD. in discharge of any moral duty he might owe him. In his wake he left a divided community, scarred by the open hostility and contempt in which father and son held each other. The relationship between the deceased and Peter was unusual by any standard. Leaving technical college at an early age to run the main farm for his father, Peter never basked in the glory of his father's affection who, on one occasion, introduced him to a neighbour as his employee. In return for his labours he received bed and board but no remuneration. While Peter and his brother had run-ins with their father regarding the family land, matters only came to a head when Peter married into a family for whom his father had a serious dislike. Matters spiralled seriously out of hand after that event – from pitchfork battles and the blockading of kennels by the sons to the institution of ejectment proceedings by the deceased against Peter in relation to the main farm, which ultimately

---

[72]*ibid.* at 33.
[73][1999] 4 I.R. 301 (H.C. & S.C.).

resulted in Peter's attachment in Mountjoy for a period of eleven months. The deceased took advantage of this spell to repossess some of his property, transferring one holding to his younger son, Thomas and selling the other to a third party. Following his release from prison, the relationship between father and son hit a new low. Peter resumed his occupation of his father's lands and continued to work them for his own benefit despite a court order against him. Neighbours took sides and what can only be described as a campaign of intimidation and terror was waged against the deceased (by this time in his seventies and in ailing health), the N. family and the purchasers of the McD. farm. Abusive graffiti, threatening phone calls, letting loose of livestock and the burning out of equipment owned by the new owner of the McD. holding were only some of the appalling activities in which the applicant, although not directly involved, acquiesced. McCracken J. in the High Court dismissed the plaintiff's claim under section 117. In his view, the fulfilment of the deceased's moral duty to provide for the plaintiff was affected by the latter's behaviour towards his father. While it did not fall directly within section 120, the plaintiff's conduct and the benefits acquired by force and enjoyed by him during his father's lifetime were pertinent factors in the court's finding that no breach of moral duty arose in this case.

In allowing the son's appeal, the Supreme Court commenced its examination of the case by restating the extent of a parent's moral duty under section 117 in the following terms:

> "[I]t is an obligation which exists from the relationship between the parties and is one which is continuous from the date of birth of the child until the date of death of the parent unless in the meantime it has been satisfied or extinguished."[74]

Barron J., delivering the judgment of the court (*nem. diss.*), found that the ejection of the plaintiff from the family lands *per se* amounted to a breach of the testator's moral duty, "whatever the legalities of the matter may have been".[75] In ascertaining the extent of the duty owed the judge posed three questions for consideration:

(1) what would satisfy the moral obligation in the particular circumstances of this family?;

(2) should Peter's behaviour be taken into account in either extinguishing or diminishing his father's obligation?; and finally,

(3) what benefits, if any, had Peter received already in satisfaction of his moral claim against his father?

---

[74] [1999] 4 I.R. 301 at 317.
[75] *ibid.*

In dealing with the first and third questions Barron J. held that provision capable of satisfying a child's moral claim should take the form of advancements – leading either to the education of the latter or his establishment in life. In Peter's case, any advancement received by him had been temporary in nature or amounted to *ad hoc* benefits that had never been passed on.[76] In the judge's mind, all else being equal, the plaintiff would have been entitled to expect a bequest of half his father's land, amounting to 250 acres, in light of his choice of farming as his livelihood and his work to date on the farm.

Turning to the matter of the plaintiff's conduct, the court started from the premise that bad behaviour can affect the moral duty owed to a child.[77] While in line with the finding of McCracken J. in this respect, the fundamental difference between the High Court and Supreme Court on this issue was Barron J.'s emphasis on the importance of putting such behaviour in context. According to the learned judge:

> "It should not be overlooked that parents and children have the same genes and that an uncompromising stubbornness in the one is likely to be mirrored in the other."[78]

The court held that while one could not justify the plaintiff's atrocious conduct, neither could one ignore the reason for it. Attributing the initial blame for the vendetta to the deceased's irrational animosity to his son's wife and her family, Barron J. was of the view that the testator's breach of moral duty to his son preceded and was, in fact, the catalyst for Peter's subsequent behaviour towards him. In light of these facts, his conduct had not extinguished his moral claim on his father's estate.[79] However, it did diminish the size of the moral obligation owed. The farm, referred to by the court as Peter's "birthright", existed at the date of the testator's death as a result of Peter's efforts – without him the probability was that the lands would have been dissipated. Taking into consideration the help afforded to the N. family during the testator's lifetime, any moral obligations he may have felt towards them for their support were well satisfied at the date of his death and certainly were not such as would

---

[76]The court classified both the plaintiff's rent-free occupation of his father's land and his profits from the quarry as advancements, while judicial note was taken of the fact that the court order awarding the plaintiff £11,000 for his work on the farm had never been satisfied.

[77]This is in line with the *obiter dicta* of Finlay C.J. in *In the Estate of I.A.C. deceased: C. and F. v. W.C. and T.C.* [1989] I.L.R.M. 815 at 820 where he commented that "quite different considerations may apply...where a marked hostility between a testator and one particular child is established to the satisfaction of the court."

[78]*McD. v. N.*, above, n.74 at 319.

[79]Reference was made to the fact that the plaintiff's brother, Tom, had initially enjoyed less than cordial relations with his father also and that hostility between them only ceased when the testator made over one of his farms to Tom, during the plaintiff's term in prison.

justify a will favouring them to Peter's detriment.[80] In giving judgment in his favour, the Supreme Court awarded the remaining 170 acres to Peter on condition that a pecuniary legacy be paid to the N. family in some recognition of the testator's wishes.

The Supreme Court's decision in *McD. v. N.* is commendable. Addressing the realities of family dissension, it focuses on the net issue of how bad feeling between parent and child can affect the moral obligations owed under section 117. In examining the conduct of the child, the court takes that conduct outside the realm of the parent/child relationship and examines whether the conduct would have been the same had a stranger been involved. The advantage of such an approach is that it allows the court to be an objective onlooker in determining whether the bad behaviour counts as disqualifying behaviour for the purposes of section 117. Thus, when such an approach is adopted in the *McD.* case it becomes evident that the testator's attitude towards his son in treating him as an employee and in disparaging his wife and her family certainly helped to fuel the bad relations between them. While undoubtedly one could not in any way condone Peter's behaviour, one can understand why he felt unfairly treated by his father, in comparison to his brother (who was given land) and his cousins (who benefited greatly from the sale of McD. land, the proceeds of which were used to clear their debts). The court's approach is reminiscent of the sentiments expressed by Scollin J. in *Re Bartel* and cited above.[81] It is worthy of note that Barron J. gave judgment for the Court in *McD.* The hallmark of his previous decisions has been that of pragmatism. In *In the goods of J.H. deceased* Barron J. showed himself willing to consider relevant factors arising after the death of the testator in determining the issue of moral duty,[82] while in *Browne v. Sweeney* the judge was prepared to consider an expanded definition of "child" in an attempt to ensure a pragmatic distribution of wealth.[83]

---

[80]The facts indicate that during his stay with them the testator had greatly assisted the N.s' in their financial difficulties and that large capital sums realised on the sale of his land and cattle had been applied by the testator in clearing their debts, *ibid.* at 319.

[81](1982) 16 Man. R. (2d) 29 at 31. See n. 72 above and accompanying text.

[82][1984] I.R. 599 (H.C.). This approach was adopted by Blayney J. in *In the Estate of J.H. de B. decd* [1991] 2 I.R. 105 (H.C.) who praised Barron J.'s very clear analysis of section 117(2). In his book, *Succession Law in Ireland* (2nd ed., Dublin, 1995) Professor Brady makes the point that in the absence of special factors such as those pertaining in *In the goods of J.H.*, the crucial time for determining the testator's provision for the applicant will remain the date of the testator's death.

[83]See n. 60 above and accompanying text.

6. CONCLUSION: TESTAMENTARY AUTONOMY *VERSUS* PRIMA FACIE RIGHTS OF PATRIMONY

"[T]he possibilities of variations in the facts of every case are so infinite that very little assistance can be obtained from the quotation of cases."[84]

There is a certain truth to this and the Irish courts have in the past subscribed to such a view, emphasising the importance of studying each case on its own facts. Nevertheless, there are trends and principles which do emerge from the myriad of cases and which therefore deserve recognition in so far as they inform us as to the changing nature of the concept of moral duty and as to what society expects from and will tolerate in terms of the behaviour of the next generation. It has been long established that a section 117 applicant carries a heavy burden of proof in satisfying the court that the deceased failed in his moral duty towards him. What is clear from the cases considered above is that an equally high threshold exists where a testator wishes to disinherit a child on the basis of their fractious relationship.

Moreover, it appears that the court will welcome both lost sheep and black sheep back into the fold. Attempts to disenfranchise them will be very difficult to sustain in the absence of evidence that proper provision was already made for them during the testator's lifetime or evidence that their behaviour brings them within the provisions of section 120 of the Succession Act 1965. The balance drawn by the court between testamentary autonomy and patrimony is more likely to manifest itself in the diminution of the size of the share to which the applicant would have been entitled had he been good. The *raison d'être* for this approach, which is adopted across the commonwealth jurisdictions, lies in the fact that in most cases our children become what we make them. This non-negotiable moral obligation imposed upon parents to make proper provision for their offspring endures and in most cases where the applicant succeeds in his application to vary the will notwithstanding his prior bad conduct, it will be because of the lack of advancement received by him during the testator's lifetime.

Thus, whether your child is a drunk or a drug addict, whether his nature is volatile or vitriolic, whether as a latchkey kid or a lame duck you view your responsibilities towards him as lessened, the moral of the story is that he may still have a claim on your estate, even if not on your affections.

---

[84] *In re Holmes (dec'd)* [1936] N.Z.L.R. 26 at 35 (C.A.).

UNBUNDLING CONSTRUCTIVE TRUSTEESHIP

JOHN BRESLIN

1. INTRODUCTION

Equity's enhanced modern role in the resolution of commercial disputes is a result, of course, of its inherent flexibility, which enables it to be adapted to the complexities of modern business problems. Accordingly, the law of trusts still continues to play an indispensable role in the regulation and administration of pension schemes; and equitable principles have inhibited the excesses of mortgagees,[1] and informed statutory control of receivers.[2] The recovery of the proceeds of corporate fraud and corrupt payments[3] have been facilitated by the equitable doctrine of constructive trusts[4] (formerly referred to as liability for knowing receipt and knowing assistance). This is an attractive method of tackling white-collar crime for the following reasons. First, the cases need be proved on the balance of probabilities, and not beyond a reasonable doubt. Secondly, cases are tried before a judge alone, and not before a jury – where there is a perception that the tedium of a long fraud trial can lead to perverse decisions.[5] Thirdly, unlike the criminal law, if a plaintiff/victim is successful in his action he can expect a measure of compensation: this contrasts with the criminal process whereby a successful prosecution will generally only result in punishment/ retribution. Fourthly, unlike the law of tort, equitable compensation can sometimes go beyond actual losses, lead to enhanced awards of interest on judgments, and liability in Equity is not necessarily dependent upon establishing a duty of care owed by the defendant to the plaintiff.

---

[1] *Downsview Nominees Ltd. v. First City Corporation Ltd.* [1993] A.C. 295.
[2] S. 316A of the Companies Act 1963: see Breslin, *Banking Law in the Republic of Ireland* (Dublin, 1998) pp. 865-867. See *Re Edenfell Holdings* [1999] 1 I.R. 458.
[3] *Attorney General of Hong Kong v. Reid* [1994] 1 A.C. 324.
[4] See, generally, Breslin *op. cit.*, above, n.2 at pp. 251-271; Delany, *Equity and the Law of Trusts in Ireland* (2nd ed., Dublin, 1999) pp. 218 *et seq.*; Oakley, *Constructive Trusts* (3rd ed., London, 1997) chapters 2, 3 and 4; Pearce and Stevens, *The Law of Trusts and Equitable Obligations* (London, 1998) chapter 30; Harpum, "The Stranger as Constructive Trustee" (1986) 102 *L.Q.R.* 110, 267; Gardner, "Knowing Assistance and Knowing Receipt: Taking Stock" (1996) 112 *L.Q.R.* 56.
[5] Paragraph 1 of the Fraud Trials Committee Report (chaired by Lord Roskill, 1986 HMSO) stated that the criminal justice system in England and Wales was incapable of bringing the perpetrators of serious fraud expeditiously and effectively to book.

In working out the principles upon which liability for constructive trustee-ship should be imposed, a single head of liability (or at least a form of liability with two potential "limbs") has effectively been unbundled into two distinct causes of action. This "unbundling" of constructive trusteeship has led to much needed clarity under the sub-heading of "knowing assistance" – although there are some apparent difficulties in application of the new principles upon which liability should be based. However, unbundling constructive trusteeship has, in the case of knowing receipt, manifested itself in tension between the applica-tion of traditional equitable principles, and the rapid extension of restitution law to new areas where it is perceived to be useful. The growing preference for supplanting equitable principles with restitution reflects dissatisfaction with the shortfalls of the law of Equity – in the main, its relative vagueness (the downside of flexibility) and unpredictability. But is restitution a reliable sub-stitute for Equity?

In order to analyse the current state of play in this important area it is useful to plot the course to date of constructive trusteeship.

2. The Development of Constructive Trusteeship Liability

For present purposes, a constructive trust is a form of trust which is declared by the court (rather than by the intention of a settlor) in circumstances where it is just and equitable to do so. The constructive trust has, in practical terms, been utilised by plaintiffs as a remedy to fix a solvent defendant with personal liabil-ity for the wrong (often fraud) of a third party, where the third party is a man of straw or is beyond the reach of the court. However, unlike liability in tort and contract, where liability is (in general terms) imposed on a person who is in some manner primarily liable as a principal actor in the saga, this is not neces-sarily the case with regard to constructive trusteeship. Invariably, this class of constructive trusteeship concerns situations where the defendant has been on the fringes of the fraud or other wrong. So, what are the circumstances in which a secondary actor in the factual matrix can be held liable to account for the wrongdoing of the primary actor? This is the complex legal and commercial-moral task which the law of Equity performs: the answer is as complex as the factual settings in which the question has often been debated.

Constructive trustee liability has its primary source in the decision of *Barnes v. Addy*[6] which formulated the general principle that:

> "strangers are not to be made constructive trustees merely because they
> act as the agents of trustees in transactions within their legal powers ...
> unless those agents receive and become chargeable with some part of the

---

[6] (1874) 9 Ch. App. 244.

trust property, or unless they assist with knowledge in a dishonest and fraudulent design on the part of the trustees."[7]

Accordingly, there are two ways in which one can become a constructive trustee: first, knowingly assisting in a breach of trust, and secondly, knowingly receiving property with knowledge that it has been transferred in breach of trust. These heads of liability became labelled by way of shorthand as liability for knowing assistance, and liability for knowing receipt.

The case law has naturally focused on the principles applicable so as to identify the precise state of mind required to found liability. An abundance of authority has given rise to considerable confusion as to the parameters of the *mens reus* required to found liability. For this reason, it is helpful to identify certain landmark decisions along the way.

In *Selangor United Rubber Estates Ltd. v. Craddock*[8] Ungoed-Thomas J. held as follows:[9]

> "The knowledge required to hold a stranger liable as constructive trustee in a dishonest and fraudulent design, is knowledge of circumstances which would indicate to an honest, reasonable man that such a design was being committed or would put him on inquiry, which the stranger failed to make, whether it was being committed."

The case concerned a complex scheme to "asset strip" a company. A bank was implicated by being used to process and route payments by which, in effect, the company's own assets were being used to fund the purchase of shares in the company by the defendants in breach of the then UK equivalent of section 60 of the Companies Act 1963. Equally, in *Karak Rubber Co Ltd. v. Burden (No. 2)*[10] (another case concerning the same form of corporate abuse) Brightman J. followed *Selangor* and equated the bank's negligent failure to inquire with liability in equity.[11]

The equation of the test for liability for constructive trusteeship with liability for the tort of negligence caused some consternation at the time.[12] Soon thereafter, a more sophisticated formula for testing liability emerged from the submissions of counsel in *Baden v. Societè Genérale pour Favouriser le Développement et de l'Industrie en France S.A.*[13] Five categories of state of

---

[7] *ibid.* at 251-252.
[8] [1968] 2 All E.R. 1073.
[9] *ibid.* at 1104.
[10] [1972] 1 All E.R. 1210.
[11] *ibid.* at 1231.
[12] See Megrah and Ryder (ed.), *Paget's Law of Banking* (9th ed., London, 1982) p. 225, and Goode, *Commercial Law* (London, 1982) p. 514.
[13] [1992] 4 All E.R. 161.

mind were identified by counsel, and summarised and adopted by the trial judge (Peter Gibson J., as he then was):

1. Actual knowledge;

2. Wilfully shutting one's eyes to the obvious;

3. Wilfully and recklessly failing to make such enquiries as an honest and reasonable man would make;

4. Knowledge of facts that would indicate the facts to an honest and reasonable man;

5. Knowledge of circumstances which would put an honest and reasonable man on inquiry.

As can be seen, the five states of mind were formulated in terms of decreasing culpability.

Before considering how constructive trusteeship has been analysed, with particular reference to counsel's formulation in the *Baden* case, the following general comments may be made. First, the formulation of shades of guilty knowledge has not always been accepted as useful.[14] Secondly, there has been widespread disagreement as to whether the shades of liability towards the less culpable end of the spectrum can ground liability in a given case – to use a sporting analogy, "line calls" are still difficult to make even if the court is equipped with the *Baden* formula. And thirdly, the "various categories of mental state identified in *Baden's* case are not rigid categories with clear and precise boundaries. One category may merge imperceptibly into another."[15]

3. THE DEVELOPMENT OF ACCESSORY LIABILITY

The first instance decision of Millett J. (as he then was) in *Agip (Africa) Ltd. v. Jackson*[16] reversed the trend towards over-sophistication characterised by *Baden* and asserted that the true basis for liability for knowing assistance was dishonesty. In so classifying this test, Millett J. stated that this was "a jury question", a question of fact, to be judged on the basis of the circumstances of the case. The decision of Millett J. in that case was affirmed by the Court of Appeal.[17]

---

[14]Notably with regard to "knowing assistance" liability, Lord Nicholls in *Royal Brunei Airlines v. Tan* [1995] 3 W.L.R. 64 at 76, indicated that the *Baden* criteria were "best forgotten".

[15]*Per* Scott L.J. in *Polly Peck International plc v. Nadir* [1992] 4 All E.R. 769 at 777. Or, as Ungoed-Thomas J. put it in *Selangor* "the shaded area between clear honesty and black dishonesty": [1968] 2 All E.R. 1073 at 1085.

[16][1990] Ch. 265.

[17][1991] Ch. 547.

However, the learned appellate judges' resort to the complications of the *Baden* formula caused their decisions to be overshadowed by the attractive conceptual simplicity of Millett J.'s approach.

In spite of its attractions, the "dishonesty"/"jury question" test advocated in *Agip* did not find universal favour among the UK courts. And so, the judges took an *à la carte* approach, applying versions of the *Baden* formula, and sometimes shading towards the "dishonesty" test. The conceptual disarray in such an important area of the civil law clearly caused much concern among commentators[18] and finally the Privy Council took the opportunity in *Royal Brunei Airlines v. Tan*[19] to affirm Millett J.'s approach.

The Privy Council gave its decision through Lord Nicholls of Birkenhead. The opinion is striking for its clarity and refreshing departure from somewhat mechanistic thinking that had bedevilled this area for well over a century. The Privy Council, first, consigned the cliché "knowing assistance in a breach of trust" to history by deprecating it as displaying, and propagating, a dangerous confusion in the principles which should underlie liability. *Barnes v. Addy*, Lord Nicholls stated, had been applied mechanistically as though it were a statute. The Privy Council held that the cliché should be avoided as it focused on the state of mind of the trustee (the absent or insolvent rogue) and not the defendant. Furthermore, and as a consequence, the defendant should henceforth be referred to as the "accessory" and this class of equitable liability (for knowing assistance in a breach of trust) should instead be labelled "accessory liability". This was the correct approach as it concentrated judicial evaluation on the actions and motives of the relevant party. Lord Nicholls said this:[20]

> "... in the context of the accessory liability principle acting dishonestly, or with a lack of probity, which is synonymous, means simply not acting as an honest person would in the circumstances. This is an objective standard. . . . To enquire ... whether a person dishonestly assisted in what is later held to be a breach of trust is to ask a meaningful question, which is capable of being given a meaningful answer. This is not always so if the question is posed in terms of 'knowingly' assisted. Framing the question in the latter form all too often leads one into tortuous convolutions about the 'sort' of knowledge required, when the truth is that 'knowingly' is inapt as a criterion when applied to the gradually darkening spectrum where the differences are of degree and not kind."

Furthermore, the judgment of Millett J. (as he then was) in *Agip* was affirmed

---

[18]Hoffman, "The redundancy of knowing assistance" in Birks (ed.), *The Frontiers of Liability* (Oxford, 1994) Vol. 1 p. 27.
[19][1995] 2 A.C. 378.
[20]*ibid.* at 391.

as stating the true benchmark of liability: i.e. the "jury question" of whether or not the defendant had acted honestly or dishonestly. Whether or not the defendant acted honestly or dishonestly was to be judged by an objective standard, and not the subjective standards of the particular defendant. Lord Nicholls said:[21]

> "... dishonesty is an essential ingredient here. There may be cases where, in the light of the particular facts, a third party will owe a duty of care to the beneficiaries. As a general proposition, however, beneficiaries cannot reasonably expect that all the world dealing with their trustees should owe them a duty to take care lest the trustees are behaving dishonestly."

However, Lord Nicholls indicated that "commercially unacceptable conduct"[22] could in certain circumstances amount to "dishonesty." On its face, this notion appeared to extend the notion of dishonesty to its very limits, as it would appear that there may be instances where a defendant might act honestly albeit in a commercially unacceptable manner.

4. POST-*TAN*: ACCESSORY LIABILITY IN SUBSEQUENT CASES

While the guidance of the Privy Council has been welcomed by most commentators (but not all[23]), the application of the principles in subsequent case law has, perhaps not surprisingly, proved problematic. While the philosophical underpinnings of liability have been clarified, there still remain immense difficulties in putting into practice even a test built on the solid objective criteria as put forward in *Tan*. There has been some reluctance to abandon entirely the *Baden* criteria, even in the context of accessory liability. Accordingly, there are considerable differences of opinion among the major Common Law jurisdictions as to precisely how far down the *Baden* scale it is permissible to go in order to find liability.[24] In other words, how careless must the defendant be before he faces the prospect of liability: when does recklessness become dishonesty (as defined)? Dishonest recklessness has been sufficient in some cases,[25] and the

---

[21] *ibid.* at 392.
[22] A phrase coined by Knox J. in *Cowan de Groot Properties Ltd. v. Eagle Trust plc* [1992] 4 All E.R. 700 at 761 – a knowing receipt case.
[23] Berg, "Accessory Liability for Breach of Trust" [1996] 59 *M.L.R.* 443.
[24] For instance, in New Zealand the courts have indicated that liability for knowing receipt can be imposed on the basis of any of the five categories of state of mind in *Baden*: *Westpac Banking Corp v. Savin* [1985] 2 N.Z.L.R. 41. In Australia, some courts will only find liability where the defendant's state of mind falls within one of the first four of the categories: *Gertsch v. Atsas* unreported, Supreme Court of New South Wales, Foster AJ, October 1, 1999.
[25] *Twinsectra Ltd. v. Yardley* [1999] Lloyd's Law Rep. Banking 438l; followed by *Bank of America v. Arnell* [1999] Lloyd's Rep. Banking 399 (Q.B.)

Privy Council's formulation of objective dishonesty has been applied domesti-
cally in the English courts:[26] but it is clear that some courts will be unwilling to
impose liability on the basis of mere carelessness.[27]

Another issue is the question as to what, if any, level of knowledge must be
demonstrated on the part of the defendant as to the details of the original wrong
by the trustee or fiduciary? This was a key issue in *Brinks Ltd. v. Abu-Saleh et
al.*[28] That case concerned whether the victim of the notorious Brinks Mat robbery near Heathrow Airport in London could impose accessory liability on the
wife of a person who assisted in the laundering of the proceeds of the robbery.
Mrs. E had accompanied her husband, who had driven with large amounts of
cash from England to Switzerland on numerous occasions to open deposits at
banks there. Mrs. E claimed to have been unaware of the criminal origin of the
money. She claimed she thought that her husband was participating in a scheme
for a business associate of her husband's to evade tax by salting away large
sums of cash earned from his husband's associate legitimate business but in
respect of which the associate was determined not to pay tax. The plaintiff
argued that it was not necessary for it to prove that Mrs. E knew of the trust
which was being breached (*i.e.,* a breach of fiduciary duty by a security guard
employed by the plaintiff whose activities enabled the robbers to carry out their
crime). Rimer J. rejected the plaintiff's contention that it need only prove that
Mrs. E provided her assistance in furtherance of a dishonest transaction, regardless of whether she knew there was a breach of trust. Rimer J. held as
follows:[29]

> "...a claim based on accessory liability can only be brought against some-
> one who knows of the existence of the trust, or at least of the facts giving
> rise to the trust."

This sits uneasily with the speech of Lord Nicholls in *Tan*, where such a gloss
on the dishonesty test is not apparent. Lord Nicholls said this:[30]

> "A liability in equity to make good resulting loss attaches to a person
> who dishonestly procures or assists in a breach of trust or fiduciary obli-

---

[26] *Dubai Aluminium Co Ltd. v. Salaam* [1999] 1 Lloyd's Rep. 415; *Brinks Ltd. v. Abu Saleh, The
Times*, October 23, 1995.

[27] See *Beach Petroleum NL v. Abbott Tout Russell Kennedy,* unreported, New South Wales Court
of Appeal, November 5, 1999, where the court deprecated the appellant's failure to distinguish
between imprudence (which would not trigger liability) and dishonesty (which would).

[28] *The Times*, October 23, 1995: Ch. D., Rimer J. His statements in this regard were *obiter* as he
had already found that Mrs. E could not be made liable as she had not assisted in any "relevant"
way in the security guard's breach of trust.

[29] At p. 22 of Lexis transcript.

[30] [1995] 2 A.C. 378 at 392.

gation. It is not necessary that, in addition, the trustee or fiduciary was acting dishonestly, although this will usually be so where the third party who is assisting him is acting dishonestly."

If the state of mind of the trustee is irrelevant to the question of the accessory's liability, and if dishonesty – in the general terms expounded by the Privy Council – is the trigger for liability, it seems illogical to require the potential accessory to have knowledge of the precise nature of the trust, or breach of trust. This is because while the dishonest nature of the transaction might be all too apparent to the trustee and his accessory, they might have no idea that, as a matter of law, it could be classed as a breach of trust. Indeed, in *Brinks Ltd.*, whether or not the security guard was acting in breach of trust was the subject of careful judicial analysis by Rimer J. It is unreasonable to expect the defendant to undertake the same legal evaluation as a precondition to his liability as an accessory. If, however, something less than this is required, it is unclear what it should be, and does not, in any event, appear to be mandated by the Privy Council's analysis in *Tan*.

Moreover, the gloss imposed by Rimer J. is wholly inconsistent with this observation by Millett J. (as he then was) in *Agip Africa*:

> "… it is no answer for a man charged with having knowingly assisted in a fraudulent and dishonest scheme to say that he thought that it was 'only' a breach of exchange control or 'only' a case of tax evasion."[31]

Heinl v. Jyske Bank (Gibraltar) Ltd.,[32] a recent decision of the Court of Appeal in England and Wales, illustrates the difficulties judges can undergo at the interface between carelessness and dishonest recklessness. It also, it is submitted, demonstrates that *Tan* is being interpreted as requiring some specific knowledge on the part of the defendant as to the details of the breach of trust before the court will find liability. This case concerned the activities of H and others whom the plaintiff bank alleged had conspired with one of its senior officers, S, to defraud it of several million pounds by making bogus loans to companies controlled by S and others. The decision of the Court of Appeal centred on the trial judge's finding that H had been guilty of a breach of constructive trust in assisting the defrauding of the bank. One of the activities in respect of which H was alleged to have been instrumental was the "laundering" of several hundred thousand pounds by apparently pointless transfers between the respective accounts of different companies controlled by him, which accounts were held at

---

[31] [1990] Ch. 265 at 295.
[32] [1999] Lloyd's Law Reports: Banking 511, reversing in part the decision of Evans-Lombe J. [1992] 2 B.C.L.C. 101.

a branch of a bank in Ireland. The fact that H did not have the resources to
secure legal representation during the entirety of a long fraud trial clearly gave
the learned judges in the Court of Appeal considerable grounds for concern.
However, their decision does indicate, with the greatest respect, a degree of
lack of appreciation of the tenets of "accessory liability."

Colman J. appears to have accepted that while the alleged "laundering"
activities had the appearance of illegality, this was not necessarily recognised
by H: accordingly, this could not be a ground for finding him liable as accessory. It is clear from the judgment of Lord Nicholls in *Tan*, that the subjective
attitude of the defendant is close to irrelevant. Yet Colman J. said this:[33]

> "It is important in this analysis to be very clear that the material question
> is not the objective test whether he ought as a reasonable businessman to
> have appreciated that the funds subject to his control had been fraudu-
> lently procured from the Bank or that there was a real probability that
> they had been, but the subjective test whether he did indeed appreciate
> that the funds had been or probably had been so procured."

It would appear that Colman J. applied an objective test of dishonesty to the
facts of which the defendant was actually aware (hence the "subjective" element).[34] Yet a defendant's pretended perception of what occurred cannot be
the starting point for the type of objective evaluation envisaged by the Privy
Council in *Tan*. Indeed, a sufficiently skewed or incredible account by a defendant of his perception of the transaction may be the best evidence of dishonesty the court will find. This is not to say that the defendant's account of what
he knew is irrelevant. Far from it. However, it appears to limit the court's ability to apply the objective test of dishonesty unduly if such an account is taken
at face value as the benchmark by which the defendant's honesty is evaluated.
There is a danger that the objective element of the test will be emasculated by
overemphasising the defendant's knowledge of the relevant facts.

It is clear that once the trial judge has found as a fact that a defendant had
knowledge of relevant facts (whether or not the defendant claimed in his evidence not to know them) the defendant's lack of moral standards will not avail
him. The point is well put by Gibbs J. of the High Court of Australia in *Consul
Development Pty Ltd v. DPC Estates Pty Ltd*:[35]

> "It may be going too far to say that a stranger will be liable if the circum-
> stances would have put an honest and reasonable man on inquiry, when
> the stranger's failure to inquire had been innocent and he has not wilfully

[33] [1999] Lloyd's Law Reports: Banking 511 at p. 546.
[34] A similar argument is made by Gardner, *loc. cit.* p. 67 at n. 4 above.
[35] (1974–1975) 132 C.L.R. 373 at 398.

shut his eyes to the obvious. On the other hand, it does not seem to me to be necessary to prove that a stranger who participated in a breach of trust or fiduciary duty with knowledge of all the circumstances did so actually knowing that what he was doing was improper. It would not be just that a person who had full knowledge of all the facts could escape liability because his own moral obtuseness prevented him from recognising an impropriety that would have been apparent to an ordinary man."

Human nature being what it is, most defendants, if they choose to give evidence, will proffer *ex post facto* rationalisations for what they did, and these will inevitably involve evaluating the commercial morality of their actions by a less exacting standard than the court would be inclined to apply. The explanations of the defendant in person can be relevant to the question of whether or not the defendant was "taking risks", or whether he or she was turning the "Nelsonian blind eye" and ought to have asked questions but did not.

As noted above, Colman J.'s approach in *Jyske Bank* demonstrates that *Tan* is being interpreted as requiring some specific knowledge on the part of the defendant as to the details of the breach of trust before the court will find liability. Sedley L.J. indicated at the conclusion of his short judgment that "he did not adopt Colman J.'s exegesis of [*Tan*]."[36] Colman J.'s judgment also demonstrates how an analysis of the defendant's state of mind, if not kept properly within the bounds set by the Privy Council in *Tan*, can effectively result in the application of a purely subjective test. An analysis of the defendant's state of mind is appropriate and necessary, but it is not dispositive. First, his account of what he knew has to be credible; secondly, his actions and his state of mind, are to be judged according to an objective commercial-moral standard.[37]

Standing back from the detail somewhat, on the facts of *Jyske Bank* the Court of Appeal was clearly applying something akin to a criminal standard of proof of the *mens rea* for accessory liability. The Court of Appeal stated that H was less than frank in his evidence – aspects of which the court found difficult to accept: but clearly the court had doubts as to the extent of his involvement in the fraud. This is inevitable for two principal reasons. First, the high standard of proof traditionally required by the courts, even in the context of the civil law, when an allegation of fraud is made.[38] Secondly, the very phrase "accessory" liability, carries with it overtones of degrees of involvement or participation in a criminal venture. It is also unsurprising, accordingly, that the criterion of "commercially unacceptable conduct" never featured in their Lordships analysis of the legal principles applicable to H's activities.

---

[36] *Heinl v. Jyske Bank (Gibraltar) Ltd.*, above, n.32 at 532.
[37] *Thomas v. Pearce,* unreported, Court of Appeal, February 10, 2000.
[38] *Bruno Tassan Din v. Banco Ambrosiano* [1991] 1 I.R. 569; *The National Justice Compania Naviera v. Prudential Assurance Co Ltd. ("The Ikarian Reefer")* [1993] 2 Lloyd's Rep. 68 at 71.

5. KNOWING RECEIPT

The law relating to knowing assistance/accessory liability has at least developed, albeit through tectonic shifts, towards a coherent concept of liability based on dishonesty, even if the application of that test has at times proved difficult in practice. Such difficulty is explicable by the invariably complex nature of the subject matter of such litigation, rather than any supposed defects in the legal tests as adumbrated in *Tan*. Furthermore, with some exceptions,[39] there appears to be judicial acceptance since *Tan*, that knowing receipt should be governed by different principles from knowing assistance.

Such coherence is utterly lacking in the case law dealing with knowing receipt. It can be gleaned from the plethora of contradictory dicta in this area that there has been fundamental disagreement as to whether (a) the law of Equity or Restitution should govern; (b) the *Baden* criteria have any role to play, and (c) if they are to feature in assessing liability, which degrees of knowledge should suffice. The rationale behind receipt-based constructive trustee liability has been (and continues to be) confused. Bryan[40] argues convincingly that "… the confusion reflects a basic tension between security of title, favouring equitable relief for the victims of fraud, and security of transaction, which protects the ultimate recipients of the proceeds of fraud if they have acted in good faith." This is indeed the source of the problem, and has contributed to the importation of property-related doctrines (such as undue influence, and the law of priorities) themselves bedevilled with inconsistency and complexity. Their influence can hardly be described as helpful.

(a) Millett *v.* Megarry

Lord Millett and Sir Robert Megarry V.-C. have disagreed with each other in fundamental terms as to the question of whether liability for knowing receipt should be dependent on an evaluation of the state of mind, or moral culpability, of the recipient at all. The view that the recipient's liability is determined upon equitable principles by analysing his probity (or lack thereof), which preserves the lineage back to *Barnes v. Addy*, has been favoured by Megarry V.-C. in *Re Montagu's Settlement*.[41] Lord Millett, on the other hand, has expressed the

---

[39] *Dubai Aluminium Co Ltd. v. Salaam* [1999] 1 Lloyd's Rep. 415: McGrath, "Knowing Receipt and Dishonest Assistance: a Wrong Turn" [2000] *L.M.C.L.Q.* 343. See also *Gertsch v. Atsas,* above, n. 24, and *Bankgesellschaft Berlin AG v. Makis,* unreported, Queen's Bench Division, Cresswell J., January 22, 1999.

[40] Bryan, "Cleaning up after breaches of fiduciary duty – the liability of banks and other financial institutions as constructive trustees" (1995) 7 *Bond. L.R.* 67 at 94.

[41] [1992] 4 All E.R. 308; [1987] Ch. 264; and by Hoffman L.J., as he then was, in *El Ajou v. Dollar Land Holdings* [1994] 1 B.C.L.C. 464; [1994] 2 All E.R. 685 (CA).

view extra-judicially[42] and judicially[43] that liability is rooted in the law of restitution. As such it is strict, in the sense that the defendant will be liable if he has been unjustly enriched at the expense of the plaintiff and is unable to establish the normal restitutionary defence available to him, i.e. that he has changed his position in reliance on the payment and without notice that the payment was made to him in breach of trust. In support of this, the Privy Council said (*obiter*) in *Royal Brunei Airlines v. Tan*[44] that liability for what used to be referred to as knowing receipt is "restitution based."

Although the recasting of knowing receipt liability in terms of a restitutionary remedy appears to import a notion of strict liability, a consideration of whether or not the defendant has the defence of change of position itself involves an investigation of whether or not the defendant was on notice that the circumstances of the payment to him were suspicious. Even the acceptance of the supposedly strict liability featured in the restitution-based approach does not avoid agonising over the defendant's state of mind, and has not even rendered obsolete pigeon-holing his or her state of mind into the *Baden* criteria.

(b) Knowing Receipt as a Non-Restitutionary Remedy

Megarry V.-C. in *Re Montagu's Settlement* held that a lack of probity, or, in other words, the first three of the *Baden* categories only, could ground liability for knowing receipt. That case concerned whether certain heirlooms held in trust for members of the Montagu family were received (and in some cases sold) by a descendant of the settlor in breach of trust. Because the recipient was not shown to have a lack of probity, particularly because the existence of the trust had apparently been forgotten by most family members, he was held not to be liable. Whatever of the shade of knowledge required to ground liability, *Montagu*, and indeed other authorities decided after *Tan*,[45] support a contention that the *Baden* criteria are still useful in a case of recipient liability.

As to the operation of this general formula, Megarry V.-C. in *Montagu* summarised the case law as follows:[46]

> "(1) The equitable doctrine of tracing and the imposition of a constructive trust by reason of the knowing receipt of trust property are governed by different rules and must be kept distinct. Tracing is primarily a means of determining the rights of property, whereas the imposition of a constructive trust creates personal obligations that go beyond mere property rights.

---

[42]"Tracing the proceeds of fraud" (1991) 107 *L.Q.R.* 71.
[43]*El Ajou v. Dollar Land Holdings* [1993] B.C.L.C. 735; [1993] 3 All E.R. 717 (Ch. D.).
[44][1995] 2 A.C. 378 at 386.
[45]*Johnathan v. Tilley,* unreported, Peter Gibson L.J., June 30, 1995.
[46]In the second portion of his judgment: [1992] 4 All E.R. 308 at 309–330.

(2) In considering whether a constructive trust has arisen in a case of the knowing receipt of trust property, the basic question is whether the conscience of the recipient is affected to justify the imposition of such a trust.

(3) Whether a constructive trust arises in such a case primarily depends on the knowledge of the recipient, and not on notice to him; and for the sake of clarity it is desirable to use the word "knowledge" and avoid the word "notice" in such cases.

(4) For this purpose, knowledge is not confined to actual knowledge, but includes at least types (ii) and (iii) Baden knowledge, i.e. actual knowledge that would have been acquired but for shutting one's eyes to the obvious or wilfully and recklessly failing to make such inquiries as a reasonable and honest man would make; for in such cases there is a want of probity which justifies imposing a constructive trust.

(5) Whether knowledge of Baden types (iv) and (v) suffices for this purpose is doubtful; in my view, it does not, for I cannot see that the carelessness involved will normally amount to a want of probity."[47]

It is of crucial importance to understand that in stating the basis for liability for knowing receipt, Megarry V.-C. indicated that such liability is personal, and not proprietary in nature. In the earlier judgment in the case he said:

"[The doctrine of purchaser without notice] is concerned with the question whether a person takes property subject to or free from some equity. [The doctrine of constructive trusteeship] is concerned with whether or not a person is to have imposed upon him the personal burdens and obligations of trusteeship. I do not see why one of the touchstones for determining the burdens on property should be the same as that for deciding whether to impose a personal obligation on a [person]. The cold calculus of constructive and imputed notice does not seem to me to be an appropriate instrument for deciding whether a [person's] conscience is sufficiently affected for it to be right to bind him by the obligations of a constructive trustee."[48]

The test for liability for knowing receipt (cast as a constructive trustee claim) was succinctly stated by Hoffman L.J. (as he then was) in *El Ajou v. Dollar Land Holdings*:[49]

---

[47]The passage continues with three more points which are not strictly relevant to this article.
[48]*Re Montagu's Settlement* [1992] 4 All E.R. 308 at 320.
[49][1994] 2 All E.R. 685 at 700.

"the plaintiff must show, first, a disposal of his assets in breach of fiduciary duty; secondly, the beneficial receipt by the defendant of assets which are traceable as representing the assets of the plaintiff; and, thirdly, knowledge on the part of the defendant that the assets he received are traceable to a breach of fiduciary duty."

The consensus among English judges who have applied the *Baden* criteria to knowing receipt liability, and some commentators,[50] is that the defendant should only be held to be liable if his state of mind falls within the first three of the criteria.[51] This contrasts with the approach of Australian courts, where it has been held that liability can be imposed on the basis of the first four (and possibly the fifth) of the *Baden* criteria,[52] and of the New Zealand courts, where it has been held that liability can be imposed on the basis of *any* of the *Baden* criteria.[53]

(c) Knowing Receipt Liability as a Restitutionary Remedy

Lord Millett has contended that liability for knowing receipt, on the one hand, and what has now become to be known as "accessory liability", on the other, are and should be kept distinct. As a judge in the Chancery Division of the High Court, Millett J. said this in *Agip Africa*:[54]

"The basis of liability in the two types of cases is quite different; there is no good reason why the knowledge required should be the same, and good reason why it should not. Tracing claims and cases of 'knowing receipt' are both concerned with rights of priority in relation to property taken by a legal owner for his own benefit; cases of 'knowing assistance' are concerned with the furtherance of fraud."

Millett J. expanded on this in his judgment at first instance in *El Ajou v. Dollar Land Holdings plc*:[55]

"The plaintiff seeks a personal remedy based on 'knowing receipt'. As I have previously pointed out, this is the counterpart in equity of the common law claim for money had and received. The latter, at least, is a receipt-based claim to restitution, and the cause of action is complete when the money is received."

---

[50] Oakley, *op. cit.*, above, n. 4, p. 239.
[51] *Eagle Trust plc v. SBC Securities Limited* [1992] 4 All E.R. 488.
[52] *Equitcorp Finance v. Bank of New Zealand* [1993] N.S.W.L.R. 50.
[53] *Equiticorp Group v. Attorney-General* [1996] 3 N.Z.L.R. 586.
[54] [1990] Ch. 265 at 292-293.
[55] [1993] 3 All E.R. 717 at 738.

It follows that if receipt-based liability is personal and not proprietary, then it is of no assistance *per se* where the defendant recipient is insolvent and accordingly unable to satisfy a personal judgment against it, and where a tracing remedy (or process)[56] is unavailable. In addition, as the right to trace in equity will depend on the *conscience* of the recipient,[57] a plaintiff seeking to assert a proprietary remedy against its defendant will have, in any event, to prove that the receipt by the defendant of the plaintiff's assets was unconscionable in the accepted sense of that word. It is well established that in order to be granted a remedy in restitution it is necessary for the plaintiff to prove that the defendant has been unjustly enriched at the plaintiff's expense, and that the defendant has no established defence under the law of restitution – principally, the defence of change of position.[58] Even in the context of change of position, whether the defendant can claim the defence of change of position depends on the absence of notice of facts giving rise to the plaintiff's claim.[59] Accordingly, to formulate knowing receipt liability as "strict" in this sense, is perhaps to unfairly raise hopes that by doing so one can avoid the agonising process of identifying the point on the moral spectrum occupied by the defendant.

Oakley points out:[60]

"… it is clear that a defaulting fiduciary will never be able to use the defence of change of position since he cannot have acted in good faith; consequently a constructive trustee will never be able to invoke this defence as against the constructive beneficiary."

This is perhaps to beg the question, as a person acting in good faith would not (in general) be classified as a constructive trustee in the first place. However, quite apart from the (to date) uncertainties involved in the defence,[61] it is clear that an evaluation of the availability of the defence of change of position is going to involve analysis of the bona fides (probity) of the defendant.

A consideration of two recent cases from the state of Victoria, in Australia, indicates that even if one classifies receipt liability as an element of restitution, the defendant's state of mind is highly relevant, and a commercial-moral evaluation of it is necessary.[62] Both cases involved the fraudulent pledging by a trustee in favour of a bank of trust assets without authorisation as security for personal borrowings by the trustee. Both cases also involved a consideration of the effect, under the Australian Torrens system of land registration, of knowing

---

[56] *Per* Millett L.J. in *Boscawen v. Bajwa* [1995] 4 All E.R. 769 at 776.
[57] *Westdeutsche Landesbank v. Islington London Borough Council* [1996] A.C. 669.
[58] *Lipkin Gorman v. Karpnale* [1991] 2 A.C. 548 at 579.
[59] *ibid.*
[60] *op. cit.,* above, n.4, p. 15.
[61] *South Tyneside Metropolitan B.C. v. Svenska International* [1995] 1 All E.R. 545.
[62] So much was predicted by Gardner, *loc. cit.,* above, n.4 at p. 90.

receipt on the otherwise indefeasible title to the registered holder of an interest in land. In each case the bank was registered as mortgagee and it was argued that its state of knowledge as to the trustee's lack of authority operated to deprive it of title under the land registration system. While an analysis of this aspect of the cases is beyond the scope of this article, it does, perhaps, highlight the issues which potentially arise where receipt liability is classified as proprietary rather than personal.

The first case is *Koorootang Nominees Pty Ltd. v Australia and New Zealand Banking Group Ltd.*[63] This was a meticulous judgment of Hansen J. in the Supreme Court of Victoria. Hansen J. said this:[64]

> "A question which naturally arises if one adopts the view that recipient liability is strict but subject to defences is the level of knowledge which disentitles a defendant from a restitutionary defence. In other words, is constructive knowledge (or, if there be a difference, constructive notice) of the plaintiff's interest sufficient to disentitle a defendant from successfully arguing that he is a bona fide purchaser of the legal title of the legal estate for value without notice or that he detrimentally changed his position on the faith of the receipt? How should 'constructive knowledge' be defined for this purpose?"

Hansen J. then applied the law of priorities to determine whether or not the interest of the bank, as registered mortgagee, had priority over those of the beneficiaries of the trust. He held that the bank did not enjoy such priority, in the circumstances, and, furthermore, the beneficiaries' interest overrode the otherwise indefeasible title of the bank under the land registration system.

The second case is *Macquarie Bank Ltd v. Sixty-Fourth Throne Pty Ltd,*[65] a case turning on broadly similar facts to those in *Koorootang*. However, the Court of Appeal of the Supreme Court of Victoria distinguished *Koorootang*. The Court of Appeal reversed the trial judge who had held that the bank had obtained its mortgage with such a state of mind that its interests were to be deemed to be inferior to those of the trust beneficiaries. In doing so, the Court of Appeal rejected the beneficiaries' argument that the principles as to notice of equitable interests as expounded by the House of Lords in *Barclays Bank plc v. O'Brien*[66] had no role to play in the analysis of recipient liability. Given that receipt liability was increasingly characterised as property based, there was considerable logic in the plaintiff's analogy with the doctrine of notice as developed in *O'Brien*. The Court of Appeal was forced to distinguish *O'Brien*

---

[63] [1998] 3 V.R. 16.
[64] *ibid.* at 103.
[65] [1998] 3 V.R. 133.
[66] [1994] 1 A.C. 180.

on the basis that the system of land registration in the UK is different to that applicable in Australia.

The point of referring to these cases is to highlight the inherent uncertainty of the restitution – proprietary liability approach. Like *Montagu*, applying the law of restitution also involves consideration of the probity of the recipient. Moreover, the restitution approach raises more questions than it answers. It is unclear what role the change of position defence plays in the context of receipt liability.[67] Is the defendant's state of mind to be evaluated as at the time of receipt, or as at the time of alleged change of position? It is clear that in the search for a standard by which the defendant's state of mind can be evaluated, resort is often had to complex and unpredictable aspects of the law relating to the hierarchy of proprietary interests such as the doctrines of priorities and of undue influence.

In summary, therefore, it is submitted that the role of the law of restitution, as characterised as a form of strict proprietary liability, is currently of uncertain benefit. It is perhaps because of this that the Court of Appeal in England and Wales recently took the opportunity to affirm the Megarry approach.

6. KNOWING RECEIPT – RECENT DEVELOPMENTS

BCCI v. Akindele[68] concerned a claim in the liquidation of Bank of Credit and Commerce International ("BCCI") against a Mr. A, who was alleged by the liquidators of BCCI to have received monies from BCCI in circumstances where he ought to have known that such monies were paid to him in breach of trust or fiduciary duty. The circumstances were, in summary, that Mr. A entered into a contract with BCCI whereby in consideration of a down-payment of US$10 million, A would obtain an interest in shares in BCCI, which he then had the option of selling within two to five years after the date of the contract. The attraction of the transaction was that it guaranteed a return on Mr. A's investment of 15 per cent – which the liquidators argued was an unusually high one to be offered at the time. Secondly, Mr. A never obtained an actual transfer of the shares, which were intended to remain in the names of the existing holders. The liquidators argued that these unusual features of the transaction were sufficient to render Mr. A liable for knowing receipt. The liquidators also alleged that the transaction was a "sham", and was merely designed to provide BCCI with temporary liquidity to satisfy an urgent requirement to prop up its balance

---

[67] Or, as Gardner puts it, (*loc. cit.*, n.4 at p. 87) the defence of change of position and bona fide purchaser for value may have a "purity too refined for the realities of life."

[68] [2000] 4 All E.R. 221. The judgment at first instance was given by Carnwath J. and is reported at [1999] B.C.C. 669.

sheet so as to meet regulatory capital requirements.[69]

The claim that the transaction was a sham was rejected by the trial judge and this was affirmed by the Court of Appeal. Furthermore, the trial judge, and the Court of Appeal rejected the liquidator's contention that, in the circumstances, Mr. A could be fixed with liability for knowing receipt. It held that dishonesty is not an essential ingredient for liability for knowing receipt.[70] The Court of Appeal preferred the reasoning of Megarry V.-C. in *Montagu*, as the solution to the issue, describing it as "seminal". Nourse L.J. summarised Megarry V.-C.'s decision as follows:

> "in order to establish liability in knowing receipt, the recipient must have actual knowledge (or the equivalent) that the assets received are traceable to a breach of trust and that constructive knowledge is not enough."[71]

It is not, however, clear what the difference is between the "equivalent" of actual knowledge, and "constructive knowledge". Nonetheless, the gravamen of Megarry V.-C.'s analysis of the basis for liability is that the conscience of the recipient should be affected – and this is, perhaps, and with respect, a preferable way of summarising *Montagu*.

With regard to the *Baden* categorisation, Nourse L.J. concluded that he had "grave doubts" as to its utility in cases of knowing receipt. It serves no purpose, he held, in determining whether the recipient's conscience was affected or not. He concluded:

> "For these reasons I have come to the view that, just as there is now a single test of dishonesty for knowing assistance, so ought there to be a single test of knowledge for knowing receipt. The recipient's state of knowledge must be such as to make it unconscionable for him to retain the benefit of the receipt. A test in that form, though it cannot, any more than any other, avoid difficulties of application, ought to avoid those of definition and allocation to which the previous categorisations have led. Moreover, it should better enable the courts to give common-sense decisions in the commercial context in which claims in knowing receipt are now frequently made. ..."[72]

---

[69] See Breslin *op. cit.,* above, n.2, chapter 5.

[70] *Belmont Finance Corporation. v. Williams Furniture Ltd. (No 2)* [1980] 1 All E.R. 393, which has been followed by the Irish Supreme Court in *In re Frederick Inns Ltd.* [1994] 1 I.L.R.M. 387. Nourse L.J. also indicated the importance of *Belmont Finance* in *Houghton v. Fayers* [2000] 1 B.C.L.C. 511.

[71] *BCCI v. Akindele* [2000] 4 All E.R. 221 at 234.

[72] *ibid.* at 235–236.

Nourse L.J. also made reference to the restitutionary theory of liability – *i.e.* strict liability subject to a change of position defence. He rejected the "strict" theory of restitutionary liability. It ignored questions of ostensible authority, which, he implied a recipient should be permitted to call in aid. Furthermore, if the circumstances were such that it was unconscionable for the defendant to retain the benefit, it would not necessarily be correct to permit the defendant none the less to avail of a defence of change of position. In his "footnote" to the judgment in *Akindele* he said as follows:[73]

> "I beg leave to doubt whether strict liability coupled with a change of position defence would be preferable to fault-based liability in many commercial transactions, for example where, as here, the receipt is of a company's funds which have been misapplied by its directors. Without having heard argument it is unwise to be dogmatic, but in such a case it would appear to be commercially unworkable and contrary to the spirit of *Royal British Bank v. Turquand* (1856) 6 E. & B. 327 that, simply on proof of an internal misapplication of the company's funds, the burden should shift to the recipient to defend the receipt either by a change of position or perhaps in some other way. Moreover, if the circumstances of the receipt are such as to make it unconscionable for the recipient to retain the benefit of it, there is an obvious difficulty in saying that it is equitable for a change of position to afford him a defence."

While these comments might be subject to criticism by advocates of the restitutionary approach as proceeding upon an assumption that the Megarry V.-C. approach is intrinsically correct, it is nonetheless submitted that they represent cogent arguments as to why, at its current stage of development at least, the change of defence position is not ready for the task it would have to meet in the context of receipt-based liability. Furthermore, the change of position defence provides little guidance for a trial judge upon whom it falls to resolve a knowing receipt issue. And if the change of position defence is applied so the defendant's state of mind can be evaluated in a property-based context, one must question the role to be played by these proprietary doctrines in the context of liability which is personal in nature. Inevitably, as pointed out by *Bryan*,[74] this will lead to tension between upholding commercial certainty and the protection of property rights.

---

[73] *BCCI v. Akindele* [2000] 4 All E.R. 221 at 236.
[74] Bryan, *op. cit.*, above, n.40.

7. Conclusions

Such is the volume of case law on constructive trusteeship, evaluation of which jurisdictions and courts apply particular elements of the *Baden* criteria has become an arid statistical exercise that provides no meaningful assistance either to the judge or to the adviser.[75] Analysis of case law in this area, it could be argued, merely foments confusion, inconsistency and unpredictability.

Restitution has not proved the saviour from the over-complexities of the law of Equity than one would first have hoped for, in spite of its characterisation of liability as "strict".[76] Indeed, the application of the law of restitution appears necessarily to involve the same process of analysis of state of mind as required under the old equitable approach. So while the law of restitution might commence the journey from a different station, it soon joins the tracks of the law of Equity at the crucial point of deciding the liability issue. Furthermore, the proprietary anchor of the restitutionary analysis potentially entails the importation of concepts from the law of priorities and the law of undue influence. These principles are, it is submitted, a distraction from the judge's task in hand.

In the face of the welter of case law on this topic it is perhaps natural to suppose that statutory intervention might provide an escape from the quagmire of conceptual over-complexity. After all, at least as far as Irish law is concerned, not only has statute provided for a basis for what was the former equitable liability of receivers,[77] but also the fiduciary duties of company insiders have been given statutory sanction through the provisions of Irish law which outlaw insider dealing.[78] Furthermore, through the provisions which outlaw money laundering[79] the legislature has defined the *mens reus* for criminal accessory liability. In brief, the defendant will be taken to have known the illegal source of funds which he has laundered if a reasonable person would have so concluded – subject to a reasonable doubt level of proof. However, the reduction of equitable principles to statutory form in the context of constructive trusteeship would be a momentous task, and perhaps ultimately an undesirable one, given the various types of constructive trust which exist.[80]

Undoubtedly the solution lies in simplicity. This has been achieved for accessory liability, through the opinion of the Privy Council in *Tan*. It is submitted that such simplicity, for knowing receipt, is equally found in Megarry V.-C.'s

---

[75] Although, for an effective and accessible presentation of this data see Oakley, *op. cit.,* above, n.4, pp. 198-200 (accessory liability) and 222-238 (knowing receipt).

[76] It is notable that the fifth edition of Goff and Jones, *Law of Restitution* (5th ed., London, 1998) classifies knowing receipt under the heading "Where the defendant has acquired a benefit through his own wrongful act".

[77] s. 316A of the Companies Act 1963: see n. 2 above.

[78] s. 109 of the Companies Act 1990.

[79] s. 31 of the Criminal Justice Act 1994, particularly subs. (6), (7) and (8).

[80] See, generally, Oakley, *op. cit.,* above, n.4.

approach in *Montagu*, and that of Nourse L.J. in *Akindele*. While the purportedly "strict" liability in restitution had the attraction of potentially circumventing the dismemberment of the defendant's state of mind, such attraction is illusory. An evaluation of the defendant's state of mind cannot be avoided, particularly when receipt liability is personal rather than proprietary. The role sought for the law of restitution in this area is, at the moment at least, too great for the change of position defence to bear. In any event, whilst it might be argued that the change of position defence is inherently flexible so as to accommodate the application of a *Montagu* styled evaluation of liability, it is submitted that the latter test performs the necessary function well enough and equips the trial judge with the necessary tools to do justice, in a coherent, principled and (relatively) predictable manner.

PART PERFORMANCE LIVES!

JOHN F. BUCKLEY

Jim Brady was primarily a great teacher. Of course he wrote, or co-wrote, some of the best Irish law books of recent years,[1] and was a major contributor to the Law Reform Commission's various reports on Land Law and Conveyancing but it is as a teacher of several generations of law students that he will be best remembered. My daughter, who was a student in the last undergraduate class that Jim taught, told me recently that as she was writing a sentence in answering an examination last summer she could hear Jim saying the words. He was no stuffy academic; as we waited for the members of the Law Reform Commission's Working Group to assemble there were only two topics of conversation, rugby and the latest interesting decision from the superior courts – in that order.

Every Equity textbook begins by explaining that Equity arose as a parallel system of law, operated by the Courts of Chancery, to ameliorate the harshness of the common law. Increasingly the harshness arose not only from the decisions of the common law judges but from the inflexibility of statute law. The struggle between the "black letter" lawyers who believe that precision in the law is all that is required and that certainty and predictability are achievable by skilled draftsmanship, and those other lawyers who believe that human fallibility extends to the makers of law, be they judges or legislators (in fact legislative draftsmen), continues to this day.

The doctrine of part performance was applied in the case of *Hollis v. Edwards*[2] within six years of the passing of the Statute of Frauds in England in 1677 (1695 in Ireland) and had continued to be applied in the English courts until its apparent abolition, certainly in so far as agreements for the sale of interests in land are concerned, by the Law of Property (Miscellaneous Provisions) Act 1989 which in section 2(1) provided that:

> "A contract for the sale or other disposition of an interest in land can only be made in writing, and only by incorporating all the terms which the parties have expressly agreed in one document, or where contracts are being exchanged, in each."

---

[1] *Religion and the Law of Charities in Ireland* (Belfast, 1975); *Succession Law in Ireland* (1st ed., Dublin, 1989; 2nd ed., Dublin, 1995); and with Anthony Kerr, *Limitation of Actions in the Republic of Ireland* (1st ed., Dublin, 1984; 2nd ed., Dublin, 1994).

[2] (1683) 1 Vern 189.

Section 2(8) provided that "Section 40 of the Law of Property Act 1925 (which is superseded by this section) shall cease to have effect." Section 40(2) of the 1925 Act had provided that "[t]his section applies to contracts whether made before or after the commencement of this Act and does not affect the law relating to part performance, or sales by the court."

The previous law which originated in the English Statute of Frauds only required that some written evidence of a contract be available. At the time of the passing of the statute neither the parties to an action nor anyone with an interest in the outcome of the action were competent witnesses. All of these became competent under nineteenth century legislation. Because of these changes the English Law Commission, in its 1987 Report, which led to the passing of the 1989 Act, considered the possibility of simply repealing section 40 of the Law of Property Act 1925, into which the 1677 Act had largely been transformed, but found no support for this view.[3] The Commission's alternative was to go to the other extreme and recommend that, instead of a requirement that contracts for the sale of land should be evidenced in writing, they should only be made in writing.

Its draft Bill had provided a more flexible form of wording than that used in the 1989 Act, and would probably have avoided the difficulties caused in the cases of *Commission for the New Towns v. Cooper (Great Britain) Ltd*[4] and *McCausland v. Duncan Lawrie*[5] where it was respectively held that contracts for the sale of an interest in land could not be made, or varied, in correspondence. It is far from clear that the 1989 Act cannot be used as an instrument of fraud and the ancillary abolition of the doctrine of part performance, generally perceived to have been effected by section 2(8) of the 1989 Act, is an example of the triumph of hope over experience.[6]

The Law Commission had commenced its study of the subject as a result of the uncertainty created by two conflicting Court of Appeal decisions, *Law v. Jones*[7] and *Tiverton v. Wearwell*.[8] In this jurisdiction similar difficulties arose and might have been thought to have been resolved by the Supreme Court's decisions in *Kelly v. Park Hall School*[9] and *Casey v. Irish Intercontinental Bank*,[10] particularly as applied by Keane J. in *Mulhall v. Haren*.[11] Both the

---

[3] English Law Commission, *The Transfer of Land: Formalities for Contracts for Sale etc. of Land* (1987) Law Com. No. 164.
[4] [1995] Ch. 259.
[5] [1997] 1 W.L.R. 38.
[6] In this respect see Davis, "Estoppel: An Adequate Substitute for Part Performance?" (1993) 13 *Oxford Journal of Legal Studies* 99, and Bently and Coughlan, "Proprietary Estoppel and Part Performance: Historical Confusion or Modern Dilemma?" (1988) 23 *Irish Jurist (ns)* 38.
[7] [1974] Ch. 112.
[8] [1975] Ch. 146.
[9] [1979] I.R. 340.
[10] [1979] I.R. 364.
[11] [1981] I.R. 364.

Park Hall and *Casey* cases were judgments of three-judge courts only, though two of the three judges, Kenny and Parke JJ., had been leading Chancery lawyers (the third being Henchy J.). It was therefore open to a five-judge court to review the issues of "subject to contract" and the "note or memorandum in writing" and so it did in *Boyle v. Lee & Goyns.*[12] It is in many ways an unsatisfactory judgment, exemplifying the confusion that can arise where a number of judges deliver separate judgments and (as they did in this case) do not agree with one another on all of the issues. Three of the five judges found that there was no oral agreement and went on to say that even if there had been there was no note or memorandum in writing of such agreement sufficient to satisfy the statute.[13] A strict view of the judgments in this case would be that the necessary *ratio decidendi* was that there was no oral agreement and that the comments on the note or memorandum in writing were *obiter dicta* and that the "subject to contract" issue may not be finally buried in this jurisdiction and may arise again in a case in which there clearly was an oral or partly oral and partly written agreement. Even if *Boyle v. Lee & Goyns*[14] has decided the "subject to contract" issue definitively, it was not a "part performance" case and that doctrine may still be available to the parties to an oral contract.

The principle upon which the courts of Equity developed the doctrine of part performance was that a court should not permit a statute to be used as an instrument of fraud. The Statute of Frauds, enacted in Ireland in 1695 provided that:

> "no action could be brought whereby to charge . . . any person ... upon any contract or sale of lands, tenements or hereditaments, or any interest in or concerning them . . . unless the agreement upon which such action shall be brought, or some memorandum or note thereof shall be in writing and signed by the party to be charged therewith, or some other person thereunto by him lawfully authorised."

The evil which this Act was intended to counter was the allegation by dishonest persons that an agreement to sell an interest in land had been reached. In an era when writing would largely have been the prerogative of a small class in society many contacts for the sale of interests in land would have been made verbally, and the existence of any agreement to sell land would depend on the verbal evidence available to the court, which of course excluded the parties to the alleged contract. The requirement that some written evidence of the exist-

---

[12][1992] 1 I.R. 555.
[13]Finlay C.J., O'Flaherty J. and Hederman J., concurring. McCarthy and Egan JJ. dissented in part, holding that a concluded oral agreement existed here but concurred with the majority in the finding that the proffered note or memorandum was insufficient to satisfy the Statute of Frauds 1695.
[14]See n.12, above.

ence of the agreement be available to the court was intended to remove the risk of third parties "swearing up" about alleged agreements.

The downside of the statute was that, if there were no written evidence of an agreement, the common law courts could not entertain any action to enforce it, or for damages for breach of it. The Chancery courts, implementing the principle that persons should not be able to avoid liability to perform an agreement which they had reached, simply because there was not the written evidence required by the statute, were prepared to accept collateral evidence in writing of the existence of the contract. That collateral evidence must show that "the party seeking relief has been put into a situation which makes it against conscience for the other party to insist on the want of writing so signed, as a bar to his relief."

The collateral evidence must establish that the plaintiff has an equity arising from part performance which in the words of Andrews L.J. in *Lowry v. Reid*[15] is "so affixed to the conscience of the defendant that it would amount to fraud on his part to take advantage of the absence of writing." Where a court is satisfied that there was an agreement for the sale of land and the purchaser having, to the knowledge of the vendor, taken steps which would only have been taken in the belief that there was a binding agreement, and the vendor, for reasons unconnected with the purchaser, decides to call off the transaction, it may well decide to hold that the vendor is bound under the doctrine of part performance.[16]

Such an option is no longer available to the English courts, who must now perforce rely on the doctrine of estoppel as in the case of *Yaxley v. Gotts*,[17] in which the Court of Appeal affirmed that the doctrine of estoppel is relevant to a situation where the parties have concluded an oral agreement. It is interesting that one of the judges, Beldam L.J., was chairman of the Law Commission at the time of the making of the 1987 Report.

However strong the arguments for altering the requirements for the enforceability of a contract from evidential to formal may be, those put forward by the Law Commission for the abolition of the doctrine of part performance are not compelling, and may not be relevant in this jurisdiction. The Commission's Working Paper[18] suggested that the case of *Steadman v. Steadman*[19]

---

[15] [1927] N.I. 142 at 154-155.

[16] One of the most common situations in which the doctrine is invoked in Ireland is where a promise is made by an elderly farmer to a younger person, usually a relative, that in consideration of the young person working on the land the farmer will devise the land to the younger person. This situation came before the Supreme Court in *McCarron v. McCarron*, unreported, Supreme Court, February 13, 1997.

[17] [2000] 1 All E.R. 711.

[18] Law Commission, *Transfer of Land, Formalities for Contracts for Sale etc. of Land* (Working Paper 92), at paras. 2.12 – 2.17.

[19] [1976] A.C. 536.

amounted to a judicial repeal by the House of Lords of section 40(1) of the 1925 Act. The Commission's report has a somewhat circular argument, namely that if a contract has to be in the form of writing and there is no such writing, there cannot be a contract of which there could be part performance, so part performance must necessarily disappear.

In the two Statutes of Frauds and the 1925 Act the word used is "agreement" to describe the consensus between the parties and it is suggested that only when the consensus was appropriately evidenced in writing, or was implemented by a sufficient act of part performance was it proper to apply the word "contract" to it. The Law Commission's draft Bill abandoned the word "agreement" and by saying that "[n]o contract . . . shall come into being unless the contract is in writing and all the express terms of the contract. . . ." and repeating the word "contract" throughout the draft appeared to subscribe to the Gertrude Stein school of definitions. Whatever else the legislators may have got wrong, they sensibly used the word "agree" in the passage "all the terms which the parties have expressly agreed" in section 2(1) of the 1989 Act. This recognised that agreement on the terms was highly likely to have been reached orally or, in writing not sufficient to comply with the Act, or partly orally and partly in writing. It is not at all clear why the doctrine of part performance could not have been permitted to survive so as to avoid the 1989 Act being made an instrument of fraud in situations where there was a clear agreement which one of the parties then refuses to put into the form required by the statute, and the other has engaged in acts of part performance.

Steadman, the Law Commission's bête noire, was first considered in the Irish courts in *Howlin v. Power*,[20] a judgment of McWilliam J., but only in respect of the issue whether the payment of money could be a sufficient act of part performance. Prior to *Steadman v. Steadman*[21] it had not been considered to be such. McWilliam J. referred to the circumstances of the *Steadman* case as "unusual" and accepted that there were circumstances in which the payment of money could be a sufficient act of part performance. He did not adopt any other aspect of the House of Lords judgment. No subsequent Irish case has taken a position which could be described as a judicial repeal of the statute. Indeed all recent Irish decisions treat *Lowry v. Reid*[22] as the leading Irish case on part performance.[23] In the majority of them the court held that there were not sufficient acts of part performance to establish a binding contract. Arguments are put forward from time to time that section 4 of the Statute of Frauds should be amended or replaced with an equivalent of the 1989 Act; indeed such an argument was made by one of the judges in *Boyle v. Lee and Goyns*.[24]

[20] Unreported, High Court, McWilliam J., May 5,1978.
[21] *Steadman v. Steadman*, above, n.19.
[22] [1927] N.I. 142.
[23] See, for instance, the Supreme Court decision in *Mackey v. Wilde* [1998] 1 I.L.R.M. 449.
[24] See the comments of O'Flaherty J. in Boyle above, n. 12, at 589.

The golden rule of law reform should be "if it ain't broke don't fix it", if only because there is ample evidence around that "fixing" has only made things worse. Abolishing the doctrine of part performance would be a fine example of unnecessary law reform. To cast us all afloat on the uncertain seas of promissory estoppel and constructive trusts when we have a strong jurisprudence, best exemplified by *Lowry v. Reid*, in part performance, would be foolish indeed.

The Court of Appeal in *Yaxley v Gotts*[25] considered that the difficult doctrines of proprietary estoppel and constructive trusts could be applied in appropriate cases where section 2 of the 1989 Act had not been complied with. Courts might well be happier to have part performance available to them. Irish courts are not limited by statutory limitations on the use of the doctrine of part performance and should, where appropriate, continue to make use of their freedom to invoke it.

---

[25] *Yaxley v. Gotts*, above, n.17.

ASSIGNMENT OF DEBTS AND THE RULE IN *DEARLE v. HALL*: THE JOURNEY FROM EQUITY TO LAW – AND BACK AGAIN

DERMOT CAHILL

1. INTRODUCTION

Dearle v. Hall[1] concerned a dispute between assignees, each of whom claimed to be the assignee that was rightfully entitled over the other to receive an annual payment of a sum of money payable out of a trust fund set up in a deceased's will. The right to receive the entitlement had been assigned by the beneficiary, one Zachariah Brown, to each assignee in turn (three in all), without notice of the other's interest. When first reading the case, it appears to be confined to resolving a dispute between competing *equitable* assignees in dispute over who had the right to be regarded as the assignee with the superior right to receive an equitable chose in action (an annuity out of a fund): one side arguing for priority on the grounds that their interest in the fund came into being first-in-time, as against the other side arguing for priority on account of having been the first to have notified their interest in the fund to the executors/trustees of the fund.

However, in modern times, the case has assumed a far wider significance. Although, at the time *Dearle v. Hall* was heard (the 1820s) the enforcement of assignments of debt was freely facilitated at Equity, it was not until 1877 with the adoption of the Supreme Court of Judicature (Ireland) Act (following on from the 1873 English equivalent)[2] that the law readily facilitated the enforcement of such assignments.[3] Apart from creating a new High Court of Justice in

---

[1] (1823) 3 Russ. 1, Sir Thomas Plumer M.R.; and affirmed on appeal by Lyndhurst L.C., 3 Russ 56; also reported at [1824–1834] All E.R. 28.

[2] Supreme Court of Judicature (Ireland) Act 1877 (40 & 41 Vict., chap. 57), s. 28(6). The UK equivalent is to be found in the Supreme Court of Judicature Act 1873, (36 & 37 Vict.) s. 25(6), which was subsequently replaced (with some minor changes) by the Law of Property Act 1925 (15 Geo. 5) chap 20, s. 136(1).

[3] Although it is conceded that the enforcement of assignment of debts at Law was increasingly accepted in the nineteenth century, nevertheless, it was not until the adoption of the 1877 Act (1873 in the case of England) that the assignee could sue the debtor directly without having to join the assignor: before that assignees had to resort to use of the fiction of joining the assignor as a party to the action (thereby maintaining the fiction that it was the actual original (assignor) creditor who was suing to recover, rather than the assignee).

which Law and Equity could be disbursed, both Judicature Acts provided a set of criteria which facilitated the assignee to enforce the assignment of debt at Law.[4] *Inter alia,* the form of wording used by the Judicature Acts to so provide transplanted the reasoning underlying the judgment in *Dearle v. Hall* (developed for resolving priority disputes between competing *equitable* assignees of an interest under a will) into the wider arena of solving priority disputes between competing equitable assignees (of debt) *and* assignees at law (of debt).[5] In this regard therefore, *Dearle v. Hall's* applicability was extended, as not only did it continue to apply as originally devised (to determine priority between competing equitable assignees of a chose in action) but now its application was extended to the determination of priority as between competing equitable assignees and assignees at law of a chose in action.

This development has been of particular significance in the world of corporate finance where companies typically assign their book debts to debt factors in order to raise finance. Where a company seeks to assign its book debts to a debt factor in order to raise such finance, the principles emanating from *Dearle v. Hall* shall be to the forefront of the debt factor's mind. Debt factors are painfully aware of the central importance of the principles that emanate out of this early nineteenth century judgment that centred around the resolution of a dispute between assignees fooled by a knave who was the beneficiary under a will. This is because, in debt factoring, all hinges around the importance of the giving of notice, just as it did in *Dearle v. Hall*. A major concern for the debt factor (*i.e.,* the assignee) is whether the factor has priority to the debt, or whether earlier equitable assignees of the same debt (such as other assignees (*e.g.,* other factors) have already given notice of their equitable interest to the debtor.[6] This is an issue which causes serious difficulties in the world of debt factoring and corporate finance. Priority determination is determined to this day by the rule in *Dearle v. Hall*, a rule which concerned competing assignments of equi-

---

[4] Using very similar wording: s. 25(6) in the case of the 1873 Act, and s. 28(6) in the case of the 1877 Act, respectively (see n. 2 above, and see further below at nn. 16 and 20 where the actual wording of both s. 28(6) and the replacement of s. 25(6), s. 136(1) of the Law of Property Act 1925, are set out in full).

[5] As applied in the case of the U.K. equivalent of s. 28(6), s. 25(6) Supreme Court of Judicature Act 1873 in *Marchant v. Morton Down* [1901] 2 K.B. 829 and its replacement, s. 136(1) Law of Property Act 1825 *per* Philips J. in *Pfeiffer Weinkellerei v. Arbuthnot Factors Ltd.* [1988] 1 W.L.R. 150; and *per* Mummery J. in *Compaq Computer Ltd. v. Abercorn Group Ltd.* [1991] B.C.C. 484 (though as shall be noted later below, not all commentators agree with the transplanting of *Dearle v. Hall,* or the reasoning used to so justify it, in these judgments).

[6] Apart altogether from being concerned as to whether other prior equities integral to the debt itself exist, such as the right of set-off: in *International (Factors) Ireland Ltd. v. Midland International Ltd.,* unreported, High Court, December 9, 1993, Lynch J. held that a debtor was entitled to counterclaim for damages against the factor (who was seeking payment from the debtor) as the debtor alleged that the contract goods supplied by the assignor were defective at the time of their delivery to the debtor: hence, the debtor was entitled to exercise a right of set-off as against the new owner of the contract debt, the assignee factor.

table interests under a will – and which now since the enactment of the 1873/ 1877 Acts has been transplanted into the arena of corporate finance and is used to resolve priority disputes between competing equitable and legal assignments of the same debt. This progression is but one example of the manner in which Equity continues to play as great a role as ever in an area that has now been adopted, as its own, by Law.[7]

Or as the esteemed late Professor Brady would say, "Equity and Law, bedfellows to the bitter end!" Before considering *Dearle v. Hall* any further, I wish to be allowed to record my appreciation of Professor James Brady. I first met Jim when I was being interviewed for appointment in UCD. To say our first encounter at that interview board was "combative" would be an understatement! Evidently it worked however, and over the following years I got to know him better. In particular, I admired the dedication he had, particularly for his students, in ensuring that Equity should always be part of the arsenal of the well-rounded lawyer, whether academic or practitioner. One of the last times that I had the pleasure of his company was at the Law Society during an Examiners' Lunch, held after a Solicitors' Entrance Examination exam board meeting. During that lunch, Jim regaled all with tales and legal yarns. I could see the esteem in which he was held, and how much he enjoyed his work. At table, the discussion centred on the relevance of including Equity as a subject in the modern academic curriculum. One thing he said to me on that occasion has stuck with me ever since and indeed formed the gem of an idea for this piece. He said, "whichever of them came first (historically), the funny thing you'll find with Law, is that you keep having to return to the well of Equity, time and again."

These observations by the esteemed late Professor provide an appropriate point of departure. Until the merger of Law and Equity in the High Court of Justice brought about by the adoption of section 27 of the Supreme Court of Judicature (Ireland) Act 1877 (whereby a new High Court of Justice was created which had both Common Law and Equitable jurisdiction) the Law and Equity distinction meant that, subject to certain limited instances, the Common Law courts would not readily give effect to *assignments of choses in action* whereas the courts of Equity had no such difficulty giving effect to assignments of many (though not all) *choses in action*.[8] Unlike the Chancery courts,

---

[7] Though not all commentators would agree that *Dearle v. Hall* should be given such extension. See further below.

[8] This difficulty was greatest in the case of assignments of non-negotiable forms of debt, though it must be conceded that even before 1877 the Common Law courts increasingly were facilitating enforcement of debt assignments (see for example the *dicta* of Cozens-Hardy J. in *Fitzroy v. Cave* [1905] 2 K.B. 364 where it was pointed out at 372 that the Common Law courts had in the nineteenth century begun to allow the assignee to sue the debtor in the name of the creditor), nevertheless, historically, the general position had been that until the nineteenth century, the Law and Equity distinction meant that, subject to certain limited instances, the Common Law

the Common Law courts had great conceptual difficulty in giving effect to assignments of debt. The Common Law had difficulty dealing with *intangible* property such as debts other than by purely enforcing the debt in favour of the original creditor. Thus, courts of Common Law would not readily recognise claims to enforce the assignment of a debt by an assignee because it considered the debt to be personal in nature, *i.e.*, personal as between debtor and creditor and no other party. To permit a third party (the assignee) to enforce against the debtor, what was before the purported assignment the personal right of another (the creditor assignor), was not considered palatable by the courts of Common Law.

However, Equity had no such qualms in enforcing assignments of debt. The report of *Dearle v. Hall*[9] indicates a court setting out principle whereby Equity resolved a priority dispute as between two assignees,[10] each of whom were claiming to be the rightful assignee of what was effectively a debt, a sum due by way of equitable assignment of an interest arising out of a trust set up under a will. All centred around the giving of notice to the executors (effectively the "debtor") and so some consideration of the facts of *Dearle v. Hall* is required in order to appreciate how the giving of notice is an important starting point in Equity, before proceeding to see how it is equally important in Law even after the adoption of the two Supreme Court of Judicature Acts 1873, and 1877, respectively.

2. *DEARLE V. HALL* – BACKGROUND

In *Dearle v. Hall*, Zachariah Brown, a beneficiary under his father's will, was to receive annual dividends from a trust which was set up following the implementation of instructions contained in the deceased's will. Brown's right to receive the dividends was an equitable *chose in action*, as the legal title remained vested in the executors/trustees. Brown assigned his equitable right to benefit to Dearle, but neither party gave notice to the executors/trustees of this transaction. Subsequently, Brown assigned his right to Shering, but again neither party gave notice to the executors/trustees of this transaction. (Shering of course was unaware of Dearle's prior interest). Finally, Brown assigned his interest to Hall. Before he paid Brown, Hall entered into certain inquiries with the deceased's estate as to whether there were any prior interests in the *chose*.

---

courts were reluctant to give effect to *assignments of choses in action* whereas the courts of Equity had no such difficulty giving effect to assignments of various kinds of *choses in action*.

[9] (1823) 3 Russ 1, Sir Thomas Plumer M.R., and affirmed on appeal by Lord Chancellor Lyndhurst, (1823) 3 Russ. 56; also reported at [1824–1834] All E.R. 28.

[10] In fact there were three, Shering being the third (being second-in-time), but the action was fought principally between Dearle, the assignee first-in-time, and Hall the third-in-time.

The reply was in the negative (the estate being genuinely unaware of the interest of the two previous assignees).

The Master of the Rolls, Sir Thomas Plumer, held that Hall had priority over the prior assignee, Dearle, because Hall had, by virtue of his inquiries, been the first assignee to have given notice to the executors/trustees of the equitable assignment in his favour and it would be inequitable to permit Dearle, an earlier assignee-in-time, to have priority when he had failed to give any such notice. Dearle (and also Shering, the second assignee) were therefore found, by their failure respectively to give notice, to have permitted Brown to appear to Hall as if he were entitled to transfer the *chose* free of any other interests (had either of them done so, then the executors would have been in a position to inform Hall of their prior interest(s)).

In order to place this precedent in its legal and historical context, it should be noted that this case concerned priority as between assignments effective in equity only, as the legal interest in the fund remained with the executors/trustees (Brown only ever had an equitable interest to assign). Effectively, the Master of the Rolls had created an exception to the principle that where the equities are equal, the first-in-time prevails. The "rule" in *Dearle v. Hall,* as it came to be known, originally governed the law relating to the *assignment of equitable interests* held under a trust set up in a will. Then its applicability was extended by the courts[11] such that it applied to *equitable* assignments of *choses* generally, in particular to the question of determining *priority* as between an equitable assignment and a subsequently created equitable assignment in the same *chose*. Furthermore, the rule acquired a so-called "second limb" whereby the subsequent assignee could only obtain priority by virtue of being the first to give notice provided that they were bona fide, *i.e.,* neither aware actually or constructively of earlier assignments at the time notice was given. Although this so-called second limb is not a feature of the ratio of *Dearle v. Hall* itself (if for no other reason that there was no question but that Hall was acting bona fides) it has been accepted as part of the rule in many judicial statements.[12]

3. THE SUPREME COURT OF JUDICATURE ACTS 1873/1877 – ASSIGNMENT OF DEBTS AT LAW

However, *Dearle v. Hall* was not to be confined to merely settling priority

---

[11] *e.g. Marchant v. Morton, Down & Co* [1901] 2 K.B. 829.
[12] *e.g.* the House of Lords in *Foster v. Cockerell* (1835) 9 Bl.N.S. 332. Note that De Lacy, "The Priority Rule of Dearle v. Hall Restated" [1999] 63 *The Conveyancer* 311 at p. 321 observes, having reviewed the authorities which in his view mistakenly introduced the second limb into the rule, "It appears as if the existence of the second limb owes more to the theory that if you state the rule exists for long enough people will come to believe you despite the non-existence of any articulated theory or principle to support it."

disputes as between competing *equitable* assignees. With the enactment of section 28(6) of the Supreme Court of Judicature (Ireland) Act 1877, neither the assignment of debts at law as a general proposition, nor the ability of the assignee at law to enforce them directly without recourse to having to join the original assignor as a party to the action, was in doubt any longer.[13] Section 28(6) set out the requirements to be satisfied in order to give effect to an assignment of a debt at law. An assignment that complies with the subsection's requirements is an assignment effective in law. Assignments in equity remain possible notwithstanding. The difference between the two from a substantive point of view is that the assignee in law, being the owner of all title in the debt, can sue on foot of the debt in his own name, and furthermore, notice to the debtor is required in order for an assignment at law to come into being[14] whereas it is not necessary in order for an equitable assignment to be created (though, apart from seeking to preserve priority, there are several reasons why it should be given as a matter of prudence).[15]

---

[13]This arose because s. 27 of the Judicature Act provided for Law and Equity to be administered in the High Court of Justice. There had been earlier legislative attempts to give courts of Equity a Common Law jurisdiction and Common Law courts an equitable jurisdiction (such as the Common Law Procedure Act 1854 and the Chancery Amendment Act 1858) but these were not entirely satisfactory. As a result of the adoption of the 1877 Act, the Common Law's resistance to the enforceability of assignments of debt, which historically had been regarded as enforceable by the original creditor only, was no more (such resistance admittedly weakened as the nineteenth century progressed): Equity of course had long recognised and given effect to such transactions by use of the fiction of compelling the original creditor to be joined as a plaintiff to the action, thereby maintaining the fiction that it was the original creditor who was suing to enforce the debt, when in fact the benefit of any judgment thereby obtained would in fact be the assignee's.

[14]Though the subsection does not specify which party is to give notice, the assignor or the assignee. Principally this burden will fall on the assignee.

[15]For example, a key reason why notice should be given to the debtor of the factor's existence would be to prevent the debtor from paying the assignor, rather than the factor directly. While in some situations the assignor and the factor are happy for the assignor to continue to act as debt collecting agent, there will be situations where the factor may not be happy for the assignor to be collecting debts due (such as where the assignor is in a precarious financial position). A factor who wishes to have maximum protection in the event that the debtor continues to pay assigned debts to the assignor can look to the authority of *International Factors Ltd. v. Rodriguez* [1979] Q.B. 351 where an assignor company agreed that if a debtor paid the company instead of the factor directly, then the payment was to be held on trust for the factor. When a company director breached this arrangement by ordering debtors' cheques to be lodged to the company's own account, the factor was allowed sue the director in conversion.

Another reason why notice should be given to the debtor would be to prevent the factor assignee having to assume responsibility for any equities that the debtor may seek to set up against the assignor *after* the time of the assignment (though equities that pre-date the assignment will bind the factor: *International (Factors) Ireland Ltd. v. Midland International Ltd*, unreported, High Court, December 9, 1993, *per* Lynch J. where the debtor succeeded because the equity claimed *pre-dated* the assignment; also see *Newfoundland Government v. Newfoundland Railway Co and Others* (1883) 13 App.Cas. 198).

Another reason why notice should be given is to evidence the making of the assignment in

Given that it is section 28(6) that is directly responsible for *Dearle v. Hall's* intervention into the settling of priority disputes as between equitable assignees and section 28(6) assignees, it is worth citing the subsection in full.[16] It provides that:

"Any absolute[17] assignment, by writing under the hand of the assignor (not purporting to be by way of charge only), of any debt[18] or other le-

cases where no written assignment document has been executed by the assignee. Until the adoption of the Finance Act 1992, debt factoring arrangements were subject to stamp duty, hence a common practice developed whereby assignors would execute the assignment documents (as a demonstration of their intent to assign) but assignees (*i.e.*, the factors) would not (in order to prevent a stampable event arising). However, the assignee might well insist in this situation on notifying the debtors of the assignment so that they would pay the sums due directly to the assignee rather than to the assignor, and hence such notice would help evidence existence of an assignment in the first place.

[16]While this article focuses on the importance of giving of notice in the context of the rule in *Dearle v. Hall* and its interplay with s. 28(6), the reader interested in other salient features of s. 28(6) can refer to Bell, *Modern Law of Personal Property in England and Ireland* (Dublin, 1989) chap. 15, as well as this writer's own modest contribution in Cahill, *Corporate Finance Law* (Dublin, 2000) chap 7; also see Donnelly, "Transferring Intangibles: Possibilities and Pitfalls" (2000) *Commercial Law Practitioner* 59. For discussion of the U.K. equivalent, see Salinger, *Factoring Law & Practice* (2nd ed., London, 1995); Burgess, *Corporate Finance Law* (2nd ed., London, 1992), pp. 99-128. For the interested reader's ease of reference, case law that arises based on some of the key phrases used in the subsection (consideration of which is outside the scope of this article) is briefly outlined immediately hereafter in the next three footnotes, being those pertaining to the phrases: "absolute"; whether an assignment of *part* of a debt can be effected under s. 28(6); and, "legal".

[17]The requirement that the assignment of the assignor's rights in the debt must be "absolute" means that it must not be granted subject to any conditions. Therefore, the assignor must not retain any rights to the debt as against the debtor. The assignor must alienate his rights completely. So, for example, the granting of a charge over company book debts (as opposed to selling them outright to the assignee (*i.e.*, the factor)) cannot constitute an assignment at law because a charge does not effect an outright transfer of ownership of the book debts to the factor. Instead, all that a charge does is indicate the debts out of which the charge will be satisfied if the sums which the charge secures are not repaid. This is not tantamount to a transfer of outright ownership in those debts: *Re Williams* [1917] 1 Ch. 1. Indeed the subsection itself makes this clear as it expressly provides that a charge is not an assignment.

[18]An assignment of part only of a debt causes the assignment to fall outside s. 28(6) according to a 1912 decision of the Irish Kings Bench: *Conlan v. Carlow County Council* [1912] II I.R. 535 at 542 where it was held that an assignment of part of a debt causes the assignment to fall outside s. 28(6). Gibson J. held that: "The section appears intended to make debts and legal *choses in action*, previously in equity transferable, legally assignable so as to be recoverable without joining the assignor, subject to specific conditions. 'Any debt or other legal *choses in action*' must be read as descriptive of the entire debt and *choses in action*, and not part of them." However, in the English decision of *Skipper & Tucker v. Holloway and Howard* [1910] 2 K.B. 630 Darling J. held that assignment of part of a debt was within the former U.K. equivalent of s. 28(6), s. 25(6) of the Supreme Court of Judicature Act 1873 (Bell, *op. cit.,* above, n. 16 points out that this decision, although not yet overruled, must be doubted and it has been heavily criticised in the U.K.): Bray J. did not follow it in *Forster v. Baker* [1910] 2 K.B. 636 using reasoning similar to that employed by Gibson J. in *Conlan v. Carlow County Council*; also see *Williams v. Atlantic Assurance Co. Ltd* [1933] 1 K.B. 81 and *Walter & Sullivan v. J. Murphy & Sons Ltd* [1955] 2 Q.B. 584 in this respect.

gal[19] choses in action, of which express notice in writing shall have been given to the debtor, trustee, or other person from whom the assignor would have been entitled to receive or claim such debt or chose in action, shall be and be deemed to have been effectual in law (subject to all equities which would have been entitled to priority over the right of the assignee if this Act had not passed,) to pass and transfer the legal right to such debt or chose in action from the date of such notice, and all legal and other remedies for the same, and the power to give a good discharge for the same, without the concurrence of the assignor: Provided always, that if the debtor, trustee, or other person liable in respect of such debt or chose in action shall have had notice that such assignment is disputed by the assignor or anyone claiming under him, or of any other opposing or conflicting claims to such debt or chose in action, he shall be entitled, if he think fit, to call upon the persons making claim thereto to interplead concerning the same, or he may, if he think fit, pay the same into the High Court of Justice under and in conformity with the provisions of the Acts for the relief of trustees."[20]

---

[19] In *Torkington v. Magee* [1902] 2 K.B. 427 at 430-431, Channell J. held that the word "legal" in this context means "debt or right which the common law looks on as not being assignable by reason of its being a *chose in action*, but which a Court of Equity deals with as being assignable." In other words, it refers to *choses* which were, before the enactment of s. 28(6), not assignable at law but were at equity. According to Bell, *op. cit.* at n. 16 above at p. 363 "legal" also means *choses* that were "lawfully assignable." In other words, any *chose* that can lawfully be assigned, can be assigned under the subsection, except those *choses* which the law does not permit to be assignable at all, or, those *choses* which the law prescribes must be assigned pursuant to a different legal framework. In *Torkington v. Magee,* Channell J. instanced the assignment of company shares pursuant to the Companies Acts as an example of the latter. (Note that although Channell J.'s judgment was overturned on appeal in 1903 [1903] W.N. 60, it was reversed on other grounds).

[20] Note that s. 136(1) of the U.K. Law of Property Act 1925 is similar to s. 28(6) though there are some minor differences: see Bell, *op. cit.,* above, n. 16 at pp. 362 *et seq.* where a brief comparison is made between the Irish and U.K. provisions. The U.K. courts' interpretation of s.136 or its forerunner, s. 25(6) of the Supreme Court of Judicature Act 1873 (referred to in pre-1925 cases), are of assistance in interpreting s. 28(6) in situations where no Irish authority exists. Section 136(1) states that:

"Any absolute assignment by writing under the hand of the assignor (not purporting to be by way of charge only) of any debt or other legal thing in action, of which express notice in writing has been given to the debtor, trustee, or other person from whom the assignor would have been entitled to claim such debt or thing in action, is effectual in law (subject to equities having priority over the right of the assignee) to pass and transfer from the date of such notice –
(a) the legal right to such debt or thing in action;
(b) all legal and other remedies for the same; and
(c) the power to give a good discharge for the same without the concurrence of the assignor:
Provided, that if the debtor, trustee, or other person liable in respect of such debt or thing in action has notice:
(a) that the assignment is disputed by the assignor or any person claiming under him; or

4. THE IMPORTANCE OF NOTICE TO THE DEBTOR

Before further elaborating on how section 28(6) transplants the reasoning of *Dearle v. Hall* into the arena of section 28(6) assignments, a preliminary observation may be helpful: *Dearle v. Hall* is not authority for the proposition that notice must be given to the debtor in order to *create* an equitable assignment. Notice to the debtor is *not* required in order to *create* an assignment effective in equity as between assignor and assignee. However, the giving of notice to the debtor can obtain valuable protection for the assignee of an equitable assignment. *Dearle v. Hall* demonstrates that the giving of notice to the debtor of the assignee's equitable assignment will ensure that the *bona fide*[21] assignee gets priority over *prior created* equitable assignments of the debt where the existence of the prior assignments was never notified to the debtor.[22]

By contrast, notice to the debtor is a statutory requirement to effect an assignment at law under section 28(6). The section does not actually stipulate which party should give notice to the debtor. Notice must be clear and unambiguous to the effect that the factor is now owner of the debts and is the only party who can discharge the debtor's indebtedness.[23] In practice, notice is often given by actually stamping notice of the existence of factoring arrangements on the assignor's invoices as they are issued. In *Denney Gasquet & Metcalfe v. Conklin*,[24] Atkin J. held that notice must bring to the attention of the debtor that the debt has been assigned and that the debtor is now required to discharge the debt in favour of the assignee, not the assignor. One of the issues in *Holt v. Heatherfield Trust Ltd*,[25] was whether, for the purposes of the modern U.K. equivalent of section 28(6),[26] notice became effective on the date it was sent or it was received? It was held that the assignment cannot be complete

---

(b) of any other opposing or conflicting claims to such debt or thing in action;

   he may, if he thinks fit, either call upon the persons making claim thereto to interplead concerning the same, or pay the debt or other thing in action into court under the provisions of the Trustee Act, 1925."

[21] As noted already above at n. 12 (and discussed further below at n. 34) this bona fide requirement has been adopted by the courts as being part of the rule in *Dearle v. Hall* itself though it was not part of the ratio in *Dearle v. Hall* itself (if for no other reason than that Hall was unaware of any prior assignments, hence the matter of Hall's *fides* did not arise for consideration).

[22] *Dearle v. Hall* however is of no consequence where the first created assignment of the debt was one effective at law, *i.e.,* a s.28(6) assignee. This is because, in creating an assignment effective at law under s. 28(6), the legal title to the debt is fully assigned according to the requirements of the law and there is therefore nothing left to the assignor to attempt to further assign to anybody else (whether at law or at equity). As the assignee will have in such a case given notice automatically to the debtor as required by s. 28(6), no subsequently "created" interest in the debt can take priority over the notified assignment.

[23] As Lord MacNaghten observed in *William Brandt's Sons & Co. v. Dunlop Rubber Company* [1905] A.C. 454 at 462, "If the debtor ignores such a notice he does so at his peril".

[24] [1913] 3 K.B. 177.

[25] [1942] 1 All E.R. 404.

[26] *i.e.,* s. 136(1) of the Law of Property Act 1925.

at law as between assignee factor and assignor until notice of the assignment is actually *received* by the debtor. Finding the date of receipt of notice to be the correct view, Atkinson J. continued to explain that until the debtor actually receives notice of the assignment, even if the assignment satisfies the statutory requirements in every other respect, the assignment can only take effect *in equity* as between assignor and assignee. The learned judge noted that:

> "Absence of notice to the debtor does not affect the efficacy of the transaction as between the assignor and the assignee. Until notice be given the assignment is an equitable assignment, but it is an assignment which requires nothing more from the assignor to become a legal assignment. The assignee may himself give notice at any time before action brought, and, further than that, even before notice he may sue in his own name, provided that he makes the assignor a party to the action, a plaintiff if he consents, and as defendant if he does not consent."[27]

Therefore, while the absence of notice to the debtor does not affect the *efficacy* of the transaction as between the assignor and the assignee, a failure to give such notice will prevent the assignee taking the full legal title to the debt such that, in order for the assignee to enforce the debt, it will be necessary to join the assignor to the action.

In order to be effective as a section 28(6) notice, notice to the debtor must be received by the debtor *after* the assignment has taken place and not before.[28] In what is known as whole turnover factoring, the factor agrees to buy all of the trade debt owed to the assignor or a particular section of the assignor's invoices. On the other hand, in facultative factoring the factor instead insists that each debt is offered to the factor by the assignor and the factor remains free to refuse to take an assignment of any particular debt that the assignor might offer. Salinger[29] points out that a danger inherent in facultative factoring arrangements is that while the assignor may have already notified the debtor that the debt is to be assigned to the factor, the factor's acceptance of the offered debt might only occur *after* the assignor had given notice to the debtor. This does not comply with the U.K. legislation,[30] and it is submitted that neither would it constitute compliance with the Irish section 28(6). In both provisions, the reasonable interpretation appears to be that notice must be received

---

[27] *Holt v. Heatherfield Trust Ltd.,* above, n. 25 at 407. In the earlier decision of *Gorringe v. Irwell India Rubber and Gutta Percha Works* (1887) 34 Ch. D. 128 a similar view was taken where it was held that where an equitable assignment has otherwise been created, notice to the debtor is not required to perfect the assignment.

[28] *A fortiori* the notice must be communicated to the debtor before the debt has extinguished itself: see *Lee v. McGrath* [1882] 10 L.R. (Ir) 313 (C.A.).

[29] *Factoring Law and Practice, op. cit.,* above, n. 16.

[30] Section 136(1) of the U.K. Law of Property Act 1925.

by the debtor *after* the assignment has occurred between the assignor and the assignee factor, in order to satisfy the legislative requirements for assignments of debt to be effective at law.

A further difficulty that can arise in factoring arrangements is that the factor may attempt to give notice to debtors by way of a letter of introduction stating that *future* debts that the debtors may incur by reason of their doing business with the assignor, are to be paid to the factor as owner of those future debts. The difficulty with this arrangement is that, as those debts have not yet come into existence, they are incapable of being assigned to the factor at the time the letter of introduction (i.e., notice) was sent out to the debtors. An "assignment" of a *future chose* – a debt not yet in existence – is not capable of being a present assignment because an assignment will only come into effect once the debt comes into existence. As a result, a factor in this position runs the risk that the notice letter would constitute notice given *prior* to *the assignment* of those future debts coming into existence, with the result that the letter could not be effective notice pursuant to section 28(6). Thus, the factor would be well advised to modify the factoring arrangements so that this risk is eliminated.[31]

5. *DEARLE V. HALL* AND THE DETERMINATION OF PRIORITY AS BETWEEN PRIOR EQUITABLE ASSIGNMENTS AND SUBSEQUENT ASSIGNMENTS AT LAW

At this point the issue arises as to how the reasoning of *Dearle v. Hall* was introduced into the territory occupied by section 28(6). It is submitted that the answer is to be found in the bracketed caveat contained in section 28(6) which provides that section 28(6) assignments are, "… (subject to all equities which would have been entitled to priority over the right of the assignee if this Act had not passed)… ."[32] In this context, the issue that arises here is, whether an

---

[31] See *Johnstone v. Cox* (1881) 16 Ch. Div. 571. Future debts must be distinguished from the situation where debts, *already in existence,* have been assigned although *not due* until some time in the future. These latter debts are not future debts and are capable of present assignment. However, as noted above, the factor must ensure that the debtor does not receive notice until *after* assignment in order to satisfy s. 28(6). See also Salinger; Bell; *op. cit.,* above, at n.16.

[32] Although Irish authority on whether the s. 28(6) caveat has this effect does not exist, judicial interpretation of the analogous U.K. provisions (s. 25(6) Supreme Court of Judicature Act 1873 in *Marchant v. Morton Down* [1901] 2 K.B. 829, and also of its successor, s.136 (1) Law of Property Act 1925 *per* Philips J. in *Pfeiffer Weinkellerei v. Arbuthnot Factors Ltd.* [1988] 1 W.L.R. 150; and *per* Mummery J. in *Compaq Computer Ltd. v. Abercorn Group Ltd.* [1991] B.C.C. 484) is persuasive such that an Irish court might well similarly interpret s. 28(6). Given the similarity of the language used in both the Irish and U.K. legislation, these judgments are persuasive, as are (again in the context of the U.K. subsection) academic commentators such as McCormack, "Effective Reservation of Title and Priorities" [1990] *J.B.L.* 314 and Hicks, "Retention of Title – Latest Developments" [1992] *J.B.L. 398.* However, other commentators take an opposing view, the most determined being Oditah, "Priorities: Equitable versus Legal As-

equitable assignment of a debt made by the assignor in favour of a third party *before* it was assigned to the factor pursuant to section 28(6) could affect the factor's section 28(6) title in the debt. In the case of determining priorities as between competing interests in *intangible* property such as a *chose in action* (*i.e.* a debt), *Dearle v. Hall* stipulates that interests in a debt rank in priority based not from the date of their creation, but from the date of their notification to the debtor.

Originally, the rule in *Dearle v. Hall* governed the issue of priority determination where several *equitable assignments* of the same equitable interest arising under a trust were competing for priority. It was held that priority amongst the competing equitable assignees depended not on which assignee's assignment arose first in time, but on which assignee's assignment was the first to be notified to the debtor. Accordingly, it was held that the third assignee of the chose who was the first to notify the debtors of his interest, took priority over the earlier assignees who had neglected to give any such notice of their respective interests.

The rule's application has subsequently been extended to also determine priority between prior created equitable assignments *and* subsequently created assignments effective at law in the same debt because of the "subject to equities" proviso employed in section 28(6)'s U.K. analogue, section 136(1) as will be illustrated when the *Pfeiffer Weinkellerei* case is discussed below. In effect, the proviso in this context permits *Dearle v. Hall* to apply to a priority dispute between an equitable assignment followed by a subsequently created assignment effective at law under section 28(6) in the same debt because the proviso qualifies section 28(6) – which permits assignments to be effected at law – by stating that such assignments are to be "subject to all equities which would have been entitled to priority over the right of the assignee if this Act had not [been][33] passed". Hence, a section 28(6) assignee's title in a debt will prevail against the holder of a prior existing equitable assignment of the debt provided that the section 28(6) assignee was bona fide[34] and provided that the debtor

---

signments of Book Debts" (1989) 9 *Oxford Journal of Legal Studies* 513 where that author argues that such a construction of the U.K. s.136(1) is not possible (at 516); that the cases cited above do not validly support such a construction of the subsection (at 517-521); and furthermore, that the issue of priorities should be determined not by the first to give notice rule (*Dearle v. Hall*) but rather by the bona fide purchaser for value without notice rule such that a subsequent assignee at law should triumph over a prior assignee at equity even though the assignee in equity had given notice to the debtor (at 529-531).

[33] This writer has inserted the word "been" in order to make the proviso more intelligible in to-day's language.

[34] De Lacy, "The Priority Rule of Dearle v. Hall Restated" [1999] 63 *The Conveyancer* 311 argues (probably correctly) that there is no bona fide requirement to be found in the rule in *Dearle v. Hall*, restricting the scope of the rule to merely being authority for the proposition that the first assignee to give notice gets priority: according to that commentator an analysis of the case law reveals that the courts have, over time, added a so-called "second limb" to *Dearle v. Hall* not actually found in the case itself, namely that the subsequent assignee can only benefit from the

had not received notice of any such prior equitable assignment.[35]

In other words, failure by an equitable assignee (whose interest in the debt arose first in time) to give notice to the debtor will enable the subsequent *bona fide* section 28(6) assignee to gain priority under *Dearle v. Hall* (as notice to the debtor is a mandatory requirement for section 28(6) assignments and so will be given as a matter of course).[36]

Thus, while notice to the debtor is not necessary in order to actually *create* a valid assignment of a debt *in equity,* there is therefore good reason why an equitable assignee should give notice. The rule in *Dearle v. Hall* will give such an equitable assignee who, as a matter of prudence gives notice to the debtor, priority over a subsequent section 28(6) assignee.[37] Furthermore, section 28(6) combined with *Dearle v. Hall* ensures that the prior equitable assignee of the

---

rule's invocation where they are bona fide, *i.e.* neither aware actually or constructively of the earlier assignment. However, as against this, as that commentator does point out, there are so many examples of obiter judicial statements which have effectively imported this bona fide requirement into the rule's application, that hence for practical purposes, for better or worse, it must now be regarded as part of the rule in *Dearle v. Hall.* Harman J. in *Rhodes v. Allied Dunbar Pension Services* [1987] 1 W.L.R. 1703 at 1708 explained the rationale for the so-called second limb as being "... intended to prevent sharp practice: people jumping in and taking advantage of a technical failure to give notice ... I do not believe that one needs to find anything equivalent to sharp practice to invoke the second limb in *Dearle v. Hall.* I think it is simply a rule – and a rule of a good sense, to my mind – which says that formalities are not essential and that the law will follow the ordinary morality of the matter, that the man who has had the first claim cannot be put out of his claim by somebody coming in when that person had knowledge of the first claimant's position." Oditah, *"Priorities: Equitable versus Legal Assignments of Book Debts"* (1989) 9 *Ox.J.Leg.St.* 513 on the other hand argues in the context of s. 136(1) (and, if correct, such argument could equally apply to s. 28(6) in the context of the Irish legislation given the similarity between s. 136(1) and s. 28(6)) that the rule in *Dearle v. Hall* does not apply to determine priorities at all as between equitable assignees and subsequent assignees at law, that commentator instead arguing that the bona fide purchaser for value without notice principle determines the matter, not the rule in *Dearle v. Hall* (though that commentator does concede at p. 529 that orthodox academic opinion is to the effect that *Dearle v. Hall* does apply). Judicial interpretation of s. 136(1) does not accord with Oditah's view, and holds that *Dearle v. Hall* does apply: see *Pfeiffer Weinkellerei v. Arbuthnot Factors Ltd* and *Compaq Computer Ltd v. Abercorn Group Ltd* considered below.

[35] As Atkinson J. observed in *Holt v. Heatherfield Trust Ltd.* [1942] 1 All E.R. 404 (see above at nn. 25-27) an equitable assignment does not require notice to be given to the debtor in order for it to be perfected (apart from preventing a subsequent s. 28(6) assignee taking priority), there are several other reasons why notice should be given as a matter of prudence which have already been noted earlier above at n. 15, though in practice, often the assignor may not want notice to be given to the debtor as use of a factor's services may be regarded in some quarters as a sign of credit frailty).

[36] Of course, no such priority issue can arise where the assignment effective at law is created first in time because the entire legal interest will have been assigned (and in any event, notice will have been given to the debtor as required by s. 28(6)).

[37] And of course, priority also over other prior equitable assignees who have failed to notify the debtor of their interest in the debt (as was the case in *Dearle v. Hall* itself), provided of course that the assignee was *bona fide* (*i.e.* unaware of those earlier assignments) at the time of notification (*i.e.* provided the so-called "second limb" bona fide requirements are satisfied (see the comments of Harman J. above at n. 34).

debt will not lose priority to the subsequent *bona fide* section 28(6) assignee who had no notice of the earlier equitable interest in the debt *provided* the equitable assignee had gone beyond the strict requirements demanded to effect an equitable assignment by actually giving notice to the debtor.[38] In such a situation, *Dearle v. Hall* will permit the equitable assignee's assignment to have priority over a subsequently created section 28(6) assignment at law.[39]

These issues arose for consideration in the English High Court decision of Phillips J. in *Pfeiffer Weinkellerei v. Arbuthnot Factors Ltd*[40] where consideration was given to the combination of the "subject to equities" proviso employed in the analogous U.K. legislation (section 136(1) of the Law of Property Act 1925) and *Dearle v. Hall*. The court held, applying a combination of the "subject to equities" rationale and the rule in *Dearle v. Hall,* that a prior created equitable assignment competed for, and lost, priority to a subsequently created assignment effective at law on the grounds that no notice had been given to the debtors of the prior-created equitable assignment (whereas notice of the subsequent assignment of law was).

An appreciation of the somewhat complicated background facts and arguments are necessary in order to appreciate the reasoning employed in this judgment. The plaintiff, a wine supplier, sold wine to a wine importer who subsequently entered into a factoring agreement with the defendant (a debt factor) by which the defendant agreed to purchase debts owed to the wine importer by the wine importer's wine customers (*i.e.* the debtors) for the wine. The factoring agreement was one entered into in accordance with section 136(1) of the U.K. Law of Property Act 1925 and therefore was an assignment effective in law. At the time of entering into the factoring agreement, the defendant factor was unaware that any adverse third party claims or interests might affect the wine, and indeed the wine importer had warranted to the defendant that no reservation of title by any third party affected the goods.

However, there was already such a claim because the plaintiff, the original supplier of the wine, had inserted a purported retention of title clause in the contract of sale to the wine importer. That clause purported to retain property in the wine to the plaintiff, but yet at the same time, permitted the wine importer to sell the wine provided that the wine importer passed on any proceeds collected or claims to such proceeds to the plaintiff up to the amount of the wine importer's outstanding indebtedness to the plaintiff.

---

[38] Oditah (at n. 34 above) would argue to the contrary, *i.e.* that the subsequent assignee has priority by virtue of the application of the bona fide purchaser for value of a legal interest without notice principle, that commentator taking the view that *Dearle v. Hall* does not apply on the grounds that it does not apply via s. 136(1) (and therefore, by analogy of this reasoning, via s. 28(6)).

[39] In other words, the assignee at law under s. 28(6) will not take the assignment of the debt free from the prior created equitable assignment *provided* the equitable assignee had already given notice to the debtor of the equitable assignment.

[40] [1988] 1 W.L.R. 150.

In the course of time the wine importer failed to pay the plaintiff sums due for wine. Accordingly, the plaintiff claimed under the purported retention of title clause that it was the beneficial owner of the debts arising from each sale of wine made by the wine importer. To resolve the dispute as to who had priority to the debts, the plaintiff, the wine supplier, instituted legal proceedings against the defendant, the debt factor.

The first issue was to determine the exact nature of the plaintiff's interest.[41] Phillips J. held that the terms of the purported reservation of title clause did not retain title to the plaintiff as it permitted the wine importer to sell the goods in the ordinary course of business, and that it in fact merely created a charge which was void for want of registration.[42] Phillips J. proceeded to hold

---

[41] The plaintiff submitted that the reservation of title clause retained title in the goods to the plaintiff while in the wine importer's possession, and allowed it obtain title in the debts/proceeds once the wine importer had sold the goods. The defendant claimed that the clause merely created some sort of security interest in the goods and in the proceeds/debts arising from their sale.

[42] Title to the goods and proceeds from sub-sales could only be reserved to the plaintiff where a fiduciary relationship was deemed to exist and the clause was held on its terms not to have given rise to such a relationship. Phillips J. then held that the clause gave rise to a charge over the wine while in the wine importer's possession and over the sale debts when the importer sold that wine. However, such a charge required registration under the U.K. Companies Act 1948, s. 95 (charges over book debts are also registrable in Ireland: s. 99 Companies Act 1963) and because it was never registered, it was void for want of registration (it never occurred to the plaintiff to register the clause as a charge because it thought it had a totally different effect, *i.e.* that of reserving title). Oditah, *op. cit.,* above, at n. 32 criticises this aspect of the judgment at p. 518 arguing that Phillips J. misconstrued U.K. company legislation pertaining to avoidability of unregistered charges such that the charge should not, in that commentator's view, have been avoided as against the factor: the argument was made that s. 95 of the UK Companies legislation only rendered unregistered charges void as against "creditors" (it being argued by that commentator that the factor is not a "creditor") and furthermore, that s. 95 only comes into effect if the company is in liquidation and there is nothing in the report of the case to suggest that this was so. That commentator makes such argument in an effort to demonstrate that there was therefore no occasion which demanded that *Dearle v. Hall* apply.

Notwithstanding that U.K. company law has in the interim been amended to remove these objections (see Hicks, "Retention of Title – Latest Developments" [1992] *J.B.L.* 398 who points out that s. 399 of the Companies Act 1985 (as amended in 1989) now makes an unregistered charge void *inter alia* as against *any person* who acquires an interest in or right over property subject to the charge, such that it is submitted by that commentator that a seller's right to debts arising out of the sale of such property which in substance constitutes an unregistered charge, will be void as against a factor who has been assigned the sale debts (the point being that the amendment of the legislation no longer confines the charge to being void as against "creditors" only). To that extent therefore, while Oditah's criticism may well be accurate, it has now been overtaken by events, and furthermore, such criticism does not effectively deal with Philips J's conclusion (erroneous or not) that the unregistered charge amounted to an equitable assignment (other than to observe that it would still be defeated by the bona fide purchaser for value principle – Phillips J. rejected such contention), thereby creating an occasion *demanding* the application of *Dearle v. Hall.* McCormack, in "Effective Reservation of Title and Priorities" [1990] *J.B.L.* 314 at 323 supports the view that where a retention of title clause fails as such and thereby creates a equitable right, then the rule in *Dearle v. Hall* is properly invoked to resolve the priority dispute thereby arising; Professor Goode takes a similar view, *Commercial Law* (Harmondsworth, 1982) at p. 873.

that the clause, an unregistered security interest, *inter alia,* in effect gave rise to a form of equitable assignment by the wine importer to the plaintiff of the wine importer's rights in debts owed to the wine importer by its customers for the wine to the extent that the plaintiff could claim out of such debts up to the amount of the wine importer's indebtedness to the plaintiff *but not* that the entirety of such debts were assigned to the plaintiff absolutely.[43]

The plaintiff could not argue that, even if the clause did not reserve title to him, it constituted an assignment effective at law (thereby defeating the defendant) because the actual debts themselves were not assigned to the plaintiff absolutely by the clause. In any event, this argument was not open to the plaintiff as notice of the clause had never been given to the debtors of the wine importer (as is required by section 136(1)).[44]

The second issue therefore was to determine which party's assignment had priority. The defendant (factor)'s primary submission was that, being the holder of legal title to the debts under an assignment effective at law, its interest in the debt should defeat the plaintiff's equitable assignment even though created subsequent to the plaintiff's, purely because a legal interest is superior title to a merely equitable one (*i.e.* the bona fide purchaser for value without notice argument).

In reply, the plaintiff submitted that while section 136(1) permitted an assignee of debt to take a title effective in law, section 136(1) does not affect the determination of priorities. In other words, in so far as *priorities* between competing interests are concerned, a section 136 assignee is in no better position than if the assignment had been effective in equity because the proviso in section 136(1) states that, "Any absolute assignment . . . *shall be subject to equities having priority over the right of the assignee....* ."[45]

Thus the plaintiff submitted that the proviso to section 136(1) meant that, for priority determination purposes, an assignment in law must be considered *as if it were* an equitable assignment, and, consequently under normal equity principles the interest created first-in-time prevails (such that the plaintiff's equitable rights took priority because they were created first-in-time).

Phillips J. accepted the plaintiff's first submission (that the statutory proviso meant that an assignment in law should be regarded as an assignment in equity for priority determination purposes). In effect, therefore, the priority

---

[43] Once wine-sale debts came into existence, the clause created an assignment in equity of the sale debts' proceeds in favour of the plaintiff but only up to the amounts owing to him at any one time by the wine importer. This assignment was not the same as an outright assignment absolutely of all the wine importer's rights in those sale debts as the wine importer could retain the surplus balance of any particular debt once the sums due to the plaintiff were discharged.

[44] It is also a requirement of the Supreme Court of Judicature (Ireland) Act 1877, s. 28(6) as seen earlier above.

[45] At this point it is appropriate to point out that the proviso in the Irish legislation, s. 28(6), is even more emphatic: "Any absolute assignment . . . shall be . . . (subject to all equities which would have been entitled to priority over the right of the assignee if this Act had not passed). . . ."

rules were not altered by the enactment of section 136(1). In other words, while section 136(1) allows debt assignments to be *effective* at law, it did not, however, permit a subsequently created assignment effective in law to have priority over a prior created assignment in equity merely because the subsequent assignment was effective at law and the prior created assignment was only effective in equity. Thus, the court rejected the defendant's primary argument that a subsequently created assignment effective in law is by definition superior to a prior created assignment effective in equity when determining priorities between such competing interests in a debt.

However, the learned judge could not agree with the plaintiff's second argument for priority based on the first-in-time rule. Phillips J. held that when dealing with priorities and intangible property such as debts he would agree with the defendant's argument which was that the first-in-time rule, gave way to the rule in *Dearle v. Hall*. In accepting this argument, the learned judge held that the rule in *Dearle v. Hall* is an exception to the general principle that equitable interests take priority in the order in which they are created. It applies, in particular, where priority as between equitable assignments of choses in action versus assignments effective at law is at stake. Furthermore, he held that an assignment effective at law such as the defendant's, must be regarded, for priority determination purposes, as if it were merely an assignment effective in equity. Under the *Dearle v. Hall* rule, priority depends not on whether the interest was created first in time, but on the order in which notice of the interest is given to the party affected by it. Applying *Dearle v. Hall,* the defendant's assignment at law took priority because the defendant had notified the debtors of the wine importer of the assignment of the debts whereas no such notification had ever been given to them by either the plaintiff or the wine importer of the plaintiff's "reservation of title" clause, which itself in reality in legal substance was no more than an assignment in equity. Had notice of the plaintiff's equitable assignment been given (by either the plaintiff or the wine importer) to the wine importer's debtors, then it would have had priority instead.[46]

In *Compaq Computer Ltd v. Abercorn Group Ltd*[47] Mummery J. agreed with the decision in *Pfeiffer,* holding *inter alia* that the "subject to equities" caveat in section 136(1) displaces the *bona fide* purchaser without notice rule, such that an assignee at law does not get priority over an earlier equitable assignee on that account – and the learned judge further held that in such circumstances the priority determination is conducted within the rubric of section 136(1) which means that priority is determined by the rule in *Dearle v. Hall,*

---

[46]But of course, this never occurred to the plaintiff or the wine importer as they assumed that the clause reserved title to the plaintiff and never suspected that it was ineffective for that purpose (instead taking effect as an equitable assignment!).

[47][1991] B.C.C. 484.

i.e. whichever assignee was first to give notice to the debtor of their interest in the debt will obtain priority.

6. CONCLUSION

The statutory phrase "subject to all equities" contained in section 28(6) is a caveat of great significance. In effect it means that even though the statutory assignee may take legal title in the debt, the assignee's interest in the debt may still be subordinate to the interests of prior equitable assignees provided those assignees have notified their interests to the debtor. The interplay between equitable and statutory regimes as set out in this article would, it is submitted, be persuasive were the issue of priority determination as between competing assignments in the same debt to arise under section 28(6) of the 1877 Irish Judicature Act.

This piece began with a memorable quote from Professor Brady. Equity does indeed endure, and though the Law may appropriate an area as its own, the well of Equity will continue to be revisited time and again.

INJUNCTIONS AND FREEDOM OF EXPRESSION

JAMES CASEY

1. INTRODUCTION

The First Amendment of the United States Constitution famously protects freedom of speech and of the press:

> "Congress shall make no law . . . abridging the freedom of speech, or of the press. . . ."

In *Near v. Minnesota*[1] the Supreme Court[2] held that the purpose of this guarantee was to curtail prior restraints upon publication – as by the grant of an injunction. Forty years later, the breadth of this prohibition was re-emphasised in *New York Times Co. v. United States*[3] (the "Pentagon Papers" case).[4] Even the constitutionally protected right to a fair trial has been held not to justify a prior restraint: *Nebraska Press Association v. Stuart*.[5]

Against this background it would obviously be impossible to secure an injunction to restrain the dissemination of material alleged to be defamatory[6] or to violate individual privacy[7] or to breach a confidence.[8] Thus, despite their

---

[1] (1931) 283 U.S. 697.

[2] Hughes C.J., Holmes, Brandeis, Stone and Roberts JJ.; Butler, Van Devanter, McReynolds and Sutherland JJ. dissenting. In retrospect this decision seems most remarkable, given that the Supreme Court of this period was far from a liberal body. See Mason, *Harlan Fiske Stone: Pillar of the Law* (New York, 1956), Chaps. 19-28: White, *Justice Oliver Wendell Holmes* (New York, 1993), Chaps. 11-12.

[3] (1971) 403 U.S. 713.

[4] This was an attempt by the federal government to enjoin the publication of a classified study of U.S. policy-making on Vietnam. The Supreme Court rejected the application by a 6-3 majority – Black, Douglas, Brennan, Stewart, White and Marshall, JJ.; Burger C.J., Harlan and Blackmun JJ. dissenting.

[5] (1976) 427 U.S. 539.

[6] And, of course, the decision in *New York Times Co. v. Sullivan* (1964) 376 U.S. 254 makes it very difficult for a public official to recover damages for defamation.

[7] Even State statutes imposing liability in damages for invasion of privacy may founder on constitutional reefs: see *Florida Star v. B.J.F.* (1989) 491 U.S. 524.

[8] Note, however, that in *Snepp v. United States* (1980) 444 U.S. 507 the Supreme Court upheld a lower court's order impressing a constructive trust in favour of the federal government on all profits earned by a former C.I.A. agent from a book he had published without security clearance, in breach of his contract of employment. In *Attorney General v. Blake* [2000] 3 W.L.R. 625 the House of Lords achieved a similar result *via* the remedy of an account of profits.

frantic efforts at suppression elsewhere, the United Kingdom authorities made no attempt to enjoin the publication of Peter Wright's book *Spycatcher* in the United States.[9]

Irish law does not go so far as this; and in defamation cases at least, a blanket ban on prior restraints would hardly be compatible with the constitutional guarantee of the right to one's good name (Article 40.3.2°). Nevertheless, there is clear evidence at High Court level of a strong presumption against enjoining the publication or broadcasting of material, whether on grounds of breach of confidence, invasion of privacy or libel.

2. BREACH OF CONFIDENCE

It is well settled that Irish law offers protection against breaches of confidence,[10] and that such protection may involve the grant of an injunction. In *Attorney General for England and Wales v. Brandon Book Publishers Ltd.*[11] the plaintiff had secured an interim injunction restraining the defendant company from selling, distributing or communicating any part of the contents of the book *One Girl's War*, by Joan Miller. Ms. Miller, who had died in June 1984, was a former British intelligence officer, and the plaintiff contended that she was under a perpetual obligation of confidentiality in regard to her employment.[12] The interim injunction was granted by Blayney J. on November 27, 1986, and an application for an interlocutory injunction was heard by Carroll J. on December 1, 1986. On the following day she delivered a judgment refusing the relief sought. Carroll J. referred to Article 40.6.1°'s[13] guarantee of freedom of expression, and continued:

> ". . . the Article refers to the organs of public opinion *preserving their rightful liberty of expression* provided it is not used to undermine public

---

[9] As all the law lords noted in the *Spycatcher* case (*Attorney General v. Guardian Newspapers Ltd.* [1987] 1 W.L.R. 1248. See Lord Bridge at 1283, Lord Brandon at 1288, Lord Templeman at 1295, Lord Ackner at 1305 and Lord Oliver at 1312-1313. And in *Attorney General v. Guardian Newspapers Ltd. (No. 2)* [1990] 1 A.C. 109 Lord Keith said (at 254): "Her Majesty's government had been advised that, in view of the terms of the First Amendment to the U.S. Constitution, any attempt to restrain publication there would be certain to fail".

[10] See the Supreme Court decisions in *House of Spring Gardens Ltd. v. Point Blank Ltd.* [1986] I.R. 611 and *National Irish Bank Ltd. v. Radio Telefís Éireann* [1998] 2 I.R. 465.

[11] [1986] I.R. 597.

[12] It can hardly be accidental that these proceedings were brought while the *Spycatcher* litigation was under way in England and elsewhere. As its name suggests, Joan Miller's book dealt with events which took place during World War II, and much of the information therein was already public knowledge. But the principle of a perpetual obligation of confidentiality invoked there was also the foundation of the *Spycatcher* applications, and they might have been prejudiced had no action been taken against the Miller book.

[13] [1986] I.R. 597 at 600.

order or the authority of the State. There is no question of public order or morality being undermined here. Therefore in my opinion there is *prima facie* a constitutional right to publish information and the onus rests on the plaintiff to establish in the context of an interlocutory application that the constitutional right of the defendant should not be exercised".

Founding on Australian authority,[14] Carroll J. distinguished cases involving private confidences or trade information from those involving confidential relationships between a government and an individual. In the latter, disclosure would be restrained only where it was likely to injure the public interest. But here there was no question of the public interest of the Irish State being involved, and the only relevant considerations were that:

(a) the defendant had a constitutional right to publish information not involving a breach of copyright;

(b) the public interest in this jurisdiction was not affected;

(c) there was no breach of confidentiality in a private or commercial setting; and

(d) there was no absolute confidentiality where the parties were a government and a private individual.

Carroll J. concluded that no cause of action had been shown, and ended by saying:[15]

"The exercise of a constitutional right cannot be measured in terms of money: what is at stake is the very important constitutional right to communicate *now* and not in a year or more when the case has worked its way through the courts".

In the view of one commentator:[16]

". . . *Brandon Books* strikes an important blow for freedom of the press in Ireland. In view of the emphatic manner in which Carroll J. upheld the right to communicate, it would probably be only in exceptional circumstances that the Irish courts would restrain the publication of information which a government found embarrassing or disclosure of which was deemed contrary to the public interest".

Subsequent events suggest that this 1987 prediction might have been unduly

---

[14]*Commonwealth v. John Fairfax and Sons Ltd.* (1980) 147 C.L.R. 39.
[15][1986] I.R. 597 at 602.
[16]Hogan, "Free Speech, Privacy and the Press in Ireland" [1987] *Public Law* 509.

optimistic. After all, in the protracted litigation on abortion information[17] the Supreme Court subordinated the right to communicate to the right to life of the unborn, and it required an adverse ruling by the European Court of Human Rights[18] and a constitutional amendment[19] to change this.[20] A like subordination of the right to communicate also seems to be implicit in the Supreme Court's Government confidentiality decision,[21] which gives rise to the inference that the Attorney General could seek injunctive relief against breaches of such confidentiality, whether by memoir writers, biographers or historians.[22]

No one, of course, could have foretold these developments at the time of the *Brandon Books* decision; nonetheless that case is not quite the ringing defence of freedom to communicate suggested. For Carroll J. made it clear that no public interest of the Irish State was involved. The implication is surely that in a case involving disclosures by an *Irish* public servant matters might have been different.

An issue topical at the time of writing illustrates the problem. The Garda authorities, it seems, decline to reveal the instructions given to armed officers regarding the use of lethal force.[23] Might a former Garda be enjoined from revealing their content in a newspaper article or a broadcast? On the basis of *Brandon Books*, there would not be an absolute obligation of confidentiality in such a case. The court would then, presumably, have to balance the public interests involved – that in maintaining confidentiality (perhaps for the protection of Garda lives) against that in the citizen's "right to be informed".[24] And in regard to the latter, there must be a public interest in ensuring that the Garda instructions are in conformity with the common law, as authoritatively expounded by Hanna J. in *Lynch v. Fitzgerald*.[25]

---

[17]*Attorney General (S.P.U.C. (Ireland) Ltd) v. Open Door Counselling Ltd.* [1988] I.R. 593; *S.P.U.C. (Ireland) Ltd v. Coogan* [1989] I.R. 734; *S.P.U.C. (Ireland) Ltd v. Grogan* [1989] I.R. 753; Case C–159/60, *S.P.U.C. (Ireland) Ltd. v. Grogan* [1991] E.C.R. I–4685; *Attorney General (S.P.U.C. (Ireland) Ltd.) v. Open Door Counselling Ltd.* [1994] 2 I.R. 338; *S.P.U.C. (Ireland) Ltd. v. Grogan (No. 4)* [1994] 1 I.R. 46.

[18]*Open Door and Dublin Well Woman v. Ireland* (1992) 15 E.H.R.R. 244.

[19]Fourteenth Amendment of the Constitution Act 1992.

[20]See the Supreme Court's decision in *S.P.U.C. (Ireland) Ltd v. Grogan (No. 5)* [1998] 4 I.R. 343.

[21]*Attorney General v. Hamilton* [1993] 2 I.R. 250.

[22]The Seventeenth Amendment of the Constitution Act 1997 has inserted a new Article 28.4.3° which, with two exceptions not relevant here, proclaims that the confidentiality of discussions at Government meetings ". . . shall be respected in all circumstances. . .". Presumably, it would be the right and duty of the Attorney General to enforce this constitutional command, by injunction if necessary.

[23]*Irish Times*, June 5, 2000.

[24]As McCarthy J. put it in *Cullen v. Toibín* [1984] I.L.R.M. 577 at 582.

[25][1938] I.R. 382.

3. INVASION OF PRIVACY

That the Constitution guarantees an unenumerated right of privacy is well established,[26] even if the precise contours of the right remain to be delineated. A breach of that right may sound in damages,[27] and there would seem to be no reason in principle why an injunction should not be granted to restrain a threatened breach – such as the publication of material which is the product of privacy-invasive surveillance.[28]

A much more difficult problem arises where two persons share certain information, which one wishes to disseminate and the other wants to keep private. Such was the situation in *M. v. Drury*.[29] The plaintiff and the eleventh defendant were wife and husband, judicially separated at the instance of the wife. There were five children of the marriage, ranging in age from fifteen to seven, all living with the plaintiff in the family home. The husband claimed that the sole cause of the breakdown of the marriage was the wife's infidelity with a Roman Catholic priest. He had sold his story to the *Daily Mirror*, which published an article based thereon on June 2, 1994. The plaintiff sought an interlocutory injunction to restrain the publication of any further matter particular to her family life. On the application of her counsel, the court ordered that the five children be joined as co-plaintiffs.

O'Hanlon J. noted that the plaintiff's claim was founded on an alleged violation of the right of privacy stemming from Articles 40 and 41 of the Constitution. The wife's case was that the proposed publication amounted to a disclosure of matters related to intimate family life. But the judge did not think that this was so; the proposed publication did not relate to the intimacies of married life, or involve marital communications. Rather, it was a matter of the husband alleging an extra-marital affair on his wife's part, and seeking publicity to vent his anger and possibly to reap some financial reward. O'Hanlon J. continued:[30]

> "If the truth of the allegations were seriously challenged, the courts would certainly intervene in an appropriate case to prevent publication pending trial, and the law of libel could be invoked in aid of the plaintiff's case. Similarly, in case of a breach of the *in camera* rule, as happened in *Re Kennedy and McCann* [1976] I.R. 382, injunctive relief could be obtained under various statutes dealing with family law matters."

---

[26] *McGee v. Attorney General* [1974] I.R. 284; *Norris v. Attorney General* [1984] I.R. 36; *Kennedy v. Ireland* [1987] I.R. 587.

[27] *Kennedy v. Ireland* [1987] I.R. 587.

[28] The Law Reform Commission's *Report on Privacy* (L.R.C. 57 – 1998) recommends the creation by statute of such a remedy. See Chap. 7, para. 31. But the *Report* does not suggest that the existing law cannot deliver such relief.

[29] [1994] 2 I.R. 8.

[30] *ibid.* at p. 14.

But he was unable to conclude that there was a fair question to be tried as to whether some right of the wife's under Article 40 or 41 would be breached by the publication of further revelations of the kind in issue.

O'Hanlon J. went on to say that the situation was more complex now that the children had been joined as co-plaintiffs. Publication of this kind of material, it was claimed, was potentially harmful to them, and their constitutional rights – as distinct from the wife's – entitled them to protection against this. But the judge felt that, *absent* any statutory provision or relevant precedent, he could not grant the relief sought. He said:[31]

> ". . . the court is asked to intervene to restrain the publication of material, the truth of which has not yet been disputed, in order to save from the distress that such publication is sure to cause, the children of the marriage who are all minors. This would represent a new departure in our law, for which, in my opinion, no precedent has been shown, and for which I can find no basis in the Irish Constitution, having regard, in particular, to the strongly-expressed guarantees in favour of freedom of expression in that document".[32]

Had the question of balance of convenience arisen, O'Hanlon J. said that a factor to be taken into account was:

> ". . . the general undesirability of holding up – perhaps for years – the publication of material when the ultimate decision is likely to be that it was quite lawful to publish. Otherwise the interlocutory injunction could be used effectively to encroach in a significant manner on the freedom of the press."[33]

This decision clearly proceeds on the basis of a strong presumption against any prior restraint on the publication or other dissemination of information. O'Hanlon J.'s approach closely resembles that of Carroll J. in the *Brandon Books* case, and subsequently in the defamation case of *Connolly v. RTÉ*.[34] There the plaintiff sought an interlocutory injunction restraining any repeat broadcasts of an RTÉ film on drunk driving, used to highlight a Garda campaign against such conduct in December 1990. Her distinctive car appeared on the film, intercut with another shot of a woman driver being breathalysed and a

---

[31] *M. v. Drury*, above, n. 29 at 17.

[32] This perception of the Constitution's guarantees is not universally shared. The Constitution Review Group thought that ". . . the extent of the protection of free speech provided for by this sub-section [Article 40.6.1°i] seems weak and heavily circumscribed" (*Report*, May 1996: Pn 2632, p. 291).

[33] [1994] 2 I.R. 8 at 17-18.

[34] [1991] 2 I.R. 446.

voiceover saying that the woman was just below the limit. The plaintiff's face did not appear on the film, nor did the registration number of her car, and she was not identified. Nonetheless, she claimed that the film was defamatory of her, and that an eventual award of damages therefor would not be an adequate remedy.

Carroll J. noted that the plaintiff had founded on *Campus Oil Ltd. v. Minister for Energy (No. 2)*,[35] arguing that there was an issue to be tried, that damages would not be an adequate remedy and that the balance of convenience determined whether an injunction would issue. For RTÉ it was contended that *Campus Oil* did not apply, and that the established law in defamation cases was that injunctions were rarely granted. Carroll J. saw no reason why *both* principles should not be applied. In considering the balance of convenience, the court must take into account the right to freedom of expression balanced against the plaintiff's right to a good name and reputation, in the light of the law on injunctive relief in defamation cases. The judgment concludes as follows:[36]

> "In my opinion the balance of convenience is in favour of not granting the injunction. Despite the plaintiff's fears, there is no immediate danger of using the footage and RTÉ has promised to co-operate in bringing the matter to an early trial. It is preferable in the circumstances of this case that the alleged libel which is contested should be tried by a jury rather than that an injunction should issue."

A similar reluctance to impose prior restraints is further evident from *Weeland v. RTÉ*,[37] where Carroll J. declined to enjoin the broadcasting of material alleged to be both defamatory and a contempt of court.

4. DEFAMATION

The decisions surveyed above clearly show that the courts lean strongly against enjoining the dissemination of material alleged to be defamatory. Indeed, in *Sinclair v. Gogarty*[38] the former Supreme Court stated the principle applicable as follows:

---

[35] [1983] I.R. 88.

[36] [1991] 2 I.R. 446 at 448.

[37] [1987] I.R. 662.

[38] [1937] I.R. 377. The defendant there was the celebrated author, surgeon and wit Oliver St. John Gogarty, and the alleged libel appeared in his autobiographical work *As I Was Going Down Sackville Street*. An affidavit supporting the plaintiff's claim was sworn by another writer who had not then achieved his subsequent renown, Samuel Beckett. For an account of the trial of the substantive action, see Ulick O'Connor, *Oliver St. John Gogarty* (London, 1964), Chap. 19.

". . . an interlocutory injunction should only be granted in the clearest cases where any jury would say that the matter complained of was libellous, and where if the jury did not so find the Court would set aside the verdict as unreasonable".[39]

Nonetheless, the court upheld Hanna J.'s grant of an injunction in the instant case.

What if the defendant pleads justification? In *Bonnard v. Perryman*[40] the English Court of Appeal laid it down that no interlocutory injunction should be granted in such circumstances, and in *Sinclair v. Gogarty* the former Supreme Court had referred with approval to *Bonnard's* case. That approval, however, was for the general approach of circumspection manifested in *Bonnard's* case; since justification was not pleaded in *Sinclair's* case any approval of the 'no interlocutory injunction' rule there propounded would have been *obiter*.

This issue arose squarely for decision in *Reynolds v. Malocco*,[41] where the plaintiff sought an interlocutory injunction to prohibit the publication, in a new magazine edited by the first defendant, of an article alleged to be defamatory of him. He contended that an eventual award of damages would be an inadequate remedy, *inter alia*, because there was little possibility of actually recovering damages from any of the defendants, including the publishing company. The defendants pleaded justification, and argued that no injunction should therefore issue. The plaintiff responded by inviting the court to examine the defendants' evidence to determine whether the plea of justification had any prospect of success.

Kelly J. observed that in cases of this type, an interlocutory injunction would normally be refused if the defendant intended to plead justification. But was a bare statement of an intention to invoke that defence sufficient to debar the plaintiff from interlocutory relief? Kelly J. said that if this was the law it would hardly be consistent with the obligations imposed on the court by the Constitution.[42] Moreover, the application of so rigid a rule would provide a happy hunting ground for unscrupulous defamers. He was, accordingly, satisfied that the court was entitled to examine the evidence in order to ascertain whether the justification plea had any prospect of success. Having done so, he concluded that there was no arguable prospect of making out this defence.

Kelly J. went on to emphasise that the grant of injunctive relief was always discretionary. In cases such as this, the court must be circumspect to ensure

[39] [1937] I.R. 377 at 384, *per* Sullivan C.J., FitzGibbon, Murnaghan, Meredith and Geoghegan JJ. concurring.
[40] [1891] 2 Ch. 269.
[41] [1999] 2 I.R. 203.
[42] Kelly J. presumably meant the obligation to find the proper balance, in each concrete case, between freedom of expression and other competing constitutional interests, such as protection of reputation.

that it did not unnecessarily interfere with freedom of expression. Damages were the normal remedy for defamation and injunctions were not. In this case, however, to leave the plaintiff to his remedy in damages would be incorrect, since the evidence showed that, given the financial position of each of the defendants, it would be virtually impossible to recover any sum awarded. Kelly J. accordingly granted the interlocutory relief sought.

5. Conclusion

The approach of the United States courts, sketched in the opening paragraphs of this essay, has the undoubted merit of clarity. There seem to be no shades of grey; the 'no injunction' rule is starkly black and white. Though liability in damages may still exist, in this context of prior restraints, at least, freedom of expression trumps other constitutional values, such as privacy or reputation. The Irish approach is more *nuancé*. There is a strong presumption against granting injunctions, though it is not irrebutable. Since, as the *Reynolds*[43] case shows, an eventual remedy in damages may on occasion be illusory, this flexibility is valuable. Though it does not offer the media the clear guidance of the United States rule, it seems to strike a more just balance between media freedom and individual rights.

---

[43] *Reynolds v. Malocco*, above, n. 41.

JUDICIAL DISCRETION AND THE PLANNING INJUNCTION

TOM COONEY

1. INTRODUCTION

The idea that judges decide hard cases on the basis of legal principle has faced a harsh season of jurisprudential antagonism. Diverse critics have sought to slough off what they conceive to be an encrustation of intellectual errors to show that judges use their discretion to legislate in hard cases. Here I defend the view that the judge's task in hard cases is not to invent but to re-spin the law's thread of principle to a more coherent design. I will offer a brief defence in an examination of the law governing the planning injunction. My plan is this. I will summarise the law on the planning injunction. I will give examples of how the courts exercise discretion in cases dealing with the planning injunction. I will criticise sceptical views of legal reasoning which say, at best, that when judges run out of rules they can exercise their discretion to legislate, or, at worst, that legal reasoning is caprice. I will argue that the idea of constructive interpretation clarifies how principles form an integral part of the social practice of law.

2. SECTION 27

Section 27 of the Local Government (Planning and Development) Act 1976,[1] empowers the courts to grant injunctions to ensure, in the public interest, compliance by developers with the planning code generally and with planning conditions in particular.[2] The planning injunction is designed as "a powerful tool"[3] to enforce urgently and effectively the requirements of the planning code. It is

---

[1] As substituted by s. 19(4)(g) of the Local Government (Planning and Development) Act, 1992. Section 160 of the Planning and Development Act, 2000, restates, with modifications, s. 27 of the 1976 Act, as amended by the 1992 Act. The Act of 2000 requires ministerial orders to bring it into operation.

[2] *Cork Corporation v. O'Connell* [1982] I.L.R.M. 505.

[3] See *Mahon v. Butler* [1998] 1 I.L.R.M. 284 (Denham J.) (S.C.). The courts have clarified the concept of "development" mainly in s. 27 cases. See, for example, *Dublin Corporation v. Regan Advertising Ltd* [1986] I.R. 171 (H.C.); [1989] I.R. 61 (S.C.); and *Patterson v. Murphy* [1978] I.L.R.M. 85 (H.C.).

a summary and self-contained remedy which enables the courts to interdict and correct non-conforming development. Although section 27 does not use the term "injunction," the reference to "interim" and "interlocutory" orders in section 27(3) fortifies the inference that the provision contemplates an order in the nature of an injunction.[4]

Under section 27(1), where a development of land, being development which requires planning permission, has been carried out, or is being carried out, without such permission, or an unauthorised use is being made of land, the High Court or the Circuit Court may, on the application of a planning authority or any other person, whether or not the person has an interest in the land, by order require any person to do or not to do, or to cease to do, as the case may be, anything that the court considers necessary and specifies in the order to ensure, as appropriate, that the development or unauthorised use is not continued, and, in so far as is practicable, that the land is restored to its original condition.[5]

Section 27(2) provides that where any permitted development has been commenced but has not been, or is not being, carried out in conformity with the permission or for any other reason, the High Court or the Circuit Court may, on the application of a planning authority or any other person, whether or not that person has an interest in the land, by order require any person to do or not to do, or to cease to do, as the case may be, anything that the Court considers necessary and specifies in the order to ensure that the development is carried out in conformity with the permission.[6]

Thus, section 27 targets two general categories of non-conforming development: development or unauthorised use lacking the required permission; and permitted development which exceeds its specified limitations. Applications can be made to the High Court or to the Circuit Court. The application must be made by motion and the court has power to make such interim or interlocutory order as it sees fit. An applicant is not obliged to give an undertaking as to damages,[7] but the court may require this in an appropriate case.

As to standing, section 27 breaks new ground in the area of planning enforcement. Before its enactment only planning authorities could apply for a judicial remedy against planning violations.[8] In 1974, the Kenny Report on the price of building land recommended legislation to give planning authorities a

---

[4] See *Avenue Properties Ltd v. Farrell Homes Ltd* [1982] I.L.R.M. 21 (H.C.).
[5] See, for example, *Cavan County Council v. Eircell Ltd*, unreported, High Court, Geoghegan J., March 10, 1999.
[6] See, for example, *Fitzpatrick v. O'Connor*, unreported, High Court, Costello J., March 11, 1988.
[7] See *Dublin County Council v. Crampton Builders Ltd*, unreported, High Court, Finlay P., March 10, 1980.
[8] See *Buckley v. Holland Clyde Ltd*, unreported, High Court, Kenny J., 1969; and note Murphy J.'s comments in *The State (Haverty) v. An Bord Pleanála* [1988] I.L.R.M. 545 at 549 (H.C.).

statutory *locus standi* to restrain planning violations.[9] But section 27 goes further, granting standing to the planning authority or "any other person" to apply for a planning injunction. The underlying idea is that all people, as users and enjoyers of the environment, have a standing to seek section 27 relief.[10] An applicant for a planning injunction has no obligation to show that he or she has an interest in the land in question or has suffered any damage beyond what all citizens suffer in the teeth of non-conformity with the planning code.[11] Section 27 is thus an important section enabling anyone to take "watch dog" actions. The section enables the ordinary individual to intervene like a private attorney general to secure planning compliance. In practice, planning authorities bring most applications.

The court can grant a planning injunction against any person. Respondents have included owners and occupiers of land (such as a quarry operator acting under licence) and local authorities. The court may grant an injunction against unknown persons.[12] Applicants have secured planning injunctions against companies, and the courts have been prepared to pierce the veil of incorporation to hold company directors personally accountable for improprieties or negligence undermining the company's ability to meet its planning obligations.[13] A court will require reliable evidence of a director's culpability before affixing him or her with personal liability.[14]

The court has a wide jurisdiction to make whatever orders it judges necessary for enforcement of the planning code. A debt owed to a respondent was attached to ensure the money was available for completion of a development.[15] A waste disposal company who dumped toxic hospital waste on a landfill site in breach of its planning permission was required to provide pure and potable water to the local residents whose wells were polluted as a result.[16] A quarry operator who intensified his operations was required to repair the public roads which had been damaged by heavy trucks travelling to and from the site.[17]

The section 27 procedure is summary so an applicant can invoke the rem-

---

[9] Prl 3632, para. 141 at p. 72.

[10] *Morris v. Garvey* [1983] I.R. 319 at 323 (S.C.).

[11] See *Avenue Properties Ltd v. Farrell Homes Ltd* [1982] I.L.R.M. 21 (H.C.). Note that in *Robinson v. Chariot Inns Ltd* [1986] I.L.R.M. 21 (H.C.), a *bona fide* applicant had standing to apply for a planning injunction even though his motive was commercial self-interest.

[12] See s. 27(4) and r. 8, O.103 of the *Rules of the Superior Courts* added by *Rules of the Superior Courts (No. 1) 1996* (S.I. No. 5 of 1996).

[13] See *Dublin County Council v. Elton Homes* [1984] I.L.R.M. 297 (H.C.); *Dun Laoghaire Corporation v. Parkhill Developments Ltd* [1989] I.R. 447; [1989] I.L.R.M. 235 (H.C.).

[14] See *Dublin County Council v. O'Riordan* [1985] I.R. 159; [1986] I.L.R.M. 104 (H.C.).

[15] See *Coffey v. Hebron Homes Ltd*, unreported, High Court, O'Hanlon J., July 27, 1984.

[16] See *Meath County Council v. Thornton & Thornton Waste Disposals Ltd*, unreported, High Court, O'Hanlon J., January 14, 1994.

[17] See *Dublin County Council v. Macken*, unreported, High Court, O'Hanlon J., May 13, 1994.

edy by evidence on affidavit.[18] The summary procedure is most appropriate when a planning permission creates clear obligations which require expeditious enforcement; but when material facts, particularly the nature of the relationship between the parties and the events giving rise to the application, are a matter of vigorous dispute or profound doubt, the court may interdict the development pending clarification of the nature and extent of the disputed issues through pleadings and a full hearing.[19] Plenary proceedings are necessary when the application asserts that a company director has been responsible for some financial impropriety affecting the company.[20]

The onus of proof in section 27 proceedings lies on the applicant because the relief involved could impact upon the property rights of the respondent and potentially cause him or her loss.[21] The applicant is not required to adduce evidence of the planning authority's attitude to the impugned development.[22] The onus of proof falls on the respondent when he or she invokes an exemption to resist an application.[23] This seems defensible. An exemption from development control is a statutory privilege accorded a developer. It is for the developer to show that he or she is unambiguously entitled to this privilege.[24] Moreover, the party who asserts the existence of a state of affairs in court should, as a matter of fairness, bear the burden of proving his or her assertion.

Section 27 is a self-contained enforcement procedure. Therefore, the courts will not allow it to be frustrated or protracted by the use of collateral procedures such as the reference procedure under section 5 of the 1976 Act.[25] Moreover, the courts will not allow it to be deployed save for proper planning enforcement purposes. In this regard, the courts will not order only partial compliance with a planning permission.[26] They will not tolerate applications under section 27 in which the applicant questions the legality of a planning decision by the planning authority or Planning Board, or asks the court to usurp a function vested in the planning authority.[27]

---

[18] See s. 27(3). For the Circuit Court procedure, see O. 67A of the *Circuit Court Rules*, 1950 (S.I. No. 179 of 1950), as inserted by the Circuit Court Rules (No. 1) 1995 (S.I. No. 215 of 1995). For the High Court procedure, see O.103 of the *Rules of the Superior Courts*, 1986 (S.I. No. 15 of 1986), as amended by the *Rules of the Superior Courts* (No. 1) 1996 (S.I. No. 5 of 1996).

[19] See *Dublin County Council v. Kirby* [1985] I.L.R.M. 325 (H.C.); and *Dublin Corporation v. Lowe & Signings Holdings Ltd*, unreported, High Court, Morris J., February 4, 2000.

[20] See *Dublin County Council v. O'Riordan* [1985] I.R. 159; [1986] I.L.R.M. 104.

[21] See *Dublin Corporation v. Sullivan*, unreported, High Court, Finlay P., December 21, 1984.

[22] See *Monaghan County Council v. Brogan* [1987] I.R. 333 (H.C.).

[23] See *Lambert v. Lewis*, unreported, High Court, Gannon J., November 24, 1982; and *Dolan v. Cooke*, unreported, High Court, Morris J., January 20, 2000.

[24] *Dillon v. Irish Cement*, unreported, Supreme Court, November 26, 1986.

[25] See *Cork Corporation v. O'Connell* [1982] I.R. 505 (S.C.).

[26] See *Dublin Corporation v. McGowan* [1993] 1 I.R. 405 (H.C.).

[27] See *Dublin Corporation v. Kevans*, unreported, High Court, Finlay P., July 14, 1980; and *Dublin Corporation v. Garland* [1982] I.L.R.M. 104 (H.C.).

Section 27 does not provide for the granting of a *quia timet* planning injunction to restrain an anticipated non-conforming development. In *Mahon v. Butler*,[28] the Supreme Court allowed an appeal by the respondents against an order of the High Court restraining the holding of pop concerts in the Irish Rugby Football Union's grounds. The Supreme Court held that the High Court had no jurisdiction to restrain an anticipated breach of the planning code. For the court, Denham J. pointed out that section 27 refers plainly to events occurring in the present or which have occurred in the past but not to future events. Thus, applicants could intervene under section 27 only in present or established events. The new Planning and Development Act will allow the granting of *quia timet* planning injunctions.[29]

There is a five-year limit on applications for a planning injunction, which brings the procedure into line with the other enforcement remedies.[30]

3. LIMITED JUDICIAL DISCRETION

Subsections (1) and (2) of section 27 state that the court "may" grant a planning injunction. The word "may" as deployed here does not have a mandatory or imperative sense, and so there is no absolute requirement that the court must, on proof of a non-conforming development, grant an injunction. In equity, the courts have had a discretion as to whether they should or should not grant an injunction.[31] Section 27 is a precise statutory remedy but the word "may" imports into the court's jurisdiction at least the discretion which is an integral part of its equitable inheritance.[32]

Although this "limited discretion"[33] has an equitable tread, it must be exercised in fidelity to legal principle, confined within the ambit of the section, and designed to preserve the integrity of the planning code. The courts have emphasised that it would take "exceptional circumstances" for them to exercise their discretion. The party asserting the existence of exceptional circumstances bears the onus of proving his or her point. Examples of exceptional circum-

---

[28] [1998] 1 I.L.R.M. 284 (S.C.).

[29] See s. 160(1) of the Planning and Development Act 2000.

[30] See s. 27(6). Section 160(6) of the Act of 2000 provides that an injunction may not be sought after seven years from the commission of the unauthorised development, or the expiry of the relevant planning permission, as appropriate, unless it relates to a planning condition concerning the use of the land.

[31] See *Stafford v. Roadstone Ltd* [1980] I.L.R.M. 1 (H.C.).

[32] In *White v. McInerney Construction Ltd* [1995] 1 I.L.R.M. 373 (S.C.), the Supreme Court explicitly endorsed Barrington J.'s view in *Avenue Properties Ltd v. Farrell Homes Ltd* [1982] I.L.R.M. 21 (H.C.), that in a s. 27 case the courts should, to some extent at least, be influenced by equitable factors.

[33] See the judgment of Geoghegan J. in *Cavan County Council v. Eircell Ltd*, unreported, High Court, March 10, 1999 at p 1.

stances include genuine mistake, acquiescence over a long period, the triviality or mere technicality of the infraction, gross or disproportionate hardship, or like extenuating factors.[34]

The legislative intention is to allow the courts to exercise a context-specific discretion, which is disciplined by principle. This makes sense because applicants for planning injunctions could span the spectrum from a meddler with no interests in the matter to persons who have sustained real injury or who alert the court to blatant planning violations which ought to be stopped in the public interest.[35] In carrying out its function under section 27, a court must balance the benefit and duty of the developer against the environmental and ecological rights and amenities of the public, present and future, particularly those closely or immediately affected by the planning violation. How the courts discipline their exercise of discretion may be seen from the following examples.

(a) Delay or Lapse of Time or Acquiescence

In *Dublin County Council v. Matra Investments Ltd*,[36] Finlay P. observed that the length of time between the commencement of an unauthorised use or the making of an unlawful development and the time when application is made to the court under section 27 must always be a material factor in regard to the exercise by the court of its discretion as to whether to grant or not an injunction. Thus, the applicant's laches or undue delay or acquiescence in the violation may be a ground for refusing him or her a remedy.

In *Dublin Corporation v. Mulligan*,[37] the respondent, a solicitor, purchased a residential house located in an area zoned only for residential use. From 1972, he openly practised law there in the basement and lived in the remainder. In 1978, the planning authority served a warning notice on him. In 1979, he vacated the entire residential portion and began to use the whole house for his practice. In 1980, the planning authority applied to the High Court for a planning injunction against him. At the hearing, the respondent disputed the applicant's case in respect only of the basement. He contended that an injunction should be refused because, besides other things, of the lapse of time.

Finlay P. stated that if an applicant could be said to be guilty of laches or delay, he or she might be disentitled to relief. He was not satisfied that the applicant here had been so guilty because it was not actually aware of the breach until 1978. He accepted that it had experienced difficulties in assembling proof of the user of the premises before the operative date (October 1,

---

[34]See the judgment of Henchy J. in *Morris v. Garvey* [1983] I.R. 319 (S.C.).
[35]See the judgment of Barrington J. in *Avenue Properties Ltd v. Farrell Homes Ltd* [1982] I.L.R.M. 21 (H.C.).
[36](1980) 114 I.L.T.R. 306.
[37]Unreported, High Court, Finlay P., May 6, 1987.

1964) of the planning code. Even so, the judge opined that the respondent's argument about the lapse of time carried weight. The respondent found himself in the position, although he had violated the planning code, that after a considerable number of years without any enforcement he faced interdiction. He could not have been subjected to enforcement notice proceedings because sections 30 and 31 of the 1976 Act were subject to a time limit of five years. This justified the inference that the legislature accepted that with regard to those enforcement powers it would be unjust that a person after the lapse of five years should face injunction proceedings. Finlay P. decided to exercise his discretion to refuse to grant an injunction in regard to the basement but he ordered the respondent to discontinue the use of the remainder of the house for any purpose other than residential use within three months.

The courts will not readily hold the lapse of time against an applicant. In *Dublin Corporation v. Kevans*,[38] the first-named respondent, a solicitor, commenced his legal practice in a three-storey Georgian house. The house had been occupied as a family residence from 1949 until 1971. In 1974, he converted the basement to residential and continued to practice law in the remainder. In 1977, he moved his office elsewhere. In 1978, he leased the entire house to the second-named respondent for office use.

In an application by the planning authority for a planning injunction against the two respondents, Finlay P. examined the planning history of the house. He found that a material change of use of the house had occurred in 1972 when the first-named respondent commenced to use it as an office. He noted that a planning inspector had visited the house in 1974 and that the planning authority had then served a notice requiring the first-named respondent to cease the unauthorised use. He pointed out that the first-named respondent had not complied with the notice and that, in 1975, the planning authority had successfully prosecuted him for the planning violation. In 1977, the first-named respondent advertised the entire house for letting as an office. The planning authority wrote to him and the estate agent objecting to this advertisement. The first-named respondent replied stating that he was obtaining legal advice (from his own firm) but he made no further response. The planning authority served warning notices on him in 1978 and 1979. In the face of his persistent violation the planning authority then applied to the High Court for a planning injunction.

In resisting the application, the first-named respondent acknowledged that his user had been unlawful but claimed that he had used the house as an office for a long time with the substantial acquiescence of the planning authority. He cited the judgment of Finlay P. in *Mulligan*. However, Finlay P. decided that the consideration which arose in *Mulligan* was not present in *Kevans*. He distinguished the cases by indicating that there had been in *Mulligan* a significant

[38] Unreported, High Court, Finlay P., July 14, 1980.

delay between the commencement of an unauthorised use and an application for a planning injunction. Moreover, the planning authority had taken no enforcement steps there until 1978 although the breach had commenced in 1973. In addition, the respondent in that case had a particular vested interest in the basement of the house he was using because he had built up his solicitor's practice there and had created goodwill for his practice over the seven years before the case came to court.

In *Kevans*, Finlay P. also rejected the submission that the planning authority's conduct with regard to the house should be interpreted by the court as a partial or complete acquiescence by it in the change of use which occurred in 1972. It was significant that the planning authority had called on the respondent to stop his unauthorised use within two years from its commencement. Moreover, the respondent solicitor ought to have considered the prosecution for a criminal offence a determination of the issue. The planning authority's pursuit of the matter and its reaction to the advertisement was inconsistent with either a partial or complete acquiescence on its part. The first-named respondent held the house solely as an investment property so he lacked the merit which would have arisen had he been occupying it for professional purposes.

(b) Clean Hands

There is clear authority for the proposition that where an application seeks relief under section 27, the court in exercising its discretion may consider the past conduct of the applicant with regard to the subject matter of the proceedings. If the applicant's conduct reveals bad faith or is tainted by a lack of candour in some material respect, the court may deny him or her relief since he or she lacks "clean hands".

In *O'Connor & Spollen Concrete Group Ltd v. Frank Harrington Ltd & Ors*,[39] O'Connor, a farmer, feared that the blasting involved in quarrying operations by Rydene, the fifth-named respondent, would obstruct the movement of his cattle to and from Coney Island in County Sligo. His other concern was that the quarrying activities would interfere with his aim to build holiday homes on his land in the future. He made no effort to explore the possibility of a friendly resolution of the issue with Rydene, even though all he needed was uninterrupted passage during low tide. He was minded to institute section 27 proceedings but the costs of the action deterred him from doing so.

When Spollens learned of O'Connor's objections to Rydene's operations, they agreed to underwrite the costs of the action to be instituted in O'Connor's name. Spollens considered that Rydene, a business competitor, had obtained an unmerited commercial advantage because they had not sought planning per-

---

[39]Unreported, High Court, Barr J., April 26, 1983.

mission for their quarry and so had avoided the inevitable financial burden arising from compliance with planning conditions. In fact, Rydene had ascertained that the planning authority had no concerns about their intensifying quarrying on the site.

Spollens knew that they could have instituted proceedings in their own name against Rydene, but they preferred to become O'Connor's backers in the action. O'Connor did not reveal to the court either that Spollens were his backers or that they were Rydene's competitor. The initial application was refused but O'Connor brought the case back to court on two later occasions. Then O'Connor had to disclose Spollens' involvement to explain the delay on his part in pursuing Rydene. His explanation suggested, falsely, that Spollens' backing was recent.

Barr J. refused to grant the injunction because the applicant had not come to court with clean hands. O'Connor had failed to put before the court fairly and with candour all facts known to him which were relevant to the exercise of the court's discretion. He had failed to discharge his obligation to satisfy the court about his good faith and the true purpose of his application. Moreover, he had disentitled himself to relief because he had made no attempt to remedy the issue by negotiation.

An applicant's blighted planning history does not necessarily disentitle him or her to an injunction, but candour is essential. In *Fusco v. Aprile*,[40] the applicant, a restaurateur, sought an injunction against the respondent, a competitor, whose restaurant was next door to the applicant, restraining him from selling hot food for consumption off the premises and from exhibiting on his premises an advertisement for this takeaway business. The respondent argued in his defence that the applicant had not come to court with clean hands since he had planning problems affecting his own premises, and that the court should exercise its discretion to refuse to grant an injunction. Morris J. noted that the applicant had made no secret of his own planning problems but had, from the outset, placed them squarely before the court. Granting the applicant relief, the judge found that there was nothing in the applicant's conduct evincing a lack of good faith.

(c) Gross or Disproportionate Hardship

The court may refuse a planning injunction if to grant it would be unfair or an undue hardship on the respondent.

In *Dublin County Council v. Sellwood Quarries Ltd & Ors*,[41] the respondents were extracting rock for commercial purposes by blasting from a quarry which had before been used as a sand-and-gravel pit. On foot of complaints by

---

[40]Unreported, High Court, Morris J., June 6, 1997.
[41][1982] I.L.R.M. 23 (H.C.).

local residents, the applicants sought an injunction to restrain the respondents from carrying out an unauthorised use. The court decided not to grant or refuse the order until it heard further submissions. The court was concerned about the damaging consequences of a prohibitory order for the respondents, their employees, and those customers to whom they were contractually bound. It accepted that the respondents' failure to apply for planning permission was due to a good faith belief on the their part that permission was not required.

In *Avenue Properties Ltd v. Farrell Homes Ltd*,[42] the applicants sought to restrain the respondents from continuing to build an office block otherwise than in accordance with the planning permission, which had been obtained in 1952. They asked for an order requiring the respondents to demolish such portion of the building as was already constructed. The evidence showed that the line of the building had been moved some few feet, that projections had been omitted which could not then be added, and that the basement had been omitted.

Barrington J. noted that the applicants had not been adversely affected by these deviations. In fact, the modifications had the desirable effect of reducing the building in size. He found that the respondents were formally in the wrong, but that there was no evidence to suggest that public amenities had in any way been damaged by the differences between the constructed building and the permitted building, and judged that it would be burdensome on the respondents to grant an injunction in these circumstances. He declined to make an order but adjourned the application to give the respondents a chance to put themselves right with the planning authority by applying for a retention permission.

(d) Third Party Interests

The courts are entitled to take into account the convenience of members of the public when adjudicating upon section 27 applications.

In *Stafford v. Roadstone Ltd*,[43] the respondents had, without planning permission, intensified their quarrying activities, causing a nuisance to local residents, including the applicants. The court indicated that when a private individual comes forward under section 27 as a public watchdog, the court, in exercising its discretion, is entitled to look not only at the convenience of the parties but at the convenience of the public. The court rejected the notion that the legislative intention was that the court should be obliged on an application by someone with no interest in the lands automatically to close down, for example, an important factory, because of some technical breach of the planning code regardless of the inconvenience to employees and the public.

---

[42][1982] I.L.R.M. 21 (H.C.).
[43][1980] I.L.R.M. 1 (H.C.).

Here, the court decided not to grant an injunction because the respondents had not committed a deliberate and conscious planning violation, local residents did not want the quarry to be closed down but to be subject to proper planning limitations, and the quarry had given needed employment in the locality. Barrington J. disposed of the application on the basis that the respondents were willing to give certain undertakings to the court. They were willing to apply for planning permission as quickly as practicable and undertook to take all possible steps to ensure that, in the interim, their activities did not cause a nuisance locally.

In *Curley v. Galway Corporation*,[44] the applicants, local residents, sought an injunction to stop the respondent dumping waste for landfill on a site in their locality. The governing planning permission allowed the respondent to carry out this development, but the evidence showed that it had breached many environmentally protective planning conditions. Moreover, although the respondent was obliged to cease operations by a certain date, it had failed to do so. The respondent argued that the court should exercise its discretion to decline the application in view of the hardship it would cause it and the very considerable inconvenience it would cause the citizens of Galway in disposing of their refuse.

Kelly J. rejected the respondent's arguments in the case because it was responsible for a deliberate and conscious illegality. The court made an order restraining the use of the site for dumping save in respect of material from refuse trucks operated by the respondent. This exception was allowed for one month from the date of the judgment. The court justified this concession out of concern not for the respondent, whose behaviour it found unacceptable, but out of concern for the citizens of Galway who might have found themselves confronted with great difficulties over the Christmas period if their refuse could not be disposed of.

(e) Trivial or Technical Violations

The courts may deny relief against a non-conforming development if the violation is trivial or technical, is inadvertent on the part of the developer, and causes no adverse planning impact.

In *Leech v. Reilly*,[45] the respondent was injuncted from enlarging his workshop without permission close to the boundary of the applicant's property. He undertook not to do more work on the structure. He obtained permission to modify the structure so he resumed the work. Here the court denied the applicant relief on the basis that she had failed to co-operate with the respondent by denying him access to her property to do work on the structure when he sought

---

[44]Unreported, High Court, Kelly J., December 14, 1998.
[45]Unreported, High Court, O'Hanlon J., April 26, 1983.

to mend his hand. Moreover, the court found that the respondent had not deliberately flouted the planning code and that his breach of his undertaking to the court was purely technical on the facts.

No matter how the courts exercise their discretion under section 27, they are scrupulous about preserving the integrity of the planning code. Thus, the High Court declined to grant an injunction in *Mulligan*, but it declared that the non-conforming office use could not have the effect of rezoning the premises from residential use, which meant that the respondent could not have sold the house as an office. In another case, the High Court interdicted the respondent's non-conforming use of the wall of a premises to advertise, even though the respondent was waiting for the outcome of its planning appeal, because the court was not prepared to allow it to reap a financial profit from its illegality.[46]

4. Scepticism about Legal Reasoning

Adjudication is at the heart of our legal system. We expect judges to decide cases in light of legal principle, even in hard cases where the relevant legal materials do not unequivocally yield a single answer. The importance of this requirement seems all the more obvious where a judge's decision involves the application of state coercion. Enforcement of a planning injunction may have a far-reaching impact on the respondent's interests, and non-compliance with the injunction may attract imprisonment. Judges must have a basis in principle that enables them to say when coercive force may be exercised in the name of the community as a whole.[47] But there are perspectives which make judicial *diktat* the centrepiece.

(a) Legal Realism

Legal Realists are sceptical of the idea that legal standards provide certain answers to legal questions.[48] A proper lawyerly focus therefore will concentrate on what judges do rather than on what paper rules say. Competent lawyers will study judges' attitudes and decisions to acquire data enough to let them predict decisions for the clients, and in their advocacy they will draw on whatever materials they think will convince judges to endorse the policy arguments they make in court. In its philosophical bent, legal realism is pragmatic. On this view, arguments of principle in section 27 cases are best seen as extralegal

---

[46]*Dublin Corporation v. Maiden Posters Sites* [1983] I.L.R.M. 48.
[47]Dworkin, *Law's Empire* (Cambridge, Mass; London: Belknap Press, 1986) at pp. 93, 97, 103, & 151.
[48]See, for example, Holmes, *Collected Legal Papers* (London: Constable & Co, 1920); and Llewellyn, *Jurisprudence: Realism in Theory and Practice* (Chicago, Ill; London; University of Chicago Press, 1962).

moral arguments. But leaving aside legal realism's naive reliance of the alms of quack psychology, its pragmatic attitude is questionable.

First, it fails to consider seriously enough the proposition that legal standards are sufficiently determinate to decide legal issues. In *Attorney General (McGarry) v. Sligo County Council*,[49] the Supreme Court based its decision on a purposive reading of the relevant provisions of the 1963 Act to hold that the respondent county council could not carry out a development which involved dumping waste close to rare megalithic graves, in material contravention of its development plan. The decision evinces a close and faithful reading of the relevant sections and there is nothing to show that the court took account of extralegal factors. While legal realism professes to favour a scientific approach to decision-making, it belies its commitment by ignoring data that attest to legal standards informing judicial decisions.

Secondly, legal realism fails to take seriously the division of governmental powers one of whose cardinal ideas is that the legislature enacts future-oriented policy while the courts apply the law. A legal realist would find it hard to say that the courts should not usurp the legislative or executive role, because a realist is indiscriminate as to which institution of state achieves preferred policy changes so long as it is effective.

Thirdly, implicit in our legal tradition is the idea that a court is itself a creature of law. Properly to identify a court we must have recourse to legal standards. Realism slights the responsibility to interpret and defer to pre-existing law and so, from its perspective, what constitutes a court is not a legal question. Moreover, it cannot explain in what sense the power to grant or refuse injunctions is uniquely a judicial function. It seems paradoxical that realists are obsessed with what the courts do in fact yet they are precluded from settling principles governing the judicial function. They are like non-believers who scatter salt to ward off the spirits they do not believe in.

(b) Critical Legal Studies (CLS)

CLS asserts that law serves an unjust political order and privileges the selfish person who is able to assert his or her rights through the courts. For CLS, legal reasoning is formalistic reasoning, and formalistic reasoning is false reasoning because it pretends that justification can be got from legal standards to resolve legal questions. Judges can manipulate the law to give decisions reflecting their own ideological tilt. CLS evinces deep scepticism about the possibility of legal reasoning.[50] It has gone down into the magma of continental Deconstructionist (Derrida) and Marxist (Gramsci) thought for its intellectual

---

[49] [1991] 1 I.R. 21.
[50] Unger, "The Critical Legal Studies Movement" (1983) 46 *Harv. L. Rev.* 569. See also Kelman, *A Guide to Critical Legal Studies* (Cambridge, Mass: Harvard University Press, 1987).

rock, and what it has brought back from that descent is a corrosive anti-legal scepticism. But it bristles with threats to its coherence.

First, CLS's view that judgments are makeshift rationalisations is questionable. Most lawyers find that legal standards often afford determinate answers, and although lawyers are willing to argue for either side of a legal controversy, this does not mean that each party's claim is equally sound. The existence of hard cases does not nullify the truth that many legal questions are answerable from a purposive reading of existing legal standards. In practice, lawyers routinely advise clients about what the planning code requires in specific cases.

It is true that courts sometimes have to face hard cases. In *Mulligan*, for example, the court faced the argument that, although section 27 on its wording appeared to mandate the grant of a planning injunction, the case as a whole demanded otherwise. Here, the respondent argued that the undue delay in enforcement and the vested interests he had in pursuing his livelihood warranted not interdicting his unauthorised use of his home as an office. In interpreting section 27, the court's reasoning was not gripped by the claw of semantics. Instead, the court recognised that section 27 exists not singly but as part of a collective purposeful practice, and that its meaning in the case was a matter of argument within that practice, driven by propulsive principle. The propulsive principle in the case was justice whose weight demanded that the applicant not be unfairly disadvantaged by the applicant's inordinate delay in taking proceedings.

Secondly, CLS asserts that legal standards lack coherence because they are internally contradictory. As to section 27, its point might be that section 27 and its case law reveal both the principle that non-conforming development should be interdicted and the counterprinciple that an applicant who makes an undue or inexcusable delay in prosecuting his or her claim against the respondent should be denied a remedy. This contradiction is open to being exploited by a court to arrive at its preferred disposition of any particular case. This criticism lacks force. When principles collide in section 27 cases, the judge has to consider the relative weight of each. In *Mulligan*, the principle of fairness in the fact of undue delay prevailed, but, in *Kevans*, it lacked decisive weight. But this is not troubling for legal reasoning. The principle is still a legal principle and in a future section 27 case, when competing considerations are weaker, it may be decisive. Contrary to what CLS seems to think, weighing colliding principles is a normal part of legal reasoning.

Thirdly, CLS devalues the role of legal standards in restraining excesses of administrative power. Ordinarily, the courts defer to the specialised expertise of administrative authorities that operate the planning code. The doctrine of irrationality evinces judicial respect for those authorities' conceptions of how rationally to perform their statutory roles. If a local planning authority or the Planning Board acts within proper statutory constraints, in good faith, and fairly, and its decision can be rationally defended on an interpretation which the planning code may reasonably be judged to yield, the courts will not interfere. But the exercise of administrative discretion is amenable to judicial supervision to preserve the integrity of the law, including personal rights. In *McGarry*, when the Supreme Court enjoined Sligo County Council from violating its own development plan by dumping waste on an important archaeological site, it checked this abuse, thus preserving the integrity of the planning code and the local planning authority's own development plan, and protecting the rights of the applicants who represented the public interest against the county council.

Fourthly, CLS holds that law serves to legitimate the unjust structure of society by using its rhetoric of rights and duties to influence people into accepting that law is a source of justice. On this view, when judges say that planning issues involve three parties – the planning authority or Planning Board, the developer, and the public – this helps to cultivate a misplaced sense among people that law is a communal good which serves their interests as equals. This approach towards legitimation springs from the writings of the Italian Marxist, Antonio Gramsci. It claims that law keeps its hold on people's minds, not mainly by way of coercive force, but by promoting "false consciousness".

Law is bound to influence how people think, and contribute to political legitimacy. It can legitimate the state's various interventions into people's lives. The acceptability of this influence turns on what values the law serves. When the law interdicts the activities of a selfish developer, as it did in *Thornton*, where the respondent contaminated wells by dumping toxic medical waste, this is eminently desirable, and if the decision sends a message to other reckless waste disposal businesses, that is welcome. But CLS's point goes deeper: it argues that the "false consciousness" which the law fosters means that ordinary people are unlikely to invoke the law to protect their rights. The case law on section 27 shows – *McGarry* is a case in point[51] – that the law has not moulded a people who act slavishly in the face of unlawful development by government or the powerful and that unselfish citizens can invoke the law.

In sum, the CLS's criticisms of legal reasoning have none of the grain of true criticism. Its attitude is like a commuter bus that misses all the crucial stops along route. Intellectually, like Legal Realism's pragmatism, it covers a barren ground broken by the futile plough of scepticism.

(c) Positivism

For positivism, legal propositions make sense, but when courts run out of legal standards they exercise their discretion to make law.

HLA Hart has given us the most sophisticated theory of legal positivism.[52] Law is a systemic union of primary rules and secondary rules. Primary rules

---

[51] See also *Howard v. The Commissioners of Public Works* [1994] 1 I.R. 101.
[52] See Hart, *The Concept of Law* (2nd ed. by Bulloch & Raz, Oxford, 1994).

impose obligations or confer powers on persons to structure their legal relations to others (for example, section 24 of the 1963 Act). Secondary rules are about the primary rules of the legal system since they specify the way in which the primary rules may be identified, changed, and enforced. Three types of secondary rules stake out the transition from primitive law to a sophisticated legal system. The *rule of recognition* spells out the criteria satisfaction of which by a suggested rule is taken as establishing legal pedigree or validity. Using *rules of change* (e.g. section 4 of the 1963 Act), society may add, repeal, and amend existing valid rules. *Rules of adjudication* (e.g. section 27 itself) afford a process for conclusive determinations of whether a valid rule has been violated.

Fundamental to the concept of a legal rule is the idea of obligation. The obligatory character of legal rules, Hart says, flows from the social fact that people accept them as standards to which they ought to conform and as reasons to criticise non-conforming behaviour. Hart says that those who accept a rule as promulgating a common standard adopt "the internal point of view" towards it. Since most people lack an understanding of their legal system or its criteria of validity, what is vital for a legal system to exist is that most officials (e.g. judges) hold the internal point of view towards the rule of recognition and the rules of change and adjudication. They must accept them as common public standards of official behaviour by officials in the legal system. For others, general obedience to valid primary rules suffices.

For Hart, law and morals are logically separable, and it is not necessary that law mirror moral requirements, although laws often do so. Unjust or unfair rules which meet the applicable tests of legal validity possess legal pedigree. Once a judge runs out of valid legal rules, the law is exhausted. If a party's case is not covered by such a rule or the judge is willing to decline to apply an unjust or unfair rule, the issues raised cannot be resolved according to law. Hart explains the presence of gaps in the law by reference to the nature of language. Since rules are open-textured, they leave much room for judicial discretion in applying the law in a particular case.[53] Rules are open-textured because all natural language is indeterminate.

He thinks the quasi-legislative power of judges to fill in the interstitial gaps in the law is desirable. It would be imprudent to try to settle in advance, but in the dark, issues that can only reasonably be resolved when they arise. The disadvantage of trying to be overly determinate in drafting rules is that legislators may include in the scope of the rule cases which we would wish to exclude in order to give effect to reasonable social purposes. Open textured terms of language would have allowed us to exclude those cases appropriately. Also, very often rules incorporate general standards. A rule may include words such as "reasonable" or "fair". There will be clear cases where the standard applies

---

[53] *ibid.* at pp. 124–125.

and clear cases where it does not. In some cases, however, uncertainty obtains before an authoritative judicial decision on the question. Moreover, what a precedent stands for is liable to change over time. For this reason there is no uniquely correct formulation of a rule set down in a precedent. The holdings in cases are open to distinguishing or broadening in the face of new questions.

The upshot of this analysis is that judicial legislation is an inevitable feature of a sophisticated legal system.[54] In the open margins of hard cases judges make new rules. Hart says it is like the exercise of delegated rule-making powers by an administrative authority. This creative judicial function involves discretion because it does not depend on a search for legislative intention or pre-existing law. But Hart's view is questionable. In the hard cases where he thinks that judicial discretion operates there may be sound judicial decisions for the making.

First, although the right answer in any such case is not patent on the face of an existing rule, the judge may find the right answer by invoking legal principles which are implicit in the law. The mistake in Hart's conception of law is to assume that the law is made up only of rules whose existence is a matter of solid fact. In response, Ronald Dworkin comments that in hard cases, competing considerations are likely to pull judges in different directions. He cites the American case of *Riggs v. Palmer*.[55] A grandson murdered his grandfather to inherit his property. The grandson was a beneficiary under his grandfather's will. The will had been validly executed under existing statutory rules. The court held that in view of the principle that no person should be allowed to profit from his own fraud or to take advantage of his own wrong, the grandson had no right to the inheritance. Dworkin takes this case to illustrate the point that the law is concerned not only with settled rules but also with principles. Hart's positivism misses the importance of these principles. In cases like *Riggs* principles perform a decisive role in arguments supporting judgments about legal rights and obligations. After judgment has been given we may say that the decision articulates a new rule from existing legal principle. If the principle had been an extralegal standard lacking fit or justification in the law, then the judges would have had no basis for invoking it.[56]

Rules and principles are legal standards. They differ in how they require judges to act. Rules are applicable in an all-or-nothing way; either a rule speaks to the issue before a court or it does not. Principles operate differently. The principle that a planning injunction ought not to be granted to an applicant if doing so would cause a gross and disproportionate hardship to the respondent does not mean that it will protect respondents or members of the public in every case from the burdens caused by the grant of a planning injunction. A

---

[54] *ibid.* at p. 132.
[55] (1889) 115 N.Y. 506, 22 N.E. 188.
[56] See Dworkin, *Taking Rights Seriously* (London, 1978) at p. 41.

principle affords a reason that weighs in one direction, but does not mechanically dictate an answer. Other principles or enacted policies may argue in a different direction in a particular case and the principle may not prevail there. But the principle remains a principle and in the next appropriate case, where the competing considerations are not coercive or are less weighty, the principle may be decisive for the outcome. Principles, unlike rules, have a dimension of weight. When there is an interaction between them in a case, the judge must decide upon the relative weight of each to find a resolution. As in section 27 cases, the court must show a context-specific sensitivity to the equities of the case.

Secondly, the legal force of the principle in *Mulligan*, for example, does not derive from its satisfying any criteria set out by a rule of recognition. Hart's notion that a rule of recognition gives principles their legal pedigree is unconvincing. It is not feasible to construct a convention setting out exhaustively legal principles.[57] The basis of such principles lies not in particular legislative or judicial decisions, but in a sense of moral appropriateness and integrity within our society's practice of law. Of course, we cite cases or statutory provisions in which a principle figures in court to leaven our argument that the principle we are invoking is a legal principle. Our argument however would be that the materials involved exemplify the principle. But the legal force of the principle stems from its argumentative role in making the best moral justification for our law as a whole.

Hart might say that principles could be identified by the rule of recognition once it mirrors judicial practice in identifying the sources of law. Conventional judicial practice can include recognising moral principles for the purposes of deciding cases.[58] In *O'Connor*, for example, the court cites the principle that an applicant for a planning injunction must come to court with clean hands as a background standard against which to read section 27. In this way it justified a new reading of the statutory provision. Before this decision there was no knockdown fact of the matter that the principle ought to figure in the case, and, since the issue was the subject of adversarial legal argument, the principle was not readily identifiable as having legal force in the case. Hart might claim that the rule of recognition need do no more that state the fact that the judge is required, or at liberty, to take the principle of "clean hands" into account.

This is inadequate because it does not tell the judge how to take the principle into account. Principles are a matter of weight, and judges have to determine what weight the principle should bear in any case. The parties can point out to the judge that the principle operates in equity or some cognate segment of the law, but the problem is the judge has to make a judgment to resolve the controversy before him or her. Making judgments about which principles war-

---

[57] *ibid.* p. 36.
[58] See Hart, *op. cit.*, above n. 52 at p. 250.

rant consideration in a case and about what weight they should bear is simply not an exercise in factual description or factual discovery. It is a normative and argumentative process.

5. Constructive Interpretation

From a sceptical or a positivistic perspective, the courts in section 27 cases have merely fattened their judgments with the sediment of extralegal values and have felt the need to exercise this discretion because of the lack of guidance from the provision itself. But this view is wrong; the law on section 27 is not bloated; it is the product of constructive judicial interpretation. The core question is, when faced with an application under section 27, how does a court connect the principles with the issues arising in the case? We have already noted that the law on section 27 has a density, and the cases show that there is no hard-and-fast boundary between legal reasoning and moral or political principles. The court's finding against the applicants in *O'Connor* on the basis that they had come to court with "unclean hands" was a morally principled finding. It was a constructive view of the law because the court made a decision which advanced the purposes behind section 27.

Moral conviction is a constitutive aspect of sound adjudication. Judges have to invoke self-consciously their own moral convictions to decide cases.[59] Judges who seek to preserve the integrity of law need to decide cases in the light of principles that fit and justify the settled law and must invoke their own moral convictions to determine what those principles are. This is not a formalistic exercise. A judge has the responsibility of confronting these issues, drawing upon his or her own convictions.

This approach commences once a case begins in court. The fact-eliciting process of the trial hearing requires a sense of principle in the judge because he or she cannot separate material from non-material facts without the principle, just as a pilot cannot fly without a sense of direction. The facts of *Mulligan* do not exist in law independently of the background principles of law that gave them significance. But legal reasoning acquires its character not from the facts that find significance in statements of legal principle but from how judicial interpretation in cases constructs the meaning of such principles and their relative weight. So, what is constructive interpretation?

Constructive interpretation is a general attitude towards the practice of interpretation. It enables us to carry forward the social practice of law. The key thing to note about the social practice of law is that it is argumentative. Those who take part in legal practice, especially judges and lawyers, often disagree about what the law requires. They support their conflicting claims with argu-

---

[59] See Dworkin, *op. cit.*, above, n. 47, pp. 94, 225-275.

ments. Every participant in legal argument knows that what the law is in any case turns on the validity of legal propositions whose sense derives only from and within the practice of law. The practice consists mainly in stating and arguing about these propositions.[60]

There are two ways to examine the argumentative character of legal practice. One involves the external perspective of the sociologist or historian, the outsider's point of view. The other is the insider's point of view, the internal understanding of those who make the claims involving propositions of law. To understand legal practice, we must adopt the insider's perspective, and constructive interpretation is an attitude that tries to understand social practices, such as law (or art or literature), from the participating insider's standpoint.[61] The claims advanced by a constructive interpretation of law, for this reason, are not detached reports of what insiders think the law might require, but claims about what he or she as an internal participant is convinced it does require.

It is distinctive of the insider's perspective that it can express an interpretative attitude to a practice.[62] Dworkin explains what an interpretative attitude means by imagining a community that has a social practice called courtesy whose members argue about what the practice mandates. For example, in this imaginary society, courtesy might demand that peasants doff their hats to nobility. An interpretative attitude towards this practice depends on two assumptions: that there is more to a social practice than simply the facts of convergent behaviour since the practice is purposive; and deciding what action the practice requires in a particular case must be sensitive to this purpose.

Once a participant adopts an interpretative attitude toward a practice, his or her view of what it requires in a particular case depends ultimately on an interaction between the behaviour that constitutes that practice and his or her understanding of the point of the practice. For the citizens who practise courtesy, interpretation decides not only why courtesy exists but also what, properly understood, it now requires. Value and content have become enmeshed.[63] Constructive interpretation is a theory about the precise nature of the interplay between the behaviour that constitutes a practice and the purpose of that practice.

The process of constructive interpretation consists of three analytic stages: the pre-interpretative stage; the interpretative stage; and the post-interpretative stage.[64] At the pre-interpretative stage, the participant identifies the rules and standards that tentatively constitute the practice. At the interpretative stage, the participant offers a justification for the practice, At the final stage, the partici-

---

[60]*ibid.* at p. 13.
[61]*ibid.* at p. 64.
[62]*ibid* at pp. 46-48.
[63]*ibid.* at p. 48.
[64]*ibid.* at pp. 65-68.

pant reforms the practice in light of its point, that is, he or she adjusts his or her sense of what the practice requires so as better to serve the justification he or she accepts at the interpretative stage.[65]

The most important stage of interpretation is the interpretative stage. At this stage the participant makes a proposal about the value of the practice. This proposal must satisfy two dimensions: a descriptive dimension and an evaluative dimension. First, any proposal of value must be consistent with the pre-interpretative data that constitute the practice. The proposal need not fit every aspect or feature of the standing practice, but it must fit enough for the interpreter to be able to see himself or herself as interpreting the practice, not inventing a new one. A corollary of this is that an interpretation "can condemn some of its data as a mistake, as inconsistent with the justification it offers for the rest."[66] Second, in some situations more than one proposal of value will fit a threshold amount of the practice such that it can count as an interpretation of the practice as opposed to the invention of a new one. In such a situation, the interpreter shifts to the evaluative dimension, and, on the basis of his or her own convictions, chooses the justification that he or she believes shows the practice in its best light.

Law is an interpretative concept. What the law requires in a particular case rests ultimately on a constructive interpretation of legal practice. Dworkin considers that, of the different theories of law, "law as integrity" shows our legal practice in its best light. Integrity differs from positivism and realism in that it strikes an attitude to adjudication that instructs judges to decide cases by using constructive interpretation.[67] A judge committed to integrity is required to decide particular cases not by seeking a principle that both fits and justifies legal practice as a whole, but a principle that "both fits and justifies some complex part of legal practice, that ... provides an attractive way to see, in the structure of that practice, the consistency of principle integrity requires."[68] Thus, a judge must seek a principle that satisfies two dimensions of legal practice: it must both *fit* and *justify* a threshold amount of some complex part of legal practice. It is a central feature of law as integrity that a judge relies on his or her own political or moral convictions to decide whether a principle satisfies each of these dimensions.

Therefore, in a section 27 case, the court must first assemble the positive law bearing on the legal question requiring an answer. This comprises section 27 itself and the cases that have breathed life into it. Once the court has established its pre-interpretative starting-point, it must ask itself which principles animate these materials. This is to say that there is the bare law set out in

[65] Dworkin, *ibid.* at p. 66.
[66] *ibid.* at p. 99.
[67] *ibid.* at p. 226
[68] *ibid.* at p. 228.

section 27 and the full law comprising the principles which give it sound legal sense. This is the point where constructive interpretation does its creative work. The best interpretation of the section in any particular case flows from the set of principles that offers the best justification of the provision and its case law within the constitutional order.

Consider the principle that the court should deny section 27 relief when an inexcusable or inordinate delay on the part of the applicant in seeking redress places an unjustifiable and unfair burden on the respondent. The case law under section 27 embodies this principle, but the courts can find the background justification for this doctrine in the principles regarding constitutional rights. First, there is the right to fairness or due process. An applicant who fails to take timely enforcement proceedings creates a real and substantial risk of unfairness. With the efflux of time, vital witnesses may no longer be available, and memories may have dimmed in respect of material facts. The effect of this state of affairs may be to dilute the integrity of the fact-eliciting process, and deny the respondent meaningful participation in the hearing process. There is also the principle of justice. The respondent may have acted to his or her detriment in the face of the applicant's passivity over a substantial period. He or she may have invested money in unlocking the development potential of the property, fashioned a livelihood to sustain himself or herself and dependents, or built up a business with contractual obligations to third parties. An inordinate or inexcusable delay may have the effect of unreasonably disadvantaging such a respondent.

It follows from the view of interpretation sketched above that the best interpretation of the section must satisfy two requirements: it must fit the generality of the cases decided under the section as if the community has spoken in one voice, and it must justify that law by clarifying that it is the most coherent and morally appealing elaboration of the underlying values. This personification of the constitutional community is attractive and already finds expression in our constitutional order.[69]

A judge's political or moral convictions are relevant to the question of whether a particular principle fits legal practice. This is because it is a matter of political or moral conviction precisely what complex part, and what threshold amount, of legal practice a particular principle must fit in order to count as an interpretation of that practice as opposed to the invention of a new one.[70] A judge's convictions about fit are political or moral not mechanical. More than one principle might, consistent with law as integrity, fit a threshold amount of a complex part of legal practice. In this situation, a judge chooses the principle by which to decide a case "by asking which [principle] shows the community's

---

[69] See *Byrne v. Ireland* [1972] I.R. 241 (S.C.).
[70] Dworkin, *op.cit.*, above, n.47 at pp 255 & 257.

structure of institutions and decisions – its public standards as a whole – in a better light from the standpoint of political morality."[71] This decision directly engages the judge's own moral and political convictions.

Dworkin suggests that right answers can, in theory, be found by inquiring along two dimensions: the dimension of fit, identifying legal norms that form part of the legal record or institutional history; and the dimension of justification, constructing the moral theory that affords the best justification for using those norms as the basis for state coercion. There are sound reasons to say that judges do seek rights answers in cases. Lawyers argue their cases on the basis that they have a right answer to the questions raised. Judges give their best decisions, which they offer as the rights answers in cases. Law affords decision-makers a dense text. The value dimension of interpretative claims in law reflects a commitment to rights, so that one claim will normally be entitled to priority as a matter of principle.[72]

Constructive interpretation, I submit, puts the practice of law in its best light.[73] First, it illuminates the intellectual constraints on the judicial function. Section 27 decisions are the outcome of a public process of justification about what principles of justice and fairness require in planning enforcement cases. Such principles constrain what can be a proper purposive justification for the exercise of limited judicial discretion.

Secondly, constructive interpretation enhances section 27. Since judges have to provide a reasoned elaboration of the principles behind the planning injunction, it is always possible that they will discover a more coherent reading of the section's requirements which is more compelling than an existing reading in a decided case. The case law can be reinterpreted in light of better theories about background principles, and judges, disciplined by retrospect, can synthesise creatively.

Thirdly, principled decision-making under section 27, however, does not involve judicial legislation; rather it involves clarification. *Pace* Oliver Wendell Holmes, the life of the law is the force of principle in answer to the practical demands of justice and fairness; it is not harnessed in either bare logic or brute experience.

Finally, constructive interpretation enhances the integrity of the law. The virtue of integrity is that it expresses respect for citizens as equals. It makes a substantial contribution to legitimacy because it requires law to be more like the product of a single moral communal voice that treats people with principled consistency. The applicant in *Mulligan* got nothing more than what an applicant in similar circumstances in a future case would get.

---

[71] *ibid.* at p. 256.
[72] See *Taking Rights Seriously* at p. 286.
[73] See Dworkin, "Natural Law Revisited" (1982) 34 *University of Florida Law Review* 165.

6. CONCLUSION

In section 27 cases, the courts do not legislate, but try to construct sound decisions based on legal principle. Being a judge does not require a lawyer to impound his or her moral imagination. The law on the planning injunction is a coherent body of jurisprudence held together with the mortar of commitment to principle, and not a mere collection of cases. For judges every planning injunction case must be a venture into principle, an argumentative journey to the exposed shores of law as integrity. Principles of justice and fairness find coherent incarnation in their best decisions. The noble conviction that the integrity of these values is always worth arguing for had its home in James Brady's classes and writings on Equity.

IS THERE STILL A USE FOR TRUSTS IN TAX/ WEALTH PRESERVATION PLANNING?

ANNE CORRIGAN

1. INTRODUCTION

Anybody who knew Jim Brady knew of his interest in trusts, and in particular charitable trusts. Indeed charitable trusts were the subject of Jim's first book.[1] I remember well Jim telling me of a conference on trusts which he was invited to address in the United Kingdom, and how he had carefully chosen and delivered a paper on issues concerning charitable trusts. It transpired the conference was predominantly devoted to the use of trusts in tax planning schemes and structures and Jim felt his contribution was regarded as quaint by the majority of delegates!

Jim was not too upset to learn that this former student also ultimately ended up specialising in the taxation of trusts, recognising the fundamental importance of tax to private trusts.

2. THE IRISH TAX TREATMENT OF TRUSTS

Before looking at the issue of whether there is still a use for trusts in tax and wealth preservation planning, and if so, how they can be used, it is useful to recap on the principal tax issues that arise affecting trusts:

1. The liability of trustees to income tax is determined by their residence. There is no statutory test of residence and instead this is established by common law principles.[2] If all the trustees are resident in Ireland, they are liable to Irish income tax on the world-wide trust income from all sources. If none or only some of the trustees are resident in Ireland for tax purposes, the trustees may only be taxed on Irish source income.

2. Trustees are liable to income tax at the standard rate, currently 22 per cent.

3. If the trustees accumulate funds within most accumulation/discretionary trusts for more than 18 months after the end of the tax year in which the

---

[1] *Religion and the Law of Charities in Ireland* (Belfast, 1975).
[2] *Dawson v. I.R.C.* [1990] A.C. 1.

income has arisen, they will be liable to a surcharge of a further 20 per cent.

4. If a beneficiary has an absolute right to trust income (for example as a life tenant) or if the trustees mandate income directly to a beneficiary, the Revenue Commissioners will assess that beneficiary to tax directly, instead of the trustees. In a case where income has been mandated directly to a beneficiary, the Revenue will not be in a position to assess the trustees to Irish income tax even if they are resident in Ireland, as they have not actually received the income in question. If the beneficiary in question is resident abroad and the income is foreign source income, then the Revenue will not be in a position to assess the beneficiary to income tax either.

5. Anti-avoidance provisions exist (principally section 795 of the Taxes Consolidation Act 1997) to attribute income of a trust established for minor children to the settlor of the trust. This deeming provision can only be avoided under section 796 of the Taxes Consolidation Act 1997 if the settlement is an irrevocable capital settlement, with any income being accumulated for the benefit of the minor children. Note that if the income is so accumulated, the trustees will be subject to the 20 per cent surcharge mentioned.

6. A further anti-avoidance provision that should be borne in mind is the transfer of assets abroad legislation.[3] That legislation applies to individuals who are resident or ordinarily resident in Ireland and who have transferred assets abroad with the result that income becomes payable to persons resident or domiciled out of the State (such as foreign trustees). If the individual in question retains the power to enjoy that income within the meaning of the section, the income will be attributed to that person and taxed on him or her. Note, however, that this will not necessarily result in an Irish income tax liability arising if the settlor is a foreign domiciled person entitled to the remittance basis of tax.[4]

7. There are specific statutory provisions in section 574 of the Taxes Consolidation Act 1997 dealing with the liability of trustees to Capital Gains Tax ("CGT"). Irish CGT will be imposed if the trustees are either resident or ordinarily resident in Ireland within the meaning of the section or, if they are not so Irish resident, if they dispose of one of the specified assets such as Irish land. Note that favourable rules exist for trusts settled by a settlor who was not domiciled, resident or ordinarily resident in Ireland and where the Irish based trustees are professional trustees. In these cases even though the trustees are in fact resident in Ireland for tax purposes

---

[3] Taxes Consolidation Act 1997, s. 806.
[4] Taxes Consolidation Act 1997, s. 807(5).

under a fiction they are deemed not to be resident and therefore only subject to Irish CGT on gains from the Irish specified assets.

8. In addition to being liable to CGT on actual disposals, trustees are also subject to CGT in three instances in respect of deemed disposals:
    (a) when a person becomes absolutely entitled as against them in relation to trust assets[5] except where that occurs on the death of a person with a life interest in the property;[6]
    (b) where on the termination of a life interest in trust property, the property continues to be settled property; [7]
    (c) where the trustees cease to be resident and ordinarily resident in Ireland.[8]

9. Anti-avoidance provisions exist to prevent the avoidance of Irish tax by use of foreign trusts. The result is that:
    (a) in certain circumstances beneficiaries of a foreign trust who are domiciled and either resident or ordinarily resident in Ireland will be subject to Irish CGT in respect of gains made by the foreign trustees. This will arise where the settlor is domiciled and either resident or ordinarily resident in Ireland, or was when he made the settlement.[9]
    (b) if a beneficiary who is domiciled and either resident or ordinarily resident in Ireland receives a capital payment from a foreign trust, that individual can be subjected to Irish CGT in respect of a deemed gain equal to the amount of that capital payment.[10]

10. When a beneficiary receives an appointment of property from a trust, or becomes beneficially entitled in possession to an interest in trust property, a liability to Irish Capital Acquisitions Tax ("CAT") will arise if the property in question is located in Ireland. Alternatively a liability can arise if the settlor was domiciled in Ireland (in the case of trusts established before December 1, 1999) or if either the settlor was resident or ordinarily resident in Ireland or the beneficiary is resident or ordinarily resident in Ireland at the date of the benefit (in the case of trusts established after December 1, 1999). Note that special rules apply in the case of non-domiciliaries who will be treated as not resident and not ordinarily resident in Ireland until December 1, 2004 and then only as resident/ordinarily resident if they have been resident in Ireland for five consecutive tax years preceding the tax year in which the benefit arises, and they are either resident or

---

[5] Taxes Consolidation Act 1997, s. 576.
[6] Taxes Consolidation Act 1997, s. 577.
[7] Taxes Consolidation Act 1997, s. 577(3).
[8] Ss. 579B to 579E Taxes Consolidation Act 1997, inclusive.
[9] Taxes Consolidation Act 1997, s. 579.
[10] Taxes Consolidation Act 1997, s. 579A.

ordinarily resident in the State when the benefit arises. The rate of CAT is currently 20 per cent.

11. On the death of the settlor, assets held within a discretionary trust (as defined in the legislation) will be subject to discretionary trust tax charges if there are no principal objects (broadly speaking, children of the settlor) under the age of 21. A once-off charge of six per cent is imposed (reduced to three per cent if the trust is wound up within five years) and an annual charge of one per cent of the value of the trust assets for each year thereafter that the trust remains in existence.

12. If assets are transferred into a trust on the death of a settlor prior to December 6, 2000, probate tax of two per cent may arise.

13. If assets are transferred into a trust during the settlor's lifetime, a stamp duty liability may arise.

In view of all of the above it might be considered that trusts exist despite the tax implications, instead of for tax reasons! Nevertheless, although it is clear that Ireland is by no means a tax haven for trusts, they continue to thrive and people still have a requirement for them. Some of the situations in which trusts are used, and the tax implications flowing from that use are set out below.

3. CHANNELLING ASSETS TO MINOR CHILDREN SO CHILDREN BENEFIT FROM APPRECIATION IN VALUE

Parents are sometimes anxious that assets should be placed in the names of their children so that the children will benefit from any appreciation in value of those assets. This can certainly be beneficial to the children from a tax perspective, as highlighted below, but clearly there are practical and legal considerations involved, which the parent must consider carefully before proceeding with any such trust arrangement. If one is dealing with a very young child (for example, one as young as eight) one should caution the parent or settlor that to achieve the tax result they want, the child must legally be given access to the trust property. The child must be entitled to direct the trustees how to deal with the property and to give them a valid receipt for it should the child decide that the property is to be transferred into his or her own name. In other words, in this type of trust situation the trustees are effectively bare trustees.

Example 1

Aidan purchases shares worth IR£150,000 in a quoted technology company in January 1998. He has reason to believe that the shares will appreciate significantly in value in the coming years. He wants to gift the shares to his son Christopher who is 10 years old. He is particularly anxious to make this transfer while it is sub-threshold. Therefore he transfers the shares to Jack on trust for Christopher absolutely, with Jack specifically instructed to act in accordance with Christopher's instructions, notwithstanding that he is an infant. The trust is put in place at the end of January 1998 and by April 2000 the shares have increased in value to IR£1 million.

The consequences of that arrangement are as follows:

1. While the transfer of the shares into the trust is a disposal for CGT purposes, because Aidan disposed of the shares immediately after acquisition there was no increase in value and therefore no CGT liability;

2. A stamp duty charge of one per cent of the value of the assets (IR£1,500) arises;

3. The shares are effectively sub-threshold so no CAT liability arises for Christopher when he takes the benefit in 1998 (note that if the threshold had been absorbed by other gifts or inheritances, then to the extent that any CGT liability had arisen on the creation of the trust, Christopher could have claimed a credit against this CAT liability);

4. As the trust is a bare trust, any dealings in the shares will be taxed directly on Christopher for CGT purposes;

5. Within a very short period of time the shares have increased in value to IR£1 million. Because Christopher was beneficially entitled to the shares from the date the trust was created that appreciation in value accrues to him. If Aidan had retained the shares in his name he would now be facing a large CGT bill on transferring the shares to his son, and Christopher would be exposed to a CAT liability. Because the CGT and CAT tax rates are now roughly the same, it should be the case that the CGT credit available would absorb that CAT liability. However, as it is the gift does not trigger either a CGT or CAT liability and in fact it leaves Christopher with a partially unused CAT threshold;

6. If Christopher wishes to dispose of the shares his base cost for CGT purposes is IR£150,000;

7. Because Christopher is a minor, any income or dividends earned on the shares until he reaches the age of 18 will be attributed to Aidan, and Aidan must account for income tax on that income. However, under section 797 of the Taxes Consolidation Act 1997 Aidan is permitted to have access to the trust fund to pay the resulting tax liability. Thus his position is no worse than if he had retained the shares in his own name.

4. Protection of Substantial Wealth for Individuals with Young Families

This is one of the most common instances where individuals have a require-ment for a discretionary trust. The typical profile is that of a relatively young couple who have significant wealth. They have a young family and they are anxious to protect the interests of their children, particularly in the event of the husband and wife both dying together (for example, as a result of a car or plane accident).

Example 2

Alan and Shirley are in their mid-forties. They have three children aged from two years to eight years. They have assets totalling approximately IR£10 mil-lion. They are concerned that their children's interests should be protected in the event of both of them dying while the children are young. They are clear that in the first instance they would like the assets owned by each of them to be given to the surviving spouse, but in the event of both of them dying together or in the event of the survivor dying while the children are young, they are reluctant to specify specific shares that each child should take. The respective requirements of the children and their ability to handle money has not yet been proven and Alan and Shirley realise that the requirements of some of the chil-dren might be higher than those of others. Therefore they each execute wills whereby they give the assets owned by each of them to the other or in the event of both dying simultaneously or within 30 days of each other, the assets are to be transferred to a discretionary trust for a class of beneficiaries comprising their three children.

The making of the wills in themselves does not create any taxation liabili-ties. The wills only come into effect on the death of the testator/testatrix. To the extent that either the husband or the wife dies, and all of the assets pass to the surviving spouse, the surviving spouse will enjoy a complete exemption from tax. The surviving spouse will inherit those assets at their base cost at that time. Should both spouses die together, or where one does not survive the other by 30 days, or where the surviving spouse who has inherited the assets subse-quently dies, the discretionary trust will come into effect.

In the case of deaths prior to December 6, 2000 the assets passing under the will into the trust will be subject to probate tax at two per cent. Since the trust is a discretionary trust and none of the beneficiaries have any entitlement to a specific share of the trust property, no CAT liability will arise until such time as the trustees choose to make an appointment. As the children are all minor chil-dren, although the settlor is dead, no liability to discretionary trust tax charges arise. Indeed there is a view that the discretionary trust tax charges could never be applicable to this particular trust, even if the trustees have not appointed the property out by the time the youngest child reaches the age of 21. That view arises because of the wording of section 108 of the Finance Act 1984 which states that section 106 of that Act (the charging provision):

> "shall not apply or have effect in relation to a discretionary trust which is shown to the satisfaction of the Commissioners to have been created exclusively –
>
> ...
>
> (d) (i) for the benefit of one or more named individuals, and
>
>   (ii) for the reason that such individual, or all such individuals, is or are, because of age or improvidence, or of physical, mental or legal incapacity, incapable of managing his or their affairs . . ."

Clearly at the time the trust was created, it was for the benefit of individuals who were by reason of their age incapable of managing their affairs. Thus the view is that even after the youngest child reaches the age of 21, it is still possible to rely on the exemption provided by section 108(1)(d). I should add that the Revenue Commissioners do not necessarily agree with this view!

At the time when an appointment is made out of the trust to the beneficiaries, a deemed disposal will arise for CGT purposes. The trustees will have acquired the assets at their market value at the date the trust was established, and a CGT computation will be prepared accordingly. The beneficiary will be entitled to a credit against his or her CAT liability for the CGT borne by the trustees on the deemed disposal of the trust assets.

No stamp duty liability arises on the transfer of the assets to the beneficiary entitled to them pursuant to the terms of an appointment made under the trust instrument.

5. Maximising the Benefit of the CGT/CAT Credit

It is particularly important in the context of trust situations to maximise the availability of the credit for CGT paid against any CAT liability arising on the same event. Clearly it is important to bear this credit in mind, and to avail of it where possible, particularly since the CAT rate was reduced to 20 per cent so that it is possible the CGT paid (also at the rate of 20 per cent) might give a full matching credit against the CAT liability.

Example 3

Charles established a discretionary trust for his sons William and Harry in 1997, and transferred property worth IR£200,000 into the trust. The trustees have decided that the trust should be wound up. The land is now worth IR£600,000 and they plan to sell it and appoint IR£300,000 each to William and Harry.

The sale of the land by the trustees would be a foolish step because they would become liable to CGT on the sale without being able to avail of a credit for that liability against the CAT liability. Ignoring indexation and any miscellaneous deductions, the gain would be IR£400,000 so that the CGT liability would be IR£80,000. Assuming that Harry and William have already absorbed their thresholds they would each have a CAT liability of IR£60,000 on the benefit from the trust fund (IR£300,000 x 20 per cent). Thus by handling the winding up of the trust in the way the trustees originally propose the total tax charge will be IR£200,000 (the trustees' own CGT liability of IR£80,000 and the IR£60,000 each paid by William and Harry).

The alternative, which the trustees should consider, is appointing the property to Harry and William equally. This will still trigger a CGT deemed disposal by the trustees, and a liability of IR£80,000 as before. However that IR£80,000 will be creditable by the boys against their CAT liability totalling IR£120,000 leaving them with a balance to pay of IR£40,000. Thus in that scenario the total tax liability is restricted to IR£120,000.

6. Use of Trusts to Protect Surviving Spouse with Assets Ultimately Passing to Children

One frequently encounters cases where an individual wants to ensure that his/her spouse is comfortably and adequately provided for after his/her death, but is concerned by his/her ability to manage a business that might perhaps be quite complex. The individual would like to preserve the business to pass on ultimately to his/her children, but feels that the children are not yet ready to assume control of the business. He/she is concerned that his/her spouse should not be in any way reliant on the children, or on their ability to manage the business prudently.

Example 4

Denis is aged 65 and runs a shipping and distribution business. His wife Alice is 45 and has never been involved in running the business. They have one child Julian who is aged 22 and who recently joined Denis in the business. Denis feels that Julian is still relatively inexperienced and needs his guidance or the guidance of an experienced business manager for some time before he would feel that Julian is ready to assume full responsibility and control of the business. Denis has therefore decided that what he would like to do in his will is to give his wife a life interest in the business with Julian inheriting it absolutely on her death.

When Denis' will comes into effect on his death, his wife Alice takes a limited interest in the business, *i.e.* she is a life tenant. As such she is entitled to the income that the business produces but not to the capital of the business itself. If the trust comes into existence on Denis' death prior to December 6, 2000, a liability to probate tax of two per cent arises. Because Alice has taken a limited interest in the business, the probate tax liability is postponed until nine months after the date of Alice's death.

Because Alice has become beneficially entitled in possession to an interest in property (albeit a limited interest) she would ordinarily have a CAT liability. However, as Denis' spouse she is entitled to a full exemption. She will of course be subject to income tax on any income generated by her from the business since as life tenant she is absolutely entitled to this income.

On Alice's death, Julian will become beneficially entitled in possession to the business. Note that no CGT liability will arise for the trustees. This is because although a beneficiary (Julian) has become absolutely entitled as against them to the trust property, this occurred on the death of the life tenant entitled to an interest in that property (Alice). Thus the property will pass to Julian at its market value at the date of Alice's death free of CGT. Julian will have a CAT liability in respect of the value of the property at that date. He may have his threshold of IR£300,000 available against any liability, and indeed the property may qualify for business property relief.

7. Use of Trusts to Maximise CAT Reliefs

It may happen that individuals are interested in availing of CAT reliefs if possible, but it does not suit them to convert their existing assets during their lifetime into property that would qualify for any of the reliefs in question. However they are anxious that if their successors would otherwise suffer an onerous CAT liability, the passing of their wealth to the next generation should be structured in such a way that it is sufficiently flexible to allow their assets to be converted into assets that would qualify for a full or partial relief.

Example 5

Mary is a wealthy widow who has been left a significant portfolio of investment property by her husband. She has two children. Her daughter is married to an American citizen, is resident in the US and has acquired a US domicile of choice. Her son lives in Ireland and is extremely interested in the hotel business. He has persuaded his mother to diversify her property interests as a result of which Mary purchased a hotel a year ago which her son is running. Mary realises that the value of her property interests totalling approximately IR£10 million will result in a significant CAT liability for her children. However, she is apprehensive about selling the property to invest in other assets which might

qualify for a relief since her husband had always focussed on property investment, and she does not feel capable of evaluating other investment opportunities. She would like her children to share her estate equally. She seeks your
advice.

As Mary's property is worth IR£10 million, the probate tax liability that
would arise on her death prior to December 6, 2000 is IR£200,000. Her children stand to inherit roughly IR£4.9 million each and after allowing for their
exempt threshold of IR£300,000 their taxable inheritance would be IR£4.6
million each giving rise to a CAT liability of IR£920,000 each. Thus the total
liability of each, together with the probate tax liability, would amount to IR£2.04
million.

Mary should consider establishing a discretionary trust in favour of her
children. This could be accompanied by a letter of wishes explaining that she
would like her children to share the estate equally. If Mary left her property to
trustees on a discretionary trust with her children as the class of beneficiaries,
the probate tax liability of IR£200,000 would still arise. Furthermore, assuming that the children are over the age of 21, a discretionary trust tax liability of
six per cent of the value of the assets would arise, *i.e.* IR£588,000. However, if
the trust is wound up within five years of the date it is created, that once off
liability will be reduced to IR£294,000. For each year thereafter that the trust
remains in existence, let us assume that that gives rise to an annual discretionary trust tax liability of IR£100,000 each year.

On Mary's death, the trustees consult with her two children. They ascertain
that her daughter has no particular wish to retain a portfolio of Irish investment
property, and would rather receive cash. Her son indicates that he would be
quite happy to take the hotel valued at IR£4 million in partial satisfaction of his
share. He has further indicated that if there was some tax efficient way of chan-
nelling the balance of his share to him he would be interested in facilitating
that, even if it meant a delay in being able to deal with the property as he
wished.

If Mary died within two years of acquiring the hotel, had she simply bequeathed it to her son in her will it would not have qualified for business property relief as she would not have satisfied the two year prior ownership
requirement for inheritances. As it is, the trustees retain the hotel within the
trust for a further year after Mary's death, and as the property has then been
owned for two years in aggregate they appoint it to her son. He can now qualify
for business property relief so that he is only subject to tax on 10 per cent of the
value (IR£400,000). As against this he has his threshold of IR£300,000. His
taxable inheritance is only IR£100,000 on which the tax take is IR£20,000.
The trustees may have a small CGT liability on the appreciation in value of the
hotel from the date of Mary's death to the date of appointment and her son can
use this as a credit against his CAT liability.

In the meantime, immediately after Mary's death the trustees sell the balance of the property. They have little or no CGT to pay since there has been little appreciation in value between the date of death and the date of sale of the property. They invest IR£4.8 million earmarked for Mary's daughter into Irish Government gilts. They intend to retain those gilts for three years and then to appoint them to the daughter at which point the gilts will qualify for exemption from Irish CAT.

They have a further IR£800,000 earmarked for the son and they decide to invest that in heritage objects which they appoint to the son.

At the end of the three years the trust is totally wound up with the gilts being appointed to the daughter. The heritage objects had been appointed to the son immediately after their acquisition, and the hotel was appointed to the son one year after the date of Mary's death. Thus the total tax liabilities suffered are the once-off discretionary trust tax charge (IR£294,000); the annual discretionary trust tax charge totalling say IR£200,000 (the hotel having been appointed out one year after the date of death and the heritage objects immediately on purchase) and the son's CAT liability of IR£20,000, *i.e.* a total tax take of IR£514,000 as opposed to IR£2.04 million if Mary had simply left her property to her children in equal shares.

Clearly whether it is appropriate or feasible to convert assets in this manner will depend on the circumstances, and the attitude of the prospective beneficiaries. In some cases (such as business property relief and relief for heritage property) there will be a requirement that the beneficiary retains the property for a period of time following the date of the benefit to avoid a clawback of the relief and it will have to be clear that a beneficiary is prepared to do this.

In other instances there will be a prior holding period before the property qualifies for a relief. For example, in the case of business property passing by way of inheritance one must satisfy a two-year prior ownership requirement. In the case of heritage houses and gardens, the property must have satisfied certain conditions for three years prior to qualifying for the relief. The advantages of securing the reliefs must of course be weighed against the costs incurred (particularly those incurred on discretionary trust charges) in retaining the property for such a period as will satisfy the conditions for the relief. It is likely to be worthwhile incurring those costs if the result is that one will obtain a complete exemption from CAT. Where there is now a maximum CAT exposure of 20 per cent, it might be less worthwhile incurring discretionary trust tax charges, particularly if there is any CGT available as a credit against the CAT liability.

In some instances while the settlor may be dead, there may be minor children who have not reached the age of 21 and therefore it might be possible for the trustees to take steps to convert the assets into qualifying assets before the discretionary trust tax charges kick in, thus avoiding those charges, and thus able to ultimately appoint property out to the beneficiaries free of CAT.

8. Asset Protection Trusts – Separation and Divorce

This writer finds that an increasing concern amongst clients is a reluctance to pass on assets to their children by way of lifetime gift because of the fear that their children might be divested of a significant proportion of those assets as a result of an ill-advised marriage. Some clients would prefer that the wealth of the family be preserved within a trust, rather than being exposed to possible claims by estranged or former spouses, notwithstanding that the result might be a tax cost in terms of discretionary trust tax charges. It is important to be aware of course of the scope of the powers of the courts in relation to trusts which have been established with this purpose in mind.

Where spouses separate, the courts have extensive powers under the Family Law Act 1995 to make a range of financial orders conferring both income maintenance and assets on a financially dependent spouse. The courts can make similar orders in the context of divorce applications under the Family Law (Divorce) Act 1996. In determining the orders to be made, it is normal practice for each side to produce an affidavit of means and an affidavit of discovery, setting out their income, assets and liabilities and vouching same. The extent to which the court will take into account a beneficiary's interest in a trust will depend on the nature of that interest, and the circumstances in which it was created.

(a) Variation of Trusts in Matrimonial Cases

The courts are permitted to order:

> "the variation for the benefit of either of the spouses and of any dependent member of the family or any or all of those persons of any ante-nuptial or post-nuptial settlement (including such a settlement made by will or codicil) made on the spouses."[11]

The courts can also order "the extinguishment or reduction of the interest of either of the spouses under any such settlement."[12]

In what circumstances therefore can a court vary an existing trust in the context of a separation or divorce? There is comparatively little Irish case law on this area although this type of jurisdiction has existed since 1989 when it was contained in the Judicial Separation and Family Law Reform Act 1989. The court can only vary a trust if it amounts to an "ante-nuptial or post-nuptial settlement made on the spouses".[13]

---

[11] Section 14(1)(c) of the Family Law (Divorce) Act 1996.
[12] Section 14(1)(d) of the Family Law (Divorce) Act 1996.
[13] *ibid.*, s. 14(1)(c).

In the United Kingdom, where the courts have had this type of jurisdiction since 1973, that term has been construed as comprising only settlements made either in contemplation of or during the marriage of the husband and wife whose marriage is the subject of the proceedings.[14]

Example 6

In 1970 Jack settled IR£1 million by way of discretionary trust for a class comprising his children, their future spouses, and his grandchildren and their future spouses. At the time Jack had three children. The eldest child was aged 15 and the youngest was aged five. The oldest child, a son, married in 1985 aged 30. His marriage has recently broken up and the question arises as to whether the court can make a variation order in respect of the 1970 trust.

The view is that such an order cannot be made in a case such as this since the trust was established for a wide category of beneficiaries and the marriage which was the subject of the separation proceedings was not in contemplation at the time. In dealing with the exercise of their discretion by trustees of a discretionary trust, Lord Greene M.R. in the English Court of Appeal in *Howard v. Howard*[15] commented:

> "Trustees who have a discretion are bound to exercise that discretion, and if they do so, nobody can interfere with it. In my opinion there is no jurisdiction in the Divorce Court to make an order which will leave the husband in a state of starvation with a view to putting pressure on trustees to exercise their discretion in a way in which they would not have exercised it but for that pressure. Under discretionary trusts (as indeed, under this trust) other persons are potential beneficiaries. In many such trusts the range of potential beneficiaries is a very wide one. Here it extends to any future wife that the husband may marry and the children of any future marriage. The settlement is not being varied in that respect. On what grounds should pressure be put upon the trustees to exercise their discretion in such way as to pay the husband, in order that he may pay maintenance to his wife, sums which in their discretion, they would not otherwise have paid to him?"[16]

The court made it clear that if the trust had been established solely for the benefit of the spouses whose marriage was in question the court would be in a position to exercise a statutory power to vary the terms of the trust.

In an Irish case *D(J) v. D(D)*[17] McGuinness J. considered a trust that had

---

[14] *Loraine v. Loraine & Murphy* [1912] P. 222.
[15] [1945] 1 All E.R. 91.
[16] *ibid.* at 93.
[17] [1998] 1 Fam. L.J. 17.

been established in September 1966, shortly after the marriage of the parties to the proceedings. The trust had been established by the husband's mother. The beneficiaries comprised a class including the settlor, her children, their spouses and children and remoter issue. At the date the case was heard the prospective beneficiaries were the husband and wife to the proceedings, their five children and the husband's sister and her husband. The trust assets were worth approximately IR£600,000.

The wife's lawyers argued that the existence of the trust should be taken into account in terms of the overall financial settlement arrived at. However, McGuinness J. ruled that she did not have the power to vary the settlement under the Family Law Act 1995 because of the wide class of beneficiaries who could otherwise be affected. She also felt that it was inappropriate that an order be made putting pressure on the trustees to exercise their discretion in favour of the husband. It should be noted that in the case the wife was also amongst a class of beneficiaries of a discretionary trust which had been established by her family. The class of beneficiaries included the wife's mother, her seven siblings, her mother's 23 grandchildren and two great-grandchildren. Again the court ruled that because of the wide class of beneficiaries involved, this trust was not capable of variation under the 1995 Act.

(b) Prohibition on Use of Trusts to Defeat Financial Claims of Spouses

Both the 1995 and 1996 Acts enable the courts to set aside any disposition of property (including trust arrangements) which were made for the purpose of defeating the claim of a spouse or dependent children under the Acts. If the disposition was made within three years of the court proceedings, a presumption is raised against the disponer that he made the disposition to frustrate the financial claims of his family (although this presumption is rebuttable). If the disposition was made more than three years before the institution of the proceedings, the burden of proof will rest with the applicant to prove that the disposition was for the purpose of frustrating her claims.

This issue also arose for consideration before McGuinness J. in *D(J) v. D(D)*.[18] In that case, the wife had issued judicial separation proceedings in October 1995. Some six months later in May 1996 the husband established a trust with A.I.B. in the Isle of Man and transferred IR£148,000 from his bank account to that trust. The beneficiaries of the trust were two charities together with the husband's five children. The husband declared that he had established the trust solely for the benefit of his children. McGuinness J. was sceptical. She stated:

---

[18] *ibid.*

> "It is crystal clear that this is a reviewable disposition under section 35 [of the Family Law Act 1995]. Even were the presumption contained in sub-section (5) not included in the section, I have already made clear my view that this disposition was, in essence, an effort to reduce the monies available for distribution to the applicant. I consider that the respondent's explanation of his action as given in his evidence falls very far short of rebutting the presumption in sub-section (5)."[19]

The judge therefore made an order setting aside the disposition together with ancillary orders directed to the husband and to the relevant AIB trustee company to implement her decision.

(c) Relevance of Beneficiary's Interest in Trusts

It may be that the courts do not have jurisdiction to vary a trust because it does not amount to an ante-nuptial or postnuptial settlement within the meaning of the legislation. The trust might also pre-date the initiation of proceedings by such a period of time or have been established in such circumstances that the court is satisfied that the trust was not made for the purpose of defeating the financial claims of a spouse.

However, that does not mean that the court will ignore the existence of the trust assets or the interest that one of the parties to the proceedings has as beneficiary in a settlement.

Example 7

A wife institutes divorce proceedings against her husband. In addition to his employment income and income from investments, her husband is the life tenant in a trust fund worth IR£1 million (generating an income of IR£70,000 p.a.) established by his parents, with remainder interest over to any of his surviving siblings, and remainder to his parents' grandchildren (which may include the husband's own children).

The court will not make a variation order in relation to this trust, as it is not an ante-nuptial settlement within the meaning of the legislation. Nor was it put in place by the husband for the purpose of defeating his wife's claims. However, the trust does entitle the husband as life tenant to the income produced by the trust fund each year. The court will take this income into account in deciding on the appropriate level of maintenance that the husband should pay to his wife.

---

[19] *D(J) v. D(D)*, n.17 above, at 26.

9. CONCLUSION

As discussed above, trusts continue to prove popular in tax planning structures. It is important to emphasise the care that must be exercised in relation to them, given that any particular trust transaction has the potential to trigger numerous tax consequences. However, used in a focused way they can be a valuable device in achieving the desired result for a client either in commercial terms (such as protecting the wealth of minors) or to minimise a taxation exposure.

REGULATING THE ANTI-DISMISSAL INJUNCTION

KEVIN COSTELLO

In 1985 the *Irish Law Times* published, as a news item, an account of the *ex tempore* judgment in an interlocutory injunction application, *Fennelly v. Assicurazioni S.P.A. & General Underwriting Agreements Ireland Ltd.*[1] That short news report has now generated a mini industry, and, in comparative terms, a doctrinal innovation: the anti-dismissal injunction.

As a matter of first principle, the purpose of any interlocutory injunction is to compel, in the interval before the full trial, the observance by the defendant of those rights which the plaintiff identifies the defendant as infringing. It should, in principle, follow that a wrongfully dismissed employee is, prior to a full trial, entitled to the observance of those rights due under the contract of employment, including the right to be paid. In fact, for almost 150 years the common law refused to concede this principle.[2] Fennelly was a former Garda who had joined the defendants as an insurance claims manager, and had been dismissed on grounds of redundancy. The court accepted the argument that since one of the rights of the employee is the right to be paid, and since a wrongfully dismissed employee is being deprived of a continuing right to be paid, that it followed that an interlocutory injunction may be obtained to compel the payment of salary until the hearing of a wrongful dismissal action. Subject to the plaintiff establishing a fair case that the dismissal was wrongful, and the balance of convenience favouring the plaintiff, an interlocutory salary injunction would be granted. Here Fennelly had established a fair case that he had been dismissed in breach of a fixed term twelve-year contract. Secondly, the balance of convenience favoured the plaintiff. Costello J. (as he then was) stated:

> "it is clear that it will be some considerable time before it comes to hearing. In the meantime the plaintiff will be left without a salary and nothing to live on. The situation in which he finds himself would be little short of disastrous. It seems to me, in that situation, that the balance of convenience is in the plaintiff's favour. He should not be left in the situation

---

[1] (1985) 3 I.L.T. (*n.s.*) 73. The judgment was delivered on March 12, 1985. See, also on this topic, Redmond, *Dismissal Law in Ireland* (Dublin, 1999), pp. 137-158.

[2] *Goodman v. Pocock* (1850) 15 Q.B. 576, 117 E.R. 577; *Emmens v. Elderton* (1853) 4 H.L.C. 624, 10 E.R. 106.

between now and the action in which he would be virtually destitute with the prospect of damages at the action."[3]

The High Court having found that the two conventional conditions for the grant of an interlocutory injunction, a fair case and the balance of convenience, were in place, then ordered that the defendants continue to pay the plaintiff's salary and bonus payments until the date of the trial. The order was made subject to the condition, now conventional in orders of this kind, that the plaintiff work if requested by the employer.

Later cases have expanded the original limits of the jurisdiction. The condition that the plaintiff must show current destitution was abandoned with the result that such injunctions are now sought by employees at the upper end of the salary scale. In *Harte v. Kelly*[4] the plaintiff was an independently wealthy person, not reliant upon a salary. There was evidence that he was in receipt of royalty payments of £3,000 per month for use by the defendants of patents held by the plaintiff. The defendants argued that the dismissal was not as devastating to the plaintiff as it was in *Fennelly's* case. The High Court rejected the argument that destitution was a condition precedent to this species of injunction. All that was required was a reduction in living standards. The salary injunction was, therefore, granted.

However, attempts to use the mechanism of the injunction to compel the enforcement of employment rights, other than wages, have not been as successful. Attempts to enforce the employee's right to work through an injunction ordering reinstatement have almost always proved unsuccessful.[5] Usually, the balance of convenience is said to favour the exercise of the employer's prerogative to reorganise the administration of his business. Nonetheless, the

---

[3] *Fennelly*, above n.1 at 74.

[4] [1997] E.L.R. 125.

[5] See, *e.g. Doyle v. Grangeford Precast Concrete Ltd* [1998] E.L.R 261 (High Court declining to grant injunction restraining the defendants from filling the plaintiff's position as safety officer); *O'Malley v. Aravon School*, unreported, High Court, August 13, 1997 (High Court refusing to grant an interlocutory injunction continuing the plaintiff in her position as school principal. This case is unusual in that it appears that no application was made that the plaintiff's wages be paid pending full trial); *Courtney v. Radio 2000 Ltd.* [1997] E.L.R. 199 (High Court refusing injunction restraining the defendant appointing another to the plaintiff's position as radio presenter pending the trial of the action); *Gee v. The Irish Times, The Irish Times,* June 28, 2000, (High Court refusing an order restraining the defendants from appointing a financial controller in place of the plaintiff). See, however, *McCann v. Jury's Hotel Group, The Irish Times,* April 9, 1999, where an order was made restraining the defendants from appointing another to the post of general manager of Cardiff Jury's hotel. Likewise, see *Lonergan v. Salter Townshend* [2000] E.L.R. 15 (order restraining defendants from filling post of chief executive officer, but refusing to reinstate the defendant) and *O'Shaugnessy v. Boston Scientific, The Irish Times,* January 19, 1999 (defendants restrained from filling, on a permanent basis, the dismissed plaintiff's position).

original *Fennelly* wages injunction continues to flourish,[6] and has resulted in a substantial increase in the business of the High Court in dismissal cases.

1. THE LEGAL BASIS OF THE DISMISSAL INJUNCTION

> "He may wait till the termination of the period for which he was hired, and may then, perhaps sue for his whole wages in *indebitatus assumpsit.*"[7]

For the past 150 years this statement in the 1843 edition of *Smith's Leading Cases* has been condemned as a misunderstanding of the legal position in English law. Irish law, on the other hand, now appears to be in line with the proposition originally stated in *Smith*.

The *Fennelly* order directs the defendant to continue to pay the plaintiff's salary until the trial of action. The assumption that, post-repudiation, the contract of employment continues after dismissal, and that the right to wages also continues, is more interesting, and more of an innovation, than it seems. It contradicts two cardinal rules of traditional contract of employment theory: (i) the rule that a contract of employment is immediately determined on repudiation, and (ii) the theory that, even if the contract is maintained post-repudiation, that the duty to pay wages is definitely not one of the rights which is continued.

In conventional contractual doctrine the victim of a repudiatory breach may exercise the right to continue to hold the party in default to the terms of the original agreement until the contract is properly determined. But the contract of employment was considered *sui generis*. The contract of employment could not be perpetuated by the victim's non-acceptance. A wrongful dismissal, even if illegal, was effective; not void. Since the early 1850s the contract of employment was regarded as automatically terminated by repudiation.[8] At common law no court would have dreamt of making an order compelling the employer to continue paying salary post-dismissal. "It has long been settled that if a man employed under a contract of personal service is wrongfully

---

[6] A sample of the cases includes: *Shortt v. Data Packaging Ltd* [1994] E.L.R. 251; *Harte v. Kelly* [1997] E.L.R. 125; *Phelan v. BIC (Ireland) Ltd.* [1997] E.L.R. 208; *Courtney v. Radio 2000 Ltd.* [1997] E.L.R. 199; *Boland v. Phoenix Shannon Plc* [1997] E.L.R. 113; *Doyle v. Grangeford Precast Concrete Ltd* [1998] E.L.R. 260; *Keating v. Weir & Son, The Irish Times,* February 13 1999; *Lonergan v. Salter Townshend* [2000] E.L.R. 15; *Gee v. The Irish Times, The Irish Times,* July 17, 2000.

[7] Smith, *Leading Cases in Various Branches of the Law* (2nd ed., London, 1841), vol.2, p.20.

[8] *Ewings v. Tisdal* (1847) 1 Exch. 295; *Emmens v. Elderton* (1853) 4 HL Cas. 624, 10 E.R. 642; *Goodman v. Pocock* (1850) 15 Q.B. 576, 117 E.R. 577. Periodical treatment of the debate includes: Kerr, "Contract Doesn't Live Here Any More" (1984) 47 *M.L.R.* 30; McMullen, "A Synthesis of the Mode of Termination of Contracts of Employment" (1982) 41 C.L.J. 110.

dismissed he has no claim for remuneration due under the contract after the repudiation."[9] The contract was regarded as having automatically, and completely, determined.

In the 1980s, however, the line began to soften a little. The theory of automatic and complete termination was replaced by a modified theory of relative existence. The contract of employment was deemed to continue to exist for the purpose of the recognition of some rights, but not others. Thus, to take one example, the contract was regarded as continuing to exist for the purpose of the employee accumulating service periods necessary for qualification for employment protection rights. Or to take another example, the obligation to observe a disciplinary hearing might be continued by non-acceptance, and an injunction obtained to compel it. But one point was clear: the right to wages did not continue post-repudiation.

A number of reasons underlie the wages exception. First, that the entitlement to wages is contingent on the provision of work. The point was made by Dixon J. in the High Court of Australia[10] in 1946:

> "The common understanding of a contract of employment at wages periodically payable is that it is the service that earns the remuneration and even a wrongful discharge from the service means that wages or salary cannot be earned however ready and willing the employee may be to serve and however much he stands by his contract and declines to treat it as discharged by breach."[11]

The second objection is policy-based. Why should an employee be allowed to sit in the sun, and accumulate wages until such time as the contract is properly discharged? It is wrong in principle that an employee should be indulged in doing nothing until the contract is discharged, and discouraged from mitigating his loss.

The English position is that an employee who refuses to accept repudiation is entitled to avail of all of his outstanding rights, except the right to wages, and the right to work. The English understanding of post-repudiation wages was clearly restated in *Marsh v. National Autistic Society.*[12] Here the principal of a school established by the society was dismissed in breach of contract. The employee argued that the contract remained in existence until he accepted the repudiatory breach, or until the contract was lawfully determined. Since the contract remained in existence, the employee claimed he was entitled to an

---

[9] *Per* Lord Denning M.R. in *Denmark Productions Ltd v. Boscobel Productions Ltd* [1969] 1 Q.B. 699, at 726.
[10] In *Automatic Fire Sprinklers Pty Ltd v. Watson* (1946) 72 C.L.R. 435.
[11] *ibid.* at 465.
[12] [1993] I.C.R. 453.

order directing that his wages continue to be paid. Ferris J., refusing to deviate from the traditional line, said:

> "they [*i.e.*, the authorities] show that ... where a contract of employment has been wrongfully terminated by the employer the ordinary contractual principles relating to the acceptance of repudiatory breach apply and to some extent at least the authorities show that the contract continues to subsist ... the very same authorities show, however, ... that although it is the employer who in the circumstances is in breach of contract by having committed a repudiatory breach, the employee is not thereafter entitled to remuneration as a matter of debt."[13]

Irish and English law have now separated. Irish law grants wages to employees who may have been wrongfully dismissed until the proper termination of the contract. Is the Irish view sound? At least two arguments might support the view that wages continue to be payable following an unaccepted repudiation.

First, the proposition that the consideration for wages is the actual provision of work (so that in the absence of work wages are not payable) may not be true of Irish law. In Irish law there is some support for the proposition that the consideration for wages is willingness and ability to work. Thus, the presumption that wages continue to be paid during illness seems to be accepted in Irish law.[14] That can only be so on the understanding that willingness to work rather than the actual provision of work is the consideration for wages. Second, the English position assumes that the relationship can remain open for some purposes, but not for the purpose of wages. But, after the Payment of Wages Act 1991 there cannot be a contract of employment without a corresponding right to wages. It is not possible to have it both ways. Section 5 of the Act constitutes a general prohibition against the deduction of wages. The prohibition is activated by the existence of the relationship and not just by the provision of work by the employee.[15] Section 5 recognises two exceptions to the general princi-

---

[13] [1993] I.C.R. 453 at 459.

[14] *Flynn v. Great Northern Railway* (1955) 89 I.L.T.R. 46.

[15] The counter-argument is that there is no deduction of wages since there is no initial entitlement to wages. "Wages" are defined as including any sums "payable" to an employee. "Payable" means payable through proper performance. Since a dismissed employee is not rendering performance there is no entitlement to wages, and therefore, no withholding of wages. Accordingly, s. 5 does not apply.

  However, this restrictive interpretation of the word "wages" does not seem to be consistent with the overall scheme of the legislation. Section 5(5) (c) provides that the rules against withholding do not apply to cases where an employee has taken part in a strike or industrial action. That exclusion would have been quite unnecessary if the word "payable" meant "properly payable" following performance. An employee who is striking does not, of course, render performance. Second, the legislative intention is to regulate the administration by employers of deductions on grounds that could be categorised as involving no, or defective performance: absenteeism, or

ple. The first, subsection (1) is to the effect that a deduction may be made where an employee has assented to a deduction; or there is a provision in the contract authorising a deduction. The second, subsection (2), permits in the case of "an act or deduction" a deduction, but only where six procedural steps have been complied with. The only way in which non-payment following wrongful dismissal may be justified is where the conditions laid down in the first of these rules, subsection (1), are complied with. This is because the deduction is made not because of "an act or omission of the employee" but because of an act of *the employer*. Unless, therefore, the employer has taken the precaution of having inserted into the contract a clause providing that wages should cease to be payable upon the purported termination, whether lawful or otherwise, of the contract of employment, there is no right to withhold wages without offending subsection (2). Absent such a clause,[16] the right to wages is an automatic corollary of the existence of the relationship of employment.

2. THE TERMS AND DURATION OF THE ORDER

Distaste at the idea of an employee "sitting in the sun"[17] simply collecting wages without making any attempt at mitigation, underlies, to a great extent, the refusal to acknowledge the right to wages to an employee who has been wrongfully dismissed. Relief from the duty to mitigate is a general incident of the doctrine of unaccepted repudiatory breach. It is not unique to the law of wages. It is, however, inefficient, and may not be attractive in policy. It may be that the law should be revised and, as in the United States,[18] a duty to mitigate should arise once there has been an anticipatory repudiation. The co-existence of a right of non-acceptance, and a duty of reasonable mitigation are not incompatible. But the current position, under which the duty to mitigate is enforced (by refusing to apply the right of non-acceptance) in the case of the contract of employment, but not enforced in the case of other contracts, is not defensible. Such selective enforcement is not principled.

But there is in principle no reason why the question of mitigation should not be a factor in the discretion to grant, or in the form in which a wages

---

refusal to observe instructions to work. The range of application of the legislation would be significantly contracted were the word "wages" to be defined as confined to wages "properly payable" following proper performance. The whole point of the legislation is to introduce controls even in cases where wages may not be properly payable.

[16]There is, of course, nothing to prevent an employer inserting in the contract of employment a clause to the effect that wages shall not be payable following dismissal, or a purported dismissal. It may be, though the point has yet to be addressed, that this might provide an effective mechanism for entirely cancelling the *Fennelly* order jurisdiction.

[17]The phrase is that of Salmon L.J. in *Denmark Productions v. Boscobel Productions* [1969] 1 Q.B. 699 at 726.

[18]Uniform Commercial Code, s. 2-610a, s. 2-723 (1).

injunction is granted. The discretionary components of the interlocutory injunction contain the flexibility to accommodate the duty to take reasonable efforts at mitigation. There are two ways in which the mitigation principle may be accommodated. One technique, for which there is precedent, is to reduce the quantum ordered to be paid as wages.[19] Control of the duration of the order provides another means. The basis of the wages order is pre-trial hardship. But, in the case of an employee who is failing to mitigate, the hardship is self-induced. Where the full trial cannot be expected to take place for some time, it may be that a periodic, reviewable order may be a more balanced alternative to current practice of directing wages until the date of trial.

The full story of the proceedings in *Fennelly* is sometimes forgotten. The original High Court order directed payment until the date of the trial. The Supreme Court modified that order.[20] Acknowledging the employer's concerns that this would be to expose it to a liability in excess of its outstanding common law duties, the court substituted an order directing payment until August 20, 1985.[21] At common law an employer remains – so long as fair procedures are complied with, or the grounds are not unconstitutional, or in breach of a statutory prohibition – entitled to dismiss simply on giving notice. Therefore, post-dismissal, the length of the contract of employment (and of the obligation to pay wages) is no greater than the period of outstanding notice. Where the dismissal is administered in breach of fair procedures, or for unconstitutional reasons, the period is usually longer. The right of dismissal is, it would seem, suspended until the accrual of circumstances unconnected with the original improper dismissal, or until fair procedures have been complied with. At that point, however, the entitlement to dismiss on notice should revive. As the Supreme Court appeared to suggest in *Fennelly's* case, the length of the wages order should be determined solely by reference to the employer's outstanding notice commitments. The order cannot drag on beyond the exhaustion of those obligations. The risk is that the order in its current form, by directing wages to the trial of action, may be doing precisely that. The principle that an order should not exceed the limit of the employer's remaining obligations seems to be neglected.

3. THE BURDEN OF PROOF

When the rules governing the grant of interlocutory injunctions were re-stated

---

[19] In *Hegarty v. P.J. Hegarty and Sons, Irish Times*, January 21, 1998, the plaintiff was allowed merely half his ordinary salary prior to trial.
[20] (1985) 3 I.L.T. *(n.s.)* 125 (April 16, 1985).
[21] The date of August 20 was selected so that the order would lapse six months from the date of the employee's dismissal. The employer had argued that the plaintiff was entitled to six month's notice.

in *Campus Oil v. Minister for Industry and Energy (No. 2)*[22] the courts were in effect instructed no longer to concern themselves with the merits of the plaintiff's case, or with the strength of the defendant's case. The only concern, it was said, was with whom the balance of convenience lies. The effect of the rule is that the merits of the plaintiff's claim are no longer, even provisionally, tested. The result, of course, is that injunctions are being granted to dismissed employees who, at the trial of the action, if there were one, would not be able to establish the illegality of their dismissal; that injunctions are being granted to parties who are, in fact, lawfully dismissed.

The rules governing the grant of interlocutory injunctions in anti-dismissal cases were rehearsed by Macken J. in *Lonergan v. Salter-Townshend*:[23]

> "I have to consider the application for interlocutory relief … on the basis of several well-established principles which have been adopted into Irish law, since as early as the decision in *Campus Oil v. Minister of Industry and Commerce*[24] which, in turn, adopted the English decision in *American Cyanamid v. Ethicon*[25] in which the principles were first enunciated in a pithy and discreet manner. They may be summarised in the following terms, namely, that for the plaintiff to succeed in an application for interlocutory relief he must establish:
>
> (i)   That there is a serious issue to be tried;
> (ii) That damages would not be an adequate remedy;
> (iii) That the balance of convenience favours the granting of an injunction, rather than its refusal. . . .
>
> Insofar as the first of these is concerned, over the years a preferable description has come to be used, namely, that the plaintiff must establish that there is a fair issue to be tried. This avoids the difficulties that arise with use of the word 'serious', which tended to give the impression that the plaintiff had to establish that he had a case which was very strong. It is only where all of the requirements above are evenly balanced between the parties that the Court considers the final principle enunciated by [Lord] Diplock in the *American Cyanamid* case… the relative strengths and weaknesses of the claims made by the plaintiff and defendant. In the present case I do not consider that I have to reach any view as to the strength or weakness of the plaintiff's case."

---

[22] [1983] I.R. 88.
[23] [2000] E.L.R. 15 at 25.
[24] [1983] I.R. 88.
[25] [1975] A.C. 396.

Is a principle under which the court "does not consider the relative strengths and weaknesses of the plaintiff" not a little complacent? Adoption of *Campus Oil* principles for the granting of interlocutory injunctions means that a plaintiff seeking a salary injunction has just two relatively straightforward conditions to establish: the existence of a merely arguable case, and, that the balance of convenience is in his favour. The balance of convenience nearly always favours the employee. The inconvenience to the employer is always subordinated to the interest of the employee in maintaining his or her standard of living. There is no reported case where an application for an interlocutory injunction of the *Fennelly* variety has been refused upon the basis that the plaintiff has failed to raise a stateable case, or upon an assessment of the strength of the plaintiff's arguments in fact or in law, and there appears to be only one case where the High Court has found that one of the grounds raised by the plaintiff has failed to pass the arguable case threshold. This single exception is the finding in *Phelan v. BIC*[26] that the plaintiff did not have an arguable case that a decision to dismiss on grounds of redundancy required the provision of a hearing, and an entitlement to show cause. However, the plaintiff managed to make an arguable case on other grounds and was granted an injunction. Generally, in the absence of some decisive authority against the proposition, the plaintiff is virtually guaranteed an injunction.

This very high success rate seems artificial. Almost 45 per cent of unfair dismissal cases are unsuccessful.[27] It is unlikely that the percentage of successful wrongful dismissal claims is much higher. The injunction is granted on the assumption that the plaintiff has been wrongfully dismissed. Yet the certainty is that injunctions are being granted to plaintiffs who would not succeed were the case to come to trial. The safeguard against such miscarriages is supposed to be the trial of the action at which, if unsuccessful, the unsuccessful plaintiff's undertaking in damages may be enforced. But this does not correspond to the reality. Yet, since the jurisdiction began it seems that in only one of the cases in which interlocutory injunctions to pay salary have been granted, has the matter proceeded to full trial.[28] It is easy to see that the plaintiff may have little interest in pursuing the matter. Where the only condition to dismissal is a short notice period the plaintiff may already have been fully compensated, or, more likely over-compensated. The plaintiff may through the interlocutory wages order have received an amount in excess of the sum to which he will be entitled in damages. There may be little incentive to pursue the matter further: the plaintiff may have found alternative work, and the issue

---

[26] [1997] E.L.R. 209.

[27] See *Annual Report Employment Appeals Tribunal, 1999* which records that 56 per cent of unfair dismissal claims are successful. In that year 151 claims were allowed, while 113 were dismissed and 551 were withdrawn.

[28] The exception is *Cassidy v. Shannon Castle Banquets and Heritage Centre*, unreported, High Court, July 30, 1999.

may no longer be of any live interest. The defendants may have a real interest in pursuing the matter to trial in order to enforce the undertaking in damages. But there is something unreal about the undertaking in damages in the case of the post-dismissal salary injunction. The rationale for the order, that the defendant is "virtually destitute", that the defendant is "totally without remuneration" is not easily reconcilable with the existence of an effective right of recovery. Even where there might be a prospect of recovery, the sum involved may not justify the risk of the costs of a full action, and the temptation may be to write the matter off.

There is a further reason for intensifying scrutiny. There now appear to be two currents of dismissal litigation, and two types of dismissal litigant. There are, on the one hand, those whose only means of redress is by means of the statutory unfair dismissal remedy. Here compensation is retrospective and usually falls short of the annual industrial wage. Those who can afford to proceed by way of the dismissal injunction occupy the other current. Here redress is immediate, and the plaintiff recovers his or her full salary. Of course, there is nothing unique to dismissal about difference of access. But what does appear invidious is that in the case of the privileged group, the remedy should not merely be superior, but that it should be granted virtually without scrutiny, while in the case of the non-privileged group, the remedy should be closely contested, and often fail.

4. REASSESSING THE FAIR CASE STANDARD

The *Campus Oil* principle has the effect that once a stereotypical view of the balance of convenience crystallises, the party in whose favour the balance of convenience is felt to lie is guaranteed interlocutory relief. Such a view of the balance of convenience has developed in this area, and the plaintiff employee is almost immediately granted relief. This is not the only area of employment law where the rule may be working an injustice. The rule has had a devastating effect in the case of the labour injunction. Under the previous regime, under which the merits of plaintiffs' claims were subject to assessment, applications for an injunction were not infrequently refused. Since the enactment of the Industrial Relations Act 1990 only two injunctions have been refused on the ground that the employer has failed to raise a stateable case.[29]

There are perhaps two alternatives to the current rule. The moderate solution is to build upon the recognition that there may be exceptions to *Campus Oil*. The more radical alternative is to revise entirely the rule in *Campus Oil*.

---

[29]*Draycar v. Whelan* [1993] E.L.R 119; *Bus Éireann v. SIPTU, The Irish Times,* June 17, 1993. See generally, Kerr, "The Problem of the Labour Injunction Revisited" (1983) 18 *Ir Jur (n.s.)* 3.

In *Irish Shell v. Elm Motors*,[30] the companion case to *Campus Oil*, McCarthy J. suggested that there might be exceptions to the general rule, cases where "it might be proper for the court to express a concluded view". A catalogue of exceptions has developed in England following *American Cyanamid*.[31] One of the most prominent of these exceptions is where the interlocutory proceedings are likely to dispose of the case.[32] An example of interest, because of its high analogical value, is the approach now adopted by the English courts in injunctions to restrain breaches of restrictive covenants. Here the legal merits of the plaintiff's case are assessed, and the *Cyanamid* rule disapplied. The exception is justified because by the date of trial any restrictive covenant is likely to have exhausted itself, and the employer is unlikely to have any interest in pursuing the matter further. If an injunction restraining alleged infringement is granted the employee is unlikely to have the means to pursue the matter to court. The practical deterrent effect of legal costs was expressly recognised by the Court of Appeal in *Lansing Linde v. Kerr*.[33] Here the Court of Appeal stated that the practical effect of applying the *American Cyanamid* test would almost certainly favour the employer. On the other hand, the employee would be unlikely to press the matter much further;

> "[The defendant employee] has the support of his present employers in these proceedings for the purpose of resisting an injunction ... But we are not told that he has that support for a five day trial designed to secure damages for himself and freedom for restraint for the last 2 or 3 months of the 12 month period. In *American Cyanamid* both parties were chemical companies, no doubt with substantial resources and accustomed to litigation. Not so [the former employee against whom the plaintiffs are trying to enforce the restrictive covenant]. . . ."[34]

The position in the case of the post-dismissal injunction is similar. The employee's undertaking in damages is not likely to be recoverable, employers are unlikely to prosecute the matter to trial, and the injunction is likely to conclude

---

[30] [1984] I.L.R.M. 595.

[31] [1975] A.C. 396.

[32] See the recent decision of the Supreme Court in *Attorney General v. Lee*, unreported, October 23, 2000, where Keane C.J., *nem. diss.*, allowed an appeal from a High Court order directing the appellant to attend the inquest of her husband, commenting at p. 12 of the judgment that, "[a]lthough in form the order appealed from is an interlocutory injunction, it is obvious that, if upheld, it will finally dispose of the proceedings. It is, accordingly, not entirely logical to resolve the issue as to whether the plaintiff has established a fair question to be tried. If it should emerge at the plenary hearing of the proceedings, that, while there was a fair question to be tried, the defendant was entitled to succeed, it is difficult to see how justice could be done to the defendant where the interlocutory order has effectively disposed of the entire case."

[33] [1991] I.C.R. 428.

[34] *ibid.* at 436.

the matter. Here, applying the determination of the proceedings approach, an exception to the ordinary rule is justified. There is already one Irish employment decision, which appears to endorse this approach.[35]

In *Campus Oil v. Minister for Industry and Energy (No. 2)*[36] O'Higgins C.J. held that the proposition that a court should only dispense injunctive relief where after an appraisal of the merits the court was satisfied that the plaintiff had a substantial case, or a sound case, was "contrary to principle". It was by reference to established principle that the Supreme Court justified its arguable case standard. The court was returning the law to original principle. The source of principle in the case of the equitable remedies is the established practice of the court in administering those remedies. In a famous speech[37] Lord Blackburn described the nature of the discretion underlying the interlocutory injunction as:

"A discretion to be exercised according to the rules which have been established by a long series of decisions, and which are now settled to be the proper guides to the Judges in the Court of Equity."

What then was the settled practice of the Irish courts in dispensing or refusing an interlocutory injunction prior to the mid-1970s? A review of the practice from the 1860s establishes three general propositions: (i) firstly, by contrast with the current minimal review standard, the courts usually did confront the legal merits of the dispute, and did reach a provisional conclusion; (ii) in exceptional cases, cases either where the legal point at issue was one of exceptional complexity, or where there were insoluble disputes of fact, the courts might reserve consideration of the issues and determine the question on the balance of convenience; (iii) by contrast with the current position, under which the balance of convenience is usually decisive, under earlier practice the balance of convenience rarely figured.

A review of the reported interlocutory injunction case law shows that the general practice was to confront and decide, at least on a provisional basis, routine, medium level issues of law: the legal construction of 'trade dispute";[38]

---

[35] *Vogel v. Cheeverstown House* [1998] 2 I.R. 496. In *Vogel's* case the plaintiff sought an application to prevent a disciplinary hearing proceeding without permitting the plaintiff to cross-examine a crucial witness. Shanley J. considered the merits of the legal arguments fully. Refusing to apply conventional principles, he said: "it is recognised that there are exceptional cases in which the principles that are ordinarily applied would not necessarily have application. This is one such case." The ground presumably was that there was unlikely to be a full trial: if the injunction was refused, and the employee dismissed the matter would be a *fait accompli*. If the injunction was granted the employer would have little incentive in pursuing the matter to a full trial.

[36] [1983] I.R. 83.

[37] *Doherty v. Allman* (1878) 3 App. Cas. 709 at 728–729.

[38] *Silver Tassie Co. Ltd. v. Beirne* (1956) 90 I.L.T.R. 90.

the construction of an exclusive supply contract;[39] the right of a company to exclude a director;[40] the question of whether the make-up of an article was likely to constitute a passing off;[41] the statutory construction of the Land Act, 1881;[42] the issue of whether the Commissioners of Public Works had spent money in a manner which was *ultra vires* the Drainage Acts;[43] the issue of whether a publication was clearly defamatory;[44] the legal entitlement of the owner of a painting to restrain the publication of a photograph of that painting;[45] the construction of a commercial contract[46] were all discussed on applications for interlocutory injunctions. The courts did not just register a quick finding that the legal argument was not specious and then move on to consider the balance of convenience. The courts appeared to have considered it their function to address the legal issue. The balance of convenience hardly figures, except as a make-weight where the court has already made a provisional determination on the legal issues.[47]

However, this was not an inflexible principle. In cases of particular difficulty the courts might reserve the legal issue to the trial of the action. In *Moore v. Attorney General*[48] Kennedy C.J. writes in terms which bear a striking resemblance to the judgments in *Campus Oil* and *American Cyanamid*:

> "It is, in my view, impossible, as it would be, in my judgment wrong to accept and affirm either contention at this stage of the proceedings ... What is required before entertaining an application on the plaintiff's part for an interlocutory injunction is that the Court shall be satisfied that the plaintiff is presenting a *bona fide* claim which does not state itself out of court, that the action is a real issue to be tried, and that the Court must be careful not to prejudge the issue or anticipate the findings of any of the issues of fact, some of which must fall to be determined by a jury."[49]

However, *Moore* must be understood in its proper context: the legal issues which arose in that case, and which included the construction of a patent of James I, and of its confirmation by Charles I, were questions of exceptional interpretative difficulty, not routine questions, and it was on this basis that the Supreme Court reserved examination. Between 1870 and 1970 there appear to

---

[39] *Esso Petroleum v. Fogarty* [1965] I.R. 531.
[40] *Loubrough v. James Panton & Co. Ltd.* [1965] I.R. 272.
[41] *Polycell Products Ltd. v. O'Connell* [1959] Ir. Jur. Rep. 34.
[42] *Richardson v. Murphy* [1899] 1 I.R. 248.
[43] *Foster v. Hornsby* (1853) 2 Ir. Ch. Rep. 426.
[44] *Sinclair v. Gogarty* [1937] I.R. 377.
[45] *Turner v. Robinson* (1860) Ir. Ch. Rep. 117.
[46] *Dublin Port and Docks Board v. Britannia Dredging* [1968] I.R. 136.
[47] *Rooney v. Cork Corporation* (1881) 7 Ir. L.R. 191.
[48] [1927] I.R. 569.
[49] *ibid.* at 575.

be just four cases mentioned in the reports where the Irish courts *Campus Oil* style reserved the legal issue, and applied the balance of convenience: *Mackey v. Scottish Widows Fund Assurance Society*;[50] *Moore v. Attorney General*;[51] *Smith v. Beirne*;[52] and *Educational Company of Ireland v. FitzPatrick*.[53] In the first and third cases the ground for reserving consideration of the merits was that there were conflicts of evidence (the existence of a nuisance, as to whether there was a trade dispute) which were incapable of being resolved. In the second, third and fourth cases the ground for reserving the decision was said to be the existence of legal controversy of special difficulty (the status of the right not to join a trade union, the construction of seventeenth century patents, whether the definition of trade dispute applied to a dispute between workers and a members' club). There was (unlike the current position) no categorical rule. Instead, the general practice was prior to granting an injunction, to investigate routine issues of law or interpretation, but to reserve applications which depended upon intractable factual controversy, or points of law of particular awkwardness. Applying the principles which appear to underlie Irish practice pre- and post- Supreme Court of Judicature (Ireland) Act 1877, the immediate decision in *Campus Oil* itself was unremarkable. That case, like *Moore* and *FitzPatrick*, involved novel and difficult legal propositions which it might have been irresponsible to resolve at the stage of an interlocutory hearing. The decision to decide the matter on the balance of convenience was entirely consistent with earlier Irish practice. The departure from principle in *Campus Oil* was in promulgating a set of systematic rules and in the fettering of a discretionary jurisdiction.

It is clear that were the principles which previously regulated the grant of interlocutory injunctions still in existence, the post-dismissal salary injunction would not be the virtually automatic remedy that it now appears to have become. Post-dismissal injunctions are, typically, sought on the following grounds: that fair procedures were not complied with (predictably the most popular of the grounds); that statutory procedures under the Redundancy Payments Acts 1967–1991 have not been complied with; that insufficient notice was given; that the articles of association of the defendant had not been complied with; that the plaintiff was not guilty of the allegations complained of. Yet, were these legal issues to have arisen in the 1870s or in the 1920s or 1960s the likelihood is that (with the exception of the last of these grounds) the merits of the plaintiff's claim would have been assessed, and there would have been a consideration of the balance of argument. Underlying this approach was a con-

---

[50] (1876) I.R. 10 Eq. 114.
[51] [1927] I.R. 569.
[52] The *Irish Times,* January 30, 1953. The judgment in the full trial is reported at (1954) 88 I.L.T.R. 24.
[53] [1961] I.R. 323.

cern to avoid restraining the liberties of persons who were acting lawfully. The rule was not inflexible, and yielded to a balance of convenience approach in difficult cases where a provisional appraisal was impracticable. The practice seems to have been informed by the concern that, as a matter of natural justice, the plaintiff ought to be put to proof of his or her claim.[54]

There are indications that the law of dismissal may be in a process of evolution. The right of an employer to dismiss on notice may have contracted. The right of a wrongfully dismissed employee to disregard a purported termination as void, and to claim wages for the period until the contract is properly terminated, or the breach is accepted, seems also to have been recognised. There are, however, problems with the most popular remedy through which these new rights are being administered, the interlocutory injunction. The application of the current, limited scrutiny standard to the post-dismissal wages injunction means that defendants are being subjected to orders which are virtually unchangeable, and salary is being handed out to relatively well-to-do employees who may have been entirely lawfully dismissed. Both of these faults originate in the rule which forbids courts to fully test legal propositions made in applications for an interlocutory injunction. A study of this modern injunction adds to the argument for a return to the established Irish principles in the administration of the interlocutory injunction.

5. CONCLUSION

The anti-dismissal injunction is both an innovative, and effective, pre-trial remedy for the wrongfully dismissed employee. There may, however, be some small problems. Applications for the remedy are difficult to resist and allegations never properly tested; the order may be imposing on employers obligations in excess of their common law duties; and the remedy seems to be in tension with the mitigation rule. There are a number of ways in which this remedy might, perhaps, be better regulated: by aligning the duration of the order with the employer's outstanding notice obligations; by greater flexibility in the terms on which the order is granted; and, especially, by raising the burden of proof required of a plaintiff in order to obtain an order.

---

[54]See, in particular the judgment of Ó Dálaigh C.J. in *Esso Petroleum Co. Ltd. v. Fogarty* [1965] I.R. 531.

SUCCESSION RIGHTS UNDER THE EUROPEAN CONVENTION ON HUMAN RIGHTS

SUZANNE EGAN

1. INTRODUCTION

A notable aspect of the evolution of succession law in Ireland has been the goal of the legislature and judiciary alike to achieve an element of certainty in the formulation of the legal rules governing inheritance.[1] A premium appears to have been placed in this area of law on the value of settled rules that are not to be interpreted flexibly.[2] Given the importance of the matters that the law in this area is designed to regulate – the desire to maintain certainty is considered necessary to eliminate any risk of arbitrariness. Such adherence to form may, however, lead to injustice in individual cases.

This theme of the tension between legal certainty and the demands of justice in domestic law was a central concern of Professor Brady's scholarship.[3] In this article, an attempt is made to assess the extent to which that tension pervades adjudication of succession rights under the European Convention on Human Rights. It is argued that despite encouraging indications in its early

---

[1] In his seminal work on the subject, Professor J.C. Brady notes the strict attention to technical compliance with the Wills Act 1837 formerly adhered to by the Irish courts in relation to the execution of wills. Although some flexibility has been introduced in the application of the law by the Irish courts in relation to the execution of wills since the enactment of the Succession Act 1965, no such flexibility operates with respect to the operation of the intestacy rules elaborated under that legislation: *Succession Law in Ireland* (1st ed., Dublin, 1989) at viii.

[2] A classic example of this concern has been the reluctance of the Irish courts to give the broadest possible interpretation to the unclear legislative provisions enacted in the Succession Act 1965 relating to the admissibility of extrinsic evidence in construing the intentions of a testator. See the Supreme Court's decision in *Rowe v. Law* [1978] I.R. 55 in which the court held that s. 90 of the Succession Act 1965 could be interpreted as allowing extrinsic evidence only if it met the double test of (a) showing the intention of the testator; and (b) assisting in the construction of, or explaining any contradiction, in a will. In the view of Henchy J., any wider interpretation of the legislative intent in framing the Succession Act so as to allow the testator's intentions as expressed in a will to be tested against any available extrinsic evidence would be "fraught with possibilities for fraud, mistake, unfairness and uncertainty…": *ibid.* at 60. See more recently *In the Matter of the Estate of Mary Francis Collins deceased; Joseph O'Connell and Alma O'Connell v. Governor and Company of the Bank of Ireland and Bank of Ireland Trustee Co. Ltd.,* [1998] I.L.R.M. 465 in which the Supreme Court refused to depart from its reasoning in the earlier decision.

[3] See for example, Brady, "Legal Certainty: The Durable Myth" (1973) 8 *Irish Jurist* (n.s.) 18.

case law, the European Court of Human Rights has proved itself to be just as susceptible to governmental concerns in regard to legal certainty in this area, at the expense of the interests of the individual applicants.

2. THE EUROPEAN CONVENTION ON HUMAN RIGHTS

The European Convention on Human Rights[4] is the primary vehicle through which a human rights claim may be pursued against European States at the international level. Although predictions as to its utility were not altogether uniformly positive in its infancy,[5] it has since become commonly recognised as the most successful international human rights treaty in terms of securing effective respect for human rights at the international level.[6]

The importance of the Convention rests not only in its delineation of the rights which Contracting States are obliged to guarantee, but also in the enforcement machinery which it sets up to ensure compliance by the States with these rights. Originally, this machinery was two-tiered, consisting of a part-time European Commission of Human Rights and European Court of Human Rights. Each of these organs had a specific role to play in the investigation of individual complaints under the complaint procedure provided for in the Convention. The Commission's principal role was to decide whether the complaint was admissible according to stringent criteria set forth in the Convention[7] and, if so, to offer a non-binding opinion on the merits. The court's task was to

---

[4] The long title of the Convention is the *Convention for the Protection of Human Rights and Fundamental Freedoms*, European Treaty Series, No. 5. See Ghandhi, *International Human Rights Documents,* (London, 1995) at p. 125.

[5] Apparently, the signing of the Convention in 1950 was announced by the President of the Consultative Assembly (now the Parliamentary Assembly) of the Council of Europe in the following terms: "The Convention on Human Rights will be signed by 15 countries at 3.00p.m. at the Palazzo Barberini. It is not a very good convention but it is a lovely palace": Maxwell-Fyfe, *Political Adventure: The Memoirs of the Earl of Kilmuir* (London, 1962) at pp. 183–184.

[6] "... [t]he instrument, signed in 1950 was to become the most important step, so far taken, to translate into reality the commitment of the international community and of every one of its members to protect the dignity and worth of the human person": Schwelb, "Some Aspects of the International Covenants on Human Rights of December 1966" in Eide and Schou (eds.), *International Protection of Human Rights* [Proceedings of the Seventh Nobel Symposium, Oslo, September 25-27, 1967] (Stockholm: Almqvist and Wiksell, 1968) at p. 103.

[7] The admissibility conditions included, for example, the requirement that all domestic remedies must have been exhausted before the Commission would deal with the complaint; that the complaint would not be dealt with unless it had been made within a period of six months from the date on which the last domestic decision was taken. They also included, for example, the requirements that the complaints should not be "manifestly ill-founded", "anonymous" or an "abuse of the right of petition": See Articles 26 and 27 of the Convention, prior to its amendment by Protocol No. 11: I. Brownlie, *Basic Documents on Human Rights* (3rd ed., Oxford, 1992) 326 at p. 334.

adjudicate on the existence of a violation.[8] Recently, the machinery has been reincarnated as a full-time European Court of Human Rights[9] and the Commission has been abolished.[10] The new court has sole responsibility for investigating complaints by individuals[11] within the jurisdiction of the Contracting States who allege a breach of any of the Convention guarantees.[12] Each complaint must still satisfy the same admissibility hurdles before it will be considered on its merits by the court.[13] If the case is deemed admissible, the court must then consider the merits of the case and ultimately whether there has been a violation of the Convention by the state in question. While the Convention does not give the court the power to order remedial measures, it does give the court the power to order "just satisfaction" in the form of an award for costs or expenses and/or compensation to the applicant for pecuniary or non-pecuniary damage.[14] Failure to implement a judgment of the court may result in considerable political pressure from Member States of the Council of Europe[15] and it is generally accepted that the track record of the Contracting States in terms of compliance with negative judgments is usually favourable. Moreover, the fact that Convention guarantees have been incorporated into the domestic laws of virtually all of the Contracting States has meant that legislative change may be induced by a ruling by a domestic court that Convention rights have been violated by a state without the need for referral to Strasbourg.

---

[8] For a detailed exegesis on the procedure for implementing the Convention prior to its reform in 1998, see Harris, O'Boyle and Warbrick, *Law of the European Convention on Human Rights* (London, 1995), chapters 22-24.

[9] Hereinafter referred to as the "court". The court is composed of the same number of judges as there are contracting states to the Convention, *i.e.*, 41. The court sits in Committees of Three, Chambers of seven Judges and as a Grand Chamber of 17 judges, depending on the stage of consideration of the complaint. The plenary court does not convene to consider the substance of any complaint. Rather, it convenes only to consider procedural matters.

[10] This reform was made by the elaboration of a specific Protocol to the Convention, Protocol No. 11, which came into force in November 1998: Harris, *et al*, *op. cit.*, above, n. 8, chapter 26.

[11] There is also a provision for an inter-state complaint mechanism but this is rarely utilised: see Art. 33 of the Convention, *op. cit.*, above, n.4 at 131.

[12] The original guarantees in the Convention have been supplemented since 1950 by the elaboration of a number of Protocols, adopted at intervals since 1953. See Protocols 1, 4, 6, & 7 to the Convention: see Ghandhi, above n.4 at pp. 135-141. A further Protocol (Protocol No. 12) on the principle of non-discrimination has recently been opened for signature on June 26, 2000: see http://www.humanrights.coe.int.

[13] The original admissibility conditions referred to *supra* at n.7 have been preserved in the reformed Convention in Art. 35: Ghandhi, *op. cit.*, above, n. 4.

[14] Art. 41, *ibid.*

[15] The Committee of Ministers is charged with the task of enforcing judgments of the Court of Human Rights under Art. 46 of the Convention. In this respect, the most powerful weapon in the arsenal of the Committee of Ministers resides in Art. 8 of the Statute of the Council of Europe. Art. 8 provides that the Committee of Ministers may expel any Member State from the Council of Europe for violation of Art. 3 of that Statute which in turn requires respect for the rule of law and the protection of human rights and fundamental freedoms.

3. Succession Rights under the European Convention on Human Rights

Not surprisingly, there is no reference to succession rights specifically in the Convention. Indeed, there is no explicit reference either to a "right to property".[16] However, Article 1 of Protocol No. 1 to the Convention provides in paragraph 1 for the right to "peaceful enjoyment of possessions", which the Court has interpreted as guaranteeing in substance "the right to property".[17] The second paragraph of Article 1 goes on to provide that:

> "No one shall be deprived of his possessions except in the public interest and subject to the conditions provided for by law and by the general principles of international law".

Property rights are further qualified by the final paragraph which provides that the preceding provisions:

> "... shall not, however, in any way impair the right of a state to enforce such laws as it deems necessary to control the use of property in accordance with the general interest or to secure the payment of taxes or other contributions or penalties".

Although one might be forgiven for assuming this Article of the Convention to be the axis around which cases raising succession issues have revolved, in fact the court has rather narrowly interpreted Article 1 so as to preclude its application in many cases in which succession issues are raised. In the *Marckx* case, the court emphatically stated that Article 1 protects a person's *existing* possessions against interference. Specifically, the court stated that "it does not guarantee the right to acquire possessions whether on intestacy or through voluntary dispositions".[18] Although, as we shall see, the Article has generated some interesting jurisprudence in terms of the right to bequeath property, most of the cases which have raised succession rights have in fact been tackled by a different route than Article 1. Where inheritance issues are raised, the road to success has usually been reached through arguments based on a combination of Articles 8 and 14 of the Convention. Article 8 provides *inter alia* for the right

---

[16]The elaboration of a "right to property" has traditionally been controversial in international human rights law: Henkin, "The International Bill of Rights: The Universal Declaration and the Covenants" in Bernhardt and Jolowicz (eds.), *International Enforcement of Human Rights* (Max-Planck Institute: Reports Submitted to the Colloquium of the International Association of Legal Science, Heidelberg, August 28-30, 1985) 1 at 8. On the attempt to elaborate the substance of such a right in the European Convention on Human Rights specifically, see Harris *et al., op. cit.,* above, n. 8 at pp. 516-517.

[17]*Marckx v. Belgium* (1979) Series A 31, para. 63; (1979) 2 E.H.R.R. 330.

[18]*ibid.* para. 50.

to "respect for private and family life", while Article 14 provides for the right not to be discriminated against in the enjoyment of a Convention right on various grounds, including "sex, race, colour, language, religion, political or other opinion, national or social origin, association with a national minority, property, birth or other status".

Positive and Negative Obligations

Any analysis of the case law of the court in relation to succession must proceed with a few prefatory remarks on the structure of Articles 8 and 14 of the Convention and the manner in which each has been interpreted generally by the court.

Article 8(1) provides as follows:

> "Everyone has the right to respect for his private and family life, his home and his correspondence".

This right is qualified by a second paragraph which provides for justifiable restrictions by States on the guarantee in paragraph 1, as follows:

> "There shall be no interference by a public authority with the exercise of this right except such as is in accordance with the law and is necessary in a democratic society in the interests of national security, public safety or the economic well-being of the country, for the prevention of disorder or crime, for the protection of health or morals, or for the protection of the rights and freedoms of others".

In the *Belgian Linguistics Case (No. 2)*, the European Court of Human Rights ("the Court") held that the object of Article 8 of the Convention was "essentially that of protecting the individual against arbitrary interference by the public authorities into his private and family life".[19] If the court should find that there has been interference in the sphere of private or family life, it proceeds to analyse whether such an interference can be justified under the criteria set forth in paragraph 2 of Article 8. The methodology of the Court in analysing state justification for interference with the rights set forth in paragraph 1 is well rehearsed elsewhere.[20] It is sufficient to note here that a dominant factor in the court's reasoning is usually whether the respondent State can show that the interference is "necessary" in a democratic society for one of the stated aims.

---

[19](1968) 1 E.H.R.R. 252 at 282.
[20]An excellent analysis is to be found in Van Dijk & Van Hoof, *Theory and Practice of the European Convention on Human Rights* (3rd ed., The Hague: Kluwer, 1998) at Chap. 8, pp. 761-773; and Chap. 2, ss. 2.5 and 3.2.

Necessity implies that there must be some "pressing social need" for the interference, that the interference is "proportionate to the aim being pursued", and
that the reasons put forward for the interference were "relevant" and "sufficient".[21] In examining the question of necessity, the Court has stated that the
Convention leaves to the State a "margin of appreciation". The "margin of
appreciation" has been aptly described as a device which the court has drawn
on in its jurisprudence as a means of introducing relativity into the interpretation of Convention rights.[22] Through it, the court accepts that there may be
some instances in which the national authorities are better placed to assess the
extent of the measures necessary to protect Convention rights, having regard to
complex societal factors at work in its particular jurisdiction.[23] States do not
have unlimited powers of appreciation. Ultimately, it is up to the court to decide whether the government has exceeded its discretion in a particular case.
The scope of the margin of appreciation granted to the State varies depending
on the variety of considerations at work in a given case. In general terms, the
scope of the discretion may be influenced by, amongst other things, the right in
question, the nature of the interference complained of, and very often the aim
sought to be achieved by the interference.[24] Moreover, the existence or not of
a European consensus on a particular issue will often influence the court's
decision whether to grant a wide or narrow margin of appreciation to the State
as regards the actions taken by it at the domestic level.[25] In many cases, the
scope of the margin of appreciation granted in a particular case will prove
crucial to the ultimate decision of the court on the facts.[26]

But negative interference is not the only type of violation recognised by the
court. Indeed, the court has recognised that Article 8 not only requires the State
to *abstain* from interference in the private sphere, but also to undertake *positive obligations* inherent in effective respect for private life.[27] In other words,

---

[21] As an illustrative example, see *Norris v. Ireland* (1991) 13 E.H.R.R. 186.

[22] MacDonald, "The Margin of Appreciation" in Macdonald et al (eds.), *The European System for
the Protection of Human Rights* (London, 1993) at p. 83.

[23] The rationale for the margin of appreciation doctrine was first elaborated by the European Commission of Human Rights in *Lawless v. Ireland* (1979) Series B, para. 408; (1979-80) 1 E.H.R.R.
15. That rationale was subsequently adopted by the European Court of Human Rights and readily applied in its adjudicative function across the spectrum of Convention rights: See, in particular, the court's judgment in *Handyside v. United Kingdom,* December 7, 1976, Series A, No. 24,
1 E.H.R.R. 737.

[24] See the analysis of Van Dijk and van Hoof, *op. cit.*, above, n. 20 at pp. 87-91.

[25] In finding a violation of the right to respect for private life in Art. 8 in *Norris v. Ireland,* above,
n. 21, the Court was persuaded by the developments that had occurred in the domestic laws of
the Contracting States as regards the decriminalisation of homosexual activity between consent-
ing male adults. The fact that Irish law was out of step with the position in other Contracting
States by retaining a statutory prohibition on such activity on pain of criminal sanction, influenced the court in finding against the State, despite the normally wide margin of appreciation
granted to States in cases involving the protection of morals.

[26] See generally, MacDonald, *op. cit.*, above, n. 22.

[27] *Airey v. Ireland* (1980) 2 E.H.R.R. 305.

the Article obliges States to be pro-active in protecting a person's private and family life. This aspect of state obligation has been reiterated by the court on a number of occasions, not least in cases involving the succession rights of families based outside marriage.[28] In fulfilling their positive obligations under Article 8 of the Convention, Contracting States are also afforded a margin of appreciation by the Convention.[29] As with cases of negative interference, the scope of this margin of appreciation may also be influenced by the existence or not of a European consensus in respect of the obligation alleged to exist by the applicant.[30] Moreover, where positive obligations are concerned, the court has acknowledged that in determining the steps to be taken to ensure compliance with the Convention, a fair balance must be struck between the needs and resources of the community and of individuals.[31] Even though paragraph 2, strictly speaking, only applies to cases of negative interference, the court has stated that in striking the required balance, the aims mentioned in the second paragraph "may be of a certain relevance".[32] The difficulty, therefore, for an applicant who seeks to argue that the State has failed in its positive obligations under Article 8 is that he or she will first have to convince the court of the existence of an interest which the State has failed to respect. In the course of that analysis, the court will often assess whether there may be a legitimate basis on which the State has failed to respect the right. The simultaneous consideration of the two aspects of the claim has led to the inexorable conclusion of Warbrick, that it is usually harder for the applicant to succeed in this type of claim than it is in regard to an argument based on negative interference.[33]

Article 14 of the Convention provides for a limited basis upon which discrimination arguments can be raised before the court. It provides for a general duty of non-discrimination by Contracting States in securing the enjoyment of Convention rights. In this respect, Article 14 is not a free-standing equality norm, but rather a subordinate equality norm.[34] In order to claim that a law or

---

[28] See text accompanying nn. 37 to 62, below.

[29] *Abdulaziz, Cabales & Balkandali v. United Kingdom* (1985) 7 E.H.R.R. 471.

[30] See in this respect, for example, the recent decision of the Court in *Sheffield and Horsham v. United Kingdom* (1999) 27 E.H.R.R. 163.

[31] *Powell & Rayner v. United Kingdom* (1990) 12 E.H.R.R. 355 at para. 41.

[32] *ibid.*

[33] "The task of deciding whether there *is* a duty is different from deciding whether a duty has been breached but the court's approach does not always make this clear. Where the Art. 8(1) duty of respect involves a negative obligation, the court regards the failure of the State to comply as an 'interference' requiring justification under Art. 8(2). Where the Art. 8(1) duty of respect involves a positive obligation, the court tends to collapse the inquiry as to what the duty is with the question of whether the duty has been breached": Warbrick, "The Structure of Article 8" (1998) 1 *E.H.R.L.R.* 32 at 35.

[34] However, as noted above at n. 12, the Contracting States have recently elaborated an extra Protocol to the Convention (Protocol No. 12), by which the Contracting States may each opt to adhere to an open-ended equality norm which guarantees equality before the law in relation to the enjoyment of *any* right set forth by law. At the time of writing, the Protocol has not entered into force for any of the Contracting States.

administrative practice is discriminatory, an applicant must first show that the law or practice falls within the ambit of a Convention right. Once that condition is satisfied, the court may proceed to analyse whether the State has discriminated against the applicant in guaranteeing the right in question. That enquiry takes the form of a two-pronged assessment: first, whether there is a difference in treatment between the applicant and another similarly situated group; and if so, whether there is a reasonable and objective justification for the difference in treatment.[35] The court is prepared to accept that a difference in treatment has a "reasonable and objective justification" if it is satisfied that the difference is based on a legitimate aim and if the means used to achieve that aim is proportionate to the aim pursued.[36]

4. SUCCESSION RIGHTS IN THE STRASBOURG CASE LAW

The jurisprudence of the European Court of Human Rights to date in regard to succession rights has been concerned principally with the rights of families based outside marriage to bequeath and inherit property. In a trilogy of cases, the Court has made clear the obligations of Contracting States in this area. Indeed, it was in the first of these cases, *Marckx v. Belgium*,[37] that the dynamic interpretation of Article 8 of the Convention as imposing positive obligations on Contracting States first emerged. In *Marckx*, the court had to consider whether there had been a violation of both applicants' succession rights from two angles. First, had there been a violation of the Convention in the restricted ability of the child applicant, because of her status as a child born outside wedlock, to inherit from her mother or from near relatives on intestacy or by way of voluntary disposition? Second, did the restrictions on the mother's freedom to bequeath property to her child violate the Convention?

The first challenge for the applicants was to convince the court that their relationship did amount to "family life" within the meaning of Article 8. In a seminal judgment, the court held definitively that Article 8 did not make any distinction between the family based within or outside marriage.[38] Article 8 imposed a positive obligation on States to ensure that their domestic laws were such as to allow an unmarried mother and her child to lead a "normal life".[39]

---

[35] *Belgian Linguistics Case (No. 2)* (1968) 1 E.H.R.R. 252.

[36] The court stated the test succinctly more recently in *Fredin v. Sweden*: "A difference in treatment is discriminatory, for the purposes of Art. 14, if it has no objective and reasonable justification, that is, if it does not pursue a legitimate aim or if there is not a reasonable relationship of proportionality between the means employed and the aim sought to be realised": (1991) Series A no. 192; (1991) 13 E.H.R.R. 784, para. 60.

[37] (1979) Series A 31; (1979) 2 E.H.R.R. 330.

[38] *ibid.* para. 31.

[39] *ibid.*

This implied, in particular, that there should be legal safeguards in place to allow for the child's integration into the family.[40] As regards the child's claim to be entitled to inherit from her mother, the court did not accept that Article 1 of Protocol No. 1 of the Convention guaranteed the right to acquire possessions whether on intestacy or through voluntary dispositions.[41] While it did accept that the right of succession between children and parents was so closely related to family life that it fell within the sphere of Article 8 of the Convention, [42] the court went on to express the view that:

> "... it is not a requirement of Article 8 that a child should be entitled to some share in the estates of his parents or even of other near relatives: in the matter of patrimonial rights also, Article 8 in principle leaves to the Contracting States the choice of the means calculated to allow everyone to lead a normal family life and such an entitlement is not indispensable in the pursuit of a normal family life".[43]

Consequently, the restrictions on the second applicant's inheritance rights, or in respect of her position as regards voluntary dispositions, did not in themselves conflict with the Convention, considered independently of the reasons underlying those restrictions.[44] The latter reasons, however, were relevant for the court in deciding whether there had been any discrimination against the applicant in the enjoyment of her Convention rights under Article 8 in conjunction with Article 14. In the court's view, the difference in treatment between the "illegitimate" and the "legitimate" child as regards capacity to inherit property lacked objective and reasonable justification. Accordingly, the child was found to be a victim of a violation of Article 14 of the Convention in conjunction with Article 8, by reason both of the restrictions on her capacity to receive property from her mother and of her total lack of inheritance rights on intestacy over the estates of her near relatives on her mother's side.[45]

---

[40] *ibid.*

[41] *ibid.* at para. 50.

[42] *ibid.* at para. 52: "It held that "Matters of intestate succession – and of disposition – between near relatives prove to be intimately connected with family life. Family life does not include only social, moral or cultural relations, for example in the sphere of children's education; it also comprises interests of a material kind, as shown by, amongst other things, the obligations in respect of maintenance and the position occupied in the domestic legal systems of the majority of the Contracting States by the institution of the reserved portion of an estate (*réserve héréditaire*). Whilst inheritance rights are not normally exercised until the estate-owner's death, that is, at a time when family life undergoes a change or even comes to an end, this does not mean that no issue concerning such rights may arise before death; the distribution of an estate may be settled, and in practice fairly often is settled, by the making of a will or of a gift on account of a future inheritance (*avance d'hoirie*); it therefore represents a feature of family life that cannot be disregarded".

[43] *ibid.* at para. 53.

[44] *ibid.*

[45] *ibid.* at para. 59.

As regards the mother's limited rights to bequeath property to her daughter, the court held that while Article 8 was relevant, it did not guarantee to a mother complete freedom to give or bequeath her property to her child. In the court's view:

> "… [I]n principle, it [the Convention] leaves to the Contracting States the choice of means calculated to lead a normal family life and such freedom is not indispensable in the pursuit of a normal family life."[46]

Similarly, while Article 1 of Protocol No. 1 was relevant in relation to this aspect of succession, the restrictions in question were not sufficient to establish a violation of that Article. In the court's view, even though the right to dispose of one's property constitutes a traditional and fundamental aspect of the right to property, the provision in the second paragraph of Article 1 that allows Contracting States to "enforce such laws as it deems necessary to control the use of property in accordance with the general interest" was held to be capable of justifying the restriction.[47] In this respect, the court conceded that the "general interest" might in certain cases induce a legislature to "control the use of property in the area of dispositions *inter vivos* or by will".[48] Nonetheless, since the restriction in question again applied only to unmarried mothers as opposed to married mothers, the court ultimately found a violation of Article 14 in conjunction with Article 1 of Protocol No. 1 on the grounds that there was no objective and reasonable justification for the limitation.[49]

The second case before the court which dealt with the succession rights of a child born outside marriage was the case of *Johnston v. Ireland.*[50] However, unlike the *Marckx* case, in *Johnston* the succession issue was raised as part of a panoply of limitations on the applicant child's status which she and her natural parents claimed collectively violated the Convention. The applicants were an unmarried couple and their child. The couple had been living together for some fifteen years following the breakdown of the male applicant's marriage to another woman. The applicants could not marry each other because of the constitutional ban on divorce in operation at that time. The child's sole legal guardian was her mother and she could not be jointly adopted by her parents or legitimated by any subsequent marriage of her parents. An aspect of the third applicant's case that her succession rights were inferior to those of a child born within marriage. As is well known, the Irish Supreme Court had narrowly interpreted the word "issue" in the Succession Act 1965 as referring to chil-

---

[46] *ibid.* at para. 61.
[47] *ibid.* at paras. 63-64.
[48] *ibid.* at para. 64.
[49] *ibid.* at para. 65.
[50] (1987) 9 E.H.R.R. 203.

dren born of a lawful marriage and not to those born outside marriage.[51] As a result of this ruling, children such as the applicant had no right to inherit on the intestacy of her natural father. Neither did the Succession Act empower the Irish courts to make proper provision for a child born outside marriage where a testator had failed in his or her moral duty to make proper provision for the child, as it could in the case of a child born within marriage.[52] Finally, a child such as the applicant was also liable to pay greater capital acquisitions tax on inheriting property than a child born within marriage.[53]

The European Court of Human Rights had little difficulty in finding that all three applicants constituted a "family" for the purposes of Article 8, as a result of which they were entitled to the protection of Article 8, notwithstanding that their relationship existed outside marriage.[54] While the parent applicants failed to convince the court that there had been a breach of Article 8 in the failure of the State to establish an analogous legal status for married and non-married couples,[55] the court did find a violation of all three applicants' rights to "respect" for family life by virtue of the child's inferior status under Irish law. The court's previous *dicta* in the *Marckx* case led to the inevitable conclusion that a legal regime allowing family ties to develop normally had not been established in the instant case.[56] Although the court had expressly decided in *Marckx* that neither Article 8 nor Article 1 of Protocol No. 1 of the Convention establishes a right to inherit property, it decided in *Johnston* that the child's inferior status *vis-à-vis* succession and other matters, differed considerably from that of a child born within marriage. The state's failure to establish an appropriate legal regime reflecting the child's natural family ties amounted to a clear failure to respect her family life, notwithstanding the state's wide margin of appreciation in this area.[57]

While the *Marckx* and *Johnston* cases concerned disputes which arose directly against the state *ab initio*, the applicant's complaint in *Inze v. Austria*[58] came to light as a result of a dispute between two brothers over the distribution

---

[51] *O'B v. S* [1984] I.R. 316. For diverse commentary on the ruling of the Supreme Court, see Brady, *Succession Law in Ireland* (2nd ed., Dublin, 1995) at pp. 252-253; and Lyall, *Land Law in Ireland* (2nd ed., Dublin, 2000) pp.1006–1007.
[52] See s. 117 of the Succession Act.
[53] Further examples of the child's subordinate status cited before the court were the impossibility for her to be "legitimated" even by her parents' subsequent remarriage; the impossibility of her parents jointly adopting her; and the fact that it was impossible for her father to be appointed as her joint legal guardian. See generally para. 70 of the court's judgment, above, n.50.
[54] *Johnston v. Ireland*, above n. 50 at para. 56 of the judgment.
[55] In this respect, the court held that the positive obligations on the state in respect of Art. 8 did not stretch so far as to require it to establish a special regime for a particular category of unmarried couples, i.e. persons like the applicants who wished to marry but who were unable to do so: *ibid.,* at para. 57.
[56] *ibid.* at paras. 72-75.
[57] *ibid.* at para. 75.
[58] (1987) Series A, No. 126, 10 E.H.R.R. 394.

on intestacy of their late mother's farm. Under Austrian intestacy law, each of the brothers was entitled to an equal share of the farm. However, the law also provided that the farm itself could not be divided in the case of hereditary succession. Instead, one of the heirs was obliged to take over the entire property and pay off the other heirs. However, the Act went on to provide that children born out of wedlock must be excluded as "principal" heirs. The applicant in *Inze* had been born out of wedlock and hence did not qualify as the principal heir. He complained that he had been discriminated against on grounds of birth in the inheritance of his deceased mother's estate.[59] His brother, who had been born within marriage, was appointed as the principal heir, and hence was entitled to take over the farm.

The court found that Article 1 of Protocol No. 1 was applicable to the facts. It distinguished the case from *Marckx* insofar as the latter case had been concerned with *potential* rights of inheritance on intestacy.[60] In *Inze*, the applicant had already acquired by inheritance a right to a share in his deceased mother's estate, as a result of which the farm was now the joint property of the applicant and his co-heirs. The key question, therefore, was whether the applicant had been discriminated against in the enjoyment of his property. The government argued that the provision in favour of the legitimate heir corresponded with what could be "presumed to be the deceased's intentions". In its view, it also corresponded with a variety of other factors such as the surviving spouse's presumed preference and the likelihood that children born outside wedlock would not have been brought up on the parents' farm.[61] The court gave short shrift to these "abstract and general" considerations as providing an objective and reasonable justification for the difference in treatment based on birth.[62] Accordingly, it found that there had been a violation of Article 14 taken together with Article 1 of Protocol 1.

Legal Certainty versus Individual Rights?

The narrowest possible extrapolation of the *Marckx*, *Johnston* and *Inze* judgments, of course, is that Contracting States are not entitled to draw distinctions between "families" based within and outside marriage in their succession laws. But the judgments could perhaps be read in a slightly wider context: namely, that the traditional concern of domestic legislatures to regulate property law by reference to an inflexible concept of the family as being one based on mar-

---

[59] According to special regulations in the Carinthian Hereditary Farms Act of 1903, farms of a certain size could not be divided in the case of hereditary succession and one of the heirs was obliged to take over the entire farm and pay off the other heirs. This Act gave precedence to the legitimate heirs of the deceased estate as the principal heir.

[60] *Inze v. Austria*, above, n. 58 at para. 38 of the court's judgment.

[61] *ibid.* at para. 42.

[62] *ibid.* at para. 43.

riage, without giving sufficient consideration to the variety of other *de facto* relationships that may arise, may not be compatible with Convention obligations.[63]

Despite this progressive conceptual breakthrough, it appears that the court has not been prepared to abandon the Contracting States to the wholly uncertain results that might have obtained if it had not in some way circumscribed the potential impact of its judgments. Although the court's judgments are normally declaratory in nature, with the Contracting States being left to draw their own conclusions as to how to remedy the identified violation, the court in *Marckx* expressly stated that its judgment should be applied prospectively. In its view, the principle of legal certainty, which it professed was "necessarily inherent in the law of the Convention", dispensed the Belgian State from re-opening legal acts or situations that antedated the delivery of the judgment.[64]

This deliberate and indeed uncharacteristic restriction of the impact of its own judgment may be seen as no more than a pragmatic desire not to penalise the Contracting States for reliance on laws that they may not have foreseen to be incompatible with the Convention. Indeed, the device of limiting the impact of a groundbreaking decision by means of prospective overruling has been prayed in aid in many domestic constitutional courts.[65] Though controversial when applied to cases concerning fundamental human rights,[66] one might be prepared to concede the court's understandable concern that its ruling should not affect ownership of estates that may *already* have been irregularly distributed on foot of the old law. But one may well query whether it is acceptable to limit the effect of the *Marckx* judgment to the distribution of estates that have not been so settled. Unfortunately, the court appears to have resolved the latter question in a most ungenerous way in the subsequent case of *Vermeire v. Belgium*.[67] In that case, the applicant complained about her exclusion from the inheritance of her grandmother's estate on the basis of her birth outside marriage under the law in force at the time of the *Marckx* judgment. The applicant's grandmother had died prior to the decision of the European Court of

---

[63]"It would therefore appear that the right to respect for family life relations of the 'social, moral and cultural' kind referred to in the *Marckx* case will depend on the existence of *de facto*, real family life, whereas interests of a material kind *vis-à-vis* deceased grandparents do not depend on a prior *de facto* relationship. . . . This is to say no more than that the Convention reflects the fact that in national law rights of inheritance on intestacy and definition clauses of family ties for that purpose are generally formal rules intended to regulate the ownership of property with a high degree of certainty, and with regard to the uncertainties and vagaries of *de facto* relationships": Liddy, "The Concept of Family Life under the ECHR" [1998] 1 *E.H.R.L.R.* 15 at p. 19.

[64]*Marckx v. Belgium*, above n. 17, at para. 58.

[65]See for example the decisions of the U.S. Court of Appeal (Fifth Circuit) in *Linkletter v. Walker* (1965) 381 U.S. 618; and in Ireland, *The State (Byrne) v. Frawley* [1978] I.R. 326 and *Murphy v. Attorney General* [1982] I.R. 241. See also Nicol, "Prospective Overruling: A New Device for English Courts" (1976) 39 *M.L.R.* 542.

[66]See, for example, the dissenting judgment of Black J. in *Linkletter v. Walker*, above, n.65.

[67](1991) Series A No. 214-C, 81.

Human Rights in the *Marckx* case, but her estate was not actually distributed amongst her "legitimate" grandchildren until after the court's decision. The domestic appeal court refused to give effect to the judgment in the *Marckx* case, on the basis that it was a matter for the legislature to rectify and not the judiciary. In a terse judgment, the European Court of Human Rights relied on its dicta as to the temporal effect of its judgment in *Marckx* to deny a violation of Article 8 and 14 in the applicant's case. That judgment had provided that the principle of legal certainty dispensed the State from applying the ruling to "legal acts or situations" which antedated the delivery of the judgment. The death of the grandmother prior to the court's judgment was sufficient to open the succession issue and hence a "situation" was activated capable of disfranchising the applicant.[68]

In a trenchant dissent, Martens J. took the view that the majority had wrongly interpreted the effect of its own ruling in *Marckx* on the temporal effect of the judgment. In his view, the judgment only applied to "successions where the distribution of the estate has not yet been finalised on that date", *i.e.*, the date of the judgment.[69] In his view, the prospective application of the court's judgment was based on a concern not to interfere with estates that were already distributed to the detriment of third parties. By going beyond the confines of that premise in *Vermeire*, Martens J. believed that the majority had undermined the essential "message" of its ruling in *Marckx*, namely that discrimination against illegitimate children was "fundamentally unjust and could no longer be tolerated".[70] Moreover, the goal of legal certainty should not have been used to obfuscate that essential proposition:

> "Legal certainty should of course be taken into account where possible (in the sense of prevention of legal 'disorder') but where the price for attaining this end has to be the 'continuation of fundamental injustice' that continuation should be allowed only in so far as wholly unavoidable".[71]

It is submitted that Martens J.'s interpretation of the court's ruling in *Marckx* must surely be preferable in terms of achieving individuated justice. The court has often been criticised for favouring state interests over the interests of individuals in adjudicating on the necessity of a restriction on fundamental rights. But it difficult to see why the court would have indulged the State by deferring to its interpretation as to the appropriate date for the opening of the succession. Simply because national law designated that date to be the date of the death of

---

[68] *Vermeire v. Belgium*, above, n.67 at para. 22.
[69] *ibid.* at para. 3, dissenting judgment.
[70] *ibid.* at para. 9.
[71] *ibid.*

the deceased was sufficient for the court, without the need for objective evaluation based on Convention principles. Unfortunately, however, the majority ruling in *Vermeire* apparently took root in the former Commission's jurisprudence, leading to further repercussions for similarly situated individuals whose subsequent applications to the Commission have fallen on deaf ears.[72]

Nonetheless, in a dying gasp before its abolition in October 1999, the Commission finally appears to have given the "message" of the *Marckx* case as regards the succession rights of children born outside marriage priority over state interests in achieving legal certainty in the formation of intestacy rules. In the case of *Camp & Bourimi v. The Netherlands*,[73] the applicant child and his mother complained of a violation of Article 8 in conjunction with Article 14 of the Convention by reason of the child's exclusion from the inheritance of his deceased father's estate. The child had been conceived outside marriage and was born after the father's death. The father had died intestate and before he had legally recognised the child as his own. The mother succeeded in obtaining letters of legitimation from the domestic courts in which the child's paternity was recognised two years after the father's death. However, under Dutch law then in force, letters of legitimation did not have retroactive effect, as a result of which the child could not inherit from his father. The core of the child's claim was that he had been a victim of an unjustified difference in treatment on grounds of his birth. Whereas children who, at the time of the death of their father, had legally recognised family relationships with their father could inherit from him, children not having such legally recognised ties, like the applicant, could not.

The government argued that the limitation on retroactive effect of letters of legitimation was aimed at providing an element of legal certainty in the law as regards the true heir to an estate. Since there was no deadline for taking out letters of legitimation, the heirs to an estate have an interest in being able to have confidence that they need not spend years fearing that they will have to give up their lawful inheritance to some descendant who "may turn up unexpectedly".[74]

The Commission's reasoning in this case is to be preferred to that of the court in *Vermeire*. Rather than abdicating its function of examining the individual interests at stake in deference to domestic law, the Commission thoroughly took account of the particular facts of the case in its analysis of whether there had been a breach of the Convention. In the instant case, it observed that the other heirs to the estate had had ample warning of the applicant child's

---

[72] See, for example, *HR v. Federal Republic of Germany,* June 30, 1992, Application No, 17750/91 and *Verryt v. Belgium,* May 18, 1994, Application No. 21199/93.

[73] Application No. 28369/95, admissibility decision of September 8, 1997; Report of the Commission adopted on April 23, 1997: http://www.dhcour.coe.

[74] *ibid.* at para. 53 of the Report.

potential claim on his father's estate. His mother had applied to the domestic court for letters of legitimation very soon after the father's death.[75] Taking account of the Court's reasoning in *Marckx*, the Commission held that there had clearly been a difference in treatment.[76] It was not persuaded that there was any objective and reasonable justification for the impugned difference in treatment advanced by the government. Although the protection of the rights of heirs may in itself constitute a legitimate aim, the Commission considered that the method employed to achieve that aim (the exclusion of the child from the father's inheritance) was disproportionate in the circumstances of the present case. Having regard to the facts of the case, the applicant could not be said to have "unexpectedly turned up".[77] Accordingly, there had been a violation of Article 14 of the Convention, taken together with Article 8, with respect to the child.

At the time of writing, the judgment of the European Court of Human Rights in *Camp & Bourimi* is still pending. It is hoped that the court will retreat from the minimalist stance taken in *Vermeire* as regards the precedence to be given to legal certainty in succession law. It must be remembered that the former court itself has recognised that only the weightiest of reasons could justify a difference in treatment as between children born within and outside marriage.[78] With this background in mind, it would be incongruous for the new court to allow state concerns over legal certainty to trump individual rights to inheritance, without thoroughly taking into account all of the interests at stake.[79]

5. FRESH CHALLENGES: THE EVOLVING JURISPRUDENCE ON FAMILY LIFE AND ITS POTENTIAL EFFECT ON SUCCESSION ISSUES

The dynamic nature of the *Marckx* judgement is perhaps difficult to appreciate twenty years after the event. In the new millennium, discriminatory distinctions in domestic law between children born within or outside marriage as regards succession rights would appear to be anathema to the domestic laws of the Contracting States.[80] As noted above, the clear implication of the judg-

---

[75] *ibid.* at paras. 18-26 of the Commission's Report.
[76] *ibid.* at para. 55.
[77] *ibid.* at para. 57.
[78] *Inze v. Austria*, 28 October 1987, Series A no. 126, p. 18, para. 41.
[79] Since this article was submitted for publication, the decision of the European Court of Human Rights in *Camp & Bourimi v. The Netherlands* has been delivered. The author is pleased to note that the Court has adopted similar reasoning to that of the Commission in its opinion on the merits of the case, discussed above. Accordingly, the Court held that there had been a violation of Art. 14 of the Convention in conjunction with Art. 8 in respect of the child applicant. The full text of the Court's judgment may be accessed on the web site of the European Court of Human Rights at: www.echr.coe.
[80] See the survey of European succession laws in Hayton, *European Succession Laws* (Bristol, 1998).

ments in *Marckx*, *Johnston* and *Inze* on the substantive issue is that Contracting States are not entitled to draw distinctions between "families" based within and outside marriage in their succession laws. Pushed slightly further, the judgments could be cited for the proposition that the state's interest in ensuring legal certainty through a rigid definition of "family" cannot be used as a bar to recognition of other *de facto* relations for the purpose of succession rights. If this proposition is accepted, the logical conclusion is that the Convention may well serve as an instrument for challenging domestic laws which discriminate against individuals in alternative relationships to those arising within marriage in terms of their succession rights. As will be seen, however, tentative arguments to date in that direction have been received with very disappointing results.

(a) Intimate Relationships

> "Not everyone's personal situation fits into the paradigm case with which family law is most at home, that of the heterosexual married couple with children".[81]

This truism of Karsten's would actually seem to be somewhat of an understatement. In his extensive analysis of the property rights of cohabitants in common law jurisdictions, Mee has noted a dramatic increase in cohabitation between unmarried partners in Western societies in the second half of the twentieth century.[82] Despite difficulties in obtaining statistical information on the extent of homosexual cohabitation, he notes that there is evidence of an increase in some jurisdictions.[83] Technological developments in assisted conception in recent years have also challenged the traditional understanding of the concept of "family".[84] It has become necessary in some cases to distinguish between the "genetic" as opposed to the "social" parent in deciding who may be defined as a child's "parent" for legal purposes.[85] With these relationships in mind, it is

---

[81] Karsten, "Atypical Families and the Human Rights Act: The Rights of Unmarried Fathers, Same Sex Couples and Transsexuals" (1999) 2 *E.H.R.L.R.* 195.

[82] Mee, *The Property Rights of Cohabitees: An Analysis of Equity's Response in Five Common Law Jurisdictions* (Oxford, 1999), pp. 7-11.

[83] Mee attributes a lack of concrete statistical information on homosexual cohabitation to the social stigma which has traditionally been associated with same sex relationships: *ibid.* at pp. 11-12. Presumably, the dearth of such information may also be connected to the shortage of legal recognition of such relationships in most jurisdictions: Freeman and Lyon, *Cohabitation Without Marriage* (Aldershot, 1983) at p. 139.

[84] See generally, Hoggett, *Parents and Children* (2nd ed., London, 1981) chapter 3, pp. 45-56. In this regard, it has been claimed that male couples may one day be able to conceive their own children using genetic cloning techniques applied to produce the cloned sheep called "Dolly": the *Irish Times*, September 27, 2000.

[85] See, for example, the case of *U. v. W. (Attorney General Intervening)* [1997] 3 W.L.R. 739. In the case of *G. v. The Netherlands* (1993) 13 E.H.R.R. 38, the European Commission of Human

clear that the traditional definition of a "family" as encompassing a biological woman and man and their genetic child may be out of step with the realities of many current *de facto* relationships. In sum, developments in society have forced the pace in the development of the legal concept of "family" and in what used to be regarded as a "non law zone".[86]

Recently, for example, in *Fitzpatrick v. Sterling Housing Association Ltd.*,[87] the House of Lords was invited to consider the meaning of the term "family" in the Rent Act 1977. The case involved an application by a homosexual man for a declaration that that he was entitled to succeed to the tenancy of his deceased same-sex partner as a member of the latter's "family" under section 3(1) of the Act. In the course of their speeches, the majority of the House of Lords considered the meaning of the word "family" and what classes of relationships fell within its ambit. Lord Clyde propounded the following test:

> "It seems to me that essentially the bond must be one of love and affection, not of a casual or transitory nature, but in a relationship which is permanent or at least intended to be so. As a result of that personal attachment to each other, other characteristics will follow, such as a readiness to support each other emotionally and financially, to care for and look after the other in times of need, and to provide a companionship in which mutual interests and activities can be shared and enjoyed together. It would be difficult to establish such a bond unless the couple were living together in the same house. It would also be difficult to establish it without an active sexual relationship between them or at least the potentiality of such a relationship. If they have or are caring for children whom they regard as their own, that would make the family designation more immediately obvious, but the existence of children is not a necessary element. Each case will require to depend eventually upon its own facts."[88]

In the instant case, where the homosexual couple had lived together for many years in a stable and loving partnership, it followed that the appellant qualified as a member of the deceased tenant's "family" as the term was used in the

---

Rights held that where a person donates sperm only to enable a woman to become pregnant through A.I.D. treatment (i.e. artificial insemination by a donor), this does not of itself give rise to a right to respect for family life with the child.

[86]"More than any other area of law the development of the law relating to the family has followed the extraordinary evolution of society itself": Chauveau and Hutchinson, "A Short History of Cohabitation and Marriage" (1995) 145 *N.L.J.* 304 at 304.

[87][1999] 4 All E.R. 705. See generally, Bainham, "*Homosexuality and the Lords: Shifting Definitions of Marriage and the Family*" (2000) 59 *Cambridge Law Journal* 39; and Wikeley, "*Fitzpatrick v. Sterling Housing Association Ltd.* – Same Sex Partners and Succession to the Rent Act Tenancies" [1998] *C.F.L.Q.* 191.

[88]*ibid.* at 727-728.

Act.[89] Accordingly, the court held that the legislation should be applied to him so that he could succeed to the tenancy.

Not surprisingly, this decision has been described as marking a "profound change" in the attitude of the House of Lords to same-sex relationships.[90] Having broadened the interpretation of the legal definition of "family" in this particular legislation, the decision is set to have dramatic consequences in terms of the legal recognition of same sex relationships in domestic law, including the field of succession law.[91]

(b) Convention Jurisprudence on the Definition of Family Life

The Strasbourg organs have been wrestling with the meaning of "family life" under the Convention ever since the decision of the European Court of Human Rights in the *Marckx* case. The court has clearly confirmed since that case that the Convention understanding of "family life" is not restricted to formal relationships based on blood or marriage. For example, in *Berrehab v. Netherlands*,[92] it held that the fact that divorced parents were no longer cohabiting did not necessarily put an end to family life for parents and their children. In other words, cohabitation between parents is not a *sine qua non* of family life.[93] Even where parents are unmarried, are no longer cohabiting and where their relationship is at an end before the birth of their child, a bond amounting to "family life" may still be found to exist for the purposes of the Convention.[94] Indeed, in *Kroon v. The Netherlands* the court was prepared to hold that family life may exist where a couple is not cohabiting and where the child is born of an extra-marital relationship.[95] It would seem that the key test for establishing the existence of "family life" for the purposes of the Convention, as far as the European Court of Human Rights is concerned, is whether a sufficiently close relationship in fact can be demonstrated between the parties.[96]

The case law indicates, therefore, that it is possible for an unmarried heterosexual couple to demonstrate "family life" for the purposes of the Convention. The question of whether a homosexual relationship is capable of constituting "family life" within the meaning of Article 8 of the Convention has not yet been adjudicated upon by the Court of Human Rights.[97] However,

---

[89] Note that the majority did not believe that the appellant qualified as the "spouse" of his partner. The true construction of para. 2(2) of Schedule 1 to the 1977 Act was that the extended meaning given to the word "spouse" did not apply to same-sex partners.

[90] Roberts, "*Fitzpatrick v. Sterling* – A Case with Wider Implications?" [2000] *Fam. Law* 417.

[91] *ibid.* The author explores the implications for succession law, in particular, at 419-420.

[92] Series A, No. 138, (1989) 11 E.H.R.R. 322.

[93] *ibid.*, at para. 21.

[94] *Keegan v. Ireland*, 26 May 1994, Series A, No. 290, (1994) 18 E.H.R.R. 342.

[95] Series A, No. 297-C, (1995) 19 E.H.R.R. 263.

[96] Van Dijk and Van Hoof, *op. cit.*, above, n.20 at pp. 504-508.

[97] It should be noted, however, that the Court does not consider that the Contracting States are

the Commission has answered that question in the negative.[98] Rather, interference with such relationships or failure to respect them, may fall to be considered under Article 8 by reference to the concept of "private life".[99]

None of the above cases have directly raised succession issues. However, succession rights were indirectly in issue in one of the more controversial cases to be adjudicated upon by the court concerning the right to respect for family life under Article 8 of the Convention. In *X, Y & Z v. United Kingdom* the court was asked for the first time to assess whether family life could be said to exist in the absence of blood links or a legal nexus of marriage or adoption.[100] The first applicant, X, was a female to male transsexual who had lived in a permanent relationship with Y for some 14 years before the application was initiated in Strasbourg. The third applicant, Z, had been born to Y as a result of artificial insemination by a donor (A.I.D.). Their difficulty was that X was not permitted under British law to be registered as Z's father. Their complaint under the Convention was that this state of affairs violated their right to respect for family life under Article 8 of the Convention either alone or in conjunction with Article 14. A crucial aspect of the applicants' submission was that the child was seriously disadvantaged by X's inability to recognise her under the law: she was prejudiced, *inter alia,* in that she could not inherit from X on intestacy, nor could she benefit through him from the transmission of tenancies.[101] The court reiterated the factors normally taken into account in deciding whether family life exists - including whether a couple live together, the length of the relationship and whether they have demonstrated their commitment to each other by having children together or by any other means. It held that such a commitment surely existed in the instant case. X had jointly applied with Y for the A.I.D. treatment. X was involved throughout the process and had acted as Z's father in every respect since the birth.

However, while the court was prepared to accept that "family life" existed on the facts,[102] it was not prepared to find that there had been any violation of Convention rights. It acknowledged its constant jurisprudence since *Marckx,* to the effect that where family life has been found to exist, the state must act in a manner calculated to allow that tie to develop normally. Previously decided

---

obliged to provide for the right of homosexuals to marry. In *Rees v. United Kingdom*, the Court made plain its view that the right to marry and to found a family in Art. 12 of the Convention refers to the traditional concept of marriage based on the family: Series A, No. 106, (1987) 9 E.H.R.R. 56, para. 49.

[98] *Kerkhoven v. The Netherlands*, Commission, admissibility decision, 19.5.1992. See also *X v. United Kingdom* (1997) 24 E.H.R.R. 143.

[99] European Commission of Human Rights, admissibility decision, Application No. 9369/81, 3.5.83, vol. 32 D & R 220.

[100] (1997) 24 E.H.R.R. 143.

[101] *ibid.*, at para. 45.

[102] On this issue, see paras. 32-37 of the judgment, *ibid.*

cases, however, had all dealt with the family ties of biological parents and their children.[103] In the court's view, there was no common European standard with regard to the granting of parental rights to transsexuals or the manner in which the social relationship between a child conceived by A.I.D. and the person performing the social role of father should be reflected in law. The law was in a state of change and hence a wide margin of appreciation must be afforded to the State.[104] As regards the "fair balance" which must be struck in deciding the extent of the Contracting States' positive obligations under the Convention, the court held that the community as a whole has an interest in maintaining a coherent system of family law which places the best interests of the child at the forefront. It was unclear whether the amendment to the law sought in this case would benefit the child conceived by A.I.D. or have implications in other areas of family law. In these circumstances, the Contracting States were entitled to be cautious.[105] In sum, the disadvantages suffered by the applicants did not outweigh the general interest given the facts of the case, and in any case, these disadvantages were not insurmountable. Z's inability to inherit from X on intestacy, for example, "could be solved in practice if X were to make a will".[106]

Reasonable people may of course differ in their opinion as to the reasoning of the court in the *X, Y & Z* case. Indeed, a majority of the European Commission of Human Rights reached the opposite conclusion to that of the court in its opinion on the merits of the case.[107] It is certainly arguable that the court has taken "one step forward and two steps back" in this decision. While prepared to recognise the changing parameters of the term "family life" in the Convention, the court was not prepared to afford practical significance to this position by finding that the State had failed in its positive obligations to "respect" the family life which had been found to exist on the facts.

The weakness in the decision is more obvious when one compares it with the outcome in the *Johnston* case. The couples in both cases were in an analogous position in that they were unable to marry because of constraints in domestic law. As a result, a number of limitations were attached to the legal rights of the child applicants in both cases, including inheritance rights on intestacy. Whereas in *Johnston* the court was not prepared to accept that the child's deficient rights in the event of her father dying intestate could be cured by his

---

[103] *ibid.*, para. 43.
[104] *ibid.*, para. 44.
[105] *ibid.*, para. 47.
[106] *ibid.*, para. 48.
[107] In its opinion on the merits, the European Commission of Human Rights had, by a majority, given its view of a violation of Art. 8 in this case. It held that the government had failed to put forward any countervailing public concern which outweighed the interests of the applicants. It therefore could not agree that the margin of appreciation extended to denying effective or appropriate legal recognition where the existence of "family life" had been identified which in turn required protection: (1997) 24 E.H.R.R. 143, at 155-157.

making a will, the court in the *X, Y, & Z* case advanced this rationale as a basis for its ultimate decision against the applicants. It would seem that the reason why the court imposed a positive obligation on the State in *Johnston* and not in *X, Y, and Z* can be explained by one factor, namely that the applicants in *X, Y and Z*, unlike the applicants in *Johnston*,[108] were not able to point to a European consensus in favour of recognising their rights.[109]

In this respect, the case reveals a constant predicament for the Court of Human Rights: how to balance its task of interpreting and applying the Convention to changing social conditions,[110] without straying too far from the obligations that are explicit or obviously "implicit" in the text.[111] If the court interprets amorphous terminology in the Convention in too radical a way, it is open to the charge of over-zealous judicial activism. At worst, it runs the risk of losing credibility with the very governments whose behaviour it has been set up to regulate. On the other hand, if the court is reluctant to take on any creative role in the interpretative process, the Convention may lose its capacity to be an effective instrument of social and legal change in the Contracting States. The House of Lords in *Fitzpatrick* was conscious of a similar dilemma. In the course of his judgment, Lord Clyde acknowledged that "judicial activism certainly has to be tempered by due restraint, and the drawing of the boundary of the judicial task is often delicate and sometimes controversial." [112]

The "margin of appreciation" concept is the obvious device by which the court attempts to strike a balance between the twin challenges of activism and restraint. And as noted above, an assessment of whether a European consensus on any particular issue may be said to exist is often a factor in assessing the breadth of the margin of appreciation that is open to the Contracting States. On

---

[108] In finding for the applicants in *Johnston*, the Court's reasoning was bolstered by reference to the Preamble to the *European Convention on the Legal Status of Children born out of Wedlock* (HMSO, Cmnd. 6358, Strasbourg October 15, 1975). The latter provision specifically noted that "in a great number of member States efforts have been, or are being, made to improve the legal status of children born out of wedlock by reducing the difference between their legal status and that of children born in wedlock which are to the legal or social disadvantage of the former". Art. 9 of that Convention provides that "a child born out of wedlock shall have the same right of succession in the estate of its father and its mother and of a member of its father's or mother's family, as if it had been born in wedlock".

[109] It is also possible that the Court's negative decision may have been somewhat influenced by the "taboo" factor referred to by Maartens J. in another case dealing with the claimed violation of Art. 8 of the Convention by a transsexual: *Cossey v. United Kingdom,* Series A No. 184, (1991) 13 E.H.R.R. 622, para. 2.5. (dissenting judgment).

[110] The Court has said on many occasions that the Convention is a "living instrument" and should be interpreted accordingly: See, for example, its decisions in *Tyrer v. United Kingdom,* April 25, 1978, Series A, No. 26, (1980) 2 E.H.R.R. 1 and *Soering v. United Kingdom,* July 7, 1989, Ser. A, No. 161, (1989) 11 E.H.R.R. 439.

[111] This dilemma is thoroughly analysed by Mahoney in his article "Judicial Activism and Judicial Self-Restraint: Two Sides of the Same Coin" (1990) 11 H.R.L.J. 57.

[112] *Fitzpatrick v. Sterling Housing Association,* above n.87, at 730.

many occasions, the court has been criticised for failing to perform a thorough comparative analysis of the relevant laws in the Contracting States.[113] Others have warned that too close attention to the existence or not of a consensus in a given area may in some circumstances be irrelevant to the question of a breach. In other words, a practice may easily violate the Convention even if it is applied in the majority of the Contracting States.[114]

Unfortunately, the decision of the court in the *X, Y & Z* case has all the hallmarks of a knee-jerk reaction against an overly interventionist interpretation of the Convention. It would seem that the court was reluctant to impose obligations to the discomfort of the majority of Contracting States in an area in which there is no obviously shared approach. The decision would appear to prioritise the concern of maintaining certainty in the already established parameters of family law in this area over the interests of the particular parties at hand. One may speculate whether similarly negative results would obtain if a case arose involving the succession rights of homosexual partners[115] or even cohabiting heterosexual partners.[116] Given the apparent lack of consensus[117] amongst European states generally on the exact parameters of those rights,[118] it is likely that the court would evince a similarly cautious approach.[119]

---

[113] Van Dijk and Van Hoof, *Theory and Practice of the European Convention on Human Rights* (2nd ed., The Netherlands: Kluwer, 1990) at p. 602.

[114] "… [t]he Court needs to be aware that government and individual interests do not always coincide and that a practice may not be acceptable in human rights terms simply because it is generally followed": Harris, O'Boyle and Warbrick, *Law of the European Convention on Human Rights* (London, 1995) at p. 9.

[115] The Commission has certainly been very slow to recognise positive obligations in respect of a homosexual couple's rights under Art. 8. In *Kerkhoven v. The Netherlands,* it refused to accept that the positive obligations in Art. 8 extended so far as to require that a lesbian, who had acted as a parent to the child born of her long-term partner by artificial insemination, should be able to establish legal ties with the child: unreported, admissibility decision, May 19, 1992.

[116] Again, recent case law of the Commission is most ungenerous as regards the property rights of heterosexual cohabitants. In *Saucedo Gomez v. Spain* (Application No. 37784/97, admissibility decision, January 19, 1998), the Commission decided that the refusal of the national authorities to grant the applicant access to the family home in which she and her ex-partner had cohabited for eighteen years did not violate the Convention. As part of its reasoning, the Commission noted that the Contracting States have a wide margin of appreciation as regards their obligations to heterosexual cohabitants who live together outside marriage. Kath O'Donnell is similarly pessimistic about the court's capacity to recognise the rights of cohabiting heterosexual partners: "Discrimination against the unmarried family unit is a common feature of domestic state policy, and the case law suggests that it seems to be perpetuated in the attitudes of the Convention institutions towards such policies": "Protection of Family Life: Positive Approaches and the ECHR" (1995) 17 *Journal of Social Welfare and Family Law* 261 at p. 277.

[117] The rights of heterosexual cohabitants or homosexual cohabitants in terms of succession rights in all the European States is beyond the scope of this article. See generally Hayton, *European Succession Laws* (Bristol, 1998).

[118] There has been some development in the legal recognition given to homosexual relationships in some European States. The concept of "registered partnerships", whereby homosexual unions are accorded legal recognition parallel to that of married heterosexual couples, was first introduced by the Scandinavian countries (Denmark, Iceland, Norway and Sweden). Similar

6. CONCLUSION

The attractions of ensuring an element of legal certainty in the formulation of any legal rule cannot be underestimated. The parties to transactions affected or likely to be affected by such rules may be able to predict with a strong degree of assurance the likely outcome of any dispute arising. But in circumstances where a rule leads to obviously unjust results in individual cases, the interest in achieving certainty must surely yield to the requirements of justice. This need for flexibility in the application of legal rules of course has led to the development of many equitable doctrines which have remedied the harsh effects of the common law. Similar flexibility, one would imagine, would be desirable at the international level whenever the dramatic tension arises. As has been demonstrated above, the European Court of Human Rights has been presented with a number of cases in Strasbourg in which the desire of the national authorities to ensure an element of legal certainty in the application of succession rights has been faced down by applicants whose individual interests have been adversely affected. Unfortunately, however, in this area, the court has preferred to defer all too readily to the concerns of the Contracting States, without rigorously assessing whether those concerns can be sacrificed in favour of the often dominant interests of the individual applicants.

---

legislation has now been introduced in the Netherlands and is under consideration in Germany and France. Hungary has opened a form of "common law" marriage for same-sex couples. In all of these countries, "registered partners" are granted the same legal rights in relation to inheritance as those associated with marriage: See generally, the fact sheet compiled by the International Gay and Lesbian Human Rights Commission, *"Registered Partnership, Domestic Partnership and Marriage"*: www.iglhrc.org.

[119] This analysis is supported somewhat by Feldman: "… [t]he Court has been rather too tender towards the claims of States to institutionalise dominant moralities. While the need of an international tribunal to maintain the confidence of its client States must be acknowledged, too wide a margin of appreciation for States in deciding what is necessary to uphold national standards of morality threatens to undermine the attempt to secure pan-European respect for consistent formulations of human rights": "The Developing Scope of Art. 8 of the European Convention on Human Rights" (1997) 3 *E.H.R.L.R.* 265 at p. 273.

"A FALSE, MAWKISH AND MONGREL HUMANITY"? THE EARLY HISTORY OF EMPLOYERS' LIABILITY IN IRELAND

D.S. GREER

The general outline of the early history of employers' liability is well known;[1] what is less well documented is the working of the law in Ireland during its formative period. Given Professor Brady's interest in Irish legal history, it seemed not inappropriate to contribute to this collection of papers in his memory some observations on the impact which a law primarily developed in the context of the industrial revolution in Great Britain had on an industrial population in Ireland which had by the end of the 19th century grown to significant proportions, not least in that part of Ireland from which Professor Brady hailed.

1. A STATUTORY STRICT LIABILITY?

As early as 1833, it was acknowledged that "one of the great evils to which people employed in factories are exposed is, the danger of receiving serious and even fatal injury from the machinery".[2] Many aspects of the new industrial technology[3] put at risk a workforce which in Ireland, as in Great Britain, included many women, young persons and children. The *ex parte* evidence presented by owners or managers, however, suggested that factory machinery was generally well-fenced and that few serious accidents occurred in the cotton and flax mills of north-east Ireland.[4] Ten mills employing more than 3,000 workers

---

[1] See especially White, *Civil Liability for Industrial Accidents* (Dublin, 1993) vol. 1, chap. 1 and Binchy and McMahon, *Irish Law of Torts* (2nd ed., Dublin, 1990), Chap. 1. Greer and Nicolson, *The Factory Acts in Ireland 1802-1914* (Four Courts Press, Dublin, forthcoming) will provide a detailed examination of this legislation. For an excellent study relating to England, see Bartrip and Burman, *The Wounded Soldiers of Industry: Industrial Compensation Policy 1833-1897* (Oxford, 1983).

[2] *First Report of the Central Board of His Majesty's Commissioners appointed to collect information in the manufacturing districts, relative to the employment of children in factories . . .* 1833 B.P.P. xx, 1 at p. 31.

[3] As to which see McCutcheon, *The Industrial Archaeology of Northern Ireland* (Belfast, 1980), pp. 302 and 310.

[4] See *First Report of the Factory Commissioners, op. cit.,* above, n. 2, Appendix A.1: Reports of Examinations taken before Mr Stuart, pp. 127-134 and Appendix A.2, Evidence taken by Mr Mackintosh, pp. 89-93.

had apparently experienced only one fatal accident and few serious injuries in recent years. Messrs Boomar & Co's cotton and flax mills in Belfast, for example, employed about 600 workers; but James Campbell, the managing partner for the past 18 years, reported that "the only accidents of a serious nature which he remembers to have happened at these works resulted in one case in the loss of a hand, in another of a thumb, and in a third of two fingers . . .".[5] The fatal accident occurred in Martin's cotton mill in Killyleagh, Co. Down where "one man . . . was caught by a belt and killed" – but otherwise no serious accident had befallen any of the 250 workers there.[6] Mr Mackintosh, a commissioner for the "northern district", agreed that "the number of persons who have been killed or have lost limbs by accidents from the machinery will have been found proportionably small. . .".[7]

The more alarming evidence as to industrial conditions in England[8] led the Commissioners to conclude, however, that "in many of the mills numerous accidents of a grievous nature do occur to the workpeople".[9] Their primary solution to the regulation of textile factories generally was the appointment of inspectors with general supervisory responsibilities, which would include the power to direct the fencing of dangerous machinery. But "we apprehend that no inspector would probably be so fully conversant with all the uses of every variety of machinery as to be acquainted with all the dangers which may be provided against", and in any case "there is much that could not be made entirely safe without the reconstruction of whole manufactories." Accordingly, it was also desirable to ensure, by means of "pecuniary consequences", that the factory owners took all necessary safety precautions:

> "We conceive that it may be stated as a principle of jurisprudence applicable to the cases of evils arising from causes which ordinary prudence cannot avert that responsibility should be concentrated, or as closely as possible apportioned, on those who have the best means of preventing the mischief. Unless we are to impose on the workman the obligation of perpetual care and apprehension of danger, the nature of the injuries inflicted are of themselves evidence that all the care which can be taken by

---

[5] *First Report of the Factory Commissioners, op. cit.* above n. 2, Appendix A.1: Reports of Examinations taken before Mr Stuart, p. 129.

[6] *ibid.*, p. 133.

[7] *First Report of the Factory Commissioners, op. cit.* above n. 2, Appendix A.2, Evidence taken by Mr Mackintosh, p. 95. The chances of accidents had been much diminished by "the spaciousness of lately erected factories. . .", but "something remains to be done (especially in the smaller works, where the children come in so much closer contact with the wheels in motion) in the way of boxing parts of the machinery which might be still better secured, and which familiarity with the object of danger alone perhaps prevents".

[8] See especially *Report from the Select Committee to whom the Bill to regulate the labour of children in mills and factories of the United Kingdom was referred* 1831-1832 B.P.P. xv, 1.

[9] *First Report of the Factory Commissioners, op. cit.*, above, n. 2, pp. 72-74.

individuals attending to their work is taken by them; it is only the proprietor of the machinery who has the most effectual means of guarding against
the dangers attendant upon its use. . . . By throwing upon him a portion of
the pecuniary responsibility for those mischiefs, we combine interest with
duty, and add to the efficiency of both."[10]

In the case of all accidental injuries to children under 14, the factory owner
should therefore pay medical expenses and half wages during the period of
incapacity; similar compensation should also be paid to injured adults who
were not guilty of "culpable temerity".[11]

This early version of "general deterrence" was the brainchild of Ashley and
Chadwick; it seems to have received no support from Ireland where, as might
be expected, the factory owners were opposed even to the appointment of government inspectors.[12] In any event, such thinking was far too radical for Lord
Grey's Government. Lord Althorp, the Chancellor of the Exchequer, attacked
the compensation proposals as likely to have "very disastrous" and "unjust"
results,[13] and others vehemently criticised the whole notion of "economic deterrence". The Government measure which became the Factory Act 1833 contained no accident prevention or compensation clauses, and the notion of strict
liability for factory accidents failed to obtain any official support for the remainder of the 19th century.

2. THE COMMON LAW ALTERNATIVE

Part of the Government case against the "pecuniary consequences" principle
was that the common law would deal with negligent employers. Although there
is no recorded case, in Ireland or England, prior to 1836 of a worker suing an
employer for damages in respect of personal injury arising from an accident at
work,[14] the English courts had paved the way for this development by holding

---

[10] *First Report of the Factory Commissioners, op. cit.,* above n. 2, p. 73. The "pecuniary consequences" arising from the imposition of the proposed responsibility were to be met by the master, or by a form of accident insurance funded by "regular deductions" from the wages of the
workers.

[11] *ibid.,* on the basis that "an allowance of full wages would occasion considerable fraud in the
protraction of that period [of incapacity], especially in the cases of accidents of a less serious
nature".

[12] Thus Joseph Stevenson, the owner of a cotton spinning mill near Belfast, advised the factory
commissioners: "Let manufacturers, as commerce, be free from compulsory laws, and they will
work better than with all the restrictions that can be heaped upon them": *Supplementary Report
of the Central Board of Her Majesty's [Factory] Commissioners (Part II)* 1834 B.P.P. xx, 1 at
p. 239.

[13] 19 Parl. Debs. (3rd ser.), cols. 221-222 (July 5, 1833).

[14] Bartrip and Burman, *op. cit.,* above, n. 1, pp. 1 and 24-25, where it is contended that the casual
way in which the legal issue was approached in *Priestley v. Fowler* (1837) 3 M. & W. 1, 150

that an action in case, rather than in trespass, could lie for an accidental, direct, injury.[15] But it was not until 1837 that they explicitly accepted that an employer could in certain circumstances be liable in tort to an employee for an injury accidentally sustained in the course of his employment.[16] The first recorded claim for damages for injuries sustained in a factory accident soon followed. In 1840, thanks to the intervention of Lord Ashley, a 17-year-old girl seriously injured by an accident in a Lancashire cotton factory succeeded in obtaining damages of £100 from her employer in the case of *Cotterrell v. Samuel Stocks & Co.*[17]

There is no evidence that this case paved the way for a level of successful litigation sufficient to induce recalcitrant employers to fence dangerous machinery. On the contrary, there were already many practical and legal obstacles which generally defeated a common law claim. An injured worker had first to accept that bringing an action would in all probability lead to his or her dismissal from employment. In any event, for those earning no more than five shillings per week,[18] the expense of litigation was normally prohibitive at a time when the civil bill jurisdiction in actions on the case for negligence was limited to £10.[19] A determined plaintiff also faced the legal and evidential difficulties of proving that the employer had failed to act as "a man of ordinary prudence".[20] If he or she could only show that the injury was due to the negli-

---

E.R. 1030 suggests that "such cases had come to court before. . .". But Simpson, "A Case of First Impression: *Priestley v. Fowler* (1837)" in his *Leading Cases in the Common Law* (Oxford, 1995) at p. 108 takes the view that the court in *Priestley* "conceded, for the first time, that there might be circumstances which entitled a servant to sue his master for loss caused through an accident at work. . .".

[15] *Moreton v. Hardern* (1825) 4 B. & C. 223, 107 E.R. 1042; *Williams v. Holland* (1833) 10 Bing. 112, 131 E.R. 848. Baker, *An Introduction to English Legal History* (3rd ed., London, 1990), pp. 464-465 explains that a plaintiff proceeding in case could focus attention on the defendant's fault rather than on other aspects of the case; perhaps more importantly in factory accident claims, vicarious liability could only be imposed in an action on the case. See generally, Pritchard, "Trespass, Case and the Rule in *Williams v. Holland*" [1964] *Camb. L.J.* 234 at pp. 251-252.

[16] *Priestley v. Fowler* (1837) 3 M. & W. 1, 150 E.R. 1030.

[17] *Reports of the Inspectors of Factories . . . for the quarter ending 30th Sept. 1840*, 1841 B.P.P. x, 168-169. The case was settled; but counsel for P emphasised that "the defendant is now satisfied that the law does impose upon him such obligation; and I trust that others also will be fully convinced that the defendant has not yielded in this case without good advice, and that others who have machinery uncovered, or not fenced off, so as to expose other workpeople to great risk of injury, will forthwith cause it to be fenced off or altered". Earlier the same year, in *Dunn v. Crawford and Smith, ibid.*, p.186, a solicitor in Scotland had brought an action on behalf of a boy injured in a factory accident; the case was settled for £50 – plus £18 costs (an early example of a contingent fee?).

[18] Armstrong, "Social and economic conditions in the Belfast linen industry, 1850–1900" (1950-1951) 7 *Ir. Hist. Stud.* 235 at 264.

[19] Civil Bill Act 1836, s. 1. It is noticeable that the second edition (by Robert Longfield) of Napier's *Practice of the Civil Bill Courts and Courts of Appeal* (Dublin, 1841) contains no discussion of personal injury actions.

[20] The objective standard of care adopted in *Vaughan v. Menlove* (1837) 3 Bing. N.C. 468, 132 E.R. 490. Until the Fatal Accidents Act 1846, damages could not be claimed at all in respect of

gence of a fellow servant, the claim would invariably be defeated (at least after 1850) by the defence of common employment. If the plaintiff somehow managed to surmount this obstacle, he or she still faced the defences of contributory negligence[21] and *volenti non fit injuria.*[22] As an Irish commentator subsequently observed:

> "The old common law gave the workman only a shadowy semblance of protection – a protection which, owing to its limitations, was rather a pitfall for the unwary litigant."[23]

Put more emphatically, these legal and practical "pitfalls" undermined the Government's contention that the common law would ensure the safety of factory workers. From a purely legal perspective, they derived in essence from the prevailing judicial view of the employment relationship. In *Priestley v. Fowler*[24] Lord Abinger C.B. accepted that the employer

> "... is, no doubt, bound to provide for the safety of his servant, in the course of his employment, to the best of his judgement, information and belief."

But the master was not obliged to take more care of the servant than the servant might reasonably be expected to take of himself. In *Priestley*, the plaintiff must have known just as well as his employer, and probably better, whether the van in question was "sufficient" and whether it was overloaded; to hold the employer liable in such circumstances would encourage servants to neglect to exercise the due diligence and caution which they owed to their master, and which were also their own best protection from injury.[25]

---

fatal accidents. But an employer might still enter into some voluntary arrangement – in 1842, for example, an accident in Mulholland's linen factory in Belfast caused the deaths of Campbell, an overlooker, and Burns, a girl of 14 or 15; Inspector Stuart reported that "some pecuniary compensation was made to the parents of the girl, her funeral expenses paid, etc. Campbell's wife was set up in business": *Reports of the Inspectors of Factories . . . for the quarter ending April 30th 1842* 1842 B.P.P. xxii, 441 at p. 463. For the background to the 1846 Act see Kidner, "A History of the Fatal Accidents Acts" (1999) 50 *N.I.L.Q.* 318.

[21] *Butterfield v. Forrester* (1809) 11 East 60, 103 E.R. 926. *cf. Vaughan v. Cork & Youghal Rly. Co.* (1860) 12 I.C.L.R. 297 at 302, where Pigot C.B. explained that "if the injury occurs in consequence of the negligence of the defendant, the circumstance that the plaintiff's act, to some extent, contributed to the injury, is no defence to the action, unless the plaintiff could, at the time, have himself avoided the consequences of the defendant's neglect, by the exercise of ordinary care".

[22] See generally Ingman, "A history of the defence of *volenti non fit injuria*" [1981] *Juridical Rev.* 1.

[23] Campbell, *Workmen's Compensation under the Workmen's Compensation Act 1906 and the Employers' Liability Act 1880* (5th ed., Dublin, 1908), p. 3.

[24] (1837) 3 M. & W. 1, 150 E.R. 1030.

[25] Lord Abinger further observed (at p. 7) that if the defendant was held liable in this case, it would

This judicial philosophy was followed in Ireland. In *Potts v. Plunkett*,[26] for example, the plaintiff, in the course of his employment as a carpenter, stepped onto the raised flagstone landing of the defendant's house. Part of the landing gave way and the plaintiff fell to the ground below, badly injuring himself. Since the defendant had selected the flagstones for the landing and employed another person to set them, the plaintiff argued that the defendant had failed to take reasonable precautions to secure his safety. The Court of Queen's Bench disagreed. Lefroy C.J. began by stating that "a master is not responsible for injuries occurring to his servant in the course of his employment generally, though being a result of it; because the servant is supposed to undertake the duty, for which he is paid, subject to all the risks which may occur during its continuance". The master might properly be liable if the injury resulted not from an accidental occurrence, but by gross negligence on the part of the master. But "if the cause producing the injury is equally known and equally palpable to the servant as to the master, the servant cannot complain, for it may be said that he went into the danger with his eyes open".[27]

In short, the judges in Ireland as well as England disagreed with the factory commissioners and in effect imposed on the workman "the obligation of perpetual care and apprehension of danger" which the commissioners thought better imposed on factory occupiers – and they adhered to this philosophy even after Parliament enacted legislative provisions explicitly imposing safety obligations on employers.[28] It is, however, noticeable that few of the early common law cases involve claims arising from factory accidents, and that the prevailing judicial philosophy largely developed from what might be described as pre-industrial relationships and circumstances. Some judicial support did emerge in England for a more sympathetic view of industrial conditions; in *Clarke v. Holmes*,[29] for example, Byles J. stated that the owner of dangerous machinery should be obliged to exercise due care that it is in a safe and proper condition:

> "It is, in most cases, impossible that a workman can judge of the condition of a complex and dangerous machine, wielding irresistible mechanical power, and, if he could, he is quite incapable of estimating the degree of risk involved in different conditions of the machine; but the master

---

logically follow, given the normal rules of vicarious liability, that the master could be liable for the misconduct of fellow servants; this would carry liability "to an alarming extent". It was this observation which was to form the basis of the doctrine of "common employment" later confirmed by *Hutchinson v. York, Newcastle & Berwick Rly Co.* (1850) 5 Ex. 343, 155 E.R. 150.

[26] (1859) 9 I.C.L.R. 290. See also *Vaughan v. Cork & Youghal Rly Co.* (1860) 12 I.C.L.R. 297 at 303-304, *per* Pigot C.B.

[27] (1859) 9 I.C.L.R. 290 at 297-298.

[28] See below, p. 235.

[29] (1862) 7 H. & N. 937 at 948, 158 E.R. 751 at 755.

may be able, and generally is able, to estimate both. . . . On the other hand, to hold that the master warrants the safety and proper condition of the machine, is equally unjust to the master, for no degree of care can insure perfect safety; and it is equally inconvenient to the public, for who would employ such machines if he were an insurer?"

As in England and Wales, however, judicial support in Ireland for such an approach was not forthcoming until much later in the century.

At a more practical level, however, it appeared in 1841 that a remedy was to be provided for the particular problem of "the unavoidable expensiveness of [common] law proceedings".[30] The Select Committee set up to examine the working of the 1833 Act were in favour of giving factory inspectors a general power to require factory owners to fence dangerous machinery; if the owner did not then take appropriate action and a worker was injured as a result *and* recovered damages in a common law action, the owner was in addition to be liable to an enhanced fine. The committee acknowledged, however, that workers rarely had the means to finance civil proceedings, and therefore went on to recommend that "there be given by enactment a speedy and cheap mode of recovering compensation for injuries received in all those cases where machinery has, through negligence, been left uncovered".[31]

In its statutory form, however, this "legal aid" provision was detached from the enforcement of the fencing provision. Section 24 of the Factory Act 1844 provided that the Home Secretary could, on the report and recommendation of an inspector, empower him to bring an action for damages on behalf of any worker injured by *any* machinery in a factory. By section 25 any damages so recovered were to be paid to or for the benefit of the worker in question.

No documented case in which section 24 was invoked has been found in England or Ireland.[32] Various reasons have been suggested, including Home Office opposition[33] and the willingness of employers to pay compensation voluntarily.[34] It may, however, be that section 24 as enacted was simply redun-

---

[30]*Semble*, in addition to that already available by way of the *in forma pauperis* procedure, as to which see especially Ferguson, *A Treatise in the Practice of the Courts of Queen's Bench, Common Pleas and Exchequer of Pleas in Ireland, in Personal Actions and Ejectments* (Dublin, 1841-1842) vol. 2, p. 730.

[31]*Report from the Select Committee appointed to enquire into the operation of the Act for the regulation of Mills and Factories* 1841 B.P.P. ix, 557 at p. 577.

[32]Bartrip and Burman, *op. cit.,* above, n. 1, p. 55 found none in England and Wales, and I have not found any in Ireland. It is, perhaps, noteworthy, that in his first report in 1845, Inspector Stuart noted that "No application has been made to me . . . to take any step with a view to recover damages on behalf of any [injured] person. . .": *Reports of the Inspectors of Factories . . . for the quarter ending 30th April 1845* 1845 B.P.P. xxv, 431 at p. 488.

[33]Bartrip and Burman, *op. cit.,* above, n. 1, p. 56.

[34]In 1853 Inspector Redgrave stated that "In no one instance . . . have I felt it necessary to cause proceedings to be taken before a judicial tribunal, inasmuch as the occupiers of the factories

dant; it had been conceived as a mechanism to encourage compliance with an inspector's notice to fence dangerous machinery – but the 1844 Act effectively gave that function to a separate provision for "penal" compensation.[35]

Section 24 was not re-enacted when the Factory Acts were consolidated in 1878. By this time, claims for common law damages could be remitted from the superior courts to the county courts under the "sham actions act" – the Common Law Procedure Amendment Act (Ireland) 1870 – on the grounds that the plaintiff had "no visible means of paying the costs of the defendant should a verdict not be found for the plaintiff".[36] Since most factory workers would have failed this test, it seems likely that the few claims which were brought in the superior courts would normally have been remitted to the civil bill courts, particularly after 1877, when those courts were given unlimited jurisdiction in cases remitted under the 1870 Act.[37] It is perhaps for this reason that the 1870 Act (and its English equivalent) was advanced by Mr Charles Meldon, the MP for Co. Kildare and a barrister, as sufficient to protect employers from spurious claims when it was suggested that the factory inspectors should be required, under a new version of section 24 of the 1844 Act, to filter out "vexatious" claims by injured workers.[38]

3. PENAL COMPENSATION

Although the 1833 Act had contained no safety provisions, the new factory inspectors drew attention to the number and severity of factory accidents in

---

who were liable, have provided readily, at my suggestion, that which the law required to be obtained from them, viz., reasonable compensation for the injured person": *Reports from the Inspectors of Factories. . .for the half-year ending 30th April 1853* 1852-1853 B.P.P. xl, 533 at p. 587. But when confirming in 1869 that the power had still not been exercised, Redgrave acknowledged that "I have been frequently applied to by injured persons . . . for assistance to enable them to proceed against the occupier of a factory in which they have been injured. . . .": *Reports from the Inspectors of Factories . . . for the half-year ending 31st October 1869* 1870 B.P.P. xv, 75 at p. 99. But he does not explain why section 24 had never been invoked.

[35] s. 60 is discussed below.

[36] Under s. 6 of the Act, a case was not to be remitted if the plaintiff provided security for the costs or satisfied the court that the case was "fit to be prosecuted in the Superior Court". For a commentary on this provision, which was continued by the Supreme Court of Judicature Act (Ireland) 1877, s. 60, see Kavanagh and Quill, *The remitting of actions from the Common Law . . . Divisions of the High Court of Justice in Ireland to the County Courts* (2nd ed., Dublin, 1879), pp 55-74.

[37] County Officers and Courts (Ireland) Act 1877, s. 52. A case would not be remitted where the plaintiff satisfied the court that "his action is not a sham, frivolous, oppressive, or vexatious action, and that it has been instituted *bona fide* to enforce some real and substantial cause of action which ought to be tried in the Superior Court. . .": *Kennedy v. Baxendale* (1871) I.R. 5 C.L. 74 at 81, *per* Fitzgerald J.

[38] *Report from the Select Committee on Employers' Liability for injuries to their servants: Minutes of Evidence* 1877 B.P.P. x, 551 at pp. 666-667.

their quarterly reports.[39] As a result, the matter was considered by the Select Committee appointed to review the 1833 Act, and in due course that committee recommended a number of specific safety provisions,[40] many of which were ultimately enacted in the Factories Act 1844. In particular, section 20 provided that no child or young person "shall be allowed to clean any part of the mill-gearing in a factory while the same is in motion for the purpose of propelling any part of the manufacturing machinery . . .", and by section 21, "every fly-wheel directly connected with the steam engine or water-wheel or other mechanical power . . . and every hoist or teagle, near to which children or young persons are liable to pass or be employed, and all parts of the mill-gearing in a factory shall be securely fenced . . . while . . . in motion . . . for any manufacturing process".

Breach of these provisions *per se* made the factory owner liable to a fine not exceeding £20. But if a worker thereby suffered "bodily injury", the occupier became liable to a fine of not less than £10 and not more than £100, and "the whole or any part of such penalty may be applied for the benefit of the injured person, or otherwise as the Secretary of State shall determine".[41]

For a time, a small number of factory accident victims in Great Britain benefited from this "penal compensation" provision; but it seems that it had virtually fallen into disuse by the 1860s.[42] But even this lamentable record appears to surpass the position in Ireland, where not a single case in which section 60 was successfully applied can be found. It appears that no prosecution was brought prior to 1854 for any breach of the 1844 Act resulting in "bodily injury", and the one case which was brought in 1855 was ultimately unsuccessful.[43] By that time, the "compensation" part of the section had fallen foul of official concern that the Crown was not receiving its due share of the fines imposed by the Irish criminal courts. Section 13 of the Fines Act (Ireland) 1851 provided that "in every case . . . it shall be lawful for the court to award

---

[39]Their evidence was subsequently collected in *Special reports of Inspectors of Factories on the practicability of legislative interference to diminish the frequency of accidents to the children and young persons employed in factories . . .* 1841 B.P.P. x, 199. Little of this evidence came from Ireland.

[40]*Report from the Select Committee, op. cit.,* above, n. 31, pp. 587-590. With reference to the controversy which arose in the 1850s (see below) it should be noted that the Committee specifically recommended that shafts and gearing should be fenced or boxed off "to the height of at least seven feet from the floor. . .".

[41]1844 Act, s. 60. Bartrip and Burnam, *op. cit.* above n. 1, p. 60 explain that the Law Officers held in 1846 that compensation was not obtainable under this section in cases of instantaneous death, since it refers only to "the injured person" and not to dependants. The section was not amended to bring it into line with the Fatal Accidents Act 1846.

[42]Bartrip and Burman, *op. cit.,* above, n. 1, pp. 57-60. See also Howells, *"Priestley v. Fowler* and the Factory Acts" (1963) 26 M.L.R. 367 at 394-395, where it is suggested that the greatest need for penal compensation was in the period 1844 to 1880, when the alternative remedy of a civil action was most ineffective.

[43]See *Darkin v. Herdman's of Sion Mills,* below, p. 241.

any sum not exceeding one-third of such penalty to the prosecutor or informer, and the remainder of such penalty and all other penalties shall be awarded to the Crown, any Act or Acts to the contrary notwithstanding." In 1856 the factory inspectors advised the Home Secretary that the effect of this provision was that "penalties levied under s 60 [of the 1844 Act] . . . are not in Ireland applicable as in Great Britain for the benefit of the injured person. . . .".[44] This opinion was confirmed by the Irish Law Officers, who declared that "the object and policy of the Fines and Penalties Act . . . were to establish one general and uniform mode of collecting and accounting for fines and penalties and to constitute all a portion of the casual revenue of the Crown". They considered that it would not be desirable that "the law . . . should be altered as regards the particular subject. . .".[45] Although this policy was breached by other "particular" statutes,[46] it was not until 1878 that a provision similar to section 60 was revived in Ireland.

Section 82 of the Factory and Workshop Act 1878[47] made it clear that an injured worker was now to take precedence over the Crown, and this new "penal compensation" provision was further extended by section 13 of the Factory and Workshop Act 1895 to cover any case of death, bodily injury *or injury to health*[48] caused by the occupier's neglect to observe *any* provision of the Factory Acts.[49] This amended provision, which was re-enacted as section 136 of the Factory and Workshop Act 1901, was given significant judicial support when Kennedy J. in *Blenkinsopp v. Ogden*[50] rejected an employer's contention that a boy aged 13, who was injured by an unfenced machine as a result of his own carelessness and wilful disobedience of orders, had not been injured "in consequence of" the employer's failure to fence that machine:

---

[44] *Minutes of the Meeting of Inspectors, 11 July 1856*: P.R.O. LAB 15/4.

[45] Opinion of FitzGerald AG and Christian SG, 7 May 1857: *ibid*. When a similar argument was raised in England in 1872, it was decided that s. 60 should be considered to be still in force, with the result that a fine of £10 was paid over to the grandmother of a 16-year-old orphan killed in an accident in a tile works. Parliamentary Counsel advised that, as a precautionary measure, a suitable clause might be enacted to remove the doubt, but this could await the expected consolidation of the Factory Acts: Opinion of 22 April 1872, P.R.O. H.O. 45/9301/10684.

[46] See *e.g.* the different appropriation of fines provided by the Salmon Fishery Act (Ir.) 1863, s. 45.

[47] In particular, the new provision expressly applied to fatal accidents. Penal compensation provisions are also to be found in the Coal Mines Regulation Act 1887 (s. 70) and Metalliferous Mines Regulation Act 1872 (s. 38), both of which applied to Ireland.

[48] Provided in the case of injury to health that "the injury was caused *directly* by such neglect" – 1895 Act, s. 13 (emphasis added).

[49] Note that the Employers' Liability Act 1880, s. 5 provided that an injured employee who commenced proceedings under that Act *before* receiving any penal compensation under s. 82 was wholly disentitled as a result from receiving any such compensation, whether the action under the 1880 Act was ultimately successful or not. If he commenced proceedings *after* receiving s. 82 compensation, that amount was deducted from any 1880 Act damages.

[50] [1898] 1 Q.B. 783.

"[W]e are dealing with a section the primary object of which is not to compensate the injured person, but to provide safe machinery. It is to the interest of the State that the machinery should be safe for negligent as well as for careful people, and it is reasonable that the State should impose a penalty upon the party omitting to fence even under circumstances under which the person injured by the omission could not recover damages."[51]

This legislative and judicial support for the concept of penal compensation had little effect; the enhanced power to make such an award continued to be exercised infrequently.[52] Detailed information in respect of Ireland is available only for the period 1898-1903, when it appears that there were only five cases (one fatal and four injury) in which the possibility of penal compensation even arose.[53] The fatal case involved a 15-year-old boy killed by a gas engine in Wexford Sawmills; the factory inspector's prosecution was dismissed by the magistrates – and a civil action was also unsuccessful. Sawmill accidents also gave rise to two injury cases. William Phelan, a sawmill owner in Newcastle West, was fined five shillings when a man aged 40 suffered eye injuries from wood flying from a circular saw; the report says that "the injured man was compensated", presumably by his employer. Another sawmill owner in Dublin was fined one shilling when a man aged 29 lost his hand and part of his arm in a planing machine accident; the employers subsequently paid him compensation of £300. Dublin City Distillery were fined £25 when a man aged 70 suffered neck and shoulder strain and shock from an accident involving the gear wheels on the main shaft from a steam engine; £20 of the fine was applied to the injured man. And the Metropole Southern Hotel in Cork was fined £1 when a 26-year-old woman caught and fractured her arm in the rollers of a wringer.

These few cases suggest that penal compensation failed for much the same reasons as have bedevilled the operation of present-day "compensation or-

---

[51] *ibid.*, at 786. Grantham J.'s observation that it was "entirely" in the Home Secretary's discretion whether any of the fine was paid over to the injured worker may have been intended to suggest that the Home Secretary might be guided by common law principles in the exercise of that discretion; but in fact the whole of the fine (of £25) was paid to the injured boy: *Annual Report of the Chief Inspector of Factories and Workshops for the year 1898 (Part II)* 1900 B.P.P xi, 1 at pp. 84-85.

[52] See Howells, *op. cit.*, above, n. 42, at pp. 388 and 392, where it is suggested that the Employers' Liability Act 1880 "robbed [s. 82] of much of its importance as deterrent or compensation". But this seems unlikely, given the ineffectiveness of that Act.

[53] See the Tables of Penal Compensation Cases in *Annual Reports of the Chief Inspector of Factories and Workshops* from 1898-1903 in 1900 B.P.P xi, 1 at pp. 84-87; 1900 B.P.P. xi, 249 at pp. 288-291; 1901 B.P.P. x, 1 at pp. 44-47; 1902 B.P.P. xii, 391 at pp. 454-457; 1904 B.P.P. x, 1 at pp. 68-69 and 1905 B.P.P. x, 665 at pp. 714-717. During this period, s. 82 appears to have been invoked in Great Britain in 206 cases (40 fatal and 166 injury), resulting in the payment of penal compensation from fines of just under £1,000, with an average payment in death cases of £8 and in injury cases of £5. Publication of these detailed Tables ceased in 1903.

ders".[54] When determining the amount of a section 82 fine, the magistrates apparently took into account any compensation which the victim had received, or seemed likely to receive, from his or her employer. But it also seems likely, as Howells has suggested[55] that, in setting the amount of the fine, they had regard to the nature of the defendant's offence rather than the severity of the victim's injury – and to the means of the defendant. The infrequency of prosecutions may also have undermined the "primary object" of providing safe machinery. In 1909, Miss Galway, secretary of the Textile Operatives Society of Ireland, informed the Committee on Accidents that the factory inspectors, to her knowledge, did not bring many cases to court and get heavy penalties inflicted upon employers for having inefficient guards on machines and other things; she was sure that "the machinery would be better looked after if there were more prosecutions and efficient inspection."[56]

Inefficient as it may have been, the notion of penal compensation under the Factory Acts was not formally abolished in Northern Ireland until 1965[57] and still appears on the statute book in the Republic.[58]

4. The Action upon the Statute

By the early 1850s, the Irish linen mills had apparently become much more dangerous places:

> "Accidents occurred in every department, but the most dangerous were machine hackling and carding. The accidents which occurred in machine hackling were the more dreadful in that the victims were usually boys under 14 years of age. The function of these children was to feed the hackling machines with fibre. In many cases accidents were caused by a loose shirtsleeve or other piece of clothing being caught in the machinery, with the result that a hand or arm was drawn in against the pins which combed the fibre and mangled. . . . But the accidents which befell the machine boys were trifles compared with the frightful mutilation which was the lot of the worker, usually a young woman, who was dragged into the 'card' . . . a diabolical machine [which] consisted essentially of a cylinder about four or five feet in diameter studded with iron pins of different sizes which revolved at a rapid rate".[59]

---

[54] See *e.g.* Miers, *Compensation for Criminal Injuries* (London, 1990), chaps. 8-11.
[55] *op. cit.,* above, n. 42, p. 380.
[56] *Report of the Departmental Committee on Accidents in Places under the Factory and Workshop Acts: Minutes of Evidence* 1911 B.P.P. xxiii, 71 at p. 325.
[57] Factories Act (N.I.) 1965.
[58] See Factories Act 1955, s. 103.
[59] Armstrong, *op. cit.,* above, n. 18, p. 254. By way of example, he cites the case of Sarah Jane

The inspectors' returns of the number of reported accidents unfortunately do not give separate figures for Ireland. But it may still be the case that the factories of this period were not as dangerous as they are sometimes portrayed. That certainly appears to have been the view of the factory inspectors at the time, at least if the number of prosecutions for breaches of the 1844 Act is anything to go by. As already indicated, the first "safety" prosecution in Ireland was brought only in 1854,[60] and between then and 1878, there appear to have been only three other prosecutions for failure to fence mill-gearing or other machinery,[61] together with one of allowing a young person to clean a machine while in motion[62] and six of failing to report an accident.[63] The number of prosecutions seems unreasonably low and suggests that the 1844 Act was not adequately enforced in Ireland. But the inspectors may, of course, have achieved many necessary improvements by encouragement and advice, or by the threat of prosecution.[64]

For a while it appeared that the common law courts might fill this vacuum. In *Coe v. Platt*[65] it was accepted that a breach of the safety provisions of the 1844 Act could give rise to liability at common law in the absence of negligence on the part of the employer. In particular, Parke B. stated:

Quin, an employee of Messrs Rowan of York St., Belfast, whose head "by some means" got entangled with the carding machine, with the result that "the greater portion of the scalp was removed from the head and the skull was severely injured" – see *Belfast Newsletter*, May 1, 1854. See also Maconchy, "A comparison between the accidents which have occurred in scutch mills, and in factories subject to Government inspection" (1865) 43 *Dublin Q.J. of Medical Science* 65 and Babington, "Flax mills – their machinery: Accidents occurring therein, with suggestions for their prevention" – *ibid.*, p. 392.

[60] *Darkin v. Herdman's of Sion Mills* (1854), discussed below, p. 241.

[61] *Darkin v. James Kennedy & Son* 1856 B.P.P. xviii, 362 (Belfast flax-spinners allegedly failed to fence horizontal shaft nine feet above floor, whereby young person lost his arm; case dismissed on procedural grounds); *Steen v. Nicholas Kenny* 1859 (Sess. 2) B.P.P. xiv, 450 (Carrick-on-Suir mill owner failed to fence mill-gearing, whereby young person injured; fined £10); *Cramp v. Robert Rowan & Co* 1874 B.P.P. xiii, 146 (Belfast hemp-spinners failed to fence steam-engine; fined £5).

[62] *Steen v. Bridget Jordan* 1857 (Sess. 1) B.P.P. iii, 620 (operative mule spinner at Greenmount Cotton Factory in Dublin allowed young person to work between fixed and traversing parts of self-acting machine negligently set in motion by D, killing the young person; D fined £2).

[63] *Darkin v. Francis Ritchie & Sons* 1857 (Sess. 1) B.P.P. iii, 617 (case against felt manufacturer in Belfast dismissed – premises not a "factory"); *Darkin v. Foster Connor* 1857 (Sess. 2) B.P.P. xvi, 259 (power loom weaver in Belfast fined £2); *Darkin v. Francis Ritchie & Sons* 1857 B.P.P. xvi, 260 (case dismissed – still not a "factory"); *Darkin v. James Kennedy & Sons* 1857-1858 B.P.P. xxiv, 751 (flax-spinners in Belfast fined £2); *Darkin v. Brookfield & Doagh Spinning Co.* 1859 (Sess. 1) B.P.P. xii, 221 (fined £2); *Bignold v. James Haigh* 1870 B.P.P. xv, 449 (Dublin ironfounder fined £2).

[64] There is a voluminous literature on the enforcement practices of the factory inspectors in England – see especially Arthurs, *Without the Law: Administrative Justice and Legal Pluralism in 19th century England* (Toronto and London: University of Toronto Press, 1985).

[65] (1851) 6 Exch. Rep. 752, (1852) 7 Exch. Rep. 460 and 923; 155 E. R. 1030 and 1226.

"Though its main object may have been to afford security to children and young persons who are more likely to sustain injuries than others, yet there is a positive enactment [in the 1844 Act] that in all factories . . . when any part of the machinery is used for any manufacturing process it shall be securely fenced. Consequently if any person sustains an injury through the violation of the enactment, he has a right to bring an action."

Support for this view can be found in *Couch v. Steel*,[66] where Lord Campbell C.J. stated that "where a statute enacts or prohibits a thing for the benefit of a person, he shall have a remedy upon the same statute . . . for a recompense of a wrong done contrary to the said law." As Stanton has explained, this decision "emphasised that an action on the case founded on breach of a statute could provide a potent remedy in a society which was becoming increasingly subject to statutory regulation".[67]

But an attempt to free the "action upon the statute"[68] from one of the shackles of common law liability was rejected in *Caswell v. Worth*,[69] when Lord Campbell C.J. held that wilful misconduct by the plaintiff was a good defence to an action based on breach of section 21 of the 1844 Act:

"The Factory Acts . . . have had a very salutary effect, but they would have a most unjust and oppressive operation if this action could be maintained. . . . [I]t would be contrary to all principle to hold that the plaintiff, having himself, by his own misconduct, wilfully caused the injury to himself, may maintain an action for compensation."[70]

Further disappointment was to follow. Section 21 provided (*inter alia*) that "*all* parts of the mill-gearing in a factory shall be securely fenced"; but the factory inspectors had initially required only the fencing of those parts which were within reach of the persons employed (i.e. within seven feet of the ground).[71] Under pressure from Lord Palmerston, the Home Secretary, however, they issued a circular in January 1854 requiring *all* overhead shafts to be fenced.[72]

---

[66] (1854) 3 El. & Bl. 402, 118 E.R. 1193.

[67] *Breach of Statutory Duty in Tort* (London, 1986), pp. 2-3.

[68] As Crampton J. called this cause of action in *McCracken v. Dargan* (1856) 1 I.J. (ns) 404 at 406.

[69] (1856) 25 L.J.Q.B. 121, immediately followed and applied in *McCracken's* case, above, n. 68.

[70] *ibid.*, at 123. Coleridge J. did, however, suggest (at p. 124) that "if it had appeared that this was the case of a young person shewn to be within the policy of the Act . . . a different principle may prevail from that which applies in the case of an adult person. . . .".

[71] *Reports of the Inspectors of Factories . . . for the half-year ending 30th April 1854* 1854 B.P.P. xix, 373 at pp. 427-428. See generally Dickson, "Legal Aspects of the Factory Act of 1856" (1981) 2 *Journal of Legal History* 276 and Bartrip and Burman, *op. cit.*, above, n. 1, pp. 63-66.

[72] The inspectors also explained that the policy of non-prosecution prevented them from seeking compensation either under s. 24 or under s. 60 of the 1844 Act for persons injured in such cases;

This relatively mild change of course antagonised the factory occupiers – and for the first time brought some at least of the Irish employers to act closely in concert with their counterparts in Great Britain. A deputation representing factory owners, which included three Irish MPs,[73] persuaded Palmerston that the inspectors had gone too far, and an amended circular was issued in March 1854.

It was at this stage that the issue arose for consideration in the Irish courts. In *Darkin v. Herdman's of Sion Mills*[74] the owners had failed to ensure that a horizontal shaft (part of the mill-gearing) more than seven feet above the floor was securely fenced. There was a ladder up to the shaft "which was left there for the purpose of bringing [certain workers] within arm range to adjust the straps and oil the journals". When in the summer of 1854 a boy aged 13 climbed the ladder and was injured by the unfenced shaft, Inspector Darkin brought a prosecution under section 60 of the 1844 Act. The owners were convicted at Strabane petty sessions on September 6, 1854 and fined £10. They promptly appealed to Strabane Quarter Sessions.

The appeal was heard on October 20, 1854. The owners had obviously decided *not* to join issue on the proper scope of section 21. Instead, they contended that Inspector Darkin had failed to prove that the machinery in question was "in motion . . . for any manufacturing process". They claimed that the mill was idle at the relevant time, and that the machinery had been set in motion by three or four boys as the result of "a childish folly". A number of prosecution witnesses (including the injured boy himself) had obviously changed their stories before the appeal came on for hearing[75] and the Assistant Barrister had little alternative but to quash the conviction, having made clear his belief that many witnesses had given false testimony.[76]

The prosecution nevertheless seems to have achieved some good; Inspector Howell ended his report by stating that "since the decision all the shafts in

---

"having in our circular relieved ourselves of the responsibility of not enforcing the law, the right of an injured person to receive compensation or damages from a mill-owner who has neglected the obligation . . . will no longer be interfered with": *Memorandum to the Home Office on fencing securely horizontal shafts in factories,* February 24, 1854 P.R.O. HO45/5209.

[73] Mr J.J. Richardson (MP for Lisburn 1853-1857 and a member of a well-known linen family), Mr W. Kirk (a linen merchant and Liberal MP for Newry 1852-1859 and 1868-1876) and Mr V. Scully (Q.C. and Liberal MP for Cork Co. 1852-1857 and 1859-1867) – see P.R.O. HO45/5209 and Stenton (ed.), *Who's Who of British Members of Parliament: Volume I, 1832-1885* (Brighton, 1976).

[74] A full report of the case appears in *Reports of the Inspectors of Factories . . . for the half-year ending 31st October 1854* 1854-1855 B.P.P. xv, 275 at pp. 303-313.

[75] The injured boy was one of seven of the family employed by D, and as counsel for Darkin observed, "A manager can easily discharge factory operatives. . . .".

[76] He gave counsel for the prosecution leave to cross-examine the injured boy, whose testimony was "evidently adverse". The Assistant Barrister is also reported to have said: "I will commit these boys to Bridewell: it is a disgusting exhibition" and he replied "Certainly not" when asked to make an order for the appellant's costs.

the factory have been fenced". But the evident hostility to such prosecutions in certain quarters was reflected in the *Belfast Newsletter*: "It is but a false, mawkish and mongrel humanity which cares not though trade should go to the dogs lest an impudent little larking scamp . . . should fail to get his cut fingers salved with a ten pound note".[77]

The controversy over the true scope of section 21 was exacerbated in 1855 when *Doel v. Sheppard and Others*[78] decided that "The Act does not merely provide that machinery in factories is to be fenced where it is dangerous. All mill gearing, while in motion for a manufacturing purpose, is to be fenced."[79] This authoritative interpretation, and the continuing activities of the factory inspectorate, drove the employers into further action. In March 1855, the linen manufacturers of Belfast formed a committee affiliated to the National Association of Factory Occupiers and agreed to co-operate with the association in opposing the full enforcement of the 1844 Act and to campaign against the Factory Acts in general.[80] When the factory inspectors issued another circular requiring occupiers "to commence at once to adopt adequate means for 'securely fencing' their horizontal shafts",[81] the National Association replied by promoting a Bill to limit the scope of section 21.

The 1856 Bill was not unexpectedly supported by Richardson and Kirk,[82] two of the Irish MPs in the owners' deputation which had met Palmerson in 1854. It was strongly opposed by (amongst others) Colonel Dunne (the "very Liberal Conservative" MP for Portarlington), who believed "the measure to be the prelude to an attempt to get rid of the factory laws altogether . . .".[83] But the Bill met with the "entire approbation" of none other than Lord Campbell[84] and, perhaps for this reason, ultimately excited relatively little political interest in Ireland. The Factory Act 1856, which represents the only serious "reverse"

---

[77]*Belfast Newsletter*, September 8 and October 27, 1854.
[78](1856) 5 El. & Bl. 856, 119 E.R. 700.
[79]But the court found that the injury was due to P's own wilful misconduct, and therefore gave judgment for D. As Coleridge J. had just explained in *Caswell v. Worth* (1856) 25 L.J.Q.B. 121 at 124: "Our judgment assumes that a person sustaining an injury by the unlawful act has a common law remedy by action. That remedy, however, must be in accordance with common law principles, and one of those principles is, that a person contributing to his own injury cannot maintain an action for such injury . . .".
[80]Armstrong, *op. cit.,* above, n. 18, p. 257, citing *Belfast Newsletter*, March 19, 1855.
[81]See *Reports of the Inspectors of Factories . . . for the half-year ending 30th April 1855* 1854-1855 B.P.P. xv, 367 at pp. 428-429.
[82]See 140 Parl. Debs. (3rd. ser.) col. 1673 (Kirk) and 141 Parl. Debs. col. 444 (Richardson). Mr Richardson even went so far as to suggest that the Bill "would give increased security to the operatives".
[83]141 Parl. Debs. cols. 377 and 443 (April 3 and 4, 1856). This description of Dunne is from Stenton, *op. cit.,* above, n. 73.
[84]142 Parl Debs col. 1671 (June 19, 1856). The learned judge, who had presided in *Doel v. Sheppard*, above, n. 78, explained that he did not believe that the interpretation of s. 21 given by the court "was the meaning of the framers of the [1844] Act".

to the onward march of factory legislation during the nineteenth century, overruled *Doel v. Sheppard* by reducing the requirement to fence mill gearing to
such parts "with which children and young persons and women are liable to
come in contact, *either in passing or in their ordinary occupation . . .* ".[85]
Other transmission machinery was to be fenced only if the inspector gave notice of danger to the employer – who could then take the matter to arbitration
under section 43 of the Act; if the arbitrators agreed with the inspector then the
fencing provisions applied; otherwise they did not.

The likely impact of this arbitration provision was immediately raised by
what appears to have been the first successful employers' liability claim in
Ireland. In *MacCracken v. Dargan and Haughton*[86] a spinning master aged 22
lost an arm when he was putting a belt onto a revolving horizontal shaft situated some nine feet above the floor. Acting on his own behalf, "and not on the
report and recommendation of the inspector",[87] he brought a claim in negligence for damages of £500, alleging failure by his employers to fence the shaft
securely. The employers in turn claimed that the plaintiff, in breach of a factory
rule known to him and contrary to an explicit warning, had stood on an inse-
cure plank and attempted to put the belt on by hand, instead of standing on the
floor and using the special "crutch" which was supplied for this purpose.[88] A
special jury in the Court of Queen's Bench rejected this defence and awarded
damages of £200.

The case was heard just before the passing of the 1856 Act, and Inspector
Howell speculated on the effect of that Act in such cases:

> "If the inspector should unwarily give rise to an arbitration under the
> Factory Act of 1856 [s. 5], and if the arbitrators, looking at such machin-
> ery, should be of opinion that it was from its position harmless, and should
> adjudge that it need not be fenced, and if a young person should after-
> wards, in the course of his 'ordinary occupation' suffer a similar injury to
> that of the plaintiff MacCracken . . . from such machinery remaining
> unfenced . . . we apprehend that the formal though extra-judicial award

---

[85] 1856 Act, s. 4 (emphasis added). S. 21 had always contained this qualification with respect to
steam engines, water wheels, hoists and teagles.
[86] *Reports of the Inspectors of Factories . . . for the half-year ending 31st October 1856* 1857
(Sess. 1) B.P.P. iii, 559 at pp. 561-562. This flax-spinning factory at Chapelizod was a thorn in
the factory inspectorate's flesh, leading to an unprecedented series of at least nine prosecutions
between August 1854 and February 1858, for employing women and young persons for excessive hours – and for obstructing the inspectors in the course of their duties.
[87] A rare reference to s. 24 of the 1844 Act.
[88] See *McCracken v. Dargan* (1856) 1 I.J. (ns) 404, where P, by way of demurrer, sought to have
this defence struck out; the court, however, held that if "the mischief has grown in a certain
degree from the negligence of the plaintiff", he is not entitled to recover.

of two arbitrators . . . would materially damage the plaintiff's case before a jury, if not destroy his right of action altogether."[89]

The inspectors accordingly "refrained from giving, under the Factory Act of 1856, any notice which would call into action the imperfect extra-judicial kind of arbitration provided by that statute".[90] The Home Secretary rightly drew attention to a different inference:

"[I]f an action were brought by any person for damages on account of an injury received from machinery or mill gearing of any kind, with regard to which the inspector . . . was authorised by law to give notice to the occupier of the factory that he deemed it to be dangerous, but had purposely abstained from doing so, it might be not unreasonably argued on behalf of the defendant that it was not deemed to be dangerous by the inspector . . ."[91]

The adverse impact of the 1856 Act should not, however, be exaggerated; women, young persons and children, who in Ireland as in England accounted for the large majority of those working in textile factories, were still generally protected. Indeed, Inspector Howell was able to make a favourable report in 1857:

"I am happy to be able to state that in the important manufacturing district of the north of Ireland . . . considerable progress has been willingly made in fencing horizontal shafts for the prevention of accidents to the workpeople . . . Mr Darkin reports that of 96 factories recently visited by him, 42 are either completely fenced . . . or are promised to be completely fenced, and the fencing is in progress; 53 have the shafts in the spinning rooms fenced, and in some few cases there are partial attempts at fencing elsewhere than in the spinning rooms; and in one case only is the occupier indisposed to add to the [partial fencing] already fixed in his factory. This forms an instructive commentary on the objections of some factory occupiers in other districts."[92]

---

[89] *Reports from the Inspectors of Factories . . . for the half-year ending 31st October 1856* 1857 (Sess. 1) B.P.P. iii, 559 at p. 562.

[90] *ibid.*, p. 566. The arbitration procedure was also criticised on the grounds that the arbitrators, who had to be persons 'skilled in the construction of the kind of machinery to which the notice refers', were too closely connected with the occupiers to be regarded as unbiased; it was also said that they were not familiar with accidents and had no power to summon witnesses, particularly those workers "who were most familiar with accidents": Dickson, *op. cit.,* above, n. 71, p. 281.

[91] Letter from Waddington (Under-Secretary, Home Office) to the Inspectors, Jan. 31, 1857 PRO LAB 15/4.

[92] *Reports of the Inspectors of Factories . . . for the half-year ending 30th April 1857* 1857 (Sess. 2) B.P.P. xvi, 201 at p. 247.

Nonetheless the 1856 Act appears to have marked a temporary turning point in the development of employers' liability. After their initial enthusiasm for the tort of breach of statutory duty, the courts appear to have had second thoughts. The whole basis of the new tort was questioned as the courts began to hold that the principle enunciated by Lord Campbell C.J. in *Couch v. Steel* was too wide.[93] By the 1870s, the courts were suggesting that a common law action would lie only where the statute creating the duty failed expressly to provide a remedy for its breach.[94] This retrenchment seems to be borne out by *Norton v. Kearon*,[95] where a bye-law made under the Dublin Port and Docks Act 1869 directed that all ships discharging coal should have a gangway plank at least 22 inches wide, with a good hand rail or rope. The plaintiff was killed when he fell from a plank which did not comply with these requirements. The court stated that the 1869 Act provided its own remedy for breach and that P's dependants had therefore no right to bring an action for breach of statutory duty. This view was affirmed by Deasy L.J. in *Hildige v. O'Farrell*,[96] when he observed that the decision in *Couch v. Steel* "was afterwards greatly questioned in the Court of Appeal; the Judges went so near overruling it as judicial comity would allow".

Although none of these cases directly involved the 1844 Act, it seems[97] that their cumulative effect cast some doubt on the legitimacy of decisions such as *Coe v. Platt*, a doubt which was not put at rest until 1898.[98]

5. THE EMPLOYERS' LIABILITY ACT 1880[99]

By 1870, the Factories Acts had been extended to cover non-textile factories and a wide variety of workshops; the "protected" workforce in Ireland now exceeded 120,000, of whom roughly one-half were women over the age of 13.[100] The doctrine of common employment had by then reached its zenith[101]

---

[93] Stanton, *op. cit.,* above, n.67, pp. 3 and 34.

[94] *Atkinson v. Newcastle and Gateshead Waterworks Co.* (1877) 2 Ex. D. 441.

[95] (1871) I.R. 6 C.L. 126.

[96] (1880) 6 L.R. Ir. 493 at 497.

[97] As Cornish and Clark, *Law and Society in England, 1750-1950* (London, 1989), p. 519 say, the changed judicial attitude in the 1870s and 1880s "was bound to wash against the industrial accident claim based on breach of statute".

[98] *Groves v. Lord Wimborne* [1898] 2 Q.B. 402.

[99] See Porter, *The Law relating to Employers' Liability and Workmen's Compensation* (Dublin, 1908), pp. 19-32; Hanna, *The Workmen's Compensation Act 1897, as applied to Ireland* (1st ed., Dublin, 1898), pp. 15-21; Campbell, *Workmen's Compensation under the Workmen's Compensation Act 1906 and the Employers' Liability Act 1880* (5th ed., Dublin, 1908), pp. 17-27.

[100] See *Report of the Commissioners appointed to inquire into the working of the Factory and Workshops Acts with a view to their consolidation and amendment* 1876 B.P.P. xxix, 1 at Appendix B, pp. 5-6.

[101] See especially *Bartonshill Coal Co. v. Reid* (1858) 3 Macq. 266 and *Wilson v. Merry and Cunningham* (1868) L.R. 1 Sc. & Div. 326.

and it appears to have been applied with equal rigour in Ireland.[102] In particular, the rejection by the House of Lords of attempts to restrict the doctrine to fellow servants of the same status as the plaintiff[103] meant, as Wright J. was to acknowledge in *Carlos v. Congested Districts Board*,[104] that employers "might delegate to a competent engineer or foreman the duty of taking reasonable and proper precautions against accidents to their workmen . . . [and then] rely on the doctrine of common employment as a defence to an action founded on the negligence of the person to whom he has delegated his duties". Accordingly:

> "The doctrine of common employment operated with peculiar hardship on those workmen whose employers took little or no share in the conduct and management of their own business. Limited liability companies also availed themselves of the doctrine with great success, and the number of such companies was increasing with great rapidity."[105]

The wide ambit of common employment, and the other inhibiting factors mentioned earlier, make it unlikely that many common law claims arising from factory accidents were brought in the superior courts at this time. Unfortunately, the Civil Judicial Statistics for Ireland do not enable us to determine the number of employers' liability cases commenced or entered for trial. We are given only the *total* number of all claims for damages in respect of personal injury and death; but these figures suggest that very few employers' liability cases went to court. In 1870, for example, only 31 negligence actions of all kinds were tried, of which a mere nine resulted in judgment for the plaintiff; aggregate damages of £3,125 were awarded, representing an average award of just under £350, but including one award of £1,100.

The "unfair" protection afforded to large and wealthy employers in particular, and the adverse effect of virtual immunity from tort liability on the enforcement of safety provisions and the prevention of accidents, led to agitation in Parliament from 1862 for the abolition of common employment.[106] Although consistently and vehemently opposed on the basis that "unrestricted" common law liability for negligence would be too burdensome for employers, the movement for reform of the law had by 1876 gained considerable momentum. In that year yet another Employers' Liability Bill, on this occasion inspired by the

---

[102] *Report from the Select Committee on Employers' Liability for Injuries to their Servants* 1877 BPP x, 551, Appendix.

[103] *Wilson v. Merry and Cunningham* (1868) L.R. 1 Sc. & Div. 326 and *Allen v. New Gas Co.* (1876) 1 Ex. D. 251.

[104] [1908] 2 I.R. 91 at 95. Thus, the traffic manager of a railway company and a milesman employed by the company were held to be fellow-servants: *Conway v. Belfast & Northern Counties Rly Co.* (1875) I.R. 9 C.L. 498.

[105] Porter, *op. cit.,* above, n. 99, p. 20.

[106] Bartrip and Burman, *op. cit.,* above, n. 1, pp. 111-130.

Trades Union Congress, was introduced in the House of Commons by (amongst others) Mr Charles Meldon, MP for Kildare,[107] who was to play an active role in the reform movement. Although the Bill was opposed by the Government as too radical, there was by now wide support for *some* reform of common law liability. Accordingly, in the following year, a Select Committee (which included Meldon) was set up to inquire into the matter.[108]

In practical and political terms, the committee had to choose between a major and a minor curtailment of the defence of common employment. The majority favoured a cautious approach. In their view, the greatest safety in factories could still be achieved by relying on fellow-workers to enforce safety provisions, a strategy consistent with the "true principle of law . . . that no man is responsible except for his own acts and defaults". In any event, abolishing common employment "would effect a serious disturbance in the industrial arrangements of the country. Sooner or later the position of master and workman would find its level by a readjustment of the rate of wages, but in the meantime great alarm would be occasioned, and the investment of capital in industrial undertakings would be discouraged."[109] The committee accepted, however, that many "modern" employers often delegated the conduct of their business to "chief" managers; in such cases (but no others), "the acts or defaults of the agents who thus discharge the duties and fulfil the functions of master, should be considered as the personal acts or defaults of the principals and employers" for the purposes of common law liability.

A minority of the committee were in favour of abolishing common employment insofar as it extended to most, if not all, "supervisors". The case for such reform in the changed conditions of the 1870s was ably stated by Meldon:

> "At that time [when *Priestley v. Fowler* was decided], machinery was comparatively unused, and industrial and manufacturing operations were carried on by a small number of workmen who were under the immediate supervision of their employers. Now we have dangerous and complicated machinery in every possible industrial operation; the labourers are numbered by legions, and instead of being under the immediate eye of their employer, they are superintended by middle-men of a superior grade, whom the constantly increasing scale on which mining and manufactur-

---

[107] Charles Henry Meldon (1841-1892) was educated at Trinity College Dublin and was called to the Irish Bar in 1863. He became a QC in 1877, was MP for Co. Kildare from 1874 to 1885 and served as first whip of Butt's Home Rule Party 1874-1879. According to *The Times*, September 19, 1892, p. 9 Meldon "was never politically associated with Mr Parnell's followers". His attempt in 1881 to assimilate the Irish borough franchise with that in England only failed by eight votes.

[108] *Report from the Select Committee on Employers' Liability for Injuries to their Servants*: 1877 BPP x, 551.

[109] *ibid.*, p. 554.

ing establishments are conducted. . .has called into existence; there are more gradations of servants, more separation or distribution of duties, and more delegation of authority. . ."[110]

Employers should therefore be liable to their workers for injuries arising from the negligence of any other "servant" in a superior grade or employed in a different department of the business.[111]

There was no immediate response to either facet of the Select Committee report, but Meldon and the other reformers saw to it that the issue remained under active consideration. Common employment even became an election issue (at least in Great Britain) in 1880, and the new Liberal Home Secretary (Sir William Harcourt) took office bound to honour a campaign promise to "abolish" the defence. This he purported to do in a Bill which took the form of "a rather muddleheaded compromise"[112] along the lines recommended by Meldon in 1877, but the increased liability of employers was to be offset by a cap on the amount of compensation payable. After a lengthy debate in which Irish members, as the Land War reached its height, took little part, the Bill received the royal assent in September 1880.[113]

The 1880 Act "is not by any means a sweeping enactment. . . . Parliament went slowly and warily. . . .".[114] An injured worker could now elect to sue an employer under the Act or at common law. Under the Act, he or she still had to prove negligence.[115] The employer was prohibited from raising common employment as a defence in five specified cases[116] – but he could still rely on

---

[110] *Report from the Select Committee on Employers' Liability, op. cit.,* above, n. 108, Appendix. Mr Meldon's draft report was received too late to be considered by the committee. It was published as an article in (1877) 11 *I.L.T.S.J.* 357.

[111] *ibid.* The case for reform was supported, by reference to cases from the United States and Scotland, in two articles which appeared in (1880) 14 I.L.T.S.J. 293 and 303.

[112] Hanes, *The First British Workmen's Compensation Act, 1897* (New Haven and London: Yale University Press, 1968), p. 19. According to Pollock, *The Law of Torts* (1st ed., London, 1887), p 90, "So far as the Act has any principle, it is that of holding the employer answerable for the conduct of those who are in delegated authority under him."

[113] The Act was not formally repealed in Northern Ireland until 1948 (Law Reform (Miscellaneous Provisions) Act (N.I.)) and in the Republic until 1958 (Law Reform (Personal Injuries) Act).

[114] Campbell, *op. cit.,* above, n. 99, p. 17. Wilson and Levy, *Workmen's Compensation* (London, 1939), vol. 1, p. 47 say that: "As a first attack upon a peculiarly English conception of the workman's responsibility, the Act of 1880 does credit to its framers. To have attempted to enforce compulsory and general protection for workmen would probably have been fatal to the whole Bill." The *Irish Law Times* "do not anticipate that the Act will have a widespread consequence either in provoking antagonism between employer and employee or in handicapping industry in meeting foreign competition": (1880) 14 *I.L.T.S.J.* 521. The journal nevertheless provided a detailed analysis of the Act – see (1880) 14 *I.L.T.S.J.* 521, 531, 555, 567, 577, 589, 611 and 621.

[115] See *e.g., Noonan v. Dublin Distillery Co.* (1893) 32 L.R. Ir. 399.

[116] In particular, s. 1(1) provided that an employer was liable for "any defect in the condition of the ways, works, machinery or plant connected with or used in [his] business. . ., provided the

contributory negligence or *volenti*.[117] If the worker was successful, the damages were limited to "such sum as may be . . . equivalent to the estimated earnings, during the three years preceding the injury, of a person in the same grade employed during those years in the like employment and in the district in which the workman is employed at the time of the injury" – less any sum already recovered by way of penal compensation. There was no maximum sum imposed in cash terms; but it is generally accepted that awards under the Act would seldom, if ever, exceed £150 in practice.[118]

The most controversial aspect of the 1880 Act was that, as confirmed by *Griffiths v. Earl Dudley*,[119] it contained nothing to prevent a workman from expressly contracting away his or her right of action under the Act. In December 1880 (before the Act came into force) the *Irish Law Times and Solicitors' Journal* reported that "[A]n extensive movement [is being] made with a view to procuring the workmen to contract themselves out of the advantages conferred by the Legislature".[120] The *Journal* anticipated the decision in *Griffiths*, and put the arguments for and against the decision, without coming down on one side or the other:

> "[C]ertainly . . . workmen have reason for agitating against such a perversion of what the law would seem to recognise as their ordinary rights; though we find that . . . the Sheffield Chamber of Commerce . . . [has] resolved that such interference, as now proposed [by the TUC, to make

---

defect arose from, or had not been discovered or remedied owing to the negligence of the employer, or of some person in the service of the employer entrusted with the duty of seeing that the ways, etc were in proper condition". According to Campbell, *op. cit.* above n. 99, p. 19, " 'defect in the condition' has given rise to shoals of amusing decisions. . ." A number of cases are summarised in "Employers' Liability for Defective Ways, Means, Works, Machinery or Plant" (1887) 21 *I.L.T.S.J.* 453 and 467, and in "Employers' Liability for Defective 'Works'" (1892) 26 *I.L.T.S.J.* 177 and 201.

[117] See *e.g. M'Evoy v. Waterford SS Co. (No. 2)* (1886) 18 L.R. Ir. 159 and *Campbell v. Brennan* (1889) 23 I.L.T.R. 84 at 85, where Andrews J. anticipated the decision of the House of Lords in *Smith v. Baker & Sons* [1891] A.C. 325 by holding that "in order to enable a defence to be taken on that principle [*volenti*] it must be shown that not only was there knowledge of danger, but an adequate appreciation of the risk that was about to be experienced by bringing a man into contact with that danger".

[118] According to Armstrong, *op. cit.,* above, n. 18, p. 264, the average wage in the Irish linen industry in 1884 was 10*s.* 6*d.* per week; by 1906 it had risen to 12*s.* per week. Such a worker was, therefore, entitled under the Act to maximum compensation of £81. 18*s.* 0*d.* in 1884, rising to £91. 4*s.* 0*d.* in 1906. *cf. Campbell v. Brennan* (1889) 23 I.L.T.R. 84, 86, where the court considered £1 per week to be fair compensation for a painter's widow and two children and therefore awarded damages of £156; the family had claimed £219.

[119] (1882) 9 Q.B.D. 357. Field J. (at 363) stated: "It is said that the intention of the legislation to protect workmen against imprudent bargains will be frustrated if contracts like this one are allowed to stand. I should say that workmen as a rule are perfectly competent to make reasonable bargains for themselves."

[120] (1880) 14 *I.L.T.S.J.* 521 (referring to English examples only).

contracting out unlawful] with the right of free contract between adults would be prejudicial to the interests of commerce in this country."[121]

But the question of "contracting out" was not as straightforward as it might seem. By 1880, a number of workers were taking steps for themselves to solve the compensation problem:

> "By contributing a certain sum to a worker's pool they gradually built up their own compensation insurance funds. As the funds grew larger their management became a full-time job; reaching the stature of autonomous organisations, they became known by the generic name of Friendly Societies. These societies provided financial remuneration to the worker or his dependants in case of disability or death . . . irrespective of fault by worker or employer."[122]

As Campbell noted, "the workman may agree with the employer to look solely to a benefit society for compensation and forego his statutory remedy. . .",[123] in some cases at least on the basis that the employer made a contribution (or an increased contribution) to the accident relief fund.[124] But less benevolent employers simply made contracting out a condition of employment, so that workers had no real choice in the matter. Unfortunately, we do not yet know into which camp Irish employers tended to fall.

We do, however, know that the 1880 Act had a very limited impact on employers' liability in practice.[125] In Ireland, only 25 claims were made in the first three years, and in the period to 1896 there were on average only 19 claims per year.[126] However, since this figure represents roughly one tenth of the

---

[121] "Contracts in ouster of the Employers' Liability Act, 1880" (1882) 16 *I.L.T.S.J.* 303 at 304.

[122] Hanes, *op. cit.,* above, n. 112, pp. 22-23. Some of these schemes were already being supported by contributions from employers who, when faced with the uncertain impact of the 1880 Act, agreed to increase their contributions (to 15-25% of workers' contributions) in return for a "contracting out" agreement.

[123] *op. cit.,* above, n. 99, p.26.

[124] Bartrip and Burman, *op. cit.,* above, n. 1, p. 158.

[125] See especially Wilson and Levy, *op. cit.,* above, n. 114, vol. 1, chap. 2 and Cornish and Clark, *op. cit.,* above, n. 97, pp. 525-527.

[126] By s. 6(1), an action under the Act had to be brought in the civil bill court, where it could be tried by judge and jury – as in *Noonan v. Dublin Distillery* (1893) 32 L.R. Ir. 399. Alternatively, the judge could sit alone or with assessors "appointed for the purpose of ascertaining the amount of compensation" (s. 6(2)). In all such cases, the normal civil bill limit of £50 did not apply; but a case was removable to a superior court on application by the plaintiff or defendant; but the fact that a plaintiff was likely to obtain damages in excess of £50 was not a ground for removal, and indeed it seems that few cases were removed for any reason. See especially *M'Evoy v. Waterford Steamship Co. (No. 1)* (1885) 16 L.R. Ir. 291 at 297, where Dowse B. observed: "It would be to defeat the object of the legislature in conferring this great benefit upon workmen to remove an action from the inferior court, with all the expenses consequent upon that proceed-

Employers' Liability Act Claims 1881-1896[127]

	No of cases tried		Total amount claimed		Total amount awarded	
	E/W	Ireland	E/W	Ireland	E/W	Ireland
1881–1885	882	124	£153,648	£12,660	£34,362	£2,345
1886–1891	1,042	92	£166,552	£11,429	£44,509	£1,574
1892–1896	1,138	91	£164,083	£12,582	£50,409	£2,442

number (albeit only one twentieth of the value) of claims in England and Wales, it suggests that in proportion to the reported number of factory accidents in the two jurisdictions,[128] the Act was, relatively speaking, more used in Ireland. The high point for claims in Ireland appears to have been 1885, when 57 claims were made (as compared to 340 in England and Wales); the total amount claimed was over £6,000, but only £1,116 was awarded (as compared to £7,356 in England and Wales). Never again was the Act to reach even such lowly heights in Ireland. By the 1890s, the number of claims per year averaged only 18, leading to total payment of compensation in the region of £500.[129] This represented a relative decline in resort to the Act as compared to England and Wales at a time when the number of reported accidents in both jurisdictions was on the rise.[130]

The most important achievement of the Act may have been the fillip which it gave to the development of liability insurance;[131] it may also have given some encouragement to the judges to extend the scope of common law liability, at they finally began to do in the 1890s.[132] And, indeed, there may have been more to the Act even in Ireland than is suggested by the small number of decided cases; we do not know, for example, how many claims were settled out of court. But for whatever reason the low number of reported cases does not

---

ing, in a case like this, which presents no difficulties in point of law, and in which no special circumstances have been shown to exist".

[127] This table has been compiled from the annual statistics of compensation under the 1880 Act which were published from 1881 onwards.

[128] The number of reported factory accidents in Ireland in 1900 at 1,588 was roughly 2.5% of that in England and Wales – see *Annual Report of the Chief Inspector of Factories and Workshops for the year 1900* 1901 B.P.P. x, 1 at p. 561.

[129] In 1895, John Murphy, a member of Belfast Trades Council, commented that the 1880 Act was carried out by the Irish judges "in the most contradictory and inconsistent manner", although he allowed that some were "fair and honourable": *Report of the Third Irish Trades Congress* (Limerick, 1895), p. 39.

[130] By 1908 contested claims under the 1880 Act in respect of factory accidents had virtually died out in Ireland.

[131] Bartrip and Burman, *op. cit.,* above, n. 1, pp. 165-170.

[132] See *e.g., Smith v. Baker & Sons* [1891] A.C. 325 and *Groves v. Lord Wimborne* [1898] 2 Q.B. 402.

appear to have dampened the factory inspectors' enthusiastic support for the Act as a means of strengthening their hand when they sought to persuade employers to fence dangerous machinery. In 1881, Inspector Cameron reported from the North of Ireland:

"[U]ndoubtedly, the provisions of the Employers Liability Act are of service in illustrating the importance of fencing and of *keeping efficient* the guards which have been put up. I think that the penalties [*sic*] under the Act may probably secure a more perfect system of general supervision, and a more prompt replacement of any guard which has broken or become inefficient."[133]

6. THE SEARCH FOR AN ALTERNATIVE APPROACH

As it became clear that the Employers' Liability Act was not bringing about a major extension in the liability of employers, its critics, and in particular the TUC, sought to revitalise it by securing the total abolition of common employment and the prohibition of contracting out.[134] Bills were introduced annually during the 1880s, until in 1886 a Select Committee was appointed to review the working of the Act.[135] The committee's conclusion was optimistic:

"The operation of the Act of 1880 has been attended with no hardship to the employers, whilst it has been of great benefit to the workmen. . . . The apprehensions as to its possible results in provoking litigation and imposing heavy charges upon employers have proved groundless, while a useful stimulus has been given to the establishment of provident funds and associations, in many cases liberally supported by the employers."[136]

But some employers were not so generous, and the committee recommended that contracting out should be prohibited unless the employer made a sufficient contribution to the workers' provident fund to enable that fund to pay a level of compensation comparable to damages under the 1880 Act in the event of in-

---

[133] *Annual Report of the Chief Inspector of Factories and Workshops for the year 1881,* 1882 B.P.P. xviii, 1 at p. 12 (emphasis in original). Cameron's assessment was supported by many of the inspectors in England and Wales.

[134] Bartrip and Burman, *op. cit.,* above, n. 1, pp. 170-185; Cornish and Clark, *op. cit.,* above, n. 97, pp. 520-528.

[135] According to Hanes, *op. cit.,* above, n. 112, p. 35, the committee "was composed of men favourably disposed toward labour and genuinely concerned with the welfare of the workingman". *cf.* Wilson and Levy, *op. cit.,* above, n. 114, vol. 1, pp. 52-53, say that the committee "hardly considered" the workers' point of view.

[136] *Report from the Select Committee on the Employers' Liability Act 1880 Amendment Bill,* 1886 (Sess. 1) B.P.P. viii, 1 at p.7.

jury. This recommendation was apparently acceptable to the Conservative Government; but it did not go far enough for the TUC, who (with the support of the Liberals) continued to press for a total prohibition of contracting out. A Conservative Government Bill introduced in 1888 foundered in the face of such opposition, but continued lobbying ensured that the matter was not forgotten. In 1893 a further attempt was made by Asquith for the Liberals to prohibit the right to contract out; although the Bill managed to pass the House of Commons, the contracting-out provision was amended by the House of Lords in ways which were regarded by the inaugural meeting of the Irish Trades Congress as "destroying" it.[137] That defeat effectively ended (until well into the 20th century) legislative attempts to extend employers' liability by removing restrictions on the scope of their liability for negligence, as interest grew in more radical reform wholly independent of the common law.

---

[137] See *Report of the First Irish Trades Congress* (Dublin, 1894), p. 17. Congress called for the Bill to be reintroduced with a new provision putting the onus of proof of non-negligence on employers. Bartrip and Burman, *op. cit.,* above, n. 1, pp. 190-198 explain that the House of Lords, led by the Earl of Dudley – of *Griffiths v. Earl Dudley* fame (above, p. 249) – amended the Bill so that contracting out was permissible, albeit only on very strict conditions.

"WHAT'S IN A NAME?" – TAXONOMY AND THE LAW

RONAN KEANE

"TAXONOMY" ...

> *"1. Classification, esp. in relation to its general laws or principles; that department of science, or of a particular science or subject, which consists in or relates to classification; esp. the systematic classification of living organisms..."*[1]

Professor James Brady was a learned and thoughtful scholar, who liked to stand back from his subject and examine the wider context in which a particular branch of the law had evolved. I think particularly in that connection of his book on *Religion and the Law of Charities in Ireland*.[2] When I was asked to contribute to this collection of essays in his memory, I bore in mind that characteristic of his approach to legal problems. It is true that the study that results is largely concerned with the common law, rather than equity, trusts and succession law in which he specialised. However, the legal saga to which I will refer prompts points of general principle which, I think, might have appealed to his reflective temperament.

In the year 1866, a case which by modern standards would seem reasonably straightforward came before the Court of Common Pleas in England. A journeyman gasfitter went to the premises of a sugar refiner in order to see whether a patent gas regulator, which his employers had installed in the premises, was working properly. While he was there, and through no fault of his own, he fell down an unfenced shaft and was seriously hurt. He sued the sugar refiner for negligence and the case duly came on before Erle C.J. and a jury. The jury awarded him £400 for damages and, under the cumbersome procedures which bedevilled the courts of equity and law in both England and Ireland in those days, the legal issues had to be determined by an application being made by the defendant for leave to enter a nonsuit or to arrest the judgment. This in due course was heard by a court consisting of the Chief Justice and four other judges.

---

[1] *Oxford English Dictionary* (2nd ed.).
[2] Brady, *Religion and the Law of Charities* (Belfast, 1975).

The judgment of the court was delivered by Willes J., who was described by Lord Coleridge C.J. as "one of the greatest jurists of this or any other time."[3] The case was *Indermaur v. Dames*[4] and the judgment contains two passages which echoed through court rooms and lecture rooms all over the common law world in the centuries that followed:

> "It was also argued that the plaintiff was at best in the condition of a bare licensee or guest, who, it was urged, is only entitled to use the place as he finds it, and whose complaint may be said to wear the colour of ingratitude so long as there is no design to injure him. ... We think this argument fails because the capacity in which the plaintiff was there was that of a person on lawful business in the course of fulfilling a contract, in which both the plaintiff and the defendant had an interest, and not upon bare permission...The authorities respecting guests and other bare licensees and those respecting servants and others who consent to incur the risk being, therefore, inapplicable, we are to consider what is the law regulating the duty of the occupier of a building with reference to persons resorting thereto in the course of business upon his invitation, express or implied. . . . With respect to such a visitor, at least, we consider it settled law that he, using reasonable care on his part for his own safety, is entitled to expect that the occupier shall on his part use reasonable care to prevent damage from unusual danger which he knows or ought to know, and this where there is evidence. . . ."[5]

The jury was entitled to hold in that case that the occupier had failed to use such reasonable care and their verdict accordingly stood.

The tone is magisterial, the language spare and precise. But upon these passages, as we all know, there was erected a huge edifice of law, as the courts and academic commentators parsed, analysed and refined the distinctions between the duties owed by the occupiers of premises to licensees, invitees and trespassers. While judges and practitioners have on occasions been inclined to blame the academy for developing and refining such distinctions, thereby effectively making the law more complex than it need be, a fairer view would be that the legal community as a whole must take the responsibility. Lawyers are as prone as the practitioners of any other discipline to resort to classifications of this nature as being logical and coherent. Taxonomy appeals to the legal mind, it would seem, in much the same way as it does to the scientific mind.

Could it have been anticipated that this relish for the systematic approach, wherever it came from, would have led to such remarkable distinctions as those

---

[3] *Bowen v. Hall* (1881) 6 Q.B.D. 333 at 342.
[4] (1866) L.R. 1 C.P. 274.
[5] *ibid.* at 287.

discussed in *Boylan v. Dublin Corporation*?[6] The issue again might have appeared comparatively straightforward. The plaintiff took part in a whist drive being held in aid of a charity in the Mansion House in Dublin. While he was on his way from the Mansion House to Dawson Street along a passage which was not included in the agreement between the organisers and Dublin Corporation and which was in the possession of the corporation, a flagpole fell from the roof and struck and seriously injured him. Was he an invitee or a licensee? If he was a licensee, he could not succeed, because the corporation did not know of the defective condition of the flagpole. But if he was an invitee, they owed him a duty to take reasonable care to protect him against any danger of which they knew or ought to have known. By a majority, the Supreme Court concluded that the plaintiff was an invitee, since the corporation had a material interest in people such as he attending functions from which they derived an income *i.e.*, the fee they charged the organisers for using the premises, and that the corporation ought to have known of the flagpole's condition. The plaintiff thus succeeded.

Two members of the court – Maguire C.J. and Black J. – were concerned with whether the decision of the House of Lords in *Fairman v. Perpetual Investment Building Society*[7] was authority for the proposition that the plaintiff was only a licensee. The state which the law had reached as a result of the seminal judgment in *Indermaur v. Dames*[8] – the surely overworked adjective is for once truly applicable – is vividly illustrated by this passage from the judgment of the latter judge[9]:

> "... Lord Sumner himself declared in *Fairman's* case that it made no difference whether the plaintiff was a licensee or an invitee, for whichever she was, the defendants were not liable, in as much as there was no trap and the danger was obvious. This last consideration was the sole *ratio decidendi* of the case. The plaintiff's status – whether that of licensee or that of invitee – was not an issue, and I am at a loss to understand how a pronouncement on a matter that is not an issue can be part of the *ratio decidendi*, or anything else but an *obiter dictum*. It seems to me manifest that these pronouncements of the three Lords were only *obiter* as Scott L.J. said they were,[10] and that by no stretch of the imagination could either the decision or those pronouncements in *Fairman v. Perpetual Investment Building Society* bind this Court to hold that the present plain-

---

[6] [1949] I.R. 60.
[7] [1923] A.C. 74. In that case, the plaintiff was a lodger of a tenant in a block of flats and caught her heel in a depression on the common staircase, which was in the landlord's occupation.
[8] Above, n.4.
[9] *Boylan v. Dublin Corporation* above, n.6 at 77-78.
[10] In *Haseldine v. C. A. Daw & Co. Ltd* [1941] 2 K.B. 343.

tiff was not the Corporation's invitee, even if its position had been comparable to that of the lodger in *Fairman's* case, which I have sought to show it most certainly was not."

By 1957, the Westminster Parliament had decided that enough was enough and enacted the Occupiers' Liability Act 1957 which swept away the distinctions between invitees and licensees, although the position of trespassers was not affected. In the case of all other visitors to the premises, the occupier's duty was to take such care as in all the circumstances of the case were reasonable to see that the visitor would be reasonably safe in using the premises for the purposes for which he or she was invited or permitted to be there. At the same time, the Act recognised that the occupier must be prepared for children to be less careful than adults. Thus, another category, which had also found favour with judges, practitioners and academics alike, was preserved: that of "allurements", the existence of which may render the occupier liable as being of a nature likely to lead children into danger.

The law continued to treat adult trespassers with less indulgence. Unless it could be proved that the occupier had deliberately intended to do harm to the trespasser or had acted with reckless disregard for safety, he could not succeed. That ceased to be the law in England with the decision of the House of Lords in *Herrington v. British Railways Board*[11] and in Ireland with the decision of the Supreme Court in *MacNamara v. Electricity Supply Board*.[12] Henchy J. pointed out the anomalies which resulted from unduly rigid classifications:

"Considering that in law the word 'trespasser' covers every person who enters on another's property in circumstances in which he is neither a licensee nor an invitee, it is difficult to see why the same inferior duty should be owed by the occupier to every person who comes within that category. Why, for example, should no higher duty be owed to a child openly but innocently trespassing in pursuit of a lost ball than to a burglar furtively and knowingly trespassing for the purpose of committing a crime? But the fact is that the wide and heterogeneous selection of people who fall within the category of *'trespasser'* are compressed into a simplistic stereotype when the law says that the occupier owes a common unvarying duty to each of them."[13]

The distinction between invitees and licensees, however, persisted in Irish law until the enactment of the Occupiers' Liability Act 1995. Although in the unre-

---

[11] [1972] A.C. 877.
[12] [1975] I.R. 1. The change in the law was foreshadowed in an earlier Supreme Court decision, *Purtill v. Athlone UDC* [1968] I.R. 205.
[13] [1975] I.R. 1 at 22.

ported Supreme Court decision of *Foley v. Musgrave Cash and Carry Limited,*[14] both McCarthy J. and Griffin J. favoured a departure from the traditional categories as determining the duty of care, the distinction appeared to have been preserved by the court's decision in *Rooney v. Connolly.*[15]

The development of the law in this area has been seen as constituting more than simply a departure from over rigid classifications of legal duties. The philosophy of *Indermaur v. Dames*[16] and its huge progeny was seen by some as based on the reverence of nineteenth century English judges for the rights of property owners. On this view, the higher duty of care owed to an invitee was explicable because the occupier had a material interest in his presence on the land. If he simply allowed the visitor access and derived no material benefit from his presence, then he should not be asked to do any more than warn the visitor of concealed dangers of which he actually knew. As for trespassers, they could not expect to receive even that degree of protection.

Undoubtedly, the modern law reflects a greater emphasis on the rights of injured persons and less sensitivity to the rights of property owners and, on any view, that is surely a more just and balanced approach. But it is also fair to recall that the changes in the law reflect, not merely that shift in emphasis, but also the enormous social changes which have taken place. The urban landscape of today presents far more hazards for visitors to premises, whether invited or not and whether adults or children.

It is somewhat ironic then that when the Oireachtas came to deal with the matter, somewhat belatedly, in recent years, the taxonomic approach was again adopted, the categories now being "visitor", "recreational user" and "trespasser". It might have been preferable if the law had been developed by the courts along the course charted in *Purtill v. Athlone UDC* and *MacNamara v. Electricity Supply Board.* In his judgment in *Foley v. Musgrave Cash and Carry Limited,* McCarthy J. had said:

> "In cases of alleged occupier liability I find little assistance in the examination of different and somewhat artificial legal relationships. In my view, cases of this kind are better approached on the simple principle of foreseeable risk, of the duty to take reasonable care to avoid unnecessary risk of injury to persons who may come upon the premises."[17]

In *Rooney v. Connolly,* where a nine-year-old girl was severely burned when she was lighting a candle in a church, the majority of the Supreme Court dealt with the case on the basis on which it was argued both in that court and in the

---

[14] Judgments delivered December 20, 1985.
[15] [1987] I.L.R.M. 768.
[16] Above, n.4.
[17] *Foley v. Musgrave Cash and Carry Limited,* above n.14 at pp. 4-5.

High Court, *i.e.*, that the duty, if any, owed by the defendant was to an infant licensee. However, McCarthy J. in the course of his judgment said:

> "In my view, a more fundamental question is involved than the application of *MacNamara* to the case of an infant licensee; that question is whether or not the judicially-created set of categories of entrant on premises forms part of the law. . . . For my part, where the law has been made by judges, it can be unmade by judges. Indeed, it is somewhat invidious to invite the legislature to effect a change in judge-made law; presumably such law was based upon the perceived demands of justice."[18]

Or, as Lord Denning M.R., said pithily in *Pannett v. McGuinness & Company:*[19]

> "The long and short of it is that you have to take into account all the circumstances of the case and see then whether the occupier ought to have done more than he did."

The moral, I think, is that legislators and judges alike should be careful of succumbing to the attractions of taxonomy. The law, of its nature, cannot always be as precise as the natural sciences in defining categories. In the areas of law in which Professor Brady had a particular interest, such as equity, examples could also be cited of the dangers of excessively rigid classifications. Take, for example, the position of beneficiaries under a will or an intestacy. Until such time as the personal representative assents to the bequest or, in the case of the residue, until he has completed the administration of the estate by paying all the debts and legacies, the legal ownership is vested in the personal representatives: the only right of the beneficiaries is their right to require them to complete the administration of the estate in accordance with law. But it does not follow that personal representatives who are not beneficiaries under a will or on intestacy are during that interim period in some sense the beneficial owners as well as the legal owners. As Viscount Radcliffe pointed out in *Stamp Duties Commissioner (Queensland) v. Livingston,*[20] it is not the law that

> ". . . for all purposes and at every moment of time the law requires the separate existence of two different kinds of estate or interests in property, the legal and the equitable. . . . Equity in fact calls into existence and protects equitable rights and interests in property only where their recog-

---

[18]*Rooney v. Connolly*, above, n.15 at 787.
[19][1972] 2 Q.B. 599 at 606.
[20][1965] A.C. 694 at 712.

nition has been found to be required in order to give effect to its doctrines."

What's in a name? Sometimes, it would seem, so far as the law is concerned, far too much.

RECENT DEVELOPMENTS IN THE LAW ON THE LIMITATION OF ACTIONS

ANTHONY KERR

"For his post-graduate examination he had submitted a thesis on 'Probate and the Validity of Wills', in which he'd argued that testamentary capacity should be strictly limited, and as his cross questioner at the *viva* had led him on to talk nonsense, he had done so at great length while the examiners had remained inscrutable. Then, as bad luck would have it, Prescription had turned up as the topic for exposition. Deslauriers had launched into quite outrageous theories: old claims were to be given no more weight than new ones; why should an owner be denied his property merely on the grounds that he can't furnish proof of title until thirty one years have elapsed? It amounted to giving the heir of a thief the same security as an honest man. Any extension of this right would sanction every kind of injustice; it would be a tyrannical abuse of power."

Flaubert, *A Sentimental Education*[1]

1. INTRODUCTION

One doubts that Deslauriers' anticipated *magnum opus* on "Positive and Negative Prescription considered as the basis of Civil and Natural Law" would have found much favour with Jim Brady, had it been submitted to him. Jim believed that there were compelling policy reasons for the law's insistence that redress for wrongs be sought expeditiously and we attempted to consider those reasons in our collaboration on *The Limitation of Actions.*[2]

It is hoped that a third edition of that work will be commissioned by the Law Society of Ireland because there have been a number of significant developments since the publication of the second edition in 1994. Not least has been the enactment of amending legislation extending the definition of "disability" as contained in section 48 of the Statute of Limitations 1957 to circumstances in which a person is suffering from a significant "psychological injury" as a

---

[1] Parmee translation (Oxford, 1989) pp. 120–121. I am very grateful to Dr Frank Callanan SC for alerting me to this passage.
[2] First edition, Dublin, 1984; second edition, Dublin, 1994.

result of being sexually abused during childhood so "that his or her will or his or her ability to make a reasoned decision" to institute civil proceedings in respect of such abuse is "substantially impaired".[3] The scope of this legislation is considered elsewhere in this volume.[4] This essay focuses on four areas of particular interest to Jim where the courts have been particularly active over the past six years.

2. ACTIONS IN RESPECT OF THE ESTATES OF DECEASED PERSONS

This was an aspect of the law of limitations that perhaps more than any other excited Jim intellectually. Section 45 (1) of the Statute of Limitations 1957, as amended by section 126 of the Succession Act 1965, provides that no action in respect of any claim to the estate of a deceased person or to any share or interest in such estate, whether under a will or an intestacy, shall be brought after the expiration of six years from the date when the right to receive the share or interest accrued.

In *Drohan v. Drohan*[5] McMahon J. expressed the view that section 45 had no application to a claim by a personal representative to recover assets of the deceased from a person, whether a beneficiary or a stranger, holding adversely to the estate. The applicable period, McMahon J. concluded, was the period of twelve years provided by section 13(2) of the Statute of 1957. Jim found this reasoning to be "compelling" and went on to write:

"If a personal representative recovers land belonging to the deceased's estate within twelve years of the accrual of the right to action, but more than six years after the date of the death of the deceased, the vesting of such land in the next-of-kin or those otherwise entitled who are statute-barred would clearly be at odds with the policy considerations underlying the limitation period of six years in the new section 45(1). Indeed the facts of a particular case may reveal that the personal representative is acting at the behest of next-of-kin who are statute barred and the question

---

[3] Statute of Limitations (Amendment) Act 2000 (No. 13 of 2000). The Law Reform Commission has now issued a Consultation Paper on *The Law of Limitation of Actions arising from Non-Sexual Abuse of Children* CP16-2000. Their provisional recommendation is that plaintiffs, in cases concerning non-sexual abuse of children, should have a fixed period of time from the date of their majority within which to bring an action and that the approach adopted in the 2000 Amendment Act as regards cases of sexual abuse should not be adopted. In other words, there would be separate limitation regimes for cases of sexual abuse and cases of non-sexual abuse of children. The Commission saw the virtue of their proposal as going some distance towards accommodating a plaintiff's incapacity to commence proceedings, while also importing certainty and clarity into this area of law.
[4] See Paul Ward at p. 344 *infra*.
[5] [1981] I.L.R.M. 473.

arises whether the limitation period can be circumvented in this fashion."[6]

Such a question did arise in *Gleeson v. Feehan,*[7] where the plaintiff was both the personal representative of James Dwyer, deceased, who was the registered owner of Folios A and B in the register of County Tipperary, and the personal representative of Edmond Dwyer, deceased, who was the registered owner of Folio C in that register. James Dwyer had died intestate on November 27, 1937 leaving a widow and six children including the said Edmond Dwyer and Josephine Dwyer, the natural mother of one Jimmy Dwyer. Only Edmond and Jimmy had remained on the lands and the widow and other children of James Dwyer were all dead. Edmond had died on October 22, 1971, a bachelor and intestate, and after his death Jimmy had remained in possession of the lands enjoying the rents and profits. In 1975 Jimmy Dwyer sold the lands in Folio C to the first named defendant for £5,000 and the lands in Folios A and B to the second named defendant for £12,000.

The plaintiff, acting under a power of attorney for the next-of-kin of the registered owners who were resident in the United States, obtained a Grant of Administration Intestate to the estate of James Dwyer and a grant to the estate of Edmond Dwyer and instituted proceedings by ejectment civil bill on the title against the defendants with respect to the lands contained in Folios A, B and C. The defendants replied that the plaintiff was statute-barred and had been since the expiry of six years from Edmond Dwyer's death, which latter date was the crucial one since James Dwyer had died in 1937 and his title to the lands would have been effected by section 24 of the Statute of Limitations which, subject to formalities, extinguishes title to land after twelve years.

Judge Sheridan found for the defendants in the Circuit Court on the grounds that the rights of Edmond Dwyer's next-of-kin to share in his estate accrued on his death and were barred after the expiry of six years from that date. Section 45(1) had no direct application to an action by a personal representative but the facts, as agreed, revealed that the plaintiff was acting at the behest and authority of the next-of-kin of the registered owners who were statute-barred and this fact led Judge Sheridan to the conclusion that it would appear to defeat the purpose of section 45(1) if his personal representative could acquire Edmond Dwyer's assets and vest them in his next-of-kin outside the six-year limitation period.

Judge Sheridan's decision was appealed to the High Court where Barron J. stated a case for the Supreme Court pursuant to the provisions of section 38 (3) of the Courts of Justice Act 1936. The question of law for the determination of the Supreme Court was whether section 45 of the Statute of Limitations 1957,

---

[6] *The Limitation of Actions* (2nd ed., Dublin, 1994) at p. 147.
[7] *(No. 1)* [1993] 2 I.R. 113; *(No. 2)* [1997] 1 I.L.R.M. 522.

as amended by section 126 of the Succession Act 1965, barred the claim of the plaintiff to the property in his aforesaid capacity.

The Supreme Court (Finlay C.J., McCarthy, O'Flaherty and Egan JJ., Hederman J. concurring) answered the question posed in the case stated in the negative, holding that the limitation period of six years laid down by the provisions of section 45 of the Statute of 1957, as substituted by section 126 of the Succession Act 1965, did not apply to an action by a personal representative of a deceased owner of land seeking recovery of such land in succession to the owner. The court held that the relevant period of limitation in such a case was the period of twelve years laid down by section 13(2) of the Statute of 1957, and approved the *dicta* of McMahon J. in *Drohan* to that effect.

The case was remitted back to the Circuit Court where the plaintiff was granted a decree for possession. The defendants appealed to the High Court where, following certain concessions by both sides, it was agreed that the only issue to be determined was whether Jimmy Dwyer was entitled to be registered as owner of the lands comprised in Folios A, B and C to the exclusion of Edmond Dwyer's next-of-kin. By way of case stated Morris J. (as he then was) posed the following questions for the Supreme Court:

1. (a) Where, prior to the Succession Act 1965, several next-of-kin in actual occupation of lands of a deceased person acquired title to those lands by adverse possession against the personal representative, was the title so acquired the title to which they would have been beneficially entitled on due administration?
   (b) Where such next-of-kin acquired title by adverse possession against other next-of-kin not in occupation, was such title acquired as joint tenants?

2. Where such next-of-kin in actual occupation shared such occupation with persons other than next-of-kin, was the possession of such other persons adverse possession against (a) the personal representative or (b) next-of-kin not in occupation?

3. If the answer to 1(a) or 1(b) is yes, was such title acquired jointly with the next-of-kin in occupation as (a) joint tenants or (b) tenants in common?

The Supreme Court, in an unanimous judgment delivered by Keane J. (as he then was) (Blayney and Barrington JJ. concurring) answered question 1(a) in the negative and 1(b) in the affirmative. The answer to question 2 was "the personal representative" and that to question 3 was "joint tenants".

Any third edition will be all the poorer without Jim's analysis of the judgment.[8] Keane J. summarised the submissions of both parties as follows:

---

[8] The judgment would also have to feature in any further edition of Jim's *Succession Law in*

"On behalf of the defendants, it is submitted that, on the death of James Dwyer, the registered owner, in 1937, the lands became vested in the President of the High Court pending the extraction of a grant of letters of administration. The next-of-kin, it was said, acquired no legal or equitable interest on the death of James Dwyer to any particular assets which happened to form part of his estate. In those circumstances, it was urged that the occupation by Edmond, or anyone else, of the lands was unlawful and could have been restrained by the legal owner, *i.e.,* the President of the High Court. Since Edmond and Jimmy had acquired title as disseisors, it followed that they acquired that title as joint tenants and that, on the death of Edmond in 1971, Jimmy, as the surviving joint tenant, became entitled to the land.

On behalf of the plaintiff, it was submitted that, on the death intestate of the owner of the lands, the beneficial interest vested immediately in the next-of-kin entitled under the Statute of Distributions (Ireland) 1695 and that any of them who remained on in possession were equitable tenants in common of the land and not trespassers. Prior to the Administration of Estates Act 1959 and the Succession Act 1965 the personal representative (or the President of the High Court before the raising of administration) could only eject the next-of-kin in possession if a sale of the lands was required for the payment of debts. Moreover, the beneficiaries were entitled to call on the personal representatives to vest the land in them. In the present case, the lands vested in the six children of James Dwyer to the exclusion of anyone else, whether in possession or otherwise. The claims of the remaining five tenants in common were statute barred at the time of Edmond's death and, accordingly, he was solely entitled to the land at that stage. It thereupon devolved on his next-of-kin of whom Jimmy was not one."[9]

The sheet anchor of the plaintiff's case was *Martin v. Kearney*,[10] a decision of Palles C.B. in which the Chief Baron held that next-of-kin remaining in possession without any administration having been taken out to the deceased's estate were equitable tenants in common. This view of the law, as Keane J. pointed out, derived from the decision of the House of Lords in *Cooper v. Cooper*,[11] where Lord Cairns expressed the view that the interest of the next-of-kin in the estate of an intestate is a defined and tangible interest in specified property. That view, however, was not in accord with that of the House of

---

Ireland (Dublin, 1st ed., 1989; 2nd ed., 1995) and one can only speculate as to how it would have affected his analysis of Barron J.'s decision in *H. v. M.* [1983] I.L.R.M. 519: see 2nd ed. at pp. 259–261.

[9] [1997] 1 I.L.R.M. 522 at 528–529.
[10] (1902) 36 I.L.T.R. 117.
[11] (1874) L.R. 7 H.L. 53.

Lords subsequently in *Lord Sudeley v. Attorney General*[12] and *Doctor Barnardo's Homes v. Special Income Tax Commissioners*[13] or that of the Judicial Committee of the Privy Council in *Stamp Duties Commissioner (Queensland) v. Livingston*[14] or that of the Supreme Court of Canada in *Minister of National Revenue v. Fitzgerald*.[15]

Keane J. was satisfied that *Martin v. Kearney* was wrongly decided and should be overruled and that the possession of both Jimmy Dwyer and Edmond Dwyer of these lands was at all times adverse to the title of the true owner, the President of the High Court, in whom the entire estate in the land was vested pending the raising of representation.[16] It was conceded on behalf of the plaintiff that, in the event of both Edmond and Jimmy being regarded as in adverse possession, they would have acquired title as joint tenants and that, accordingly, the interest of Edmond would have devolved by survivorship on his death to Jimmy. What was extinguished by virtue of section 24 was not the title of the next-of-kin (whom the court had found to have no proprietary interest in the land pending the administration of the estate) but the title of the President of the High Court and his right to bring an action to recover the land.[17]

It was urged upon the court, without much impact, that, having regard to the longstanding practice in rural Ireland of not raising representation to the estates of deceased persons, particularly when they consist of small farms, the conclusions arrived at in the judgment of the court would lead to considerable uncertainty as to the title to such properties.

The problem still remains, however, as Hourican[18] has pointed out, that, although a personal representative has *twelve* years from the date of death in which to recover land to which the estate is entitled, the entitlement of the beneficiaries to have that land vested in them expires *six* years after the date of death. So, if a personal representative recovers land after the expiration of six years and within the twelve-year period, in respect of which land no claim has been made by the beneficiaries within the six-year period, their claim is statute-barred.

Such a conclusion would undoubtedly have commended itself to Deslauriers.

---

[12] [1897] A.C. 11.

[13] [1921] 2 A.C. 1.

[14] [1965] A.C. 1.

[15] [1949] S.C.R. 453.

[16] Section 15 of the Probate and Letters of Administration (Ireland) Act 1859 provided that, after the death of a person dying intestate and until letters of administration were granted in respect of his estate, the person's estate and effects of that person would vest in what is now the President of the High Court. This provision was replaced by s. 13 of the Administration of Estates Act 1959 which in turn was replaced by s. 13 of the Succession Act 1965.

[17] See Keane J. at 540.

[18] "The Running of Time in Succession Law" (2000) 5 *Conveyancing and Property Law Journal* 34.

3. LIMITATION PERIODS AND THE CONSTITUTION

> "In legislation creating a time limit for the commencement of actions, the time provided for any particular type of action; the absolute or qualified nature of the limit; whether the Court is vested with a discretion in certain cases in the interests of justice; and the special instances, if any, in which exception from the general time limit are provided, are with others, all matters in the formulation of which the legislature must seek to balance between, on the one hand, the desirability of enabling persons with causes of action to litigate them, and on the other hand, the desirability of finality and certainty in the potential liability which citizens may incur into the future."[19]

The constitutionality of certain provisions of section 11 of the Statute of 1957, namely those which provided for a six-year limitation period for actions founded on simple contract or tort, has now been considered by the Supreme Court in *Tuohy v. Courtney.*[20]

The plaintiff in 1978 instructed the defendant solicitors to act on his behalf in the purchase of premises in Mallow in the County of Cork. The plaintiff believed that he was purchasing a freehold interest in the premises whereas what he in fact purchased was the unexpired term of a lease for 99 years, in respect of which there was no right of renewal or of conversion into a freehold interest. This was a title of substantially less value than the purchase price which he had paid. The plaintiff only became aware of the true nature of the title he had acquired in 1985 but, under the provisions of section 11, the plaintiff's right of action, whether in tort or contract, became barred at the latest in December 1984.[21]

The plaintiff's challenge to the constitutionality of section 11 was thus based on the proposition that the section had operated in his case as to time bar his action before he could reasonably be expected to have appreciated that he had any worthwhile or significant claim against the defendant.

Having satisfied themselves that the plaintiff did have *locus standi* to maintain his challenge to the constitutionality of the legislation, the Supreme Court then considered the nature of the constitutional right which the plaintiff claimed had been wrongfully invaded. The court was of the opinion that it was not the

---

[19] *Per* Finlay C.J. in *Hegarty v. O'Loughran* [1990] 1 I.R. 148 at 156.
[20] [1994] 3 I.R. 1.
[21] The trial judge (Lynch J.) found that the plaintiff could not take steps, which he reasonably might have expected to take before he became aware of the true position and his true loss, before the summer of 1985. The Supreme Court refused to interfere with this finding of fact. See further *Irish Equine Foundation Ltd v. Robinson* [1999] 2 I.L.R.M. 289 at 291 where Geoghegan J. said that "discoverability, as such, cannot be relevant in considering what is the appropriate commencement date in respect of the limitation period."

constitutional right of access to the courts and adopted the analysis of Henchy
J. in *O Domhnaill v. Merrick*[22] that the Statute of Limitations did not bear on a
plaintiff's right to sue but on a plaintiff's right to succeed "if the action is
brought after the relevant period of limitation has passed and if a defendant
pleads the statute as a defence." Rather the court accepted that the true legal
effect of section 11 was to restrict the right of a person to litigate, which was in
the nature of an unenumerated personal constitutional right, and, as such, attracted the protection of Article 40.3.1° whereby the State guaranteed in its
laws to respect and, as far as practicable, to defend and vindicate such rights.

The court did not find it necessary to decide whether the plaintiff's right to
litigate was also a property right which attracted the protection of Article 40.3.2°,
and thus to resolve the apparent incompatibility between, on the one hand,
O'Brien v. Keogh[23] and *O'Brien v. Manufacturing Engineering Co Ltd*[24] and,
on the other, *Foley v. Irish Land Commission*[25] and *Attorney General v. Southern Industrial Trust Ltd.*[26] This was because the court was satisfied that there
was no "material difference in the constitutional protection which would apply
to this right to litigate if it were on the one hand considered to be exclusively an
unenumerated right or on the other hand if it were considered to be exclusively
a constitutional property right or indeed if it were considered to be both."[27]

The court accepted that the Oireachtas, in legislating for time limits on the
bringing of actions, is essentially engaged in a balancing of constitutional rights
and duties. What had to be balanced, the court said, was the constitutional right
of the plaintiff to litigate against the other contesting rights namely

> ". . . the constitutional right of the defendant in his property to be pro-
> tected against unjust or burdensome claims and, secondly, the interest of
> the public constituting an interest or requirement of the common good
> which is involved in the avoidance of stale or delayed claims."[28]

In any challenge to the constitutional validity of a statute in the enactment of
which the Oireachtas has been engaged in such a balancing function, the traditional role of the courts has been not to impose their view of the correct or
desirable balance but rather to determine whether the balance contained in the
statute is so contrary to reason and fairness as to constitute an unjust attack on
the plaintiff's constitutional rights.

---

[22][1984] I.R. 151 at 158.
[23][1972] I.R. 144.
[24][1973] I.R. 334.
[25][1952] I.R. 118.
[26](1957) 94 I.L.T.R. 161.
[27][1994] 3 I.R. 1 at 46.
[28]*ibid.* at 47.

It cannot be disputed that a person, whose right to seek a legal remedy is barred by a statutory time limit before he or she, without fault or neglect, becomes aware of the existence of that right, has suffered a severe apparent injustice. The court, however, did not conclude from that that the section was inconsistent with the Constitution. Any time limit statutorily imposed upon the bringing of actions is potentially going to impose some hardship. What the Supreme Court saw its task as being was to ascertain whether the nature and extent of such hardship were so undue and so unreasonable, having regard to the objectives of the legislation, as to make it constitutionally flawed.[29]

The primary purpose of a statute of limitation is to protect defendants against stale claims and to avoid the injustices which might occur if they were asked to defend themselves from claims which were not notified to them within a reasonable time. They were also designed to discourage plaintiffs from delaying in instituting proceedings and to promote expeditious trials so that a court might have before it, as the material upon which it must make its decision, "oral evidence which has the accuracy of recent recollection and documentary proof which is complete" and a certainty of finality in potential claims.[30]

The court felt that a period of six years "objectively viewed" was a "substantial period", a period unchanged since 1853[31] "notwithstanding the very significant increase in literacy, understanding of legal rights and sophistication" which has occurred since then. Moreover the Statute of 1957 contained extensions of the periods of limitation in cases of disability, fraud and mistake which constituted "a significant inroad on the certainty of finality" provided by the Statute.

The court concluded that, for the Oireachtas to reach a decision not to add to these extensions an extension relating to discoverability, was a decision which could be supported by just and reasonable policy decisions and was not a proper matter for judicial intervention. Consequently the court declined to declare the provisions inconsistent with the Constitution.

In their Consultation Paper on *The Statutes of Limitation: Claims in Contract and Tort in Respect of Latent Damage (other than Personal Injury)*,[32] the Law Reform Commission indicated that they were firmly of the opinion that the existing law was in urgent need of reform. Palpable injustice occurred in cases of latent damage and accordingly they provisionally recommended that a discoverability test should be introduced to deal with cases in tort and contract where the loss or damage was latent. However, in an effort to minimise any adverse consequences from the point of view of potential defendants, the Commission went on to provisionally recommend the introduction of a "long stop"

---

[29] *ibid.* at 48.
[30] *ibid.*
[31] Common Law Procedure Amendment Act (Ireland) 1853 (16 & 17 Vict c 113).
[32] November 1998.

or ultimate limitation period beyond which no action could lie, irrespective of whether the cause of action was discoverable at the expiration of this period.[33]

4. DISCOVERABILITY TEST FOR PERSONAL INJURIES

In the area of personal injuries, a discoverability test was introduced by the Statute of Limitations (Amendment) Act 1991.[34] The fundamental change brought about by this Act was that the limitation period began to run from the "date of knowledge" of the person injured. Under section 2(1) of the Act a reference to a person's "date of knowledge" is a reference to the date on which he or she first had knowledge of certain causally relevant facts essential to the cause of action namely:

(a) that the person alleged to have been injured had been injured;

(b) that the injury in question was significant;

(c) that the injury was attributable in whole or in part to the act or omission which is alleged to constitute negligence, nuisance or breach of duty;

(d) the identity of the defendant; and

(e) if it is alleged that the act or omission was that of a person other than the defendant, the identity of that person and the additional facts supporting the bringing of an action against the defendant.

This definition is in terms similar to that in the English Limitation Act 1980 except that the English Act goes on to provide that an injury is significant "if the person whose date of knowledge is in question would reasonably have considered it sufficiently serious to justify his instituting proceedings for damages against a defendant who did not dispute liability and was able to satisfy a judgment".[35]

The first occasion in which these provisions of the 1991 Act were considered was in *Whitely v. Minister for Defence*.[36] Quirke J. said that, because the Act expressly avoided any attempt to define what was meant by "significant", it was thus the legislative intention to avoid confining the sense in which the

---

[33] The length of the "long stop" was provisionally recommended to be 15 years. The Commission further provisionally recommended that there should be no judicial discretion to extend or disapply the long stop.

[34] This legislation was introduced following the Law Reform Commission's Report on *The Statute of Limitations: Claims in Respect of Latent Personal Injuries* (LRC 21-1987).

[35] On which see *McCafferty v. Metropolitan Police District Receiver* [1977] 1 W.L.R. 1073 where Geoffrey Lane L.J. said that the test was partly subjective and partly objective.

[36] [1998] 4 I.R. 442. See also *Gallagher v. Minister for Defence* [1998] 4 I.R. 457 (O'Higgins J.) and *Bolger v. O'Brien* [1999] 2 I.L.R.M. 372 (S.C.).

word "significant" ought to be understood to the terms of the definition in the English Act. It followed that the test to be applied was "primarily subjective" and that the court should take into account "the state of mind of the particular plaintiff at the particular time having regard to his particular circumstances at that time".[37] Quirke J. went on to say, however, that, although the appropriate test was primarily subjective, it was qualified by the provisions of section 2(2) of the 1991 Act which require the additional consideration of whether the particular plaintiff ought reasonably to have sought medical or other expert advice, having regard to the symptoms from which he or she was suffering and the other circumstances in which he or she then found himself. This introduced "a degree of objectivity into the test".

It is interesting to note that, when the Law Reform Commission considered the nature of the discoverability test for non personal injuries latent damage cases, the members of the Commission were divided as to whether the test should be purely objective or whether it should involve a hybrid objective/subjective formulation.[38] Were the Commission to ultimately recommend the latter approach, it remains to be seen whether they will recommend that there be a difference in the degree of objectivity between the *Whiteley* test for personal injuries and the test in relation to latent building and other defects.

5. DISMISSAL FOR WANT OF PROSECUTION

"The draconian penalty of dismissing proceedings as against a particular defendant in circumstances which will wholly defeat that claim of the plaintiff is not an Order which is made with a view to punishing a party for his dilatoriness in proceeding with the action or for his failure to meet some artificial regime. The Order is made only where it is necessary to protect the legitimate interests of the party sued and in particular his constitutional right to a trial in accordance with fair procedures."[39]

Applications to dismiss proceedings for want of prosecution have occupied much time of the courts over the last six years both as regards cases where there has been delay in instituting proceedings and cases where there has been delay in prosecuting them.[40]

---

[37] *Whitely v. Minister for Defence,* n.36, above, at 453.

[38] November 1998 Consultation Paper, para. 4.24.

[39] *Per* Murphy J. in *Hogan v. Jones* [1994] 1 I.L.R.M. 512, 518.

[40] Apart from the cases mentioned in the text, see also *Carroll Shipping Ltd v. Matthews Mulcahy & Sutherland Ltd* unreported, High Court, McGuinness J., December 18, 1996; *Reidy v. National Maternity Hospital* unreported, High Court, Barr J., July 31, 1997; *Whearty v. Agriculture Credit Corporation Ltd* unreported, High Court, McCracken J., October 31, 1997; *Robert McGregor & Sons (Ireland) Ltd v. The Mining Board* unreported, High Court, Carroll J., October

The leading case is now undoubtedly *Primor plc v. Stokes Kennedy Crowley*,[41] where the defendants had acted as auditors for the plaintiff in 1978 and the sums claimed by way of damages made the claim one of the highest of its kind ever brought. Proceedings were instituted by Plenary Summons issued on 21 December 1984 and a Statement of Claim was delivered on 8 January 1986. The motion to dismiss was issued in March 1993. Having reviewed the relevant authorities,[42] Hamilton C.J. said that the relevant principles of law could be summarised as follows:

"(a) the courts have an inherent jurisdiction to control their own procedure and to dismiss a claim when the interests of justice require them to do so;

(b) it must, in the first instance, be established by the party seeking a dismissal of proceedings for want of prosecution on the ground of delay in the prosecution thereof, that the delay was inordinate and inexcusable;

(c) even where the delay has been both inordinate and inexcusable the Court must exercise a judgment on whether, in its discretion, on the facts the balance of justice is in favour of or against the proceeding of the case;

(d) in considering this latter obligation the court is entitled to take into consideration and have regard to:

(i) the implied constitutional principles of basic fairness of procedures,

(ii) whether the delay and consequent prejudice in the special facts of the case are such as to make it unfair to the defendant to allow the action to proceed and to make it just to strike out the plaintiff's action,

(iii) any delay on the part of the defendant – because litigation is a two party operation the conduct of both parties should be looked at,

---

5, 1998; *Superwood Holdings plc v. Scully* unreported, Supreme Court, November 4, 1998; *Brennan v. Western Health Board* unreported, High Court, Macken J., May 18, 1999; *Hughes v. Moy Contractors Ltd (No. 1)* unreported, High Court, Carroll J., July 29, 1999; *Dunne v. The Electricity Supply Board* unreported, High Court, Laffoy J., October 19, 1999; *Truck and Machinery Sales Ltd v. General Accident Fire and Life Assurance Corporation plc* unreported, High Court, Geoghegan J., November 12, 1999; *Hughes v. Moy Contractors Ltd (No. 2)* unreported, High Court, Morris P., January 25, 2000; *Glynn v. Rotunda Hospital* unreported, High Court, O'Sullivan J., April 6, 2000; *In re Verit Hotel and Leisure (Ireland) Ltd* unreported, High Court, O'Donovan J., July 27, 2000. See further Delany "Dismissal for want of Prosecution" (1996) 14 *I.L.T (n.s.)* 240 and "Dismissal for Want of Prosecution or on Grounds of Inordinate and Inexcusable Delay" (2000) 2 *Practice and Procedure* 2.

[41] [1996] 2 I.R. 459.

[42] *Dowd v. Kerry County Council* [1970] I.R. 97; *Rainsford v. Limerick Corporation* unreported, High Court, Finlay P., July 31, 1979; *O Domhnaill v. Merrick* [1984] I.R. 151; *Celtic Ceramics Ltd v. Industrial Development Authority* [1993] I.L.R.M. 248; and *Hogan v. Jones* [1994] 1 I.L.R.M. 512.

(iv) whether any delay or conduct of the defendant amounts to acquiescence on the part of the defendant in the plaintiff's delay,

(v) the fact that conduct of the defendant which induces the plaintiff
to incur further expense in pursuing the action does not, in law,
constitute an absolute bar preventing the defendant from obtaining a striking out order but is a relevant factor to be taken into
account by the judge in exercising his discretion whether or not
to strike out the claim, the weight to be attached to such conduct
depending upon all the circumstances of the particular case,

(vi) whether the delay gives rise to a substantial risk that it is not
possible to have a fair trial or is likely to cause or have caused
serious prejudice to the defendant,

(vii) the fact that the prejudice to the defendant referred to in (vi) may
arise in many ways and be other than that merely caused by the
delay, including damage to a defendant's reputation and business."[43]

In the High Court both O'Hanlon J. and Johnson J. in separate motions had
held that, even though there had been inordinate and inexcusable delay on the
part of the plaintiff, the actions should be allowed to continue. Both judges
held that the defendants had compromised their positions by participating in
the discovery process. O'Hanlon J. had specifically relied on the English Court
of Appeal decision in *County and District Properties v. Lyell* [44] to the effect
that, whenever a defendant has induced a plaintiff to believe that the case is to
go to trial, he or she must be taken to have made a representation that the action
is to be allowed to proceed to trial. However *Lyell* was overruled by the House
of Lords in *Roebuck v. Mungovin*,[45] where it was held that a defendant's subsequent conduct was merely a factor to be taken into account.

In *Primor* O'Flaherty J. was of the opinion that the reasoning of the House
of Lords accorded with our jurisprudence in the matter. The fact that a party
had availed of his rights under the Rules of Court could not be advanced so as
to evoke some form of estoppel against him. Hamilton C.J. said that the "fundamental ingredient" to be taken into account was the prejudice caused to a
defendant by inordinate and inexcusable delay on the part of the plaintiff. If the
prejudice was such that a fair trial between the parties could not be held then
the proceedings should be dismissed. Since *Primor* the matter has been twice
further considered by the Supreme Court. In *In re Southern Mineral Oil Ltd*,[46]

---

[43] [1996] 2 I.R. 459 at 475. See also *Collins v. Dublin Bus* unreported, Supreme Court, October
22, 1999.
[44] [1991] 1 W.L.R. 683.
[45] [1994] 2 A.C. 224.
[46] Unreported, Supreme Court, July 22, 1997.

Keane J. (as he then was) said that the court in exercising its discretion should take into account not merely the prejudice "resulting from the dimming of memories, the loss of records and the death, incapacity or disappearance of witnesses" but also the prejudice suffered by particular defendants in having an action "hanging indefinitely over their heads". It was also considered by the Supreme Court in *Kelly v. Cullen*.[47] This was a case where the proceedings were commenced within the limitation period. Barron J. said that delay could not be "inordinate" if the proceedings were so instituted but he went on to say that "delay thereafter is more likely to be found to be inordinate the less excuse there is for delay in commencing the proceedings". The learned judge added that "the longer it is since the cause of action arose, the less likely it is that circumstances giving rise to delay will be regarded as excusable".[48]

6. CONCLUSION

The theme of the tension between legal certainty and the demands of justice was central to much of Jim Brady's scholarship.[49] The law on the limitation of actions reflects that tension. On the one hand, the existence of rules which serve to bar plaintiffs' claims after a particular time period has elapsed add to the objectives of certainty and finality. On the other hand, to bar plaintiffs with meritorious claims merely because of the date of institution of proceedings is a strong sanction to apply and may cause injustice to individual plaintiffs. One sees this tension particularly in the Law Reform Commission's discussions on whether to introduce a discoverability test in cases of latent damage in non personal injuries cases and, if so, whether to introduce a "long stop". Is the injustice to the plaintiff greater than the hardship that would be caused to the defendant? I will miss the lively discussions that Jim and I would have had on this.

---

[47] Unreported, Supreme Court, July 27, 1998.
[48] At p. 10 of his unreported judgment (Hamilton C.J. and Barrington J. concurring).
[49] See, for instance, "Legal Certainty: The Durable Myth" (1973) 8 *Ir. Jur. (n.s.)* 18.

QUIA EMPTORES IN IRELAND

ANDREW LYALL

1. INTRODUCTION

In Ireland, unlike England,[1] a holder of a leasehold estate may grant the whole term to a grantee and the grant may nevertheless create leasehold tenure between the parties, rather than take effect as an outright assignment of the term. The present position is contained in section 3 of the Landlord and Tenant Law Amendment, Ireland, Act 1860, known in Ireland as Deasy's Act:

> "3.—The relationship of landlord and tenant shall be deemed to be founded on the express or implied contract of the parties and not upon tenure or service, and a reversion shall not be necessary to such relation, which shall be deemed to subsist in all cases in which there shall be an agreement by one party to hold land from or under another in consideration of any rent."

In *Pluck v. Digges*[2] the British House of Lords in 1831 had refused to recognise the Irish doctrine, overruling the Irish Court of Exchequer Chamber, which itself had followed, by a majority of seven to three,[3] the Irish Court of Common Pleas in reaffirming the Irish rule. Section 3 restored the law in Ireland to the position before *Pluck v. Digges*.[4] The following article explores the origins of this curious and apparently insignificant difference in doctrine. It seeks to show that, far from being insignificant, the doctrinal difference can be traced all the way back to the origins of freehold, in particular to the statute *Quia Emptores* 1290 and to the different application of that statute in Ireland which emerged after 1290. This in turn allows one to reconstruct the main outlines of the distinct history of land law in Ireland, many of the details of which were

---

[1] Megarry, Wade, and Harpum, with Grant and Bridge, *The Law of Real Property* (6th ed., London, 2000) para. 14-110: "… if the tenant disposes of the whole residue of his estate, the transaction must operate as an assignment even though the parties intend it to operate as a sub-lease."

[2] (1828) 2 Hud. & Br. 1, (1832) 5 Bli. N.S. 31, 5 E.R. 219 (Exchequer Chamber, Ir.), 2 Dow. & Cl. 180, 6 E.R. 695 (British House of Lords).

[3] O'Grady C.B., Lord Plunket C.J., Bushe C.J., Torrens J., Moore J., McCleland B., Smith B. (Vandeleur, Jebb, and Johnson JJ. dissenting). Of the panel of twelve judges, Pennefather B. was absent on the day judgment was delivered and Burton J. was absent both then and during argument due to illness – see (1828) 2 Hud. & Br. 1, at 36, note (b).

[4] *Gordon v. Phelan* (1881) 15 I.L.T.R. 70.

probably lost forever with the destruction of the original materials in the fire that consumed the Public Records Office in the Four Courts in 1922.

2. THE TENURE/REVERSION CONTROVERSY

The controversy which occurred at the beginning of the nineteenth century in Ireland concerning the relationship between reversion and tenure has been dealt with elsewhere[5] and is fairly clear. Before the Union of 1801 it had been the practice in Ireland, apparently from time immemorial, for lessors to grant their whole term to lessees, the grant being held to create leasehold tenure between the parties despite the fact that no reversion had been retained by the lessor. In other words, if A held a term of 10 years he could grant a term to B for 10 years, the same length as the remainder of his own term and the grant could operate to create tenure between A and B. It was not necessarily an outright assignment of A's term. The distinction is important because the practical result was that A remained liable on his covenants to his landlord and furthermore covenants could be created between A and B which would not be purely personal but would bind their successors in title.

The above explanation is oversimplified in two respects. First, the owners of the fee simple would often be absentee landlords and the "lessors" would be the absentee head landlords' agents in Ireland, "middlemen" who held leasehold terms from the head landlords and made grants tenants locally and were in the habit, before the Union, of doing so for the whole term and were considered in Ireland as retaining tenure, *i.e.* they were the immediate landlords of the local tenant despite the fact that they retained no reversion. The second complication is that the leases that were granted for the whole term were not always leasehold terms, but "leases" for lives renewable forever, *i.e.* freehold estates *pur autre vie* with multiple *cestuis que vie*, the lives being renewable indefinitely. I shall return to this complication later.

3. BEFORE QUIA EMPTORES

Before 1290 a grant of land in fee simple could create tenure without at the same time creating a reversion. This would occur when A, a holder of a fee simple estate, subinfeudated to B in fee simple for a particular tenure, such as knight service or socage.[6] A became the feudal lord of B, entitled to whatever

---

[5] Lyall, *Land Law in Ireland* (2nd ed., Dublin, 2000) pp. 566-567; Wylie, *Irish Land Law,* (3rd ed., Dublin, Charlottesville, Va: Butterworths, 1997) para. 17.005.

[6] Challis and Sweet, *Challis's Law of Real Property Chiefly in Relation to Conveyancing,* (3rd ed., London, 1911) p. 18; *Delacherois v. Delacherois* (1859) 8 Ir. C.L.R. 1, Irish Ex. Ch., at p. 8, on appeal at (1864) 11 H.L.C. 62.

feudal services, such as rent, the grant provided for and to whatever incidents the law attached to the tenure concerned. Since there was tenure, the grant could also create covenants concerning the land which would bind not only A and B but their successors in title as well. The grantor had instead created a *seignory*, or lordship, in himself. A had a seignory in fee simple. A became feudal lord of B. One of the incidents of tenure was escheat, whereby, if B's heirs died out, the land returned to A or his heirs if they still existed by that time.

At this time there was probably no clear distinction between an escheat and reversion. As Bean[7] has pointed out, in his excellent book on the decline of feudalism in England, the distinction may have been one of the consequences of *Quia Emptores* itself. Lawyers by the time of Littleton[8] in the 15th century would say that there was not, either before or after *Quia Emptores*, a reversion on the grant of a fee simple. One could never have a reversion on a fee simple. It was the largest estate known to the common law. There was tenure, and an escheat, but no reversion. If, on the other hand, A, who had a fee simple, granted B a mere life estate, A then retained a reversion, a part of his estate which he had not granted and which remained with the grantor.[9] If, instead of creating a new layer of tenure by subinfeudation, the tenant substituted a new tenant in his place, no new tenure was created, but that would generally require the consent of the tenant's own lord.

4. QUIA EMPTORES, 1290

The statute *Quia Emptores*, 1290,[10] so called after the opening words of the preamble, "*Quia emptores terrarum…*" *i.e.* "Because purchasers of lands…" was enacted to solve the problem of alienation which had developed up to that time. Freehold tenants, under the guise of subinfeudation, had been selling land, *i.e.* receiving a lump sum for the grant while reserving only nominal services for the tenure which itself had become a mere form. This had two adverse effects on the superior lords of such tenures. First, the tenants might grant away so much land in this way that they became less able to perform the services of their own tenure to the superior lord. They still remained legally

---

[7] Bean, *The Decline of English Feudalism, 1215-1540* (Manchester, 1968).

[8] "For if tenant in general tail dieth without issue, the donor or his heirs may enter as in their reversion." Littleton *Tenures*, s. 18.

[9] "A reversion is where the residue of the estate always doth continue in him that made the particular estate, or where the particular estate is derived out of his estate, as here in the case of Littleton [see n. 8 above]." Co. Litt. 22b.

[10] Statute of Westminster III, 18 Edw. I cc. 1, 2; Bean *op. cit.*, above, n. 7, pp. 79-103; Digby and Harrison, *An Introduction to the History of the Law of Real Property: With Original Authorities* (5th ed., Oxford, 1897), pp. 236-268.

liable to do so, but less able to do so in fact. Secondly, superior lords lost the value of wardships and escheats. If the tenure of the tenant was suspended, as in the case of wardship, or came to an end, as in the case of escheat, the superior lord would find that he was only entitled to the nominal services. The king lost and never gained, since he was always a lord but never a tenant. The statute prohibited subinfeudation in future, but allowed the substitution of one tenant by another. It also gave the right to do so without the consent of the superior lord. The statute has been called one of the pillars of land law[11] and was so radical in its effect that an understanding of it is still necessary for a proper understanding of the common law system of land law. The relevant part of the statute is as follows[12]

> "... the King in his parliament at Westminster after Easter in the eighteenth year of his reign, that is, a fortnight after the feast of St. John the Baptist, at the request of the magnates of his realm, conceded, provided and decreed as follows:
>
> (i)   That in future it should be lawful for any free man to sell at will his land or tenement or part of them, provided the feoffee holds that land or tenement of the same chief lord and by the same services and customs, by which his feoffor previously held it.
>
> ...
>
> (iii) Provided that by such purchases or sales of lands or tenements or parts of the same, no lands or tenements, in part or in whole, may come into mortmain, against the form of the earlier statute on that point.
>
> (iv) This statute is to apply only to lands sold to be held in fee simple."

Despite what some later commentators say about it, one might note that the statute in general did not prohibit the creation of tenure without a reversion. That was simply a *consequence* of the statute in England. It expressly prohibited the creation of freehold tenure on the grant of a fee simple estate.

5. TENANTS IN CHIEF

The statute was held not to bind the Crown in the sense that the Crown could create new tenures by grant.[13] However, the statute was not clear as to whether

---

[11] Megarry, Wade, and Harpum *op. cit.,* above, n.1, para. 2-043; Plucknett, *A Concise History of the Common Law* (4th ed., London, 1948) p. 29.
[12] See n.10, above.
[13] Co. Litt. 43b; Challis and Sweet *op. cit.,* above, n. 6, p. 20.

the new freedom of alienation applied to tenants in chief.[14] Fitzherbert[15] implies as much, and also that the crown could licence alienations by such tenants, when he says that if a tenant in chief alienated without a licence from the crown, the crown could distrain for a fine on the land. As Challis comments:[16]

"Blackstone seems to have thought that the statute did not extend to the tenants of the crown *in capite,* in the sense that they might subsequently create *de novo* a tenure in fee simple to be holden of themselves (2 Bl.Com. 91.) But it is perhaps uncertain whether he adverted to the distinction between the different senses which the words 'extend to' may bear. The statute has two aspects, one in so far as it enables the tenant to alienate, the other in so far as it disables him from creating *de novo* a tenure in fee simple to be held of himself. The statute did not enable the tenants *in capite* to alienate as against the Crown; and in this sense it may be said that the statute did not 'extend to' the tenants *in capite,* though it would be more strictly correct to say, that the statute did not extend to the Crown. . . . But it does not follow that the statute did not extend to the tenants *in capite,* meaning thereby that it failed to restrain them from creating *de novo* a tenure in fee simple. The question seems to **[21]** be at this day of no practical importance; for Blackstone held that in any case the effect of the statutes 17 Edw. 2, *De Prærogativa Regis,* c. 6, and 34 Edw. 3, c. 15, is to invalidate all sub-infeudations by the tenants *in capite* of later date than the commencement of the reign of Edward I."

The practice grew up after the statute of the Crown granting licences to tenants in chief to alienate.[17] In so far as the Crown granted licences to tenants in chief to make grants by substitution, it was simply acting as if the statute did not grant to them the freedom of alienation which was granted to mesne lords. There is some evidence, indeed, that at this time, in England at least, the crown insisted on substitution, so that if a tenant in chief wished to grant a fee tail or life estate, which were not subject to the general prohibition in *Quia Emptores* against subinfeudation, the Crown nevertheless insisted that they did so by substitution and not subinfeudation.[18] It was, of course, one thing for the Crown to grant permission to tenants in chief to do something which all other tenants were permitted to do by the statute, but quite another thing for the Crown to give permission for them to do what all other tenants were prohibited from

[14]Bean *op. cit.,* above, n.7, pp. 81-85; *Re Holliday* [1922] 2 Ch. D. 698, *per* Astbury J.
[15]Fitzherbert and Hale, *The New Natura Brevium* (7th ed., London, 1730) p. 175a.
[16]Challis and Sweet *op. cit.,* above, n.6, pp. 20-21.
[17]Bean *op. cit.,* above, n.7, pp. 81-82. See also the discussion in *Verschoyle v. Perkins* (1847) 13 Ir. Eq. R. 72, by Smith M.R., at 76-77.
[18]Bean *op. cit.,* above, n.7, p. 82, especially n. 2.

doing. The latter was an exercise of the dispensing power, *i.e.* the power to exempt an individual from a statute. I shall return to this later, since it was central to the issue of *non obstante* grants in Ireland.

6. MANORS

Some of the grants discussed later use the phrase "create manors" or some such phrase. In the language of real property law this implies that the person who thus becomes lord of a manor has the power to create new freehold tenures, *i.e.* to subinfeudate for freehold estates, including the fee simple. As Pollock and Maitland[19] pointed out, "manor" is not a technical term. They quote Scriven[20] as saying:

> "A manor . . . is the district . . . granted by the ancient kings of this realm to the lords or barons, with liberty to parcel the land out to inferior tenants, reserving such duties and services as thought convenient, and with power to hold a court (from thence called a court baron), for redressing misdemeanours, punishing the offences of their tenants and settling any disputes of property between them."

Manor may not be a technical term, but the two main types of rights of which it was composed clearly were matters of law: the right to create new tenures within the manor and the right to hold manorial courts.[21]

The view is often expressed, especially by English commentators, that new manors could not be created after *Quia Emptores*. However, the views are far from unanimous. *Quia Emptores* may have prohibited it, but could not the king licence subinfeudations by tenants in chief by granting them a new manor? Sir Matthew Hale, in a manuscript published only in recent years but written in the 1640s, was curiously ambiguous on the creation of new tenures after *Quia Emptores*:[22]

> "*A Manor* cannot be but by prescription or act of parliament. 33 H. *8*, Brooke, *Comprise* 31;[23] 44 E. 3, 14.[24] And although the king may licence the erecting of a tenure notwithstanding the statute of *quia emptores*

---

[19] Pollock and Maitland, *The History of English Law Before the Time of Edward I* (2nd ed., Cambridge, 1898) 1.596.

[20] *ibid.*; Scriven, *Copyholds* 1.1.

[21] Hence Sir Matthew Hale writes of manors existing by prescription or act of parliament only: see n. 22, below.

[22] Yale (ed.), Hale, *Sir Matthew Hale's The Prerogatives of the King* (London, 1976) pp. 249-250.

[23] Brooke's Abridgement, citing 33 Hen. 8.

[24] YB (1370), Pasch. 44 Edw. 3, fo. 14, pl. 33.

terrarum and consequently by such licence a man that hath a manor may create new freeholders *tenendum de manerio,* or **[250]** dying seised and the manor descending to two daughters by partition thereof the manor multiplied, yet a manor cannot be created at this day by the king's grant. To a manor there is incident a court baron. But by the king's grant the court may be severed from the manor. 12 Eliz., Dyer 288."[25]

Is the distinction between a *non obstante* grant and a manor, or between an express licence and a mere grant of land without an express licence? Challis comments on the issue:[26]

"The inference may, perhaps, be too hasty, that 'all manors existing at this day must have existed as early as King Edward the first.' (2 Bl. Com. 92.) Charters have been granted by the crown, and confirmed by parliament, empowering subjects to create manors since that date; of which an example is to be found in the case of *Delacherois v. Delacherois,* 11 H. L. C. 62. In that case the land to which the charter had reference was in Ireland, and the confirmation was of course by the Irish parliament. There can be no doubt that, if aided by the confirmation of the English or British parliament, a charter authorising the creation *de novo* of manors in England would be valid. Nor is it at all clear, that such confirmation is necessary. Lord Coke expressly affirms, that the statute may be dispensed with, by consent of the crown and all the mesne lords. (Co. Litt. 98b; 2 Inst. 501.)"

It is curious that Challis, writing in 1911, should repeat Coke's argument. The premise on which it was based was always dubious, since it ignored the ambiguous position of intermediate lords. The statute was only to their advantage in so far as they were lords in relation to the tenure below them, but in so far as they were themselves tenants of a higher lord, it was against their interests. As far as the King was concerned, his right to grant exemptions from a statute was really based on the dispensing power, a point we shall return to later.

7. QUIA EMPTORES IN IRELAND

There is no record of *Quia Emptores* being expressly extended to Ireland at the time it was enacted or shortly thereafter,[27] although there is evidence that within a few years it was regarded as in force in Ireland. In a case before the justiciar

---

[25] *Sir Robert Acton's Case* (1570) 3 Dyer 288b, 72 ER 647.
[26] Challis and Sweet *op. cit.,* above, n.6, p. 21.
[27] Hand, *English Law in Ireland, 1290-1324* (Cambridge, 1967) p. 162 .

and the Irish council in 1302, the King's serjeant pleads "the statute by which it is enacted that no one may alien a tenement in fee, to hold of the feoffor, or of any others, than the chief lords of the fee."[28] This certainly seems to be a reference to *Quia Emptores*, as Donaldson[29] notes, and was successful in that the purported mesne tenancy was held invalid and the new tenant "did fealty to the King here in full Court."[30] Donaldson also notes that the point may have been (almost certainly was) regarded as important because it was transferred from the Cork eyre to the justiciar and the council. That might also indicate that the King's representatives did not trust the Cork eyre to apply *Quia Emptores*. It certainly seems to be an affirmation that *Quia Emptores* in general applied in Ireland, in cases which did not fall within the exemption statute of 1293, which is dealt with below, such as attempted subinfeudations by tenants who were not tenants in chief. *Quia Emptores* would probably have been applied in 1495 by Poynings' Act,[31] a statute of the Irish parliament which applied English statutes generally to Ireland, although there must be some doubt since it referred, with extraordinary vagueness, to statutes "late made" in England. That is not in any case to say that lords in Ireland immediately conformed to the statute, if they had not done so earlier, and doubtful titles may have continued to be created.

(a) The Statute of 1293

The statute[32] sent to Ireland by Edward I in 1293 contains a partial exemption for Irish tenants in chief from *Quia Emptores*. It is worth reproducing section 2 of the Act in full. The original is in Norman French and is reproduced in Berry.[33] The text here is that as translated in Berry:

> "II. Concerning the lands held in chief of the King, which are alienated without licence of the King, as to which those of Ireland say that they have full power to do, and always, have done so, it is agreed that as soon as they are alienated, they be taken into the hand of the King by the Escheator, so as in England, and so remain until they have made satisfaction to the King; and that the Justiciar, the Treasurer, and the Council

---

[28] *Cal. Just. Rolls Ir. 1295-130*, p. 384 (no name); Donaldson, "The Application in Ireland of English and British Legislation Made Before 1801" (PhD dissertation, Queen's University, Belfast, 1952) p. 80.

[29] Donaldson, *op. cit.* above, n.28, p. 80.

[30] *Cal. Just. Rolls Ir. 1295-130*, p. 385.

[31] 10 Hen VII c. 22 (Ir).

[32] 21 Edward I, 1293. Ireland, Parliament and Berry (ed.), *Statutes and Ordinances and Acts of the Parliament of Ireland: King John to Henry V* (Dublin, 1907) p. 193; see also Hand *op. cit.,* above, n.27, p. 162; Donaldson *op. cit.,* above, n.28, pp. 80, 84.

[33] Ireland, Parliament and Berry *op. cit.,* above, n. 32, p. 192.

jointly have power to take, such kind of fines; and that henceforth none have power to enfeoff another of land which is held in chief of the King, save to hold of the King in chief, and that by leave of the King or of the Justiciar, if it be not in land of war or in the marches, and that there the lords that hold of the King have full power to enfeoff others to hold of them for the defence of the land, to their profit and to the increase of the lordship of the King and of his peace, and that the lords have such power in this last case to make feoffments, until the King advises at another time or until he wish to recall it. So nevertheless that the feoffments which have been made before this recall, shall be and are firm and established."

The statute recognises that tenants in chief in Ireland had apparently ignored *Quia Emptores* and had done so in two respects. First, they had alienated without consent of the King, or his representative in Ireland, the justiciar, and secondly they had alienated to grantees to hold of themselves, not of the King, *i.e.,* by subinfeudation notwithstanding *Quia Emptores*. Existing subinfeudations are recognised as valid, as the final words of the statute show, but in future there are to be no subinfeudations, and no alienations without consent, except as provided. The prohibition presumably refers to subinfeudations for fee simple estates. There is nothing to indicate that the statute was to *extend* the scope of *Quia Emptores*. But then there is the exemption: "if it be not in land of war or in the marches and that there the lords that hold of the King have full power to enfeoff others to hold of them ...", or in the original French: "*si il ne seyt en tere de gerre ou de marche e la eyent bien poer les seygnurs qe tengt del Rey a feffer autres a tenyr de eus ...*". As to such lands they may continue to subinfeudate and apparently without the need of obtaining consent in each case. One may also note that the King reserves the power to retake the privilege or exemption granted: "until the King advises at another time or until he wish to recall it". Being a medieval statute, it was in effect made by the King, not by a parliament, and at that time the King in theory could repeal it, although it is not clear whether he would have to issue another statute to do so.

The exemption itself must have been quite considerable in relation to both the extent and proportion of land in Ireland granted by English kings up to that time. Much land in Ireland was probably held in chief and much of it would have been in a state of warfare or something like it. The exemption would apply to land beyond the Pale and any other land in a state of warfare. Much land remained in a state of war, or arguably so, up to the end of Tudor rule.

The interpretation of the statute must have given rise to some problems, the solution to which may well have had the effect of extending the exemption even further. What would constitute war? Would intermittent attacks on English castles qualify the land for the exemption? What of occasional attacks? Even if the land was indisputably in a state of war at the time when the exemption was granted, it might cease to be so later. As to land in the marches, *i.e.* the borders beyond the Pale, those borders changed from time to time depending on who had the upper hand in warfare, the Anglo-Normans or the native Irish. The question might have arisen as to whether land which had once been on the border, but was now some way inside the Pale because its boundaries had been extended by conquest, would retain the right to the exemption. There would be the difficulty of determining at what time exactly the land had ceased to be in a state of war. Would the lord or his descendants ever lose the privilege? If so, there would be the difficulty of determining at exactly what time the privilege was lost and conveyancing, even in the Middle Ages, required certainty. Was the grant a subinfeudation or a substitution? Did the grantor retain the right to services or were they due directly to the King? In order to achieve certainty it may well have been decided that once a lord had the exemption then he or his descendants would retain it as to that particular piece of land permanently, or at least until such time in the future as the King should repeal the statute. The need for certainty could only have been met by holding that, once the exemption had applied, it remained regardless of later changes in conditions which were impossible to define with exactness. One can speculate, although it must remain speculation, that lords who had up to then ignored *Quia Emptores* entirely would be likely to interpret the exemption widely. They would continue to generate grants and therefore titles whose validity might not be called into question until many years later, and to undo them would cause major problems and disruption. In fact the statute may have been little more than an exercise in politics: an apparent assertion of control and power to influence the practice in Ireland which the King largely lacked or at least did not possess to the degree that he asserted.

It seems likely, therefore, that the statute probably entrenched the general disregard of *Quia Emptores* which had applied up to that time and that subinfeudation in fee simple continued to be a common feature of Irish land law after 1293. The case in 1302[34] is certainly some evidence inconsistent with this, but the exemption expressly applied only to tenants in chief, however numerous. The case itself may have disposed of an argument that might have been made by mesne lords after 1293 in favour of their being able to subinfeudate in fee simple: that the statute of 1293 was in force in Ireland *instead* of *Quia Emptores*. That argument would have been that tenants in chief under *Quia Emptores* in England did not have the benefit of free alienation granted by the statute to other tenants and that the object of the statute of 1293 was simply to make a different rule in Ireland as to tenants in chief, that it was not concerned with prohibiting subinfeudation by mesne lords which continued to be possible in Ireland. If so, the case apparently disposed of the point. The reference in the case is to *Quia Emptores*, not to the statute of 1293. If the grantor was a tenant

---

[34]See n. 28 above.

in chief, but the land concerned was not on the marches or not in a state of war, then the King's serjeant would hardly have referred, as he did, to a general prohibition on subinfeudation in fee, *i.e.* to *Quia Emptores*. He would surely have cited the statute of 1293. This almost certainly indicates that the grantor in the case was a mesne lord who had attempted to subinfeudate in fee.

(b) Non obstante grants

It is not clear how long the general disregard of *Quia Emptores*, if that is what it was, lasted in Ireland. One way of detecting the point when *Quia Emptores* came to be, or came to be regarded as, generally in force in Ireland is to deduce it from other measures or laws that assumed its general validity. One such marker is the practice of the Crown making grants in Ireland that expressly gave exemption from *Quia Emptores*, *i.e.* the so-called *non obstante* grants. These were grants by the Crown to a grantee, a tenant in chief, in fee simple, with a licence to further subinfeudate in fee simple, something which *Quia Emptores* certainly did prohibit expressly. It was therefore permission to create tenure without a reversion. There would hardly be any point in doing so if tenants in chief still had the benefit of a general exemption. The practice of making such grants seems to date from the plantations.

There are numerous examples of *non obstante* grants from the time of Charles I. Clearly, there would have been no point in the King expressly exempting a grantee, who by definition was to become a tenant in chief, from *Quia Emptores* if the general exemption in the 1293 statute still applied. Either the Crown at some time had withdrawn the privilege, and that could be James I, or it came to be the view that the statute of 1293 had become obsolete because by that time there was no longer any land to which it applied, *i.e.* there were no "marches" any longer and no land subject to war.

The calendar of state papers contains many examples of such grants, and they are not confined to the north of Ireland. From the time of Charles I there is the grant in 1633 to Lord Burke of Brittas of "the castle, town and lands of Brittas" and "the castle, town and lands of Grinanbeg, Enishilawras, and Knockroe with all their appurtenances in the Co. Limerick." Then the grant continues: "He may make them into a manor in spite of the statute *Quia Emptores Terrarum* and have the usual manorial rights."[35] In 1637 the marquis of Hamilton was granted lands "lying on the seashore between high and low water mark, called or known by the names of Lough Cong or Lough Cone and Lough Down, and some royal fishings there or in the bays of Strangford and Killagh" and the grant then provides that: "the Marquis may make manors of the lands and make leases of English tenures notwithstanding the statute *Quia Emptores*

---

[35]March 12, 1633, *Cal. St. Papers Ir. 1633-1647,* p. 4.

Terrarum."[36] "Make manors of the lands" implies that the grantee in turn may make grants to tenants by subinfeudation in fee simple,[37] as in the case of an instruction by Charles I to the lord deputy ordering him to confirm the Earl of Roscommon and his two sons in possession of their lands, the grant to permit "the creation of manors notwithstanding the *Quia Emptores Terrarum*".[38]

There is an example of a commission of Queen Elizabeth[39] which appointed Sir Richard Bingham, chief commissioner of Connaught and Thomond, and others "to call before them the chiefs and lords of several baronies" and to divide the baronies into manors. It provided for the creation of manors to be confirmed by act of parliament. Presumably, this is because it would otherwise offend against *Quia Emptores*. In 1633 Charles I ruled without parliament in England, and with a strong belief in the prerogatives of the King, and so he purported to dispense with *Quia Emptores* by royal fiat alone. However, he did have a parliament in Ireland, and one wonders why the grants did not recite that they were to be confirmed by the Irish parliament. Nevertheless, that is what happened, since the Irish parliament passed several Settlement of Ireland Acts confirming the grants. Charles II and James II made similar grants without express recital of the need for parliamentary approval, but the dispensing power, as it was known, was not abolished in England by statute until the Bill of Rights of 1689 and in any case no Bill of Rights was enacted in Ireland.[40]

While some of the grants purport to re-establish the grantees in manors which they held, or claim to have held before the wars of the 1640s, many of the grants provide that the lands granted should be consolidated into a new manor or manors. Judging from the grants in the calendar of state papers, the purpose of *non obstante* grants was not to create manors for their own sake, although social prestige was probably an element. One of its purposes was seemingly to create a system of local manorial courts. One such grant in which manorial rights are set out in full is that to the Duke of Albemarle, to whom land in Co. Wexford was granted in 1668. The lands are to be formed into, *inter alia*, the "manor of Limerick" on the following terms:[41]

"The Duke of Albemarle, &c. shall have leave to keep as many acres as he likes in these manors for the respective demesne lands thereof, and may aliene so much of the said lands as he, &c., thinks fit to others in fee

[36]March 4, 1637, *Cal. St. Papers Ir. 1633-1647*, p. 152.
[37]There reference to "leases" is odd, in conjunction with "English tenures" which implies free-hold grants. It may be that any kind of tenure by this time was thought of as a "lease", as in the case of "leases for lives".
[38]*Cal. St. Papers Ir. 1625-1632, No. 985*, p. 326, no date, follows grant dated April 23, 1628.
[39] *Irish Fiants of the Tudor Sovereigns*, vol. 2 1558-1586 No. 4745, July 15, 1585.
[40]Osborough, "The Failure to Enact an Irish Bill of Rights: a Gap in Irish Constitutional History" (1998) 33 *Irish Jurist (n.s.)* 392-416.
[41]February 8, 1668, *Cal. St. Papers Ir. 1669-1670*, p. 594-597.

simple, fee farm, in tail for lives or for any other estate. They shall hold in free and common socage *non obstante* the Statute *Quia Emptores Terrarum, &c.,* or by suit of **[597]** court or any other lawful services whatsoever. He may hold a court leet, view of frankpledge and court baron, and all that thereto appertains, within each of the said manors by such seneschals as he shall appoint; the court leets [*sic*] to be kept twice a year and the court barons [*sic*] as often as the Duke, &c., shall think fit; and the court barons shall hold plea of all debt or damage not exceeding £20. …he shall have a grant of all privileges, immunities, &c., usually attaching to the grant of such courts, with full power to nominate and appoint such officers as are usually belonging to such courts. …"

The duke was granted, *inter alia*, the right to hold three fairs a year and "may hold courts of Pye Powder [pie powder][42] on the said fair days, and the power to take reasonable toll and other rights usual in such cases." He also had the right to appoint a clerk of the market. Before the manorial and other courts were established the duke was given the right "to hold one or more Courts of Record in his manor before such persons as he appoints, with jurisdiction in personal actions up to £100, with all the privileges, &c. usually attaching to such courts." Several other grants, or instructions to make grants, confer full manorial rights although they are not set out in the transcription in the calendar, to avoid repetition. Examples of grants of manorial rights are as follows:

4 April 1600 [42 Eliz.], to Hubert Fox.[43]

6 December 1628, Sir Tirlogh O'Neill, "the Fues" in Armagh.[44]

8 June 1629, to John Burnett, "manor of Drumloghlen".[45]

6 September 1664, to Robert Maxwell, bishop of Kilmore, "manor of Farnham".[46]

28 September 1664, to Robert Kennedy, "manor of Mount Kennedy" in Co. Wicklow.[47]

24 October 1664, to Sir George Lane, "manor of Lanesborough".[48]

31 March 1665, to Colonel Richard Grace, to be named by him.[49]

---

[42]*i.e.,* a court merchant at a fair, from the French *pie poudre*, dusty feet, supposedly referring to the condition of the suitors to the court: see Baker, *Manual of Law French,* (2nd ed., Aldershot, 1990) p. 168 "pepoudrous".

[43]Cal. Pat. Close Rol. of Chancery Ir., vol. 2, No. 82 p. 575. The grant was "by the ancient service of four footmen at every general hosting, as Hubert and his ancestors were accustomed to furnish."

[44]*Cal. St. Papers Ir., No. 1247,* p. 412.

[45]*Cal. St. Papers Ir. 1625-1632,* No. 1395, p. 453.

[46]*Cal. St. Papers Ir. 1663-65,* p. 433-35.

[47]*Cal. St. Papers Ir. 1663-65,* p. 438.

[48]*Cal. St. Papers Ir. 1663-65,* p. 442-45.

[49]*Cal. St. Papers Ir. 1663-65,* p. 560-61.

25 July 1665, to Sir George Lane.[50]

14 April 1668 to Sir Milo Power, lands at the discretion of the lord lieutenant.[51]

29 May 1668, to Sir St. John Broderick.[52]

3 May 1669, lord chancellor (Michael Boyle, then archbishop of Dublin),[53] "manor of Blessington".[54]

25 August 1669, to Robert Leigh, "manor of Rosegarland", Co. Wexford.[55]

28 October 1669, to Francis Leigh, lands in Kildare and Co. Meath.[56]

28 October 1669, to James Barnwall, lands in Co. Dublin (Bremore and Drumnagh) and Co. Meath.[57]

26 April 1670, to Sir St. John Broderick, the "manor of Middleton".[58]

10 June 1670, Earl of Orrery, "manor of Charleville".[59]

1 November 1686, to Sir Arthur Gore, "manor of Castlegore".[60]

Several of the grants carry with them the right to hold fairs and markets and expressly mention courts of pie powder.[61] The grant of the manor of Blessington expressly mentions that the seneschals of the courts shall have "full jurisdiction to inquire into all felonies, trespasses, deceits, nuisances and other offences arising within the manor" and the seneschals of the court baron were to have "full authority to hold pleas … in all actions of debt, covenants, trespasses, accounts, contracts and detinues and all other maters whatsoever."[62]

Many of the grants had defects according to the law of the time, sometimes merely misnaming the lands, which usually meant making mistakes over the Irish names, but in many cases of a more substantive kind. Ffoliot Wingfield of Powerscourt was granted land in Wicklow "as of our castle of Wicklow in common socage" and land in Glencap "as of our castle of Dublin in common socage. He may create any tenures he likes on the lands…"[63] Grants to be held

---

[50]*Cal. St. Papers Ir. 1663-65*, p. 611.

[51]*Cal. St. Papers Ir. 1663-65*, p. 60.

[52]*Cal. St. Papers Ir. 1666-1669*, p. 607.

[53]Ball, *The Judges in Ireland, 1221-1921* (Blackrock, Co. Dublin: 1993) 1.351.

[54]*Cal. St. Papers Ir. 1669-1670*, p. 720.

[55]*Cal. St. Papers Ir. 1669-1670*, p. 779.

[56]*Cal. St. Papers Ir. 1669-1670*, p. 19-20.

[57]*Cal. St. Papers Ir. 1669-1670*, p. 20.

[58]*Cal. St. Papers Ir. 1669-1670*, p. 116-17.

[59]*Cal. St. Papers Ir. 1669-70*, p. 154.

[60]*Verschoyle v. Perkins* (1847) 13 Ir. Eq. R. 72.

[61]Viscount Massereene, *Cal. St. Papers Ir. 1663-65*, p. 599, where it is spelled "pipower"; Arthur Viscount Ranelagh, *Cal. St. Papers Ir. 1663-65*, p. 352-53; William Hamilton, *Cal. St. Papers Ir. 1666-1669*, p. 532; Lord Chancellor, *Cal. St. Papers Ir. 1669-1670*, p. 720; and n. 57.

[62]*Cal. St. Papers Ir. 1669-1670*, p. 721.

[63]*Cal. St. Papers Ir. 1663-65*, p. 62; and see Lane, *Cal. St. Papers Ir. 1663-65*, p. 611.

"of our castle of Dublin",[64] or a similar phrase, rather than of the king, were held to be invalid by the judges giving opinion in the *Case of Tenures upon Commission of Defective Titles.*[65] The Settlement of Ireland Act 1634, passed by the Irish parliament, attempted to remedy these defects not only by declaring existing grants to be valid but also, more extraordinarily, declaring any future grants to be valid despite whatever defects they might have,[66] but this does not seem to have been regarded as curing all defects of whatever kind, because further Settlement of Ireland Acts were passed to deal with specific defects in titles.[67] One of the Acts passed in 1634[68] validates in section 1 defects including: "…lack or omission of sufficient and special *non obstantes* of particular statutes, whereby the said letters patents or grants may be impeached…" Some grants in the tenure of knight service were defective because they failed to mention by what number of knight's fees the land was held. In such cases the Settlement of Ireland Act 1639[69] provided that they should be held by one knight's fee.

(c) Leases for lives renewable forever

The origin of leases for lives renewable forever is obscure, but there were probably two reasons. The earliest examples date from the 1660s.[70] At that time and up to the end of James II's rule not every tenant in chief had a *non*

[64] See, in addition to the example just mentioned: Viscount Massereene, *Cal. St. Papers Ir. 1663-65*, p. 599.

[65] Ireland, Judges, *The Case of Tenures Upon Commission of Defective Titles, Argued by All the Judges of Ireland, With Their Resolution, and the Reason of Their Resolution.* (Dublin: Printed with the 1720 edition of Wm. Molyneux, *The Case of Ireland's Being Bound by Acts of Parliament in England, Stated.*).

[66] Settlement of Ireland Act 1634 (10 Chas 1 sess. 1 c. 3, Ir): "Whereas … divers … subjects, having mannors, lands, tenements, and hereditaments in use, possession, remainder, or reversion, are notwithstanding subject to much question and exception, either because they can derive no title from the crown, or because the letters patents wherein any mannors, lands, tenements, and hereditaments, are mentioned to be passed or granted are insufficient in the law, defective, doubtful or not so plain, but that both for the present and in future times, much trouble loss and disquiet may arise and happen to the owners, or pretended owners of such mannors, [etc.] …Be it therefore enacted… that all and every person or persons, bodies politique and corporate, as well spiritual as temporal, shall and may have, hold, use, possess and enjoy all such mannors, [etc.] of what nature soever, according to the purport of the said letters patents…II. and be it further enacted … that the said patents, and every one of them to be contained, shall stand and be ratified, allowed approved and confirmed…"

[67] Settlement of Ireland Act 1634 (10 Chas. I sess. 3 c. 2, Ir.); Settlement of Ireland Act 1634 (10 Chas. I sess. 3 c. 3, IR.); Settlement of Ireland Act 1639 (15 Chas. I sess. 2 c. 6, Ir.); Settlement of Ireland Act 1665 (17 & 18 Chas. II c. 2, Ir.); Settlement of Ireland Act 1695 (7 Wm. III c. 3, Ir.).

[68] The Settlement of Ireland Act 1634 (10 Chas I sess. 3 c 2, Ir.).

[69] (15 Chas I sess. 2 c 6, Ir.) 2 St. Large p. 197.

[70] The lease in *Boyle v. Lysaght* (1787) 1 Ridg. P.C. 384 was dated 1660; and see Lyall *op. cit.*, above, n.5, p. 242.

obstante grant, and even then there may have been doubts about the validity of the licence. Furthermore, as to those who had such grants, the licence only permitted the grantee to subinfeudate. If grantee subinfeudated, no further subinfeudation by sub-grantee was authorised by the licence. Leases for lives renewable forever provided the next best thing to a subinfeudation in fee simple. It was almost as good, or even better, than a subinfeudation: a virtually perpetual freehold estate providing an income to the grantor in the form of rent but also fines, *i.e.* lump sums payable by the tenant to renew one of the measuring lives. It did not contravene the letter of *Quia Emptores* since the statute only applied to grants in fee simple. A "lease" for lives renewable forever was the grant of an estate pur autre vie with multiple, renewable cestuis que vie. This was a brilliant invention and solved the legal problem of the time. It was a device to avoid *Quia Emptores*.

After the end of James II's rule, the constitutional change brought about by the Bill of Rights in England meant that no further exercise of the dispensing power was possible there. Licences in mortmain continued to be given, but only under the authority of statute. In Ireland, although heads of an Irish Bill of Rights, including a declaration that the dispensing power was illegal, were presented to the lord deputy in 1695, it was never enacted.[71] Nevertheless, it may have been regarded as no longer constitutionally respectable. In 1697 the Duke of Ormonde obtained a private act of the English parliament[72] authorising him to grant leases for lives renewable forever, which would hardly have been necessary if he could have obtained a *non obstante* grant instead.

8. THE ENGLISH AND IRISH DOCTRINES

In England, there were no *non obstante* grants at least after the medieval period. The idea then gained ground that there was some necessary connection between tenure and reversion. If A had a fee simple and granted it to B, he or she could only do so by substitution. There was no reversion, so there could be no tenure. The English doctrine was evident by the time of Henry VIII. One of the tracts reproduced by Hargrave from that time says:[73]

> "... there is a maxime by the lawe, that a reservation of rente shall not stand in effect, unles he that maketh a reservation have a reversion in him, or else that[74] the lande may be holden of him by that rent reserved

---

[71] Osborough *op. cit.,* above, n.40, p. 416.
[72] 8 & 9 Wm. III c 5, 1697 (England).
[73] "Little Treatise Concerning Writs of Subpoena" in Hargrave, *Law Tracts* 335, cited in 2 Hud. & Br. 41.
[74] *i.e.* otherwise.

as it mighte have been before the saide statute of *Quia Emptores Terrarum*."

"Tenure" and "reversion" became synonymous terms in England. For example, section 44 of the Conveyancing Act 1881 speaks of a "rent incident to a reversion".[75] Rent was never incident to a reversion: it was a service of tenure. The notion gained such acceptance that it was applied to leaseholds as well. If A had a lease for 10 years and made a grant in favour of B for 10 years, that was necessarily a "substitution", or in the language of leaseholds, an assignment and not a sub-letting. If A wanted to sublet to B, so that A would become the landlord of B, then A would have to grant a term less than 10 years, even if only a day less.[76] Leaseholds were developed often by analogy to freehold tenure, and it was as if the analogy was to freeholds after *Quia Emptores*, and, naturally, to freeholds in England.

In Ireland, it was otherwise. There had always been exceptions to *Quia Emptores*, from the statute of 1293 to the *non obstante* grants from the Tudor period up to the reign of James II. Tenure without reversion was far from unknown in the case of freeholds. It is not known how early the distinct Irish rule as to leaseholds developed, but it may have been as early as the medieval period. The analogy would be to freeholds in Ireland at the time and the "no reversion, no tenure" mantra did not hold good here. There were other arguments in favour of the Irish view. *Quia Emptores* never applied to leaseholds. As to freeholds, it only applied to fees simple, not to lesser estates.[77] The statute did not in terms prohibit tenure without a reversion, only freehold subinfeudation in fee simple.

---

[75] Even Williams sometimes falls into this terminology: "Rent service, being incident to the reversion, passes by a grant of such reversion…", Williams, *Principles of the Law of Real Property*, (23rd ed., London, Toronto, 1920) p. 369.

[76] There is one curious apparent exception which still applies: concurrent leases. If B holds a lease from A for 10 years, then A grants another lease to C to take effect at the same time, the second lease is valid and C becomes the landlord of B and the tenant of A: Sheppard's *Touchstone* 275, 276; *Neale v. Mackenzie* (1836) 1 M. & W. 747, 150 E.R. 635, Megarry, Wade, and Harpum *op. cit.*, above, n.1, para. 14-104, and perhaps even if the second lease is the same length or even shorter than B's lease: *Birch v. Wright* (1786) 1 T.R. 378 at 384, 99 E.R. 1148 at 1152; *Re Moore & Hulm's Contract* [1912] 2 Ch. 105; Megarry, Wade, and Harpum *op. cit.*, above, n.1, para. 14-104 and n. 63. But concurrent leases, of the same or greater length than the first lease were void at common law unless validated by the attornment of B and the rule that the second lease could be of the same length or shorter came about, if at all, as a result of the statute of uses; *Birch v. Wright* (1786) 1 T.R. 378 at 384; 99 E.R. 1148 at 1152.

[77] Torrens J. in the Irish Exchequer Chamber in *Pluck v. Digges* (1828) 2 Hud. & Br. 19 at pp. 22-23: "At common law, before the statute of *Quia Emptores*, where a tenant in fee granted in fee to hold of himself, he had no reversion; yet there was tenure; and the statute itself proves this, for if there was no tenure, in that case, the statute would have been unnecessary, since it was introduced to destroy subinfeudation, and to preserve to the chief lords of the fee the escheats and other incidents belonging to the tenure of their fees. That statute has only operated upon estates in fee simple; 2 Co. Inst. 504; and does not apply to the case now before us."

9. SUB-GRANTS OF LEASES FOR LIVES

One complication needs to be mentioned. The issue in *Pluck v. Digges*[78] did not arise in relation to terms of years, but in relation to leases for lives renewable forever and the issue was whether a grant for the same renewable lives could take effect as a sub-grant, creating tenure, or whether it was necessarily an outright assignment. To reduce that to a simpler question, on the answer to which the issue as to leases for lives must surely depend: if A holds an estate pur autre vie for the life of X, can A make a grant of the land to B for the same life, X, the grant taking effect as a sub-grant creating tenure between A and B, *i.e.* tenure without reversion, but on the grant of an estate less than a fee simple? In the House of Lords in *Pluck v. Digges* it was recognised that there was no direct authority on the point.[79] The judgment notes that *Jenison v. Lord Lexington*[80] decided the somewhat obvious point that a tenant *pur autre vie* who granted his whole estate to another did not retain a reversion, but the grantor nevertheless reserved a rent and it was also held, which is significant, that it passed to his heirs. The case does not state that the rent was created by rentcharge and so it would seem to be an authority for the view that freehold tenure could exist in an estate *pur autre vie* on the grant of the whole term. There seems to be no pre-Union Irish authority on the point, or no surviving one, but, to be consistent, one would expect that Irish courts would have held that tenure could be created in such cases. The point was raised, but not decided, in the case of *Walker v. Williamson*,[81] but was regarded by the Bar at the time as having settled the issue. It seems that the Irish courts by the end of the century had come to regard the landlord and tenant relationship, of whatever sort, as based upon contract rather than on tenure and so section 3 of Deasy's Act 1860 on that view was not enacting anything new in Ireland.

  Hogan v. Fitzgerald,[82] decided in 1825, after the Union but before the British House of Lords decision in *Pluck*, concerned a lease for the same three lives as that held by the grantor. The twelve common law judges, Burton J. dissenting, held that a reversion was not necessary for the plaintiff to maintain ejectment under the statute 56 Geo. III c. 88. The Court of King's Bench had come to the same conclusion, unanimously, in *Jack d. Morrison v. Little*.[83] Some Irish cases[84] after *Pluck v. Digges*, and before Deasy's Act 1860, held

---

[78](1828) 2 Hud. & Br. 1, (1831) 5 Bli. N.S. 31 at 65, 5 E.R. 219 at 236.
[79](1831) 5 Bli. N.S. 31 at 65.
[80](1719) 1 P. Wms. 555; 2 Eq. Cas. Ab. 430 pl. 10; 24 E.R. 515, M.R.
[81](1794) Ir. T. Rep. 271.
[82](1825) 1 Hud. & Br. 77, noted.
[83]Hudson, *Statute Law of Landlord and Tenant*, 489 (1817) n. 2; *Pluck v. Digges* (1831) 5 Bli. N.S. 59, 5 E.R. 219 at 233, per Lord Plunket C.J.
[84]*Porter v. French* (1847) 9 Ir. C.L.R. 519; *Roberts v. Mayne* (1859) 8 Ir. Ch. R. 523; *Tobin v. Redmond* (1861) 11 Ir. Ch. R. 445.

that a grant of a lease for lives renewable forever for the same lives was necessarily an outright assignment and created no tenure, but they were bound by the
British House of Lords decision in *Pluck v. Digges*[85] which had overruled the
Irish Court of Exchequer Chamber. However, other Irish cases confined *Pluck*
to the issues directly raised in it. In *Lessee of Walsh v. Feely*[86] the Court of
Exchequer, following *Lessee of Coyne v. Smith,*[87] confined *Pluck* to the remedy of distress at common law and allowed an action in ejectment despite the
absence of a reversion. The case concerned a holder of an estate *pur autre vie*
who demised it for the life of the same *cestui que vie*, reserving a rent. Ferguson[88]
commented:

> "The Court of Exchequer in Ireland, however, still contend for a different
> construction of the Statute of *Quia Emptores,* holding, that when enact-
> ing that there should be no tenure without a reversion, it applied only to
> alienations in fee, and that a demise for the same term as the lessor him-
> self has, though it may operate as an assignment, in respect of the head
> landlord... as between the parties themselves, creates the relation of land-
> lord and tenant, and operates as a lease, and re-entry being for a condi-
> tion broken requires no reversion; that even the very enactment of the
> Statute demonstrates, that at common law no reversion was necessary to
> constitute tenure or rent service, (as Littleton expressly says[89]), and the
> case of lessee for life or years alienating now, is as that of tenant in fee
> before the Statute, not being regulated or affected by it, but expressly
> exempted, and so strongly did the court entertain this opinion, that, though
> coerced by the decision of the House of Lords, in the case of a *replevin,*
> they refused to recognise its authority any further, or to extend its princi-
> ple to ejectments."

In *Brady v. Fitzgerald*[90] the Chancery held that a remedy was available in
equity even if in common law one existed but was difficult to obtain. It was
argued that "since *Quia Emptores* neither relation of landlord and tenant, nor
any remedy incident to it" could arise out of the grant, "that ejectment would
not now lie on the condition of re-entry; and neither action of debt nor covenant could be maintained."[91] Nevertheless the Lord Chancellor held that: "The
operation in law of the deed is an assignment, and of course there is no rever-

[85](1828) 2 Hud. & Br. 1, (1832) 5 Bli. N.S. 31, 5 ER 219, 2 Dow. & Cl. 180, 6 E.R. 695.
[86](1835) 1 Jones 413.
[87](1826) Batty 90, n.
[88]W.D. Ferguson, *A Treatise on the Practice of the Queen's Bench, Common Pleas, and Exchequer Of Pleas, in Ireland, in Personal Actions and Ejectments.* 2 vols. (Dublin, 1841), 1.105.
[89]Littleton, *Tenures* 216.
[90](1848) 12 Ir. Eq. R. 273.
[91]*ibid.* at 275.

sion, but still it operates in some sense as a lease. . . ." It operated as a lease between the parties on the familiar ground that a tenant is estopped from denying the landlord's title. This was in fact the same ground on which Lord Plunket C.J. had based his judgment in the Irish Exchequer Chamber in *Pluck v. Digges*[92] and which had been overruled by the British House of Lords. The estoppel argument, though sufficient to dispose of the cases mentioned, created the awkwardness alluded to by Ferguson, that the grant was only a sub-lease as between the parties, but as far as the head landlord was concerned it was an assignment. That problem was only resolved by Deasy's Act 1860.

---

[92](1831) 5 Bli. N.S. 31 at 73, 5 E.R. 219 at 241.

PRAYERS UNANSWERED: HOW CONTRACT LAW VIEWS RELIGION

1. INTRODUCTION

A student once posed the following philosophical question on the way out of a particularly onerous (though, of course, perfectly fair) contract exam – "Why is it that in contract law, your prayers are never answered?" Perhaps in part due to the haunted look on the student's face, this question has troubled my conscience ever since. For anyone with even a lapsed knowledge of contract law will be familiar with such rules as the one which holds that prayers do not amount to sufficient consideration or the one to the effect that religious arrangements generally do not involve an intention to create legal relations. But why should this be so? Why is it that the law of contract holds such a sceptical view of religion, a subject that plays such a large role in so many peoples everyday lives and transactions? This can be contrasted with the law of equity which has long recognised religious trusts and where Cross J. once proclaimed that "As between different religions the law stands neutral, but it assumes that any religion is better than none."[1] The purpose of this article is to attempt to answer the student's question. It will examine the role of religion in three areas of contract law; consideration, intention to create legal relations and undue influence. The approach of contract law to the wider spirit world will also be addressed. Finally the issues of Faustian pacts and damages will be considered.

2. CONSIDERATION[2]

The traditional rule is that in order to be enforceable, a promise must be either contained in a deed under seal, or made in exchange for some sufficient consideration.[3] Consideration is the mechanism that the common law uses to dis-

---

[1] *Neville Estates Ltd v. Madden* [1962] Ch. 832 at 853.
[2] See generally Atiyah, "Consideration: A Restatement" in *Essays on Contract* (Oxford, 1986) at p.185.
[3] However it is now apparent that contract is only one way in which a promise may be upheld by the courts. Equity may intervene to enforce a promise that is not backed up by consideration through principles such as estoppel or, if the promise was made by a public body, legitimate

tinguish promises that are to be enforced from promises which are not to be enforced. If there is no consideration the promise will be unenforceable at law.[4] Sir Frances Pollock defined consideration as:

> "An act or forbearance of the one party, or the promise thereof, is the price for which the promise of the other is bought, and the promise thus given for value is enforceable."[5]

The question arises as to whether prayers can ever amount to consideration for a contract. The key to answering this question lies in the distinction the law draws between sufficiency and adequacy of consideration. It is a basic principle of contract law that while consideration must be sufficient, it need not be adequate.[6] Adequacy refers to the situation where the price paid by a person is out of proportion to what he obtains in return. Thus, if I pay £1 for a brand new canary yellow Mercedes it can be said that I have not paid an adequate consideration. This is not something that that can affect the validity of the consideration. If someone wants to sell a Mercedes at a gross undervalue that is their business not the court's. In *Kennedy v. Kennedy*[7] Ellis J. stated: "once there is consideration its adequacy in this sort of case is irrelevant to its validity and enforceability if the agreement itself has been proved."[8]

The requirement that consideration be sufficient means that it must be something that is capable of being recognised as consideration by the courts. Another way of stating this is that the consideration must be something of value in the eyes of the law.[9] Whilst it is easy to survey the cases that have held something to be insufficient consideration, it is less easy to draw any general principles from them. Burrows, speaking in the context of New Zealand contract

---

expectation. It is possible to view the development of such remedies as a response to the perceived inadequacies of consideration. See Furmston and Others, *The Law of Contract* (London, 1999) para 2.16.

[4] For example in *Aga Khan v. Firestone and Firestone* [1992] I.L.R.M. 31 at 48 Morris J. found that a promise of first refusal on the sale of a property was unenforceable for want of consideration:

> "... it was a voluntary document given by Mr Firestone in the hope of cementing business relationships. Nowhere in the evidence can I find any suggestion of it forming part of the overall deal. . . . Accordingly it follows that the agreement being a voluntary agreement is unenforceable."

A recent example of a promise which was held to be unenforceable in the absence of consideration is *Allied Irish Banks v. Fagan* unreported, High Court, November 10, 1995.

[5] Winfield (ed.), *Pollock's Principles of Contracts* (13th ed., London, 1950) at p.133.

[6] Whilst the adequacy of the consideration is not relevant to whether it is a valid consideration, its adequacy may be relevant to other issues. For example if an allegation is made that the contract was the result of fraud or was an improvident or unconscionable bargain, then obviously the adequacy of the consideration will become a central issue.

[7] Unreported, High Court, January 12, 1984.

[8] *ibid.,* at p.38.

[9] Furmston and Others, *op. cit.*, above, n.3, para 2.42.

law, also accurately summarises the position in this jurisdiction when he suggests:

> "It is, indeed, not without significance that these controversies are, for the most part, carried on outside the courts. The judges have been content to deny the name of consideration to certain acts or promises without attempting to generalise the grounds of their prohibition; and it may well be that the process of judicial thought is purely empirical and does not lend itself to *ex post facto* rationalisation."[10]

Prayers as consideration

The leading case on prayers as consideration is *O'Neill v. Murphy*[11] where it was alleged that a builder had done certain work in return for prayers. The builder had written a letter to one Father Murphy in which he stated "Now I think I will be well paid for anything I did if you can arrange with the Mother General to have daily prayers offered up for myself and family together with Mrs O'Neill and my brother J.K." Andrews L.J. held that the builder had not received any consideration in exchange for his promise to waive his fee:

> "Now, whilst expressly disclaiming any opinion which might be construed as in the slightest degree derogatory of the real value and efficacy of prayer, I can only say that no case cited to us or which I have found, can properly be relied upon as an authority for the proposition that a mere promise by one person to say prayers or to cause prayers to be said for another amounts in law to a good and valuable consideration for a contract not under seal."[12]

It should be noted that *O'Neill* is a Northern Irish case and would not necessarily be followed in this jurisdiction. It is not clear why prayers should not be recognised as sufficient consideration. If the builder had agreed to take one penny for the work that would have been regarded as sufficient consideration. Yet a promise of daily prayers for him and his family was not regarded as sufficient. Andrews L.J. gives no reason for his decision other than the bald assertion that he could find no authority to support such a proposition. But there seems to be no good reason why the promise in the case was not enforceable. The builder clearly placed a high value on the prayers. There was no uncertainty as to the nature or subject of the prayers, they were to be said daily and were for the builder and his family together with Mrs O'Neill and his

---

[10]Burrows, Finn & Todd *Law of Contract in New Zealand* (Wellington: Butterworths, 1997) 101.
[11][1936] N.I. 16.
[12]*ibid.* at 31.

brother J.K. There was no mention of how long the prayers were to continue to be said for, but a term of reasonable time could easily have been implied in by the court on the basis of the officious bystander test. The Mother General would no doubt have regarded the saying of the prayers as a serious obligation and one of value. She was under no pre-existing duty to pray for the said persons and by promising to ensure that such prayers were said on a daily basis she could be said to have undertaken an onerous obligation.

Even if one were to take the view that prayers are worthless it is well-established in contract law that worthless consideration will not be regarded as insufficient merely because it is worthless. For example, in *Haigh v. Brooks*[13] the defendant received, as per his request, a worthless piece of paper in return for a promise made by him to pay £10,000. It was held to be sufficient consideration. It is bizarre that a worthless piece of paper may be regarded as sufficient consideration, but not an onerous and clear undertaking to offer prayers for certain persons. Perhaps the real explanation for the decision in *O'Neill* lies in the fact that the builder was able to set his promise aside on the basis of undue influence which he successfully claimed had been exerted on him by his spiritual adviser. This may have influenced the Court against accepting prayers as sufficient consideration and it is possible to speculate that if no issue of undue influence had arisen in the case the Court might have taken a different view of the promise of prayers. It is submitted that were the issue to arise again before our courts, it deserves more careful analysis than it was given in *O'Neill*.

Different considerations apply if the prayers are required to produce some material result. This is because the efficacy of prayer cannot be proved in court. Authority for this proposition is to be found in the decision of the Supreme Court of New York in *Pando v. Fernandez*.[14] The plaintiff, who was a deeply religious minor, sought a share of the defendant's lottery win of $2.8 million. He claimed that he had purchased the winning one dollar ticket with the defendant's money pursuant to her promise that she would share the prize money equally with him if he prayed to "Saint Eleggua"[15] to cause the lottery numbers he selected for her to win. The Supreme Court of New York held that the plaintiff could not prove compliance with the contract as he could not prove that his prayers were efficacious and that the saint caused the numbers to win. The Court emphasised that the contract in question was not that the numbers

---

[13](1839) 10 Ad. & E. 309, 113 E.R. 119.

[14](1984) 127 Misc. (2d) 224; 485 N.Y.S. (2d) 162.

[15]The Court was unable to ascertain the identity of "Saint Eleggua". The closest it could come was Saint Eligius (immortalised on television as St. Elsewhere), the patron saint of goldsmiths, who before his canonisation served under French kings in the Seventh Century as master of the mint, and who showered his riches on the poor who turned to him in overwhelming numbers. He possessed the gifts of miracles and prophecy and is reputed to have broken open the chains of prisoners by his prayers. As the court pointed out *ibid.* at 230 "No wonder defendant sought to invoke his aid as the means to overwhelming riches."

would win but that the saint would make the numbers win.[16] Greenfield J. explained the difficulties of proof in an elegant passage worth quoting in full:

"How can we really know what happened? Is a court to engage in the epistemological inquiry as to the acquisition of knowledge and belief through proof or through faith? Faith is the antithesis of proof. It is a belief which is firmly held even though demonstrable proof may be lacking. It is instinctive, spiritual, and profound, arrived at not through a coldly logical appraisal of the facts but, in Wordsworth's phrase, by 'a passionate intuition'.

'[Faith] is the substance of things hoped for, the evidence of things not seen.' (Paul, Epistle to Hebrews: xi, 1.) How, then, in a court of law, set up to require tangible proof, in a mundane setting, can a litigant establish that his faith and his prayers brought about a miracle? Perhaps they did, but there is no way to prove that in a modern courtroom.

In ages past, controversies were not determined by marshalling an array of rational probative proof. Under Roman law, there was acceptance of divine testimonies, omens, auguries or oracles and the power of dreams. In Medieval law the demonstration of miracles in the courtroom and a show of divine intervention were grist for the judicial mill, and trial by combat and trial by ordeal constituted proof of God's will. But in those days, the function of the secular and the ecclesiastical courts was not sharply separated, and the distinction was not drawn between the *ius soli*, the law of earth, and *ius poli,* the law of heaven. Up to the 18th Century, testimony of the power of spells was received in cases where a defendant was accused of witchcraft – the charge that invocation of the

---

[16]It is of interest to note that the defendant's attempt to rely on the Statute of Frauds failed. The Court held that the contract was not one to be performed outside of one year since the alleged obligation of the defendant to share the prize with the plaintiff became fixed when the winning numbers were drawn. Greenfield J. held at 226 that:

"In this case ... the contract could be performed well within one year. Defendant was to furnish the funds with which to purchase the ticket. Plaintiff had to purchase the ticket, select the numbers, return it to defendant, and pray. The winning numbers were scheduled to be drawn, and were drawn, within days, and at that time the obligations of the parties became fixed. The defendant would then have to notify a third party, the State Lottery Division, that all future payments were to be divided equally between herself and the plaintiff, a task which she could perform within days. At that point the obligations of each side would have been performed.

Greenfield J. held , at 227 that the clock stopped running once the contractual obligation became fixed :

"The actual computation of the amount due, even if it were to take more than a year, was of no significance, since this was a mere ministerial act. The controlling criterion is the time at which the obligation becomes, or could become fixed. If all the contingencies can occur, and all conditions can be performed within the one-year period, with nothing remaining to be done thereafter except the act of payment, there is no violation of the Statute of Frauds."

spirits caused temporal disasters. The question of the efficacy of prayer is just the converse. Are we to accept testimony or argument that invoking the power of Heaven rather than of the nether world, followed by a beneficial rather than a sinister result should result in a court decision? In this more workaday and pragmatic era, shaped by tragic experience, the chasm between the temporal and the spiritual world has become unbridgeable. Theology is to be protected against the law, just as the law is to be protected from theology." (footnotes omitted)[17]

Greenfield J. held that it was incumbent on the plaintiff to prove that under the agreement as he alleged it, every condition which had to occur to entitle him to payment did occur, and thereupon defendant's obligation came into being. The condition was not that the numbers chosen would win, but that the saint was to make the numbers win. Establishing that this occurred was simply not susceptible to forensic proof. It called for matters which transcend proof – the existence of saints, the power of prayer, and divine intervention in temporal affairs. But judges and jurors must decide issues based on what they have seen and heard, not on what faith leads them to believe. Greenfield J. concluded that causation could never be proved in the present case:

"If a rainmaker exacts a promise from a group of farmers to be paid if he makes it rain, he can collect if the trier of facts finds he seeded supercooled clouds with silver iodide and an expert testifies that was the cause of the rain. On the other hand, if the rainmaker performs chants and dances and incantations and it rains within 24 hours, he cannot demonstrate by accepted judicial modes of proof that his acts caused the desired event. The distinction is that in the first example the claimant is shown to have caused something; in the second we do not know if he has.

The distinction must always be made between evidence based on knowledge and conclusions based on belief. This court has no desire to denigrate the power of prayer, matters of spirit, or the workings of the hand of God, but such matters, not susceptible of rational courtroom proof, are for theology and not jurisprudence. Concededly, 'there are more things in heaven and in earth ... than are dream't of in [our] philosophy'."[18]

The two cases can be distinguished. In *Pando* the prayers were required to produce a lottery win. By contrast, in *O'Neill* no particular result was requested from the prayers. No doubt the builder hoped that the prayers said by the Mother General would confer some benefit on his family if not in this life then in the next, but the conferring of such benefit was not an express part of the transac-

[17] *ibid.* at 230–231.
[18] *ibid.* at 231-232.

tion. Thus, if the builder and his family had experienced a miserable time after the prayers commenced the builder would not be entitled to renege on the deal. By contrast in *Pando* unless the defendant's lottery ticket won as a result of the prayers, the contract had not been performed. Thus there is nothing in the judgment in *Pando* which would prevent prayers from being sufficient consideration in an *O'Neill*-type scenario.

The decision in *O'Neill* reveals that there is sometimes little logic behind the doctrine of consideration and it is tempting to agree with the conclusion that:

> "... a finding of 'consideration' or 'no consideration' is an *ex post facto* rationalisation of an a priori decision based on considerations of the perceived morality, justice or commercial convenience of a particular outcome. Thus, if a court wishes to enforce a promise it must find that it was given for good consideration, whilst if it wishes to hold a promise unenforceable it may justify its decision by finding that there was no consideration for it, and there is sufficient flexibility in the 'doctrine' to allow it to do so."[19]

3. INTENTION TO CREATE LEGAL RELATIONS

The doctrine of consideration is used to filter out those promises that are contractual in nature from those that are unenforceable. However, even if consideration is present, there are certain promises that will not be given contractual effect on the basis that there was no intention to create legal relations.[20] In the words of Sir William Scott, contracts "must not be the sports of an idle hour, mere matters of pleasantry and badinage, never intended by the parties to have any serious effect whatever."[21] The principle is explained in the following passage by Scrutton J. which has been followed by the Irish Supreme Court:

> "... it is quite possible for the parties to come to an agreement by accepting a proposal with the result that the agreement concluded does not give rise to legal relations. The reason of this is that the parties do not intend

---

[19]Furmston and Others, *op. cit.*, above n.3, para. 2.26. See also Atiyah who has complained that from being merely a reason for the enforcement of a promise consideration has come to be regarded as "a technical requirement of the law which has little to do with the justice or desirability of enforcing a promise, or recognising obligations." Atiyah "Consideration: A Restatement" in *Essays on Contract* (Oxford, 1986) at p.135.

[20]See generally Hepple *"Intention to Create Legal Relations"* (1970) 28 *C.L.J.* 122; Hedley *"Keeping Contract in its Place: Balfour v. Balfour and the Enforceability of Informal Agreements"* (1985) 5 *O.J.L.S.* 391.

[21]*Dalrymple v. Dalrymple* (1811) 2 Hag. Con. 54 at 105; 161 E.R. 665 at 683.

that their agreement shall give rise to legal relations. This intention may be implied from the subject matter of the agreement, but it may also be expressed by the parties. In social and family relations such an intention is readily implied, while in business matters the opposite result would ordinarily follow."[22]

The courts have tended to view religious arrangements as not being intended to create legal relations. Spiritual matters are not regarded as being subject to the law of contract. An example from Ontario will illustrate this point. In *Zecevic v. The Russian Orthodox Christ the Saviour Cathedral*[23] a priest and his church were sued after failing to perform a funeral service. The plaintiff and his wife had emigrated to Canada from Yugoslavia where they had been baptised in the Serbian Orthodox Church. When his wife died the plaintiff arranged for a memorial service and a funeral service to be held in the local Russian Orthodox Church in Montreal. The local Serbian Orthodox priest viewed this as an infringement of his territory and made it clear to Father Nicholas, the Russian priest, that the plaintiff and his deceased wife were "his people." In fact the plaintiff had only ever attended the Serbian Church for funerals although he had occasionally dropped into the Serbian Church Community Hall for unspecified entertainment. It appeared that a minor turf war had recently occurred between the neighbouring Serbian and Russian Churches. Upon discovering that he had unwillingly encroached upon Serb territory, Father Nicholas prudently decided to cancel the funeral service. Unfortunately he made this announcement to the plaintiff just before the commencement of the memorial service thereby causing some confusion and disruption (the extent of which was disputed by the parties). Although the memorial service proceeded, the funeral mass which had been due to take place the next day was cancelled. The plaintiff alleged that the trauma of this incident had caused him to suffer from sleep loss and confusion.

In the Ontario High Court Gray J. considered whether an agreement to perform a funeral service could be the subject of a contract. He concluded that it could not:

"In my view the Panihida prayer service or the funeral involve spiritual matters, not the subject of the law of contract. There was no intention on the part of Father Nicholas to enter into any legal relationship and the same can probably be said of the plaintiff as of [the date of the memorial service]."[24]

---

[22] *Rose and Frank v. Crompton* [1943] 2 K.B. 261 at 288, cited by O'Dalaigh C.J. in *Rogers v. Smith* unreported, Supreme Court, July 16, 1970.
[23] Unreported, Ontario High Court, August 10, 1988.
[24] *ibid.* at p.31.

Gray J. proceeded to consider whether there had been any consideration given in exchange for the promise to hold the service. The plaintiff asserted that he had intended to pay Father Nicholas $150 and to pay $150 to the Russian Church itself at a later time. The evidence of the priest was that it was traditional and expected that a funeral would result in a payment to him or the church. There were no set fees and in his experience a funeral payment could range from $800 to nil dollars. In the present case the subject of money never came up. Gray J. could find no consideration in this type of arrangement:

> "There was no legal consideration involved. There was no payment prom-
> ised or made, nor was there any communication from the plaintiff of any
> intention to compensate. The payment, if one had been made, would have
> been gratuitous. A subsequent promise to pay out of moral gratitude does
> not found consideration ... Similarly, 'one cannot imply a promise to pay
> for services if the supplier did not intend to charge or be remunerated for
> the services'..." (footnotes omitted).[25]

There is some merit in the view that no legal relations were intended and it may have been true on the facts of the case, but it cannot be a universal principle. No doubt devout members of a church may well believe that a marriage or a funeral service is a purely spiritual affair far removed from the black letter rules of contract law. But many people, for whom a marriage or a funeral may be their only visit to their local Church, take a more business-like view of the arrangements. If a fee and the nature of the service are clearly agreed in advance, is there any reason why a contractual remedy should not lie if the contract is not performed or is incompletely or inadequately performed?

Difficulties also arise in assigning an intention to create contractual relations to charitable endeavours undertaken by religious groups. In *Biddle v. Bentley*[26] an agreement under which members of a church would cut scrub in return for donations to a charity by the defendant was held never to have been intended to have contractual status. Thomson J. in the Auckland Compensation Court held that:

> "The circumstance which to me seems particularly relevant in the present
> case is that the aim and object of the persons who worked on the fence
> line was to make a donation of their time and labour to Corso. That was
> the real transaction and I do not think that they would have thought of
> entering into a contract with anyone. Although it may not be important to
> the existence of a contract between A and B that moneys payable by A
> are to go not to B but to C, it does make a difference to the substance of

---

[25] *Zecevic v. The Russian Orthodox Christ the Saviour Cathedral*, above, n.23 at p.32.
[26] [1967] N.Z.L.R. 1047.

the transaction that C happens to be a charity and that no money at all is to pass except to the charity."[27]

Attempting to bring the transaction into the area of contract law would cause a number of difficulties. There was no fixed group of people engaged in the work. It was fanciful to suppose that the Church group formed itself into a partnership for the single adventure of cutting the scrub. There was simply a call for volunteers. Some volunteers would turn up every day, others might just turn up for one day or a part of a day. As there was no fixed group to whom the offer was made or by whom it might be accepted one would therefore have to look for a series of individual contracts resulting from the acceptance of the offer made by the defendant by the people who turned up from time to time. On the facts of the case, this had not been contemplated by anyone and Thomson J. was "reasonably confident that the attitude of each worker was that he was contributing a certain amount of labour as a charitable gift and so far as he was concerned that was the end of the matter."[28]

It is not clear why any of these reasons should pose an insurmountable bar to contractual relations. The context of the decision was that one of the volunteers had been injured whilst cutting gorse and sought to recover damages from the defendant and it may be that the Court was concerned about opening up a wide field for potential claimants.

The imposition of a separate requirement of intention to create legal relations over and above those of offer, acceptance and consideration has been criticised. For example one leading English text states that:

> "... [it] is unnecessary to impose a separate requirement of 'intention to create legal relations' over and above those of offer, acceptance and consideration. A proposal cannot properly be regarded as an offer unless it indicates an intention to undertake a legal obligation if its terms are accepted and the requested consideration is furnished by the offeree. Thus a proposal in which the maker indicates, expressly or impliedly, that he does not intend to undertake a legal obligation cannot properly be regarded as an offer. Similarly, if an offer is made and the offeree responds agreeing to the terms of the offer but indicating that he does not intend to create a legal relationship, the offeree's response cannot properly be regarded as an acceptance of the offer ... If the parties agree but neither intends a legal relationship there is neither offer nor acceptance. If this view is accepted, 'intention to create legal relations' is not a separate, additional requirement, but an aspect of the rules relating to offer, acceptance and consideration."[29]

---

[27] *ibid.* at 1048.
[28] *ibid.* at 1049.
[29] Furmston & Others, *op. cit.*, above n.3, para 2.165.

While there is some merit in this view, the existence of a separate requirement of intention to create legal relations is probably too firmly established in Irish law to be challenged. Nevertheless, when a religious transaction is made in circumstances where it cannot be accused of being too vague, incomplete or ambiguous it should be open to a court to conclude in an appropriate case that there was an intention to create legal relations.

4. Undue Influence

The equitable doctrine of undue influence is intended to provide relief to persons who enter into transactions in circumstances where there are potential or actual grounds for believing that improper pressure has been brought to bear on one of the contracting parties. In respect of certain relationships, the relationship itself raises the presumption (*e.g.* trustee/agent, doctor/patient, solicitor/client, parent/child, guardian/ward). In such cases the party in whom trust and confidence is placed will have to show that the transaction was fair and freely assented to. One of the relationships that automatically raises the presumption of undue influence is that of religious association/devotee. The definition of a religious relationship is a wide one and includes spiritual mediums. The Supreme Court of California has offered the following guidance as to the scope of the concept:

> "The rule applies with peculiar force to the relationship of one and his priest, confessor, clergyman, or spiritual adviser, and certainly with no less force to the relation between one who is a firm believer in, not to say monomaniac upon, the subject of spiritualism, and the medium in whom he has confidence, and upon whom he habitually relies."[30]

The presumption arises even if the religious minister does not receive the gift himself. Authority for this is to be found in *Good v. Zook*[31] where the Supreme Court of Iowa stated:

> "The relation of clergyman and parishioner, as the books term it, or,

---

[30] *Conor v. Stanley* (1887) 72 Cal. 556; 14 P. 306. See also *Gilmore v. Lee* (1908) 237 Ill. 402 where the Supreme Court of Illinois stated at 411 that: "It is a universal rule, founded upon public policy, that where a confidential relation exists, if a gift is made to the person in whom the confidence is reposed by reason of the relation it is prima facie void. The law will presume, from the mere existence of the relation, that the gift was obtained by undue influence or improper means, and the burden of proof rests upon the donee to show that it was the free and voluntary act of the donor." On the facts of the case a gift by a parishioner to a priest was set aside.

[31] (1901) 116 Iowa 582; 88 N.W. 376.

perhaps more properly, of spiritual adviser and the subject of his ministrations, is of a confidential nature, and raises a presumption of undue influence on the part of the former in the case of a contract between them. Or, stating it differently, where such spiritual adviser obtains a devise or grant or gift from a member of his flock, the burden is upon him to show the entire good faith of the transaction. It makes no difference in the rule that the minister received no personal benefit from the transaction. The principle cannot be evaded by giving interests to third persons instead of reserving them to the one who exercises the undue influence, or who is presumed to do so."[32]

A number of cases have considered the religious relationship and they reveal that it is viewed more suspiciously by the courts than almost any other relationship. One of the earliest cases is *Whyte v. Meade*.[33] The plaintiff, then aged 18, entered into Ranelagh Convent as a lodger. Her friends were averse to her becoming a nun and thus it was envisaged that if the plaintiff decided at a later date to take holy orders she could do so after being allowed to consult with her friends. Two years later the defendants, who took what might be described as a vigorous approach to recruitment, prevailed on the plaintiff to take holy orders while actively preventing her from seeking guidance from her brother-in-law. Two years after that, the Order, also managed to get the plaintiff to transfer £1,100 to the Order. Later that same year, when the plaintiff was very ill, the Order took the opportunity to induce her to make over her real property. The Order's attorney prepared the deed of transfer but the plaintiff did not have the assistance of any professional friend. Some nine years later the plaintiff quitted the convent.

In the Equity Exchequer Pennefather B. had no hesitation in setting the transfer aside. He stated:

> "Can it seriously be said that a transaction like this ought to stand? that a deed executed by a person placed at a convent like this person – placed in a situation where that undue influence is more likely to be exercised than in any other, which Courts of Equity should interfere to prevent; and shall it not be presumed, beyond almost a doubt so strong as not to be rebutted, that the documents in question were executed by the plaintiff under undue influence."[34]

Pennefather B. was less than impressed with the conduct of the Order's attorney in the whole affair and did not mince his words:

---

[32] (1901) 116 Iowa 582 at 587.
[33] (1840) 2 Ir. Eq. R. 420.
[34] *ibid.* at 422.

"... the deed was got up by Mr Dolan, the professional friend of the convent, without the presence of any professional friend, or of any friend at all, of the infant; and this gentleman takes upon himself to swear that these ladies are so incapable of erring, that all this young woman has done, was without the slightest influence having been exercised over her – the spontaneous effusion of her own mind! When we find him thus volunteering to swear what the Searcher of Hearts alone could tell, is it not plain that he gave his heart and mind, not to the unfortunate victim upon whom he was about to practice as far as he was able, but to the defendants in this cause?"[35]

Pennefather B. then turned his displeasure on the Order who in his opinion "ought not to be engaged in secular pursuits, but ought to have been devoted to the instruction of the plaintiff's mind."[36] Perhaps Pennefather B. was concerned that his strident attack on the defendants might create too narrow a precedent for he subsequently added an addendum to his judgment in which he emphasised that the Court "did not intend to lay down any general rule; but that the particular circumstances of this case brought it within that class of cases which decide that transactions ought not to stand. There are cases in which dealings between guardian and ward are upheld, but it lies upon the party seeking to uphold them to prove that such transactions have been *bona fide*."[37] Despite this rider, *Whyte* laid the seeds of the suspicion of religious relationships which later cases would reap.

It was quickly established that it is not necessary to show that the religious order practised coercion. It is enough to show that the religious devotee was unable freely to consent to the transaction because he or she was incapable of exercising independent judgment. The case of *Allcard v. Skinner*[38] shows that even if a court does not impute improper motive or unconscionable behaviour to the party taking under the contract or transfer, the transaction will be set aside unless it can be shown to be fair and freely consented to. The plaintiff was a woman of 27. She was introduced by her spiritual adviser to the defendant, a lady superior of a Protestant enclosed sisterhood called "The Sisters of the Poor". This sisterhood was a voluntary association of ladies who resided together in Finsbury. The spiritual adviser was one of the founders of the sisterhood. After some years, the plaintiff entered the sisterhood and in furtherance of her vows gave property to it which was used for charitable purposes. Under the rules of the sisterhood, obedience to the defendant was a central tenant. After eight years, the plaintiff left the sisterhood. Some six years later, she

---

[35](1840) 2 Ir. Eq. R. 420 at 423.
[36]*ibid.*
[37]*ibid.*
[38](1887) 36 Ch. D. 145.

sought the return of that portion of her donated property that was unspent on the date of her departure from the sisterhood. While no pressure had been placed upon the plaintiff other than the ordinary rules and vows of poverty and obedience, and no improper use had been made of the monies, undue influence was presumed. In a well-known passage Lindley L.J. explained the theoretical basis of the doctrine of undue influence:

> "What then is the principle? Is it that it is right and expedient to save persons from the consequences of their own folly? – or is it that it is right and expedient to save them from being victimised by other people? In my view the doctrine of undue influence is founded upon the second of these two principles. Courts of Equity have never set aside gifts on the ground of folly, imprudence or want of foresight on the part of donors."[39]

Lindley L.J. noted that on earlier occasions the plaintiff had wished to leave the sisterhood but did not feel that she could do so. He also noted that although the vow of poverty did not require her to give her property to the sisterhood, she could for instance give it away to her family, in his view she would feel that she ought to give at least some of it to the sisterhood. He concluded that "no pressure except the inevitable pressure of the vows and rules, was brought to bear on the plaintiff; that no deception was practised upon her; that no unfair advantage was taken of her; that none of her money was obtained or applied for any purpose other than the legitimate objects of the sisterhood."[40] Despite this, the presumption of undue influence still arose. Lindley L.J. explained that this was because of the great power inherent in religious influence:

> "... the influence of one mind over another is very subtle, and of all influences religious influence is the most dangerous and the most powerful, and to counteract it Courts of Equity have gone very far. They have not shrunk from setting aside gifts made to persons in a position to exercise undue influence over the donors, although there has been no proof of the actual exercise of such influence; and the courts have done this on the avowed ground of the necessity of going this length in order to protect persons from the exercise of such influence under circumstances which render proof of it impossible."[41]

For his part, Bowen L.J. firmly identified the presumption of undue influence in such cases as a rule of public policy:

---

[39] (1887) 36 Ch. D. 145 at 182 –183.
[40] *ibid.* at 179.
[41] *ibid.* at 183.

"... it is plain that equity will not allow a person who exercises or enjoys a dominant religious influence over another to benefit directly or indirectly by the gifts which the donor makes under or in consequence of such influence, unless it is shewn that the donor, at the time of making the gift, was allowed full and free opportunity for counsel and advice outside – the means of considering his or her worldly position and exercising an independent will about it. This is not a limitation placed on the action of the donor; it is a fetter placed upon the conscience of the recipient of the gift, and one which arises out of public policy and fair play."[42]

This necessity for independent advice arose even in circumstances where if given it would probably have been disregarded.[43] On the facts of the case the Order had not fulfilled the onus of proving that the donor could have obtained independent advice and that she knew that she would have been allowed to obtain such advice had she wished to do so.

However the delay in seeking relief and acts of affirmation carried out during the six-year interval prevented the plaintiff from recovering her property. Lindley L.J. stated:

"So long as the relation between the donor and the donee which invalidates the gift lasts, so long is it necessary to hold that lapse of time affords no sufficient ground for refusing relief to the donor. But this necessity ceases when the relation itself comes to an end; and if the donor desires to have his gift declared invalid and set aside, he ought, in my opinion, to seek relief within a reasonable time after the removal of the influence under which the gift was made."[44]

In the Court of Appeal, the majority spoke in terms of a requirement that the donor knew she would have been allowed to obtain independent advice had she wished to do so. At first instance Kekewich J. seemed to go further and require that such advice actually be obtained. It is submitted that it would be prudent for a religious organisation receiving a gift from a devotee to follow Kekewich J. This is because of the decision of the English Court of Appeal in *Credit Lyonnais Bank Nederland NV v. Burch*[45] that a bank which had constructive notice of a relationship where undue influence was a possibility should not only have advised the weaker party to seek independent legal advice but should have ensured that she *actually received* such advice. Another relevant case in this context is *Caspari v. The First German Church of the New Jerusa-*

---

[42](1887) 36 Ch. D. 145 at 190.
[43]*Per* Kekewich J. *ibid.* at 159.
[44]*ibid.* at 187.
[45][1997] 1 All E.R. 144.

lem[46] where the Missouri Court of Appeals set aside a gift which had been made by an aged widow to the defendant church at the solicitation of the church's pastor. Thompson J. focused on the fact that the widow had not received any independent advice and held that the church had:

> "... not only failed to show that at the times when Mrs Caspari took the various steps in this donation ...she had competent and disinterested advice; but on the contrary, all the testimony shows that, during this long period she had no such advice, nor any communication with any one upon the subject, except the pastor and other influential members of the church, all of whom were interested in obtaining the gift for the church. So far from procuring for her such advice, the testimony shows, on the part of the pastor, a studied attempt and the greatest pains to conceal from the step-children of Mrs Caspari, from her neighbours, and even from the members of the congregation, except those who were taken into the secret, the fact of the making of this gift ..."[47]

It is not necessary for the representative of the religious organisation to be the confessor of the donor in order for the presumption to arise. In the Northern Ireland case of *O'Neill v. Murphy*[48] it was alleged by the defendant that the plaintiff builder had done certain work in return for prayers. The builder pleaded that if he had made the alleged agreement he was induced to do so by the undue influence of his spiritual adviser, one Canon Murphy, who was the defendant in the case. The jury found that undue influence had been exercised over the builder by the Canon. In the Court of Appeal Andrews L.J. noted that the case presented many difficult features. The Canon had not been the confessor of the builder, and had not administered the sacraments to him or given him religious instruction. In addition, the builder was not resident in the Canon's parish, but in the adjoining parish. At the time of the alleged undue influence the builder was a businessman in the prime of life and in full possession of his faculties. However Andrews L.J. concluded that whilst he would probably have reached a different conclusion to the jury, their verdict should not be interfered with.[49] Andrews L.J. identified the following evidence, which was capable of supporting their verdict:

> "... they had the plaintiff's evidence that he had met Canon Murphy twenty years before in Ballinalea, where he was parish priest; that Canon Murphy

---

[46](1881) 12 Mo. App. 293.

[47]*ibid.* at 316.

[48][1936] N.I. 16.

[49]Best L.J. also expressed doubts as to the correctness of the jury's verdict. However, he was not prepared to overturn it; *ibid.* at 42. In particular he noted that the plaintiff had been perfectly free to consult his legal advisors or friends.

told him on many occasions he would get all sorts of spiritual benefits from the work, and from the masses and prayers which would be said for him; that he had had spiritual conversations with Canon Murphy who had said that he would be repaid well over; that, metaphorically speaking, Canon Murphy had held a stick over his head; that he understood by it all that he would not get spiritual benefits if he could not fall in with all that Canon Murphy wanted him to do, and that he believed that he would get benefit from the prayers of the nuns. Finally, there was the important evidence, which it was for the jury to accept or reject, that Canon Murphy had actually dictated to the plaintiff the major portion of the plaintiff's letter [in which he had offered to accept prayers in lieu of payment]"[50]

One of the few reported Irish cases in which a gift was upheld in the face of an allegation of undue influence in a religious context is *Kirwan v. Cullen.*[51] In that case a Catholic lady had transferred a sum of £3,000 to the Archbishop of Dublin under a trust instrument. One of the trustees was a priest who had previously been the lady's spiritual confessor. On the lady's death her brother sought to have the transaction set aside on the ground, *inter alia*, that it was the result of undue influence. Lord St. Leonards L.C. noted that at the time of the gift the donor had been a lady of full age and competent understanding who moved in the world and lived with her family. The lady had never complained to anyone after making the gift. Whilst one of the trustees had formerly been her spiritual confessor "the relation between them had ceased two years before the transaction occurred, and she had been before this [gift] perfectly independent of him." The Archbishop of Dublin had had no knowledge of the transaction until after it had been made. Lord St. Leonards L.C. suggested that the transaction might have taken on a different aspect had the claim of undue influence been made by the lady herself during her lifetime and if she had contradicted the evidence of the Archbishop or other trustees.

The decision in *Kirwan* is not without its difficulties. Admittedly it can be distinguished from the other cases in this area in that the alleged victim of the undue influence was dead and had never complained about the gift in her lifetime. On the other hand the onus should have been on the Church to satisfy the Court that the donor had felt able to obtain independent advice on the matter. In addition, *O'Neill v. Murphy*[52] makes it clear that there is no need for the

---

[50][1936] N.I. 16 at 33.

[51](1854) 2 Ir. Ch. Rep. 322. For another case in which a bequest to a religious minister was upheld see *Marx v. McGlynn* (1882) 88 N.Y. 357 where the Court of Appeals of New York stated at 373–374 that "To refuse probate of this will ... would be to hold that a will influenced and controlled by affection shall not stand; that where one person has such an affection for another as to induce her to give her property to such person at death, the affection producing such result shall be regarded as undue influence."

[52][1936] N.I. 16.

other party to be the spiritual confessor of the donor at the time of the gift. Therefore, the fact that the relationship between the lady and her spiritual confessor had ceased two years before the gift was made should not have been a decisive factor.

The presumption of undue influence against religious gifts does not breach the constitutional protection of freedom of religious belief. In *Re The Bible Speaks*[53] three gifts to the defendant church totalling $6.5 million by the plaintiff, who was heir to the Dayton-Hudson fortune, were considered by the United States Court of Appeals for the First Circuit. The Church ran radio and television ministries as well as operating a missionary boat in the Caribbean. The founder of the Church, Carl Stevens, gave the plaintiff advice on religious, financial and personal matters. She was told that she had to obey Stevens because he was the highest authority on earth. The first gift of $1 million was upheld by the Court as no direct solicitation had been made for it under circumstances where the plaintiff was emotionally isolated from all outside advice. However, the second two gifts were given in bizarre circumstances. One was given after the plaintiff was told that her first gift of $1 million had cured Stevens' wife of severe migraine headaches which she had been suffering from. The plaintiff was subsequently informed that another $5 million was needed to rescue a member of the Church from detention in Romania. The Court had little hesitation in setting these gifts aside without raising any presumption of undue influence. It held that attempts by a recipient to isolate a donor from her former friends and relatives can be considered in determining undue influence. Finally the Court rejected the defendant's claim that the constitutional right to free exercise of religion shields the solicitation of funds by a religious organisation from attack. The Court held that:

> "Neither our decision in this case nor the proceedings below implicates the religious tenets of TBS or the beliefs of its adherents. The findings and rulings rest solely on secular statements and actions. The facts relied upon have not been derived from an inquiry into the religious principles of TBS or the truth and sincerity of its adherents' beliefs.... Those who run TBS may freely exercise their religion, but they cannot use the cloak of religion to exert undue influence of a non-religious nature with impunity."[54]

5. THE SPIRIT WORLD

The courts' reluctance to become involved in religious disputes extends to

---

[53] (1989) 869 F. (2d) 628.
[54] *ibid.* at 645.

disputes over spirits and ghosts. In 1999, a judgment in Britain's first super-natural court case since the Middle Ages went some way to deciding the legal status of ghosts in contract law.[55] A 250 year-old cottage in Staffordshire was said by its new owners, Mr and Mrs Smith, to be possessed by spirits which caused walls to weep and objects to be moved, and which sometimes attacked the occupants. Mrs Smith told the Court that one ghostly attack had left her feeling as though she had been raped. The Smiths refused to pay the final instalment of the purchase price claiming that the sisters who sold it to them had known of the ghost and failed to disclose it. The case came on before Derby County Court and in a five-minute ruling Judge Peter Streeton stated that "I do not accept that [the house] is haunted now or has been at any other time." The judge described the plaintiffs' stories of spectral molestation as "hysterical reactions" and found that invisible presences, foul smells and ghostly footsteps were "far more likely to have been created by a man than a ghost." However the case may not have laid the issue to rest for the judge did not rule on the reality of hauntings in general. As a postscript it may be noted that according to one report the house rose above its pre-ghost value once the judge had ruled that it was not haunted.[56]

A more adventurous line was taken by the Supreme Court of New York in *Stambovsky v. Ackley.*[57] The plaintiff purchaser sought rescission of a contract to purchase a house in the village of Nyack on the basis that it was possessed by poltergeists. The plaintiff, who hailed from New York, stated that as he was not a local he could not have been expected to have any familiarity with the house's growing reputation (it had been the subject of an article in Reader's Digest, perhaps the ultimate accolade for any socially ambitious haunted house). The Supreme Court of New York held that no divination was required to con-clude that it was the defendant's own promotional efforts in publicising her close encounters with the spirits that had fostered the home's reputation in the community. In 1989 the house was included in a five-home walking tour of Nyack and described in a newspaper article as a "riverfront Victorian (with ghost)." The applicant contended that the reputation thus created went to the very essence of the bargain between the parties, greatly impairing both the value of the property and its potential for resale. Rubin J. (Ross and Kassal JJ. concurring) held that whilst the plaintiff did not have a ghost of a chance of establishing fraudulent misrepresentation on the part of the vendor, neverthe-less he was "moved by the spirit of equity to allow the buyer to seek rescission of the contract of sale and recovery of his down payment." The route by which he reached this conclusion is of some interest.

---

[55] See *The Times*, January 19, 1999. For a discussion of the case see the article by David Fickling, *The Times,* February 24, 1999.
[56] David Fickling, *The Times*, February 24, 1999.
[57] (1991) 19 A.D. (2d) 254, 572 N.Y.S. (2d) 672.

Rubin J. rejected the notion that a haunting is a condition that should be ascertained upon reasonable inspection of the premises and thus held that *caveat emptor* could not apply:

> "From the perspective of a person in the position of plaintiff herein, a very practical problem arises with respect to the discovery of a paranormal phenomenon: 'Who you gonna' call?' as a title song to the movie 'Ghostbusters' asks. Applying the strict rule of *caveat emptor* to a contract involving a house possessed by poltergeists conjures up visions of a psychic or medium routinely accompanying the structural engineer and Terminix man on an inspection of every home subject to a contract of sale. It portends that the prudent attorney will establish an escrow account lest the subject of the transaction come back to haunt him and his client – or pray that his malpractice insurance coverage extends to supernatural disasters. In the interest of avoiding such untenable consequences, the notion that a haunting is a condition which can and should be ascertained upon reasonable inspection of the premises is a hobgoblin which should be exorcised from the body of legal precedent and laid quietly to rest."[58]

Rubin J. held that "where a condition which has been created by the seller materially impairs the value of the contract and is peculiarly within the knowledge of the seller or unlikely to be discovered by a prudent purchaser exercising due care with respect to the subject transaction, non-disclosure constitutes a basis for rescission. The vendor attempted to exclude liability on the basis of an "as is" clause. However Rubin J. held that such a clause was limited to physical or tangible matters and did not extend to paranormal phenomena. In any event, he concluded that the existence of the poltergeists meant that the seller had not delivered vacant possession of the house in accordance with her obligations under the provisions of the contract.

In an terse dissent, Smith J. (Milonas J.P. concurring) was of the view that if the doctrine of *caveat emptor* was to be discarded by the Court it should be for a reason more substantive than a poltergeist. He stated that "the existence of a poltergeist is no more binding on the defendants than it is upon this court."

6. FAUSTIAN PACTS

So far we have been considering arrangements with God, or at least with his earthly representatives. This leads onto the question as to whether a Faustian

---

[58] *Stambovsky v. Ackley*, above, n.57 at 257.

pact would have any more chance of recognition before a court. Some guidance may be gathered from the decision of the US District Court for the Western District of Pennsylvania in *United States v. Satan and His Staff.*[59] The plaintiff sought leave to file a complaint for violation of his civil rights. He alleged that Satan had on numerous occasions caused him misery and unwarranted threats, had placed deliberate obstacles in his path and had generally caused his downfall. He alleged that these acts by Satan had deprived him of his constitutional rights. Weber J. was concerned that even if the plaintiff's case revealed a prima facie violation of his civil rights he could not obtain jurisdiction over the defendant in the District of Pennsylvania. He noted that the plaintiff had failed to include with his complaint the required form of instructions for the United States Marshall for directions as to exercise of service of process.

7. DAMAGES

If religious arrangements were held to be subject to contract law, the question of damages for breach of contract would arise. At this point an objection might be raised. How could the courts place a value on the cancelled funeral, the spoilt wedding or the unsaid prayers? In fact the recovery of contract damages for emotional suffering and inconvenience is well established. In *Mason v. Westside Cemeteries Ltd*[60] the defendant had in 1979 made arrangements for the ashes and cremated remains of his parents' bodies to be transferred from a funeral home to a cemetery. He paid £50 for the internment of his parents' ashes at the graveyard. In 1993 the plaintiff, wishing to transfer the ashes to another place, requested their delivery, but they could not be found despite an intensive search by the cemetery. The plaintiff sued the cemetery for damages for emotional distress. The General Division of the Ontario Court held that a contract of bailment had been created between the plaintiff and the cemetery. The Court found the idea of putting a monetary value on the ashes distasteful and therefore assigned the nominal value of $1 to the ashes and $2 for the loss of both urns. The Court accepted that the plaintiff was genuinely distressed at the loss of the ashes. The point was made on cross-examination that the plaintiff had not required any professional care or meditation as a result of this alleged emotional distress to which the plaintiff responded that he had survived four years in a prisoner of war camp in the Second World War and was not the sort of person who breaks down. Perhaps impressed by such fortitude, the Court held that damages were recoverable for mental distress. Molloy J. stated that "If damages are recoverable for upset over the loss of a dog or for

---

[59] (1971) 54 F.R.D. 282.
[60] (1996) 135 D.L.R. (4th) 361.

the disappointment of a ruined holiday, surely the distress caused by the loss of the remains of someone's deceased parents is likewise compensable."[61] He awarded the plaintiff $1,000 for mental distress.

8. CONCLUSION

We have seen that contract law prefers to keep a respectful distance from religious matters. It refuses to recognise prayers as sufficient consideration and it views religious arrangements as generally not being intended to create legal relations. These principles are of long-standing vintage and are almost never questioned by commentators. Yet when one examines the cases that are cited as authority for these principles one struggles to find convincing reasons for the decisions. It is submitted that if the rules are to remain relevant to modern religious practices, the courts will have to devise more coherent reasons for their retention than were devised for their creation. These rules developed at a time when the concept of contract damages was not very sophisticated, but now that recovery of contract damages for emotional suffering and inconvenience is well-established there seems no reason why religious arrangements cannot be subject to a contractual analysis in appropriate cases.

In contrast, it is submitted that the courts have provided sufficient justifications for the retention of the presumption of undue influence in the relationship of religious association/devotee. The strength of instincts that drive people into religious relationships justifies the law in intervening to ensure that this energy is diverted away from transactions that benefit the religion and unfairly disadvantage the donor. In particular, the prevalence of so-called "cults", which place an emphasis on property transfer to the organisation as an act of devotion, requires the courts to be extra-vigilant in protecting the weaker party. This same suspicion should not necessarily attach to prayers or religious ceremonies, where a real benefit, albeit an intangible one, does pass. In future it should be possible for a contract student leaving an exam to proclaim that in contract law prayers are occasionally answered.

---

[61](1996) 135 D.L.R. (4th) 361 at 379.

EXTRAMURAL PURSUITS OF THE EIGHTEENTH-CENTURY BENCH

W.N. OSBOROUGH

Whether by descent, marriage or purchase many members of the eighteenth-century Irish judiciary were destined to become the proprietors of considerable landed estate. Not in every instance did the responsibilities attaching present a challenge actually accepted – to utilise the wealth thereby generated to promote social and economic betterment in the interests of the larger community. But in a finite number of cases they most certainly did. That property had its duties as well as its rights represented a proposition with which the individuals concerned would by no means have been inclined to disagree. To revisit the period now will enable us to make the acquaintance of the judges in the van of this movement of social and economic improvement. Their initiatives constituted no minor extramural pursuits, and the capacity of these to deflect the persons in question from giving proper attention to their function as judges (for which, after all, they were remunerated by the crown) necessarily invites examination.

Information is sparse on the non-judicial and non-political activities of the Irish bench in the seventeenth century. An English traveller, Sir William Brereton, has left us a tantalisingly brief glimpse of the country retreat of one of the century's chief barons of the exchequer. This was Sir Richard Bolton, made chief baron in 1625 and promoted to the lord chancellorship in 1639. Brereton passed close to Bolton's residence on his three-week visit to Ireland in July 1635. His diary records the occasion thus:[1]

> "About two or three miles from Swordes, my Lord Chief Baron hath a dainty, pleasant high-built wood house, and much rich and brave land about it, this placed on the right hand."

This, of course, is the barest of glimpses and we enter the realm of speculation when we ponder the possibility – indulging the luxury of seeking to put flesh on the bones – that Brereton's reference to the "rich and brave land" surrounding Bolton's dacha in north Co. Dublin carries the connotation that its owner did a spot of farming himself.

---

[1] Sir William Brereton, "Travels in Holland, the United Provinces, England, Scotland and Ireland", ed. Edward Hawkins, *Chetham Society*, 1 (1844), 1 at 136.

We are on much surer ground as regards activity of a comparable kind for the eighteenth century, in the case of Marmaduke Coghill, for instance. Coghill succeeded his father as judge of the prerogative and faculties in 1699, holding the office until his death in 1738. Around 1725, Coghill built a fine Georgian mansion for himself on the north side of Dublin. This was Drumcondra House, which survives today as the centrepiece in the campus of All Hallows College. Both at Belvedere House, a stone's throw away (now incorporated within St. Patrick's College), where he had grown up, and at Drumcondra House, Coghill took great interest in the lay-out of the gardens. Little is known of Coghill's work as a judge, but there is an additional detail regarding his extracurricular activities that merits setting down. He is reported to have erected a manufactory for the bleaching of linen half-way between Glasnevin and Drumcondra, and probably at some point close to the banks of the River Tolka.[2]

The achievements of Coghill pale into insignificance when there is set beside them the major changes wrought by Michael Ward in one part of Co. Down. Ward was born in 1683, and after years at the Bar and in Parliament, was appointed a judge of the court of King's Bench in 1727. He died in 1759. As is the case with Coghill and with so many of the Irish judges appointed in the first two-thirds of the eighteenth century, we know little of Ward's work as a judge, whether in Dublin or travelling on the assize circuits. If Ward's thirty-odd years on the bench show a comparative blank, we know a great deal more about him as an agriculturist and as an entrepreneur. In 1709, Ward married an heiress, a Miss Hamilton. And their joint wealth enabled him to attend to the development of the estate to which he was destined to devote so much of his energies. This was Castle Ward, situated between Downpatrick and Strangford in Co. Down, and now owned by the National Trust.[3] The embellishment at Castle Ward owed much to Ward and his wife. This we learn from Walter Harris who published two accounts of Ward's achievements, in 1740 and 1744, and from the surviving Ward papers.[4] The grounds were landscaped, a good mix of trees grown, and a walled garden designed and planted, Ward's wife occupying a key role in the last of these projects. Ward also saw to the excavation of the impressive ornamental lake known as Temple Water. Other innovations undertaken by Ward were of more practical benefit, in particular the corn mill constructed by him on the Castle Ward estate adjacent to an inlet of Strangford Lough. In 1744 Walter Harris described the arrangement made by

[2] Campbell, "Two memorable Dublin houses", *Dublin Historical Record,* 2 (1939-40), 141.
[3] Ball, *The judges in Ireland, 1221-1921,* 2 vols. (London, 1926), ii, 200; National Trust, *Castle Ward, Co. Down* (Plaistow, 1979).
[4] [Walter Harris], *The topographical and chorographical survey of the county of Down* (Dublin, 1740); Harris, *The ancient and present state of the county of Down* (Dublin, 1744); PRONI, D/2092,/ 3735,/ 4216. See, too, Stevenson, *Two centuries of life in Down, 1600-1800* (Belfast, 1920), ch.11: "Michael Ward – landowner, trader, judge".

Ward to supply the new mill with motive power. This sounds like a triumph of engineering:[5]

> "On the bay that opens to the garden is a singular contrivance for supply-
> ing a mill with water. A dead wall is carried across the gut in which are
> two arches, and in them two flood-gates fixed, the one to admit the tide,
> and the other to keep it in or let it out, as occasion serves. By this means
> a corn-mill is perpetually supplied with water, which can never fail as
> long as the tide flows here."

The entire Ward inheritance benefited from what R.H. Buchanan has termed, with ample justification, the judge's business acumen and management skills.[6] Ward thus planned and developed the new settlement at Killough, Co. Down in the 1730s and 1740s. He opened a salt pan, built mills and warehouses, and constructed a harbour and quays. The harbour, Harris wrote in 1744, was now abundantly more safe and commodious, but there remained natural hazards which not even the enterprising judge was capable of neutralising. "A small degree of caution is necessary to sail into this harbour," Harris wrote:

> "... for a rock stands in the middle of the entrance, covered at half-flood,
> commonly called the water rock: upon which a perch is to be fixed for
> the safety and direction of sea-faring men."[7]

The captains of Ward's own trading vessels utilising the new harbour at Killough doubtless learnt to heed this advice.

Marl, useful as a fertiliser, had been uncovered in the neighbourhood around 1707, and Ward was to promote its employment amongst his tenants. The local economy flourished. As Buchanan has put it, Ward:

> "by skilfully lobbying for the provision of government subsidies for Irish-
> grown wheat, ... established a profitable new arable economy based on
> the export of wheat and barley to Dublin and to the ports of north-west
> England."[8]

And there was yet another side to the judge's activities. At Killough, Ward also established a charter school. Close by he set apart twelve acres of land at low rent for accommodation of the children, adding a benefaction of £20 a year for

---

[5] Harris, *Ancient and present state of Co. Down*, p.41.
[6] Buchanan, "The Lecale peninsula, county Down", in Aalen, Whelan and Stout (ed.), *Atlas of the Irish rural landscape* (Cork, 1997), p. 277 at 282.
[7] Harris, *Ancient and present state of Co. Down,* p. 123.
[8] Buchanan, *op. cit.* n. 6, p. 282.

seven years in support. Harris, who supplies this information, tells us that the school was designed

> "for the reception and constant imployment of twenty poor popish children, trained up to useful labour, and carefully educated in the principles of the protestant religion."[9]

In June 1731, a 14-man steering group met in Trinity College in Dublin to project the establishment of what was to become the Royal Dublin Society, but which was first known as the Dublin Society for Improving Husbandry, Manufactures, and other Useful Arts. Ward was a member of this original steering group.[10] Aside from Marmaduke Coghill, several other judicial figures of the period took out membership: Thomas Wyndham, Lord Chancellor (1726-39), Thomas Marlay, Chief Baron of the Exchequer (1730-41; in the latter year he became Chief Justice of King's Bench), John Wainwright, Baron of the Exchequer (1732-41), Thomas Carter, Master of the Rolls (1731-54). One future Chief Justice also took out membership: Henry Singleton, who became Chief Justice of Common Pleas in 1740.[11] One is hard put to it to avoid the conclusion that these individuals became members of the society not just because they sensed that, by virtue of their social standing, this was no inappropriate departure for them, but also because they genuinely wanted to acquire knowledge themselves as regards "improving husbandry, manufactures and other useful arts."

For the latter years of the eighteenth century most of the information touching the extramural pursuits of the Irish bench comes from the pen of Arthur Young. Young first came to Ireland in 1776. Returning in February 1777, he accepted the post of agent to Lord Kingsborough in Co. Cork, which post he retained until 1779. Differences that year with his employer caused him to return to England. During his months in Ireland Young travelled extensively. In June-July 1776, for example, we know he visited Slane, Mullingar, Carton, Wexford and Courtown, and in July-October of the same year, a second tour took in Drogheda, Collon, Armagh, Belfast, Antrim, Derry, Ballyshannon, Cavan, Longford, Roscommon, Sligo, Mayo, Galway, Cork, Kilkenny and Limerick.[12]

Young's impressions of the country were published in London in 1780 under the title, *A tour in Ireland*. In 1787, 1788 and 1789, he paid a similar series

---

[9] Harris, *Ancient and present state of Co. Down*, p.17.
[10] Berry, *A history of the Royal Dublin Society* (Dublin, 1915), pp. 6-7. Ward can thus be included among what Berry terms (at p.5) that "small band of patriotic reformers, actuated by the purest and noblest motives".
[11] See the list of members in 1734 reproduced in Berry's *A history of the Royal Dublin Society*, pp 24–27.
[12] Gazley, *The life of Arthur Young, 1741-1820* (Philadelphia, 1973), ch. 3.

of visits to France, which resulted in a further volume published in 1792, *Travels in France*. Young's biographer, J.G. Gazley, observes that *A tour in Ireland* "lacks the charm of his later masterpiece on France". A further comparison is drawn and is worth noting. "As a single work", Gazley writes, *A tour of Ireland* "is only surpassed in permanent value by his *Travels in France*".[13] A modern work has retraced Young's journeyings on the continent: Dyer, *La France revisitée sur les traces d'Arthur Young*.[14] No comparable exercise for Ireland has as yet been attempted.

Thirteen years after Young's return from Ireland, in 1793, Young became secretary to the Board of Agriculture established in England by William Pitt. Long before his arrival in Ireland, Young had acquired considerable knowledge of farming, and this bias to his interests entailed that he was very different from the general run of earlier visitors to the country. This bias is to the fore in Young's account of the improvements being undertaken on the estates of the various Irish judges he was to encounter in the course of his travels.

One such estate on which Young was to present a report was that at Woodford, three or so miles to the north of Listowel in Co. Kerry. The owner at the time was Robert Alexander, who acted as the admiralty judge from 1756 to the year of Young's visit. The report exemplifies Young's broad approach:[15]

> "Woodford is an agreeable scene; close to the house is a fine winding river under a bank of thick wood, with the view of an old castle hanging over it. Mr Fitzgerald is making a considerable progress in rural improvements; he is taking in mountain ground, fencing and draining very completely, and introducing a new husbandry. He keeps 30 pigs, which stock he feeds on potatoes, and has built a piggery for them. Turnips he cultivates for sheep, and finds them to answer perfectly. Not being able to get men to understand hoeing, he thins them by hand. He has five acres of potatoes put in drills with the plough, and designs ploughing them out: they look perfectly well, and promise to be as good a crop as any in the trench way."

Earlier in the same year of 1776, Young also visited the properties of two judges situated in the east of the country and rather closer to the capital. Here an early port of call was Hampton Hall, the estate of George Hamilton located near the coastal village of Balbriggan in Co. Dublin.

Hamilton had just been named a baron of the court of exchequer, a post he

---

[13] *ibid.* pp. 120, 95.

[14] Dyer, *La France revisitée sur les traces d'Arthur Young* (Paris, 1989).

[15] Young, *A tour in Ireland, 1776-1779,* ed. Hutton with introduction by Ruane, 2 vols. (Shannon, 1970), i, 372-373. (There are several editions of Young's *Tour*; references here are made to the 1970 Shannon edition).

held until his death in 1793. His tenure, as we shall see, was not unmarked by controversy. Connected through his mother and his wife with gentry families in Co. Down, Hamilton was set to acquire Hampton Hall.[16] Here, before as well as after his elevation to the bench, Hamilton took very seriously his role both as proprietor and landlord. Young's account of his meeting with Hamilton furnishes detail on improvements the baron had inaugurated. Near Hampton Hall itself, Young relates, Hamilton had taken in

> "150 acres, mountain land, covered with scutch grass (*triticum repens*), furz (*ulex europaeus*) and a little heath (*erica vulgaris*), stubbed it up, ploughed it four times, … limed it 140 to 150 barrels each acre."[17]

By such methods, land, previously reckoned barren, had been substantially improved. The rental income Hamilton enjoyed on his estate had been progressively increased in consequence.

Following the example set by Michael Ward at Killough earlier in the century, Hamilton had also set about the construction of a "very fine pier" at Balbriggan. A considerable engineering project, the pier's construction had presented innumerable difficulties. With unconcealed admiration, Arthur Young tells how Hamilton had tackled the problem of sinking large stones, some of them weighing as much as eight or ten tons, to protect the finished pier against the ravages of the sea.[18] Hamilton first had the stones spread along the beach, between high and low watermark. The fundamental challenge, however, was to arrange the stones into the desired precise position. Here what Hamilton organised was to lash puncheons to them at low water, which floated them when the tide came in, and conveyed them over the spot where wanted. Fresh snags arose in disengaging the casks from each stone. To remedy this state of affairs, Young relates, Hamilton

> "…had a contrivance very simple and ingenious, which answered the purpose completely. The puncheons were hooped strongly with iron near each end, and between these irons was a chain, from the centre of which went an iron tongue. The stones, at low water, were lashed round with a chain with open irons that correspond with those tongues in the cask chains, the one went into the other, and when closed had a female screw through all three; through the two jaws of the one, and the tongue of the other, a male screw at the end of a bar was then screwed in when the stone was ready to move. One of 8 tons required 10 puncheons. Upon being floated over the spot where wanted, these bars were unscrewed,

---

[16]Ball, *op. cit.*, above, n.3, ii, p. 218.
[17]Young, *op. cit.*, above, n.15, at 107.
[18]*ibid.*, i, 107-08.

and the stone and casks disengaged at once without trouble, the one sinking, and the casks floating away with the chain that was lashed round the stone."[19]

Anthony Foster served as chief baron of the exchequer from 1766 until 1777. He died in 1779. That his interests and enthusiasms extended far beyond the law was plain for all to see long before Young met him, at Collon, Co. Louth, in 1776. Thirty years before, Foster had been awarded a prize for his cider, and he had over many years given stalwart service to the linen industry.[20] He also built the residence known as Merville near Stillorgan, Co. Dublin, the grounds of which, like the house itself, now form part of the Belfield campus of University College Dublin. The association is preserved in the name of the adjacent road: Foster's avenue.[21]

Young is unstinting in his praise of what Foster had accomplished at Collon, reclaiming for agriculture an estate of 5,000 acres, previously deemed irreclaimable – "a waste sheep-walk, covered chiefly with heath, some with dwarf furz and fern".[22] The liming of Foster's lands in Louth witnessed a resort to operations, the magnitude of which Young had never heard tell of before. Foster apparently had:

"... for several years 27 lime-kilns burning stone, which was brought four miles with culm from Milford Haven. He had 450 cars employed by these kilns, and paid £700 a year for culm: the stone was quarried by from 60 to 80 men regularly at that work; this was doing the business with incomparable spirit – yet had he no peculiar advantages."[23]

But there was even more to what Foster had been determined to achieve:

"While this vast business of liming was going forwards, roads were also making, and the whole tract inclosed in fields of about 10 acres each, with ditches 7 feet wide, and 6 deep, at 1s. a perch, the banks planted with quick and forest trees. Of these fences 70,000 perches were done."[24]

The outcome had been entirely beneficial. "This great improver", to employ Young's concluding accolade,

---

[19] Young, *op. cit.*, above, n.15, at p.108.
[20] Ball, *The judges in Ireland*, ii, pp. 213-14.
[21] The house was subsequently owned by William Downes, who became chief justice of the court of king's bench on Kilwarden's murder in 1803. It was reported at one time to have possessed the finest garden in Ireland.
[22] Young, *op. cit.*, above, n.15, at p. 110.
[23] *ibid.* at p. 111.
[24] *ibid.*

"a title more deserving estimation than that of a great general or a great minister, lives now to overlook a country flourishing only from his exertions. He has made a barren wilderness smile with cultivation, planted it with people, and made those people happy. Such are the men to whom monarchs should decree their honours, and nations erect their statues."[25]

Later thinking, it is only right to point out, was to draw attention to the dangers of over-liming.[26]

As the end of the eighteenth century approached, it was becoming evident that the task of the judiciary had got much more onerous, certainly much more intellectual in the light of the expectation that written judgments would routinely be produced for incorporation in new series of law reports. The work of the judge was seen to become full-time, one that afforded less opportunity for the realisation of personal programmes of estate improvement that had fired the imaginations and tested the skills of men such as Michael Ward, George Hamilton and Anthony Foster. The professionalism of the legal profession, coupled with the favourable view taken of the advantages of a more marked division of labour, contributed to an end-result over which most lawyers, perhaps, were unlikely to have expressed their regrets. Yet, as the law became more complex and in individual areas more uncertain, those of a philosophical cast of mind may have felt tempted to ask the question: might not the intellectual talent that had manifested itself been otherwise and better employed? The king whom Lemuel Gulliver met in Brobdingnag was in no doubt as to the answer, even if Ward, Hamilton, and Foster, answering from their graves, would have doubtless felt, paradoxically enough, honour-bound to disagree. The response is well known:[27]

"Whoever could make two ears of corn or two blades of grass to grow upon a spot of ground where only one grew before would deserve better of mankind, and do more essential service to his country than the whole race of politicians put together."

The destruction of legal records and the absence of law reports until the last decade of the century make it impossible to establish whether any benefit accrued to the individual judge acting in his judicial capacity from knowledge or expertise acquired by him whilst pursuing his own personal extramural interests, whether in harbour construction, road making, agricultural improvement, or in any other field.

---

[25] *ibid.* at p. 113.
[26] Bell, "The improvement of Irish farming techniques since 1750: theory and practice", in O'Flanagan, Ferguson and Whelan (ed.), *Rural Ireland: modernisation and change* (Cork, 1987), p. 24 at pp. 33-36.
[27] Swift, *Gulliver's Travels*: "A voyage to Brobdingnag".

There is a further possibility, however, which has to be faced – that individual judges may have neglected their official duties out of a desire to spend more time, for example, on improving their estates. Foster, in conversation with Arthur Young, conceded that the risk was certainly there. He did not hide his distaste for absences from Collon, necessitated, as he put it, primarily by his regular attendance at the exchequer in Dublin.[28] This permitted him to see Collon "but by starts". The changes he was responsible for introducing there, he confided, "were necessarily left to others at a time that he would have wished constantly to have attended them". The case is not proven against any individual judge. But the black mark that Fitzgibbon, as Lord Chancellor, entered against Hamilton, the hero of the construction of the pier at Balbriggan, invites suspicion. Hamilton sat as a member of the court of delegates in the case of *Goodwin v. Giesler*, an ecclesiastical appeal about a contested will. The decision of the delegates to affirm that of the prerogative court was set to incur Fitzgibbon's wrath as much if not more than the original decision itself. In Fitzgibbon's view, the delegates had ill-advisedly disallowed an entirely reasonable procedural request made by Goodwin, the appellant. The upshot was that he took the unprecedented step of recommending the issuance of a commission of review which in theory would have facilitated the reversal of the decision of both of the lower tribunals.[29] In a letter to London explaining the action he had taken in the case, Fitzgibbon castigated the conduct of Hamilton in particular. Hamilton, Fitzgibbon wrote, "was at times induced to expedite the decision of a court somewhat more than was perfectly consistent with due attention to its merits".[30] There, for the moment at any rate, and, perhaps, in perpetuity as well, the case against Hamilton must rest.

---

[28] Young, *A tour in Ireland*, i, 111.
[29] *Goodwin v. Giesler* (1794) Irish Term Reports 371.
[30] Quoted, Kavanaugh, *John Fitzgibbon, earl of Clare: protestant reaction and English authority in late eighteenth-century Ireland* (Dublin, 1997), p. 184.

THE EIGHTEENTH-CENTURY ORIGINS OF THE IRISH DOCTRINE OF GRAFT

ALBERT POWER

1. INTRODUCTION

The evolution of that equitable principle, which in the Irish courts of the nineteenth century came to be known as the doctrine of graft,[1] derives from a succession of eighteenth-century cases in the English courts, treating of the renewal of leases under settlement, either by those occupying a fiduciary relation to the beneficiaries under the settlement, or those owning a limited interest in the lease itself. The essential issue in such cases was to ascertain to whom the benefit of such renewed lease should accrue – whether the party who had actually renewed the lease, or those enjoying a beneficial future interest.

It is a fundamental principle of equity that one standing in a fiduciary relation to another in respect of property cannot be permitted to derive a personal advantage therefrom.[2] This, of course, is the classic constructive trust concept, stemming as the textbooks aver, from the decision of Lord King L.C. in *Keech v. Sandford*,[3] described only 60 years later as "the first and most notorious case on the subject."[4]

As shall be seen, *Keech v. Sandford* was neither the first nor the most notorious case, although it is that which, in the estimation of later generations of lawyers and judges, is generally associated with the first vigorous assertion of the constructive trust principle.

Throughout the lengthy gestation of graft the nub of judicial emphasis seems

---

[1] For example, *Nesbit v. Tredennick* (1808) 1 Ball & Beatty 29, *Eyre v. Dolphin* (1813) 2 Ball & Beatty 290, *Jones v. Kearney* (1841) 4 Ir. Eq. 74, *McAuley v. Clarendon* (1858) 8 Ir. Ch. Rep. 121, *O'Brien v. Egan* (1880) 5 L.R. Ir. 633, *Gabbett v. Lawder* (1883) 11 L.R. Ir. 295, *Dempsey v. Ward* [1899] 1 I.R. 463.

[2] Memorably expressed by Lord Redesdale L.C., in *O'Herlihy v. Hedges* (1803) 1 Sch. & Lef. 123 at 126-127, thus: "The rule in equity that a Trustee shall gain no Benefit to himself by any act done by him as Trustee, but that all his acts shall be for the Benefit of his Cestui que Trust . . . is established in order to keep Trustees in the line of their duty. . . ."

[3] (1726) Sel. Cas. Chan. 61; 2 Eq. Cas. Abr. 741; Cas. Temp. King 61; 25 E.R. 233; 1 Wh. & Tud. Leading Cases 39; [1558-1774] All E.R. 230, also known occasionally as *The Rumford Market Case*.

[4] *Per* Lord Loughborough L.C. in *Stone v. Theed* (1787) 2 Brown 243 at 247.

to have been focused upon the peculiar nature of a lease in settlement, and the concomitantly strong likelihood of renewal.[5]

2. RENEWAL OF LEASES AND THE ETYMOLOGY OF GRAFT

Perhaps the earliest[6] reported case on this topic is *Holt v. Holt,*[7] set against the backdrop of the Great Fire of London and the Restoration of King Charles II. In this, executors renewed one of their testator's leases under the See of Canterbury, and then built houses on the property. Inevitably, the issue arose as to the benefit of the renewed lease. In a judgment of the Court of Chancery, recorded *ex tempore*, it was held that the beneficiaries under the will were entitled to the renewal, provided that they paid the renewal fine and reimbursed outlays already expended on improvements. Towards the end of the case the Court made an unanimous general pronouncement, "that in the case of an Executorship in Trust, the Renewal of such a Lease shall go to the Benefit of Cestuy que Trust."[8]

One particular case worthy of mention as providing a clue to the etymological origin of graft is *Seabourne v. Powell.*[9] The facts of this are somewhat diffuse and perhaps badly reported. It appears that one Mrs. Austin took a lease of building lands, and thereafter obtained a loan by way of mortgage. Subsequently it emerged that Mrs. Austin's title was not as sound as she had believed, and a new lease was made to her by the person holding the superior interest. It was then recommended that she should sue the plaintiffs on their bond, as sureties. The plaintiffs, in turn, sued for equitable relief, on the basis of the argument that:

> ". . . the mortgagee had therefore a plain equity to have the benefit of that title, which was but a graft into that stock from which he derived . . . and . . . the plaintiffs being but sureties in the bond had an equity to have the benefit of the mortgage, and of that new acquired title, to save them harmless against the bond."[10]

---

[5] In the eighteenth century statutory limitations were imposed on church, Crown and charitable leases, so that no such lease could be created for in excess of three lives or 21 years. Gradually the practice evolved of "filling up" leases for lives with the dropping of every life, and renewing twenty-one year leases at the expiration of every seven years. *Vide. Report of the Select Committee on Church Leases* (1839) and Cretney: "The Rationale of *Keech v. Sandford*" (1969) 33 *Conv.* 161 at pp. 163-168.

[6] Suggested by Lord Bathurst L.C. in *Rawe v. Chichester* (1773) 2 Ambler 715 at 719.

[7] (1670) 1 Chan. Cas. 190.

[8] *ibid.* at 191.

[9] (1686) 2 Vernon 10.

[10] (1686) 2 Vernon 10 at 11. The converse position of the mortgagor was canvassed by the shortly reported decision in *Rushworth's Case* (1676) 2 Freeman 14, in which it was held that "if a

The Master of the Rolls decreed as requested by the plaintiffs, regrettably without any recorded comment.

Throughout the eighteenth century one can discern a steady stream of cases treating of the issue of renewed leases in settlement. In *Lock v. Lock*,[11] which preceded *Keech v. Sandford* by some 16 years, Sir Nathan Wright, the Lord Keeper, observed that in a devise by a testator of a term for 21 years to his wife for life, with remainders over to his son, the very fact of such devise itself implied "that the widow should renew and keep the term on foot", and that, accordingly, any such renewal must enure to the benefit of the remainderman, and could, in fact, be compelled by his personal representative.[12]

The case of *Keech v. Sandford* is, rightly or wrongly, regarded as the *locus classicus* in such matters. In its contemporary context, however, perhaps the principal significance of this decision is the adversion by Lord King L.C. to the practical reality that, if a trustee could with impunity renew for his own benefit a lease of which a renewal had been refused to his *cestui que trust*, then few trust estates would ever be renewed for the benefit of the *cestui que trust*.[13]

In *Addis v. Clement*[14] the unusual circumstance arose of a testator who, having both a freehold and a leasehold interest in the same property, bequeathed "all" his estate to his wife for life, with tail remainder to various brothers. After the testator's death his widow renewed the lease, claiming the benefit of it for herself, on the grounds that:

1. it was accepted precedent that, where the freehold estate was adequate to satisfy the bequest, then the leasehold estate passed to the testator's widow as personalty;

2. it was inconsistent with the nature of the lease, being for a term of only 21 years, that the testator could have intended it to pass under a trust settlement or to support contingent remainders.

Lord King L.C. held, despite this, that the renewed lease must enure for the benefit of those entitled in remainder. Counsel's first point he disposed of on

---

college lease be mortgaged, and the mortgagee renews his lease, then this shall be for the benefit of the mortgagor, paying the mortgagee his charges . . . the mortgagee here doth but graft upon his stock, and it shall be for the mortgagor's benefit."

[11] (1710) 2 Vernon 666.

[12] *ibid.* Similarly, in *Verney v. Verney* (1750) Ambler 88, Lord Hardwicke L.C. implicitly affirmed the practical significance of customary renewals when he observed that leases for lives are often "looked upon by testators as continuing estates, and are devised as such with remainders over; therefore the intention is, that they should be kept filled up from time to time."

[13] *Keech v. Sandford*, above n.3. Consequently, said Lord King L.C., *ibid.,* "the trustee should rather have let the lease run out, than to have had it to himself . . . for it is very obvious what would be the consequence of letting trustees have the lease on refusal to renew to cestui que use."

[14] (1728) 2 P. Wms. 456.

the basis of contrary authority. Of the second he observed that the lease, though for twenty-one years, being a church lease was "always renewable", so that the lessee might legitimately regard himself "from the right he had to renew, as having a perpetual estate therein, a kind of inheritance."[15]

Shades of a near automatic right of renewal emerge again in the decision of Lord Hardwicke L.C. in *Crop v. Norton*.[16] In this a lessee, who was also the last life in a lease for lives, agreed to surrender his lease in lieu of another lease for lives, comprising his own life and two others, which he undertook to hold in trust for a son of the person who paid the renewal fine on his behalf. In an action after the lessee's death, Lord Hardwicke L.C. repudiated the suggestion that there could be a resulting trust in favour of the person who had advanced the renewal fine, on the grounds that valuable consideration had moved from the lessee through his exercising his right of renewal to procure a lease for lives now held on trust for that other's son. This was a right, said the Lord Chancellor, which, though not *per se* enforceable, must be regarded by those coming in under it "as a right and interest, and the person who comes in under the new lease has always been looked upon in this court as deriving from the person who had the old lease."[17]

Nevertheless, in *Abney v. Miller*,[18] Lord Hardwicke L.C. refused to countenance the contention that a bequest of leasehold property could also serve to pass any renewal of the term obtained by the testator himself after the date of execution of the will. However, it is clear from Lord Hardwicke L.C.'s judgment that his decision is based primarily on the construction of the testator's will.[19] In the course of his judgment the Lord Chancellor drew a distinction between renewals by an executor and renewals by the testator himself: in the former case the "custom of renewal" would be of relevance in fastening the trusts pertinent to the old lease on the new; whereas, in the latter case the trust principle should not extend to bind the testator in his own life-time.

Implicitly, however, Lord Hardwicke L.C. ignored the pervasive logic of counsel's argument, that the testator by renewing was not purporting to effect an ademption, but was doing no more than he had often done before, and which the nature of the estate (a college lease for 14 years, renewable at the end of every seven) almost obliged him to do. Counsel had urged that:

"... in point of law, the surrender makes it a new and independent origi-

---

[15]*ibid.* at 459.
[16](1740) 2 Atk. 74.
[17]*ibid.* at 75.
[18](1743) 2 Atk. 593.
[19]*ibid.* at 596: "Where a testator expresses himself in the present tense, it must relate to what is in being at the time of making the will, and can mean only the first lease and the term to come in it."

nal lease, yet, in equity, it is considered only as an ingrafting upon the old, and to be regarded as one consolidated interest."[20]

Despite such judicial reticence, however, in a wide-sweeping dictum in the later case of *Edwards v. Lewis*,[21] Lord Hardwicke L.C. extended the equitable principle in theory[22] to include a situation where the original lease had expired before the renewal was granted, and also where the person taking the new lease was not the original lessee, but took "in right of him who was the owner of the old lease", in which case "he must take subject to all the equity to which the original lease was liable."[23]

Further etymological pointers are furnished by the case of *Taster v. Marriott*,[24] in which Sir Thomas Sewell M.R. regarded a renewal obtained by the limited owner of a lease as an "ingraftment" upon the old lease, and made an order "that the renewed lease was to be considered as an engraftment on the leasehold interest in the premises comprized in the assignment," and that the limited owner "was to be considered as a trustee thereof, for the benefit of the persons entitled to the original lease."[25]

As the eighteenth century progressed one can discern the evolving constructive trust being applied to situations other than those concerning leasehold renewals in the strict sense. Hence, in the case of *Owen v. Williams*,[26] almost half a century after *Keech v. Sandford*, the widow of a testator, having a life estate in lands held under a Crown lease, who accepted a gratuity of three thousand pounds from an influential neighbouring landowner, in the reasonable expectation that the Treasury would prefer his application for a reversionary lease over hers, was held by Lord Bathurst L.C. to be obliged to hold the sum in trust for the benefit of those entitled in remainder.

Likewise, in *Blewett v. Millett*,[27] an analogy with leasehold renewals was drawn in the case of a trustee purchasing partnership shares in his own name, after his proposal that they be bought on behalf of the infant beneficiary had been rejected by his co-trustees. Counsel for the quondam infant, who was now seeking an account of profits accrued on his share, and in whose favour a decree was eventually granted, contended that the constructive trust principle

---

[20](1743) 2 Atk. 593 at 595-596.
[21](1747) 3 Atk. 538.
[22]The dictum to this effect not being strictly necessary on the facts of the case.
[23]*Edward v. Lewis*, above, n.21 at 538. One might note the resemblance between Lord Hardwicke L.C.'s expression "subject to all the equity" and the phrase familiar in Land Registry parlance, "subject to equities", which initially found expression in s. 29(3) of the Local Registration of Title (Ireland) Act, 1891, a sub-section which also incorporated a reference to graft, albeit in a modified sense.
[24](1768) 2 Ambler 668.
[25]*ibid.* at 668.
[26](1773) 2 Ambler 734.
[27](1774) 7 Brown P.C. 120.

was "a doctrine founded upon general policy, to prevent frauds" and that the classic case of *Keech v. Sandford* had "established it as a rule of equity", suggesting as a rationale for this phenomenon that:

> "[t]he trustee's situation in respect of the estate, gives him access to the landlord; and it would be dangerous to permit him to make use of that access for his own benefit."[28]

In *Rawe v. Chichester*[29] Lord Bathurst L.C. made his oft-quoted observation:

> "It may be laid down as a rule, that whoever has a lease has an interest in the renewal"[30]

and applied the *Keech v. Sandford* principle in a case where a testator's widow, having been bequeathed a life interest in a lease for years "during so many years of the term granted as she shall happen to live", obtained two successive renewals, of which the second was granted, not on the basis of the bequest in the will, but on the basis of the first renewal, both renewals containing additional lands to those comprised in the original lease – though these were expressly exempted from the constructive trust.[31]

A further development is represented by *Lee v. Lord Vernon*,[32] in which counsel adverted to the theoretical distinction between renewals obtained by limited owners and renewals obtained by persons occupying a fiduciary relation:

> "[T]he cases which have hitherto occurred have principally been of two kinds; some being cases of persons not having any beneficial interest in the old lease, as guardians and executors; and others being cases of persons having only partial and limited interests, as tenants for life, mortgagors and mortgagees . . ."[33]

in each of which cases the courts have invariably regarded the person obtaining the renewal as a trustee for those entitled in remainder:

---

[28] *ibid.* at 128.
[29] (1773) 2 Ambler 715.
[30] *ibid.* at 719.
[31] On the question of a similarly worded will, see *Phillips v. Phillips* (1885) 29 Ch. D. 673 and *Re Brady's Estate* [1920] 1 I.R. 710. On the question of additional property being included in the renewed lease, see *Acheson v. Fair* (1843) 2 Dr. & War. 512, *Giddings v. Giddings* (1826) 3 Russell 241 and *Re Morgan; Pillgrem v. Pillgrem* (1881) 18 Ch. D. 84.
[32] (1776) 5 Brown P.C. 10.
[33] *ibid.* at 15.

" . . . ever presuming that the new lease was obtained by means of the connection with, and a reference to the interest in the ancient one, without in the least regarding whether the persons renewing intended to act as trustees, or merely for their own emolument."[34]

Though the right of renewal claimed for in that case was accepted neither by the Court of Exchequer nor by the High Court of Parliament, due to the absence of manifest fraud or misrepresentation on the part of the person who obtained the renewal, yet the distinction drawn by counsel seems to have been endorsed implicitly by Lord Loughborough L.C. in *Pickering v. Vowles*,[35] where he observed that it was "the opportunity of renewal from being in possession"[36] that attracted the imposition of the constructive trust.

Similar language was employed by the same Lord Chancellor in the later case of *Stone v. Theed*.[37] Speaking of a tenant for life, Lord Loughborough L.C. said:

"... where such a tenant has renewed, then the court has said, that the estate given him being, from its nature, capable of renewal, the tenant for life, in renewing for his own use, would be making an unconscientious benefit of the estate . . ."[38]

and, as a result, is obliged to hold the renewed estate in trust for the remaindermen.

3. RENEWAL FINES

A corollary of the inevitable inter-relation between limited owners and those in remainder, and the judicial acceptance of their mutual duties, is afforded by the progressive relaxing of the rules about respective contributions to the costs of renewal – known as the "renewal fine".

Initially there seems to have been a tendency to oblige the life tenant to make a one-third contribution. Yet even this imposition, on scrutiny, was not as categorical as it might have appeared. Hence, even though in the case of *Lock*

---

[34] *ibid.* at 15.
[35] (1783) 1 Brown 197.
[36] *ibid.* at 198. "The right of renewal has obtained the name of a tenant right. The rule has obtained with respect to a tenant for life, who has the opportunity of renewal from being in possession, that he shall not obtain the reversion for his own use only. The Court has therefore obliged him to stand seised as a trustee to the uses of the settlement."
[37] (1787) 2 Brown 243.
[38] *ibid.* at 247.

v. Lock[39] Lord Cowper L.C. directed the widow to renew and pay a one-third contribution towards the renewal fine, it happened that the length of the renewed term was 21 years and there were still seven years to run of the existing term. Likewise in *Verney v. Verney*[40] Lord Hardwicke L.C. observed that, where a life tenant was also the last *cestui que vie* under a lease for lives, he should not be obliged to make any contribution towards the renewal fine, since, theoretically, he could never benefit from it.[41]

Similarly, in *Lawrence v. Maggs*[42] Sir Robert Henley, then the Lord Keeper,[43] postulated that "the renewing of the lease with any other life than that of the tenant for life is for the benefit of the remainderman"[44] and he alone, in such a case, should be accountable for the renewal fine. For that reason, under similar circumstances in *Adderley v. Clavering*[45] Lord Loughborough L.C. directed that the costs of renewal, plus interest from the date of advancement, must be deemed a charge on the estate, and that if the remaindermen were not prepared to accept this, they must agree to surrender the lease on the best terms they could. In that case counsel's argument that one should wait, before charging the renewal fine on the estate, to ascertain whether in fact the remaindermen would benefit from the renewal (in practical terms, to see if the life tenant should predecease the two newly appointed *cestuis que vies*) was expressly repudiated.

In the slightly earlier case of *Nightingale v. Lawson*[46] Lord Loughborough L.C. disapprobated the strict proportion rule, on the grounds that circumstances might transpire in which the life tenant would derive no benefit from the renewal: for example, if there were a long period of time still to elapse on the original lease. In the facts of the instant case the life tenant obtained a renewal of a lease for years for a term of 28 years, to commence in 1766. She died in 1775. The Lord Chancellor directed that the proportionate contribution payable by the remainderman was the ratio that the 19 years left to him to enjoy bore to the entire term of the renewed lease, with compound interest payable from the date of commencement.

Stone v. Theed[47] concerned a settlement in which the trustees had been directed to keep the leasehold interest alive by frequent renewals, and the question arose whether the renewal fine should be paid from the general trust fund, or by the life tenant alone, or by the life tenant with contributions from the

---

[39] (1710) 2 Vernon 666.
[40] (1750) Ambler 88.
[41] A one-third contribution was applied in this case also, but by consent.
[42] (1759) 1 Eden 453.
[43] Afterwards Lord Northington L.C.
[44] (1759) 1 Eden 453 at 455.
[45] (1789) 2 Cox C.C. 192.
[46] (1785) 1 Brown 440.
[47] (1787) 2 Brown 243.

remainderman. Lord Loughborough L.C. opted for the first option, on the grounds that, even after renewal, the life tenant would still only be a life tenant, and therefore would derive no benefit; then, having reviewed the constructive trust principle, observed "that so much as the life tenant took for himself, he should pay for; so much as he took for the benefit of another, he should be paid for by that other . . . the proportion should follow the benefit."[48]

By the turn of the nineteenth century, therefore, the principles governing proportionate contributions had become, in a sense, systematic, reflective of the equitable rule governing leasehold renewals generally, and were pithily embodied in a dictum of Lord Eldon L.C.: " . . . . it is better to determine the proportion upon fact than speculation."[49]

4. EXCEPTIONS TO THE APPLICATION OF CONSTRUCTIVE TRUSTS

It would be erroneous to suppose that the development of the constructive trust principle was free from exception or inconsistency. Exceptions there undoubtedly were, but these are most often bound up with marriage settlements, and show a marked affinity with the time-hallowed device of barring entailed estates.

(a) Barring the Entail

In the briskly reported case of *Cann v. Cann*,[50] from 1687, a life tenant, under a marriage settlement, with remainder to his wife for life, and further remainder to the heirs male of his body, successfully levied a fine and barred the entail, bequeathing his estate to a son of his second wife. In an action by the son of the first marriage to enforce the settlement, Lord Jeffries L.C. held that, since the life tenant was effectively a tenant in tail, it was within his capacity to bar the entail, as he had done.[51]

The case of *Cordwell v. Mackrill*,[52] in 1766, involved a similar situation, but here both the tenant for life and his wife levied a fine to such uses as they should appoint, and eventually agreed to execute a conveyance in fee to the defendant. On a technical point, Lord Northington L.C. felt that the defendant did not have sufficient notice of the articles of settlement to be bound by their terms, and also that the marriage articles themselves had not been sufficiently

---

[48] *ibid.* at 247.
[49] *White v. White* (1804) 9 Ves. 554 at 559.
[50] (1687) 1 Vernon 480.
[51] Though the actual *ratio* of the case is difficult to extract, it seems to have been of some significance that the original settlor had appointed the life tenant his executor, who in turn had made his second wife his own executrix.
[52] (1766) 2 Eden 344.

proven. Nevertheless, despite that the earlier case of *Cann v. Cann* was not cited, the Lord Chancellor seems implicitly to have adhered to a kindred reasoning in that part of his summing-up where he commented: "I cannot see any reason to lay it down as an universal rule, that in all cases of articles, the husband is to be only tenant for life."[53]

Blake v. Blake,[54] a case decided by the Chancery Division of the Court of Exchequer, is one in which the earlier decision of *Cann v. Cann* was relied on, but, it is arguable, incorrectly. A tenant in tail of property held under a church lease for lives, with remainders over in default of issue, successfully suffered a recovery, then informally surrendered his lease and took a new one. On an application by the remainderman to enforce the trusts of the settlement, the tenant in tail having died without issue and having attempted to dispose of the lease by will, it was held that the trust estate created by the original settlor had been "devested"; that the estate granted by the new lease for lives was quite different from that which had been put into settlement; and that, since the deceased tenant in tail could not have been called upon to execute a trust in his lifetime, no greater equity could prevail against his personal representative.[55]

It is respectfully submitted that, in the context of the overall thrust of the leasehold renewal cases which have been examined, an argument can be made that *Blake v. Blake* was incorrectly decided, and that the earlier case of *Cann v. Cann*, decided a hundred years earlier, was neither binding – due to the interim accretion of the constructive trust principle – nor even germane to the discussion.

(b) Acquisition of the Fee Simple Reversion

In the early years of the nineteenth century, two decisions of Sir William Grant M.R., *Hardman v. Johnson* and *Randall v. Russell*,[56] are associated with the emergence of the proposition that the acquisition of the fee simple reversion by the owner of a limited interest under a lease was not to be considered in the same way as the securing of a renewal of the lease by that limited owner.

In his judgment in *Randall v. Russell*, Sir William Grant M.R. regarded himself as bound by a decision of Lord Hardwicke L.C., from 1743, in the case of *Norris v. Le Neve*.[57] Of this case Sir William Grant M.R. observed: "There never was a stronger case for turning the purchaser of a reversion into a trustee for those who had the antecedent interest in the estate . . ." yet he concluded that Lord Hardwicke L.C. was simply unable to "find a ground for declaring

[53] *Cordwell v. Mackrill*, above, n.52 at 345.
[54] (1786) 1 Cox C.C. 266.
[55] *ibid.* at 268.
[56] (1815) 3 Merivale 347 and (1817) 3 Merivale 190, respectively.
[57] (1743) 3 Atk. 26.

the purchase to be a trust for those who had nothing to do with the reversion."[58]

It is by no means clear, however, that the decision in *Norris v. Le Neve* is in fact supportive of the proposition for which Sir William Grant M.R. ostensibly cited it. Indeed, upon examination of the facts in *Norris v. Le Neve* it becomes manifest that the Lord Chancellor could have done little else than decide as he did. The specific facts are complex, involving a title dispute that seems to have endured for the better part of seventy years. In 1674 one Oliver Neve executed a settlement, by which various properties were settled on himself for life, with remainder to his wife for life, remainder to his cousin Oliver, then an infant, for ninety-nine years, should he so long live, remainder in tail male to Oliver's heirs, remainder successively to Peter Neve for life and Francis Neve for life, with further remainder in tail to their respective heirs, and ultimate remainder in fee to the right heirs of the settlor. All this was done on the advice of one John Norris, the settlor's confidential attorney. The very next day after executing the settlement, the settlor executed a will in which he devised the settled property to John Norris, the attorney, for ten years, for the purpose of paying off estate debts. The settlor died in 1678, and in 1679 John Norris, while holding under the ten-year lease in trust to pay the estate expenses, and while the first life tenant, Oliver the cousin, was still in infancy, sought out the remainderman in fee and bought the reversion from him. Problems arose when this remainderman purported to convey the reversion a second time to Peter Neve, one of the beneficiaries under the settlement of 1674, through whom the present defendants were claiming. The plaintiff was the great-grandson of John Norris.[59]

The suit, reduced to its simplest terms, was to set aside the conveyance to Norris, as being a breach of trust on the part of Norris, and to give effect instead to the later conveyance to Peter Neve. Lord Hardwicke L.C., after summarising the facts, observed:

> "This is a transaction extremely to be disapproved, and I must say that a counsel or agent taking a conveyance from the right heir, for his own benefit, and which he discovered by his being a trustee, does a very wrong thing. . . . But this is a case *primae impressionis*, for it would be difficult to say for whom he is a trustee, and yet I should be extremely desirous of considering him as a trustee only, if I could be warranted in so doing."[60]

---

[58] (1817) 3 Merivale 190 at 198–199.

[59] The reason for the apparent inversion of the parties' roles in the title of the case derived from the fact that Norris had succeeded in recovering possession and profits in an earlier action instituted in 1741, and the present action was essentially an application by the Le Neve family to file a bill of review, adducing the fact, hitherto unknown, that they were the actual heirs-at-law to the original heir-at-law under the settlement, and various other circumstances which evinced the degree of confidence reposed by the settlor in John Norris, his attorney.

[60] (1743) 3 Atk. 26 at 37-38.

The Lord Chancellor, distinguishing *Keech v. Sandford* and the leasehold renewal cases, went on to give as his further opinion that, since there were several persons with successive life interests under the settlement, it was impossible to say that Norris, having purchased the reversion, should hold it in trust for any one of them, or that any one of them could have been deemed to have an expectation of the fee simple.

Although it is arguable that Lord Hardwicke L.C. could perhaps have adduced a fuller analogy between leasehold renewals and the purchase of the reversion, yet *Norris v. Le Neve* is significant in showing the Lord Chancellor's adversion to a general principle, which, on account of the peculiar fact circumstances, he felt himself not at liberty to apply.[61]

The decision of Lord Hardwicke L.C. was appealed to the House of Lords, which affirmed the Lord Chancellor's order, without further comment.[62] It is arguable that due consideration was not given by the House of Lords to the proposition of counsel for the petitioners, that Norris had abused the privileged position in which he found himself as a "country lawyer" to a large estate, such lawyers being "commonly left guardians and trustees", and having the capacity "to purchase for themselves any dormant titles or remote reversions of the estates of those families for whom they are concerned."[63] Counsel had further observed:

> "That public convenience (which is a source of equity from whence many and varied determinations have been drawn) required, that such a purchase as this should be held to be a trust; for otherwise no family in England could be safe."[64]

It would appear that this statement of principle conforms with that enunciated by Lord Hardwicke L.C., and it is to be regretted that the House of Lords did not specifically address it.

5. OTHER RELATIONSHIPS THAN TENANT FOR LIFE AND REMAINDERMAN

Although the development of the constructive trust throughout the eighteenth century was principally in the context of the renewal of leases and the respective rights of tenants for life and tenants in remainder, there were also cases in which the doctrine was successfully applied in other types of relationship –

---

[61] Lord Hardwicke L.C. also observed that the doctrine of laches would attenuate the merits of any case which the defendants might otherwise have had.

[62] (1744) 4 Brown 465.

[63] *ibid.* at 466.

[64] *Norris v. Le Neve* above, n.62 at 480.

particularly those which, in the legal language of the nineteenth and twentieth centuries, were said to attract a fiduciary or quasi-fiduciary duty. It behoves us, briefly, to turn to consider some of these.

(a) Mortgagors and Mortgagees

The foremost case on mortgages appears to be *Seabourne v. Powell*,[65] from 1686, in which it was held that a mortgagee had a "plain equity" to call for the benefit of a more perfect title subsequently obtained by the mortgagor, and not to rely instead, as a first alternative, on enforcing a surety bond.

In *Taylor v. Wheeler*[66] Sir Nathan Wright, the Lord Keeper, held, after expressing some doubt on the matter,[67] that a mortgagee by equitable deposit of copyhold deeds, which, however, had not been presented to the Court in good time (to satisfy a requirement analogous to the modern system of registration), had still a better equity than that of the mortgagor's assignees in bankruptcy. A mortgagee, averred the Lord Keeper, "was in the nature of a purchaser by a defective conveyance" and had, in the event, "contracted and agreed for a security on those lands, which the other creditors had not."[68]

The case of *Rakestraw v. Brewer*[69] perhaps embodies the clearest assertion of the developing constructive trust principle to mortgages. This concerned a lease for years of Chambers in Gray's Inns, the entire term of which had been mortgaged. The mortgagee, being a fellow Bencher of the Inns, contrived to procure a renewal for his own benefit to commence in 1731, the year the existing term was to expire. On an application by the mortgagors to redeem, it was contended by the mortgagee:

1. that the mortgagors, being women, and not having any connection with the Inns, would have been unable to obtain the renewal for themselves;

2. · that the second term was quite independent of the first, since it was not to commence till the first had ended.

Rejecting both these arguments, the Master of the Rolls observed:

"This additional term came from the old root, and is of the same nature,

---

[65] (1686) 2 Vernon 10. However, in relation to the corresponding right of mortgagors, see *Rushworth's Case* (1676) 2 Freeman 14, above, n.10.

[66] (1706) 2 Vernon 564.

[67] The Lord Keeper at first inclined to think that the mortgagee had been remiss in permitting a situation to arise in which the mortgagor's creditors might have been disposed to allow him further loans on the basis of an artificially appearing creditworthiness, his title deeds remaining undeposited.

[68] (1706) 2 Vernon 564 at 565.

[69] (1728) 2 P. Wms. 511.

subject to the same equity of redemption, else hardships might be brought upon mortgagors by the mortgagees getting such additional terms more easily, as being possessed of one not expired, and by that means worming out and oppressing a poor mortgagor."[70]

(b) "Guardian" and Infant

The conventional understanding of this relationship belongs to the more general body of trust law. For present purposes, there are two aspects warranting particular attention.

(i) The imputation of "guardianship"

This arose, essentially, in situations of unwarranted interference with the property of an infant by a stranger. The seminal authority is *Newburgh v. Bickerstaffe*,[71] in which the Lord Keeper observed: "if a man intrude upon an infant, he shall receive the profits, but as guardian; and the infant shall have an account against him in this court, as against a guardian", subject to the qualification that where the title was in dispute the infant would have to establish it. A similar pronouncement was made by Lord Hardwicke L.C. in *Morgan v. Morgan*,[72] a case in which the Lord Chancellor also pointed out that such accounts of rents and profits could be continued even after the infancy had determined, unless there were evidence that the infant, after coming of age, had expressly waived the account, but that the court should be especially zealous where the interfering party was the infant's father, since "the parental authority might hinder the bringing any bill or ejectment to recover the possession."

In a later case, *Dormer v. Fortescue*,[73] Lord Hardwicke L.C., attempting to ascertain the appropriate commencement date for an account of rents and profits, suggested that in cases involving infants, widows' dower or fraud, misrepresentation, or concealment on the part of the defendant occupier, accounts should be drawn from the accrual of the plaintiff's title.[74] Only under exceptional circumstances, such as where there was laches on the part of the plaintiff, or where the defendant did not have notice, or the deeds of the property were not available, should the account be limited from the date of bringing the bill only.[75]

---

[70] *ibid.* at 513.
[71] (1684) 1 Vernon 295.
[72] (1737) 1 Atk. 489.
[73] (1744) 3 Atk. 123.
[74] *ibid.* at 130.
[75] *Dormer v. Fortescue*, above, n.73 at 129. See generally in this context, *Griffin v. Griffin* (1804) 1 Sch. & Lef. 352, *Ex Parte Grace* (1799) 1 Bos. & Pul. 376, *Bloomfield v. Eyre* (1845) 8 Beav. 250, *Quinton v. Frith* (1868) 1 Ir. Eq. 396.

(ii) Cases involving an infant's death after a renewal by his trustee

This particular phenomenon might be regarded as a by-product of the constructive trust, since, on first appearances, the cases arrive at contradictory conclusions. *Mason v. Day*[76] concerned a lease for three lives which a mother took for herself and her heirs. The mother dying, the guardians of the infant heir obtained a renewal of the lease in the infant's name. In due course the infant herself died, and the question arose whether the renewed lease should devolve to the heirs of the infant's father (through the death intestate of the infant herself) or the heirs of the mother (in accordance with the trusts in the original lease for lives). The Master of the Rolls decided that the lease was a new acquisition, vesting in the daughter as purchaser, and that it should pass, therefore, to her own heirs, through her father.

Similar facts arose in the case of *Pierson v. Shore*,[77] in which Lord Hardwicke L.C. came to the same conclusion, although he did observe, *obiter*, that "in the case of a lease in trust, whatever new alterations are made, it is still subject to the old trust",[78] from which one might infer that, in cases of this general kind, the question whether a new lease is subject to the trusts governing the old lease depends very much on the peculiar circumstances of each case.

Such a view is borne out by *Witter v. Witter*,[79] in which a lessor agreed to renew a lease in settlement only on condition that it be transferred from years to lives. This had the effect of changing the nature of the estate from personalty to realty. Upon the death intestate of the infant, Lord King L.C. held that in equity the renewed lease should devolve, not as realty to the infant's heir, but as personalty to his administrator, "since the renewed lease, though for lives, comes in the place and stead of the original lease which was for years."[80]

In conclusion, despite that the dicta enunciated respectively by Lord Hardwicke L.C. in *Pierson v. Shore* and by Lord King L.C. in *Witter v. Witter* are conformable with the principle in *Keech v. Sandford*, it would appear from the above cases that renewals obtained by settlement trustees on behalf of infants were regarded as an exception – being looked upon, by and large, as new and independent purchases, exempt from the trusts of the governing settlement.

(c) Joint Tenants

This was a relationship which, during the eighteenth century, rarely arose in

---

[76](1711) Prec. Chan. 319.
[77](1737) 1 Atk. 479.
[78]*ibid.* at 480.
[79](1730) 2 P. Wms. 99.
[80]*ibid.* at 102.

the context of leasehold renewals. The *fons et origo* appears to be the tersely reported seventeenth century decision of *Palmer v. Young*,[81] in which it was decided that where "[O]ne of the three that held a lease under a dean and chapter, surrenders the old lease and takes a new one to himself . . . it shall be a trust for all."

A variant of this issue arose in the early twentieth century, in *Re Biss; Biss v. Biss*,[82] during the course of which Romer L.J., in the Court of Appeal, took the trouble of having unearthed and rechecked the original trial transcripts of Registrars Edwards and Devenish, from the Court of Chancery, in *Palmer v. Young*, to supplement the scant account in Vernon's Reports. From these transcripts it emerged that there had been a substantial degree of fraud not manifest from Vernon, the defendant joint tenants having wilfully concealed the title deeds, and not disclosing on their application for renewal that the plaintiff had also a joint interest. Consequently, it was decreed that the plaintiff was entitled at all times to an equal benefit of any renewals, subject to his paying a due proportion of the renewal charges.[83]

A further illustration is afforded by *Ex Parte Grace*.[84] In this a widow and administratrix, being entitled with her infant son to a joint interest in leasehold property owned by her late husband, remarried, and her second husband duly obtained a renewal in his own name. On an application by the son, after attaining his majority, for the benefit of his share under the renewed lease, it was argued on behalf of the step-father that there was no covenant for renewal and that, since he had been obliged to outlay money in obtaining the renewal, without knowing whether the infant would assent to it or not, the effect of a decision in the infant's favour would be to enable infants generally to claim the benefit of a renewal only in cases where the renewal transpired to be beneficial, and otherwise "to throw the whole burden on the trustee".

Eyre C.J., in the Court of Common Pleas, dismissed this contention as being incidental to the burdens of trusteeship. Such a duty the Chief Justice deemed to arise when one obtained a renewal of a lease in which an infant also had a joint interest.[85] Accordingly, the infant was entitled to a joint interest in the

---

[81] (1684) 1 Vernon 276.

[82] [1903] 2 Ch. 40.

[83] In *Re Biss* the Court of Appeal relied on the newly found fraudulent coloration in the facts of *Palmer v. Young* to distinguish that authority from the case they were deciding. However, it is arguable that the evidence of fraud does not detract from the general fiduciary principle as exemplified by *Ex p. Grace, cf.* n. 84 below.

[84] (1799) 1 Bos. & Pul. 376.

[85] "The point has been decided at least 40 times. Grace took the lease at his own peril; if it had not turned out beneficial he must have sustained the loss, but as it is a beneficial lease it must be for the benefit of the trust. This is the peculiar privilege of the unprotected situation of an infant." *Ex p. Grace*, at 377. Unfortunately, it is not wholly clear from the decision whether the overriding consideration was the fact of the joint entitlement, or the renewing party having married the executrix, and, as it were, having stepped into her shoes, or the mulcted party being at the

renewed lease, subject to the payment of a contribution towards the renewal fine.[86]

(d) Executors

Several of the cases already discussed have treated of life tenants and trustees who were also executors.[87] However, one case which succinctly demonstrates the application of the constructive trust principle to executors in particular is *Killick v. Flexney.*[88]

In this, the executor, having proved his testator's will, arranged for a valuation to be carried out of certain properties, then purchased them in his own name, securing also a personal promise for renewal in relation to such of the land as was leasehold. On an application by the infant beneficiary to have the sale set aside as fraudulent and a breach of trust, the High Court of Chancery acknowledged a dilemma:

> "The defendant, as executor, not only had a right to . . . assign the farm, and discontinue the cultivation of it on the account of the infant, but it was his duty so to do; he has sold it to himself and charged his own price, but shall he therefore be a trustee for the infant, for whom he could not, without a breach of trust, have held it . . .?"[89]

Following deliberation, the Lords Commissioners concurred that, in this instance, even after purchase the executor held the lands as trustee for the infant, especially since he had already worked them himself, though without being so obliged, for the period of 13 years beforehand.

6. Conclusion

In the early years of the nineteenth century, during the Lord Chancellorship of Lord Eldon, the principle that one occupying a fiduciary relationship could not

---

time of the renewal an infant. See the conflicting interpretations suggested by Buckley J., Collins M.R. and Romer L.J. in *Re Biss* [1903] 2 Ch. 40.

[86] See generally, *Hamilton v. Denny* (1809) 1 Ball & Beatty 199 (joint tenants), *Kieran v. McCann* [1920] 1 I.R. 99 (tenants in common), *Kennedy v. DeTrafford* [1896] 1 Ch. D. 762 and [1897] A.C. 180 (tenants in common) and *Dunne v. English* (1874) L.R. 18 Eq. 524 (partners).

[87] *e.g. Holt v. Holt* (1670) 1 Chan. Cas. 190, *Keech v. Sandford* (1726) Sel. Cas. Chan. 61, *Abney v. Miller* (1743) 2 Atk. 593, *Ex p. Grace* (1799) 1 Bos. & Pul. 376. See also *Walley v. Walley* (1687) 1 Vernon 484.

[88] (1792) 4 Brown P.C. 161.

[89] *Per* Eyre C.J. at 162.

be permitted to traffic for himself in property the subject of the trust was asserted with even greater rigidity and emphasis.[90]

In the Irish courts, at around the same time, the principle of the constructive trust, whose emergence over the preceding 100 years we have briefly traced, found itself both described and developed, in the context – of peculiarly Irish relevance – of leases and their renewal, and the respective rights of tenants for life and tenants in remainder, as the doctrine of graft. The elaboration of the doctrine, the zenith of significance that it achieved, its eventual disappearance in the middle years of the twentieth century, and the possible causes of its failure to achieve its potential as an uniquely Irish restitutive remedy, are worthy subjects of exploration in another paper than this. Even so, it is hoped that the foregoing analysis at least makes some case that the emergence of the constructive trust as an equitable doctrine in the English courts of the eighteenth century, and the peculiar nomenclature which often attended its development, provided the first tentative milestones on that vigorous voyage of discovery which eventually came to be known as the Irish doctrine of graft.

---

[90]See, *e.g. Campbell v. Walker* (1800) 5 Ves. 677, *Ex Parte Lacey* (1802) 6 Ves. 625, *Ex p. James* (1803) 8 Ves. 337, *Lord Milsington v. Musgrave and Portmore* (1818) 3 Maddock 491, and *Lord Selsey v. Rhodes* (1824) 2 Sim. & Stu. 49.

STATUTE OF LIMITATIONS (AMENDMENT) ACT 2000 AND ACTIONS FOR CHILD SEXUAL ABUSE

PAUL WARD

1. INTRODUCTION

"The damages wrought by incest are particularly complex and devastating, often manifesting themselves slowly and imperceptibly, so that the victim may only come to realise the harm she (and at times he) has suffered, and their cause, long after the statute of limitations has ostensibly proscribed a civil remedy. It has been said that the statute of limitations remains the primary stumbling block for adult survivors of incest. . . ."[1]

This statement by La Forest J., at the opening of his judgment in the Supreme Court of Canada decision on the limitation of actions for child sexual abuse claims arising from incest, is apt in describing the problems surrounding the bringing of such actions by adult survivors of child sexual abuse. Whilst *M.(K.). v. M.(H.)*[2] specifically concerned an action arising from incest, the judgments of the court are equally applicable to child sexual abuse arising from other relationships between victim and perpetrator. The degree and variety of psychological injury is not confined to sexual abuse arising from an incestuous relationship.[3]

The purpose of this contribution is to speculatively examine the Statute of Limitations (Amendment) Act 2000 ("the 2000 Act"), and to assess the extent to which it will provide an adequate avenue to victims of child sexual abuse in instituting actions against their abusers or those vicariously liable, in light of the issues faced by courts in other jurisdictions. The 2000 Act came into effect on June 21, 2000.

---

[1] La Forest J., *M.(K.) v. M.(H.)* (1992) 96 D.L.R. (4th) 289 at 293.

[2] *ibid.*

[3] See *P. v. T.* [1997] 2 N.Z.L.R 688, involving an adult victim of sodomy who claimed to have suffered eating disorders, repressed memory and psychological problems amounting to, according to the psychiatric evidence, a Post Traumatic Stress Disorder (PTSD); *H. v. H.* [1997] 2 N.Z.L.R. 700 involving the sexual abuse of a 10-year-old girl for two years by her mother's partner resulting in depression, blackouts, anxiety, low self esteem, anorexia and suicidal thoughts; *H. v. R.* [1996] 1 N.Z.L.R. 299 involving the abuse of a seven-year-old boy until he was 15 resulting in mood disturbances, self harm and self mutilation, hypersensitivity, feelings of persecution, outbursts of anger, drug and alcohol abuse and sexual dysfunction.

To appreciate why an amendment to the Statute of Limitations 1957 and the Statute of Limitations (Amendment) Act 1991 (the 1957 and 1991 Acts) was necessary, the effects of sexual abuse perpetrated upon a child need explanation. There is considerable academic writing on the effect, specifically of incest, upon adult survivors of child sexual abuse.[4] The act of committing sexual abuse upon a child may have a twofold effect. First, there is the obvious immediate physical invasion of the child amounting to an assault and battery. Secondly, the child will suffer immediate and latent psychological harm. The former psychological harm manifests itself in the child being coerced by the abuser's threats to assume responsibility for engaging initially and later instigating sexual activity and ultimately to maintain secrecy. Further the child is infected with feelings of shame and guilt which are maintained by the fear of disclosure and adverse consequences for the child and his or her family. This harm is compounded if the child's attempt to reveal the abuse is met with disbelief, scepticism or anger from persons in authority. The latter psychological harm manifests itself in depression, self-mutilation, eating disorders, drug or alcohol abuse, sexual dysfunction, inability to form intimate relationships, promiscuity, prostitution and vulnerability to re-victimisation.[5] Such consequences amount to Post-Traumatic Stress Disorder (PTSD) or, in lawyer's terminology, "nervous shock".

In tortious terms, the injury or damage caused by child sexual abuse readily falls within the concept of personal injuries.[6] More difficult is the issue of pigeonholing child sexual abuse into a recognised tort for the purpose of limitation periods within which to bring a successful action. The not necessarily appropriate, but obvious tort under which to classify child sexual abuse is assault and battery[7] but this has been described by La Forest J. in *M.(K.) v. M.(H.)*[8] as "a crude legal description" who stated that in order to fully understand the elements of the tort in this context, it was necessary to examine the complex

---

[4] Gelinas, "The Persisting Negative Effects of Incest" (1983) 46 *Psychiatry* 312; Summit, "The Child Sexual Abuse Accommodation Syndrome" (1983) 7 *Child Abuse & Neglect* 177; Finklehor and Browne, "The Traumatic Impact of Child Sexual Abuse: A Conceptualisation" (1985) 55 *Amer. J. Orthopsychiat.* 530; Handler, "Civil Claims of Adults Molested as Children: Maturation of Harm and the Stature of Limitations Hurdle" [1987] *Fordham Urb. L.J.* 709; DeRose, "Adult Survivors and the Statute of Limitations: The Delayed Discovery Rule and Long Term Damages" (1985) 25 *Santa Clara L. Rev.* 191; Lamm, "Easing Access to the Courts for Incest Victims: Toward an Equitable Application of the Delayed Discovery Rule" (1991) 100 *Yale L.J.* 2189.

[5] La Forest J., *M.(K.) v. M.(H.)* (1992) 96 D.L.R. (4th) 289 at 300-301 citing the authors at n. 4, above.

[6] s. 2(1) of the Statute of Limitations 1957 provides that personal injuries "includes any disease and any impairment of a person's physical or mental condition."

[7] Sexual abuse has been accepted as an assault and battery in Canada in *K.(M.) v H.(M.)* (1992) 96 D.L.R. (4th) 289; in New Zealand in *S. v. G.* [1995] 3 N.Z.L.R. 681 and in England and Wales in *Stubbings v. Webb* [1993] A.C. 498.

[8] (1992) 96 D.L.R. (4th) 289 at 299.

nature of abuse and its consequential harms. Cooke P. in *T. v. H.*,[9] referring to the consequential harm of child sexual abuse, stated that civil actions for such were "of a special nature justifying a distinct legal classification or approach."

2. ASSAULT AND BATTERY

McMahon and Binchy define assault[10] as "an act that places another person in reasonable apprehension of an immediate battery being committed upon him." Battery is defined by the authors as "the direct application of physical contact upon the person of another without his or her consent, express or implied, may constitute a battery."[11] The advantages of maintaining an action for personal injuries in assault and battery are that the tort is actionable *per se*, an onus rests upon the defendant to show that he acted neither intentionally nor negligently and that the direct consequences rule as opposed to the reasonable foreseeability rule in terms of remoteness of damage applies.

An action for assault and battery accrues for limitation purposes, in the case of personal injuries arising from the physical invasion of the child, when the tort is committed upon the child. This involves establishing that there was physical contact and that such occurred without the consent of the child. In this regard, the tort will not be complete until the child establishes that no consent was given. The New Zealand Court of Appeal decision in *S. v. G.*[12] is instructive in this regard. This case concerned a tortious action against the defendant for sexually abusing the plaintiff between 1978 and 1980 when she was aged between 14 and 16. Gault J., for the court, accepted the proposition set out in *K.(M.) v. H.(M.)*[13] that the reasonable discoverability rule applicable in torts that require proof of damage should apply to a case where consent is a necessary element in the proof of the tort. It is only when the plaintiff reasonably discovers the causal link between the psychological harm and the perpetration of sexual abuse by the defendant that the cause of action accrues. In other words, not until the plaintiff appreciates and understands that the abuse suffered by him or her is the cause of the adverse psychological consequences of the abuse, is the plaintiff in a position to understand that he or she did not consent to the battery. It is then that the tort of battery is complete and actionable and when, for limitation purposes, time begins to run. This realisation or understanding of the causal link between abuse and psychological harm may only occur some time after the child has reached the age of majority and often

---

[9] [1995] 3 N.Z.L.R. 37 at 42-43.
[10] *Irish Law of Torts* (2nd ed., Dublin, 1990) at p. 405.
[11] *ibid.* at p. 46.
[12] [1995] 3 N.Z.L.R. 681.
[13] (1992) 96 D.L.R. (4th) 289 at 299.

does not occur until the then adult undergoes some form of therapy which reveals the causal link in the mind of the abused. This in effect would postpone not the limitation period commencing to run, but fundamentally more important the accrual of the cause of action which is a necessary prerequisite for the limitation period to commence. Further, as Hammond J. in *H. v. R.*,[14] stated "'consent', that word, has its ordinary everyday meaning: such must be a rational decision by a person who is in a position to make an informed decision. Generally, under-age children cannot make such decisions."[15] These comments speak for themselves.

If an Irish court were to adopt this approach in interpreting the 1957 and 1991 Acts, it would afford the victims of child sexual abuse the opportunity to avail of an indefinite limitation period which would only commence to run when the tort of assault and battery was complete, and thereafter, the plaintiff would have a six-year period within which to commence an action for damages. The plaintiff, of course, would have to satisfy the court that the necessary consent was not given by providing psychiatric and psychological evidence to the effect that the mental appreciation of the causal link between abuse and harm did not materialise until the time asserted by the plaintiff. The only English authority, *Stubbings v. Webb*,[16] a House of Lords decision, did not consider the role of reasonable discoverability in relation to consent in assault and battery owing to the fact that the date of discoverability test only applied to actions for personal injuries based on breach of duty, negligence and nuisance. The House of Lords, on the facts of the case, were of the opinion that the plaintiff, upon reaching the age of majority, was aware that she had been raped, sexually assaulted and abused; and time began to run for the purposes of the plaintiff's action in assault and battery from that time. Lord Griffith stated "... I have the greatest difficulty in accepting that a woman who knows that she has been raped does not know that she has suffered a significant injury."[17] The House of Lords adopts what can be said to be an objective assessment of the plaintiff's state of mind on reaching the age of majority. This approach would present prospective plaintiffs with considerable difficulty in establishing their cause of action.

This of course presupposes that an Irish court would be willing to adopt such reasoning and further that a claim for personal injuries may be brought in assault and battery to which the six-year limitation period applies from the time when the tort is complete, rather than requiring all actions for personal injuries to be brought within a three-year period based upon the broad notion of a breach

---

[14] [1996] 1 N.Z.L.R. 299.
[15] *ibid.* at 305.
[16] [1993] A.C. 498.
[17] *ibid.* at 506.

of duty not to cause injury to another.[18] *Long v. Hepworth*[19] decided that the phrase "breach of duty"[20] encompassed all actions in tort, whether intentional or unintentional, where the claim was for damages for personal injuries. Were this to be followed in this jurisdiction it would require all plaintiffs seeking damages for personal injuries to bring their claim within three years of the date on which the action accrued. Brady and Kerr[21] query the correctness of the decision in *Long v. Hepworth*,[22] as the court did not differentiate between actions in negligence, nuisance and breach of duty on the one hand and actions in trespass to the person on the other hand, despite the glaring omission of the parliamentary draftsman to specifically include actions such as false imprisonment, assault, battery and malicious prosecution along with the particularly identified actions of negligence, breach of duty and nuisance as provided for in section 11(1) of the Limitations Act 1980.

In *Stubbings v. Webb*,[23] which involved a claim for damages for sexual abuse by a stepfather and stepbrother, the House of Lords overruled *Long v. Hepworth*[24] on the basis of the above reasoning. The advantage of this decision for a plaintiff is that a six-year limitation period applies, the disadvantage is that the date of discoverability does not apply to actions for personal injuries based on an intentional tort and specifically that of assault and battery.

There are obvious problems in following the House of Lords approach where the action for damages lies in assault and battery. The New Zealand approach would afford the plaintiff much wider scope in bringing an action but one must bear in mind that the damages that a plaintiff could recover would be limited to the direct physical invasion of the body or physical injury as opposed to damages for the adverse and latent psychological and psychiatric damage caused to the plaintiff. Needless to say, recovery for such injury is more important to the plaintiff. A possible avenue for a plaintiff would be to attempt to bring an action under the rule in *Wilkinson v. Downton*.[25] This tort amounts to the intentional or reckless infliction of emotional suffering upon the plaintiff and is

---

[18]s. 3(1) of the Statute of Limitations (Amendment) Act 1991 provides:
"An action, other than one to which s. 6 of this Act applies, claiming damages in respect of personal injuries to a person caused by negligence, nuisance, breach of duty (whether the duty exists by virtue of a contract or a provision made by or under a statute or independently of any contract or any such provision) shall not be brought after the expiration of three years from the date on which the cause of action accrued or the date of knowledge (if later) of the person injured."

[19][1968] 1 W.L.R. 1299.

[20]s. 11(1) of the Limitation Act 1980 is in identical terms to s. 3(1) of the Statute of Limitations (Amendment) Act 1991.

[21]*The Limitation of Actions* (2nd ed., Dublin, 1994) at p. 59.

[22][1968] 1 W.L.R. 1299.

[23][1993] A.C. 498.

[24][1968] 1 W.L.R. 1299.

[25][1897] 2 Q.B. 57.

generally classed amongst the torts that fall under trespass to the person. There is no Irish authority concerning this tort or any judicial indication it would be adopted in Irish law. In any event, the elements of this tort do not appear to require the plaintiff to establish that no consent was given, and thus the mechanism utilised by the court in *S. v. G.*[26] would not have to be adopted to enable an action to be brought. It would, however, require a court to adopt a date of reasonable discoverability of psychological damage to the plaintiff to enable an action to be brought and not to fall foul of the limitation period. Such would be a novel development not just in Irish law but in the common law world, and such a departure is fraught with difficulty and uncertainty.

3. NEGLIGENCE AND BREACH OF DUTY

The most accommodating tort in which to recover for both physical and psychological damage is negligence. Section 3(1) of the 1991 Act[27] expressly provides an action for personal injuries arising from negligence shall be brought within three years from the date on which the action accrued or the date of knowledge of the person injured. Negligence actions, which require proof of damage, are actionable when the plaintiff suffers damage. Physical damage or injury to the plaintiff and the commission of a negligent act often coincide. However, certain physical injuries are latent and whilst provable to be manifest at a time in and around the commission of the negligent act or omission, are not discoverable until a considerable time after the limitation period has either commenced or expired. Prior to the introduction of the 1991 Act, the 1957 Act would bar the bringing of claims resulting in latent personal injury to a plaintiff. The Supreme Court in *Hegarty v. O'Loughran*[28] acknowledged that, in tortious actions based upon breach of duty and negligence, damage may occur to a plaintiff, which would commence the limitation period running, but that the plaintiff could be unaware the damage had occurred until some time after the limitation period had expired.[29] Brady and Kerr describe the effects of pneumoconiosis and asbestosis on the lungs[30] which are apt examples of latent damage. A more recent example are the army deafness decisions which shed some light on the interpretation of the 1991 Act.[31] In this regard the condition,

---

[26][1995] 3 N.Z.L.R. 681.

[27]See n.18, above.

[28][1991] 1 I.R. 148.

[29]*ibid., per* Griffin J. at 158 and *per* McCarthy J. at 164, who advocated that particularly in medical negligence actions, the date of discovery should not be limited to knowledge of injury or damage but further to discovery of an actionable cause, that is knowledge of the facts sufficient to put him on notice of an invasion of his legal rights.

[30]*The Limitation of Actions, op. cit.,* above, n.21 at p. 62.

[31]Some recent cases to consider the "date of knowledge" provision under s. 3(1) of the Statute of

"tinnitus", a recurring ringing in the ears, is a direct injury to the plaintiff caused by exposure to excessive noise levels without protection. The condition is usually immediately apparent to the plaintiff. A consequential and latent, but invariably discoverable injury to such plaintiffs, is hearing loss. This typically only reveals itself when brought to the attention of the plaintiff by family members and friends and often is only verified after the plaintiff has undergone audiogram testing. Hearing loss can be a direct consequence of exposure to excessive noise whereby the loss in hearing ability coincides with the negligent act but the loss gradually becomes worse over time and is exacerbated by ageing and the natural deterioration of hearing.

The judgment in *Whitely v. Minister for Defence*[32] analyses section 3(1) of the 1991 Act. Quirke J. was of the opinion that the section was primarily subjective but was subject to the objective qualifying criteria set out in section 2(2).[33] He noted that the term "significant" in section 2(1)(b) was not defined, unlike in the equivalent English Act,[34] which in Quirke J.'s view attracted a

---

Limitations (Amendment) Act 1991 are: *Kerwick v. Minister for Defence*, unreported, High Court, March 19, 1999; *Cremins v. Minister for Defence*, unreported, High Court, February 17, 1999, both O'Donovan J.; *Gallagher v. Minister for Defence* [1998] 4 I.R. 457 and *Whitely v. Minister for Defence* [1998] 4 I.R. 442.

[32] [1998] 4 I.R. 442.

[33] s. 2 of the Statute of Limitations (Amendment) Act 1991 provides:
2.–(1) For the purposes of any provision of this Act whereby the time limit within which an action in respect of an injury may be brought depends on a person's date of knowledge (whether he is the person injured or a personal representative or dependant of the person injured) references to that person's date of knowledge are reference to the date on which he first had knowledge of the following facts:
(a) that the person alleged to have been injured has been injured,
(b) that the injury in question was significant,
(c) that the injury was attributable in whole or in part to the act or omission which is alleged to constitute negligence, nuisance or breach of duty,
(d) the identity of the defendant, and
(e) if it is alleged that the act or omission of a person other than the defendant, the identity of that person and the additional facts supporting the bringing of an action against the defendant:
and knowledge that any acts or omissions did or did not, as a matter of law, involve negligence, nuisance or breach of duty is irrelevant.
(2) For the purposes of this section, a person's knowledge includes knowledge which he might reasonably have been expected to acquire:
(a) from facts observable or ascertainable by him, or
(b) from facts ascertainable by him with the help of medical or other appropriate expert advice which it is reasonable for him to seek.
(3)Notwithstanding subsection (2) of this section-
(a) a person shall not be fixed under this section with knowledge of a fact ascertainable only with the help of expert advice so long as he has taken all reasonable steps to obtain (and, where appropriate, to act on) that advice; and
(b) a person injured shall not be fixed under this section with knowledge of a fact relevant to the injury which he has failed to acquire as a result of that injury.

[34] s. 14 of the U.K. Limitation Act 1980 provides for a "date of knowledge". The injury to the plaintiff must be "significant" which is defined in s. 14(2) as: "if the person whose date of

broader meaning than the definition afforded under the corresponding English legislation. He concluded that the test to be applied was "primarily subjective and that the court should take into account the state of mind of the particular plaintiff at the particular time having regard to his particular circumstances at that time."[35] On the facts of the particular case, it was found that the plaintiff had stated that he suffered from tinnitus and hearing loss from 1979, which was a year after his leaving the army. Quirke J. considered a number of personal factors that may have affected the plaintiff's knowledge of his tinnitus and hearing loss but was of the view that the plaintiff was aware, subjectively, that he had suffered a significant injury by 1979 and 1981 at the latest.[36] Turning to the objective criteria set out in section 2(2), Quirke J. was satisfied that only section 2(2)(a) need be addressed, in that the plaintiff was fixed with knowledge of a significant injury from facts observable or ascertainable by him, namely that he was aware that he had a ringing in his ears and that he had daily difficulty in hearing in 1979. Time began to run from that date which barred his bringing of the action.

Quirke J.'s analysis has been followed in *Gallagher v. Minister for Defence*[37] by O'Higgins J., where the defence was defeated. There the plaintiff was aware that he had been injured in 1989 when the army doctor informed him that his hearing was impaired and that he would not be permitted to play in the army band until examined by a specialist. Whilst the plaintiff was aware that he was injured in 1989, he did not realise that this was significant until 1990 when he was examined by a specialist who revealed the extent of the plaintiff's injury. Here it would appear that section 2(2)(b) was of considerable importance to the plaintiff's inferred knowledge, in that it was only on the advice of a specialist that he acquired knowledge that his injury was significant or, in the words of section 2(2)(b), the plaintiff had facts ascertained by him with the help of medical advice. It is the obtaining of specialist medical advice,[38] as opposed to the advice of the army doctor which was of a preliminary and precautionary nature, that fixed the plaintiff with knowledge that his injury was significant.

---

knowledge is in question would reasonably have considered it sufficiently serious to justify his instituting proceedings for damages against a defendant who did not dispute liability and was able to satisfy a judgment."

[35] [1998] 4 I.R. 442 at 453.

[36] *ibid.*, at 454-455, Quirke J. noting the plaintiff's direct evidence as to his symptoms.

[37] [1998] 4 I.R. 457.

[38] Similar facts arose in *Cremins v. Minister for Defence*, unreported, High Court, O'Donovan J., February 17, 1999, but in *Kerwick v. Minister for Defence*, unreported, High Court, O'Donovan J., March 19, 1999, the plaintiff's tinnitus claim was held to be statute barred owing to his knowledge of the injury two years after leaving the army in 1983 and about which he did nothing until 1989. In relation to the plaintiff's hearing loss claim, this was held not to be statute barred as the significance of the injury was only realised by the plaintiff after he was referred by his solicitor to a doctor for audiogram testing.

The Supreme Court has considered the "date of knowledge" provision in *Bolger v. O'Brien and Ors*[39] in a unanimous and single judgment of the court. The case involved a road traffic accident in March 1990, of which the immediate injuries to the plaintiff were that he was rendered unconscious, suffered extensive cuts, bruising and lacerations for which he received medical treatment at the time of the accident. The plaintiff required physiotherapy and was unable for manual labour on returning to work. In addition the plaintiff claimed that he was unaware that he had suffered an undisplaced fracture of his sacrum until re-examination and x-ray confirmed such in October 1992. The plaintiff had been x-rayed at the time of the accident but the medical opinion on whether there was an undisplaced fracture was not definitive.[40] Hamilton C.J. stated the injuries sustained by the plaintiff, including the undisplaced fracture of the sacrum, were known to the plaintiff at the time of the accident and that further the injuries were known to be significant.[41] The test was "when he knew or ought reasonably to have known *from facts observable or ascertainable by him* that he had suffered a significant injury."[42] Hamilton C.J. stressed that the trial judge failed to have regard to the injuries sustained by the plaintiff at the time of the accident and his knowledge of such at that time and thereafter. The trial judge had erred in finding that the plaintiff was unaware of the full significance of his injuries in that he did not understand them until October 1992, which was the incorrect test, as opposed to whether the injuries were significant at the time of the accident, which was the correct test.[43] This was the case irrespective of whether an objective or subjective test was applied. In this regard the court did not expressly approve or disapprove of the approach adopted by Quirke J. *in Whitely v. Minister for Defence*[44] Hamilton C.J. noted, however, that counsel for both parties accepted the statement by Quirke J. as the correct test to be applied.

The date of knowledge of the plaintiff was established by reference to his knowledge of his injuries immediately following the accident. No weight was given to the plaintiff's assertion that he was only aware of the full significance of his undisplaced fracture at the time of his re-examination in October 1992.[45] What appears to be determinative of the plaintiff's knowledge of significant injury is the fact that his concussion, lacerations and bruising were manifest

---

[39][1999] 2 I.L.R.M. 372, Hamilton C.J., Denham, Barrington, Keane and Lynch JJ. concurring.

[40]*ibid.* at 372., where Hamilton C.J. refers to McGuinness J.'s judgment, unreported, High Court, April 24, 1998, where she accepted that the orthopaedic surgeon's view as to the undisplaced sacrum was in doubt.

[41]*ibid.* at 380, stating the evidence to this effect was uncontested.

[42]*ibid.* at 380, (as emphasised by Hamilton C.J. in the unreported version of the judgment.)

[43]*ibid.* at 380–381.

[44][1998] 4 I.R. 442.

[45][1999] 2 I.L.R.M. 372, Hamilton C.J. at 379-380 cites the transcript of the plaintiff's cross-examination in which he accepts that he was told that he had an undisplaced fracture of the sacrum on examination after the accident.

and apparent to him immediately after the accident. The court appears to hold that he was at least aware that he may have suffered an undisplaced fracture to the sacrum as a result of his examination at the time of the accident and this appears sufficient to fix the plaintiff with knowledge that this too was a significant injury. Further, the consequences of these identified injuries resulted in him requiring physiotherapy and that he was unable for manual labour on return to work. In this regard it can be said that he was aware that he had suffered injury and that such injuries were significant. The injuries suffered by the plaintiff were physical in nature and were inflicted as a direct result of the accident.

The problem facing an Irish court would be the application of the existing case law on the "date of knowledge" test to an adult victim of child sexual abuse. To draw an analogy between physical latent damage and latent psychological damage may be misguided and in itself form an uncertain basis for analysis. In any event, the injuries would have to be divided into physical and psychological damage to the plaintiff.

4. PHYSICAL INJURY

In relation to a claim for damages for personal injury based in negligence[46] for the infliction of physical injury resulting from sexual abuse, a child turned adult plaintiff would firstly benefit from the disability provision in section 48 of the Statute of Limitations 1957. On reaching the age of majority and without reference to the "date of knowledge" proviso, the action would accrue, and a plaintiff would have three years within which to bring an action.[47] If the "date of knowledge" proviso were to be relied upon by a plaintiff seeking to bring an action beyond the expiration of the three year limitation after the plaintiff had ceased to be under a disability, the issue for the court would be when was the plaintiff aware that he or she had suffered a significant injury. Much would depend upon the psychological state of the plaintiff in determining this issue but some guidance can be found from the common law jurisdictions. In *Stubbings v. Webb*[48] the House of Lords held, albeit in relation to a claim based on assault and battery from which the injuries suffered may be said to be a direct consequence, that the plaintiff was aware that she had suffered a significant injury when she reached the age of majority in January 1975. The fact that the plaintiff was aware that she had been raped, sexually assaulted and abused,

---

[46]Breach of duty would be an alternative basis on which to maintain an action and nuisance in this regard would have a very limited if not redundant role.

[47]s. 5(1) of the Statute of Limitations (Amendment) Act 1991 amended s. 49(1)(a) of the Statute of Limitations 1957 by providing a three-year limitation period within which to bring an action based upon s. 3 of the 1991 Act.

[48][1993] A.C. 498.

commenced the limitation period running when she reached the age of majority. As she did not institute proceedings until August 1987, her action was statute barred. Similarly in *S. v. G.*[49] the New Zealand Court of Appeal held that "where some recognised damage flows immediately from the alleged conduct, the limitation period commences to run."[50]

The decisions of the Supreme Court, the House of Lords and the Court of Appeal in New Zealand[51] all hold that the plaintiff's knowledge of direct and immediate physical injury arises at the time injury is inflicted and time begins to run from that date or from the time that the plaintiff ceases to be under the disability of minority status. Once the plaintiff is aware that an injury has been suffered or in sexual abuse cases, that sexual abuse occurred, it is sufficient for the limitation period to commence. If an action is not therefore brought within three years of the date on which the action accrued,[52] the claim for damages for direct physical injury resulting from the sexual abuse would be statute barred. Such a finding is obviously fatal to the claim for direct personal injury, but may also be fatal in relation to a claim for latent psychological injury depending on what influence the common law authorities may have on an Irish court's approach to this issue.

5. LATENT PSYCHOLOGICAL INJURY

The consequential psychological injuries suffered by a child turned adult victim are causally linked to the infliction of sexual abuse. The date upon which an action for damages based in negligence would accrue to a plaintiff, without reference to the "date of knowledge", would be when the child ceases to be a minor. In this regard, the claim for psychological injury resembles that of a nervous shock action. Broadly speaking, nervous shock actions fall into two main categories of how the shock is caused. The first category involves the plaintiff suffering both physical injury and consequential psychological injury, the latter of which traditionally Irish courts have never had difficulty in compensating.[53] Indeed as far back as 1884, even apprehension of the infliction of

---

[49][1995] 3 N.Z.L.R. 681.

[50]*ibid.*, at 687 *per* Gault J. for the court stating that the physical injuries to the plaintiff, namely the infliction of anal and vaginal warts, could not be said to be wholly latent such that no cause of action should arise until later therapy linked the consequential psychological damage to the abuse.

[51]*Bolger v. O'Brien and Ors* [1999] 2 I.L.R.M. 372; *Stubbings v. Webb* [1993] A.C. 498; and *S. v. G.* [1995] 3 N.Z.L.R. 681 respectively.

[52]That is the date on which the negligent act of sexual abuse occurred or the date on which the plaintiff reaches the age of majority.

[53]*Hogg v. Keane* [1956] I.R. 155 and more recently *MacCarthy v. Murphy*, unreported, High Court, McCracken J., February 10, 1998, in which the plaintiff recovered damages for depression as a result of a road traffic accident.

physical injury with consequent psychological injury was recoverable.[54] The second category of nervous shock injuries result from what is described as the "aftermath doctrine", towards which the Irish Superior Courts,[55] and indeed the Circuit Court,[56] have adopted a flexible approach. A claim for psychological injury, of which the plaintiff was aware, would thus fall within the former category of "nervous shock" actions for which a plaintiff could institute proceedings within three years of reaching the age of majority. Where, however, the psychological injury is claimed to be unknown at the time the action accrued, the plaintiff would have to seek to rely upon sections 2 and 3 of the 1991 Act. This may prove to be a difficult task in light of section 2(2)(a) and (b). These sections in effect provide for inferred knowledge of a significant injury. The central issue would appear to be what significance would a court place upon a plaintiff's knowledge that he or she had been sexually abused? Would knowledge of this fact alone be sufficient to trigger sections 2(2)(a) and (b)? Further, sexual abuse victims may be aware of symptoms of the sexual abuse, but may not realise the connection between those symptoms and the sexual abuse. Being aware of either the abuse or the symptoms may lead a court to enquire as to why a plaintiff did not seek "appropriate expert advice", from which a court could infer a date of knowledge. The House of Lords in *Stubbings v. Webb*[57] held that because the plaintiff knew she had been sexually abused she had knowledge that she had suffered a significant injury. Further, Lord Griffiths stated that, if he had to decide whether the date of knowledge were to apply, he would not have found it easy to agree with the Court of Appeal.[58] The adoption of such an approach would probably result in an action being statute barred.

Alternatively, an Irish court could embrace the stance adopted by the Su-

---

[54] *Byrne v. Southern and Western Railway Company* unreported, Court of Appeal, February, 1884, discussed in *Bell v. G.N. Railway Co.* (1890) 26 LR (IR) 428, at 441-442.

[55] *Mulally v. Bus Éireann* [1992] 2 I.L.R.M. 722; *Kelly v. Hennessy* [1995] 3 I.R. 253, in which in the High Court, Mr Justice Lavan found as a fact that the plaintiff suffered an immediate nervous shock on being informed by phone that her family had been involved in a road traffic accident. In *McLoughlin v. O'Brian* [1983] 1 A.C. 410, the House of Lords categorically stated that nervous shock in aftermath cases must be caused by the plaintiff directly witnessing by their own senses the injury sustained to a relative and that a third party communication would not suffice as a means of communicating the shock to the plaintiff. This stance has been adhered to in subsequent cases such as *Ravenscroft v. Rederiaktiebolaget Transatlantic* [1991] 3 All E.R. 73 and *White v. Chief Constable of the South Yorkshire Police* [1999] 1 All E.R. 1. In *Kelly v. Hennessy*, however, the plaintiff did attend the hospital where she witnessed the injuries to her family..

[56] *Curran v. Cadbury (Ireland) Ltd* [2000] 2 I.L.R.M. 343, Judge McMahon, which contains an excellent analysis of the law on this topic in both Ireland and England.

[57] [1993] A.C. 498, the case was based upon assault in which the plaintiff was seeking to invoke a date of knowledge which she claimed only accrued when she underwent therapy for her psychiatric and psychological problems.

[58] *ibid.*, at 328.

preme Court of Canada in *M.(K.) v. M.(H.)*,[59] where La Forest J. held that, when the plaintiff, here an incest victim, discovers the connection between the harm she has suffered and her sexually abusive childhood, the cause of action crystallises. Further, the majority held[60] that there is a presumption that such victims do not realise the connection between the consequential adverse psychological harm and the infliction of sexual abuse until receiving therapeutic assistance either professionally or in the general community.[61] A court could interpret the phrase "knowledge which he might reasonably have been expected to acquire"[62] in line with the Canadian and New Zealand approaches and justify this by acknowledging that such actions are of a special nature requiring special accommodation[63] within law and by adopting a conscientious stance against child sexual abusers availing of the defence afforded by limitations periods.[64] If Quirke J.'s[65] primarily subjective approach were to be given considerable weight, with particular subjective regard to the plaintiff's state of mind, such an approach may overcome the difficulties the plaintiff encountered in *Stubbings v. Webb*.[66] Further, the New Zealand Court of Appeal[67] approach could be adopted which is in essence that of the Canadian Supreme Court's test but without the benefit of the presumption attaching. The absence of the presumption makes relevant the time at which a plaintiff seeks therapeutic assistance in light of the plaintiff's knowledge of his or her abuse and symptoms related thereto.

The varying American approaches would also be a basis for determining whether an action is statute barred.[68] La Forest J., however, was not prepared

---

[59] (1992) 96 D.L.R. (4th) 289.

[60] Sopinka and McLachlin JJ. dissenting.

[61] (1992) 96 D.L.R. (4th) 289 at 306.

[62] s. 2(1) of the Statute of Limitations (Amendment) Act 1991.

[63] As noted by La Forest J. in *M.(K.) v. M.(H.)* (1992), 96 D.L.R. (4th) 289 at 299; Cooke P. in *T. v. H.* [1995] 3 N.Z.L.R. 37 at 42-43 and Sir Nicolas Browne-Wilkinson V-C in *Stubbings v. Webb* [1992] Q.B. 197, at 212.

[64] See La Forest J.'s sentiments in this regard at (1992) 96 D.L.R. (4th) 289 at 302, 304 and 315.

[65] *Whitely v. Minister for Defence* [1998] 4 I.R. 442.

[66] [1993] A.C. 498. The House of Lords heard the appeal on October 12 and 13, 1992 and gave judgment on December 16, 1992. The *M.(K.) v. M.(H.)* decision was handed down on October 29, 1992 and, apparently, was not brought to the attention of the House.

[67] *S. v. G.* [1995] 3 N.Z.L.R. 681 at 687, Gault J. for the court adopting the *M.(K.) v. M.(H.)* test whereby the plaintiff's cause of action in negligence will not accrue until the link between psychological harm and past sexual abuse is reasonably discovered.

[68] In *Tyson v. Tyson* (1986) 727 P. (2d) 226 the Washington Supreme Court refused to apply the delayed discovery rule; *De Rose v. Carswell* (1987) 242 Cal. Rptr. 368 (Cal. App. 6 Dist.) suggested that the delayed discovery rule should be adopted; *Mary D. v. John D.* (1989) 264 Cal. Rptr. 633 (Cal. App. 6 Dist.) applied the rule; *Hammer v. Hammer* (1978) 418 N.W. (2d) 23 (Wis. App.) likewise applied the delayed discovery rule; *Raymond v. Ingram* (1987) 737 P. (2d) 314 (Wash. App.) followed *Tyson*; *Whatcott v. Whatcott* (1990) 790 P. (2d) 578 (Utah App.) likewise refused to apply the delayed discovery rule as did the Nevada court in *Petersen v. Bruen* (1990) 727 P. (2d) 18 (Nev.).

to embark upon the categorisation of victims into Type 1[69] and Type 2[70] categories as had occurred in the United States with varying approaches as to how the limitation periods should operate in sexual abuse and incest cases.

The evidence in these cases supporting the claim that the plaintiffs were unaware of the connection between psychological injury and the infliction of sexual abuse is of interest. In *M.(K.) v. M.(H.)*[71] the plaintiff was sexually abused by her father from the age of eight until 16. She married in 1974 at the age of 18 and had three children. The marriage broke down in 1983 because the plaintiff could no longer engage in a sexual relationship with her husband. She was referred to a psychologist to assist with her depression and marital problems. It was at this stage that the psychologist was aware that the plaintiff had been sexually abused but no therapy commenced, as the necessary trust between patient and therapist had not been established. In 1983 the plaintiff disclosed to her new partner her childhood sexual abuse. She participated in self-help incest groups and proceeded in 1984 and 1985 to undergo therapy. It was only at this stage that the plaintiff understood that she was not responsible for the sexual abuse. Of significance was the evidence that her disclosures of abuse at the age of 11 and 16 identified that the plaintiff had an intellectual awareness of the sexual abuse and its effect, but the plaintiff did not have an emotional awareness of the connection between cause and effect. It can be said of these facts the plaintiff was both aware that abuse had been inflicted upon her and that she was at least aware of some of the adverse psychological symptoms associated with that abuse. Crucially, however, she was not aware of the causal link between these symptoms and the infliction of abuse.

Similarly in *S. v. G.*[72] awareness of sexual abuse and its symptoms were insufficient to amount to reasonably knowing the link between psychological damage and the sexual abuse. Here, however, the plaintiff was found to have been aware of the necessary causal link in September 1990, which barred her bringing of her action for exemplary damages in October 1993. In the course of a counselling session, the plaintiff disclosed the abuse to an experienced counsellor. The court held that at that stage the plaintiff's action accrued. The court also noted that the plaintiff had a year earlier received psychiatric assistance for her symptoms of abuse, during which it was reasonable for the plaintiff to have disclosed her abuse to an experienced professional. Here it would appear that knowledge of both the abuse and the symptoms of that abuse coupled with the seeking of assistance for those symptoms amounted to inferring that the plaintiff had the requisite knowledge for her action to accrue. The

---

[69] Such a plaintiff is aware that and has always known that he or she has been sexually abused but has never been aware that physical or psychological problems were caused by the abuse.

[70] Such a plaintiff, due to the trauma of sexual abuse, has no recollection of the abuse until shortly before the institution of proceedings.

[71] (1992) 96 D.L.R. (4th) 289.

[72] [1995] 3 N.Z.L.R. 681.

plaintiff's action was also barred in *H. v. H.*,[73] and another New Zealand case involving claims for exemplary damages based upon a claim for assault and battery, was barred by applying the reasonable discovery test to the issue of consent.[74]

The above approaches, at best, in terms of clarity and certainty, signal the statute barring of actions in negligence for latent psychological injury and at worst the possible adoption of a flexible approach to such claims defeating a limitations defence.

One further speculative approach would be reliance upon section 2(3)(a) and (b) of the 1991 Act.[75] Here a plaintiff may attempt to claim that he or she failed to acquire knowledge of a relevant fact, namely the causal connection between psychological injury and the infliction of sexual abuse, as a result of the injury, namely the infliction of sexual abuse. Such an example is the Type 2 category of psychological injury identified by the United States courts where, as a result of the trauma of sexual abuse, the plaintiff has no recollection of the sexual abuse until shortly before the institution of proceedings. Needless to say, if only this category were entitled to maintain proceedings whereas the Type 1 category were not, such would be an unjust and arbitrary discrimination against those plaintiffs who are aware of the abuse and possibly of the conse-quential psychological symptoms of the abuse, but are unaware of the causal connection between symptoms and abuse. Of course, this speculation is sub-ject to the wording of section 2(3)(a) which imposes an obligation upon a plaintiff to take all reasonable steps to obtain expert advice to ascertain the relevant fact. A strict application of this subsection would prevent both Type 1 and 2 plaintiffs maintaining successful actions.

---

[73] [1997] 2 N.Z.L.R. 700, the plaintiff disclosed the abuse to her doctor in May 1992 and under-went therapy. She also sought accident compensation. In February 1993, the plaintiff made a complaint to the police and did not institute proceedings until March 1996. Her claim was held to have accrued in August 1992 and was thus statute barred.

[74] *P. v. T.* [1997] 2 N.Z.L.R. 688 involved an adult victim of sexual abuse committed in 1980 whose cause of action accrued in 1986, when she informed a fellow patient of the abuse and wrote to her doctor concerning the abuse, having the preceding year undergone therapy for her symptoms; but in *H. v. R.* [1996] 1 N.Z.L.R. 299, the plaintiff was sexually abused by the defendant when aged seven in 1967 until 1975. In 1991, aged 31, the plaintiff first admitted the abuse but claimed he only became aware of the link between the abuse and his psychological problems in 1992 and instituted proceedings in 1994, which the court held to be within the limitation period.

[75] s. 2(3) provides: "Notwithstanding subsection (2) of this section –
   (a) a person shall not be fixed under this section with knowledge of a fact ascertainable only with the help of expert advice so long as he has taken all reasonable steps to obtain (and where appropriate, to act on) that advice; and
   (b) a person injured shall not be fixed under this section with knowledge of a fact relevant to the injury which he has failed to acquire as a result of that injury."

6. DISABILITY

On the basis of the law prior to the introduction of the 2000 Act, the disability provisions in section 48 and 49 of the 1957 Act would appear to afford victims of child sexual abuse the best opportunity of defeating a limitations defence. Some plaintiffs in the cases decided to date have attempted to fall within the tolling effect of disability provisions commonly provided for in limitation statutes. Specifically, plaintiffs have claimed that the psychological injury inflicted results in the plaintiff suffering from a disability or is "of unsound mind" and is thereby incapable of instituting proceedings. In *T. v. H.*,[76] the plaintiff claimed that the infliction of the sexual abuse resulted in psychological injury to the plaintiff to the extent that she was under a disability and thus incapable of instituting proceedings. The New Zealand Court of Appeal accepted that a disability could arise from inflicting sexual abuse and tolls the limitation period until the disability ceased.[77] Tipping J. stated the requirement as follows:

> "A plaintiff claiming a disability by way of unsoundness of mind must, in my judgment, show two things: first the alleged unsoundness pertains to a part or facet of the mind relevant to and sufficiently inhibiting the capacity to sue; and second that the alleged unsoundness results from a demonstrable and recognised mental illness or disability rather than being just an inability to face up to the process of suing."[78]

Here a plaintiff need not be incapacitated, in a general sense to the extent that they are unable to manage their affairs entirely, but are particularly or relevantly incapacitated to the extent that they cannot institute proceedings.

This approach would accord with the views and language of Barron J. in *Rohan v. Bord na Mona*[79] where, in relation to sections 48 and 49 of the 1957 Act, he stated:

> "The purpose of the provision is to save a cause of action for someone to whom it has accrued but because of a disability may be unable to pursue it. If so, it is immaterial whether the plaintiff was at the date of the accident or immediately as a result thereof became of unsound mind. He requires the same protection in either case."[80]

---

[76] [1995] 3 N.Z.L.R. 37. See also *P. v. T.* [1997] 2 N.Z.L.R. 688 where the plaintiff failed to establish that she was suffering from a disability.
[77] *ibid. per* Hardie-Boys J. at 48-49, Casey and Gault JJ. concurring.
[78] *ibid.* at 61.
[79] [1990] 2 I.R. 425
[80] *ibid.* at 430.

All that an Irish court would have to do is accept psychological and psychiatric evidence that a plaintiff suffered from a psychological disability inflicted by the sexual abuse to the extent that it prevented the plaintiff from instituting proceedings. The plaintiff need not prior to the infliction of sexual abuse causing the psychological disability be shown to be of "unsound mind". The "unsoundness of mind" may arise as a result of the tortious conduct of the defendant. Indeed, this is the approach adopted by the legislature in the 2000 Act whereby the disability of the plaintiff must be established by reference to the plaintiff suffering from any psychological injury.[81]

7. THE STATUTE OF LIMITATIONS (AMENDMENT) ACT 2000

The effect of the 2000 Act is to confer the status of disability upon a plaintiff. Section 48 of the 1957 Act is amended by the insertion of section 48A. This enables a plaintiff to sue either the person responsible for committing the sexual abuse in tort[82] or to sue in negligence or breach of duty a person who the plaintiff claims to have been negligent or in breach of duty which resulted in damage to the plaintiff arising from the committing of sexual abuse.[83] The status of disability only arises for a plaintiff where the injury to the plaintiff results from sexual abuse. Sexual abuse is broadly defined in section 2[84] and must have been committed when the plaintiff was not of full age,[85] that is eighteen years of age after the commencement of the Age of Majority Act

---

[81] s. 2 of the Statute of Limitations (Amendment) Act 2000.

[82] s. 2 of the Statute of Limitations (Amendment) Act 2000 inserting s. 48A(1)(a) into the Statute of Limitations 1957.

[83] s. 2 of the Statute of Limitations (Amendment) Act 2000 inserting s. 48A(1)(b) into the Statute of Limitations 1957. This in essence will enable a plaintiff to sue those vicariously responsible for the conduct of the person committing the sexual abuse. In the case of State run institutions, the relevant Minister and the appropriate defendants.

[84] s. 2 of the Statute of Limitations (Amendment) Act 2000 inserting s. 48A(7)(a)-(c) into the Statute of Limitations 1957 provides:
"In this section–
"an act of sexual abuse" includes-
    (a) any act of causing, inducing or coercing the person to participate in any sexual activity,
    (b) any act of causing, inducing or coercing the person to observe any other person engaging in any sexual activity, or
    (c) any act committed against, or in the presence of, a person that any reasonable person would, in all the circumstances, regard as misconduct of a sexual nature."

[85] s. 2 of the Statute of Limitations (Amendment) Act 2000 inserting s. 48A(7) into the Statute of Limitations 1957 defines full age as:
    (a) in relation to a person against whom an act of sexual abuse was committed before the commencement of the Age of Majority Act 1985, 21 years, and
    (b) in relation to a person against whom an act of sexual abuse was committed after such commencement, full age within the meaning of that Act.

1985 and 21 years of age prior to the commencement.[86] Further and more importantly, the disability status only arises where the plaintiff is suffering from any psychological injury that is caused by the committing of sexual abuse by the defendant or any other act of the defendant and must be of such significance that the plaintiff's will, or his inability to make a reasoned decision, to bring such action is substantially impaired.[87]

How the courts will determine if the plaintiff's will or the ability to make a reasoned decision is substantially impaired by any psychological injury of significance will be of concern. The assessment of such cannot be wholly subjective or objective. It must involve both a subjective and objective approach for the psychological trauma caused by sexual abuse cannot be of universal degree of impairment to all plaintiffs. Of note is that the term "significant" is not defined and, unlike section 2(1), (2) and (3) of the 1991 Act, there are no objective criteria by which to assess the significance of the psychological injury.

The disability approach provides for greater certainty than the various approaches outlined above. Fundamentally the 2000 Act recognises that one of the symptoms of sexual abuse is the inability to institute legal proceedings against the perpetrator of the abuse.[88] The other symptoms of being unable to acknowledge the abuse or even to disclose it to a third party, be it a professional or other person, pervade the Canadian and New Zealand decisions. Indeed, in the Dáil, the Minister for Justice, Equality and Law Reform, Mr O'Donoghue, expressly acknowledged this symptom as a fundamental reason for amending the law.[89]

The 2000 Act preserves the cause of action until the disability ceases whereas the above approaches provide a defendant with the opportunity to establish the requisite elements of the tort were in being, or should have been to known to be in existence at a given time, thereby commencing the limitation period and defeating a cause of action by the technical operation of the law. Only the Canadian approach in *K.(M.) v. H.(M.)*[90] would provide a plaintiff with cer-

---

[86] March 1, 1985.

[87] s. 2 of the Statute of Limitations (Amendment) Act 2000 inserting s. 48A(1)(i) and (ii) into the Statute of Limitations 1957.

[88] *T. v. H.* [1995] 3 N.Z.L.R. 37 at 43 Cooke P. expressly accepting such. The other members of the court accepted the general proposition that sexual abuse results in a psychological injury amounting to a disability, which preserves the cause of action.

[89] 505 *Dáil Debates* Col. 1026. The Minister stated "We now know better, that these feelings of shame and self-blame can paralyse the will and the ability of otherwise rational people when it comes to dealing with the consequences of the abuse they have suffered. Apart altogether from entering on the path of litigation, many such victims will have difficulty in bringing themselves to avail of the counselling and psychotherapeutic services they need. Often until they have availed themselves of such services over a considerable period they are unable psychologically even to consider what remedies may be available through the courts. The Government's view is that the case for changing the law of limitation as it applies to child sexual abuse cases is unanswerable."

[90] (1992) 96 D.L.R. (4th) 289.

tainty that an action could be instituted. Indeed, in theory, the 2000 Act goes further than the Canadian approach by acknowledging that sexual abuse affects the plaintiff's capacity to institute proceedings rather than postponing the accrual of the action. The distinction between knowledge that the injury has been sustained, and incapacity to institute proceedings is important. A plaintiff may undergo therapy and then realise that a significant injury has been sustained, in which case a cause of action accrues, but, if because of that injury, a plaintiff's will or the ability to make a reasoned decision to bring an action is substantially impaired, then the plaintiff is under a disability which preserves the cause of action and the limitation period commencing until the disability ceases. The time lapse between knowledge of the injury and the ability to institute proceedings may prove to be the contentious issue in any attempt by a defendant to defeat the disability provision. If a defendant can establish that a plaintiff was not under a disability, then the plaintiff cannot avail of the provisions of the 2000 Act. The requirements of disability will turn on the following issues. First, whether the plaintiff is suffering from *any* psychological injury.[91] This is sufficiently broad to cover a broad spectrum of psychological injury, which from a defendant's perspective will operate as a considerable initial hurdle in raising a limitation defence. Secondly, the plaintiff must establish that the injury is of such significance that either the will of the plaintiff or the ability to make a reasoned decision to bring an action is substantially impaired. Here a defendant will attempt to establish that the injury is not of the necessary degree of significance, but this may also prove to be a difficult hurdle to overcome. Alternatively, a defendant may attempt to establish that neither the will nor the ability to make a reasoned decision was impaired or if it was that it was not substantially impaired. Defendants who have attempted to avail of the limitation defence in relation to either the cause of action accruing or the issue of disability have received little or no sympathy from the courts[92] but at the same time have benefited from a strict application of the law on limitations.[93] Whilst a court should strictly apply a limitation statute, particularly one specifically introduced to provide a remedy, it can be envisaged that a defendant, who is proven to have committed a tort in inflicting sexual abuse upon a child, may attract little sympathy in attempting to disprove the disability status by challenging and scrutinising the evidence of the plaintiff. It is, of course, the right of every defendant to defend an action. The reality is that once a plaintiff establishes disability, the cause of action is established.

---

[91] My emphasis.

[92] See the views of the Supreme Court of Canada in *K.(M.) v. H.(M.)* (1992) 96 D.L.R. (4th) 289; the Court of Appeal in *Stubbings v. Webb* [1992] Q.B. 197 and the New Zealand Court of Appeal *in S. v. G.* [1995] 3 N.Z.L.R. 681.

[93] In particular the House of Lords in *Stubbings v. Webb* [1993] A.C. 498 and the New Zealand Court of Appeal in *S. v. G.* [1995] 3 N.Z.L.R. 681.

8. DELAY

The danger for a plaintiff in maintaining a successful action and the advantage for the defendant in defending such under the 2000 Act is section 3. This expressly reserves to a court the power to dismiss an action for delay.[94] The section is clear and precise and entitles a court to dismiss an action owing to the delay between the accrual and the bringing of the action. The section mirrors the Supreme Court decision in *Toal v. Duignan (No. 2)*[95] which held that, notwithstanding both the fact that proceedings had been instituted within the limitation period provided and the absence of culpable negligence on the part of the plaintiff for the delay, a court, in the interest of justice, may dismiss a plaintiff's action. Finlay C.J. stated, however, that the inherent jurisdiction to dismiss should not be exercised frequently or assumed lightly.[96] The reasoning for this stems from the judgment of Henchy J. in *O Domhnaill v. Merrick*[97] where he stated that the problem for a court was to strike a balance between a plaintiff's need to carry on his or her delayed claim and the defendant's basic right not to be subjected to a claim which he or she could not reasonably be expected to defend.[98] Henchy J. in his judgment did stress the need for the delay to be inordinate and inexcusable and that the plaintiff was personally culpable in this regard. In *Toal v. Duignan (No. 1)*[99] and *Toal v. Duignan (No. 2)*[100] the Supreme Court rejected that the plaintiff's own culpable negligence for the delay was an essential ingredient for the exercise of the jurisdiction to dismiss an action. Of interest in these cases is to what the court identifies as the period of delay relates to. In *O Domhnaill v. Merrick*[101] Henchy J. objected to the defendant defending an allegation of negligence 24 years later in a trial stating: ". . . a trial after such a remove in time from the cause of action would be essentially unfair. . . ."[102] Here the cause of action had accrued to the plaintiff and that as a complete action it should be prosecuted with expedition. The plaintiff sustained severe personal injuries as an immediate consequence of a road traffic accident. The injuries were not latent in any respect. In both the *Toal* cases, Finlay C.J. identified the period of delay as being the "time which has elapsed between the events out of which it arises and the time

---

[94] s. 3 provides: "Nothing in s. 48A of the Statute of Limitations, 1957 shall be construed as affecting any power of a court to dismiss an action on the ground of there being such delay between the accrual of the cause of action and the bringing of the action as, in the interests of justice, would warrant its dismissal."

[95] [1991] I.L.R.M. 140.

[96] *ibid.* at 143, Griffin J. concurring.

[97] [1984] I.R. 151.

[98] *ibid.* at 157.

[99] [1991] I.L.R.M. 135.

[100] [1991] I.L.R.M. 140.

[101] [1984] I.R. 151.

[102] *ibid.* 158.

when it comes for hearing. . . ."[103] This suggests that it is the answering of the allegations relating to the defendant's conduct after such a lapse of time that makes it unjust to oblige the defendant to defend the action. Here the injury to the plaintiff was latent, but discovered by the plaintiff within the limitation period. As the issue of the discoverability of the plaintiff's injury was not an issue in any of these cases, the relevant courts were not called upon to consider this issue in relation to delay.

The *Toal (No. 2)* decision post dates the Supreme Court decision in *Hegarty v. O'Loughran*[104] by five months in which the Chief Justice acknowledged that legislation providing for discoverability of injury was "possibly very desirable"[105] and McCarthy J. strongly advocated the adoption of such in his judgment.[106] One could say, with hesitation as the issue was not raised, that the Supreme Court in *Toal (No. 2)* was mindful of the earlier decision in *Hegarty v. O'Loughran*[107] in formulating the position as regards delay. What is clear from these decisions is that it is the period of delay from the acts complained of, without reference to the issue of injury, latent or discovered, to the trial of the action that is important. In this regard, a court dealing with a child sexual abuse claim based in tort involving the same lapse as either *Toal v. Duignan (No. 1)*[108] or *O'Domhnaill v. Merrick*[109] may feel bound by those decisions to dismiss for delay. Further, the culpability of the plaintiff for the delay is clearly stated to be irrelevant. These factors could be fatal to the bringing of an action which in all reality will match if not exceed the time lapse of the above decisions.

A review of the law relating to delay concerning child sexual abuse cases may be necessary. In this regard the existing authorities may be distinguished. First, the statement of Finlay C.J. in *Toal v. Duignan (No. 2)*[110] concerning delay contains the usual escape clause that it is "in all the circumstances"[111] unjust to defend the action. This in itself may enable a court to avoid a strict application of these decisions to actions for child sexual abuse. Secondly, a court may take cognisance of the introduction of the "date of discoverability" introduced by the 1991 Act which was motivated by the criticisms in *Hegarty v. O'Loughran*.[112] A court may lean to the view that no delay can arise where the plaintiff is unaware of the injury in that the action has not accrued and thus

[103] [1991] I.L.R.M. 135 at 139 and [1991] I.L.R.M. 140 at 142 respectively.
[104] [1990] 1 I.R. 148.
[105] *ibid.* at 157.
[106] *ibid.*, at 164.
[107] [1990] 1 I.R. 148
[108] [1991] I.L.R.M. 135, a period of 25-26 years in relation to all the defendants save the fifth defendant where the period was 16 years.
[109] [1984] I.R. 151, a period of 24 years.
[110] [1991] I.L.R.M. 140.
[111] *ibid.* at 142.
[112] [1990] 1 I.R. 148.

time has not commenced running,[113] and adopt the strong views expressed by McCarthy J., that where a limitation period is provided by statute, as the 1991 Act so provides, once the action is commenced within that period, then the action cannot be statute barred.[114] Thirdly, certain specific facts were found in both *Toal* cases which would make it unjust to defend the action. The first named defendant was sued in his official capacity as Master of the Coombe hospital but at the time of the allegations of negligence neither was he a member of the staff of the hospital nor a qualified doctor. The third named defendant was deceased at the time of the hearing. The fourth named defendant was sued as the widow of a deceased paediatrician who was a consultant at the hospital at the relevant time. The fifth named defendant was a general practitioner whose alleged negligence would revolve around a telephone conversation in 1971. The same circumstances involved the alleged negligence of the eighth named defendant. Further the hospital administration, the second named defendant, was prejudiced by the loss of documentation in a physical move of the hospital some years after the birth of the plaintiff. Here the essence of the prejudice against these defendants was the availability of essential oral and documentary evidence to defend the allegations of negligence. The same prejudice would affect the plaintiff in attempting to obtain discovery of relevant documents. In a child sexual abuse action, such complexities will not arise. The oral evidence of the parties will determine the issues of fact. There may be documentary evidence lost or unavailable to the defendant, but it is impossible to imagine how this may be of significance in raising a defence.

Further, in this regard, a court may be susceptible to the arguments raised by the Canadian Supreme Court in in *K.(M.) v. H.(M.)*,[115] concerning the evidentiary principle underlying the rationale for limitation periods.[116] Finally, the wording of section 3 of the 2000 Act may itself curtail the existing law on delay. The section expressly defines the period of delay as between the accrual of the action and the bringing of the action. If a court accepts the reasonable discoverability principle in relation to the intentional torts and the issue of consent, and in relation to negligence actions and the reasonable discoverability of psychological injury, neither action will accrue until it shown that no consent was given or the psychological injury has been reasonably discovered. If this approach were adopted, no issue of delay would arise. This, of course,

---

[113] *Hegarty v. O'Loughran* [1990] 1 I.R.148 at 164.

[114] *O Domhnaill v. Merrick* [1984] I.R. 151 at 165–166.

[115] (1992) 96 D.L.R. (4th) 289.

[116] *ibid.* at 302 *per* La Forest J., who also rejected the application of the other two underlying principles for limitation periods in sexual abuse cases, namely: that a defendant must have a reasonable expectation that he will not be held accountable for his ancient obligations was of no public benefit and inequitable to allow such individuals go on with life while the plaintiff continued to suffer; that plaintiffs should not be allowed to sleep on their rights and should litigate in a timely fashion was inappropriate where the plaintiff was unaware of the injury.

presupposes that section 3 is intended to reflect the "inherent jurisdiction" that the courts possess and the courts do not interpret this as independent of their inherent jurisdiction to dismiss an action for delay.

9. FRAUD

Section 71(1)(b) of the 1957 Act provides that where the right of action is concealed by the fraud of the defendant, the period of limitation does not run until the plaintiff has discovered the fraud or could with reasonable diligence have discovered the fraud. This may be of considerable assistance to a plaintiff who falls foul of the limitation period or where there is a delay in the institution of proceedings. In *M.(K.) v. M.(H.)*[117] the Canadian Supreme Court unanimously accepted that fraudulent concealment could apply with the effect of tolling the limitation period. Specifically in relation to incest cases and by accepting the psychological effect that incest has upon the victim, La Forest J. reasoned as follows:

> "Incest takes place in a climate of secrecy, and the victim's silence is attained through various insidious measures. As we have seen, these actions by the perpetrator of the incest condition the victim to conceal the wrong from herself. The fact that the abuser is a trusted family authority figure masks the wrongfulness of the conduct in the child's eyes, thus fraudulently concealing her cause of action."[118]

By adopting a subjective interpretation of "could with reasonable diligence have discovered the fraud" and by accepting La Forest J.'s view, section 71 of the 1957 Act could prevent a defendant from defeating a plaintiff's claim. It could with relative ease apply to incest cases and, by extension, to all cases of child sexual abuse where the victim is coerced by the abuse itself to conceal it. Of course, if a court were to accept such a proposition, it would in turn be accepting the concept of the reasonable discoverability rule whereby an action is found not to have accrued, be it in relation to consent in assault and battery or the knowledge of a significant injury in negligence.

Recently in *Behan v. Bank of Ireland*[119] the Supreme Court considered section 71 of the 1957 Act. Barron J., with whom O'Flaherty J. concurred,

---

[117] (1992) 96 D.L.R. (4th) 289.

[118] *ibid.* at 320.

[119] [1998] 2 I.L.R.M. 507. See also *Heffernan v. O'Herlihy*, unreported High Court, Kinlen J., April 3, 1998, where a solicitor was held to have fraudulently concealed the plaintiff's cause of action first, by indicating that the summons had issued at a time when it had not, and secondly, by failing to disclose to the plaintiff that the action was then statute barred.

approved of the interpretation given by Lord Denning M.R. in *Archer v. Moss*[120] where the term "fraud" was to be interpreted in the equitable sense of unconscionable conduct, rather than in a common law sense. Here, the bank agreed to accept a lesser sum in discharge of a debt owed to it by the plaintiff. The bank, however, failed to inform the plaintiff of the credits made to his account which would result in the bank recouping a greater sum in discharge of the debt owed than the plaintiff had agreed to. This failure to inform concealed his cause of action. Further, it was significant that the plaintiff could not have discovered such credits.

Sexual abuse cases and the above approach may accord. Certainly the infliction of sexual abuse is unconscionable conduct. Further the concealment arises at the time the cause of action arises or as La Forest J. phrased it "incest is a double wrong – the act of incest itself is followed by an abuse of the child's innocence to prevent recognition or revelation of the abuse . . . the abuser compels the complicity of the victim in denying the harm done to her . . .",[121] concluding that "the courts will not allow a limitation period to operate as an instrument of injustice."[122]

10. BREACH OF FIDUCIARY DUTY

The 1957, 1991 and 2000 Acts may be entirely circumvented by a plaintiff basing an action for damages in equity by claiming breach of fiduciary duty. It is the breach of the duty that gives rise to the cause of action without the need to establish any particular damage. The provisions of the 1957 Act do not apply to actions for equitable relief which is governed by section 2(2)(a)(i).[123]

Whether a plaintiff is owed a fiduciary duty depends upon the relationship with the defendant. In the decided child sexual abuse cases the parent/child relationship,[124] medical practitioner and child patient relationship[125] and de facto partner of the child's mother relationship[126] have been held to amount to fiduciary relationships. The wider familial and non-professional relationships

---

[120][1971] 1 All E.R. 747.
[121](1992) 96 D.L.R. (4th) 289 at 321.
[122]*ibid.*
[123]s. 2(2)(a)(i) provides: "In this Act, "trustee" does not include–
(i) a person whose fiduciary relationship arises merely by construction or implication of law and whose fiduciary relationship is not deemed by any rule of law to be that of an express trustee."
[124]*M.(K.) v. M.(H.)* (1992) 96 D.L.R. (4th) 289 and *Evans v. Eckelman,* (1990) 365 Cal. Rptr. 605; *Daniels v. Thompson* [1998] 3 N.Z.L.R. 22 comprising four conjoined appeals to the New Zealand Court of Appeal.
[125]*S. v. G.* [1995] 3 N.Z.L.R. 681.
[126]*H. v. H.*[1997] 2 N.Z.L.R. 700.

have not been decided and the New Zealand Court of Appeal was reluctant to declare such in *H. v. R.*[127]

But there may be scope to further extend the classes of fiduciary relationships. In *M.(K.) v. M.(H.)*[128] La Forest J. cited the identifying characteristics for a fiduciary relationship as proposed by Wilson J. in *Frame v. Smith*[129] as:

1.   The fiduciary has the scope for the exercise of some discretion or power.

2.   The fiduciary can unilaterally exercise that power or discretion so as to affect the beneficiary's legal or practical interests.

3.   The beneficiary is peculiarly vulnerable to or at the mercy of the fiduciary holding the discretion or power.

These criteria were subsequently adopted by the Canadian Supreme Court in *Hodgkinson v. Simms*[130] and recently by McGuinness J. in *McMullen v. Clancy.*[131] La Forest J. was satisfied that the parent/child relationship fell within these characteristics and particularly so the third. Further, the fiduciary duty can extend beyond non-economic interests[132] and oblige the fiduciary to act or refrain from acting according to the nature of the relationship to the extent that a not irrebutable but strong presumption of fiduciary relationship arises. Such an approach would enable a court to extend the fiduciary relationship beyond that of the parent child one to such where the child is placed in a vulnerable position.

Were a breach of fiduciary relationship to arise, it would be subject to the defendant relying upon recognised defences. The 1957 Act would be of no avail to a defendant in these circumstances. Equity would be called upon to adopt by analogy the common law statutory limitation period. Here divergence has arisen between the Canadian and New Zealand courts. La Forest J. in *M.(K.) v. M.(H.)*[133] reasoned that no such analogy should be made. First, having adopted the reasonable discoverability rule, the operation of such, by analogy in equity would defeat the defendant's claim. Secondly, where the claim falls exclusively within equity's jurisdiction, then no analogy will be made. Thirdly, if an analogy were to be made, in this case it would be governed by the doctrine of laches, which La Forest J. indicated would not defeat the plaintiff's claim. In any event, were the analogy to be drawn, any application of a limitation period

---

[127] [1996] 1 N.Z.L.R. 299, where the court was reluctant to hold that a neighbour child relationship amounted to a fiduciary relationship.

[128] (1992) 96 D.L.R. (4th) 289.

[129] (1987) 42 D.L.R. (4th) 81 at 99.

[130] [1994] 3 R.C.S. 377.

[131] Unreported, High Court, September 3, 1999.

[132] *LAC Minerals v. International Corona Resources Ltd.* (1989) 61 D.L.R. (4th) 14 at 28 *per* La Forest J.

[133] (1992) 96 D.L.R. (4th) 289.

would be nullified by the equitable application of the doctrine of fraudulent concealment.[134]

By contrast, the New Zealand Court of Appeal in *S. v. G.*[135] was willing to adopt a limitation period by analogy for a claim of breach of fiduciary duty. The central reason for such was that the plaintiff's claim in equity was an alternative claim arising from the same conduct.[136]

An Irish court, however, might incline to the adoption of a limitation period in equity. In both *Murphy v. Ireland*[137] and *McDonnell v. Ireland*[138] Carroll J. applied section 11(2) of the 1957 Act to claims for breach of constitutional rights where there existed a parallel claim in tort. Equitable claims, however, attract the exclusive jurisdiction of equity and the application of its doctrines. In particular, it will not allow common law or statutory rules to infiltrate its jurisdiction or usurp the application of its principles.[139]

The success of a claim in equity will also be subject to the doctrine of laches.[140] The operation of the doctrine requires more than mere delay. La Forest J. considered the application of the doctrine to a claim for equitable relief in sexual abuse cases.[141] Neither of the two branches of the doctrine was considered applicable. The defendant could not have altered his position detrimentally in reasonable reliance on the plaintiff's acceptance of the *status quo*. The operation of laches had to centre on the plaintiff's acquiescence.[142] Here of central importance was the plaintiff's knowledge of her rights, which comprises knowledge of both the facts supporting the claim in equity and the facts that give rise to that claim. Such an inquiry was to be measured by an objective standard and the issue was whether it was reasonable for the plaintiff to be ignorant of her legal rights given her knowledge of the underlying facts relevant to a possible equitable claim. Such an inquiry was very similar to the analysis of the reasonable discoverability rule in tort. It was in the circumstances reasonable that the plaintiff was unaware that a wrong had been com-

---

[134] *ibid.* at 330.

[135] [1995] 3 N.Z.L.R. 681 and reaffirmed in *Daniels v. Thompson* [1998] 3 N.Z.L.R. 22.

[136] *ibid.* at 689.

[137] [1996] 2 I.L.R.M. 461.

[138] [1998] 1 I.R. 134 (H.C. and affirmed on appeal by S.C.).

[139] *Ryan v. Connolly,* unreported, High Court, February 29, 2000 relying upon *Doran v. Thompson Ltd.,* [1978] I.R. 223.

[140] s. 5 of the Act acknowledges equity's jurisdiction in this regard. The section provides: "Nothing in this Act shall affect any equitable jurisdiction to refuse relief on the ground of acquiescence or otherwise."

[141] (1992) 96 D.L.R. (4th) 289 at 333-336, citing *Lindsay Petroleum Co. v. Hurd* (1874) L.R. 5 P.C. 221, Lord Blackburn's approval of same in *Erlanger v. New Sombrero Phosphate Co.* (1887) 3 App. Cas. 1218.

[142] *ibid.* at 335 citing Meagher, Gummow and Lehane, *Equity Doctrines and Remedies* (2nd ed., Butterworths: Sydney, 1984) at 755, the three meanings of acquiescence as: a type of estoppel whereby the plaintiff fails to enforce his rights; having been deprived of his rights and in full knowledge of them, delays; a hybrid of the first and second branch of the doctrine.

mitted and the medical evidence supported this.[143] La Forest J., however, concluded that such a plaintiff was incapable of acquiescing or having knowledge of the wrongfulness of the defendant's conduct. He noted that in the event that the plaintiff had such knowledge, in equity time did not begin to run for the purpose of laches until it was further established that the plaintiff had acquiesced in the defendant's conduct of committing sexual assaults, that is in the knowledge that the conduct was in itself wrongful. In this regard each case would depend upon its own facts, but La Forest J. observed that such would require particularly compelling evidence that the plaintiff acquiesced in the sexual assaults.[144]

11. Conclusion

The approaches of the Canadian, New Zealand and English courts exemplify why certainty is necessary. The decisions vary from the rigorously strict to the fluidly liberal application of the existing limitations legislation to deal with these actions which the framers of the legislation could never have envisaged being relied upon by such defendants. The Canadian approach provides virtual certainty of success in instituting proceedings by victims of child sexual abuse who suffer genuine adverse psychological affects. By accepting the medical opinion of the consequences of such abuse and in essence formulating such into a legal presumption operable both at common law and equity, the Canadian approach provides the prospective plaintiff with near certainty that an action will not be statute barred when instituted as a common law tortious claim. Lest there be any doubt of such success, equity will ensure the availability of a remedy that the common law may fail to provide.

The 2000 Act had been introduced specifically to enable child sexual abuse victims bring actions without such being statute barred. If the legislative intent of providing a forum for such plaintiffs to litigate their grievance is to be fulfilled, then a purposeful interpretation of the Act will ensure that objective. The 2000 Act only enables an action in tort to be instituted. It rests with the plaintiff to establish the tort relied upon and prove that on the balance of probabilities that the tort has been committed with consequent injury where such is a necessary proof. Limitation legislation should be strictly interpreted and in the event that the 2000 Act does present a limitation obstacle to prospective plaintiffs, an action framed in equity may provide the remedy.

---

[143] Namely; denial, memory repression and self-guilt.
[144] (1992) 96 D.L.R. (4th) 289 at 336.

THE REFORM OF IRISH LAND LAW

J.C.W. WYLIE

1. Introduction

The title of this paper is prompted by a number of considerations. The first is that, until his untimely death, Jim Brady, as one of the original appointees, had been amongst the longest-serving members of the Republic's Law Reform Commission's Working Group on Land Law and Conveyancing Law. This Group was established many years ago by the Commission following the then Attorney General's request[1] that it should formulate proposals for reform in a number of areas. This included "conveyancing law and practice in areas where this could lead to savings for house purchasers." The Commission took the view that a comprehensive review of land law and conveyancing law was not feasible within its limited resources and established the Working Group to identify areas for reform, concentrating initially on areas where recommendations could be made for changes which would remove anomalies or redundant provisions.[2] Since then, the Commission has published a steady stream of Reports based upon the Working Group's work.[3] From the beginning, the Working Group has had one of the Commissioners as convenor and its membership has comprised largely judges, barristers and solicitors with extensive land law and conveyancing experience, plus one or two academic lawyers. At this stage, the writer must declare an interest as a current member.[4]

Another consideration, which leads from the first, is that, as we head into the new millennium, the issue which has been raised in the past is likely to be raised again, *viz.*, should we not have the "comprehensive review" which the

---

[1] Made on March 6, 1987 under s. 4(2)(c) of the Law Reform Commission Act 1975.

[2] See the Introduction (Ch. 1) in the Commission's first report based on the Working Group's deliberations: *Land Law and Conveyancing Law: (1) General Proposals* (L.R.C. 30 – 1989).

[3] *e.g.* the further reports on land law and conveyancing law, nos. (2) *Enduring Powers of Attorney* (L.R.C. 31 – 1989), (3) *The Passing of Risk from Vendor to Purchaser*, (4) *Service of Completion Notices* (L.R.C. 39 – 1991), (5) *Further General Proposals* (L.R.C. 44 –1992), and (6) *Further General Proposals including Execution of Deeds* (L.R.C. 56 – 1998). Other reports based on the Working Group's work include the *Report on Interests of Vendor and Purchaser in Land during the Period between Contract and Completion* (L.R.C. 49 – 1995), and the *Report on Gazumping* (L.R.C. 59 – 1999).

[4] It must also be emphasised that the views expressed in this paper are those of the writer alone and they must not be taken as representing in any way those of the Working Group, still less of the Commission itself.

Law Reform Commission felt unable to undertake some years ago? In particular, the point is made regularly that we have yet to have in Ireland the kind of comprehensive reform which occurred in England so very long ago with the enactment of the Birkenhead property legislation in 1925.[5] Again, the writer should declare an interest, for much of his career has been spent participating in just such a review for Northern Ireland.[6] Notwithstanding that experience (or, perhaps, partly as a consequence of it), the writer is sceptical of the merits of a similar review for the Republic of Ireland. One purpose of this paper is to explain why that view is taken. Another purpose is, however, to elaborate upon what sort of review and reform programme would be beneficial. As will be outlined, some of this would have substantial elements, but, while they might be described as comprehensive in the sense that they would involve a radical overhaul of particular areas of the law, they would not involve the sort of co-ordinated overview that was carried out prior to enactment of the English 1925 legislation.

A third consideration is that the future programme of the Working Group is likely to involve consideration of larger scale projects. For the most part, the reports hitherto based upon its deliberations have concentrated on net points and particular features of our land law and conveyancing system which cause difficulties.[7] If these were all acted upon, there is no doubt that they would have a considerable impact upon the day-to-day working of the system.[8] However, it is also the purpose of this paper to demonstrate that there is much more which would be necessary, if we are to have a modern system worthy of the new millennium.

---

[5] For general discussion of this, see Underhill, "Property 1885-1935" (1935) 51 *L.Q.R.* 221; Hargreaves, "Modern Real Property" (1956) 19 *M.L.R.* 14; Megarry, "Change But Not Decay: A Century of the English Law of Real Property" (1960) 35 *N.Y.U.L.R.* 1331; Grove, "Conveyancing and Property Acts of 1925" (1961) 24 *M.L.R.* 123; Offer, "The Origins of the Law of Property Acts, 1910-1925" (1977) 40 *M.L.R.* 505.

[6] Initially as a member of the QUB Land Law Working Party which was established by the Office of the Director of Law Reform in 1967 and issued its report in 1971, *Survey of the Land Law of Northern Ireland* (HMSO). The writer was then a member of the Land Law Working Group appointed in 1980 by the Northern Ireland Office to review the 1971 *Survey*. Following publication of various discussion documents and an interim report, the Group finally issued a three-volume report in 1990, *The Final Report of the Land Law Working Group* (HMSO). These reports have resulted in a number of enactments, *viz.*, Commission on Sales of Land Act (N.I.) 1972, Property (N.I.) Order 1978, Wills and Administration Proceedings (N.I.) Order 1994, and Property (N.I.) Order 1997. For obvious reasons, this paper is not concerned with reform of the law of Northern Ireland.

[7] Above, n. 3.

[8] The most disappointing aspect of the Working Group's work is how many of its recommendations have still to be acted upon by the Oireachtas. A recent encouraging sign, however, is the proposal to introduce a "Miscellaneous Provisions" Bill to include many of the "non-controversial" proposals made in recent years.

2. THE CONTEXT OF REFORM

It is important to begin with some statement of the context in which the reform programme envisaged by this paper would take place. Reference was made earlier to the English 1925 legislation, and the suggestion made from time to time that Ireland needs the equivalent of this. However, there are some crucial points to be borne in mind. One is that the English 1925 legislation was for the most part only the culmination of a reform programme which had commenced some forty to fifty years earlier. Arguably, the real watershed of "modern" land law and conveyancing was the enactment of the Conveyancing Acts 1881-1911 and Settled Land Acts 1882-1890. These Acts remain in force in Ireland. Much of the English Law of Property Act 1925 and Settled Land Act 1925 was a consolidation of provisions contained in that earlier legislation.[9] Of the other legislation which was part of the 1925 package, considerable doubts must exist about its relevance now to Ireland. The Land Charges Act 1925 established two new registry systems,[10] the central Land Charges Registry now located in Plymouth, which deals with registration of certain encumbrances on unregistered land, and local land charges registries maintained by local authorities for registration of certain public charges on land, whether the title is registered or not. While the latter system has worked well, the former has long been recognised as suffering from fundamental defects.[11] It is very doubtful whether it would ever have been sensible to introduce a similar system in Ireland, not least because a universal registry of deeds system has operated here since the early eighteenth century.[12] Apart from that, the English central land charges registration system is rapidly being phased out with the extension of registration of title throughout England and Wales.[13] The registration of title system there remains grounded on the Land Registration Act 1925,[14] another of the

---

[9] See the articles referred to in n. 5, above; also Anderson, *Lawyers and the Making of English Land Law 1832-1940* (Oxford, 1992); Offer, *Property and Politics 1870-1914* (Cambridge, 1981).

[10] Now governed by the Land Charges Act 1972 and Local Land Charges Act 1975.

[11] *e.g.* being based on a "names" index rather than a land (address) index, and not requiring registration of all the encumbrances which may affect land (thereby failing in one of its primary objectives, *viz.*, removal of reliance upon the doctrine of notice to determine priorities); see, *e.g.* Harpum, Megarry and Wade: *The Law of Real Property* (6th ed., London, 2000), para. 5-085 *et seq.*

[12] Introduced by the Registration of Deeds Act (Ir.) 1707. On operation of this see Lyall, *Land Law in Ireland* (2nd ed., Dublin, 2000), Chap. 5; Wylie, *Irish Land Law* (3rd ed., Dublin, 1997), Chap. 22. There was no universal system in England, but only localised systems such as those operating under the Yorkshire Registry Acts 1703-34 and Middlesex Registry Act 1708.

[13] All land in England and Wales has been subject to compulsory registration of title since 1990: see Registration of Title Order 1989 (S.I. No. 1347) and generally the Land Registration Act 1997. As to the future, see the Law Commission's Consultation Paper, *Land Registration in the Twenty-First Century* (Law Com. No. 254, 1998).

[14] It has, however, been subject to several amending Acts and is likely, in due course, to be re-

1925 Acts, but the system which operated in Ireland for decades under the Local Registration of Title (Ireland) Act 1891 was, of course, the subject of modern legislation in the Republic, with the enactment of the Registration of Title Act 1964.[15] Of the other English 1925 Acts, the Trustee Act was to some extent a consolidation of provisions contained in the Trustee Act 1893, which remains in force in the Republic.[16] Lastly, an equivalent of the Administration of Estates Act 1925 became no longer necessary here with the enactment of the Succession Act 1965.[17] Indeed, the 1965 Act went much further than the English Act because it also dealt comprehensively with the law of wills, replacing earlier legislation like the Wills Act 1837.[18] The conclusion must be, therefore, that a land law reform programme for the Republic of Ireland based on the English 1925 Legislation would make very little sense in the twenty-first century. It should also be noted that this conclusion is reached without taking into account the limited resources likely to be available for such a programme.

Another important consideration for any future reform programme is that account must be taken of what might be referred to as the "administrative" and "procedural" aspects of our land law and conveyancing system.[19] By the former, one is thinking particularly of the Land Registry. As has been said many times, the history of the registration of title system in Ireland has been a particularly depressing one. It is a story of decades of neglect by successive governments, and a continuing reluctance to allocate the resources necessary to ensure that it realises its full potential. The lack of progress on conversion of the Land Registry and Registry of Deeds into a semi-state body which was announced a decade ago,[20] and the recent reappearance of huge delays and backlog in processing transactions, has had an all-too-familiar ring to it. The contrast with the position in England and Wales could hardly be more stark.[21] Yet the fact remains that it is extremely unlikely that any system with greater potential for

---

placed by a much modified Act as envisaged by the Consultation Paper referred to above, n.13. See also Megarry and Wade, *op. cit.,* above, n.11, Chap. 6.

[15] See McAllister, *Registration of Title in Ireland* (Dublin, 1973); Fitzgerald, *Land Registry Practice* (2nd ed., Dublin, 1995).

[16] It is, however, suggested later that a modern Trustee Act is a prime candidate for a future reform programme, see p. 379 below.

[17] See Brady, *Succession Law in Ireland* (2nd ed., Dublin, 1995); Keating, *Probate Law and Practice* (Dublin, 1999); Pearce, *McGuire: The Succession Act 1965: A Commentary* (2nd ed., Dublin, 1986).

[18] It was one of the curious features of the English 1925 legislation that it did not cover some areas of real property like the law of wills. Another example is the law of easements and profits, so that the Prescription Act 1832 remains in force. See further p. 379 below.

[19] This subject was discussed by the writer in the first Frances E. Moran Memorial Lecture entitled *"Irish Land Law in the Next Century"*, given at Trinity College, Dublin in December 1980; see also "The 'Irishness' of Irish Land Law" (1995) 46 *N.I.L.Q.* 332.

[20] See the Land Registry publication, *Land Registry Centenary 1892-1992* (1992); also *The Statement of Strategy: Safeguarding the Social and Economic Fabric of Land Ownership* (1996).

[21] See again the Law Commission Consultation Paper, *op. cit.,* above, n. 13.

simplifying the law and facilitating land transactions will be developed in the foreseeable future. A crucial new element in realising this potential is, of course, the rapid advances in recent times of computer technology. The application of this to registration systems could transform them in terms of speed and efficiency, as has clearly been realised on the other side of the Irish Sea. There are signs of some progress in this area here,[22] but it remains to be seen whether a total commitment to this sort of development, accompanied by the necessary funding and resources, will be forthcoming. Technological advances could also transform the procedural aspect of our land law and conveyancing system, by which is meant things like the conveyancing process. This remains a relatively slow and cumbersome process, partly because the registration of title system has never been applied comprehensively to urban land and partly because of the need to gather information about a particular property from a variety of resources, each operating independently and keeping the information in different ways. One of the most interesting developments in England in recent times has been the realisation that computer technology makes it possible to create large-scale databases for storage of huge amounts of information, capable of being accessed instantaneously through systems like the Internet. Work there is already far advanced in creating a national land information database, co-ordinating information held by the Land Registry, local authorities and other public bodies, with a view to facilitating "electronic" conveyancing.[23] Proposals have already been made for amending legislation to facilitate this,[24] yet in Ireland the e-commerce legislation recently introduced by the Government in the Oireachtas expressly excludes property transactions from its scope.[25] This is understandable given the current state of play, but it is to be hoped that the powers-that-be realise that, if the objectives which underlie this sort of legislation are to be achieved, what is needed is not just some advances in technology,[26] but a revolution in the approach to funding public services like the Land Registry. This must be accompanied by a comprehensive and consistent application of technology throughout the public service and other providers of information for public use – until there are truly "joined-up" databases, developments like electronic conveyancing will remain a pipe dream. On the

---

[22] See the publications referred to in n. 20 above.

[23] Law Commission, Consultation Paper, *op. cit.*, above, n. 13.

[24] *ibid.* Pt XI.

[25] Electronic Commerce Act 2000, s 10(1)(b). In so doing the Government availed of the right in Art. 9.2 of the EC Directive on certain legal aspects of information society services, in particular electronic commerce, in the Internal Market ("Directive on electronic commerce") 2000/31/EC to exclude contracts creating or transferring rights in real property. Readers might note that s. 10(1)(b) of the Irish Act seems to allow for a broader exclusion in relation to "leasehold interests" than that originally envisaged by Art. 9.2(a) of the Directive, which simply referred to "rental rights".

[26] *e.g.* in terms of the integrity of electronic signatures and other forms of authentication of transactions.

other hand, if substantial progress were ever made in such matters, the impact would be likely to far outweigh that of any traditional law reform programme which is outlined in the remainder of this paper.

3. A PROGRAMME OF REFORM

It is suggested that there is a wide range of matters which are ripe for reform. The need for reform stems from a variety of factors. One is that our law is still weighed down by an historical baggage that should have been jettisoned long ago. Another is that, in some respects, the law never developed properly or developed in such a way that it causes unnecessary complications or does not allow landowners to achieve perfectly legitimate aims. These sorts of problems are not confined to the common law, but also afflict legislation of the past which now needs a radical overhaul. Each of these factors will be illustrated by the following suggested programme for reform. Given the limited space available, this can be set out in outline only.

(a) Historical baggage

A brief reflection upon the existing state of our land law indicates that it is still riddled with historical concepts which ceased to be relevant not just decades, but centuries ago. An obvious example is the continuance in force of the Statute of Uses (Ireland) 1634. That statute was enacted to protect the Crown from loss of feudal dues and by the time the Irish version was enacted it was already largely an anachronism![27] It is absurd that it should survive almost four centuries later and that Irish conveyancers should still have to concern themselves with conveyances to uses.[28] Equally ridiculous is the fact that, in theory,[29] it is still possible to have in Ireland conveyances in the ancient form of a feoffment with livery of seisin, and a bargain and sale, plus associated concepts like a covenant to stand seised. Another example of historical nonsense in the modern world are rules like the rule in *Shelley's Case*.[30] Getting rid of this sort of

---

[27] See Wylie, *Irish Land Law* (3rd ed., Dublin, 1997), para. 3.015 *et seq.*

[28] See Laffoy, *Irish Conveyancing Precedents*, (Dublin, 1992) p. E16.

[29] Note the contortions of the Northern Ireland judges concerning the conveyance under consideration in *Re Sergie* [1954] N.I. 1.

[30] (1581) 1 Co. Rep. 88b, 76 E.R. 199. The Law Reform Commission has already recommended the abolition of the need for words of limitation in conveyances of unregistered land, as was done for transfers of registered land by s. 123 of the Registration of Title Act 1964: see *Report on Land Law and Conveyancing Law: (5) Further General Proposals* (L.R.C. 44 –1992), pp. 6-7. Note also as regards easements concerning registered land, *Report on Land Law and Conveyancing Law: (6) Further General Proposals* (L.R.C. 56 – 1998), p. 9.

historical baggage is one of the features of the English 1925 legislation[31] which should surely be adopted.[32]

(b) Future interests

The law of future interests is notorious for its complexity, as generations of law students can testify.[33] The Republic of Ireland remains burdened with the ancient rules in all their common law glory, such as the rule in *Whitby v. Mitchell*[34] and, of course, the rule against perpetuities. The latter, as developed over the centuries by the courts, became encrusted with all manner of absurd features,[35] which led many jurisdictions to introduce legislative reform.[36] This legislation may have removed some of the more absurd features of the common law rule, but a study of the more comprehensive examples, such as the English Perpetuities and Accumulations Act 1964[37] and the Perpetuities Act (NI) 1966[38] suggests that, if anything, the result has been to make the rule even more complicated.[39] This raises the fundamental question of whether the exercise was worth the candle and arguably it was not. Not only is the rule, as it still

---

[31] See Law of Property Act 1925, ss. 60 and 131.

[32] Many would argue that the same should apply to the fee tail estate, but the Law Reform Commission in the end decided against so recommending, confining its recommendation to requiring registration of a disentailing assurance in the Registry of Deeds or Land Registry, as appropriate, instead of in the Central Office of the High Court as required by s. 39 of the Fines and Recoveries (Ir.) Act 1834: see *Report on Land Law and Conveyancing Law: (1) General Proposals* (L.R.C. 30 – 1989), p.6. The fee tail estate was not abolished in England either by the 1925 legislation; this did not occur until enactment of the Trusts of Land and Appointment of Trustees Act 1996, Schedule 1, para. 5.

[33] The writer still recalls with very mixed feelings the classes given by one of his tutors at Harvard, the late Professor Barton Leach, then the world's leading expert on the subject: see Morris and Leach, *The Rule against Perpetuities* (2nd ed., London, 1962).

[34] (1890) 44 Ch. D. 85. Variously described as the old rule against perpetuities and the rule against double possibilities: see Wylie, *Irish Land Law* (3rd ed., Dublin, 1997), para. 5.042 *et seq.*

[35] Professor Leach (above, n. 33) took a particular delight in pointing them out in a series of articles referring to features like the "fertile octogenarian" and "precocious toddler" cases: see, *e.g.* "Perpetuities in a Nutshell" (1938) 51 *H.L.R.* 638; "Perpetuities in Perspective: Ending the Rule's Reign of Terror" (1952) 65 *H.L.R.* 721; "Perpetuities: Staying the Slaughter of Innocents" (1952) 58 *L.Q.R.* 35.

[36] See further articles by Professor Leach such as "Perpetuities Legislation: Massachusetts Style" (1954) 67 *H.L.R.* 1349; "Perpetuities Reform by Legislation" (1954) 70 *L.Q.R.* 478; "Perpetuities: New Absurdity, Judicial and Statutory Corrections" (1960) 73 *H.L.R.* 1318; "Perpetuities Legislation: Hail, Pennsylvania!" (1960) 108 *U. Penn. L Rev.* 1124; "Perpetuities: New Hampshire Defertilises the Octogenarians" (1963) 77 *M.L.R.* 379; "Perpetuities Reform: London Proposes, Perth Disposes" (1963) 6 *A.L.R.* 11. See also Maudsley, *The Modern Law of Perpetuities* (London, 1979).

[37] See also Morris and Wade, "Perpetuities Reform at Last" (1964) 80 L.Q.R. 486.

[38] See Gibson, "Perpetuities Act (N.I.) 1966" (1966) 17 *N.I.L.Q.* 30.

[39] See the English Law Commission's Consultation Paper No. 133 (1993), *Rules against Perpetuities and Excessive Accumulations*. See also Sparkes, "How to Simplify Perpetuities" (1995) 59 *Conv.* 212.

applies in this jurisdiction, blighted by absurdities and complexities, it also suffers from uncertainties as to its scope, especially in relation to commercial transactions[40] and commercial aspects of land transactions.[41] Perhaps its most pernicious aspect is that it is a trap for the unwary lawyer drawing up a will or trust, which, if it is fallen into, can have disastrous consequences for the client's family and other relations. There is much to be said for the view that the rule has outlived its usefulness and that, conversely, much relief would result from its total abolition, along with associated rules like the rule in *Whitby v. Mitchell* and rule against accumulations.[42] The risk of abuse of the freedom of disposition which would result is likely to be very small, as modern taxation systems tend to exact very severe penalties on attempts to tie up property for successive generations.[43] Of course, it is possible that some testators or settlors might ignore such penalties, with the consequence that future generations might find themselves locked into a particularly burdensome disposition not of their own making. However, there are other ways of dealing with this, such as legislative provision for variation of trusts.[44]

(c) Settlements and Trusts

Mention of variation of trusts prompts the thought that there are certain aspects of the law of settlements and trusts in need of attention. There is no need for a major overhaul because the law, including the nineteenth century legislation still in force, is basically sound. However, there are some difficulties which should be dealt with. One obvious one is the muddled treatment of trusts for sale which resulted from the nonsensical provision for such trusts inserted in section 63 of the Settled Land Act 1882, and the flawed attempt to correct this in section 6 of the Settled Land Act 1884.[45] Indeed, ultimately the dichotomy

---

[40] *e.g.* share dealing restrictions which are a common feature of joint venture arrangements: see *Attorney General v. Jameson* [1904] 2 I.R. 644 (K.B.), [1905] 2 I.R. 218 (Ir. C.A.).

[41] The Law Reform Commission recommended some years ago that the rule should no longer affect interests like options, easements and other incidents: see *Report on Land Law and Conveyancing Law: (1) General Proposals* (LRC 30 –1989), pp. 7-8.

[42] This is of limited application only in Ireland, because the English Accumulations Act of 1800 (which resulted from the notorious case of *Thelluson v. Woodford* (1799) 4 Ves. 227, (1805) 11 Ves. 112) did not apply here; *cf.* the amending Act, the Accumulations Act 1892. See Keeton, "The Thelluson Case and Trusts for Accumulation" (1970) 21 *N.I.L.Q.* 131; Polden, "Panic or Prudence? The Thelluson Act 1800 and Trusts for Accumulation" (1994) 45 *N.I.L.Q.* 13.

[43] See the discussion in Bohan, *Capital Acquisitions Tax* (Dublin, 1995), especially chs. 16 and 17.

[44] In effect enabling the courts to agree to variations on behalf of beneficiaries who are incapable of agreeing for themselves, so that the rule in *Saunders v. Vautier* (1841) Cr. & Ph. 240 cannot apply. See p. 379 below.

[45] See Lyall, *Land Law in Ireland* (2nd ed., Dublin, 2000), pp. 412 - 413 and 854 - 855; Wylie, *Irish Land Law* (3rd ed., Dublin, 1997), para. 8.043 *et seq.*

of strict settlements and trusts for sale of land ought to be abolished, as has been done recently in England[46] but that would involve substantial legislation.

So far as the law of trusts is concerned, the problem in the Republic of Ireland is that the legislation still in force is the old Trustee Act 1893. That Act is perfectly sound so far as it goes, but its provisions are limited and the replacement legislation in other jurisdiction contains some very useful provisions.[47] For example, the statutory powers of appointment of trustees and vesting trust property could be extended,[48] as could the trustee powers of delegation[49] and advancement.[50] One particular gap is the lack of any legislative provision for variation of trusts generally,[51] such as was introduced by the English Variation of Trusts Act 1958.[52]

(d) Appurtenant Rights

One of the most unsatisfactory features of our land law is the law relating to appurtenant rights, *i.e.*, interests in land which exist as between neighbouring landowners. One obvious example is the law relating to easements and profits *à prendre*. The rules governing acquisition of such rights where no express provision has been made are far from clear, *e.g.* the rule in *Wheeldon v. Burrows*,[53] and the operation of statutory provisions like section 6 of the Conveyancing Act 1881.[54] The law relating to prescription is a hopeless muddle.[55] It is frankly ridiculous that the courts in the twenty-first century may find themselves being asked to apply fictions like the doctrine of lost modern grant.[56] The Prescription Act 1832,[57] which was applied to Ireland by the Prescription (Ireland) Act 1858, rejoices in the unenviable reputation of being "one of the

---

[46] See the Trusts of Land and Appointment of Trustees Act 1996, which introduces a single system of trusts of land. This was based on the Law Commission's Report, *Transfer Of Land: Trusts Of Land* (Law Com. No. 181), but such a system had been suggested much earlier by the N.I. Land Law Working Party (see above, n. 6) in its *Survey of the Land Law of Northern Ireland* (HMSO, 1971), Chap. 3. See also Harvey, *Settlements of Land* (London, 1973), Chap. 8.

[47] See, *e.g.* the Trustee Act (N.I.) 1958, fully annotated in Carswell, *Trustee Acts (Northern Ireland)* (Belfast, 1964).

[48] See Wylie, *Irish Land Law* (3rd ed., Dublin, 1997), paras. 10.005–010.

[49] *ibid*, paras. 10.033-034 and 10.038.

[50] *ibid*, paras. 10.048-049.

[51] *i.e.* other than exists for particular cases such as family breakdown where the courts have extensive power to make property adjustment orders: see Family Law Act 1995, Pt. II and Family Law (Divorce) Act 1996, Pt. III.

[52] *cf.* Trustee Act (N.I.) 1958, ss. 56 and 57: see Wylie, *op. cit.,* above, n. 48, paras. 10.095-096.

[53] (1878) Ch. D. 31.

[54] See Bland, *The Law of Easements and Profits à Prendre* (Dublin, 1997), Chap. 12.

[55] The English Law Reform Committee subjected it to a scathing critique many years ago: see its 14th Report, *Acquisition of Easements and Profits by Prescription* (1966; Cmnd. 3100).

[56] See Bland, *op. cit.,* above, n. 54, Chap. 13.

[57] It is one of the curious features of the English 1925 legislation that this statute was left in force and not replaced by that legislation.

worst drafted Acts on the Statute Book".[58] This is an area of the law which is long overdue a radical overhaul.

The same applies to the law relating to freehold covenants. The essential problem here is that the law never developed fully, so that it remains restricted by the limitations of the rule in *Tulk v. Moxhay*.[59] The most disastrous feature of this is that a positive covenant, such as a covenant to repair, does not, in general,[60] run with freehold land. This has resulted in considerable inconvenience for conveyancers over the centuries and explains why modern developments like blocks of flats and apartments have had to be confined to leasehold tenure.[61] This is clearly an area where legislative reform is needed urgently.[62]

(e) Multi-occupied Buildings

The previous paragraph referred to one particular feature of modern life, namely the creation of large buildings designed for occupation and ownership by numerous people. The obvious examples are blocks of flats and apartments and office buildings. Such developments create special problems from the conveyancing point of view and considerable care and skill must be exercised if the scheme is to work satisfactorily for all concerned.[63] The problems stem from a variety of sources. One is that the current state of the law relating to freehold covenants renders it impracticable to create freehold developments, because, for example, it is difficult, if not impossible, to ensure that positive obligations relating to vital matters like repairs and maintenance will bind successive owners.[64] Another, related problem is that any such development involves a high degree of interdependence between the various owners and occupiers. All sorts of mutual rights and obligations must be created on a permanent basis, relating to vital matters like support and shelter for each part of the building and enjoyment of common or shared facilities (like entrances, lobbies, stairs, passageways, lifts etc) and services (water, gas, electricity etc). Provision must be made for repairs and maintenance, insurance and general management of the building. All too often, even with leasehold developments, these are found to be

---

[58]Law Reform Committee, *op. cit.,* above, n. 55, para. 40.
[59](1848) 2 Ph. 744, 41 ER 1143. See Lyall, *op. cit.,* above, n. 12, Ch. 21; Wylie, *op. cit.,* above, n. 12, Chap. 19.
[60]The various ways around this problem do not provide a satisfactory solution, see *ibid.*
[61]Note the discussion in *Metropolitan Properties Ltd v. O'Brien* [1995] 1 I.R. 467.
[62]Note the provisions in Art. 34 of the Property (N.I.) Order 1997: see Wylie, *op. cit.,* above n. 12, paras 19.48-49.
[63]Note again the discussion in the *Metropolitan Properties* case, above, n. 61, and see Wylie, *Irish Conveyancing Law* (2nd ed., Dublin, 1996), para. 19.11 *et seq.* See also George, *The Sale of Flats* (5th ed., London, 1984); Cawthorn and Barraclough, *Sale and Management of Flats* (2nd ed., London, 1996).
[64]See (d) above.

either non-existent or inadequate. The consequences for individual owners or occupiers of parts of the development can be disastrous.

It is one of the great mysteries of the development of land law and convey-ancing in this part of the world that these problems have not been dealt with. They were solved decades ago by special legislation in several jurisdictions further afield. In Australia, what is known as strata titles legislation was en-acted to deal specifically with the problems, and this was adopted in other jurisdictions like Singapore and parts of the Caribbean, such as the Bahamas, Jamaica and Barbados. Similar legislation exists in Canada and the USA, where it is known as condominiums legislation,[65] and has been proposed for Eng-land[66] and Northern Ireland.[67] Given the rapid increase in such developments in this jurisdiction in recent times, the enactment of such legislation should be viewed as an urgent priority.

(f) Landlord and Tenant Legislation

At first sight, this may appear to be a somewhat odd candidate for a reform programme. No area of our land law has been the subject of more legislative interference than the relationship of landlord and tenant.[68] Much of this has been beneficial and some of it was well ahead of its time. A good example is the fact that Ireland did not suffer the problems created by the doctrine of priv-ity of contract, in particular the risk of continuing liability for a tenant after he had assigned his interest to a new tenant.[69] This was because of the special provision relieving the tenant-assignor of continuing liability enacted as long ago as 1860.[70] Therein, however, lies the clue as to one of the major problems with the legislation. This is that the legislation is seriously outdated as we enter the new millennium. The cornerstone of the law remains Deasy's Act, which was enacted during the mid-nineteenth century when the prevailing social and economic conditions were quite different. Thus, much of that Act relates to agricultural tenancies which largely disappeared as a result of the Land Pur-chase Acts. Furthermore, this problem of being out-of-step with modern times does not apply only to such nineteenth-century legislation, it also applies to the

---

[65]The writer drafted the Condominiums Act 1981 enacted in Trinidad and Tobago.

[66]A "commonhold" scheme, as recommended by the Lord Chancellor's Working Group in its 1987 Report, *Commonhold: Freehold Flats and Freehold Ownership of Other Interdependent Buildings* (C.M. 179). See also LCD's Consultation Paper, *Commonhold* (C.M. 1345, 1990), which included a draft Bill. Regrettably much delay has since occurred and the Commonhold and Leasehold Reform Bill has been published in draft form only at the time of writing.

[67]Final Report of the Land Law Working Group (HMSO, 1990), Vol. 1, Pt. 3.

[68]See generally Wylie, *Irish Landlord and Tenant Law* (2nd ed., Dublin, 1998).

[69]This created major problems in England until they were tackled by the Landlord and Tenant (Covenants) Act 1995. See Megarry and Wade, *op. cit.*, above, n. 11, Chap. 15.

[70]Landlord and Tenant Law Amendment Act Ireland 1860 (invariably known as "Deasy's Act"), s. 16.

Landlord and Tenant Acts enacted in more recent times, especially in their application to commercial leases. Far too much of this later legislation is based upon the rationale that it is needed to protect defenceless tenants against rapacious landlords. This may have made sense when the legislation was first introduced,[71] when the vast majority of commercial tenants were private individuals running small businesses on the premises. What has not made any sense in recent times has been the blanket application of the same protective legislation to the numerous, large commercial organisations and financial institutions which are such an important feature of the Irish economy nowadays.

This is not the only major problem with this legislation. Another stems from the way it has developed. It comprises numerous Acts, which have built a substantial edifice of legislation, created layer upon layer as each new Act amends the earlier ones. The result is that it is sometimes difficult to reconcile all the provisions[72] and overall the entire scheme is a nightmare to digest and interpret. Arguably the underlying aims of this legislation should be reviewed, and provisions which are judged still relevant to modern commercial conditions should be incorporated into a (hopefully much shorter) consolidating Act.

4. Conclusion

It is very doubtful whether, even if the resources were available, a comprehensive review of our land law and conveyancing system, such as led to the English 1925 legislation, would be sensible or beneficial. Rather, this brief paper suggests that certain areas of the law are in need of reform. In the case of some of those areas, the legislative provisions required could be very brief and quickly drafted, *e.g.* abolition of old historical rules and rules like the rule against perpetuities. Other areas identified in the paper would undoubtedly require something much more comprehensive, but that job is worth doing if we are to create a system worthy of the new millennium.

---

[71] The original Act, the Landlord and Tenant Act 1931, was clearly based to some extent on the earlier Town Tenants (Ir.) Act 1906: see Wylie, *op. cit.*, above, n. 68, para. 1.15 *et seq.*

[72] The Law Reform Commission has already drawn attention to various individual points which need dealing with: see *Report on Land Law and Conveyancing Law: (1) General Proposals* (L.R.C. 30 – 1989), Ch. 5 (to some extent adopted in the Landlord and Tenant (Amendment) Act 1994); *Land Law and Conveyancing Law: (5) Further General Proposals* (L.R.C. 44 - 1992), Ch. 4; *Land Law and Conveyancing Law: (6) Further General Proposals Including the Execution of Deeds* (L.R.C. 56 – 1998), pp. 10-17.

APPENDIX I

The James C. Brady Memorial Trust

In light of the affection in which students, practitioners and academics held Jim Brady, it was decided in 1999 to establish a memorial trust fund as a fitting tribute to his life and work.

The objectives of the trust fund include the award of an annual prize in the final Equity examination, known as "the Professor James C. Brady Memorial Prize", and the promotion of legal research by the award of scholarships, bursaries or maintenance allowances for the study of law to persons who are in need of such assistance.

The trust has been recognised by the Revenue Commissioners as a charity under Reference No. CHY 13572, and the initial trustees appointed under the deed are:

Professor James Casey, Faculty of Law, UCD.

Dr Albert Power, The Institute of Chartered Accountants in Ireland.

Ms Anne Corrigan, Faculty of Law, UCD.

Mr Tony Kerr, Faculty of Law, UCD.

Ms Oonagh Breen, Faculty of Law, UCD.

The trustees wish to take this opportunity to acknowledge most sincerely the many donations they have received since the creation of the trust. A list of those donors, as at the date of publication, is provided below. Contributions are still welcome and those interested should contact Oonagh Breen, at the Faculty of Law, University College Dublin.

APPENDIX II

Memorial Trust Fund Contributors

Mr Thomas J. Ainsworth
Mr Roughan Banim
Mr Anthony Barr
Beauchamps, Solicitors
Ms Noeline Blackwell
Mrs Sarah Brady
Dr P.A. Brand
Mr Michael Brennan
Mr Conan Budds
Mr David Burke
Ms Nuala Butler
Mr Malcolm Byrne
Ms Niamh Caffrey
Mr John Caldwell
Ms Sara Callanan
Ms Mary P. Cantrell
Mr Declan C. Carroll
Ms Brona Carton
Professor James Casey
Mr Dermot A. Clarke
Ms Inge Clissmann, SC
Ms Aedamar Comiskey
Mr Ciaran Connolly
Mr Enda Connolly
Mr Niall Corr
Ms Anne Corrigan
Ms Bernadette Corrigan
Ms Eithne Coughlan
Ms Eimear Cowhey
Arthur Cox, Solicitors
Ms Jacqueline Cross
Ms Caroline Cummings
Ms Emile Daly
Mr Dominic Dowling
Mr Gerard Durcan, SC
Mr Patrick J.M. Durcan
Ms Suzanne Egan
Mr Paddy Fagan
Mr Eugene Fanning

Ms Mary Finlay, SC
The Hon Mr Thomas A.
 Finlay
Mr Hugh M. Fitzpatrick
Mr John Fitzpatrick
Mr Declan Foley
Mr Paul Gallagher, SC
Professor Conor Gearty
Mr John T. Gibbons, SC
Mr Paul Gilligan, SC
Mr Dermot Gleeson, SC
F.P. Gleeson & Co.,
 Solicitors
Ms Marie Griffin
Mr Patrick J.P. Groarke
Dr Eamonn G. Hall
Mr Conor Halpenny
Ms Mary M. Heslin
Ms Anne Hughes
Mr John G. Jordan
Mr Esmonde Keane
Mr Patrick E. Keane, SC
Mr Eamonn Kelly
Mr Paul Kerrigan
Ms Christine Lavelle
Mr Patrick McCann
Mr David McCann
Ms Ella McCarthy
Mr Ciaran McCourt
Ms Deirdre McDermott
Mr Rory McEntee
Mr Michael G.
 MacGrath, SC
Mr Declan McHugh
Ms Mary Macken
Ms Cathy Maguire
Ms Imelda Maher
Ms Jacqueline Maloney
Ms Anne Markey

Mr Damien Martyn
Ms Helen Meenan
Mr Alan Mitchell
Mr Ronan Moloney
Mr Brian Morgan
Mr David Murphy
Mr P. Gerry Murphy
Ms Isobel M. Murray
Mr Craig Nethercott
Ms Sinéad Ní Chúlacháin
Ms Úna Ní Raifeartaigh
Mr Luán Ó Braonáin
Mr John O'Carroll
Mr Patrick O'Connor
Mr Donal O'Donnell, SC
Mr Turlough O'Donnell,
 SC
Mr Donal O'Donoghue
Mr T. John O'Dowd
Professor David
 O'Keeffe
Mr John O'Leary
Ms Geraine O'Loughlin
Mr Michael O'Mahony
Mr Robert O'Mahony
Mr Fintan O'Reilly
Mr James O'Reilly, SC
Mr Phelim A. O'Reilly
Mr Frank O'Riordan
Mr Andrew O'Rorke
Mr John S. O'Sullivan
Mr Joseph O'Sullivan
Mr Ciaran Oakes
Dr Albert Power
Mr John Power
Professor Dan Prentice
Ms Joan Quinn
Mr Oisín Quinn
Mr Patrick Quinn

Ms Margaret Reynolds
Ms Patricia T. Rickard-
    Clarke
Ms Margaret Rowe
Ms Mary Ryan
Mr Michael Ryan
Mr Oliver Ryan
Mr Kevin Seagrave
Mr Laurence K. Shields

Vincent Shield, Solicitors
Ms Rosemarie Sisk
Ms Sinead Smith
Mr Peter Sparkes
Ms Aisling Sweeney
Mr Terence D. Sweeney
Mr Joseph M. Swords
Mr Joe Thomas
Mr John Trainor, SC

Mr Noel J. Travers
Mr Brendan J. Twomey
Mr Patrick Wallace
Ms Muriel Walls
Mr Peter Ward
Ms Darina White
Judge Michael White
Mr Liam Young

SUBJECT HEADING INDEX

abortion,
information on, 142
art law, French law and, 3 *et seq.*
anti-seizure law, 10-14
conditions to be met under,
cultural objects, must be, 11
identity of lender, 11
lender must be foreign, 11
objects be loaned to French
state, 11
objects be on temporary loan,
11
special decree by Minister of
Culture and Minister of
Foreign Affairs
UNIDROIT Convention and, 14,
15
French Revolution Declaration of
Human Rights, 7, 8
La Danse, influence of on, 3 *et seq.*,
5, 15, 16
Mattéoli Commission, creation of,
13
Pompidou Centre, exhibition at, 5
Russian Revolution, 4
Tribunal de Grande Instance, 5, 6 *et
seq.*
Trubetskoy Palace, 3
assault, *see* **child abuse**

battery, *see* **child abuse**
Brady, James, 3, 115, 123, 138, 171,
172, 203, 227, 254, 259, 261,
274
address at funeral mass, 1, 2
"Equity and Law, bedfellows to the
bitter end", 123
family, 2
Law Reform Commission
original appointee to, as, 371
school, at, 1

Brady, James—*contd.*
university, at, 2
law, studying at, 2
medicine, studying, at, 2
writings of, 18, 19n, 53n, 92n, 171,
172, 203n, 213n, 348, 349,
374n

charities, 3, 254
creation of contractual relations to
charitable endeavours,
303
child abuse, Statute of Limitations
(Amendment) Act 2000, and,
344 *et seq.*
assault and, 345, 346
damages and, 348
definition of, 346
limitation purposes and, 346,
347
battery,
damages and, 348
definition of, 346
limitation purposes and, 346,
347
consent, 347
delay in bringing actions for, 363 *et
seq.*
disability provision, 353, 361 *et seq.*
duty, breach of, 349 *et seq.*
effects of, 345
fiduciary relationship, breach of in
instances of, 367-369
fraud and the bringing of an action
for, 366, 367
incest, 344
knowledge, date of, 352-354
laches, doctrine of, 369
limitation periods for actions, 346,
347
negligence, 349 *et seq.*

child abuse—*contd.*
  physical damage, 349 *et seq.*, 353 *et seq.*
    disability provision, 353, 359 *et seq.*
    latent, examples of, 349
      army deafness cases, 349 *et seq.*
      asbestosis on the lungs, 349
      pneumoconiosis, 349
  Post-Traumatic Stress Disorder (PTSD), 345
  psychological injury and, 262, 344-346 *et seq.*, 349, 357
    latent, 354 *et seq.*
      aftermath doctrine, 355
    types of,
      alcohol abuse, 345
      depression, 345
      drug abuse, 345
      eating disorders, 345
      prostitution, 345
      re-victimisation, 345
      self-mutilation, 345
      sexual dysfunction, 345
  symptoms, awareness of, 357, 361
children, *see also* **child abuse, graft, occupiers' liability, succession, tax**
confidence, *see also* **freedom of expression**
  breach of, 139, 140 *et seq.*
    injunctive relief against, 142
    protection against, 140
contract law, *see also* **part performance, restitution**
  religion and, 296 *et seq.*
    consideration, 296, 301
      adequacy of, 296
      intention to create legal relations, prayers and, 301 *et seq.*
      prayers amounting to, 296, 297-301

contract law—*contd.*
  religion and—*contd.*
    consideration—*contd.*
      sufficiency of, 296
      worthless, 298
    damages and, 315
    Faustian pacts, 31 *et seq.*
    spirit world, 312-314
    subject to contract, 315
  repudiatory breach, 190
  undue influence, *see* **equity**

debts, assignment of, 121 *et seq.*
  absolute, 127, 136
  assignments of choses in action, 123, 127, 128
  corporate finance and, 122
  Dearle v Hall, rule in, 121, 124 *et seq.*, 131
  debt factor, 122-131
  debtor, notice to, 124, 129 *et seq.*, 133
  enforcement of, 121
  equitable assignees, 121, 126, 127, 132
  equitable choses in action, 124, 125, 132
  equitable interests in a will, assignment of, 122-124
  law, at, 125 *et seq.*
  prior equitable assignments v subsequent assignments at law, 131 *et seq.*
  "subject to all equities", 131, 132, 134, 138
defamation *see also* **freedom of expression,** 145
  Constitution of Ireland, 140
    defamation cases and 140, 145
  defamatory material, 139
    injunction to restrain, 139
  discretionary relief, 146
  interlocutory injunction, granting of, 146
  remedy for, 147

dismissal,

anti,

injunction, interlocutory, 188 *et seq*, 195

applications for as remedy, 188, 202

caselaw, 199 *et seq*.

conditions for,

balance of convenience, 189

fair case, 189

fair case standard,

reassessment of, 197 *et seq*.

principles for granting of, 201

proof, burden of, 194 *et seq*.

rules for granting of, 195-197

terms and duration of order, 193 *et seq*.

post,

injunction, 198, 199

wrongful, 188, 190,

divorce, *see* **tax**

employment, *see* **dismissal, employers' liability**

common employment,

abolishing, 247

ambit of, 246

doctrine of, 246

contract of, 190, 191

employee's right

to wages, 189-191 *et seq*.

to work, 189, 192

rights, enforcement of, 189

termination of,

automatic, 191

complete, 191

employers' liability

action upon statute, 238 *et seq*.

common law alternative, 229 *et seq*.

contracting out, 250

Employers' Liability Act 1880, 245 *et seq*.

claims under, 251

history of, 227 *et seq*.

legal aid provision, 233

employers' liability—*contd.*

penal compensation, 234 *et seq*.

statutory strict liability, 227

equity, 3, 104, 115, 121-123, 171

choses in action, 123, 124 *et seq*., 132

clean hands, 155, 156

commercial disputes, 94, *see also* **trusts**

debts, assignment of, *see* **debts assignment of,** 121

graft, doctrine of, *see* **graft**

laches, doctrine of, 369

merger of law and, 123

part performance, *see* **part performance**

"subject to all equities", 131, 132, 134, 138

tracing, doctrine of, 105

unclean hands, 166

undue influence, doctrine of, 305 *et seq*.

presumption of in certain cases, doctor/patient, 305

guardian/ward, 305

parent/child, 305

religious association/devotee, 305 *et seq*.

solicitor/client, 305

trustee/agent, 305

estoppel, doctrine of, 118, 121, 294

European law, *see* **legitimate expectation, succession**

family, *see* **succession**

freedom of expression, 139 *et seq*.

abortion, *see* **abortion**

confidence, *see* **confidence**

confidential relationships

government and an individual, between, 141

private and commercial, between, 141

Constitution, Irish, guarantee of under, 140, 144

constitutional right to, 141

defamation, *see* **defamation**

freedom of expression—*contd.*
freedom of press in Ireland, 141, 42
information publication of,
injunctions and, 139 *et seq.*, 144
libel, 140
privacy, *see* **privacy**
protection of in United States
    Constitution, 139, 147
restraints on publication, 139
rightful liberty of expression, 140,
    141

graft, Irish doctrine of, 326 *et seq.*
barring the entail, 334, 335
    acquisition of the fee simple
        reversion, 335-337
constructive trusts, 334 *et seq.*, 343
    see also **trusts**
    exceptions to application of,
etymology of, 327 *et seq.*
    renewal of lease and, 327
        et seq.
executors, 342
gestation of, 326
guardian,
    imputation of guardianship,
        339
infant, 339
    death of, after renewal by trustee,
        30
joint tenants, 340-342
mortgagees, 338
mortgagors, 338
remaindermen, 337
renewal fines, 332
tenant for life, and, 337

injunctions, *see also* **dismissal,**
    freedom of expression and
    planning injunction
interlocutory, *see* **dismissal**
legal basis of, 190 *et seq.*
intestacy, 222, 259
rights of inheritance on, 214
Irish bench,
extramural pursuits of
    seventeenth century in, 317

Irish bench—*contd.*
extramural pursuits of—*contd.*
    eighteenth century in, 317 *et seq.*
    Arthur Young, impressions of,
        320 *et seq.*
    members of,
        Carter, Thomas, 320
        Forster, Anthony, 320, 324,
            325
        Hamilton, George, 321,
            322, 324, 325
        Marlay, Thomas, 320
        Marmaduke Coghill, 318
        Singleton, Henry, 320
        Wainwright, John, 320
        Ward, Michael, 318-320,
            322, 324
        Wyndham, Thomas, 320
    Royal Dublin Society, *see*
        Royal Dublin Society

land law, *see also* **equity, part**
    performance, Quia Emptores,
    succession and **trusts**
reform of Irish, 371 *et seq.*
    areas for,
        conveyancing, 371 *et seq.*
        Land Registry, conversion into
          semi state body, 374,
          375
        Registry of Deeds, conversion
          into semi-state body,
          374
    context of, 373 *et seq.*
        Land Registry, 374
        Registry of Deeds, 374
        registry systems, 373
    programme for, 376 *et seq.*
        appurtenant rights
          doctrine of lost modern
            grant, 379
          easements, 379
          freehold covenants, 380
          prescription, 379
          profits à prendre, 379
        future interests, 377, 378
        historical baggage and, 376

land law—*contd.*
   reform of Irish—*contd.*
      programme for—*contd.*
         landlord and tenant legislation,
            381, 382
         multi-occupied buildings, 380,
            381
         settlements, 378, 379
         trusts, 378, 379
legitimate expectation, 17 *et seq.*
   autochronous doctrine of, 18 *et seq.*,
      see **European Community**
      law, *infra*
   definition of, 19
   factors towards legitimising an
      expectation under, 53 *et
      seq.*
   conduct justifying the expectation,
      55-57
   absence of misconduct, 60
   requirement of an expectation,
      57-59
   reliance on the expectation,
      59-60
   European Community law of, 18 *et
      seq.*
   definition of, 19
   factors towards legitimising an
      expectation in,
      conduct justifying expectation,
      33
   Mulder cases, 34, 45-48
   origins of, 49-53
   principle of, 21 *et seq.*
      general principles of, 22-26
      legitimate expectation as,
         27-30
   reliance on the expectation, 44
      absence of misconduct, 44
   requirement of an expectation, 41
   retroactive legislation, 35-40
   weighing up of interests, 45-48,
      60-61
      procedure versus substance
         debate, 61-69
   what is legitimate expectation for
      purposes of, 30-33

limitation of actions, 261 *et seq., see
   also* **child abuse**
   actions in respect of estates of
      deceased persons, 262
   dismissal for want of prosecution,
      271 *et seq.*
   introduction, 261
   law reform, 269, 274
   limitation periods and the
      Constitution, 267 *et seq.*
      substantial periods, 269
   personal injuries
      date of knowledge, 270
      discoverability test, 270 *et seq.*
      significant, 270
   psychological injury, 261, *see also*
      child abuse
   recent developments, 261 *et seq.*
   Statute of Limitation,
      purpose of, 269

mortgages, *see* **graft**

occupiers' liability, 257 *et seq., see also*
   taxonomy
   allurements, 257
   injured persons, rights of, 258
   invitees, 256, 257
   licensees, 256, 257
      infant, 259
   property owners, rights of, 258
   recreational user, 258
   trespassers, 257, 258
      adult, 257
   visitor, 258

part performance, doctrine of, 115 *et
   seq.*
   agreements for sale of interests in
      land, 115-118
      breach of, 118
   apparent abolition of, 115,
      120
   development of, 117 *et seq.*
   enforceability of contract, 118
   estoppel, doctrine of, 118,
      120

part performance, doctrine of—*contd.*
　oral agreement, 117, 118
　Statute of Frauds and, 115-117,
　　119
　subject to contract, 117
　sufficient act of, 119
　　collateral evidence of, 118
　written evidence of contract,
　　116-118
planning injunction, 148 *et seq.*
　application for, 150
　　plenary proceedings for, 151
　　time limit on, 152
　enforcement of, 159
　grant of by court, 150
　judicial diktat, 159 *et seq.*
　　perspectives for,
　　　critical studies (CLS),
　　　　160-162
　　　legal reasoning, 159
　　　positivism, 162-166, 168
　judicial discretion and, 148 *et seq.*,
　　152 *et seq.*
　　context-specific discretion,
　　　153
　　examples of,
　　　acquiescence, 153
　　　clean hands, 155, 156
　　　delay, 153, 169
　　　gross hardship, 156, 157
　　　inappropriate hardship, 156,
　　　　157
　　　laches, 153
　　　lapse of time, 153, 154
　　　technical violations, 158
　　　third party interests, 157
　　　trivial violations, 158
　　　unclean hands, 166
　　exceptional circumstances and,
　　　152
　　limited, 152
　　refusal to grant injunction, 154,
　　　156, 158
　Kenny report, 149
　　planning violations, restraining of,
　　　149, 150
　law governing, 148 *et seq.*

planning injunction—*contd.*
　non-compliance with, 159
　planning violations, restraint of, 150
　planning code,
　　enforcement of, 148
　　integrity of, 152
　purpose of, 148
　quia timet,
　　granting of, 152
　"section 27", 148
　　Circuit Court, application to
　　　under, 149
　　constructive judicial interpretation
　　　of, 166 *et seq.*, 170
　　development of land and, 149
　　High Court, application to under,
　　　149
　　non-conforming development and,
　　　149
　　onus of proof, 151
　　plenary proceedings, 151
　　purpose of, 148, 149
　　self contained enforcement
　　　procedure, 151
　　summary procedure of, 150
　　unclean hands, 166
　　watchdog actions and, 150
　statutory remedy as, 152
privacy, *see also* **freedom of
　expression**
　invasion of, 139, 140, 143 *et seq.*
　unenumerated right of, 143
　　alleged violation of, 143
　　breach of, 143
proprietary estoppel, 120

Quia Emptores, 275 *et seq.*
　application of in Ireland, 275, 281 *et
　　seq.*, 290 *et seq.*
　cestuis que vie, 276, 293
　England, doctrine in, 290 *et seq.*
　fee tail, 279
　freehold estates *pur autre vie,* 276
　freehold tenants, 277
　introduction, 275
　leaseholds, non-application to,
　　291

Quia Emptores—*contd.*
  leases for lives renewable forever,
      289, 290
  licences in mortmain, 290
  life estate, 279
  manors, 280, 281, 285
      creation of, 280
  manorial rights,
      examples of, 287, 288
  mesne lords, 279, 284
  non obstante grants, 280, 281,
      285-289, 290, 291
  pre, 276 *et seq.*
  reversion, 290, 291, 292
  sub-grants of leases for lives, 292-
      294
  subinfeudation, 277, 279, 284, 285,
      286, 290, 291
  tenant *pur autre vie*, 292, 293
  tenants *in capite*, 279
  tenants in chief, 278, 279, 282-285,
      289
  tenure, 290-292

religion, *see* **contract law**
restitution, 104, 105, 112
  non-restitutionary remedy, 105
  strict liability in, 114
Royal Dublin Society
  establishment of, 320

succession, 3, *see also* **intestacy,**
      limitations of actions
  children, 73 *et seq.*
      born outside marriage, rights of,
          212, 214, 218
      proper provision for, 76, 79
  European Convention of Human
      Rights and, 204 *et seq.*, 221 *et
      seq.*
      importance of, 204
  European Court of Human Rights,
      204, 205
      European Commission of Human
          Rights, 204, 205, 221,
          222
      role of, 204, 206

Succession—*contd.*
  European Court of Human Rights—
      contd.
      rights under, 203 *et seq.*, 206 *et
          seq.*, 210 *et seq.*
      negative obligations,
          207-210
      positive obligations,
          207-210
  family, constitution of, 213
      definition of, 220, 221 *et seq.*
      genetic parent, 219
      homosexual cohabitation, 219,
          220, 221
      jurisprudence, relating to, 218 *et
          seq.*
      social parent, 219
  issue, interpretation of, 212, 213
  legitim, 74, 75
  moral duty, concept of, 76-80
      breach of, 79
  moral obligation of parents under, 73
      et seq., 76
      comparative analysis of, 73
  proper provision under, 79, 80
  quotité disponible, 75
  section 117, 73 *et seq.*
      adequate provision under,
          79
      disqualifying conduct of
          applicants, under, 81
      alternative lifestyles, 83-87
          drugs, 83-87
          prodigal children, 83-87
          sex, 83-87
      criminal conduct, 87
      hostile relations, 87-92
      lack of love and affection,
          81-83
      lesser evils, 87
  testamentary autonomy versus rights
      of patrimony, 93

Tax
  children, 179
      channelling assets to minor
          children, 175 *et seq.*

tax—*contd.*
    trusts, 172 *et seq.*
        anti-avoidance provisions, 173,
            174
        asset protection, 183 *et seq.*
            beneficiary's interest, relevance
                of in, 186, 187
            CAT reliefs, maximise by, 180-
                182
            CGT/CAT credit benefit, 178
            discretionary, 177, 178
            divorce, 183
                separation and, 183
            matrimonial cases, variation of
                in, 183-185
            prohibition of to defeat
                financial claims of
                spouses, 185
        beneficiary's liability to Capital
            Acquisitions Tax (CAT),
            173, 176
            liability of to Capital Gains
                Tax (CGT), 173, 176
        beneficiary's right to income of
            trust, 173
        protection of surviving spouses,
            by, 179
        trustees,
            liability to tax, 172
        wealth preservation planning, 172 *et
            seq.*
taxonomy, 254 *et seq.*

taxonomy—*contd.*
    attractions of, 259
    legal mind, appeal of to, 255
    occupiers' liability and, *see*
        occupiers' liability
    scientific mind, appeal to, 255
trusts, 94, *see also* **graft, Irish doctrine
    of, tax**
    accessory, 97 *et seq.*, 99 *et seq.*, 107,
        see also **restitution**
        Baden types, 106-107, 113
        carelessness, 101
        dishonest recklessness, 99 *et seq.*
        dishonesty, 97-99, 102
        jury question, 97, 98, 99
        knowing receipt, 104, 105, 107 *et
            seq.*, 111
        mens rea, proof of, for, 103, 104
            et seq.
    charitable, 172
    constructive trusteeship, 94 *et seq.*,
        120
        definition of, 95
        liability, 95 *et seq.*, 104
            general principle of, 95
            test of, 96, 97
        tracing, doctrine of, 105
        various type of, 113
    discretionary trusts, 177

will
    beneficiary under, 259